The Age of Migration

About the Authors

Stephen Castles, DPhil, is Research Professor of Sociology at the University of Sydney. He was previously Director of the International Migration Institute at the University of Oxford. His books and articles have been translated into many languages and have been highly influential in the development of international migration studies.

Hein de Haas, PhD, is Co-Director of the International Migration Institute, University Lecturer in Migration Studies, and James Martin Fellow at the University of Oxford. He is also Professor of Migration and Development at Maastricht University.

Mark J. Miller, PhD, is the Emma Smith Morris Professor at the University of Delaware. He edited the *International Migration* Review from 1983 to 2005. He is a recipient of the Francis Alison award, the highest honor extended to faculty by the University of Delaware.

The Age of Migration

International Population Movements
in the Modern World

Fifth Edition

Stephen Castles

Hein de Haas

and

Mark J. Miller

THE GUILFORD PRESS
New York   London

Published in the United States of America by
The Guilford Press
A Division of Guilford Publications, Inc.
370 Seventh Avenue, New York, NY 10001
www.guilford.com

Printed in the United States of America

Published in North America under license from Palgrave Macmillan

Last digit is print number: 9 8 7 6 5 4 3 2

Library of Congress Cataloging-in-Publication Data

Castles, Stephen.
    The age of migration : international population movements in the modern
world / Stephen Castles, Hein de Haas, and Mark J. Miller.— Fifth edition.
        pages cm
    Summary: "The leading text in the field, this authoritative work offers a
global perspective on the nature of migration flows, why they occur, and their
consequences for both origin and destination societies. Chapters provide up-to-
date descriptions and comparative analyses of major migration regions in the
North and South. The role of population movements in the formation of ethnic
minority groups is examined, as is the impact of growing ethnic diversity on
economies, cultures, and political institutions. Useful pedagogical features include
accessible boxed examples, tables, maps, and suggestions for further reading. The
companion website features an online-only chapter, additional case studies, links
to relevant resources, and periodic updates"– Provided by publisher.
    Includes bibliographical references and index.
    ISBN 978–1–4625–1311–6 (pbk.)
    1. Emigration and immigration. I. Haas, Hein de, 1969– II. Miller,
Mark J. III. Title.
JV6032.C37 2014
304.8′2—dc23   2013027895
ISBN: 978–1–4625–1311–6

Contents

v

List of Illustrative Material

Tables

Figures

Boxes

Maps

Preface to the Fifth Edition

The Age of Migration was originally published in 1993, with the aim of providing an accessible introduction to the study of global migrations and their consequences for society. It was designed to combine theoretical knowledge with up-to-date information on migration flows and their implications for states as well as people everywhere. International migration has become a major theme for public debate, and *The Age of Migration* is widely used by policy-makers, scholars and journalists. It is recommended as a textbook in politics and social science all over the world.

For this new edition, Hein de Haas has joined Stephen Castles and Mark J. Miller as an author. As with previous editions, the fifth edition is essentially a new book. It has been thoroughly revised and updated. Its revised structure now comprises three thematic clusters. After the introductory chapter, Chapters 2, 3 and 4 are concerned with theories as well as the history of migration and ethnic diversity. Chapters 5, 6, 7 and 8 then present overviews of migration in specific world regions. Chapters 9, 10, 11, 12 and 13 are devoted to the effects of migration upon societies, especially in immigration countries.

The fifth edition provides a systematic and comprehensive discussion of migration theories. It also features in-depth analysis of two new issues. A major focus in Chapter 11, but also within each regional chapter, concerns the effects of the global economic crisis since 2008 for international migration. A second major innovation is the analysis of climate change and its effects upon migration and security. Although some have viewed climate change as having dire implications for international migration, we found no evidence of large-scale international migration as a result of climate change. Another key change already came with the fourth edition and the creation of a website. This is designed as a resource for students and other users. It contains internet links, and additional information and examples to complement the text of the book. (For more detail see the guide to further reading at the end of each chapter.)

The fifth edition examines recent events and emerging trends anew. Labour migration to new industrial economies is growing fast, while violent conflicts are leading to vast movements of displaced people, especially in less developed regions. Improvements in transport and communication facilitate temporary, circular and repeated movements. New types of mobility are emerging as increasing numbers of people move for education, marriage or retirement, or in search of new lifestyles.

The fifth edition analyses and updates the migration effects of the 2004 and 2007 enlargements of the European Union, and the role of migrant labour in the 'new economy' of highly developed countries. Demographic changes in immigration countries are raising awareness of future demand for migrant labour, while, at the same time, public concern about ethnic diversity is leading to measures to increase social cohesion, for instance through 'integration contracts' and citizenship tests.

Much has changed in the world since the publication of the first edition, yet the book's central argument remains the same. International population movements are reforging states and societies around the world in ways that affect bilateral and regional relations, economic restructuring, security, national identity and sovereignty. As a key dynamic within globalization, migration is an intrinsic part of broader economic and social change, and is contributing to a fundamental transformation of the international political order. However, what sovereign states do in the realm of migration policies continues to matter a great deal. The notion of open borders remains elusive even within regional integration frameworks, except for European citizens circulating within the European Union.

The authors thank the following for help in preparing the fifth edition. Several doctoral candidates at the University of Sydney provided expert research assistance to Stephen Castles. Magdalena Arias Cubas made a major contribution to Chapter 6, Migration in the Americas; Chulhyo Kim provided significant input to Chapter 7, Migration in the Asia–Pacific Region; Derya Ozkul, Elsa Koleth and Rebecca Williamson provided crucial assistance with the preparation of country studies for Chapter 12, New Ethnic Minorities and Society. All made important contributions to the *Age of Migration* website.

Hein de Haas is indebted to Mathias Czaika, Agnieszka Kubal, Lucia Kureková, Ronald Skeldon, Simona Vezzoli and María Villares Varela for giving valuable feedback on various drafts of Chapters 2, 3, 5 and 8. He also expresses gratitude to the European Research Council (ERC), which has enabled him to do essential background research on migration theories and recent migration trends in Europe, Africa and the Middle East as part of a Starting Grant to the DEMIG (Determinants of International Migration) project under the European Community's Seventh Framework Programme (FP7/2007–2013, ERC Grant Agreement 240940).

Mark Miller is deeply indebted to James O'Neill Miller, not only for research and typing assistance, but also for his valuable editorial suggestions. He is also thankful for the assistance he received from Barbara Ford, Lynn Corbett, Cindy Waksmonski and Tony Valentine from the Department of Political Science and International Relations at the University of Delaware.

We would like to thank our publisher, Steven Kennedy, above all for his patience, but also for his editorial and substantive advice. Stephen Wenham of Palgrave Macmillan has also given a great deal of support on the fifth edition, as on the fourth.

We are indebted to Oliver Bakewell, Robin Cohen, Jock Collins, Evelyn Ersanilli, Fred Halliday, Gunvor Jónsson, Thomas Lacroix, Sako Musterd,

Christina Rocha, Stuart Rosewarne, Martin Ruhs, Patrick Simon, John Solomos, Carlos Vargas-Silva and Catherine Wihtol de Wenden for their constructive comments. The authors wish to acknowledge the many valuable criticisms of earlier editions from reviewers and colleagues, although it is not possible to respond to them all. We are also grateful to Olinka Caunerova who did essential work on preparation of the bibliography and the final book manuscript.

Stephen Castles would like to thank Ellie Vasta for all her intellectual engagement with the contents of this book and her critique and input, as well as her constant support.

Hein de Haas would like to thank Bouchra Arbaoui for her support and the countless inspiring discussions, as well as Selma and Dalila, for adding so much optimism and energy.

Mark Miller wishes to thank his wife, Jane Blumgarten Miller, for her understanding and support especially during the unexpected and trying circumstances in which the fifth edition was written.

STEPHEN CASTLES
HEIN DE HAAS
MARK J. MILLER

Note on Migration Statistics

When studying migration and minorities it is vital to use statistical data, but it is also important to be aware of the limitations of such data. Statistics are collected in different ways, using different methods and different definitions by authorities of various countries. These can even vary between different agencies within a single country.

A key point is the difference between *flow* and *stock* figures. The *flow* of migrants is the number of migrants who enter a country (*inflow, entries* or *immigration*) in a given period (usually a year), or who leave the country (*emigration, departures* or *outflow*). The balance between these figures is known as *net migration*. The *stock* of migrants is the number present in a country on a specific date. Flow figures are useful for understanding trends in mobility, while stock figures help us to examine the long-term impact of migration on a given population.

Until recently, figures on immigrants in 'classical immigration countries' (the USA, Canada, Australia and New Zealand) were mainly based on the criterion of a person being *foreign-born* (or *overseas-born*), while data for European immigration countries were mainly based on the criterion of a person being a *foreign national* (or *foreign resident, foreign citizen, foreigner* or *alien*). The foreign-born include persons who have become *naturalized,* that is, who have taken on the nationality (or citizenship) of the receiving country. The category excludes children born to immigrants in the receiving country (the *second generation*) if they are citizens of that country. The term 'foreign nationals' excludes those who have taken on the nationality of the receiving country, but includes children born to immigrants who retain their parents' nationality (see OECD, 2006: 260–1).

The two ways of looking at the concept of immigrants reflect the perceptions and laws of different types of immigration countries. However, with longer settlement and recognition of the need to improve integration of long-term immigrants and their descendants, laws on nationality and ideas on its significance are changing. Many countries now provide figures for *both* the foreign-born and foreign nationals. These figures cannot be aggregated, so we will use both types in the book, as appropriate. In addition, some countries now provide data on children born to immigrant parents, or on ethnicity, or on race, or on combinations of these. For example, when using statistics it is therefore very important to be aware of the definition of terms (which should always be given clearly in presenting data), the significance of different concepts and the purpose of the specific statistics (for detailed discussion see OECD, 2006, Statistical Annexe).

The Age of Migration Website

There is an accompanying website – **www.age-of-migration.com** – for *The Age of Migration*. This is freely accessible and is designed as a resource for students and other users. It contains web links and additional case studies to expand the analysis of the book. It also includes a web-only chapter, The Migratory Process: A Comparison of Australia and Germany. The website will also contain updates to cover important developments that affect the text.

The guides to further reading at the end of most chapters draw attention to the specific case material relevant to each chapter on the AOM5 website. This material is numbered for ease of navigation, i.e. case material for Chapter 4 is called Case 4.1, Case 4.2, and so on.

List of Abbreviations

A10	The ten new member states that gained accession to the EU on 1 May 2004: Cyprus, Czech Republic, Estonia, Hungary, Latvia, Lithuania, Malta, Poland, Slovakia and Slovenia
A8	The new Central and Eastern European member states (the A10 minus Cyprus and Malta)
ABS	Australian Bureau of Statistics
AFL-CIO	American Federation of Labor–Congress of Industrial Organizations
ALP	Australian Labor Party
ANC	African National Congress
AOM	Age of Migration
AMU	Arab Maghreb Union
DHS	Department of Homeland Security (USA)
DIAC	Department of Immigration and Citizenship (Australia)
DRC	Democratic Republic of the Congo
EC	European Community
ECOWAS	Economic Community of West African States
EU	European Union
EU2	The two new member countries (Bulgaria and Romania) that joined the EU in January 2007
EU10	The 10 new member countries (Cyprus, Czech Republic, Estonia, Hungary, Latvia, Lithuania, Malta, Poland, Slovakia and Slovenia) that joined the EU in May 2004
EU15	The 15 member states of the EU up to April 2004
EU25	The 25 member states of the EU from May 2004 to December 2006
EU27	The 27 member states of the EU since January 2007
FN	Front National (National Front, France)
FRG	Federal Republic of Germany
GEC	global economic crisis
GCIM	Global Commission on International Migration
GDP	Gross Domestic Product
IDP	internally displaced person
ILO	International Labour Organization
IMF	International Monetary Fund
IMI	International Migration Institute (University of Oxford)
IOM	International Organization for Migration
IRCA	Immigration Reform and Control Act 1986 (USA)

MENA	Middle East and North Africa
MERCOSUR	Latin American Southern Common Market
NAFTA	North American Free Trade Agreement
NELM	New Economics of Labour Migration
NGO	non-governmental organization
NIC	newly industrializing country
OECD	Organisation for Economic Co-operation and Development
OMA	Office of Multicultural Affairs
SADC	Southern African Development Community
SGI	Société Générale d'Immigration (France)
TEU	Treaty on European Union
TFW	temporary foreign worker
UAE	United Arab Emirates
UN	United Nations
UNDP	United Nations Development Programme
UNDESA	United Nations Department of Economic and Social Affairs
UNHCR	United Nations High Commissioner for Refugees
UNPD	United Nations Population Division
WTO	World Trade Organization

Chapter 1

Introduction

Migration and the resulting ethnic and racial diversity are amongst the most emotive subjects in contemporary societies. While global migration rates have remained relatively stable over the past half a century, the political salience of migration has strongly increased. For origin societies, the departure of people raises concern about the 'brain drain' on the one hand, but it also creates the hope that the money and knowledge migrants gather abroad can foster human and economic development. For receiving societies, the settlement of migrant groups and the formation of ethnic minorities can fundamentally change the social, cultural, economic and political fabric of societies, particularly in the longer run.

This became apparent during the USA presidential election in 2012. The burgeoning minority population of the USA voted overwhelmingly in favour of Obama whereas the Republican presidential candidate Mitt Romney won most of the white non-Hispanic vote. According to analysis of exit polls, 71 per cent of Latino voters voted for President Obama compared to 27 per cent for Romney. Latinos comprised 10 per cent of the electorate, up from 9 per cent in 2008 and 8 per cent in 2004. Hispanics make up a growing share of voters in key battleground states such Florida, Nevada and Colorado (Lopez and Taylor, 2012). A recent study estimated that 40 million Latinos will be eligible to vote in 2030, up from 23.7 million in 2010 (Taylor *et al.*, 2012).

The magnitude of Obama's victory seemed to reflect the increasing estrangement of the Republican Party from the daily lives and concerns of many Latino voters. This particularly relates to the inability of President George W. Bush to secure immigration reforms and, more generally, strong Republican opposition with regard to immigration reform allowing the legalization of the approximately 11 million irregular migrants living in the USA, who are primarily of Mexican and Central American origin (see also Box 1.1).

Similarly in Europe, the political salience of migration has increased, which is reflected in the rise of extreme right-wing, anti-immigrant and anti-Islam parties and a subsequent move to the right of the entire political spectrum on migration and diversity issues (cf. Davis, 2012). Growing hostility towards immigration has sometimes engendered racist attacks. On 22 July 2011, Anders Breivik, a 32-year-old Norwegian far-right radical, attacked government buildings in Oslo, causing eight deaths, and then carried out a mass shooting at a youth camp of the Norwegian Labour Party on the island of Utøya, where he killed 69 people and wounded hundreds,

1

mostly teenagers. His motive for the atrocities was to draw attention to his Islamophobic and anti-feminist manifesto *2083: A European Declaration of Independence*, which he published on the internet on the day of the attack. He regarded Islam as the enemy and advocated the deportation of all Muslims from Europe. He directed his attack against the Labour Party because he accused them of bearing responsibility for the deconstruction of Norwegian culture and the 'mass import' of Muslims. On 24 August 2012, Breivik was found guilty of mass murder and terrorism, and will probably remain in prison for life (*New York Times*, 24 August 2012).

A few months earlier, immigration had become a central issue in the French Presidential election. The incumbent centre-right president, Nicolas Sarkozy, called for a halving of immigration, saying that France could no longer integrate the many newcomers. This looked like a desperate ploy to play the 'race card' in an election in which the increasingly unpopular Sarkozy was being squeezed between a resurgent Socialist Party and the far right *Front National* (FN) candidate, Marine Le Pen. Then on 11 March 2012, a paratrooper was killed by a gunman in the city of Toulouse. Four days later two more paratroopers were shot dead, and on 19 March three children and a Rabbi were murdered at a Jewish school. The police identified the killer as Mohamed Merah, a French citizen of Algerian descent. Merah had visited Afghanistan and claimed to have received training from a group linked to al-Qaeda. In a siege at his apartment, Merah was shot dead on 21 March (BBC News, 22 March 2012). The presidential elections were thrown into turmoil, and Sarkozy was back in the spotlight, with his calls for tough new laws against terrorism. Throughout his political career, Sarkozy had campaigned for more immigration control and had portrayed the growing diversity of the French population as a security threat. Now he had a cause that he hoped would propel him back into office. Yet he failed: French voters put economic and social issues above fears about diversity and security, and the Socialist candidate François Hollande emerged as victor in the presidential election of May 2012 (France 24, 7 March 2012).

These are stark reminders of the continuing political salience of immigration and ethnic diversity – but also of the political risks of playing the 'race card'. There are many other such reminders. After Spain and Italy introduced visa requirements for North Africans in the early 1990s, migration did not stop but became increasingly irregular in nature. Each year, tens of thousands of Africans attempt to make the dangerous crossing across the Mediterranean in small fishing boats, speedboats or hidden in vans and trucks on ferries. Although this frequently leads to public outcries about 'combating illegal migration', further border controls did not stop migration but rather reinforced its irregular character and diverted flows to other crossing points.

At the time of the onset of Arab Spring in 2011, some European politicians portrayed the flight of people from violence in Libya as an invasion. Most migrant workers in Libya returned to their African or Asian homelands, and the numbers arriving in Italy remained relatively small. Nevertheless, the Berlusconi Government declared a state of emergency. Italy reached an agreement on temporary residence for Tunisians, sparking a public outcry amongst European leaders and fears that Tunisians could move on to other European Union (EU) countries. Contrary to the Schengen Agreement on free movement in Europe, France even temporarily introduced symbolical controls on its border with Italy.

While the USA remains deeply divided by race, immigration too, especially of Mexicans across the long southern border, remains controversial. The failure of Congress to pass a comprehensive immigration reform in 2006 opened the door for restrictive state legislation, with Arizona taking the lead in introducing strict controls. The USA, with over 11 million irregular immigrants, relies heavily on their labour in agriculture, construction and the services, yet has been unable to move towards legal forms of immigration and employment for this group, even though it also has the largest legal immigration programme in the world. At the same time, post-9/11 restrictions in immigration policies have made it increasingly difficult to obtain visas and residence permits (Green Cards) even for the high-skilled (see Box 1.1).

Divisive issues can be found in new immigration destinations too: In Dubai in March 2006, foreign workers building the Burj Dubai, the world's tallest building, demonstrated against low wages, squalid dormitories and dangerous conditions. Their main grievance was that employers often simply refused to pay wages. Dubai is one of the oil-rich United Arab Emirates, where the migrant workforce – mainly from South and South-East Asia – far outnumbers the local population. Lack of worker rights, prohibition of unions and fear of deportation have forced migrant workers to accept exploitative conditions. Women migrants, who often work as domestic helpers, are especially vulnerable. In Japan and Korea too, politicians often express fears of loss of ethnic homogeneity through immigration. The government of multiracial Malaysia tends to blame immigrants for crime and other social problems, and introduces 'crack downs' against irregular migrants whenever there are economic slowdowns.

Indeed, economic woes often lead to anti-immigration politics. In the global economic crisis (GEC) which started in 2008, many states tightened up immigration control measures and sought to send migrants home. These measures had little impact on migrant stocks, but they did stir up popular resentment of immigrants. In fact, as will be discussed later in this book, the GEC has had only a limited structural effect on migration. Some rather surprising new trends have emerged, such as the new flows of young Europeans to older destination countries: Greeks, Italians and Irish to Germany and Australia; Portuguese to Brazil; Spaniards to Latin America; and all of these groups to the USA.

Quite literally, international migration has changed the face of societies. The commonality of the situations lies in the increasing ethnic and cultural diversity of many immigrant-receiving societies, and the dilemmas

Box 1.1 How migration shaped US and Mexican politics in the twenty-first century

The elections of George W. Bush and Vicente Fox in 2000 appeared to augur well for US–Mexico relations. Both presidents wanted to improve relations, especially through closer cooperation on migration issues. President Bush's first foreign visit was to President Fox's ranch and the US–Mexico immigrant initiative topped the agenda. However, there was significant Congressional opposition. Then, after the terrorist attacks on 9/11, the migration initiative was put on the back-burner as securitization of US immigration policy ensued. With the re-election of President Bush in 2004, comprehensive immigration reform became a priority for the second term. But deep divisions between Republicans doomed reform in the Bush presidency with perhaps fateful long-term consequences for the Republican Party.

In 2008, newly elected Mexican President Calderón sought to de-emphasize the centrality of migration in US–Mexican relations whereas newly elected US President Barack Obama continued to support reform, albeit tepidly. In the absence of comprehensive immigration reform at the federal level, pro and anti-immigration activists launched initiatives at the state and municipal levels. Several states adopted restrictive measures which led to an important US Supreme Court ruling in 2012 that upheld the paramount prerogatives of the US federal government in determination of immigration law and policy. Nonetheless, the rules adopted in Arizona and other states led to many deportations of Mexican undocumented workers and contributed to a decline in Mexico–US migration.

President Obama too was unable to secure comprehensive immigration reform in his first term. However, he proclaimed it a principal goal of his second term after his re-election in 2012. The magnitude of his victory appeared to underscore the long-term significance of President Bush's inability to secure reform. The burgeoning minority population of the USA voted overwhelmingly in favour of Obama whereas the Republican presidential candidate Mitt Romney won most of the white non-immigrant vote. Gender also played a key role: 55 per cent of all women voters chose Obama over Romney, while for black women the figure was a massive 96 per cent, and for Latino women 76 per cent. A key question for the future is: can the Republican Party increase its appeal to minority populations, especially to Latinos?

Sources: Calmes and Thee-Brenan, 2012; Lopez and Taylor, 2012; Suzanne, 2012.

that arise for states and communities in finding ways to respond to these changes. Young people of immigrant background are protesting against their feeling of being excluded from the societies in which they had grown up (and often been born). By contrast, some politicians and elements of the media claim that immigrants are failing to integrate, deliberately maintaining distinct cultures and religions, and have become a threat to security and social cohesion.

The challenges of global migration

Migration has gained increasing political salience over the past decades. That is why we have called this book *The Age of Migration*. This does not imply that migration is something new – indeed, human beings have always moved in search of new opportunities, or to escape poverty, conflict or environmental degradation. However, migration took on a new character with the beginnings of European expansion from the sixteenth century (see Chapter 4), and the Industrial Revolution from the nineteenth century, which set in motion a massive transfer of population from rural to urban areas within and across borders.

A high point was the mass migrations from Europe to North America from the mid-nineteenth century until World War I. Between 1846 and 1939, some 59 million people left Europe, mainly for areas of settlement in North and South America, Australia, New Zealand and South Africa (Stalker, 2000: 9). Some scholars call this the 'age of mass migration' (Hatton and Williamson, 1998) and argue that these international movements were even bigger than today's.

The 1850–1914 period has been perceived (by Western scholars at least) as mainly one of transatlantic migration, while the long-distance movements that started after 1945 and expanded from the 1980s involve all regions of the world. Newer studies show great mobility in Asia, Africa and Latin America in the nineteenth and early twentieth centuries. Nonetheless, mobility has become easier as a result of new transport and communication technologies. This has enabled migrants to remain in almost constant touch with family and friends in origin countries and to travel back and forth more often. International migration is thus a central dynamic within globalization.

A defining feature of the age of migration is the challenge that some politicians and analysts believe is posed by international migration to the sovereignty of states, specifically to their ability to regulate movements of people across their borders. The relatively unregulated migration prior to 1914 was generally not seen as a challenge to state sovereignty. This would change over the course of the twentieth century. Many migrants cross borders in an irregular (also called undocumented or illegal) way. Paradoxically, irregularity is often a result of tighter control measures, which have blocked earlier forms of spontaneous mobility. While most governments have abolished the exit controls of the past, efforts by governments to regulate *immigration* are at an all-time high and involve intensive bilateral, regional and international diplomacy. A second challenge is posed by 'transnationalism': as people become more mobile, many of them foster social and economic relationships in two or more societies at once. This is often seen as undermining the undivided loyalty some observers think crucial to sovereign nation-states.

While movements of people across borders have shaped states and societies since time immemorial, what is distinctive in recent years is their global scope, their centrality to domestic and international politics and their considerable economic and social consequences. Migration processes may become so entrenched and resistant to governmental control that new international political forms may emerge, such as the attempts to regulate migration at the regional level by the EU and by regional bodies in other parts of the world. Novel forms of interdependence, transnational societies and international cooperation on migration issues are rapidly transforming the lives of millions of people and inextricably weaving together the fate of states and societies.

For the most part, the growth of diversity and transnationalism is seen as a beneficial process, because it can help overcome the violence and destructiveness that characterized the era of nationalism. But international migration is sometimes directly or indirectly linked to conflict. Events like 9/11 (the 2001 attacks on the World Trade Center in New York and the Pentagon in Washington, DC), and the attacks by Islamic radicals on trains, buses and airports in Spain in 2004 and in the UK in 2005 and 2007 involved immigrants or their offspring. Such events have given rise to perceptions that threats to security of states are somehow linked to international migration and to the problems of living together in one society for culturally and socially diverse ethnic groups. This has increased the political salience of issues like immigration, diversity and multiculturalism, and this partly explains the rise of anti-immigration and anti-Islam parties in Europe – whose main narrative is to represent immigrants as a security and cultural threat. It is in this political climate that extreme-right violence like the July 2011 killings in Norway could occur.

These developments in turn are related to fundamental economic, social and political transformations that shape today's world. Millions of people are seeking work, a new home or simply a safe place to live outside their countries of birth. For many less developed countries, emigration is one aspect of the social crisis which accompanies integration into the world market and modernization. Population growth and the 'green revolution' in rural areas lead to massive 'surplus populations'. People move to burgeoning cities, where employment opportunities are often inadequate and social conditions miserable. Violence, oppressive governments and denial of human rights can lead to forced migrations within states or across their borders. Massive urbanization outstrips the creation of jobs in the early stages of industrialization. Some of the previous rural–urban migrants embark on a second migration, seeking to improve their lives by moving to newly industrializing countries in the South or to highly developed countries in the North.

However, most migration is not driven by poverty and violence: international migration requires significant resources, and most 'South–North' migrants come neither from the poorest countries nor from the poorest social classes. Many migrants benefit from the opportunities of a globalized economy for mobility as highly qualified specialists or entrepreneurs. Class plays an important role: destination countries compete to attract the highly skilled through privileged rules on entry and residence, while manual workers and refugees often experience exclusion and discrimination. New forms of mobility are emerging: retirement migration, mobility in search of better (or just different) lifestyles, repeated or circular movement. The barrier between migration and tourism is becoming blurred, as some people travel as tourists to check out potential migration destinations. Whether the initial intention is temporary or permanent movement, many migrants become settlers. Family reunion – the entry of dependent spouses, children and other relatives of previous primary migrants – remains the largest single entry category in many places. Migration networks develop, linking areas of origin and destination, and helping to bring about major changes in both. Migrations can change demographic, economic and social structures, and create a new cultural diversity, which often brings into question national identity.

This book is about contemporary international migrations, and the way they are changing societies. The perspective is international: large-scale movements of people arise from the process of global integration. Migrations are not isolated phenomena: movements of commodities, capital and ideas almost always give rise to movements of people, and vice versa. Global cultural interchange, facilitated by improved transport and the proliferation of print and electronic media, can also increase migration aspirations. International migration ranks as one of the most important factors in global change.

There are several reasons to expect the age of migration to endure: persistent inequalities in wealth between rich and poor countries will continue to impel large numbers of people to move in search of better living standards; political or ethnic conflict in a number of regions is likely to lead to future large-scale refugee movements; and the creation of new free trade areas will facilitate movements of labour, whether or not this is intended by the governments concerned. But migration is not just a reaction to difficult conditions at home: it is also motivated by the search for better opportunities and lifestyles elsewhere. Economic development of poorer countries generally leads to greater migration because it gives people the resources to move. Some migrants experience abuse or exploitation, but most benefit and are able to improve their lives through mobility. Conditions may be tough for migrants but are often preferable to poverty, insecurity and lack of opportunities at home – otherwise migration would not continue.

According to the United Nations Department of Economic and Social Affairs (UNDESA), the world total stock of international migrants (defined as people living outside their country of birth for at least a year) grew from about 100 million in 1960 to 155 million in 2000 and then to 214 million in 2010. This sounds a lot, but is just 3.1 per cent of the world's 7 billion people (UN Population Division, 2010; see also Figure 1.2). The number of international migrants has grown only slightly more rapidly than overall global population since 1960. Although international migration has thus not increased in relative terms, falling costs of travel and infrastructure improvements have rapidly increased non-migratory forms of mobility such as tourism, business trips and commuting. Most people remain in their countries of birth, while internal migration (often in the form or rural–urban movement) is far higher than international migration, especially in some of the world's population giants like China, India, Indonesia, Brazil, and Nigeria. It is impossible to know exact numbers of internal migrants, although the UN Development Program estimated some 740 million in 2009 (UNDP, 2009). Internal and international migration are closely linked and both are driven by the same transformation processes (DIAC, 2010a). However, this book focuses on international migration.

The illustrations that follow show some main characteristics of international migrant populations. Figure 1.1 traces how total international migration has evolved since 1990. It shows that international migrant populations have increasingly concentrated in wealthy, developed countries. Figure 1.2 shows that in 2010 international migrants represented over 10.3 per cent of highly developed receiving country populations on average, up from 7.2 in 1990. In developing countries, these shares are now well under 3 per cent and have been decreasing. The figure also shows that migrants represent about 3 per cent of the world population, and that this percentage has remained stable over the past decades.

Figure 1.3 shows the evolution of migrant stocks in the various continents from 1990–2010, revealing the large and fast-growing numbers in the industrial regions of Asia, Europe and North America. According to

Figure 1.1   *World immigrant populations, by levels of development*

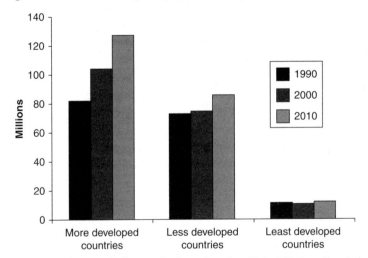

Source: World Development Indicators database, based on United Nations Population Division data.

Figure 1.2   *International immigrants as a percentage of total population, by level of development*

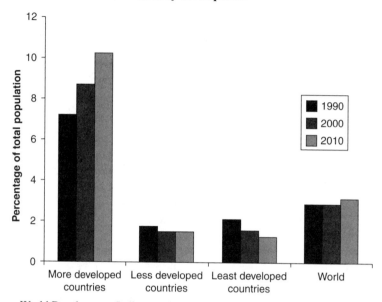

Source: World Development Indicators database, based on United Nations Population Division data.

Figure 1.3   *Estimated population of international immigrants by continent, 1990–2010*

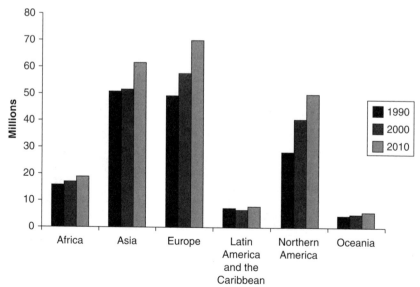

Source: World Development Indicators database, based on United Nations Population Division data.

these estimates, migrant populations have hardly been growing in Africa, Latin America and Oceania. Figure 1.4 examines migrant stocks as a percentage of the total population of the various continents. The population share of immigrants is highest in Oceania, mainly reflecting high immigration rates in Australia and New Zealand. Oceania is followed by North America and then Europe, where these rates have been increasing fast. By contrast, the population share is much lower and fairly stable in Asia, while it has actually declined in Africa and Latin America. Finally, Map 1.1 gives a very rough idea of the major migratory flows since 1973.

Some of those who move are 'forced migrants': people compelled to flee their homes and seek refuge elsewhere. The reasons for flight include political or ethnic violence or persecution, development projects like large dams, or natural disasters like the 2004 Asian Tsunami. According to UNDESA data, the total number of refugees was 16.3 million in 2010, which is an increase from the 15.6 million refugees in 2000, but still lower than the 1990 estimate of 18.4 million refugees worldwide. This figure includes the some 5 million Palestinian refugees worldwide (see Chapter 10), The decline after the early 1990s was partly due to a decline in the number of conflicts, and partly due to states' unwillingness to admit refugees. The number of internally displaced persons (IDPs) – forced migrants who remain in their country of origin because they find it impossible to cross an international border to seek refuge – grew to about 27.5 million in 2010 (see Chapter 10).

Figure 1.4   *International immigrants as a percentage of the population by continent, 1990–2010*

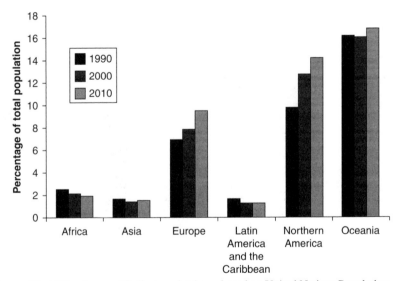

Source: World Development Indicators database, based on United Nations Population Division data.

11

Map 1.1 *International migratory movements from 1973*

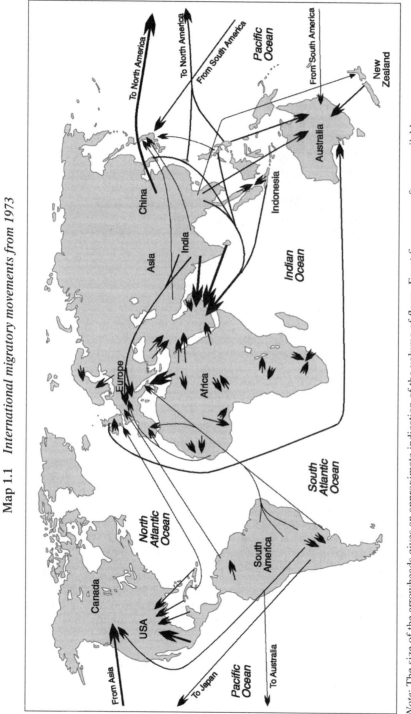

Note: The size of the arrowheads gives an approximate indication of the volume of flows. Exact figures are often unavailable.

Figure 1.5   *Estimated number of refugees by major area, 1990–2010*

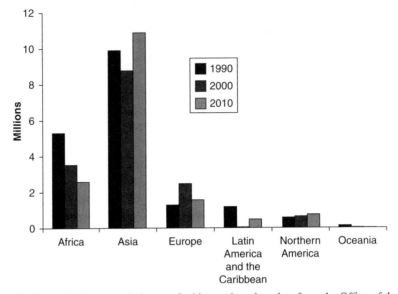

Note: Estimated refugee population as of mid-year, based on data from the Office of the United Nations High Commissioner for Refugees (UNHCR) and from the United Nations Relief and Works Agency for Palestinian Refugees in the Near East (UNRWA).

Source: United Nations Population Division.

Figure 1.5 represents refugee data by continents. This data also includes the roughly 5 million Palestinian refugees, which are not covered by the United Nations High Commissioner for Refugees (UNHCR). The distribution of refugees is quite different from that of other migrants: most refugees remain in the poorest areas of the world, while other migrants – especially high-skilled migrants – often go to the rich areas. While the numbers of refugees have considerably gone down in Africa partly due to a decreased level of conflict, they have recently increased in Asia. This partly reflects the consequences of the US-led invasions of Iraq and Afghanistan. According to the UNDESA data represented in Figure 1.6, refugees represent 13.3 per cent of the total international migrant population in Africa, down from 33.5 per cent in 1990. In Asia, this share is 17.7 per cent and has remained more or less stable. Elsewhere, these shares are much lower. In 2010, refugees now represent an estimated 7.6 per cent of the global migrant population, down from 11.9 per cent in 1990.

The vast majority of people remain in their countries of birth. Yet the impact of international migration is considerably larger than such figures suggest. The departure of migrants has considerable consequences

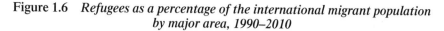

Figure 1.6 *Refugees as a percentage of the international migrant population by major area, 1990–2010*

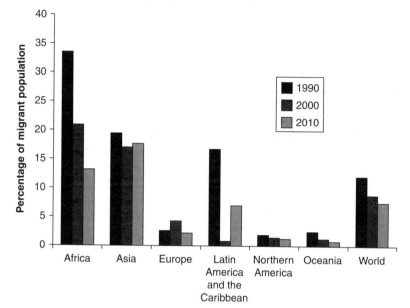

Source: United Nations Population Division.

for areas of origin. Remittances (money sent home) and investments by migrants may improve living standards, encourage economic development and create employment, but can also undermine growth and fuel inflation in remittance-dependent, non-productive and migration-obsessed communities.

In the country of immigration, settlement is closely linked to employment opportunities and is mainly concentrated in industrial and urban areas, where the impact on receiving communities is considerable. Migration thus affects not only the migrants themselves but the sending and receiving societies as a whole. There can be few people in either industrial or less developed countries today who do not have personal experience of migration or its effects.

Contemporary migrations: general trends

International migration is part of a transnational shift that is reshaping societies and politics around the globe. The old dichotomy between migrant-sending and migrant-receiving countries is being eroded – if this dichotomy was ever valid at all. Most countries experience both emigration and immigration (although one or the other often predominates). The differing ways in which such trends have affected the worlds' regions is a major theme throughout this book. Areas such as the USA, Canada, Australia, New Zealand or Argentina are considered 'classical countries of immigration'. Their current people are the result of histories of large-scale immigration – to the detriment of indigenous populations. Today, migration continues in new forms. Virtually all of Northern and Western Europe became areas of labour immigration and subsequent settlement after 1945. Since the 1980s, Southern European states like Greece, Italy and Spain, which for a long time were zones of emigration, have also become immigration areas, although in recent years emigration has been increasing in response to the global economic crisis. Today Central and Eastern European states are experiencing both significant emigration and immigration.

The Middle East and North Africa (MENA), the vast area stretching from Morocco to Iran, is affected by complex population movements. Some countries, like Turkey, Jordan and Morocco, have been major sources of migrant labour, while Turkey is now also an immigration country. The Gulf oil states experience large, officially temporary, inflows of workers. Iran has been a major receiving country for refugees from Afghanistan, along with Pakistan. In Africa, colonialism and European settlement led to the establishment of migrant labour systems for plantations and mines. Decolonization since the 1950s has sustained old migratory patterns – such as the flow of mineworkers to South Africa and Maghrebis to France – and started new ones, such as movements to Kenya, Gabon, and Nigeria. Although economic migration predominates, Africa has more refugees and IDPs relative to population size than any other region of the world. Asia and Latin America have complicated migratory patterns within their regions, as well as increasing flows to the rest of the world. An example of recent developments is discussed in Box 1.2 to give an idea of the complex ramifications of migratory movements for both North and South.

Box 1.2 Migration and revolution: the Arab Spring

The wave of political unrest that began in Tunisia in December 2010 and spread throughout the Arab world has caused the deaths of thousands of people, while millions of others had been forced to leave their homes by mid-2012. While the violence in Tunisia and Egypt remained relatively limited, the violent conflicts in Libya and Syria generated large flows of refugees.

In early 2011, the violence in Libya led to large-scale outflows of Libyan citizens and of more than one million African, Asian and European migrant workers, most of whom moved back home or were hosted in neighbouring

→

→

countries. The fate of hundreds of thousands of sub-Saharan workers in Libya exposed the scale of intra-African migration to the global public. Many African workers who lacked the means to return and feared attacks because of (largely false) accusations that they were 'mercenaries' working for the Gaddafi regime, became trapped in Libya.

The extremely violent conflict in Syria engendered an even bigger refugee crisis. In March 2013, according to the UNHCR, about four million Syrians were internally displaced and one million refugees had been registered in other countries. In the wake of the Arab Spring, European politicians sowed panic that these people would cross the Mediterranean to land on European shores in huge numbers. In 2011, the Italian government warned of an exodus of 'biblical proportions' from Libya while in 2012 Greek politicians announced that Greece should fortify itself against a massive wave of irregular migrants from Syria.

Such panic had no basis, as most people stayed within the region or returned home. Only 4 per cent of all people fleeing Libya (27,465 persons out of 790,000) ended up in Italy or Malta (Aghazarm *et al.*, 2012). The large majority of them found refuge in neighbouring Egypt and, particularly, Tunisia. UNHCR and IOM in collaboration with the Tunisian government helped hundreds of thousands of migrant workers to return home. After the death of Gaddafi in October 2011, most Libyans returned and migrant workers started to come back, although Africans migrants in particular continued to experience racist violence. The overwhelming majority of Syrian refugees have found refuge in Turkey, Jordan, Lebanon, Iraq, Egypt, and other North African countries.

Eurocentric accounts of the Arab Spring ignore the profound impact of the crisis on countries of origin. This pertains not only to the role of returnees in political violence in countries like Mali but also to the fact that many families in extremely poor countries such as Chad and Niger were now deprived of vital remittance income since migrant workers returned home.

Nevertheless, the Arab Spring has not radically transformed long-term migration patterns in the Mediterranean. Mass flight has been largely confined to Libya and, particularly, Syria, and there has been no major increase of emigration from other North African or Middle East countries. The increase in Tunisian emigration to Lampedusa, an Italian island 113 km off the Tunisian coast, was stimulated by reduced policing in Tunisia during the revolution but stood in a long-standing tradition of irregular boat migration to Europe that has existed since southern European countries introduced visas for North Africans around 1991.

So, the idea that emigration will stop is as unlikely as the idea of a 'mass exodus' towards Europe. At the same time, the processes that created the conditions for revolutionary change are also conducive to emigration. The coming of age of a new, educated and aspiring generation, which is frustrated by mass unemployment, dictatorial rule and corruption, has increased both the emigration and revolutionary potential of Arab societies.

Source: de Haas and Sigona, 2012; Fargues and Fandrich, 2012.

Throughout the world, long-standing migratory patterns are persisting in new forms, while new flows are developing in response to economic, political and cultural change, and violent conflicts. Yet, despite the diversity, it is possible to identify certain general tendencies:

1. The *globalization of migration*: the tendency for more and more countries to be significantly affected by international migration. Moreover, immigration countries tend to receive migrants from an increasingly diverse array of source countries, so that most countries of immigration have entrants from a broad spectrum of economic, social and cultural backgrounds.
2. The *changing direction of dominant migration flows*: while for centuries Europeans have been moving outward to conquer, colonize, and settle foreign lands elsewhere, these patterns were reversed after World War II. From a prime source of emigration, Europe has been transformed into a major global migration destination. As part of the same pattern, Europeans represent a declining share of immigrants in classical immigration countries such as the USA, Canada, Australia and New Zealand, along with an increase of 'South–North' migration. This also coincided with the appearance of a new global pole of attraction for migrant workers in the Gulf region.
3. The *differentiation of migration*: most countries are not dominated by one type of migration, such as labour migration, family reunion, refugee movement or permanent settlement, but experience a whole range of types at once. Migratory chains which start with one type of movement often continue with other forms, despite (or often just because of) government efforts to stop or control the movement.
4. The *proliferation of migration transition*: this occurs when traditional lands of emigration become lands of immigration. Growing transit migration is often the prelude to becoming predominantly immigration lands. States as diverse as Poland, Spain, Morocco, Mexico, the Dominican Republic, Turkey and South Korea are experiencing various stages and forms of a migration transition. But other countries, for example in Latin America, have experienced reverse migration transitions as they changed from immigration to emigration countries.
5. The *feminization of labour migration*: in the past many labour migrations were male-dominated, and women were often dealt with under the category of family reunion, even if they did take up employment. Since the 1960s, women have not only played an increasing role in labour migration, but also the *awareness* of women's role in migration has grown. Today women workers form the majority in movements as diverse as those of Cape Verdeans to Italy, Filipinas to the Middle East and Thais to Japan.
6. The *growing politicization of migration*: domestic politics, bilateral and regional relationships and national security policies of states

around the world are increasingly affected by international migration. This growing political salience of this issue is a main reason for our argument that we live in an age of migration.

International migration in global governance

Globalization has challenged the sovereignty of national governments from above and below. The growth of transnational society has given rise to novel challenges and has blurred formerly distinctive spheres of decision-making. Trends are contradictory (see Castles, 2004b): on the one hand, politicians cling to national sovereignty, with such slogans as 'British jobs for British workers'. On the other hand the complexity and fragmentation of power and authority that have resulted from globalization typically require governments (whether national, regional or local) to cooperate with other organizations and institutions, both public and private, foreign and domestic. An important manifestation of global governance is the significant expansion of regional consultative processes within bodies like the EU or the Association of South East Asian Nations (ASEAN) focusing on international migration.

Until recently, governments generally did not see international migration as a central political issue. Rather, migrants were divided up into categories, such as permanent settlers, foreign workers or refugees, and dealt with by a variety of special agencies, such as immigration departments, labour offices, aliens police, welfare authorities and education ministries. This situation began to change in the mid-1980s. The Paris-based Organization for Economic Cooperation and Development (OECD) convened the first international conference on international migration in 1986 (OECD, 1987). The OECD had found evidence of growing convergence in migration policy concerns and challenges faced by its member states. As most European Community (EC) countries started to remove their internal boundaries with the signature of the Schengen Agreement in 1985 and its full implementation in 1995, they became increasingly concerned about controlling external borders. By the 1990s, the mobilization of extreme-right groups in Europe over immigration helped bring these issues to the centre of the political stage. In the USA, the Clinton Administration ordered the Department of State and the Central Intelligence Agency (CIA) to include international migration in their assessments.

The adoption of the 1990 Convention on the Rights of Migrant Workers and Their Families by the UN General Assembly brought into sharp relief global tensions and differences surrounding international migration. Immigration countries refused to sign the convention, and it did not come into force until 2003. By October 2012 it had been ratified by just 46 of the UN's 193 states – virtually all of them countries of emigration.

Globalization has coincided with the strengthening of global institutions: the World Trade Organization for trade, the International Monetary Fund for finance, the World Bank for economic development, and so on. But the will to cooperate has not been as strong in the migration field. There are international bodies with specific tasks – such as the UNHCR for refugees and the International Labour Office (ILO) for migrant workers – but no institution with overall responsibility for global cooperation and for monitoring migrant rights. The International Organization for Migration (IOM) does have wider terms of reference, but it is a non-UN body and lacks the capacity to bring about significant change. The key issue is the unwillingness of labour-importing countries to enforce migrant rights and to adopt more liberal immigration regimes that might improve migrants' lives and outcomes for countries of origin.

In 2003, following consultation with UN Secretary General Kofi Annan, a Global Commission on International Migration (GCIM), consisting of prominent people advised by migration experts, was set up. Its report (GCIM, 2005) emphasized the potential benefits of migration for development. The UN General Assembly held its first High-Level Dialogue on International Migration and Development in 2006. The Secretary General's report on this meeting recommended a forum for UN member states to discuss migration and development issues. The Global Forum on Migration and Development (GMFD) has met annually since, although its role has been purely advisory and it is hard to see concrete results of the dialogue (see Castles, 2011).

Ethnic diversity, racism and multiculturalism

Governance of international migration is one of the two central issues arising from the population movements of the current epoch. The other is the effect of growing ethnic diversity on the societies of immigration countries. Settlers are often distinct from the receiving populations: they may come from different types of societies (for example, agrarian-rural rather than urban-industrial) with different traditions, religions and political institutions. They often speak a different language and follow different cultural practices. They may be visibly different, through physical appearance (skin colour, features and hair type) or style of dress. Some migrant groups become concentrated in certain types of work (sometimes of low social status) and live segregated lives in low-income residential areas. The position of immigrants is often marked by a specific legal status: that of the foreigner or non-citizen.

The social meaning of ethnic diversity depends to a large extent on the significance attached to it by the populations and states of the receiving countries. The classic immigration countries have generally seen immigrants as permanent settlers who were to be assimilated or integrated. However, not all potential immigrants have been seen as suitable: the USA, Canada and Australia all had policies to keep out non-Europeans and even some categories of Europeans until the 1960s. Countries which emphasized temporary labour recruitment – Western European countries in the 1960s and early 1970s, more recently the Gulf oil states and some of the fast-growing Asian economies – have tried (often unsuccessfully) to prevent family reunion and permanent settlement. Despite the emergence of permanent settler populations, such countries have declared themselves not to be countries of immigration, and have generally denied citizenship and other rights to settlers. Between these two extremes is a wealth of variations, which will be discussed in later chapters.

Culturally distinct settler groups often maintain their languages and some elements of their homeland cultures, at least for a few generations. Where governments have recognized permanent settlement, there has been a tendency to move from policies of individual assimilation to acceptance of some degree of long-term cultural difference. The result has been the granting of minority cultural and political rights, as embodied in the policies of multiculturalism introduced in Canada, Australia, the Netherlands and Sweden since the 1970s. However, the post-9/11 era has witnessed a retreat from multiculturalism in many democracies. Governments which reject the idea of permanent settlement often also oppose pluralism, which they see as a threat to national unity and identity.

Whatever the policies of the governments, immigration often leads to strong reactions from some sections of the population. Immigration sometimes takes place at the same time as economic restructuring and far-reaching social change. People whose conditions of life are already changing in an unpredictable way may see the newcomers as the cause of insecurity. One of the dominant, but empirically unjustified, images in highly developed countries today is that of masses of people flowing in from the poor South and the turbulent East, taking away jobs, pushing up housing prices and overloading social services. Similarly, in other immigration countries, such as Malaysia and South Africa, immigrants are blamed for crime, disease and unemployment. Extreme-right parties have grown and flourished through anti-immigrant campaigns. In fact, migrants are generally a symptom of change rather than its cause. For many people, immigration is the most concrete manifestation of rather intangible processes such as globalization and neoliberal economic policies. It should therefore not come as a surprise that the blame for social and economic problems is often shifted on to the shoulders of immigrants and ethnic minorities.

International migration does not always create diversity. Some migrants, such as Britons in Australia or Austrians in Germany, are virtually indistinguishable from the receiving population. Other groups, like Western Europeans in North America, are quickly assimilated. 'Professional transients' – that is, highly skilled personnel who move temporarily within specialized labour markets – are rarely seen as presenting an integration problem, although, ironically enough, such groups often hardly integrate.

More fundamental is the challenge that migration poses for national identity. The nation-state, as it has developed since the eighteenth century, is premised on the idea of cultural as well as political unity. In many countries, ethnic homogeneity, defined in terms of common language, culture, traditions and history, has been seen as the basis of the nation-state. This unity has often been fictitious – a construction of the ruling elite – but it has provided powerful national myths. Immigration and ethnic diversity threaten such ideas of the nation, because they create a people without common ethnic origins. The classical countries of immigration have been able to cope with this situation most easily, since absorption of immigrants has been part of their myth of nation-building. But countries which place common culture at the heart of their nation-building process have found it difficult to resolve the contradiction.

One of the central ways in which the link between the people and the state is expressed is through the rules governing citizenship and naturalization. States which readily grant citizenship to immigrants, without requiring common ethnicity or cultural assimilation, seem most able to cope with ethnic diversity. On the other hand, states which link citizenship to cultural belonging tend to have exclusionary policies which marginalize and disadvantage immigrants. It is one of the central themes of this book that continuing international population movements will increase the ethnic diversity of more and more countries. This has already called into question prevailing notions of the nation-state and citizenship. Debates over new approaches to diversity will shape the politics of many countries in coming decades.

Aims and structure of the book

The Age of Migration sets out to provide an understanding of the emerging global dynamics of migration and of the consequences for migrants and non-migrants everywhere. That is a task too big for a single book. Our accounts of the various migratory movements must inevitably be concise, but a global view of international migration is the precondition for understanding each specific flow. The central aim of this book is therefore to provide an introduction to the subject of international migration and the emergence of increasingly diverse societies, which will help readers to put more detailed accounts of specific migratory processes in context.

Our first specific objective is to describe and explain contemporary international migration. We set out to show its enormous complexity, and to communicate both the variations and the common factors in international population movements as they affect more and more parts of the world.

The second objective is to explain how migrant settlement is bringing about increased ethnic diversity in many societies and how it affects broader social, cultural and political change in destination *and* origin societies. Understanding these changes is the precondition for political action to deal with problems and conflicts linked to migration and ethnic diversity.

The third objective is to link the two analyses, by examining the complex interactions between migration and broader processes of change in origin and destination societies. There are large bodies of empirical and theoretical work on both themes. However, the two are often inadequately linked. The linkages can best be understood by analysing the migratory process in its totality.

The Age of Migration is structured as follows. A first group of chapters (2–4) provides the theoretical and historical background necessary to understand contemporary global trends. Chapter 2 examines the theories and concepts used to explain migration and emphasizes the need to study the migratory process as a whole and to learn to understand migration as an intrinsic part of broader processes of change rather than a 'problem to be solved'. Chapter 3 focuses on how migration has fundamentally transformed societies in both destination and origin areas. In destination areas, we examine complex issues arising from ethnic and cultural diversity, in origin areas the debates on migration and development. Chapter 4 describes the history of international migration from early modern times until 1945.

A second group of chapters (5–8) provides descriptive accounts and data on contemporary migrations around the world. In this fifth edition we seek to provide a better overview of emerging migration processes by providing a chapter on movements within, to and from each of the world's main regions. Chapter 5 is concerned with migration to and from Europe. It examines the patterns of labour migration which developed during the post-1945 boom, and discusses changes in migratory patterns after the 'Oil Crisis' of 1973 and the 2004 and 2007 enlargements of the EU as well as the GEC since 2008. Chapter 6 examines the migratory patterns affecting the Americas, which includes both major immigration countries (USA, Canada), emigration areas like much of Central America, the Andean Region, and countries that combine the role of origin-, destination- and transit-areas for migrants, like Mexico, Brazil, Argentina and Chile. Chapter 7 deals with the Asia–Pacific region – home to 60 per cent of the world's population. It is hard to even summarize the immensely varied and complex migratory patterns rooted both in history and in the often breathtakingly rapid contemporary transformations taking place in Asia and Oceania. Chapter 8 addresses two other diverse, fast-changing and closely interlinked regions: Africa and the Middle East, where movements of people are linked to rapid transformations in economic and political conditions.

A third group of chapters (9–13) is concerned with the political, economic and social meaning of migration and ethnic diversity, especially for immigration countries. Chapter 9 examines migration and security. Such questions are not new but the 9/11 events in the USA and subsequent attacks in Europe led to a securitization of migration which has had profound effects. The chapter also includes a section on the relationship between climate change and migration. It is often claimed that this has significant implications for the security of destination counties; we argue instead that climate change has a complex relationship with other factors in the migration process, and that migration may be a valuable adaptation to change. Chapter 10 assesses the capacity of industrial states to regulate international migration. It examines irregular migration, human trafficking and the policies designed to curb them. It also discusses regional integration frameworks (the EU and NAFTA) for control of migration. This chapter also discusses the various types of forced migration and how states respond to them.

Chapter 11 considers the economic position of migrant workers and the meaning of migration for the economies of destination countries. It goes on to discuss the key role of migration in labour market restructuring and the development of a 'new economy' based on employment practices such as sub-contracting, temporary employment and informal-sector work. Although the effects of the GEC are discussed in the regional chapters, a section of Chapter 11 provides an overarching analysis. Chapter 12 examines the social position of immigrants within the societies of highly developed immigration countries, looking at such factors as legal status, social policy, formation of ethnic communities, racism, citizenship and national identity. Boxes provide short country case-studies (for space reasons some of these are to be found on the Age of Migration website). Chapter 13 examines the political implications of growing ethnic diversity, looking both at the involvement of immigrants and minorities in politics, and at the way mainstream politics are changing in reaction to migrant settlement.

Chapter 14 sums up the arguments of the book, reviews current trends in global migration and speculates on possible migration futures. With new major migration destinations such as Brazil, Turkey and China appearing on the horizon, the global migration map is likely to witness fundamental changes over the next few years. Meanwhile, international mobility of people seems to imply greater ethnic diversity in many receiving countries, and new forms of transnational connectivity. We discuss the dilemmas faced by governments and people in attempting to find appropriate responses to the challenges of an increasingly mobile world, and point to some of the major obstacles blocking the way to better international cooperation.

Guide to further reading

Extra resources at www.age-of-migration.com

There are too many books on international migration to list here. Many important works are referred to in the guide to further reading for other chapters. A wide range of relevant literature is listed in the Bibliography.

Important information on all aspects of international migration is provided by several specialized journals, of which only a selection can be mentioned here. *International Migration Review* (New York: Center for Migration Studies) was established in 1964 and provides excellent comparative information. *International Migration* (IOM, Geneva) is also a valuable comparative source. *Population and Development Review* is a prominent journal on population studies with many contributions on migration. *Social Identities* started publication in 1995 and is concerned with the 'study of race, nation and culture'. A journal concerned with transnational issues is *Global Networks*. *Migration Studies* is a new journal focusing on the determinants, processes and outcomes of migration. Some journals, which formerly concentrated on Europe, are becoming more global in focus. These include the *Journal of Ethnic and Migration Studies*, the *Revue Européenne des Migrations Internationales, Race and Class* and *Ethnic and Racial Studies*. Important non-European or North American journals include: The *Journal of Intercultural Studies* (Melbourne: Swinburne University), the *Asian and Pacific Migration Journal* (Quezon City, Philippines: Scalabrini Migration Center). *Frontera Norte* (Mexico: El Colegio de la Frontera Norte) and *Migración y Desarrollo* (Autonomous University of Zacatecas) include articles in Spanish and English.

Several international organizations provide comparative information on migrations. The most useful is the OECD's annual *International Migration Outlook*. Earlier annual reports on international migration to OECD member states from 1973 to 1990 were known as SOPEMI reports. The IOM published its *World Migration Report* for the first time in 2000, and the latest appeared in 2011.

Many internet sites are concerned with issues of migration and ethnic diversity. A few of the most significant ones are listed here. These and others are also provided as hyperlinks on *The Age of Migration* fifth edition (AOM5) website. Since they are in turn linked with many others, this list should provide a starting point for further exploration:

Centre on Migration, Policy and Society, University of Oxford: http://www.compas.ox.ac.uk/
Institute for Migration and Ethnic Studies (IMES), Amsterdam: http://www.imes.uva.nl
International Migration Institute, University of Oxford: http://www.imi.ox.ac.uk/
International Network on Migration and Development, Autonomous University of Zacatecas, Mexico: http://www.migracionydesarrollo.org/
International Organization for Migration: http://www.iom.int/
Migration Information Source, Migration Policy Institute, Washington DC: http://www.migrationinformation.org/
Migration News: http://migration.ucdavis.edu/
Migration Observatory, University of Oxford: http://migrationobservatory.ox.ac.uk/

Migration Policy Centre, European University Institute, Florence:
  http://www.migrationpolicycentre.eu/
Refugee Studies Centre, University of Oxford: http://www.rsc.ox.ac.uk/
Southern African Migration Project: http://www.queensu.ca/samp/
Sussex Centre for Migration Research:
  http://www.sussex.ac.uk/migration/
United Nations High Commission for Refugees (UNHCR):
  http://www.unhcr.org

Chapter 2

Theories of Migration

Migration is hardly ever a simple individual action in which a person decides to move in search of better life-chances, pulls up his or her roots in the place of origin and quickly becomes assimilated in a new country. Much more often migration and settlement are a long-drawn-out process that will be played out for the rest of the migrant's life, and affect subsequent generations too. Migration can even transcend death: members of some migrant groups arrange for their bodies to be taken back for burial in their native soil (see Tribalat, 1995: 109–11). Migration is often a collective action, arising out of social, economic and political change and affecting the whole society in both sending and receiving areas. Moreover, the experience of migration and of living in another country often leads to modification of the original plans, so that migrants' intentions at the time of departure are poor predictors of actual behaviour.

Conventional wisdom holds that migration is driven by geographical differences in income, employment and other opportunities. Although this sounds logical, it reflects a limited understanding of the causes of migration. Most migrants do not move from the poorest to the wealthiest countries. Wealthy, industrialized societies tend to experience simultaneous high immigration, substantial emigration and internal movement. The volume and complexity of migration often *increases* with development. This is because improved access to education and information, social capital and financial resources increases people's *aspirations* and *capabilities* to migrate, while improved transport and communication also facilitate movement.

At the same time, it would be naïve to deny that global inequalities in income, political freedom and quality of life play an important role in explaining migration. However, if it is true that both development and global inequality boost migration, how can we then explain that the volume of international migration as a percentage of the world population has remained remarkably stable at levels between 2 and 3 per cent over the past decades? Such paradoxes show that the relation between migration and broader processes of development and global change is an intrinsically complex one.

In order to achieve a better understanding of migration processes, this chapter reviews the basic insights offered by various migration theories on the causes of migration. This will help to understand the more descriptive accounts of migration, settlement and minority formation in later chapters. However, the reader may prefer to read those first and come back to the theory later.

Since the late nineteenth century, several theories have been developed in various social science disciplines, which aim at understanding the processes that drive migration. These theories differ with regard to their assumptions, thematic focus, and level of analysis, ranging from global accounts of shifting migration patterns to theories of migrant transnational identities. Often, theoretical and disciplinary divides are artificial. For instance, it does not seem very useful to develop separate theories for internal and international migration. Although international migration is more often (albeit not always) subject to control by states, both forms of migration are often driven by the same processes of social, economic and political change. In most countries internal migration is far larger than international. The two are often closely linked, and internal rural–urban migration may be a prelude to cross-border movement (King and Skeldon, 2010; Skeldon, 1997).

It is also debatable whether it is useful to develop separate theories for different categories of migrants, such as for 'forced' and 'voluntary' or for refugee, family or economic migration. Motives for migrating are often manifold. Migrants who primarily move for economic reasons may also flee political oppression. It is difficult to separate economic from social, cultural and political causes of migration. For instance, because of social inequality or oppression, certain disadvantaged ethnic or class groups in origin societies often have fewer opportunities to migrate internationally, which also disadvantages them economically.

To gain a deeper understanding of migration processes, it important to see migration as an *intrinsic part* of broader processes of development, globalization and social transformation rather than 'a problem to be solved'. To do this, we need to redress the 'receiving-country bias' – the tendency of migration studies to focus on the consequences of immigration in wealthy, migrant-receiving societies, and to ignore the causes and consequences of migration in origin countries.

It is useful to make a basic distinction between theories on the *causes of migration processes*, and theories on the *impacts of migration for sending and receiving communities and societies* (compare Massey *et al.*, 1998: 3). This chapter will focus on the first set of theories, while Chapter 3 will focus on the second set of theories.

Any migratory movement can be seen as the result of interacting macro- and micro-structures. Macro-structures refer to large-scale institutional factors, such as the political economy of the world market, inter-state relationships, and efforts by the states of sending and receiving countries to control migration. Micro-structures embrace the practices, family ties and beliefs of the migrants themselves. These two levels are linked by a number of intermediate mechanisms, referred to as 'meso-structures': examples include migrant networks, immigrant communities, new business sectors catering to migrants and the 'migration industry' (see below). In looking at causes of migration, it is therefore useful to also make a distinction between theories on macro-level causes of migration and meso-level theories on the continuation of migration, which focus on feedback mechanisms such as migrant networks to explain why migration can become a self-perpetuating process.

However, it is important to link theories on causes and consequences of migration in order to develop an understanding of migration as a dynamic process which is in constant interaction with broader change processes in destination and origin societies. In this book, we use the term 'migration studies' in the widest sense, to embrace both bodies of investigation.

Explaining the migratory process

The concept of the *migratory process* sums up the complex sets of factors and interactions which lead to migration and influence its course. Migration is a process which affects every dimension of social existence, and which develops its own complex 'internal' dynamics. The great majority of people in the world (around 97 per cent) are not classified as international migrants, yet their communities and way of life are often changed by migration. The changes are generally much bigger for the migrants themselves.

Research on migration is interdisciplinary: sociology, political science, history, economics, geography, demography, psychology, cultural studies and law are all relevant (Brettell and Hollifield, 2007). Within each discipline a variety of approaches exist, based on differences in theory and methods. For instance, researchers who base their work on quantitative analysis of large data-sets (such as censuses or surveys) will ask different questions and get different results from those who do qualitative studies of small groups. Those who examine the role of migrant labour within the world economy using historical and institutional approaches will again reach different conclusions. Each of these methods has its place, as long as it lays no claim to be the only correct one. As interest in migration research has grown in recent years, theoretical approaches have proliferated and interacted. This chapter will *not* review migration theories along disciplinary lines. This is done on purpose, because such distinctions are often artificial and can obstruct a more comprehensive understanding of migration processes. Different disciplines and theories provide different views on migration, which are more often complementary than mutually exclusive.

Migration theories can be grouped together into two main paradigms, following a more general division in social sciences between 'functionalist' and 'historical–structural' theories. Functionalist social theory tends to see society as a system, a collection of interdependent parts (individuals, actors), somehow analogous to the functioning of an organism, in which an inherent tendency toward equilibrium exists. Functionalist migration theory generally treats migration as a positive phenomenon serving the interests of most people and contributing to greater equality within and between societies.

Rooted in neo-Marxist political economy, historical–structural theories emphasize how social, economic, cultural and political structures constrain and direct the behaviour of individuals in ways that generally do not lead to greater equilibrium, but rather reinforce such disequilibria. They argue that economic and political power is unequally distributed, and that cultural beliefs (such as religion and tradition) and social practices tend to reproduce such structural inequalities. They see migration as providing a cheap, exploitable labour force, which mainly serves the interests of the wealthy in receiving areas, causes a 'brain drain' in origin areas, and therefore reinforces social and geographical inequalities.

Functionalist theories: push–pull models and neoclassical theory

An early contribution to migration studies consisted of two articles by the nineteenth-century geographer Ravenstein (1885; 1889), in which he formulated his 'laws of migration'. Ravenstein saw migration as an inseparable part of development, and he asserted that the major causes of migration were economic. 'Gravity' models developed by geographers from the early twentieth century were derived from Newton's law of gravity and predict the volume of migration between places and countries on the basis of distance, population size and economic opportunities in destination and origin areas. Lee (1966) argued that migration decisions are determined by 'plus' and 'minus' factors in areas of origin and destination; intervening obstacles (such as distance, physical barriers, immigration laws, and so on); and personal factors.

These types of analytical frameworks are commonly referred to as 'push–pull' models (Passaris, 1989). Push–pull models identify economic, environmental, and demographic factors which are assumed to push people out of places of origin and pull them into destination places. 'Push factors' usually include population growth and population density, lack of economic opportunities and political repression, while 'pull factors' usually include demand for labour, availability of land, economic opportunities and political freedoms.

At first sight, the push–pull framework seems attractive because of its apparent ability to incorporate all major factors affecting migration decision-making (Bauer and Zimmermann, 1998: 103). However, its value is limited and it can be misleading. It is a purely descriptive model in which factors assumed to play a role in migration are enumerated in a relative arbitrary manner, without specifying their role and interactions. As Skeldon put it:

> The disadvantage with the push-pull model is that ... it is never entirely clear how the various factors combine together to cause population movement. We are left with a list of factors, all of which can clearly contribute to migration, but which lack a framework to bring them together in an explanatory system ... The push–pull theory is but a platitude at best. (Skeldon, 1990: 125–6)

Push–pull models have difficulties explaining return migration and the simultaneous occurrence of emigration and immigration. They are also deterministic in assuming that demographic, environmental and economic factors 'cause' migration, without taking account of the role of other factors. For instance, population growth or environmental degradation do not necessarily result in migration, because 'population pressure' can also encourage innovation, (such as the introduction of irrigation, terraces or fertilizers), enabling farmers to maintain or even increase productivity (cf. Boserup, 1965). Scarcity and impoverishment can actually *impede* long-distance migration if people cannot afford the costs and risk of migrating (Foresight, 2011; Henry *et al.*, 2004). As we will argue in Chapter 9, this is also why ideas that environmental degradation due to climate change will lead to mass migration can be very misleading.

Environmental or demographic factors should not be isolated from other social, economic, political, and institutional factors affecting people's living standards. For instance, while Eastern European countries have very low fertility and low or negative population growth, they have experienced large-scale emigration. At the same time, the Gulf countries have combined high fertility with low emigration and very high immigration. Improved education and media exposure may increase feelings of relative deprivation, and may give rise to higher aspirations and, therefore, *increased* migration, without any change in local opportunities. People may also be so poor or repressed that they are deprived of the capability to migrate. This partly explains why most migration is *not* from the poorest to the wealthiest countries, as predicted by push–pull models.

Neoclassical and human capital theories

Neoclassical migration theory is also based on the assumption that social forces tend towards equilibrium. Rooted in modernization theory (Rostow, 1960), it sees migration as a constituent or intrinsic part of the whole development process, by which surplus labour in the rural sector supplies the workforce for the urban industrial economy (Lewis, 1954; Todaro, 1969: 139). Neoclassical theory sees migration as a function of geographical differences in the supply and demand for labour. The resulting wage differentials encourage workers to move from low-wage, labour-surplus regions to high-wage, labour-scarce regions. At the micro-level, neoclassical theory views migrants as individual, rational actors, who decide to move on the basis of a cost-benefit calculation, maximizing their income. Migrants are expected to go where they can be the most productive and can earn the highest wages. In this context, Borjas (1989; 1990) developed the idea of an international immigration market, in which potential migrants base their choice of destination on individual, cost-benefit calculations.

At the macro-level, neoclassical theory views migration as a process which optimizes the allocation of production factors. Migration will make labour less scarce at the destination and scarcer at the sending end. Capital is expected to move in the opposite direction. This process will eventually result in convergence between wages (Harris and Todaro, 1970; Lewis, 1954; Ranis and Fei, 1961; Schiff, 1994; Todaro and Maruszko, 1987). In the long run, migration should therefore help to make wages and conditions in sending and receiving countries more equal, lowering the incentives for migrating.

Neoclassical migration theory was advanced by Todaro (1969) and Harris and Todaro (1970) to explain rural–urban migration in developing countries but has also been applied to international migration (cf. Borjas, 1989; Todaro and Maruszko, 1987). Harris and Todaro elaborated a model to explain rural-to-urban labour migration in developing countries despite rising unemployment in cities. They argued that, in order to understand this phenomenon, it is necessary to extend the wage differential approach by adjusting the 'expected' rural–urban income differential for the probability of finding an urban job (Todaro, 1969: 138). As long as income differences remain high enough to outweigh the risk of becoming unemployed, migration would continue (Todaro, 1969: 147). Later, this Harris–Todaro model was refined (Bauer and Zimmermann, 1998: 97) to include other factors, such as the financial and social costs of migration.

An alternative, but complementary approach was proposed by Sjaastad (1962), who viewed migration as an investment that increases the productivity of 'human capital' – such as knowledge and skills. Human capital theory helps to explain the 'selectivity' of migration (the phenomenon that migrants tend to come from particularly sub-sections of populations), by pointing to the importance of the structure of labour markets, skills and income distributions in sending and receiving societies. People vary in terms of personal skills, knowledge, physical abilities, age and gender, so there will also be differences in the extent to which they can expect to gain from migrating. People decide to invest in migration, in the same way as they might invest in education, and they are expected to migrate if the additional lifetime benefits (primarily derived from higher wages) in the destination are greater than the costs incurred through migrating (Chiswick, 2000). Differences in such expected 'returns on investments' can partly explain why the young and the higher skilled tend to migrate more (Bauer and Zimmermann, 1998: 99).

Critique of neoclassical migration theory

Although neoclassical theory is valuable in understanding the selective nature of migration, it has been criticized because of the unrealistic nature of its central assumptions. The first assumption is that people are rational actors who maximize income or 'utility' based on a systematic comparison of lifetime costs and benefits of remaining at home or moving to an infinite range of potential destinations. The second, related assumption is that potential migrants have perfect knowledge of wage levels and employment opportunities in destination regions. The third assumption is that (capital, insurance, and other) markets are perfect and accessible for the poor. Because these assumptions are unrealistic, neoclassical theories are often incapable of explaining real-life migration patterns, particularly if migration occurs in conditions of poverty and high constraints.

Neither push–pull nor neoclassical theories have much room for *human agency*, which is the limited, but real ability of human beings to make independent choices and to change structural conditions. They portray human beings as socially isolated individuals who passively and uniformly react to external factors, while people's aspiration and capability to migrate actually depends on factors such as age, gender, knowledge, social contacts, preferences, and perceptions of the outside world. These theories generally do not consider how migrants perceive their world and relate to their kin, friends, and community members. As far as they deal with structural factors, such as government policies or recruitment practices, at all, neoclassical approaches see them as distortions of perfect markets which affect migration costs rather than as migration drivers *in their own right*.

Structural constraints such as limited access to money, connections and information have proven to be crucial factors in determining actual migration decisions. Historians, anthropologists, sociologists and geographers have shown that migrants' behaviour is strongly influenced by historical experiences and connections such as colonial ties, as well as by family and community dynamics (Portes and Böröcz, 1989). This explains why real-life migration patterns often deviate enormously from neoclassical predictions. Instead of a random process, migration is a strongly *patterned* process because people's individual choices are constrained by structural factors such as social stratification, market access, power inequalities as well as cultural repertoires affecting their preferences.

Historical–structural theories

An alternative explanation of migration was provided in the 1970s and 1980s by what came to be called the *historical–structural approach*. Historical–structuralists interpret migration as one of the many manifestations of capitalist penetration and the unequal terms of trade between developed and underdeveloped countries (Massey *et al.*, 1998: 34–41). While neoclassical theories focus on migrations, which are seen as largely 'voluntary', like that from Europe to the USA before 1914, or within Europe, historical–structural accounts tend to focus on large-scale recruitment of labour, whether of indentured Indian workers by the British for the railways in East Africa, Turks and Moroccans for the factories and mines of Germany, France, Belgium and the Netherlands, or Mexicans for the agribusiness of California. The availability and control of labour is both a legacy of colonialism and the result of war and international inequalities (cf. Cohen, 1987).

Historical–structuralists criticized neoclassical approaches by arguing that individuals do *not* have a free choice because they are fundamentally constrained by structural forces. Within this perspective, people are forced to move because traditional economic structures have been undermined as a result of their incorporation into the global political–economic system and concomitant processes such as mechanization of agriculture, concentration of landownership, increasing indebtedness and dispossession of smallholder peasants. Through these processes, rural populations become increasingly deprived of their traditional livelihoods, and these uprooted populations become part of the urban proletariat to the benefit of employers in urban areas and wealthy countries that rely on their cheap labour.

Historical–structural theory assumes that economic and political power is unequally distributed among wealthy and poor countries, that various classes and groups have highly unequal access to resources, and that capitalist expansion has the tendency to *reinforce* these inequalities. Within this context, historical–structural theory sees migration as a way of mobilizing cheap labour for capital, which primarily serves to boost profits and deprives origin areas of valuable labour and skills. In total opposition to neoclassical theory, migration is therefore seen as deepening uneven development, exploiting the resources of poor countries to make the rich even richer, leading to *increased* instead of less disequilibria (Castles and Kosack, 1973; Cohen, 1987; Sassen, 1988).

The intellectual roots of such analyses lay in Marxist political economy – especially in *dependency theory*, which became influential in Latin America in the 1960s. This theory saw the underdevelopment of 'Third World' (developing) countries as a *result* of the exploitation of their resources (including labour) through colonialism, while in the postcolonial period dependency was being perpetuated by unfair terms of trade with powerful developed economies (Baeck, 1993; Frank, 1969). Andre Gunder Frank (1966; 1969) argued that global capitalism contributed to the 'development of underdevelopment', so that migration is seen as one of the very *causes* of underdevelopment (see also Chapter 3 below).

In the 1970s and 1980s, a more comprehensive *world systems theory* developed (Amin, 1974; Wallerstein, 1974; 1980; 1984). It focused on the way less developed 'peripheral' regions have been incorporated into a world economy controlled by 'core' capitalist nations. The incorporation of the peripheries into the capitalist economy and concomitant penetration of multinational corporations accelerated rural change and deprived peasants and rural workers, leading to poverty, rural–urban migration, rapid urbanization and the growth of informal economies.

Dependency and world systems theory were at first mainly concerned with internal migration (Massey *et al.*, 1998: 35), but from the mid-1970s, as the key role of migrant workers in wealthy economies became more obvious, world systems theorists began to analyse international labour migration as one of the ways in which relations of domination were forged between the core economies of capitalism and its underdeveloped periphery. Migration was seen as reinforcing the effects of military hegemony and control of world trade and investment in keeping the 'Third World' dependent on the 'First'.

Globalization theory

Dependency and world systems theories can be seen as precursors of the globalization theories that emerged in the 1990s, which also stressed the need to understand migration as an intrinsic part of much broader relationships between societies. Although there are many definitions, one approach is to characterize globalization as 'the widening, deepening and speeding up of worldwide interconnectedness in all aspects of contemporary social life' (Held *et al.*, 1999: 2). A key indicator of globalization is a rapid increase in *cross-border flows* of all sorts, starting with finance and trade, but also including democratic values, cultural and media products, and – most important in our context – people.

Globalization is often portrayed primarily as an *economic process* associated with the upsurge in foreign direct investment (FDI) and the liberalization and deregulation in cross-border flows of capital, technology and services, as well as the emergence of a new international division of labour (Petras and Veltmayer, 2000: 2). The concept of a scientific and technological revolution, led by computerization, is central to the idea that globalization is both new and inevitable.

However, globalization is not just about technological and economic change: it is also a *political process*, conceived in normative or ideological terms. Critics of globalization argue that it is not a unique new world order, but rather the latest phase in the evolution of the capitalist world economy, which, since the fifteenth century, has penetrated into every corner of the globe (cf. Petras and Veltmayer, 2000). The current globalization paradigm emerged in the context of neoliberal strategies – initiated in the 1980s by the Reagan administration in the USA and the Thatcher government in the UK – designed to roll back the welfare states and decrease government intervention in labour and capital markets. The opening of markets and transfer of industrial production to low-wage economies – like the *maquiladoras* of Mexico or the offshore production areas of South-East Asia – weakened the political left and trade unions in industrial countries and shored up authoritarian regimes in the South (cf. Froebel *et al.*, 1980). Thus far from weakening the nation-state, globalization is seen as a new form of imperialism, designed to reinforce the power of core Northern states, their ruling classes and multinational corporations whose interests they serve (Hardt and Negri, 2000; Petras and Veltmayer, 2000; Weiss, 1997).

Globalization is therefore also seen as an ideology about how the world should be reshaped – summed up in the 'Washington consensus' on the importance of market liberalization, privatization and deregulation (Gore, 2000; Stiglitz, 2002: 67). International institutions, especially the International Monetary Fund (IMF), the World Bank and the World Trade Organization (WTO) are seen as key instruments to impose this new neo-liberal economic world order, for instance through 'structural adjustment programmes'.

Globalization has led to pervasive processes of *social transformation* all around the world. The idea of *transformation* implies a fundamental change in the way society is organized that goes beyond the continual, incremental processes of social change that are always at work (compare Polanyi, 1944; Polanyi, 2001). Globalization has uneven effects. Indeed, it can be seen as a process of inclusion of particular regions and social groups in world capitalist market relations, and of exclusion of others (Castells, 1996). Penetration of poor, weak economies by 'northern' investments and multinational corporations leads to economic restructuring, through which some groups of workers and producers are included in the new economy, while other groups find their livelihoods and workplaces destroyed and their qualifications devalued.

It is often thought that globalization has spurred migration as a consequence of revolutions in transport and communication technology. However, such improvements also increase the scope for trade, outsourcing of production, commuting and teleworking, and thus potentially replace some forms of migration (de Haas, 2009; Skeldon, 2012; Zelinsky, 1971). This may partly explain why the number of international migrants as a percentage of the world population has hardly changed since World War II (cf. Zlotnik, 1999), and why *non-migratory mobility* in the form of commuting, business trips and tourism has soared.

We need to seek the main migratory impacts of globalization in transformations in production structures, labour markets and social inequalities. Historically, such transformations have often started in agriculture. This was the case in nineteenth- and twentieth-century Europe, but also currently in many African, Asian and Latin American countries. For instance, in many developing countries, the post-1945 'green revolution' involved the introduction of new strains of rice and other crops, which gave higher yields, but required big investments in fertilizers, insecticides and mechanization. This often led to a concentration of ownership in the hands of richer farmers. Poorer farmers lost their livelihoods and agricultural workers their employment, and often migrated into burgeoning cities like São Paolo, Shanghai, Calcutta or Jakarta. Although urban growth offers better livelihoods for some, others scrape a living through irregular and insecure work in the informal sector. Such conditions are powerful motivations to seek better livelihoods abroad. However, international migration is selective: only those with the financial capital and education to cover the high costs of migrating and to be eligible for visas or with the social capital to link up with opportunities abroad can make the move.

Despite some claims about the erosion of the nation-state, the *national* dimension remains vital to understand migration. Nation-states remain the main location for policies on cross-border movements and non-migration policies such as citizenship, public order, labour markets, taxation, social welfare, health services and education, which have large, albeit predominantly indirect, effects on migration. States and interstate organizations (such as the EU) have set up differentiated migration regimes, which encourage the highly skilled to be mobile, while low-skilled workers and people fleeing persecution are often denied rights. Bauman argued that, in the globalized world, 'mobility has become the most powerful and most coveted stratifying factor', 'The riches are global, the misery is local' (Bauman, 1998: 9 and 74). Control of migration and differential treatment of various categories of migrants have become the basis for a new type of transnational class structure. While immigration regimes fail to curb migration as long as labour demand persists, they lead to an increase in irregular migration and the increased vulnerability of migrants for exploitation on labour markets (Castles *et al.*, 2012).

Segmented labour market theory

Historical–structural theories view the *control and exploitation of labour* by states and corporations as vital to the survival of the capitalist system. While neoclassical and other 'functionalist' theories reduce state regulation to one of the 'intermediate' factors influencing migration costs, historical–structural theories see states, multinational corporations and employment agencies as key causes and drivers of migration processes.

Dual (or segmented) labour market theory helps to understand how the demand for high- and low-skilled immigrant labour is structurally embedded in modern capitalist economies. Piore (1979) argued that international migration is caused by structural demand within advanced economies for both highly skilled workers and lower-skilled manual workers to carry out production tasks (e.g., assembly line work or garment manufacture) and to staff service enterprises (catering, cleaning, care, etc.). This challenges the popular idea that wealthy nations only need high-skilled migrant workers. Changes in the economic and labour market structure of receiving countries drive the demand for particular labour skills. While demands of manufacturing industries in Europe and North America were met by inflows of manual workers until the early 1970s, the growing importance of the tertiary (service) sector has triggered a demand for both highly qualified and low-skilled workers over recent decades.

Through outsourcing, international corporations can move the production process to cheap labour. However, particularly in the service sectors as well as in construction, not all work processes can be outsourced.

Domestic supply for low-skilled labour has dramatically decreased because many women have entered the formal labour market and youngsters continue education for much longer, which explains why employers have increasingly relied on low-skilled migrant labour.

Dual labour market theory shows the importance of institutional factors as well as race and gender in bringing about labour market segmentation. A division into primary and secondary labour markets emerges (Piore, 1979), while the most dynamic 'global cities' are marked by economic polarization – a growing gulf between the highly paid core workers in finance, management and research, and the poorly paid workers who service their needs (Sassen, 2001). The workers in the primary labour market are positively selected on the basis of human capital, but also often through membership of the majority ethnic group, male gender and, in the case of migrants, regular legal status. Conversely, those in the secondary labour market are disadvantaged by lack of education and vocational training, as well as by gender, race, minority status and irregular legal status. The growth of the secondary sector has been reinforced through neoliberal reforms and the concomitant deregularization of labour markets.

Segmented labour market theory is also useful to understand how migration can continue even under circumstances of high unemployment, and how the irregular status of migrants may actually serve employers' interests, as it creates a vulnerable and usually docile workforce. In this perspective, public racism, xenophobic discourses by politicians and restrictive immigration policies not only fulfil a symbolic function (such as to rally voters), but actually serve to facilitate and legitimize exploitation of migrants on the labour market by depriving them of their basic rights.

Critique of historical–structural approaches

Historical–structural theories stress structural constraints and the limited extent to which migrants are free to make choices. This has led to the criticism that some historical–structural views largely rule out human agency by depicting migrants as victims of global capitalism who have no choice but to migrate in order to survive. Such deterministic views often do no justice to the diversity of migration and the fact that many people do make active choices and succeed in significantly improving their livelihoods through migrating. It would be just as unrealistic to depict all migrants as passive victims of capitalism as it would be to depict them as entirely rational and free actors who constantly make cost-benefit calculations. Nevertheless, several historical–structural accounts have paid attention to migrants' agency by emphasizing the role of migrant workers in trade unions and industrial disputes (Castles and Kosack, 1973: see Chapter 4; Lever-Tracey and Quinlan, 1988).

With their assumption of capitalism uprooting stable peasant societies, historical–structural views are often based on the 'myth of the immobile peasant' (cf. Skeldon, 1997: 7–8) the implicit assumption that pre-modern societies consisted of isolated, stable, static, homogeneous peasant communities, in which migration was exceptional. Skeldon (1997: 32) pointed out that the whole idea that the Industrial Revolution uprooted peasants from their stable communities for the first time was based on a romanticized elitist view of peasant life. Historical research has shown that peasant societies were rather mobile (de Haan, 1999; Moch, 1992). Views that capitalism has 'uprooted' peasants and ruined egalitarian and self-sufficient communities also ignore that pre-modern societies were often characterized by high mortality, conflict, famines and epidemics as well as extreme inequalities, in which entire classes, castes, ethnic groups, women and slaves were often denied the most fundamental human freedoms.

For instance, Vecoli (1964) argued that the notion that southern Italian peasants (*contadini*) living in the USA were 'uprooted' from the Italian countryside was based on the myth of the Italian village as an harmonious social entity based on solidarity, communality, and neighbourliness. In reality, typical Italian peasants lived in dismal and highly exploitative conditions. For them, migration to the USA did provide unprecedented opportunities. In such cases, migration was an active choice and an opportunity to escape from the constraints put on them by 'traditional' societies. This makes it difficult to portray migrants unilaterally as victims of global capitalism.

Putting migrants first: agency, identity and the perpetuation of migration

Both neoclassical and historical–structural perspectives are too one-sided to understand adequately the complexity of migration. Neoclassical approaches neglect historical causes of movements and downplay the role of the state and structural constraints, while historical–structural approaches put too much emphasis on political and economic structures, and often see the interests of capital as all-determining. In fact, both approaches are deterministic in portraying human beings as rather passive. Since the 1980s, an increasing body of studies has highlighted the diversity of migration and stressed the role of migrants' agency by describing the various ways in which migrants try to actively and creatively overcome structural constraints such as immigration restrictions, social exclusion, racism and social insecurity. Most of these theories focus on the micro- and meso-level and are interested in what motivates people and social groups to migrate, how they perceive the world and how they shape their identity during the migration process. They also show how migrants' agency can create social structures, such as social networks, which can make migratory processes partly self-perpetuating.

New economics and household approaches

The *new economics of labour migration* (NELM) emerged as a critical response to neoclassical migration theory (Massey *et al.*, 1993). Stark (1978; 1991) argued that, in the context of migration in and from the developing world, migration decisions are often not made by isolated individuals, but usually by families or households. NELM highlights factors other than individual income maximization as influencing migration decision-making. First, this approach sees migration as *risk-sharing* behaviour of families or households. Such groups may decide that one or more of their members should migrate, not primarily to get higher wages, but to diversify income sources in order to spread and minimize income risks (Stark and Levhari, 1982), with the money remitted by migrants providing income insurance for households of origin. For instance, the addition of an extra source of income can make peasant households less vulnerable to environmental hazards such as droughts and floods (see also Chapter 9). This risk-spreading motive is a powerful explanation of the occurrence of migration *even in the absence of wage differentials.*

Second, NELM sees migration as a family or household strategy to provide resources for investment in economic activities, such as the family farm. NELM examines households in the context of the imperfect credit (capital) and risk (insurance) markets that prevail in most developing countries (Stark and Bloom, 1985; Stark and Levhari, 1982; Taylor, 1999; Taylor and Wyatt, 1996). Such markets are often not accessible for non-elite groups. In particular through remittances, households can overcome such market constraints by generating capital to invest in economic activities and improve their welfare (Stark, 1980). Third, NELM also sees migration as a response to *relative deprivation*, rather than *absolute poverty,* within migrant sending communities and societies. While the absolutely poor are often deprived of the capability to migrate over larger distances, the feeling of being less well-off than community members can be a powerful incentive to migrate in order to attain a higher socio-economic status.

With NELM, migration economists began to address questions of household composition traditionally posed by anthropologists and sociologists (Lucas and Stark, 1985: 901). NELM has strong parallels with so-called *livelihood approaches* which evolved from the late 1970s among geographers, anthropologists, and sociologists conducting micro-research in developing countries. They observed that the poor cannot be reduced to passive victims of global capitalist forces but exert human agency by trying to actively improve their livelihoods despite the difficult conditions they live in (Lieten and Nieuwenhuys, 1989).

This went along with the insight that – particularly in circumstances of uncertainty and economic hardship – people organize their livelihoods not individually but within wider social contexts. The household was often seen as the most appropriate unit of analysis, and migration as one of the main strategies households employ to diversify and secure their livelihoods

(McDowell and de Haan, 1997). Rather than a response to emergencies and crises, research showed that migration is often a pro-active, *deliberate* decision to improve livelihoods and to reduce fluctuations in rural family incomes by making them less dependent on climatic vagaries (de Haan *et al.*, 2000: 28; McDowell and de Haan, 1997: 18).

This shows that migration cannot be sufficiently explained by focusing on income differences alone. Household approaches show that factors such as social security, income risk and inequality, the chances of secure employment, access of the poor to credit, insurance and product markets, can also be important migration determinants. For instance, as Massey *et al.* (1987) point out, Mexican farmers may migrate to the USA because, even though they have sufficient land, they lack the capital to make it productive. Migration can then become a mechanism to maintain the productivity of their farms while working in the USA.

Household approaches seem particularly useful to explain migration in developing countries and also of disadvantaged social groups in wealthy countries, where the lack of social security and high income risks increase the importance of mutual help and risk sharing within families. They seem less relevant to explain migration of the high-skilled and the relatively well-off. Household models have been criticized because they tend to obscure intra-household inequalities and conflicts of interest along the lines of gender, generation, and age (de Haas and Fokkema, 2010). It is thus important not to lose sight of intra-household power struggles. For instance, instead of a move to help the family, migration can also be an individual strategy to escape from asphyxiating social control, abuse and oppression within families.

Network, transnationalism and migration systems theories

These approaches focus on the ties, networks and distinct identities that are forged between sending and receiving countries through constant flows of information, ideas, money, and goods. What unites these theories is that they analyse how migrants' *agency* creates social, economic and cultural structures at the micro- and meso-levels, and how this provides feedback mechanisms which tends to perpetuate migration processes. In this way, and through their individual and collective agency, migrants can actively challenge structural constraints such as poverty, social exclusion and government restrictions.

Migration network theory

Migration network theory explains how migrants create and maintain social ties with other migrants and with family and friends back home, and how this can lead to the emergence of social networks. Such networks are meso-level social structures which tend to facilitate further migration. Factors such as warfare, colonialism, conquest, occupation, military service and labour recruitment, as well as shared culture, language and geographical proximity often play a crucial role in the *initiation* of migration processes (Massey *et al.*, 1998; Skeldon, 1997). However, once a critical number of migrants have settled at the destination, other forces come into play. The choices made by pioneer migrants or recruiters influence the location choices of subsequent migrants. Research on Mexican migrants in the 1970s showed that 90 per cent of those surveyed had obtained legal residence in the USA through family and employer connections (Portes and Bach, 1985).

The idea that migration is a path-dependent process because interpersonal relations shape subsequent migration patterns is quite old (cf. Franz, 1939; Lee, 1966; Petersen, 1958). Earlier scholars used the concept of 'chain migration' (Kenny, 1962; Price, 1963). In the recent literature, the term 'network migration' has gradually replaced chain migration. Migrant networks can be defined as sets of interpersonal ties that connect migrants, former migrants, and non-migrants in origin and destination areas through bonds of kinship, friendship, and shared community origin (Massey *et al.*, 1993: 448). Migrant networks are a form of location-specific *social capital* that people draw upon to gain access to resources elsewhere (Massey *et al.*, 1998). Bourdieu (1979; translated in Bourdieu, 1985) defined social capital as 'the aggregate of the actual or potential resources which are linked to the possession of a *durable network of* more or less institutionalized relationships of mutual acquaintance and recognition – or in other words, *to membership in a group*' (Bourdieu, 1985: 248, emphasis in original French version). Migrant networks tend to decrease the economic, social and psychological costs of migration. Migration can therefore be conceptualized as a diffusion process, in which

> expanding networks cause the costs of movement to fall and the probability of migration to rise; these trends feed off one another, and over time migration spreads outward to encompass all segments of society. This feedback occurs because the networks are created by the act of migration itself ... Once the number of network connections in an origin area reach a critical level, migration becomes self-perpetuating because migration itself creates the social structure to sustain it (Massey, 1990: 8).

Thus, besides financial and human capital, social capital is a third resource affecting people's capability and aspiration to migrate. Already settled migrants often function as 'bridgeheads' (Böcker, 1994), reducing the risks and costs of subsequent migration and settlement by providing information, organizing travel, finding work and housing and assisting in adaptation to a new environment. Migrant groups develop their own social and economic infrastructure: places of worship, associations, shops, cafés, professionals (such as lawyers and doctors), and other services. The formation of a migrant community at one destination therefore increases the likelihood of more migration to the same place.

Such social processes embrace non-migrants too: employers stimulate formal and informal recruitment and seek to retain capable workers. Certain individuals, groups or institutions take on the role of mediating between migrants and political or economic institutions. Krissman (2005) therefore argued that studies of migration networks should include the employers that demand new immigrant workers, as well as the smugglers and other actors that respond to this demand. A 'migration industry' emerges, consisting of employers, recruitment organizations, lawyers, agents, smugglers and other intermediaries (see Chapter 10) who have a strong interest in the continuation of migration. The cost and risk-reducing role of migration networks together with the emergence of a migration industry have often frustrated governments in their efforts to control migration (Castles, 2004a).

Transnational and diaspora theories

In recent decades a new body of theories on *transnationalism* and *transnational communities* has emerged, which argues that globalization has increased the ability of migrants to maintain network ties over long distances. Although rapid improvements in technologies of transport and communication have not necessarily increased migration, they have made it easier for migrants to foster close links with their societies of origin through (mobile) telephone, (satellite) television and the internet, and to remit money through globalized banking systems or informal channels. This has increased the ability of migrants to foster multiple identities, to travel back and forth, to relate to people, to work and to do business and politics simultaneously in distant places.

Debates on transnationalism were stimulated by the work of Basch *et al.* (1994), who argued that 'deterritorialized nation-states' were emerging, with important consequences for national identity and international politics. Portes defines transnational activities as 'those that take place on a recurrent basis across national borders and that require a regular and significant commitment of time by participants' (Portes, 1999: 464). Many researchers argue that globalization has led to a rapid proliferation of transnational communities (Vertovec, 1999: 447). Transnationalism can extend face-to-face communities based on kinship, neighbourhoods or workplaces into far-flung virtual communities, which communicate at a distance. Portes and his collaborators emphasize the significance of transnational business communities, but also note the importance of political and cultural communities. They distinguish between *transnationalism from above* – activities 'conducted by powerful institutional actors, such as multinational corporations and states' – and *transnationalism from below* – activities 'that are the result of grass-roots initiatives by immigrants and their home country counterparts' (Portes *et al.*, 1999: 221).

A much older term for transnational communities is *diaspora*. This concept goes back to ancient Greece: it meant 'scattering' and referred to city-state colonization practices. Diaspora is often used for peoples displaced or dispersed by force (e.g. the Jews; African slaves in the New World), but it has also been applied to certain trading groups such as Greeks in Western Asia and Africa, the Lebanese, or the Arab traders who brought Islam to South-East Asia, as well as to labour migrants (Indians in the British Empire; Italians in the USA; Maghrebis and Turks in Europe) (Cohen, 1997; Safran, 1991; Van Hear, 1998).

Although the term diaspora is now popularly used to denote almost any migrant community, researchers stress that diaspora communities have particular features which set them apart from other migrant communities. Cohen (1997) established a useful list, which include: dispersal from an original homeland, often traumatically, to two or more foreign regions; the expansion from a homeland in pursuit of work or trade, or to further colonial ambitions; a collective memory, and myth about the homeland; a strong ethnic group consciousness sustained over a long time; and a sense of empathy and solidarity and the maintenance of 'transversal links' with co-ethnic members in other countries of settlement.

Glick-Schiller (1999: 203) suggests the use of the term *transmigrant* to identify people who participate in transnational communities based on migration. Levitt and Glick-Schiller (2004: 1003) state that 'the lives of increasing numbers of individuals can no longer be understood by looking only at what goes on within national boundaries'. However, there is a danger of overstating this point. First of all, it would be misleading to think that past migrations could be entirely understood within the context of the state. Although modern technology may have increased its scope, transnationalism as such is anything but a new social phenomenon, as the historical cases of the Jewish and Armenian diasporas show.

Guarnizo *et al.* (2003: 1212) argue that the growing use of the term transnational has been accompanied by 'mounting theoretical ambiguity and analytical confusion'. Based on their survey of transnational political engagement among three Latin American immigrant groups (Colombians, Dominicans and Salvadorians) in four US metropolitan areas, Guarnizo *et al.* (2003) concluded that the number of immigrants regularly involved in cross-border political activism is relatively small. Their study also found that transnational political activity is far from being 'deterritorialized' or undermining the nation-state, and that there was no contradiction between transnational activism and participation of immigrants in the political institutions of the USA (Guarnizo *et al.*, 2003: 1239). Transnational political activities are generally not the refuge of the marginalized, but often include migrants with relatively high social status. This is an important observation, because politicians and academics often argue that transnational links can undermine integration in the receiving country.

Inflationary use of such terms as 'diasporas' and 'transnational communities' should be avoided. The majority of migrants probably do not fit the transnational pattern. Temporary labour migrants who sojourn abroad for a few years, send back remittances, communicate with their family at home and visit them occasionally are not necessarily 'transmigrants'. Nor are permanent migrants who leave forever, and retain only loose contact with their homeland.

Migration systems theory and cumulative causation

While migration network theories focus on the role of social capital, and transnational and diaspora theory on the role of identity formation, *migration systems theory* looks at how migration is intrinsically linked to other forms of exchange, notably flows of goods, ideas, and money; and how this changes the initial conditions under which migration takes place, both in origin and destination societies. Migration systems theory therefore allows us to deepen our understanding of how migration is embedded in broader processes of social transformation and development.

The geographer Mabogunje (1970), who pioneered migration systems theory, focused on the role of flows of information and new ideas (such as on the 'good life' and consumption patterns) in shaping migration systems. He stressed the importance of feedback mechanisms, through which information about the migrants' reception and progress at the destination is transmitted back to the place of origin. Favourable information would then encourage further migration and lead to situations of 'almost organized migratory flows from particular villages to particular cities.... In many North-African cities, for instance, it is not uncommon for an entire district or craft occupation in a city to be dominated by permanent migrants from one or two villages' (Mabogunje, 1970: 13). Migration systems link people, families, and communities over space. This encourages migration along certain spatial pathways, and discourages it along others. 'The end result is a set of relatively stable exchanges; yielding an identifiable geographical structure that persists across space and time' (Mabogunje, 1970: 12).

Information is not only *instrumental* in facilitating migration by increasing people's migratory *capabilities*, but new ideas and exposure to new life styles conveyed by migrants may also change people's cultural repertoires, preference and *aspirations*. Levitt (1998) coined the term 'social remittances' to capture this flow of ideas, behavioural repertoires, identities and social capital from receiving to sending communities. The migration systems approach highlights the need to examine both ends of migration flows and to study all linkages between the places concerned – not just migration.

While Mabogunje focused on rural–urban migration within Africa, Kritz *et al.* (1992) and others applied this framework to international migration. International migration systems consist of countries – or rather places within different countries – that exchange relatively large numbers of migrants, and concomitant flows of goods, capital (remittances), ideas, and information (see also Fawcett, 1989; Gurak and Caces, 1992). Migration systems can be conceptualized at various levels of analysis. In the South Pacific, West Africa or the Southern Cone of Latin America we can identify regional migration systems (Kritz *et al.*, 1992). However, more distant regions may also be interlinked, such as the migration systems embracing the Caribbean, Western Europe and North America; or those linking Egypt, Sudan, Jordan, and Yemen to the Gulf countries.

The key implication of migration systems theory is that one form of exchange between countries or places, such as trade, is likely to engender other forms of exchange such as people, *in both directions.* Migratory movements generally arise from the existence of prior links between countries based on colonization, political influence, trade, investment or cultural ties. Thus migration from Mexico originated in the south-westward expansion of the USA in the nineteenth century and the recruitment of Mexican workers by US employers in the twentieth century (Portes and Rumbaut, 2006: 354–5). Both the Korean and the Vietnamese migrations to the USA were consequences of US military involvement (Sassen, 1988: 6–9). The migrations from India, Pakistan and Bangladesh to Britain are linked to the British colonial presence on the Indian sub-continent. But it also works the other way around: large-scale migration between two countries tends to boost trade, capital flows, investment, travel and tourism between the same countries. This questions the popular assumption that migration can be reduced by increasing trade with origin countries, as both processes can actively reinforce each other.

In a seminal paper, Massey (1990) reintroduced Myrdal's (1957) concept of *cumulative causation* to express 'the idea that migration induces changes in social and economic structures that make additional migration likely' (Massey, 1990: 4–5). We can conceptualize such broader migration-affected changes in the communities and societies, which is their turn affect migration, as 'contextual feedback' mechanisms (de Haas, 2010b). The money remitted by migrants is a good example of such a contextual feedback mechanism. Remittances can increase income inequality in origin communities, which can subsequently increase feelings of relative deprivation and, hence, migration aspirations among non-migrants. Relative deprivation and migration-facilitating network effects often reinforce each other, while remittances may also be used to pay for new journeys. While pioneer migrants are often *relatively* well-off, such feedback mechanisms can make migration more accessible for poorer groups and lead to a diffusion of migration within and across communities (de Haas, 2010b; Jones, 1998b; Massey, 1990).

If migration becomes strongly associated with success, migrating can give rise to a 'culture of migration' in which migration becomes the norm and staying home is associated with failure (Massey *et al.*, 1993). Such migration-affected cultural change can further strengthen migration aspirations (de Haas, 2010b). Other examples of contextual feedback include the formation of immigrant-specific economic niches in destination countries

Table 2.1 *Important feedback mechanisms perpetuating migration processes*

Level	Domain		
	Social	*Economic*	*Cultural*
Intermediate (migrant group)	Migrant networks; 'Migration industry'	Remittance-financed migration	Transfers of migration-related ideas and information
Origin community (contextual)	Social stratification and relative deprivation	Income distribution, productivity and employment	Social remittances; culture of migration
Destination community (contextual)	Patterns of clustering, integration and assimilation	Demand for migrant labour generated by clusters of migrant businesses and sectors where immigrants concentrate	Transnational identities, demand for marriage partners from origin countries

Source: Adapted from de Haas (2010b).

which create a specialized demand for co-ethnic workers (e.g., Chinese cooks, Kosher or Halal butchers, musicians and clergymen). Table 2.1 summarizes the main contextual feedback mechanisms which have been identified in the literature; it shows the large extent to which social, economic and cultural transformation processes associated to migration are interrelated.

Understanding migration system breakdown

Theories on migrant networks, transnationalism, diasporas and migration systems are useful to understand the crucial role of migrants' agency in creating meso-level social, cultural and economic structures which tend to make migration processes self-sustaining. However, these theories also have a number of weaknesses. First, they cannot explain why most initial migration by pioneers does *not* lead to the formation of migration networks and migration systems (de Haas, 2010b). Through their exclusive focus on migration-facilitating mechanisms, they also have difficulties explaining the stagnation and weakening of migration systems over time. This is linked to their circular logic, according to which migration goes on *ad infinitum* (Böcker, 1994; de Haas, 2010b; Massey *et al.*, 1998). They do not specify under what general conditions migrant networks and migration systems weaken, or 'spontaneous' (pioneer) migration to *new* destinations occurs (de Haas, 2010b).

In order to understand these matters better, it is important to develop a more critical understanding of the role of social capital in migration processes (de Haas, 2010b). Portes (1998) criticized one-sided, positive interpretations of social capital by arguing that strong social capital can also have negative implications, such as exclusion of non-group members and other outsiders, excessive social and material claims on successful group members and freedom-restricting pressures for social conformity (Portes, 1998). These 'downsides' of social capital can be applied to understand non-formation and breakdown of migration networks. Tight networks may be extremely useful in facilitating migration of group members, but tend to exclude outsiders. Particular ethnic, religious or class groups can monopolize the access to migration opportunities, and this can explain the limited diffusion of migration within and across communities. Recent studies on Somali refugees and Moroccan migrants showed that constant claims by family and friend in origin communities on support by migrants can lead to social distancing and a declining appetite for network assistance (de Haas, 2010b; Lindley, 2012).

This may eventually lead to the breakdown of networks. Migration assistance does not automatically happen. After all, migrants have limited resources and might not always see the arrival of more immigrants as beneficial, particularly if they are perceived to compete for jobs, housing and other resources. This can explain why settled migrants can evolve from being 'bridgeheads' to 'gatekeepers', who are hesitant or outright reluctant to assist prospective migrants (Böcker, 1994; Collyer, 2005).

Migration transition theories

The danger of focusing on meso-level theories which explain the continuation of migration is to lose sight of how *macro-level* political and economic factors continue to affect migration processes. These include the structure of labour markets, inequality, interstate relationships and migration policies. Such macro-level factors (for instance, a worsening of economic conditions in destination countries) can be another reason why networks break down or migration diverts to new destinations. This highlights the need to connect theories focusing on agency and identities of migrant and the continuation of migration with macro-level theories on the structural causes of migration.

Despite their many differences, functionalist and historical–structural theories share the underlying assumption that migration is primarily an outgrowth of geographical inequalities. This assumption, which also predominates in the media and policy circles, informs the common idea that migration is a 'problem to be solved', and that this can be achieved by reducing inequality and stimulating development in origin societies. However, empirical observations have shown that development often increases emigration (*cf.* de Haas, 2010c; Skeldon, 1997; Tapinos, 1990). This is partly because people need resources to migrate. It is no coincidence that important emigration countries such as Mexico, Morocco and the Philippines are not amongst the poorest; and that emigrants from the poorest countries often come from relatively well-off families. The poorest usually only migrate if forced to by conflict or disasters, and then mainly move over short distances, while the extremely poor are often deprived of the capabilities to move at all. For instance, when Hurricane Katrina hit New Orleans in 2005, many of the (car-less) poor got trapped in the city.

A further explanation why development can lead to increased migration is provided by *migration transition theories*. These theories see migration as an *intrinsic* part of broader processes of development, social transformation and globalization. Transition theories conceptualize how the migration patterns tend to changes over the course of development processes. In opposition to most other migration theories, they argue that development processes are generally associated with increasing levels of migration, but they also stress that this relation is complex and fundamentally *non-linear*. This idea was initially developed by Zelinsky (1971), who linked the several phases of the demographic transition (from high to low fertility and mortality) and concomitant development processes (which he called the 'vital transition') to distinctive phases in a 'mobility transition'. He argued that there has been a *general* expansion of individual mobility in modernizing societies, and that the specific character of migration processes changes over the course of this transition.

While pre-modern societies are characterized by limited circular migration, Zelinsky (1971) argued that all forms of internal and international mobility increase in early transitional societies due to population growth, a decline in rural employment and rapid economic and technological development. This was the case in early nineteenth-century Britain, just as it was in late nineteenth-century Japan, Korea in the 1970s and China in the 1980s and the 1990s. In late transitional societies, international emigration decreases with industrialization, declining population growth and rising wages, and falling rural-to-urban migration. As industrialization proceeds, labour supply declines and wage levels rise; as a result emigration falls and immigration increases (see Figure 2.1). In 'advanced societies' with low population growth, residential mobility, urban-to-urban migration and circular movements increase, and countries transform into net immigration countries.

Skeldon (1990; 1997) elaborated on and amended Zelinsky's seminal work and applied his model to actual patterns of migration at local, regional and global levels. The core of his argument was that

> there is a relationship between the level of economic development, state formation and the patterns of population mobility. Very generally, we can say that where these are high, an integrated migration system exists consisting of global and local movements, whereas where they are low the migration systems are not integrated and mainly local. (Skeldon, 1997: 52)

Figure 2.1   *The migration transition*

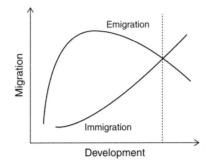

Source: de Haas (2010c).

Skeldon also emphasized the vital role of state formation, for instance through processes of colonization and decolonization, in forging social, economic and political connections which tend to boost migration. He distinguished five global migration and development 'tiers': the old and new core countries (e.g., Western Europe, North America, Japan, South Korea) characterized by immigration; the 'expanding core' (e.g., Eastern China, Southern Africa, Eastern Europe) with high immigration *and* emigration as well as rural-to-urban migration; the so-called 'labour frontier' (e.g., Mexico, Morocco, Egypt, Turkey), which experience high emigration and rural-to-urban migration; and the 'resource niche' (e.g., many sub-Saharan countries, parts of Central Asia), with variable, weaker forms of migration and low international migration (Skeldon, 1997).

Skeldon emphasized the functional relations between adjacent migration and development tiers. For instance, the 'labour frontier' countries generating migration to the USA and EU tend to be middle-income, moderately developed countries such as Mexico, Turkey and Morocco. In such countries, rapid economic and demographic transitions coincide with a temporary surplus of young, often unemployed, adults who are often prone to migrate. Such countries are also better connected to wealthy countries in terms of infrastructure and flows of information, capital, goods and tourists. This combination of factors is likely to foster the emergence of migration systems between such societies.

Historical and contemporary experiences support the idea that countries go through such migration transitions as an intrinsic part of broader development processes. In their important study on European migration to North America between 1850 and 1913, Hatton and Williamson (1998), found support for the idea that development initially boosts migration. The relatively developed North-western European nations initially dominated migration to North America, with lesser developed Eastern and Southern European nations following suit only later. They found that migration was driven by the mass arrival of cohorts of young workers on the labour market, increasing income, a structural shift of labour out of agriculture and the facilitating role of migrant networks (see also Hatton and Williamson, 1998; Massey, 2000a).

More recently a study based on World Bank data confirmed that countries with medium levels of development generally have the highest emigration rates (de Haas, 2010c). Studies of migration flows from southern Europe between 1962 and 1988 (Faini and Venturini, 1994) and from Asia and Africa to Germany from 1981 to 1995 (Vogler and Rotte, 2000) showed that development loosens financial restrictions on migration.

Historical experiences support the idea that beyond a certain level of development, societies transform from net emigration into net immigration countries (Massey, 2000b). The migration transition of Southern European countries such as Spain and Italy (since the 1970s), Asian countries such as Malaysia, Taiwan, and South Korea (see DeWind *et al.*, 2012), and currently Turkey, Brazil and China seem to fit within this model.

The concept of migration transitions should be distinguished from the theory of the *migration hump*. Transition theory focuses on *long-term* associations between development and migration. The idea of the migration hump primarily refers to *short- to medium-term* hikes in emigration in the wake of trade reforms and other economic shocks, such as the post-communist reforms in Central and Eastern Europe and Russia. Within the context of the North American Free Trade Agreement (NAFTA), Martin (1993) and Martin and Taylor (1996) argued that adjustment to new economic market conditions is never instantaneous. While the negative impacts of liberalization (particularly on unemployment in previously protected sectors such as agriculture) are often immediate; the expansion of production even in sectors *potentially* favoured by trade reforms always takes time (Martin and Taylor, 1996: 52). So, we can expect more short-term migration even if the long-term effects of free trade would be beneficial.

The danger of transition theories is to think that development and demographic change *automatically* leads to certain migration outcomes or that migration transitions are *inevitable* or *irreversible*. Whether countries will transform from emigration into immigration countries depends on many factors such as political reform needed to create the conditions for sustained social and economic development (Castles and Delgado Wise, 2008; Nayar, 1994). Unequal terms of trade, higher productivity and economics of scale in wealthy countries may harm the competitiveness of poorer countries. Under such circumstances, liberalization can lead to further concentration of economic activities in wealthy countries along with sustained migration of labourers to support them. This may result in a 'migration plateau' of sustained out-migration (Martin and Taylor, 1996), which seems to be the case in countries such as Morocco, Egypt, and the Philippines. Migration transitions may also be reversed, if countries transform from net immigration into net emigration countries, as happened in many South American nations over the second half of the twentieth century, and which seems to be happening in Ireland and southern Europe in response to the GEC.

Structure, capabilities, aspirations and migration

Transition theories argue that development *drives* migration and that developed societies generally experience higher levels of internal and international mobility. But transition theories are less strong in explaining why individual people would actually migrate more with increasing development. In order to reach a better understanding of how development processes affect people's propensity to migrate, it may be useful to conceptualize individual migration as a function of *capabilities* and *aspirations* to move (*cf.* Carling, 2002; de Haas, 2003).

Amartya Sen defined human *capability* as the ability of human beings to lead lives they have reason to value, and to enhance the substantive choices (or 'freedoms') they have (Sen, 1999). Sen's capabilities framework can be successfully applied to migration to develop a richer understanding of human mobility (de Haas, 2009). Income growth, improved education and access to information as well as improved communication and transport links increase people's capabilities to migrate over increasingly large distances. The same factors are also likely to increase awareness about lifestyles and opportunities elsewhere, which increase *aspirations* to migrate if local opportunities no longer match rising life aspirations. With development, both *capabilities* and *aspirations* to migrate can increase fast, explaining the paradox that 'take-off' development often coincides with 'take-off' emigration (de Haas, 2010c). While migration *capabilities* will further increase with development, we can expect that migration *aspirations* are likely to decrease beyond a certain level of development, particularly when opportunity gaps with destination countries decrease significantly.

There are other, structural reasons why migration and mobility in highly developed societies tend to remains high. Besides the expansion of transport and communication infrastructure, increasing levels of education and occupational specialization generate migration of people who seek to match their particular skills and preferences to particular jobs. The specialization and segmentation of labour markets typically increases with education and economic development, and migration therefore remains an essential mechanism to make demand meet supply both domestically and internationally. Obviously, this labour market complexity argument is related to several elements of *human capital theory*, *globalization theory* and *segmented labour market theory*. Such factors help to understand why high emigration and immigration remains a structural feature of developed countries and does not decrease as push–pull models, neoclassic and historical–structural theories predict.

Conceptualizing migration as a function of capabilities and aspirations to move within a given set of structural constraints may also help us to bridge certain distinctions between migration categories. An example is the dichotomy between 'forced' and 'voluntary' migration. Rather than applying such dichotomous classifications, it seems more appropriate to conceive of a continuum running from low to high constraints under which migration occurs, in which all migrants have agency and deal with structural constraints, although *to highly varying degrees* (see de Haas, 2009). From a capabilities perspective, the term 'forced migration' can therefore be an oxymoron, because people need to have a certain level of agency in order to move. In situations of violent conflict, economic crisis, environmental degradation or natural disaster, the most deprived are typically the ones 'forced to stay'. In the same vein, restrictive migration policies decreases capabilities to migrate among people who aspire to do so, and this can create situations of 'involuntary immobility' (Carling, 2002).

Conclusion

This chapter has reviewed the most important migration theories. One central argument is that we should conceptualize migration as an *intrinsic* part of broader processes of development, social transformation and globalization. Instead of reducing migration to more or less passive or predictable responses to poverty and spatial equilibria, as predicted by push–pull models, neoclassical and historical–structural theories, development processes tend to *drive* migration by increasing capabilities and aspirations to move.

A second argument is that migration processes have internal dynamics based on social networks and other contextual feedback mechanisms, which often give migration processes their own momentum. These internal dynamics are a testimony to the *agency* of migrants, leading to the formation of immigrant communities in receiving countries, the emergence of international networks and the rise of new transnational identities, which facilitate reverse flows of money (financial remittances) and ideas (social remittances) to origin societies. By lowering social, economic and psychological costs and risks, such feedback mechanisms can facilitate more migration between particular places and countries. In this way, migrants are frequently able to defy and circumvent government restrictions, often making migration notoriously difficult for governments to control.

A third argument is that the acknowledgment of migrants' agency should not obscure the real constraints migrants face. While theories on networks, transnationalism, diasporas and migration systems help us to understand how migrants can actively overcome structural constraints, they cannot explain why not all migrants are eager to help others to come, how migrants can behave like *gatekeepers* instead of *bridgeheads* and why networks decline. It would also be naïve to assume that migration continues irrespective of changes in macro-level conditions such as political transformation, economic growth or labour market dynamics. Examination of historical and contemporary migrations (see Chapters 4–8) shows that sending and receiving states continue to play a major role in initiating and shaping movements.

In their important survey of migration theories, Massey *et al.* (1993) argue that the various theories operate at different levels of analysis and focus on different aspects of migration, but that they all provide important insights into migration. However, this does not mean that all theories can be combined. For instance, neoclassical and historical–structural and neo-Marxist theories are based on different assumptions on what causes migration. However, insights from both theories can be useful to understand particular manifestations of migration occurring in particular contexts or at different levels of analysis.

For instance, while neoclassical theories seem useful to understand much migration of the highly educated within and among wealthy countries, historical–structural theory and the new economics of labour migration and livelihood approaches seem useful to understand migration taking place under conditions of poverty and oppression. It may be possible to perceive irregular migration between Mexico and the USA or between Morocco and the EU as part of a labour exploitation mechanism on the macro-structural level which mainly benefits employers, while at the same time acknowledging that, for the migrants themselves, it can be a rational strategy as remittances may enable them to significantly improve the living conditions of their families. This example shows that there is a danger in subscribing to one particular train of theoretical thought when we try to understand migration.

It is regularly argued that attempts at theorizing migration are futile because migration is such a diverse and complex process. This is not a very convincing argument, because, after all, almost all social processes are complex by nature. Complexity does not imply that there are no patterns and that no regularities can be discerned. One can even argue that migration is actually a strongly patterned process, with most people migrating along a select number of specific spatial pathways as a result of networks and other migration system dynamics.

The differing theoretical approaches lead to different ideas for migration policy. Neoclassical economists sometimes advocate 'open borders' and 'freedom of migration', believing that this will increase efficiency and lead to a global equalization of wage levels and opportunities in the long run. However, critics argue that immigration mainly serves the interest of capital by depressing wage levels – especially for low-skilled work – and undermining the bargaining power of trade unions. This is why left-wing parties and trade unions have historically opposed recruitment of guest workers and other low-skilled workers, or demanded safeguards, such as equal pay and conditions so as not to undermine the position of local workers. Historical–structural perspectives also argue that migration deprives poor countries of vital human resources through the *brain drain* (see Chapter 3). This is why, until recently, many developing countries have tried to limit or prevent emigration.

The new economics and livelihood approaches explain migration occurring within and from developing countries due to economic insecurity, inequality (relative deprivation) and market failure. Within this perspective, policies concerned merely with controlling exit or entry are unlikely to succeed, but origin country governments could perhaps affect migration indirectly through progressive taxation and other policies decreasing income inequality and increasing the access of the poor to insurance, credit, public health, education, state pensions and other social benefits (see also Massey *et al.*, 1998: 27). As Kureková (2011) has shown for post-communist migration from Central and Eastern Europe, social spending and increased social security may reduce forms of migration that are primarily driven by inequality and livelihood insecurity.

Segmented labour market theory focuses on the demand-side, emphasizing that migration is driven by a demand for immigrant labour that is structurally embedded in modern capitalist economies. Strong employer demand for cheap migrant labour that is easy to control and exploit (such as irregular migrants) creates black markets for migrant labour and opportunities for smugglers and recruitment agents, which, in combination with the migration-facilitating role of networks, is likely to undermine restrictive immigration policies. Governments could counteract undocumented migration mainly through measures to increase labour market regulation, improve workers' protection and to remove incentives for employing irregular or temporary workers. However, this could render unviable important sectors of business, such as agriculture, food processing and labour-intensive services by pushing up labour costs.

While states do often play a key role in initiating migration processes, network, migration systems and segmented labour markets theories help to explain why migration processes tend to gain their own momentum, often frustrating states' efforts to control migration (see Chapter 10). This seems particularly true for liberal democracies, which have limited legal means to control migration, in particular of family migrants. World systems, globalization and, particularly, transition theories argue that social transformation and development processes drive migration, and that it is very difficult to significantly affect long-term migration trends, unless states and multinational organizations introduce rather radical changes in their political and economic systems. The key lesson is perhaps that while states are in many ways shaping migration processes, this influence is primarily felt through non-migration policies.

Guide to further reading

Some valuable overviews of migration theory are available: Massey *et al.* (1993; 1998) provide an important overview and discussion of most theories, while Brettell and Hollifield (2007) brings together contributions of several social scientific disciplines. Skeldon (1997) is an excellent introduction into the relation between migration and broader development processes. Important collections on migration theory can be found in special issues of the *Journal of Ethnic and Migration Studies* (Castles *et al.*, 2010) and *Population, Space and Place* (Smith and King, 2012), and the *International Migration Review*.

Sassen (1988) gives an original perspective on the political economy of migration, while Borjas (1990; 2001) presents the neoclassical view. Kritz *et al.* (1992) is an excellent collection on migration systems theory. Good introductions to transnational communities include Basch *et al.* (1994), Cohen (1997), Portes *et al.* (1999), Vertovec (1999; 2004) and Faist (2000). Van Hear (1998) discusses transnational theory from the perspective of refugee movements. Amongst the many works on globalization and social transformation, the following are useful as introductions: Castells (1996; 1997; 1998), Held *et al.* (1999), Bauman (1998), Stiglitz (2002) and Cohen and Kennedy (2000).

Chapter 3

How Migration Transforms Societies

Migration raises high hopes and deep fears: hopes for the migrants themselves, for whom migration often embodies the promise of a better future. At the same time, migration can be a dangerous undertaking, and every year thousands die in attempts to cross borders. Family and friends are often left behind in uncertainty. If a migrant fails to find a job or is expelled, it can mean the loss of all family savings. However, if successful, migration can mean a stable source of family income, decent housing, the ability to cure an illness, resources to set up a business and the opportunity for children to study.

In receiving societies, migration is equally met with ambiguity. Settler societies, nascent empires and bustling economies have generally welcomed immigrants, as they fill labour shortages, boost population growth, and stimulate businesses and trade. However, particularly in times of economic crisis and conflict, immigrants are often the first to be blamed for problems, and face discrimination, racism and sometimes violence. This particularly applies to migrants who look, behave or believe differently than majority populations.

While Chapter 2 analysed how larger processes of development, social transformation and globalization affect migration, this chapter turns the analysis around and discusses how migration transforms societies of destination and origin. The first half focuses on processes of migrant settlement and incorporation, the formation of ethnic communities and minorities, and how this process transforms receiving societies. (However, the effects of immigration on labour forces and the economy are discussed in Chapter 11.) The second half of Chapter 3 focuses on the impacts of migration on development in origin societies. The two topics need to be linked with each other, because the relation between migration and broader change is a reciprocal one. Some of the theories discussed in Chapter 2 are therefore relevant here too.

Migration researchers have traditionally focused on the implications of migration for receiving societies. This 'receiving country bias' is unfortunate, because the impacts on origin societies are equally, if not more profound (Portes, 2010). There is also a need to shift away from views in which Western (or 'Northern') countries are automatically defined as receiving societies, and developing 'Southern' countries as sending or 'origin' countries. In reality, many countries both receive and send significant numbers of migrants. It is important to realize that many other countries, such as Argentina, Venezuela, Brazil, South Africa, Côte d'Ivoire, Nigeria, Libya, Egypt, Yemen, Turkey, India, Russia, Malaysia, Singapore, Thailand and the entire Gulf region host significant immigrant communities and also deal with issues of settlement and ethnic minority and community formation.

The transformation of receiving societies: from migration to settlement

Although each migratory movement has its own specific historical patterns, it is possible to generalize on the social dynamics of the migratory process. It is necessary, however, to distinguish between migration that is primarily economically motivated and forced migration. Most economic migrations start with young, economically active people. They are often 'target-earners', who want to save enough in a higher-wage economy to improve conditions at home, by buying land, building a house, setting up a business, or paying for education or dowries. After a period in the destination country, some of these migrants return home, but others prolong their stay, or return and then remigrate. The latter pattern is known as 'circular migration'. As time goes on, many erstwhile temporary migrants get their spouses to join them, or find partners in the new country. With the birth of children, settlement generally takes on a more permanent character.

It is these powerful internal dynamics of migration processes that often confound the expectations of the migrants and undermines the objectives of policy-makers (Böhning, 1984; Castles, 2004a). In many migrations, there is no initial intention of family reunion and permanent settlement. However, when governments try to stop flows they may find that the movement has become self-sustaining through the network and migration system dynamics discussed in Chapter 2. What started off as a temporary labour migration is often transformed into family reunion, undocumented migration or asylum-seeker flows. This is a result of the maturing of the migratory movement and of the migrants themselves as they pass through the life cycle.

The failure of policy-makers and analysts to see international migration as a dynamic social process is at the root of many political and social problems. The source of this failure is often a one-sided focus on neoclassical economic and push–pull models, which see migration as an individual response to market factors. This has led to the belief that migration can be turned on and off like a tap, by changing policy settings which influence the costs and benefits of mobility for migrants. But migration may continue due to social factors, even when the economic factors which initiated the movement have been completely transformed.

Such developments are illustrated by the Western European experience of settlement following the 'guest-worker'-type migration from 1945 to 1973. Similar outcomes arose from movements from former colonies to the UK, France and the Netherlands, and migration from Europe, Latin America and Asia to the USA, Canada and Australia (see Chapters 5 and 6).

One lesson of the last half-century is that it is very difficult for countries with democratic rights and strong legal systems to prevent migration turning into settlement. The situation is somewhat different in labour-recruiting countries which lack effective human rights guarantees, such as the Gulf states or some East and South-East Asian countries, where restrictions may hinder family reunion and settlement. But even these countries find it increasingly difficult to prevent long-term settlement (see Thiollet, 2010, and Chapters 7 and 8).

The initial migration dynamics are somewhat different in the case of refugees and asylum seekers, but the outcomes may be similar. Forced migrants primarily leave their countries because persecution, human rights abuse or generalized violence made life there unsustainable. Most remain in the neighbouring countries of first asylum – which are usually poor and often politically unstable themselves. Onward migration to countries which offer better opportunities is only possible for a small minority – mainly those with financial resources, knowledge and social networks in destination countries (Zolberg and Benda, 2001). Onward migration is motivated by the imperative of flight from violence, but also by the hope of building a better life elsewhere. Attempts by policy-makers to make clear distinctions between economic and forced migrants are often hampered by these 'mixed motivations'.

The formation of ethnic minorities

The long-term effects of immigration on society emerge particularly in the later stages of the migratory process when migrants settle more permanently. Outcomes can be very different, depending on migrants' characteristics and the actions of the receiving state and society. At one extreme, openness to settlement, granting of citizenship and gradual acceptance of cultural diversity may allow the formation of *ethnic communities*, which are seen as part of a multicultural society. At the other extreme, denial of the reality of settlement, refusal of citizenship and rights to settlers, and rejection of cultural diversity may lead to formation of *ethnic minorities*, whose presence is widely regarded as undesirable.

Critics of immigration portray ethnic minorities as a threat to economic well-being, public order and national identity. Yet these ethnic minorities may in fact be the creation of the very people who fear them. Ethnic minorities may be defined as groups which

(a)   have been assigned a subordinate position in society by dominant groups on the basis of socially constructed markers of phenotype (that is, physical appearance or race), origins or culture;

(b)   have some degree of collective consciousness (or feeling of being a community) based on a belief in shared language, traditions, religion, history and experiences.

An ethnic minority is therefore a product of both 'other-definition' and of 'self-definition'. *Other-definition* means ascription of undesirable characteristics and assignment to inferior social positions by dominant groups. *Self-definition* refers to the consciousness of group members of belonging together on the basis of shared cultural and social characteristics. The relative strength of these processes varies. Some minorities are mainly constructed through processes of exclusion (which may be referred to as *racism* or *xenophobia*) by the majority or dominant group. Others are mainly constituted on the basis of cultural and historical consciousness (or *ethnic identity*) among their members. The concept of the ethnic minority always implies some degree of marginalization or exclusion.

Ethnicity

In popular usage, ethnicity is usually seen as an attribute of minority groups, but most social scientists argue that everybody has ethnicity, defined as a sense of group belonging based on ideas of common origins, history, culture, experience and values (Fishman, 1985: 4; Smith, 1986: 27). These ideas change only slowly, which gives ethnicity durability over generations and even centuries. But that does not mean that ethnic consciousness and culture within a group are homogeneous and static. Rather, ethnicity is based on the linguistic and cultural practices through which a sense of collective identity is 'produced and transmitted from generation to generation, *and is changed in the process*' (Cohen and Bains, 1988: 24–5, emphasis in original).

Scholars differ in their explanations of the origins of ethnicity; one can distinguish primordialist, situational or instrumental approaches. Geertz, for example, sees ethnicity as a *primordial attachment*, which results 'from being born into a particular religious community, speaking a particular language, or even a dialect of a language and following particular social practices. These congruities of blood, speech, custom and so on, are seen to have an ineffable, and at times, overpowering coerciveness in and of themselves' (Geertz, 1963, quoted from Rex, 1986: 26–7). In this approach, ethnicity is not a matter of choice; it is pre-social, almost instinctual, something one is born into.

Other anthropologists use a concept of *situational ethnicity*. Members of a specific group decide to 'invoke' ethnicity as a criterion for self-identification. This explains the variability of ethnic boundaries at different times. The markers chosen for the boundaries are also variable, generally emphasizing cultural characteristics, such as language, shared history, customs and religion, but sometimes including physical characteristics (Wallman, 1986: 229). In this view there is no essential difference between the drawing of boundaries on the basis of cultural difference or of phenotypical difference (or race).

Some sociologists reject the concept of ethnicity altogether, seeing it as 'myth' or 'nostalgia', which cannot survive against the rational forces of economic and social integration in large-scale industrial societies (Steinberg, 1981). Yet it is hard to ignore the continued significance of ethnic mobilization. Studies of the 'ethnic revival' of the 1960s by the US sociologists Glazer and Moynihan (1975) and Bell (1975) emphasized the instrumental role of ethnic identification: phenotypical and cultural characteristics were used to strengthen group solidarity, in order to struggle for market advantages, or to make claims for increased allocation of resources by the state. This notion of ethnic mobilization as *instrumental* behaviour has its roots in Max Weber's concept of 'social closure', whereby a status group establishes rules and practices to exclude others, in order to gain a competitive advantage (Weber, 1968: 342). This does not imply that markers, such as skin colour, language, religion, shared history and customs, are not real, but rather that the decision to use them to define an ethnic group is a 'strategic choice'.

Whether ethnicity is seen as 'primordial', 'situational' or 'instrumental', the key point is that ethnicity leads to identification with a specific group, but its visible markers – phenotype, language, culture, customs, religion, behaviour – may also be used as criteria for exclusion by other groups. Ethnicity only takes on social and political meaning when it is linked to processes of boundary-drawing between dominant groups and minorities. Becoming an ethnic minority is not an automatic or necessary result of immigration, but rather the consequence of marginalization processes.

Race and racism

The visible markers of a phenotype (skin colour, features, hair colour, and so on) correspond to what is popularly understood as *race*. Most scientists agree that classification of humans into races is unsound, since genetic variance within any one population is greater than differences between groups. Race can therefore be seen as a social construct produced by racism (Miles, 1989). *Racism* may be defined as the process whereby social groups categorize other groups as different or inferior, on the basis of phenotypical or cultural markers. This process involves the use of economic, social or political power, and generally has the purpose of legitimating exploitation or exclusion of the group so defined.

The use of the term 'race' varies from country to country. In Anglo-American usage, race and racism historically referred to differences of skin colour, but have now been extended to include all types of 'visible minority' (the latter originally a Canadian term), including those distinguished by cultural markers like clothing (e.g. Islamic head scarves). In continental Europe, race and racism have been used for colonial and post-colonial situations, as well as with regard to anti-semitism, but generally not for negative attitudes towards recent immigrants – here the terms 'xenophobia', 'hostility to foreigners' or, most recently, 'Islamophobia' are used. In non-European destination countries, race and racism are often applied to attitudes towards visibly different groups whatever the skin colour of both local and migrant populations. In view of this confusion, we tend to use terms like race, racism, xenophobia, discrimination and exclusion according to the practices of the places being discussed.

In any case, the debate over the label seems sterile: it is more important to understand the phenomenon and its causes. Racism (or xenophobia) towards certain migrant (and non-migrant) groups is to be found in virtually all countries. Racism means making predictions about people's character, abilities or behaviour on the basis of socially constructed markers of difference. The power of the dominant group is sustained by developing structures (such as laws, policies and administrative practices) that exclude or discriminate against the dominated group. This aspect of racism is generally known as *institutional or structural racism*. Racist attitudes and discriminatory behaviour on the part of members of the dominant group are referred to as *informal racism*. Some social scientists now use the term *racialization* to refer to public discourses which imply that a range of social or political problems are a 'natural' consequence of certain ascribed physical or cultural characteristics of minority groups (Murji and Solomos, 2005).

The historical background for racism in Western Europe and in post-colonial settler societies (like the USA or Australia) lies in traditions, ideologies and cultural practices, which have developed through ethnic conflicts associated with nation-building and colonial expansion (compare Miles, 1989). An important reason for the persistence of racism lies in current fundamental social transformations: economic restructuring, deregulation and privatization have been experienced by many sections of the population as a threat to their livelihoods and social conditions. Since new ethnic minorities have emerged at the same time, their presence is often linked to the perceived threat. These shifts also question the dominance of previously privileged groups, leading to a reactive reassertion of nationalism and its symbols (Hage, 1998). The tendency has been to perceive the newcomers as the cause of the threatening changes: an interpretation eagerly encouraged by the extreme right, but also by many mainstream politicians and parties, often leading to more restrictive policies (Davis, 2012).

Since the events of 11 September 2001 and the proclamation of a 'global war on terror', racism has been oriented increasingly towards both Muslim minorities within Western countries and Muslim countries deemed to threaten Western security. Moreover, the neoliberal economic policies which threaten disadvantaged sections of the population have also weakened the labour movement and working-class cultures, which might otherwise have provided some measure of protection. The decline of working-class parties and trade unions and the erosion of local community networks may have created the social space for racism to become more virulent (Vasta and Castles, 1996; Wieviorka, 1995).

Gender and migration

Racial and ethnic divisions are crucial dimensions of social differentiation affecting migrants. Others include gender, social class, position in the life cycle, generation, location and legal status. None of these aspects of social differentiation are reducible to any other, yet they constantly cross-cut and interact, affecting life-chances, lifestyles, culture and social conscious-ness. Immigrant groups and ethnic minorities are just as heterogeneous as the rest of the population.

Since the nineteenth century, a large proportion of migrant workers have been female. As Phizacklea (1983) pointed out, it was particularly easy to ascribe inferiority to women migrant workers, just because their primary roles in patriarchal societies were defined as wife and mother, dependent on a male breadwinner. They could therefore be paid lower wages and con-trolled more easily than men. Today, migrant women still tend to be over-represented in the least desirable occupations, such as repetitive factory work and lower-skilled positions in the personal care and other services sectors, although there has also been increased mobility into white-collar jobs. Complex patterns of division of labour on ethnic and gender lines have developed. How gender affects work experiences of migrant women will be discussed in Chapter 11, but it would be mistaken to reduce the experi-ence of migrant women to the arena of work. Many women do migrate for other reasons: as refugees, for education, for marriage or through family reunion. These types of migration are examined in other chapters. Of par-ticular importance is the current growth of marriage migration in Asia, which frequently leads to situations of dependency and exploitation for women from poorer countries (see Chapter 7).

The role of gender in ethnic closure is evident in immigration rules which still often treat men as the principal immigrants while women and children are mere 'dependants'. Britain used gender-specific measures to limit the growth of the black population. In the 1970s, women from the Indian subcontinent coming to join husbands or fiancés were subjected to 'virginity tests' at Heathrow Airport. The authorities also sought to prevent Afro-Caribbean and Asian women from bringing in husbands, on the grounds that the 'natural place of residence' of the family was the abode of the husband (Klug, 1989: 27–9). Today, in many countries, women who enter as dependants or marriage migrants do not have an entitlement to residence in their own right and may face deportation if they get divorced.

Anthias and Yuval-Davis (1989) analyse links between gender rela-tions and the construction of the nation and the ethnic community. Women are not only the biological reproducers of an ethnic group, but also the 'cultural carriers' who have the key role in passing on the language and cultural symbols to the young. Racism, sexism and class domination are three specific forms of 'social normalization and exclusion' which have developed in close relationship to each other (Balibar, 1991: 49). Racism and sexism both involve predicting social behaviour on the basis of allegedly fixed biological or cultural characteristics. Essed argued that racism and sexism 'narrowly intertwine and combine under certain conditions into one, hybrid phenomenon. Therefore it is useful to speak of *gendered racism* to refer to the racist oppression of black women as structured by racist and ethnicist perceptions of gender roles' (Essed, 1991: 31, emphasis in original).

However, gender can also become a focus for migrant women's resistance to discrimination (Vasta, 1993). Some feminist studies suggest a more positive interpretation of female migration: it can reinforce exploitation of women, but can also help women from patriarchal societies to gain more control over their own lives (Phizacklea, 1998). This frequently makes women reluctant to return to their countries of origin because this could involve losing new-won rights and freedoms (de Haas and Fokkema, 2010; King *et al.*, 2006: 250–1).

Other forms of social differentiation: life cycle, location, legal status

The stages of the life cycle – childhood, youth, maturity, middle age, old age – also affect economic and social positions, culture and consciousness (King *et al.*, 2006). Typically it is young people of migrant background who are most affected by youth unemployment, as the experience of the global economic crisis (GEC) showed. Older migrants are often laid off due to changes in technology, especially because they are frequently concentrated in the branches most affected. They may not appear in unemployment statistics, as ill health or lack of suitable work opportunities may cause them to withdraw from the workforce.

There is often a gulf between the experiences of the migrant generation and those of their children, who have grown up and gone to school in the new country. Many young people are aware of the contradiction between the ideologies of equal opportunity and the reality of discrimination and racism in their daily lives. This consciousness can lead to the emergence of counter-cultures and political radicalization. In turn, ethnic minority youth may be perceived by the majority population as a 'social time bomb' or a threat to public order (see Chapters 12 and 13).

Location becomes an issue when migrants and their children become concentrated in areas of disadvantaged housing, whether in run-down inner city areas or peripheral housing estates. Such areas often lack jobs, and have poor amenities and transport. Job applicants have reported discrimination by prospective employers when they give addresses of disadvantaged areas. Conflicts with the police and riots by minority youth in France, Britain and other countries have originated in such areas of marginality.

Legal status has become one of the key factors of differentiation. In many countries a hierarchy of vulnerability can be observed: irregular migrants get the worst jobs and conditions; migrants with temporary residence permits are also susceptible to pressure from employers and officials; migrants with secure residence status are better off, but may experience discrimination and do not always have access to all social services. The liberal ideal of a society based on fair competition and equal opportunity is far from the reality experienced by many migrants and members of ethnic minorities.

Culture, identity and community

In the context of globalization, culture, identity and community often serve as a focus of resistance to centralizing and homogenizing forces (Castells, 1997). As already outlined, cultural difference serves as a marker for ethnic boundaries. Ethnic cultures play a central role in community formation: when ethnic groups cluster together, they establish their own neighbourhoods, marked by distinctive use of private and public spaces. In turn, ethnic neighbourhoods are perceived by some members of the majority group as confirmation of their fears of a 'foreign takeover'. They symbolize a perceived threat to the dominant culture and national identity. Dominant groups may see migrant cultures as static and regressive. Linguistic and cultural maintenance is taken as proof of backwardness and inability to come to terms with an advanced industrial society. Those who do not assimilate 'have only themselves to blame' for their marginalized position.

For ethnic minorities, culture plays a key role as a source of identity and as a focus for resistance to exclusion and discrimination. Identification with the culture of origin helps people maintain self-esteem in a situation where their capabilities and experience are undermined. But a static culture cannot fulfil this task, for it does not provide orientation in a new and sometimes rather hostile environment. Migrant or minority cultures are constantly changing and taking on new aspects according to the needs and experience of the groups concerned and their interaction with the social environment (Schierup and Alund, 1987; Vasta *et al.*, 1992). An apparent regression, for instance to religious fundamentalism, may be a reaction to a form of modernization that has been experienced as discriminatory, exploitative and destructive of identity.

It is therefore necessary to understand the development of ethnic cultures, the stabilization of personal and group identities, and the formation of ethnic communities as facets of a single process. This process is not self-contained: it depends on constant interaction with the state and the various institutions and groups in the country of immigration, as well as with the society of the country of origin. Immigrants and their descendants do not have a static, closed and homogeneous ethnic identity, but rather dynamic *multiple or hybrid identities*, influenced by a variety of cultural, social and other factors.

Culture is becoming increasingly politicized in most countries of immigration. As ideas of racial or ethnic superiority lose their ideological strength, exclusionary practices against minorities increasingly focus on issues of cultural difference. At the same time, the politics of minority resistance crystallize more and more around cultural symbols – the political significance given to Islamic dress in France, Britain and the Netherlands and other immigration countries illustrates this trend.

State and nation

Large-scale migrations and growing diversity may have important effects on political institutions and national identity. In the contemporary world, the approximately 200 nation-states are the predominant form of political organization. They derive their legitimacy from the claims of providing security and order and representing the aspirations of their people (or citizens). The latter implies two further claims: that there is an underlying cultural consensus which allows agreement on the values or interests of the people, and that there is a democratic process for the will of the citizens to be expressed. Such claims are often dubious, for most countries are marked by diversity, based on ethnicity, class and other cleavages, while only a minority of societies consistently use democratic mechanisms to resolve value and interest conflicts. Nonetheless, the democratic nation-state has become a global norm, and practices of accountable government and the rule of law are gaining ground (Giddens, 2002; Habermas and Pensky, 2001; Shaw, 2000).

Immigration of culturally diverse people presents nation-states with a dilemma: incorporation of the newcomers as citizens may undermine myths of cultural homogeneity; but failure to incorporate them may lead to divided societies, marked by severe inequality and conflict. Pre-modern states based their authority on the absolute power of a monarch over a specific territory. There was no concept of a national culture which transcended the gulf between aristocratic rulers and peasants. By contrast, the modern nation-state implies a close link between cultural belonging and political identity (Castles and Davidson, 2000).

A *state* can be defined as, '... a legal and political organization, with the power to require obedience and loyalty from its citizens' (Seton-Watson, 1977: 1). In this traditional view, the state regulates political, economic and social relations in a bounded territory. Most modern nation-states are formally defined by a constitution and laws, according to which all power derives from the people (or nation). It is therefore vital to define who belongs to the people. Membership is largely marked by the status of citizenship, which lays down rights and duties. Non-citizens are excluded from at least some of these. Citizenship is the essential link between state and nation, and obtaining citizenship is therefore of central importance for newcomers to a country.

A *nation* by contrast may be defined as 'a community of people, whose members are bound together by a sense of solidarity, a common culture, a national consciousness' (Seton-Watson, 1977: 1). Such subjective phenomena are difficult to measure, and it is not clear how a nation differs from an ethnic group, which is defined in a similar way (see above). Anderson provides an answer with his concept of the nation: 'it is an imagined political community – and imagined as both inherently limited and sovereign' (Anderson, 1983: 15). The implication is that an ethnic group that attains sovereignty over a bounded territory becomes a nation and establishes a nation-state.

Gellner (1983) argues that nations could not exist in pre-modern societies, owing to the cultural gap between elites and peasants, while modern industrial societies require cultural homogeneity to function, and therefore generate the ideologies needed to create nations. However, both Seton-Watson (1977) and Smith (1986) argue that the nation is of much greater antiquity, going back to the ancient civilizations of East Asia, the Middle East and Europe. All these authors seem to agree that the nation is essentially a belief system, based on collective cultural ties and sentiments. These convey a sense of identity and belonging, which may be referred to as national consciousness.

Mainstream political science still argues that the linking of national consciousness with the principle of democracy is a specific characteristic of the modern nation-state as it evolved in Western Europe and North America: every person classified as a member of the national community has an equal right to participate in the formulation of the political will. This conflicts with the historical reality of nation-state formation, in which being a citizen depended on membership in a certain national community, usually based on the dominant ethnic group of the territory concerned. Thus a *citizen* was always also a member of a nation, a *national*. Nationalist ideologies demand that ethnic group, nation and state should be facets of the same community and have the same boundaries – every ethnic group should constitute itself as a nation and should have its own state, with all the appropriate trappings: flag, army, Olympic team and postage stamps. In fact, such congruence has rarely been achieved: nationalism has always been an ideology trying to achieve such a condition, rather than an actual state of affairs.

The historical construction of nation-states has involved the spatial extension of state power, and the territorial incorporation of hitherto distinct ethnic groups. These may or may not coalesce into a single nation over time. Attempts to consolidate the nation-state have often meant exclusion, assimilation or even genocide for minority groups. It is possible to keep relatively small groups in situations of permanent subjugation and exclusion from the 'imagined community'. This has applied, for instance, to Jews, Catholics and Roma in various European countries, to indigenous peoples in settler colonies and to the descendants of slaves and contract workers in some areas of European colonization. Political domination and cultural exclusion are much more difficult if the subjugated nation retains a territorial base, like the Scots, Welsh and Irish in the UK, the Basques in Spain, the Kurds in Turkey or the Imazighen (Berbers) in North Africa.

But the traditional model of the relationship between state and nation is even more challenged by international migration and the growth of ethnic diversity. The pervasive fear of 'ghettos' or 'ethnic enclaves' indicates that minorities are generally perceived as most threatening when they concentrate in distinct areas. For nationalists, an ethnic group is a potential nation which does not (yet) control any territory, or have its own state. Most modern states have made conscious efforts to achieve cultural and political integration of minorities. Mechanisms include citizenship itself, the propagation of national languages, universal education systems and creation of national institutions like the army, or an established church (Schnapper, 1991; 1994). The problem is similar everywhere: how can a nation be defined, if not in terms of a shared (and single) ethnic identity? How are core values and behavioural norms to be laid down, if there is a plurality of cultures and traditions?

Citizenship

The states of immigration countries have devised policies and institutions to respond to increased ethnic diversity (see Aleinikoff and Klusmeyer, 2000; 2001). The central issues are: defining who is a citizen, how newcomers can become citizens and what citizenship means. In principle, the nation-state only permits a single membership, but immigrants and their descendants have a relationship to more than one state. They may be citizens of two states, or they may be a citizen of one state but live in another. These situations may lead to 'transnational consciousness' or 'divided loyalties' and undermine the nationalist ideal of cultural homogeneity. Thus large-scale settlement inevitably leads to a debate on citizenship.

Citizenship designates the equality of rights of all citizens within a political community, as well as a corresponding set of institutions guaranteeing these rights (Bauböck, 1991: 28). However, formal equality rarely leads to equality in practice. In many societies, women have been excluded from the rights of citizenship in the past and sometimes still are today. Moreover, the citizen has generally been defined in terms of the cultures, values and interests of the majority ethnic group. Finally, the citizen has usually been explicitly or implicitly conceived in class terms, so that gaining real rights for members of the working class (such as the right to vote or to be a member of parliament) has been one of the central historical tasks of the labour movement.

The first concern for immigrants, however, is not the exact content of citizenship, but how they can obtain it, in order to achieve a legal status formally equal to that of other residents. Access has varied considerably in different countries, depending on the prevailing concept of the nation. We can distinguish the following ideal types of citizenship:

1. The *imperial model*: definition of belonging to the nation in terms of being a subject of the same power or ruler. This notion pre-dates the French and American revolutions. It allowed the integration of the various peoples of multi-ethnic empires (the British, the Austro-Hungarian, the Ottoman, etc.). This model remained formally in operation in the UK until the Nationality Act of 1981. It also had some validity for the former Soviet Union. The concept almost always has an ideological character, as it helps to veil the actual dominance of a particular ethnic group or nationality over the other subject peoples.

2. The *folk* or *ethnic model*: definition of belonging to the nation in terms of ethnicity (common descent, language and culture), which means exclusion of minorities from citizenship and from the nation. Germany came close to this model until the introduction of new citizenship rules in 2000.

3. The *republican model*: definition of the nation as a political community, based on a constitution, laws and citizenship, with the possibility of admitting newcomers to the community, providing they adhere to the political rules and are willing to adopt the national culture. This assimilationist approach dates back to the French and American revolutions. France is the most obvious current example.

4. The *multicultural model*: the nation is also defined as a political community, based on a constitution, laws and citizenship that can admit newcomers. However, in this model they may maintain their distinctive cultures and form ethnic communities, providing they conform to national laws. This pluralist or multicultural approach became dominant in the 1970s and 1980s in Sweden, the Netherlands, Australia and Canada, and was also influential elsewhere, although there has been a recent backlash against multiculturalism.

All these ideal types have one factor in common: they are premised on citizens who belong to just one nation-state. Migrant settlement is seen as a process of transferring primary loyalty from the state of origin to the new state of residence. This process is symbolically marked by naturalization and acquisition of citizenship of the new state. Transnational theory (see Chapter 2) argues that this no longer applies for growing groups of migrants. Thus an additional ideal type of citizenship may be emerging:

5. The *transnational model*: identities of the members of transnational communities transcend national boundaries, leading to multiple and differentiated forms of belonging. Transnationalism could have important consequences for democratic institutions and political belonging in future.

The applicability of these models to specific countries will be discussed in Chapter 12. Such models are neither universally accepted nor static even within a single country (Bauböck and Rundell, 1998: 1273). Moreover, the distinction between citizens and non-citizens is becoming less clear-cut. Immigrants who have been legally resident in a country for many years often obtain a status tantamount to 'quasi-citizenship' or 'denizenship' (Hammar, 1990). This may confer such rights as permanent residence status; rights to work, seek employment and run a business; entitlements to social security benefits and health services; access to education and training; and limited political rights, such as voting rights in local elections. Such arrangements create a new legal status, which is more than that of a foreigner, but less than that of a citizen.

A further element in the emergence of quasi-citizenship is the development of international human rights standards, as laid down by bodies like the UN, the International Labour Organization (ILO) and the World Trade Organization (WTO). A whole range of civil and social rights are legally guaranteed for citizens and non-citizens alike in the states which adopt these international norms (Soysal, 1994). However, the legal protection provided by international conventions can be deficient when states do not ratify them or do not incorporate the norms into their national law, which is often the case with international measures to protect migrant rights.

The EU provides the furthest-going example for a new type of citizenship. The 1992 Maastricht Treaty established Citizenship of the European Union, which includes the right to freedom of movement and residence in the territory of member states and to vote and to stand for office in local elections and European Parliament elections in the state of residence (Martiniello, 1994: 31). (This is discussed in detail in Chapter 10).

The meaning of citizenship may change, and the exclusive link to one nation-state will become more tenuous. Dual or multiple citizenship is becoming increasingly common. Nearly all immigration countries have changed their citizenship rules over the last 40–50 years – sometimes several times. Countries of emigration like Mexico, India, Morocco and Turkey have also changed their rules on citizenship and nationality, in order to maintain links with their nationals abroad. More and more countries accept dual citizenship (at least to some extent) although such practices remain contested (Faist, 2007).

The transformation of origin societies

People often decide to leave their area of origin because conditions have changed to the point where previous modes of work and social life have become unviable or unattractive, and because of the awareness of better opportunities elsewhere. Emigration often arises through development and social transformation, but in turn brings further change in origin societies. That is the theme of the second half of this chapter.

The fact that many migrants maintain strong transnational social ties even several decades after permanent settlement illustrates that migration is seldom an individual act of people seeking to maximize their own income. In many cases, the main motivation for migrating is to improve the living conditions of the families remaining behind. The money migrants remit often enables families to improve housing, nutrition, clothing, medical care and education. Many migrants aspire to return once they have saved enough money to invest in an enterprise, such as the family farm, a store, a truck or minibus, a workshop or a factory. Migration may also serve cultural or religious purposes, for instance to perform the *hadj,* the religious pilgrimage to Mecca.

The migration and development debate

A key question today is *whether migration encourages development of the countries of origin or, conversely, hinders such development.* Over the past decades, this issue has sparked heated debate in policy and research, opposing 'migration optimists', who argue that migration brings growth and prosperity to origin countries, to 'migration pessimists', who argue that migration undermines development through draining origin countries of their scarce human and financial resources. While the pessimists predict a 'brain drain', the optimists predict a 'brain gain'. This division reflects the more general division between historical–structural and neoclassical migration theories (see Chapter 2).

The debate about migration and development has swung back and forth, from optimism in the post-1945 period, to pessimism since the 1970s, to renewed optimism since 2000 (cf. de Haas, 2012). This section will review how the migration and development debate evolved. It will also examine the theoretical foundations of optimistic and pessimistic views and summarize the main insights from the empirical literature on this topic.

However, we first need to ask: what is development? This is a highly contested concept, and there are many definitions. Although there is no room in this book for a full discussion, it seems useful to adopt a broad definition of human development. Amartya Sen defined development as the *process of expanding the substantive freedoms that people enjoy* (Sen, 1999). In order to make this concrete, Sen uses the concept of *human capability*: the 'ability of human beings to lead lives they have reason to value and to enhance the substantive choices they have' (see also Chapter 2). Sen argued that (average) income growth – which can hide huge inequalities – should not be the focus of analysis, but rather the question of whether the real capabilities of people to control their own lives have expanded.

This micro-level concept of development embodies the idea of individual *progress*, and needs to be differentiated from the macro-level concept of *social transformation*, which refers to a fundamental change in the way society is organized, such as through the industrial revolution, colonialism, warfare, revolutions, and globalization (see also Chapter 2). Such processes can bring positive development for particular social groups, regions or countries, but can deprive others. It is important to be aware that impacts of any social transformation *are* always socially and geographically differentiated, and therefore inevitably create new forms of inequality, tensions and conflict which may replace or supersede previous ones.

During the 1950s and 1960s, development economists stressed that labour migration was an integral and positive part of modernization. The reduction of labour surpluses (and hence unemployment) in areas of origin and the inflow of capital through remittances was expected to improve productivity and incomes in origin societies (Massey *et al.*, 1998: 223). Many governments shared this view, and considered migration as a key instrument to promote development (Adler, 1981; Heine-meijer *et al.*, 1977; Penninx, 1982). Sending and receiving states signed recruitment agreements as they both saw mutual benefits in temporary or 'guest worker' migration. In Western Europe most workers initially came from Southern Europe, Finland, and Ireland, but from the mid-1960s they were increasingly replaced by migrants from Turkey, Algeria, Morocco, Tunisia and (former) colonies. On the other side of the Atlantic, Mexican workers were actively recruited through the 1942–64 US *Bracero* Program.

Migration optimists saw migration from the European periphery to North-West Europe as a process that stimulated growth in origin and destination countries (Adler, 1981; Kindleberger, 1967; Penninx, 1982). It was widely thought that 'large-scale emigration can contribute to the best of both worlds: rapid growth in the country of immigration ... and rapid growth in the country of origin' (Kindleberger, 1967: 253). While migration provided the industries of destination countries with much needed labour, *remittances* and the modern ideas and entrepreneurial attitudes migrants would bring back were expected to help origin countries in their modernization and economic take-off.

Such views largely fit within neoclassical migration theory (see Chapter 2), which perceives unconstrained migration as a process contributing to a more optimal allocation of production factors and hence to greater productivity in both sending and receiving areas. This would lead to convergence of economic conditions between origin and destination countries (Massey *et al.*, 1998). Such optimism also reflected the evolutionary assumptions of modernization theory (Rostow, 1960). Freshly de-colonialized nations in Africa and Asia were expected to quickly follow the same path of modernization, industrialization, and economic growth as Western countries before them. It was thought that large-scale capital transfer (whether through loans, aid, or remittances) would enable poor countries to jump on the bandwagon of rapid industrialization. Migration and remittances were ascribed an important and positive role in this process.

However, even in the 1950s and 1960s, such views were not uncontested. In contrast to Western-aligned countries, communist or socialist countries such as Algeria, Egypt (until Sadat rose to power in the early 1970s) and Cuba saw emigration as a threat to independence and development and actively discouraged it. But also in Mediterranean origin countries, the long-term results of labour recruitment schemes were often disappointing, as they brought limited economic benefits for origin countries and did little to resolve structural development problems (Abadan-Unat, 1988; De Mas, 1978; Heinemeijer *et al.*, 1977; Martin, 1991; Paine, 1974). In the 1970s and 1980s, there was disillusionment with policies linking return migration and development through departure bonuses and investment programmes for return migrants (Entzinger, 1985; Penninx, 1982). At the same time awareness was growing that many temporary migrants would settle permanently.

After the Oil Crisis of 1973, the Western world entered a period of recessions, industrial restructuring and increasing unemployment. This also marked a turning point in thinking on migration and development, which coincided with the growing influence of historical–structural (neo-Marxist and dependency) theories (see Chapter 2). Over the 1970s, pessimistic views became predominant according to which 'migration undermines the prospects for local economic development and yields a state of stagnation and dependency' (Massey *et al.*, 1998: 272). *Migration pessimists* did not just argue that migration had negative effects, but saw it as one of the *very causes* of underdevelopment of origin countries. As Papademetriou (1985:111–12) argued, migration contributed to 'an uncontrolled depletion of their already meagre supplies of skilled manpower – and the most healthy, dynamic, and productive members of their populations'.

Migration was believed to go along with a *brain drain*, which deprived poor countries of their scarce professional resources (GCIM, 2005: 23–5; IOM, 2005: 173). Increasing student migration can be seen as part of this brain drain. Foreign students pay high fees, and support the education systems of developed countries (Khadria, 2008), while receiving countries increasingly encourage foreign graduates to stay. Indian and Chinese PhDs form the scientific backbone of Silicon Valley and other high-tech production areas. Another loss is known as *brain waste*: many migrants are unable to get their qualifications recognized or fail to find employment commensurate with their skills. The image of surgeons working as waiters or engineers driving taxis reflects reality for some.

A growing number of empirical studies contributed to such pessimism. The dominant view was that remittances fuelled consumption and that migrants rarely invested their money productively. The 'lost labour' and dependency on remittance income would encourage rural families to abandon their farms or to cease other local economic activities. Empirical studies suggested that remittances were primarily spent on (often conspicuous) consumption of goods and on 'non-productive' enterprises such as housing (Entzinger, 1985: 268; Lewis, 1986; Lipton, 1980; Rhoades, 1979). Since many of these goods (e.g. TV sets, mobile phones, household appliances, stylish clothing, fertilizers, manufactured foodstuffs) had to be imported, this had the double effect of crowding out local production, while strengthening the economies of wealthy countries.

Because international migrants were often from relatively well-off groups, remittances were thought to increase inequality (Lipton, 1980; Zachariah *et al.*, 2001). At the same time, the migration-related decline of traditional economies deprived non-migrant community members of work and income (e.g., in agriculture, crafts and small industries). Remittance-fuelled consumption and land purchase by migrants could lead to inflation (cf. Russell, 1992) and soaring land prices (Appleyard, 1989; Rubenstein, 1992), from which the non-migrant poor suffered most.

The socio-cultural effects of migration were also often seen negatively. Exposure to the relative wealth of (return) migrants and the goods and ideas they imported led to changes in rural tastes (Lipton, 1980, 12). This further increased demand for imported goods (such as processed food and wheat instead of fresh vegetables and traditional grains) and undermined local production. Migration was often held responsible for the disruption of traditional kinship systems and care structures (King and Vullnetari, 2006) and the breakdown of traditional institutions regulating village life and agriculture (de Haas, 1998). Together, these changes made traditional lifestyles less appealing, and demotivated youth to work in agriculture or other local occupations. This could give rise to a 'culture of migration' (Heering *et al.*, 2004; Massey *et al.*, 1993), in which youth could only imagine a future through migrating.

Through these mutually reinforcing social, economic and cultural effects, migration fostered the development of remittance-dependent, non-productive and migration-obsessed communities. These negative views can be amalgamated into what Reichert (1981) called the 'migrant syndrome', or the vicious circle of

migration → more underdevelopment → more migration, and so on

As an ILO official interviewed in the 1990s commented: 'migration and development – nobody believes that anymore'(Massey *et al.*, 1998: 260). Yet in the early twenty-first century, there was another swing in

Figure 3.1 *Remittances and official development assistance to lower- and middle-income countries*

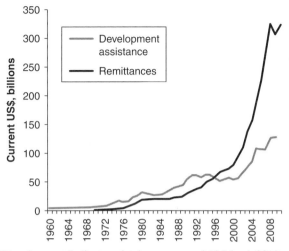

Source: World Development Indicators database, accessed 18 March 2013.

assessments. After years of seeing South–North migration as a problem, politicians and officials now emphasize the potential of international migration to foster economic and social development in the countries of origin. Particularly remittances have become a new 'development mantra' (cf. Kapur, 2003), and are now widely seen as an ideal 'bottom up' source of development finance, and an effective safety net for poor areas and countries (cf. Jones, 1998a).

This renewed optimism about migration and development was partly related to a spectacular increase in remittances. According to World Bank statistics, in 1990 migrants sent back the equivalent of US$29 billion to lower- and middle-income countries: this amount had more than doubled to US$79 billion in 2000 and reached US$321 in 2010. Although this partly reflects better measurement of remittances – itself a result of the growing interest in the issue –there is little doubt that remittances have increased and are now several times the amount of official development assistance (ODA) (see Figure 3.1). Moreover, unrecorded flows through informal channels may add 50 per cent or more to recorded flows (World Bank, 2007). In dollar terms, India and China are the largest remittance receivers, although international migration is relatively small compared with their huge populations. Next come Mexico, Philippines and Bangladesh, where a large proportion of the population emigrate. However, as the data on remittances as a share of GDP show, many smaller, poor countries have extremely high levels of economic dependence on migrant remittances (see Table 3.1).

Table 3.1   *Top 10 remittance-receiving developing countries (2009) by billions of US dollars and by share of Gross Domestic Product (GDP)*

Country	Remittances: US$ billions (2009)	Country	Remittances as share of GDP (2008)
India	49	Tajikistan	50
China	48	Tonga	38
Mexico	22	Moldova	31
Philippines	20	Kyrgyz Rep.	28
Bangladesh	11	Lesotho	27
Nigeria	10	Samoa	26
Pakistan	9	Lebanon	25
Egypt	7	Guyana	24
Lebanon	7	Nepal	22
Vietnam	7	Honduras	20

Source: Ratha *et al.* (2011).

This 'remittance euphoria' coincided with growing optimism about the development contributions of migrants through counter-flows of money, investment, trade relations, innovations, entrepreneurial and innovative attitudes and information (de Haas, 2006a; Lowell and Findlay, 2002). This led to several policy initiatives by governments and international organizations to enhance the development impact of migration and remittances (e.g., DFID, 2007; GCIM, 2005; UNDP, 2009; World Bank, 2006).

The question is how to explain such rather sudden swings in thinking about migration and development. Such changes should not be seen in isolation from ideological changes. The recent shift to optimistic views also reflects a broader ideological shift towards neoliberal principles. Kapur pointed to the ideological roots of remittance euphoria by arguing that remittances exemplify the principle of self-help, in which 'Immigrants, rather than governments, then become the biggest provider of "foreign aid"' (Kapur, 2003: 10). This also fits within the 'Washington consensus' – the World Bank and IMF-led development ideology which advocates market liberalization, privatization and deregulation (Gore, 2000; Stiglitz, 2002: 67). Or, to put it less positively, the idea is that some of the world's most exploited workers should provide the capital for development, where aid programmes have failed.

This raises the following question: to what extent are optimistic and pessimistic claims justified? What do research findings tell us about the development impacts of migration? Fortunately, there has been a rapid increase in the number of empirical studies in recent years, which has improved our insight into this issue, and has given rise to much more nuanced perspectives, which will be reviewed in the following section.

The development impacts of migration

Both pessimistic and optimistic views on migration and development represent rather extreme views, and in most cases the reality is somewhere in between. Since the 1990s a growing number of empirical studies have highlighted the diversity of migration impacts. This shift towards more nuanced views partly reflected the growing influence of the *new economics of labour migration* (NELM) (Stark, 1991; Taylor, 1999) as well as network and transnationalism theories, which emphasize the capability (or agency) migrants have to overcome structural constraints (such as failing markets, economic insecurity and immigration restrictions) but also emphasize that this capability is fundamentally limited (see Chapter 2).

Recent research insights based on qualitative fieldwork and quantitative surveys emphasize that the impacts of migration depend on the more general development context. Several reviews of the rich empirical material (Agunias, 2006; de Haas, 2007a; Katseli *et al.*, 2006; Özden and Schiff, 2005; Papademetriou and Martin, 1991; Taylor *et al.*, 1996a; 1996b; UNDP, 2009) indicate that, despite its significant benefits for individuals and communities, migration alone cannot generally remove structural development obstacles.

Most empirical studies support the view that migration in and from developing countries is an attempt by families to improve their social and economic status. Remittances are a relatively stable source of income which often help to diversify and raise household income, to improve living conditions, nutrition, health and education, as well as to finance weddings, funerals and other ceremonies. On the national level, remittances provide a less volatile and more reliable source of foreign currency than other capital flows to developing countries. However, this does not mean that remittances automatically alleviate poverty. As migration is a selective process, *most* international remittances neither flow to the poorest members of communities nor to the poorest countries. However, some poor people do migrate (though primarily internally) and remit money. The poor may also benefit *indirectly*, because of the employment and income generated by expenditure of remittances on housing, services and local products.

The effects of migration on inequality in origin communities primarily depend on *who* migrates (the 'selectivity' of migration). For instance, if migrants are from relatively wealthy families, migration and remittances tend to reinforce socio-economic inequality (Jones, 1998b). If migrants are from less wealthy sections of the population, or if 'selectivity' decreases because the relatively poor are increasingly able to migrate through the establishment of migrant networks, the effects can be neutral or positive. In South Moroccan oases, migration has been an important avenue for upward socio-economic mobility for the *haratin*, a low-status ethnic group mainly consisting of black peasants and sharecroppers (de Haas, 2006c). Migration also affects the position of women in sending communities. Such impacts can be positive or negative, depending on whether women have access to remittance income and whether they can migrate themselves (Gammage, 2004; Taylor, 1984).

Remittances potentially enable households to invest in enterprises such as the family farm or small industry. There is also reason to cast migrants' inclination to spend money on consumption in a more positive light than is usually done. For instance, it is difficult to dismiss expenditure on education, health, food, medicines and housing as 'non-developmental' if we realize that this can enormously improve people's well-being. Moreover, even such expenditures can have significant 'multiplier' effects by generating employment. In many emigration regions, construction of houses is known to stimulate economic growth and create significant employment and income for non-migrants. Even expenditure on lavish weddings and funerals can have economically beneficial multiplier effects by stimulating local demand (cf. Mazzucato *et al.*, 2006). Remittance-fuelled regional growth partly explains why several emigration regions in countries like Mexico, Morocco and Turkey have become destinations for internal migrants.

Some migrants, such as Mexicans in the USA or Nigerians in Britain, have set up 'hometown associations', through which migrants club together to send money home for community improvements, such as refurbishing churches or community facilities, or improving health provision. However, the volume of such collective remittances is far smaller than that of individual transfers (Orozco and Rouse, 2007).

Criticism of migrants' ways of spending money often reveals an inability to comprehend the difficult conditions that prevail in migrant-sending countries. For instance, policy-makers and researchers have often castigated migrants for building large, richly ornamented houses which they consider 'exaggerated' (Ben Ali, 1996: 354), reflecting an 'irrational' (Aït Hamza, 1988) use of money on unnecessary status symbols. This is typically accompanied by a call for policies to divert remittances to productive sectors of the economy by guiding migrants towards more 'rational' investment behaviour. However, this misses the point that houses are often a relatively secure and, hence, rational investment in generally insecure investment environments. In his study on remittance use in rural Egypt, Adams concluded that 'from the standpoint of the individual, housing expenses should be classified as an "investment", since new and improved housing offers possible future economic returns to the individual' (Adams, 1991: 705). In addition, better housing can add to the safety and quality of life and the social status of families. Dismissive views about migrants' supposedly irrational consumption patterns also tend to be patronizing. For instance, by suggesting that migrants' families should stay in their traditional houses, policy-makers apply different standards to others than they would probably do to themselves.

Debates on the brain drain have also become more nuanced. Only in a limited number of smaller countries, primarily in the Caribbean, the Pacific and some smaller African states, does the brain drain includes a big share of professionals (cf. Adams, 2003; Gibson and McKenzie, 2011). Furthermore, if large-scale emigration of the highly skilled occurs, this can be a symptom of development failure rather than its main cause (Lowell and Findlay, 2002: 30–1). For instance, recent studies suggest that low health staffing levels in some sub-Saharan African countries are primarily the result of unattractive working conditions and the failure to provide basic health services, which do not require highly trained personnel (Clemens, 2007), and that most elite health workers would not have provided basic health care to those most in need if they had stayed (DRC, 2006).

This casts doubt on the assumption that emigration *automatically* represents a permanent loss. Established migrants may support families over sustained periods, and migrants' ability to engage socially, politically and economically in countries of origin actually *increases* as their occupational situation in destination societies improves (Guarnizo *et al.*, 2003). In fact, many governments deliberately create surpluses of certain categories of the highly skilled as part of a 'labour export' strategy. For instance, the Philippines government encourages education of nurses, for the explicit purpose of generating remittances.

A brain drain can be accompanied by *brain gain*, which occurs when the prospect of moving abroad motivates those staying behind to continue education, through which the net effect of emigration on education levels may actually be positive (Lowell and Findlay, 2002; Stark *et al.*, 1997). However, this only seems to occur if the opportunity to migrate increases the economic returns to education. Migration can also create *negative* incentives for education in cases of low-skilled, often irregular migration, where few positive returns on education can be expected (McKenzie, 2006), and a significant *brain waste* occurs. For instance, if Moroccan university graduates end up working as irregular migrants picking tomatoes in Spanish greenhouses, this provides little incentive for prospective migrants to continue education.

The political impacts of migration are ambiguous. Largely depending on who migrates, migration can either challenge or reinforce the status quo. Migrants are often from middle-class or elite groups (Guarnizo *et al.*, 2003), who generally do not represent the views of the poor and the oppressed. Under certain circumstance, however, migrants can be a potential force for structural political change in poor and fragile states, for the better or worse. Migrants and refugees can play a significant role in political reforms and post-conflict reconstruction in countries of origin. In 2011, Tunisian, Egyptian and Libyan political exiles and emigrant communities were swift in organizing themselves to support the revolutions from abroad. Migrants may also contribute to violent conflicts, for instance by providing support for warring parties in countries such as Sri Lanka and Somalia (Nyberg-Sorensen *et al.*, 2002; Van Hear, 2004).

Reform *as a* condition for migration and development

To summarize a very rich and diverse literature, we can conclude that migration has enabled numerous families and communities around the world to secure and enhance their livelihoods. This is a testimony to the willpower of migrants to improve their own destinies, and the agency they deploy to achieve these goals. Yet this does not mean that migration *alone* can set in motion processes of national economic and human development. The extent to which migration can play a positive role in change in origin countries depends on more general development conditions, which individual migrants cannot change fundamentally. Under unfavourable conditions migration may actually undermine prospects for development.

In the poorest countries migration often remains a prerogative of the relatively better off and may therefore actually deepen socio-economic inequalities. Governments of middle-income countries such as Morocco, Tunisia, Egypt, Mexico, and the Philippines have used migration as a political 'safety valve' to reduce unemployment, poverty and political unrest (Castles and Delgado Wise, 2008; de Haas and Vezzoli, 2010; Gammage, 2006). Migration then becomes an instrument to diminish pressure for structural reform and to sustain the position of elite groups, although authoritarian governments typically remain nervous that emigrants may raise their voice from abroad.

The broader conditions under which migration occurs largely determine the extent to which the development *potential* of migration can be fulfilled. Migration can give migrants enhanced access to social, human and financial resources. It is this very capabilities-enhancing potential of migration that also increases the freedom of migrants either to invest in or to withdraw from origin countries. What will happen in practice largely depends on the political and economic situation in origin countries and the position of migrants in destination countries. If origin countries offer little hope of progress, experiences are more likely to reflect the pessimistic paradigm. Under unfavourable conditions, emigration may also undermine the growth of a critical mass necessary to enforce structural change, which is exactly why ruling elites have often encouraged emigration.

However, if development in origin countries takes a positive turn, if fundamental political reform happens, if trust in governments increases and economic growth starts to take off, migration is more likely to play the positive role predicted by the migration optimists. Migrants are likely to be among the first to recognize such new opportunities, and reinforce and accelerate these positive trends through investing, trading, circulating and returning. Over the past decades, such mutually reinforcing interactions between migration and development have occurred in several countries such as Spain, Ireland, Taiwan, South Korea, India, China, and, more recently, Turkey (see Chapters 5–8). For instance, Taiwan experienced substantial loss of high-skilled people in the 1960s and 1970s, but when Taiwan's high-tech sector took off, the government was able to attract back experienced nationals from the USA (see Newland, 2007). Similarly, India set up Institutes of Technology from the 1950s on to support national development, but many of the graduates emigrated to the USA and other rich countries. However, many IT experts later returned which boosted growth of India's own fast-growing IT sector (Khadria, 2008).

The important point to stress here is that migration was not the factor that triggered national development but, rather, that development enabled by structural political and economic reform unleashed the development potential of migration. So, it is essential to get the causality right. As Heinemeijer *et al.* (1977) already observed, development is a *condition* for investment and return by migrants rather than a *consequence* of migration.

Policy considerations

Since the 1960s, governments have attempted to stimulate remittances and enhance the development impacts of migration, but such policies seem to have marginal effects as long as general investment environments remain unattractive. Policies to 'channel remittances into productive uses' are often based on rather condescending views that migrants behave irrationally, and miss the point that migrants have good reasons *not* to invest if investment conditions are unfavourable. Such discourses also arrogantly presume that remittances can be 'tapped' by governments; in fact remittances are private money – the result of migrants' hard work and frugal lifestyles under often difficult conditions. In addition, many migrants have a deep-seated and justified distrust of governments. It would therefore be naïve to assume that governments can deploy this money.

It is also important to be aware of the neocolonial ideas underlying policy discourses which celebrate migrants as development pioneers. The idea that the transfer of the 'right' – that is, Western – attitudes and forms of behaviour ('social remittances') would bring about positive change goes back to the nineteenth-century idea of the 'civilizing mission' of Europe in the colonies. It was also central to the modernization theories of the 1950s and 1960s, according to which: '[d]evelopment was a question of instilling the 'right' orientations – values and norms – in the cultures of the non-Western world so as to enable its people to partake in the modern wealth-creating economic and political institutions of the advanced West' (Rostow, 1960: 230). More recently, neoliberal ideologies also assume that Western models of privatization and deregulation are the key to development.

A certain scepticism about the assumed benefits of importing 'Western' attitudes therefore seems justified.

Governments and international organizations often advocate temporary migration as a 'win-win-win' strategy benefiting origin and destination countries as well as the migrants themselves. However, the stated development intentions of such programmes often camouflage an agenda of expelling irregular immigrants or rejected asylum seekers after providing them some modest financial assistance or rapid and often ineffective vocational training (Weil, 2002).

Return is also notoriously difficult to enforce, and linking restrictive immigration policies to development can paradoxically *reduce* return by pushing migrants into permanent settlement (Castles, 2004b; 2006). More generally, it is also questionable whether temporary migrants have the highest potential to contribute to development. In fact, long-term and well-integrated migrants possess the resources to invest in and engage with origin countries (see Guarnizo *et al.*, 2003). Because development is a condition for attracting migrants' investments rather than a consequence of it, governments would be wise to start improving general conditions in origin countries. They should be asking how they can design immigration and integration policies that empower migrants and that maximize their ability to contribute to development in origin countries.

From this, we can draw some policy lessons. First, policies to facilitate remittances, to engage 'diasporas' (de Haas, 2006a; Gamlen, 2006), and to encourage investment and return by migrants will have marginal (if any) effects if they are not accompanied by general reform in origin countries. Discourses celebrating migration, remittances and transnational engagement as self-help development 'from below' are partly driven by neoliberal agendas and shift attention away from structural constraints and the limited ability of individual migrants to overcome these. Policies that improve infrastructure, legal security, governmental accountability and macro-economic stability while countering corruption and improving access to public education, health and credit, are crucial not only for creating positive conditions for development, but also for encouraging migrants to return and invest. This exemplifies the crucial role that states continue to play in shaping favourable conditions for human development.

Second, immigrant-receiving governments can increase the development potential of migration by lowering thresholds for immigration, particularly of the lower- and middle skilled, and through favouring the socio-economic integration of migrants by countering discrimination and racism on the labour market and giving them access to housing and education as well as residency and (dual) citizenship rights. By deterring the relatively poor from migrating or, rather, forcing them into irregular and vulnerable positions, current immigration policies damage the potential of migration to alleviate poverty and stimulate development in origin countries.

Conclusions

This chapter has discussed how migration simultaneously transforms societies of origin and destination countries, and how these changes are interrelated. A wide variety of theoretical perspectives has evolved to understand processes of settlement, ethnic minority formation and growing diversity in destination countries on the one hand, and the impact of migration on development and social transformation in origin countries on the other. What brings the various theories together is the importance they ascribe to the social, economic and cultural ties migrants maintain with origin societies, and which provide a crucial link between change occurring simultaneously in origin and destination countries.

One central argument is that migration and settlement are closely related to other economic, political and cultural linkages between different countries. Migration simultaneously affects social transformation in origin and receiving societies, which in turn changes the conditions under which migration takes place. This highlights the central argument that migration is an *intrinsic part* of broader processes of change, and that we need to simultaneously take into account processes in sending and receiving countries.

A second argument is that the migratory process has internal dynamics which often lead to developments not initially intended either by the migrants themselves or by the states concerned. The most common outcome of a migratory movement, whatever its initial character, is settlement of a significant proportion of the migrants, and formation of ethnic communities or minorities. Thus the emergence of more diverse societies must be seen as an inevitable result of initial settlement. When settlement and ethnic minority formation take place at times of economic or social crisis, they can become highly politicized.

The third argument focuses on the significance of immigration for the nation-state. Increasing ethnic diversity often contributes to changes in central political institutions, such as citizenship, and may affect the very nature of the nation-state. This helps to explain the growing political salience of issues around migration and ethnic minorities in immigration countries all over the world. Migrants often maintain links in two or more countries, and sometimes form transnational communities which live across borders. This is evident in the growing salience of dual citizenship, which some see as a threat to national identity.

A fourth argument is that migrants contribute significantly to securing and improving the livelihoods of families and communities in origin societies. Particularly, remittances fulfil an increasingly important function in improving conditions in origin countries. Migrants can also contributed to development by investing, by setting up 'home town associations' or by contributing to political change.

However, a fifth argument is that migrants and remittances can neither be blamed for a lack of development, nor be expected to trigger take-off development in generally unattractive investment environments. Despite

its benefits for families and communities, migration alone cannot generally remove structural development obstacles such as corruption, nepo-
tism and failing institutions. Rather, migration seems to reinforce already
existing development trends – whether these are negative or positive; and
is unlikely to *reverse* such general development trends. If states fail to
implement reform, migration is unlikely to fuel national development –
and can actually sustain situations of dependency, underdevelopment and
authoritarianism. In that case, migrants are also more likely to settle permanently and to reunify their families. However, if development in origin countries takes a positive turn, migrants often reinforce these positive
trends through investing and returning.

The sixth argument is that recent views celebrating migration as self-
help development 'from below' are partly driven by neoliberal ideologies,
which shift the attention away from structural development constraints
and, hence, the responsibility of origin states to pursue political and economic reform. In turn, destination countries can increase the development
potential of migration by creating legal channels for migration and integration policies that favour socio-economic mobility of migrants and avoid
their marginalization.

The latter argument shows the importance of linking theories on immigrant settlement and incorporation to theories on migration and development. As much as conditions in origin societies affect migrants' decisions
to stay or return, conditions in receiving societies will affect migrants' capabilities and aspirations to engage with or return to origin societies. Here, it
is important to emphasize that 'integration' and transnational engagement
are not necessarily substitutes as policy-makers often suggest, but can actually reinforce each other, since a better position of migrants in receiving
societies will also empower them to contribute to development in origin
societies.

In this globalizing world, migrants are increasingly linked to and
simultaneously affect change in two or more societies. The migratory
movements of the last 60 years have led to irreversible changes in sending and receiving countries around the world. Continuing migrations will
cause new transformations, both in the societies already affected and in
further countries now entering the international migration arena. The
following chapters will provide a basis for further discussion of these
ideas.

Guide to further reading

Two general studies on Europe (Penninx *et al.*, 2006) and the USA (Portes
and Rumbaut, 2006) provide valuable background on migration and settlement. Analyses of the relationship between migration and citizenship are
to be found in Bauböck (1994a; b); Bauböck and Rundell (1998); Bauböck

et al. (2006a; b), Aleinikoff and Klusmeyer (2000; 2001) and Castles and Davidson (2000). Useful works on gender and migration include Lutz *et al.* (1995), Andall (2003), Pessar and Mahler (2003) and Phizacklea (1998). Goldberg and Solomos (2002) and Murji and Solomos (2005) are comprehensive collections of essays on racial and ethnic studies, while an earlier compendium, Rex and Mason (1986), is still useful. Anderson (1983) and Gellner (1983) provide stimulating analyses of nationalism, while Smith (1986; 1991) discusses the relationship between ethnicity and nation.

The 2009 Human Development Report *Overcoming Barriers: Human Mobility and Development* (UNDP, 2009) gives a comprehensive overview on how migration affects development and growth in receiving and origin societies. De Haas (2010a) provides an overview of theories on migration and development and de Haas (2012) critically discusses policy approaches. Taylor *et al.* (1996a and 1996b) (both appeared later as chapters in Massey *et al.* (1998), Agunias (2006) and Katseli *et al.* (2006) provide reviews of the development impacts of migration and remittances. Castles and Delgado Wise (2008) examines the experience of five major emigration countries. Stark (1991) is a collection of papers which established the new economics of labour migration (NELM), while Taylor (1999) provides a useful introduction. The Migration and Remittances website of the World Bank contains useful data and research on remittances (see http://go.worldbank.org/). Adams (2011), Chami *et al.* (2008), Stark (2009) and Yang (2011) provide good discussions of the determinants and impacts of remittances. Ruiz and Vargas-Silva (2009) and Jha *et al.* (2009) provide insights into the impact of the GEC on remittances. The Web Anthology on Migrant Remittances and Development (www.ssrc.org/programs/web-anthology) is a useful online resource giving overviews of research insights and access to articles.

Chapter 4

International Migration before 1945

The post-1945 migrations may be new in scale and direction, but population movements in response to demographic change, and the development of production and trade, have always been part of human history. Indeed, recent evidence from a range of scientific disciplines, including archaeology, genetics, historical linguistics and anthropology, has shown that all human beings originated in evolutionary processes that started some 7 million years ago in Africa. The spread of *Homo erectus* – a new hominid species with superior brain capacity – out of East Africa started about 2 million years ago. *Homo erectus* was able to colonize large areas of Africa and went on to establish settlements as far afield as the Middle East, the Caucasus, Java and South China. Then, about 200,000 years ago, a new hominid species – *Homo sapiens* – emerged in Africa. *Homo sapiens* – the modern human – had superior adaptive capacities, and was able to displace all other hominids, moving stage by stage to people the entire earth (see Goldin *et al.*, 2011; also Manning, 2005, chapter 2).

Warfare, conquest, formation of nations, the emergence of states and empires, and the search for new economic opportunities have all led to migrations, both voluntary and forced. The enslavement and deportation of conquered people was a frequent early form of forced labour migration. This applies to all regions of the world (Hoerder, 2002; Manning, 2005; Wang, 1997). However, our account here focuses on the migrations of the last 600 years: from the end of the Middle Ages, the development of European states and their colonization of the rest of the world gave a new impetus to international migrations of many different kinds.

In Western Europe, 'migration was a long-standing and important facet of social life and the political economy' from about 1650 onwards, playing a vital role in modernization and industrialization (Moch, 1995: 126; see also Bade, 2003; Moch, 1992). The centrality of migration is not adequately reflected in prevailing views on the past: as Gérard Noiriel (1988:15–67) has pointed out, the history of immigration has been a 'blind spot' of historical research in France. This applies equally elsewhere, as shown by 'historians' repeated neglect of the scale and impact of immigration on European societies from the Middle Ages onwards' (Lucassen *et al.*, 2006: 7; see also Chapter 2 for discussion of the 'myth of the immobile peasant'). Denial of the role of immigrants in nation-building has been crucial to the creation of myths of national homogeneity. It is only recently that a new generation of European historians have questioned the nationalist orthodoxy of the past. Such approaches were obviously impossible in classical countries of immigration such as the USA and Australia (Archdeacon, 1983; Jupp, 2001; 2002).

Emigration as an escape from poverty and oppressive conditions and a way of seeking new opportunities is an important part of the history of modern societies. Millions of Europeans were able to build new lives by moving to the Americas or other settler colonies; many never returned but a lot did. Although data is sparse, it is believed that between 25 and 40 per cent came back to various origin areas, where they hoped to improve their economic and social situation, using resources gained through a sojourn abroad. Migrants and their descendants helped build new (often democratic) societies in the New World, while the broader perspectives gained through migration often proved a ferment for reform in origin areas. The movement of people was one of the great forces of change in the nineteenth and twentieth centuries. However, such change was not always positive for everyone – certainly not for the indigenous peoples of the Americas and Oceania, who experienced displacement, marginalization and even genocide through European colonization.

Individual liberty is portrayed as one of the great moral achievements of capitalism, in contrast with earlier societies where liberty was restricted by traditional bondage and servitude. Neoclassical theorists portray the capitalist economy as being based on free markets, including the labour market, where employers and workers encounter each other as free legal subjects, with equal rights to make contracts. But this harmonious picture often fails to match reality. As Cohen (1987) has shown, capitalism has made use of both *free* and *unfree workers* in every phase of its development. Labour migrants have frequently been unfree workers, either because they are taken by force to the place where their labour is needed, or because they are denied rights enjoyed by other workers, and cannot therefore compete under equal conditions. Even where migration is voluntary and unregulated, institutional and informal discrimination may limit the real freedom and equality of the workers concerned.

Since economic power is usually linked to political power, mobilization of labour often has an element of coercion, sometimes involving violence, military force and bureaucratic control. Examples are the slave economies of the Americas; indentured colonial labour in Asia, Africa and the Americas; mineworkers in Southern Africa in the nineteenth and twentieth centuries; foreign workers in Germany and France before World War II; forced labourers in the Nazi war economy; 'guest-workers' in post-1945 Europe; and irregular migrants denied the protection of law in many countries today. Trafficking of migrants – especially of women and children for sexual exploitation – can be seen as a modern form of bonded labour and, sometimes, slavery.

One important theme is not dealt with here because it requires more intensive treatment than is possible in the present work: the devastating effects of international migration on the indigenous peoples of colonized countries. European conquest of Africa, Asia, America and Oceania led either to the domination and exploitation of native peoples or to genocide, both physical and cultural. Nation-building – particularly in the Americas and Oceania – was based on the importation of new populations. Thus immigration contributed to the exclusion and marginalization of aboriginal peoples. One starting point for the construction of new national identities was the idealization of the destruction of indigenous societies: images such as 'how the West was won' or the struggle of Australian pioneers against the Aborigines became powerful myths. The roots of racist stereotypes – today directed against new immigrant groups – often lie in historical treatment of colonized peoples. Nowadays there is increasing realization that appropriate models for intergroup relations have to address the needs of indigenous populations, as well as those of immigrant groups.

Colonialism

European colonialism gave rise to various types of migration (see Map 4.1). One was the large *outward movement from Europe*, first to Africa and Asia, then to the Americas, and later to Oceania. Europeans migrated, either permanently or temporarily, as sailors, soldiers, farmers, traders, priests and administrators. Some of them had already migrated within Europe: Jan Lucassen (1995) has shown that around half the soldiers and sailors of the Dutch East India Company in the seventeenth and eighteenth centuries were not Dutch but 'transmigrants', mainly from poor areas of Germany. The mortality of these migrant workers through shipwreck, warfare and tropical illnesses was very high, but service in the colonies was often the only chance to escape from poverty. Such overseas migrations helped to bring about major changes in the economic structures and the cultures of both the European sending countries and the colonies.

An important antecedent of modern labour migration is the system of *chattel slavery*, which formed the basis of commodity production in the plantations and mines of the New World from the late seventeenth century to the mid-nineteenth century. The production of sugar, tobacco, coffee, cotton and gold by slave labour was crucial to the economic and political power of Britain and France – the dominant states of the eighteenth century – and played a major role for Spain, Portugal and the Netherlands as well. By 1770 there were nearly 2.5 million slaves in the Americas, producing a third of the total value of European commerce (Blackburn, 1988: 5). The slave system was organized in the notorious 'triangular trade': ships laden with manufactured goods, such as guns or household implements, sailed from ports such as Bristol and Liverpool, Bordeaux and Le Havre, to the coasts of West Africa. There Africans were either forcibly abducted or were purchased from local chiefs or traders in return

87

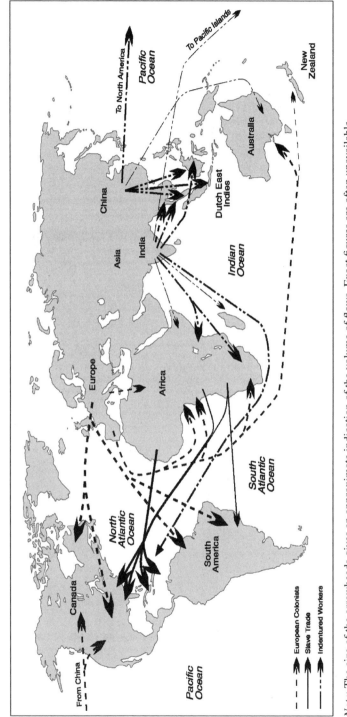

Map 4.1 *Colonial migrations from the seventeenth to nineteenth centuries*

Note: The size of the arrowheads gives an approximate indication of the volume of flows. Exact figures are often unavailable.

for the goods. Then the ships sailed to the Caribbean or the coasts of North or South America, where the slaves were sold for cash. This was used to purchase the products of the plantations, which were then brought back for sale in Europe.

An estimated 12 million slaves were taken to the Americas before 1850 (Lovejoy, 1989). For the women, hard labour in the mines, plantations and households was frequently accompanied by sexual exploitation. The children of slaves remained the chattels of the owners. In 1807, following a humanitarian campaign led by William Wilberforce, slave trafficking was abolished within the British Empire – the 200th anniversary of abolition was celebrated with great fanfare in 2007 – while other European states followed suit by 1815. A number of slave rebellions broke out – notably in Saint Domingue (later to become Haiti) (Schama, 2006). Yet slavery itself was not abolished until 1834 in British colonies, 1863 in Dutch colonies and 1865 in the Southern states of the USA (Cohen, 1991: 9). Slavery actually grew in extent and economic significance. The number of slaves in the Americas doubled from 3 million in 1800 to 6 million in 1860, with corresponding growth in the area of plantation agriculture in the South-Western USA, Cuba and Brazil (Blackburn, 1988: 544).

Slavery had existed in many pre-capitalist societies, but the colonial system was new in character. Its motive force was the emergence of global empires, which began to construct a world market, dominated by merchant capital. Slaves were transported great distances by specialized traders, and bought and sold as commodities. Slaves were economic property and were subjected to harsh forms of control to maximize their output. The great majority were exploited in plantations which produced for export, as part of an internationally integrated agricultural and manufacturing system (Blackburn, 1988; Fox-Genovese and Genovese, 1983).

In the latter half of the nineteenth century, slaves were replaced by *indentured workers* as the main source of plantation labour. Indenture (or the 'coolie system') involved recruitment of large groups of workers, sometimes by force, and their transportation to another area for work. British colonial authorities recruited workers from the Indian subcontinent for the sugar plantations of Trinidad, British Guiana and other Caribbean countries. Others were employed in plantations, mines and railway construction in Malaya, East Africa and Fiji. The British also recruited Chinese 'coolies' for Malaya and other colonies. Dutch colonial authorities used Chinese labour on construction projects in the Dutch East Indies. Up to 1 million indentured workers were recruited in Japan, mainly for work in Hawaii, the USA, Brazil and Peru (Shimpo, 1995).

According to Potts (1990: 63–103) indentured workers were used in 40 countries by all the major colonial powers. She estimates that the system involved from 12 to 37 million workers between 1834 and 1941, when indentureship was finally abolished in the Dutch colonies. Indentured workers were bound by strict labour contracts for a period of several years. Wages and conditions were generally very poor, workers were subject to rigid discipline and breaches of contract were severely punished. Indentured workers were often cheaper for their employers than slaves (Cohen, 1991: 9–11). On the other hand, work overseas offered an opportunity to escape poverty and repressive situations, such as the Indian caste system. Many workers remained as free settlers in East Africa, the Caribbean, Fiji and elsewhere, where they could obtain land or set up businesses (Cohen, 1995: 46).

Indenture epitomized the principle of divide and rule, and a number of postcolonial conflicts (for example, hostility against Indians in Africa and Fiji, and against Chinese in South-East Asia) have their roots in such divisions. The Caribbean experience shows the effect of changing colonial labour practices on dominated peoples: the original inhabitants, the Caribs and Arawaks, were wiped out completely by European diseases and violence. With the development of the sugar industry in the eighteenth century, Africans were brought in as slaves. After emancipation in the nineteenth century, former slaves generally became small-scale subsistence farmers, and were replaced with indentured workers from India. Upon completion of their indentures, many Indians settled in the Caribbean, bringing in dependants. Some remained labourers on large estates, while others became established as a trading class, mediating between the white and mixed-race ruling class and the black majority.

Industrialization and migration to North America and Oceania before 1914

The wealth accumulated in Western Europe through colonial exploitation provided much of the capital which was to unleash the industrial revolutions of the eighteenth and nineteenth centuries. In Britain, profits from the colonies were invested in new forms of manufacture, as well as encouraging commercial farming and speeding up the enclosure of arable land for pasture. The displaced tenant farmers swelled the impoverished urban masses available as labour for the new factories. This emerging class of wage-labourers was soon joined by destitute artisans, such as hand-loom weavers, who had lost their livelihood through competition from the new manufacturers. Herein lay the basis of the new class which was crucial for the British industrial economy: the 'free proletariat', which was free of traditional bonds, but also of ownership of the means of production.

However, from the outset, *unfree labour* played an important part. Throughout Europe, draconian poor laws were introduced to control the displaced farmers and artisans – the 'hordes of beggars' who threatened public order. Workhouses and poorhouses were often the first form of manufacture, where the disciplinary instruments of the future factory system were developed and tested (Marx, 1976: chapter 28). In Britain, 'parish apprentices', orphan children under the care of local authorities, were hired out to factories as cheap unskilled labour. This was a form of forced labour, with severe punishments for insubordination or refusal to work.

The peak of the industrial revolution was the main period of British migration to America: between 1800 and 1860, 66 per cent of migrants to the USA were from Britain, and a further 22 per cent were from Germany. From 1850 to 1914 most migrants came from Ireland, Italy, Spain and Eastern Europe, areas in which industrialization came later. America offered the dream of becoming an independent farmer or trader in new lands of opportunity. Often this dream led to disappointment: the migrants became wage-labourers building roads and railways across the vast expanses of the New World; 'cowboys', gauchos or stockmen on large ranches; or factory workers in the emerging industries of the North-Eastern USA. However, many settlers did eventually realize their dream, becoming farmers, white-collar workers or business people, while others were at least able to see their children achieve education and upward social mobility.

The *USA* is generally seen as the most important of all immigration countries and epitomizes the notion of *free migration*. An estimated 54 million people entered between 1820 and 1987 (Borjas, 1990: 3). The peak period was from 1861 to 1920, during which 30 million people came (see Map 4.2). Mass migration is seen by some economic historians as a crucial feature of the 'greater Atlantic economy' (Hatton and Williamson, 1998). Until the 1880s, migration was unregulated: anyone who could afford the ocean passage could come to seek a new life in America. An important US Supreme Court decision of 1849 affirmed the 'plenary power' of the federal government to regulate international migration, thereby thwarting attempts by Eastern seaboard municipalities to prevent the arrival of Irish migrants (Daniels, 2004). However, American employers did organize campaigns to attract potential workers, and a multitude of agencies and shipping companies helped organize movements. Many of the migrants were young single men, hoping to save enough to return home and start a family. But there were also single women, couples and families. Racist campaigns led to exclusionary laws to keep out Chinese and other Asians from the 1880s. For Europeans and Latin Americans, entry remained free until 1920 (Borjas, 1990: 27). The census of that year showed that there were 13.9 million foreign-born people in the USA, making up 13.2 per cent of the total population (Briggs, 1984: 77).

Slavery had been a major source of capital accumulation in the early USA, but the industrial take-off after the Civil War (1861–5) was fuelled by mass immigration from Europe. After the abolition of slavery, the racist 'Jim Crow' system (entrenched discrimination against black people) was used to keep the now nominally free African–Americans in the plantations of the Southern states, since cheap cotton and other agricultural products were central to industrialization. The largest immigrant groups from 1860 to 1920 were Irish, Italians and Jews from Eastern Europe, but there were people from just about every other European country, as well as from Mexico. Patterns of settlement were closely linked to the emerging

Map 4.2   *Labour migrations connected with industrialization, 1850–1920*

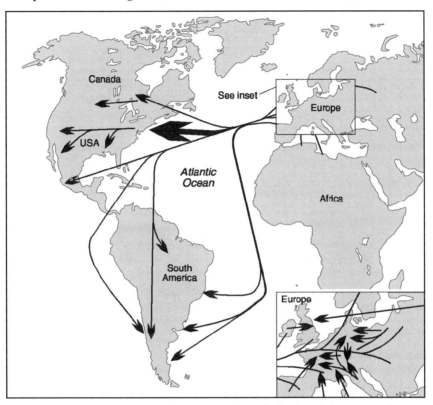

Note: The size of the arrowheads gives an approximate indication of the volume of flows. Exact figures are often unavailable.

industrial economy. Labour recruitment by canal and railway companies led to settlements of Irish and Italians along the construction routes. Some groups of Irish, Italians and Jews settled in the East coast ports of arrival, where work was available in construction, transport and factories. Chinese immigrants settled initially on the West coast, but moved inland following recruitment by railway construction companies. Similarly, early Mexican migrants were concentrated in the South-west, close to the Mexican border, but many moved northwards in response to recruitment by the railways. Some Central and Eastern European peoples became concentrated in the Midwest, where the development of heavy industry at the turn of the century provided work opportunities (Portes and Rumbaut, 2006: 38–40). The American working class thus developed through processes of chain or network migration which led to patterns of ethnic segmentation.

Canada received many loyalists of British origin after the American Revolution. From the late eighteenth century there was immigration from Britain, France, Germany and other Northern European countries. Many African–Americans came across the long frontier from the USA to escape slavery: by 1860, there were 40,000 black people in Canada. In the nine-teenth century, immigration was stimulated by the gold rushes, while rural immigrants were encouraged to settle the vast prairie areas. Between 1871 and 1931, Canada's population increased from 3.6 million to 10.3 million. Immigration from China, Japan and India also began in the late nineteenth century. Chinese came to the West coast, particularly to British Columbia, where they helped build the Canadian Pacific Railway. From 1886 a series of measures was introduced to stop Asian immigration (Kubat, 1987: 229–35). Canada received a large influx from Southern and Eastern Europe over the 1895 to 1914 period. In 1931, however, four preferred classes of immigrants were designated: British subjects with adequate financial means from the UK, Ireland and four other domains of the crown; US citizens; dependants of permanent residents of Canada; and agriculturists. Canada discouraged migration from Southern and Eastern Europe, while Asian immigration was prohibited from 1923 to 1947.

For *Australia*, immigration has been a crucial factor in economic development and nation-building ever since British colonization started in 1788. The Australian colonies were integrated into the British Empire as suppliers of raw materials such as wool, wheat and gold. The imperial state took an active role in providing workers for expansion through convict transportation (another form of unfree labour) and the encouragement of free settlement. Initially there were large male surpluses, especially in the frontier areas, which were often societies of 'men without women'. But many female convicts were transported, and there were special schemes to bring out single women as domestic servants and as wives for settlers.

When the surplus population of Britain became inadequate for labour needs from the mid-nineteenth century, Britain supported Australian employers in their demand for cheap labour from elsewhere in the Empire: China, India and the South Pacific Islands. The economic interests of Britain came into conflict with the demands of the nascent Australian labour movement. The call for decent wages came to be formulated in racist (and sexist) terms, as a demand for wages 'fit for white men'. Hostility towards Chinese and other Asian workers became violent. The exclusionary boundaries of the emerging Australian nation were drawn on racial lines, and one of the first Acts of the new Federal Parliament in 1901 was the introduction of the White Australia Policy (see de Lepervanche, 1975).

New Zealand was settled by British migrants from the 1830s. The 1840 Treaty of Waitangi between the British Crown and some 540 chiefs of the indigenous Maori people was the prelude to dispossession and marginalization of the Maori. Entry of British settlers (including white British subjects from elsewhere in the Empire) was to remain unrestricted until 1974. The government provided assisted passages virtually only for Britons, while 'non-Britons' required a special permit to enter. When quite small numbers of Chinese workers were recruited as miners and labourers from the 1860s onwards, public agitation led to strict control measures and a 'white New Zealand' policy. The great majority of the population considered themselves British rather than New Zealanders. British migrants were regarded as 'kin', and a sharp distinction was drawn between 'kin' and 'foreigners'. Maori, of course, were not 'foreigners', as the Treaty of Waitangi made them British subjects (McKinnon, 1996).

Labour migration within Europe

In Europe, *overseas emigration* and *intra-European migration* took place side by side. Of the 15 million Italians who emigrated between 1876 and 1920, nearly half (6.8 million) went to other European countries (mainly France, Switzerland and Germany (see Cinanni, 1968: 29)). As Western Europeans went overseas, often in the hope of escaping proletarianization, workers from peripheral areas, such as Poland, Ireland and Italy, were drawn in as replacement labour for large-scale agriculture and industry.

As the earliest industrial country, Britain was the first to experience large-scale labour immigration. The new factory towns quickly absorbed labour surpluses from the countryside. Atrocious working and living conditions led to poor health, high infant mortality and short life expectancy. Low wage levels forced both women and children to work, with disastrous results for the family. Natural increase was inadequate to meet labour needs, so Britain's closest colony, Ireland, became a labour source. The devastation of Irish peasant agriculture through absentee landlords and enclosures, combined with the ruin of domestic industry through British competition, had led to widespread poverty. The famines of 1822 and 1845–7 triggered massive migrations to Britain, the USA and Australia.

By 1851 there were over 700,000 Irish in Britain, making up 3 per cent of the population of England and Wales and 7 per cent of the population of Scotland (Jackson, 1963). They were concentrated in the industrial cities, especially in the textile factories and the building trades. Irish 'navvies' (a slang term derived from 'navigators') dug Britain's canals and built its railways. Engels (1962) described the appalling situation of Irish workers, arguing that Irish immigration was a threat to the wages and living conditions of English workers (see also Castles and Kosack, 1973: 16–17; Lucassen, 2005). Hostility and discrimination against the Irish were marked right into the twentieth century. This was true of Australia too, where Irish immigration accompanied British settlement from the outset. In both countries it was the active role played by Irish workers in the labour movement which was finally to overcome this split in the working class just in time for its replacement by new divisions after 1945, when black workers came to Britain and Southern Europeans to Australia.

The next major migration to Britain was of 120,000 Jews, who came as refugees from the pogroms of Russia between 1875 and 1914. Most settled initially in the East End of London, where many became workers in the clothing industry. Jewish settlement became the focus of racist campaigns, leading to the first restrictive legislation on immigration: the Aliens Act of

1905 and the Aliens Restriction Act of 1914 (Foot, 1965; Garrard, 1971). The Jewish experience of social mobility is often given as an example of migrant success. Many of the first generation managed to shift out of wage employment to become small entrepreneurs in the 'rag trade' (clothing manufacturing) or the retail sector. They placed strong emphasis on education for their children. Many of the second generation were able to move into business or white-collar employment, paving the way for professional careers for the third generation. Interestingly, one of Britain's newer immigrant groups – Bengalis from Bangladesh – now live in the same areas of the East End, often working in the same sweatshops, and worshipping in the same buildings (synagogues converted to mosques). However, they are isolated by racism and violence, and show little sign at present of repeating the Jewish trajectory. Irish and Jewish migrant workers may not be categorized as 'unfree workers'. The Irish were British subjects, with the same formal rights as other workers, while the Jews rapidly became British subjects. The constraints on their labour market freedom were not legal but economic (poverty and lack of resources made them accept inferior jobs and conditions) and social (discrimination and racism restricted their freedom of movement). It is in Germany and France that one finds the first large-scale use of the status of foreigner to restrict workers' rights.

In Germany, the heavy industries of the Ruhr, which emerged in the mid-nineteenth century, attracted agricultural workers away from the large estates of Eastern Prussia. Conditions in the mines were hard, but still preferable to semi-feudal oppression under the Junkers (large landowners). The workers who moved west were of Polish ethnic background, but had Prussian (and later German) citizenship, since Poland was at that time divided up between Prussia, the Austro-Hungarian Empire and Russia. By 1913, it was estimated that 164,000 of the 410,000 Ruhr miners were of Polish background (Stirn, 1964: 27). The Junkers compensated for the resulting labour shortages by recruiting 'foreign Poles' and Ukrainians as agricultural workers. Often workers were recruited in pairs – a man as cutter and a woman as binder – leading to so-called 'harvest marriages'. However, there was fear that settlement of Poles might weaken German control of the eastern provinces. In 1885, the Prussian government deported some 40,000 Poles and closed the frontier. The landowners protested at the loss of up to two-thirds of their labour force (Dohse, 1981: 29–32), arguing that it threatened their economic survival (see also Lucassen, 2005: 50–73).

By 1890, a compromise between political and economic interests emerged in the shape of a system of rigid control. 'Foreign Poles' were recruited as temporary seasonal workers only, not allowed to bring dependants and forced to leave German territory for several months each year. At first they were restricted to agricultural work, but later were permitted to take industrial jobs in Silesia and Thuringia (but not in western areas such as the Ruhr). Their work contracts provided pay and conditions inferior to those of German workers. Special police sections were established to deal with 'violation of contracts' (that is, workers leaving for better-paid jobs) through forcible return of workers to their employers, imprisonment or deportation. Thus police measures against foreigners were deliberately used as a method to keep wages low and to create a split labour market (Dohse, 1981: 33–83).

Foreign labour played a major role in German industrialization, with Italian, Belgian and Dutch workers alongside the Poles. In 1907, there were 950,000 foreign workers in the German Reich, of whom nearly 300,000 were in agriculture, 500,000 in industry and 86,000 in trade and transport (Dohse, 1981: 50). The authorities did their best to prevent family reunion and permanent settlement. Both in fact took place, but the exact extent is unclear. The system developed to control and exploit foreign labour was a precursor both of forced labour in the Nazi war economy and of the 'guest-worker system' in the German Federal Republic after 1955.

The number of foreigners in France increased rapidly from 381,000 in 1851 (1.1 per cent of total population) to 1 million (2.7 per cent) in 1881, and then more slowly to 1.2 million (3 per cent) in 1911 (Weil, 1991b: appendix, table 4) The majority came from neighbouring countries: Italy, Belgium, Germany and Switzerland, and later from Spain and Portugal. Movements were relatively spontaneous, though some recruitment was carried out by farmers' associations and mines (Cross, 1983: chapter 2). The foreign workers were mainly men who carried out unskilled manual work in agriculture, mines and steelworks (the heavy, unpleasant jobs that French workers were unwilling to take) (see also Rosenberg, 2006).

The peculiarity of the French case lies in the reasons for the shortage of labour during industrialization. Birth rates fell sharply after 1860. Peasants, shopkeepers and artisans followed 'Malthusian' birth control practices, which led to small families earlier than anywhere else (Cross, 1983: 5–7). According to Noiriel (1988: 297–312) this *grève des ventres* (belly strike) was motivated by resistance to proletarianization. Keeping the family small meant that property could be passed on intact from generation to generation, and that there would be sufficient resources to permit a decent education for the children. Unlike Britain and Germany, France therefore saw relatively little overseas emigration during industrialization. The only important exception was the movement of settlers to Algeria, which France invaded in 1830. Rural–urban migration was also fairly limited. The 'peasant worker' developed: the small farmer who supplemented subsistence agriculture through sporadic work in local industries. Where people did leave the countryside it was often to move straight into the new government jobs that proliferated in the late nineteenth century: straight from the primary to the tertiary sector.

In these circumstances, the shift from small to large-scale enterprises, made necessary by international competition from about the 1880s, could only be made through the employment of foreign workers. Thus labour immigration played a vital role in the emergence of modern industry and the constitution of the working class in France. Immigration was also seen as important for military reasons. The nationality law of 1889 was designed to turn immigrants and their sons into conscripts for the impending conflict with Germany (Schnapper, 1994: 66). From the mid-nineteenth century to the present, the labour market has been regularly fed by foreign immigration, making up, on average, 10–15 per cent of the working class. Noiriel estimated that, without immigration, the French population in the mid-1980s would have been only 35 million instead of over 50 million (Noiriel, 1988: 308–18).

The interwar period

At the onset of World War I, many migrants returned home to participate in military service or munitions production. However, labour shortages soon developed in the combatant countries. The German authorities prevented 'foreign Polish' workers from leaving the country, and recruited labour by force in occupied areas of Russia and Belgium (Dohse, 1981: 77–81). The French government set up recruitment systems for workers and soldiers from its North African, West African and Indo-Chinese colonies, and from China (about 225,000 in all). They were housed in barracks, paid minimal wages and supervised by former colonial overseers. Workers were also recruited in Portugal, Spain, Italy and Greece for French factories and agriculture (Cross, 1983: 34–42). Britain, too, brought soldiers and workers to Europe from its African and South Asian colonies during the conflict, although in smaller numbers. All the warring countries also made use of the forced labour of prisoners of war. Many Africans were pressed into service as soldiers and 'carriers' within Africa by Germany, Britain and other European countries. Official British figures put the military death toll in East Africa at 11,189, while 95,000 carriers died. The estimates for civilian casualties go far higher – for instance at least 650,000 in Germany's East African colonies (Paice, 2006).

The period from 1918 to 1945 was one of reduced international labour migration. This was partly because of economic stagnation and crisis, and partly because of increased hostility towards immigrants in many countries. Migration to Australia, for example, fell to low levels as early as 1891, and did not grow substantially until after 1945. An exception was the encouragement of Southern Italian migration to Queensland in the 1920s: Sicilians and Calabrians were seen as capable of backbreaking work in the sugar cane plantations, where they could replace South Pacific Islanders deported under the White Australia Policy. However, Southern Europeans were treated with suspicion. Immigrant ships were refused permission to land and there were 'anti-Dago' riots in the 1930s. Queensland passed special laws, prohibiting foreigners from owning land, and restricting them to certain industries (de Lepervanche, 1975).

In the USA, 'nativist' groups claimed that Southern and Eastern Europeans were 'unassimilable' and that they presented threats to public order and American values. Congress enacted a series of laws in the 1920s designed to limit drastically entries from any area except North-West Europe (Borjas, 1990: 28–9). This national-origins quota system stopped large-scale immigration to the USA until the 1960s. But the new mass production industries of the Fordist era had a substitute labour force at hand: black workers from the South. The period from about 1914 to the 1950s was that of the *Great Migration*, in which African–Americans fled segregation and exploitation in the Southern states for better wages and – they hoped – equal rights in the North-East, Midwest and West. Often they encountered new forms of segregation in the ghettoes of New York or Chicago, and new forms of discrimination, such as exclusion from the unions of the American Federation of Labor.

Meanwhile, Americanization campaigns were launched to ensure that immigrants learned English and became loyal US citizens. During the Great Depression, Mexican immigrants were repatriated by local governments and civic organizations, with some cooperation from the Mexican and US governments (Kiser and Kiser, 1979: 33–66). Many of the nearly 500,000 Mexicans were compelled to leave by the authorities, while others left because there was no work. In these circumstances, little was done to help Jews fleeing the rise of Hitler. There was no concept of the refugee in US law, and it was difficult to build support for admission of Jewish refugees when millions of US citizens were unemployed. Anti-Semitism was also a factor, and there was never much of a prospect for large numbers of European Jews to find safe haven before World War II.

France was the only Western European country to experience substantial immigration in the interwar years. The 'demographic deficit' had been exacerbated by war losses: 1.4 million men had been killed and 1.5 million permanently handicapped (Prost, 1966: 538). There was no return to the pre-war free movement policy; instead the government and employers refined the foreign labour systems established during the war. Recruitment agreements were concluded with Poland, Italy and Czechoslovakia. Much of the recruitment was organized by the *Société générale d'immigration* (SGI), a private body set up by farm and mining interests. North African migration to France was also developing. In addition, a 1914 law had removed barriers to movement of Algerian Muslims to Metropolitan France. Although they remained non-citizens, their numbers increased from 600 in 1912 to 60,000–80,000 by 1928 (Rosenberg, 2006: 130–1).

Foreign workers were controlled through a system of identity cards and work contracts, and were channelled into jobs in farming, construction and heavy industry. However, most foreign workers probably arrived spontaneously outside the recruiting system. The non-communist trade union movement cooperated with immigration, in return for measures designed to protect French workers from displacement and wage cutting (Cross, 1983: 51–63; Weil, 1991b: 24–7).

Just under 2 million foreign workers entered France from 1920 to 1930, about 567,000 of them recruited by the SGI (Cross, 1983: 60). Some 75 per cent of French population growth between 1921 and 1931 is estimated to

Box 4.1 Forced foreign labour in the Nazi war economy

The Nazi regime recruited enormous numbers of foreign workers – mainly by force – to replace the 11 million German workers conscripted for military service. The occupation of Poland, Germany's traditional labour reserve, was partly motivated by the need for labour. Labour recruitment offices were set up within weeks of the invasion, and the police and army rounded up thousands of young men and women (Dohse, 1981: 121). Forcible recruitment took place in all the countries invaded by Germany, while some voluntary labour was obtained from Italy, Croatia, Spain and other 'friendly or neutral countries'. By the end of the war, there were 7.5 million foreign workers in the Reich, of whom 1.8 million were prisoners of war. It is estimated that a quarter of industrial production was carried out by foreign workers in 1944 (Pfahlmann, 1968: 232). The Nazi war machine would have collapsed far earlier without foreign labour.

The basic principle for treating foreign workers declared by Sauckel, the Plenipotentiary for Labour, was that: 'All the men must be fed, sheltered and treated in such a way as to exploit them to the highest possible extent at the lowest conceivable degree of expenditure' (Homze, 1967: 113). This meant housing workers in barracks under military control, the lowest possible wages (or none at all), appalling social and health conditions, and complete deprivation of civil rights. Poles and Russians were compelled, like the Jews, to wear special badges showing their origin. Many foreign workers died through harsh treatment and cruel punishments. These were systematic; in a speech to employers, Sauckel emphasized the need for strict discipline: 'I don't care about them [the foreign workers] one bit. If they commit the most minor offence at work, report them to the police at once, hang them, shoot them. I don't care. If they are dangerous, they must be liquidated' (Dohse, 1981: 127).

The Nazis took exploitation of rightless migrants to an extreme which can only be compared with slavery, yet its legal core – the sharp division between the status of national and foreigner – was to be found in both earlier and later foreign labour systems.

have resulted from immigration (Decloîtres, 1967: 23). In view of the large female surplus in France, mainly men were recruited, and a fair degree of intermarriage took place. By 1931, there were 2.7 million foreigners in France (6.6 per cent of the total population). The largest group were Italians (808,000), followed by Poles (508,000), Spaniards (352,000) and Belgians (254,000) (Weil, 1991b: appendix, table 4). North African migration to France was also developing. Large colonies of Italians and Poles sprang up in the mining and heavy industrial towns of the north and east of France: in some towns, foreigners made up a third or more of the total population. There were Spanish and Italian agricultural settlements in the South-west.

In the depression of the 1930s, hostility towards foreigners increased, leading to a policy of discrimination in favour of French workers. In 1932 maximum quotas for foreign workers in firms were fixed. They were followed by laws permitting dismissal of foreign workers in sectors where there was unemployment. Many migrants were sacked and deported, and the foreign population dropped by half a million by 1936 (Weil, 1991b: 27–30). Cross concludes that in the 1920s foreign workers 'provided a cheap and flexible workforce necessary for capital accumulation and economic growth; at the same time, aliens allowed the French worker a degree of economic mobility'. In the 1930s, on the other hand, immigration 'attenuated and provided a scapegoat for the economic crisis' (Cross, 1983: 218).

In *Germany*, the crisis-ridden Weimar Republic had little need of foreign workers: by 1932 their number was down to about 100,000, compared with nearly a million in 1907 (Dohse, 1981: 112). Nonetheless, a new system of regulation of foreign labour developed. Its principles were: strict state control of labour recruitment; employment preference for nationals; sanctions against employers of illegal migrants; and unrestricted police power to deport unwanted foreigners (Dohse, 1981: 114–17). This system was partly attributable to the influence of the strong labour movement, which wanted measures to protect German workers, but it confirmed the weak legal position of migrant workers. Box 4.1 describes the use of forced foreign labour during World War II.

Conclusions

Contemporary migratory movements and policies are often profoundly influenced by historical precedents. This chapter has described the key role of labour migration in colonialism and industrialization. Labour migration has always been a major factor in the construction of a capitalist world market. In the USA, Canada, Australia, the UK, Germany and France (as well as in other countries not discussed here) migrant workers have played a role which varies in character according to economic, social and political conditions. But in every case the contribution of migration to industrialization and population-building was important and sometimes even decisive.

To what extent do the theories reviewed in Chapters 2 and 3 apply to the historical examples given? Involuntary movements of slaves and indentured workers do not easily fit neoclassical models and theories emphasizing migrants' agency, for the intentions of the participants played little part. Nonetheless some aspects of historical–structural models seem to fit: labour recruitment as the initial impetus, predominance of young males in the early stages, and subsequently family formation, long-term settlement and emergence of ethnic minorities. Worker migrations to England, Germany and France in the nineteenth and twentieth centuries fit the neoclassical model better. Their original intention was temporary, but they often led to family reunion and settlement.

As for migrations from Europe to America and Oceania in the nineteenth and early twentieth centuries, most migrants went by free choice, which fits better with liberal (or neoclassical) ideas on migration. Many young men and women went with the intention of permanent settlement, but quite a few went in order to work for a few years and then return home. Some did return, but in the long run the majority remained in the New World, often forming new ethnic communities. As we have seen, many of the migrants moved under difficult and dangerous conditions. Sometimes their hopes of a better life were dashed. Yet they had good reasons to take the risk, because the situation was usually even worse in the place of origin: poverty, domination by landlords, exposure to arbitrary violence – these were all powerful reasons to leave. And many – indeed most – migrants succeeded in building a better life in the new country – if not for themselves, then for their children. Thus we can see important parallels with today's migrations: migrants still experience many hardships but they often do succeed in escaping poverty and hopelessness in their place of origin and finding new opportunities elsewhere. Being a migrant can be very tough but staying at home can be worse.

Clearly the study of migrant labour is not the only way of looking at the history of migration. Movements caused by political or religious persecution have always been important, playing a major part in the development of countries as diverse as the USA and Germany. It is often impossible to draw strict lines between the various types of migration. Migrant labour systems have always led to some degree of settlement, just as settler and refugee movement have always been bound up with the political economy of capitalist development.

The period from about 1850 to 1914 was an era of mass migration in Europe and North America. Industrialization was a cause of internal rural-to-urban migration and both emigration and immigration. After 1914, war, xenophobia, economic stagnation and increased state control (such as the introduction of passports) caused a considerable decline in migration. The large-scale movements of the preceding period seemed to have been the results of a unique and unrepeatable constellation. When rapid and sustained economic growth got under way after World War II, the new age of migration was to take the world by surprise.

Guide to further reading

Additional texts, 4.1 'Migration and Nation in French History' and 4.2 'Migrations Shaping African History', are to be found on *The Age of Migration* website.

Manning (2005) gives a history of migration from the earliest times to the present, as does Part 1 of Goldin *et al.* (2011). Hoerder (2002) and

Wang (1997) both also cover the broad sweep of global migration history. Cohen (1987) provides an historical overview of migrant labour in the international division of labour. Blackburn (1988) and Fox-Genovese and Genovese (1983) analyse slavery and its role in capitalist development, while Schama (2006) charts the history of abolition and its meaning for British and US politics.

Archdeacon (1983) examines immigration in US history, showing how successive waves of entrants have 'become American'. Hatton and Williamson (1998) present an economic analysis of 'mass migration' to the USA, while their later work (Hatton and Williamson, 2005) compares pre-1920 migration with more recent patterns. Portes and Rumbaut (2006) analyse historical patterns of entry and their long-term results.

Bade (2003) and Lucassen (2005) analyse the role of migration in European history. Moch (1992) is good on earlier European migration experiences, while many contributions in Cohen (1995) are on the history of migration. Lucassen *et al.* (2006) examine the history of immigrant integration in Western European societies. French readers are referred to the excellent accounts by Noiriel (1988; 2007). Jupp (2001; 2002) provides detailed accounts of the Australian experience.

Chapter 5

Migration in Europe since 1945

This chapter and the three that follow provide overviews of migration in, to and from specific world regions: Europe; the Americas; Asia and the Pacific; and Africa and the Middle East. They cover all types of international migration, both forced and voluntary. Obviously, single chapters cannot do justice to the complexity of migration situations in such vast regions, and we encourage readers to follow up our sources for the areas that interest them most. Inevitably our accounts are selective and leave out a great deal. Some sub-regions (such as Central Asia and South Asia) are barely covered, while other areas are presented in greater detail. Although international migration transcends borders, we often have to focus on nation-states, since most data is presented and policies are formed at that level. The aim of these chapters is to show the main trends in international migration, and how global and regional patterns play out in various locations. Since historical developments and contemporary trends vary greatly, it has proved impossible to structure the regional chapters in a common way; each follows the logic of the most pressing issues of the region. Nonetheless, behind the complexity and diversity, we believe that certain global features – already discussed in earlier chapters – can be discerned.

Since the end of World War II, international migrations have changed in character and direction. While for centuries Europeans have been moving outward through conquering, colonizing, and settling in lands elsewhere on the globe, these patterns were partly reversed in the second half of the twentieth century. Under the influence of decolonization, demographic change, rapid economic growth and the creation of the European Union as a free trade and migration zone, Europe has emerged as a major global migration destination. While migration of Europeans to the Americas and Oceania rapidly declined in the 1960s and 1970s, Western European countries started to attract increasing number of migrants, mainly from former colonies and countries located on the European periphery. While they do not see themselves as immigration societies, immigration rates in many European countries now match or exceed those of the USA or other classical immigration countries.

There have been three main phases. In the first, from 1945 to the early 1970s, the chief economic strategy of large-scale enterprises was concentration of investment and expansion of production in the existing highly developed countries. As a result, large numbers of migrant workers were

102

employed or recruited from less developed countries in the Mediterranean region as well as from Ireland and Finland into the fast-expanding industrial areas of Western Europe. The end of this phase was marked by the Oil Crisis of 1973, which led to a recruitment freeze. The ensuing period of recessions gave impetus to a restructuring of the world economy, involving capital investment in new industrial areas in developing countries, altered patterns of world trade, and introduction of new technologies.

This second phase (mid-1970s to the mid-1990s) coincided with neoliberal policies which were focused on economic deregulation and flexibilization of labour markets and privatization of state companies. In this period, industrial production was increasingly relocated to low-wage developing countries. This led to the mass dismissal of factory and mine workers, including many former 'guest-workers' and other labour migrants. However, the recruitment freeze did not lead to the large-scale return of workers, as many migrant workers preferred to stay and to bring over their families. Family migration largely explained why migration was maintained at relatively high levels. From the mid-1980s, economic growth resumed, and the rapid growth of the service sectors would draw in more and more low- and high-skilled migrant workers, while labour demand in sectors such as agriculture and construction was maintained. The fall of the Berlin Wall in 1989 heralded the collapse of the Soviet Union and the rest of the Communist Warsaw Pact. The immediate effect was to precipitate flows of asylum seekers seeking refuge in Western Europe.

Although these events fell in the second phase, they were crucial to the emergence of the third phase, from the mid-1990s. The third phase (which was not a sudden shift, but rather a gradual transition building on the events of the early 1990s), saw the opening up of a new 'labour frontier' (see Chapter 2) in Central and Eastern Europe: Poland, Ukraine, Romania and Bulgaria and the Baltic republics emerged as important new source regions of migrants in Western and Southern Europe, but also became transit and immigration countries in their own right. This period was also characterized by the rise of new migration destinations on Europe's southern and western fringes, with particularly Ireland, Italy and Spain attracting many migrants from Eastern Europe, North and West Africa and Latin America. These developments coincided with further European integration, the establishment of the borderless Schengen zone and the concomitant reinforcement of border controls at EU's external borders.

The global economic crisis (GEC) which started in 2008 seems to mark the – at least temporary – end of this period of rapid economic growth, EU expansion and high immigration. Nevertheless, as after the Oil Crisis, this decline in immigration has been relatively modest, and the anticipated mass return has not occurred, because particularly non-European immigrants preferred to stay put. The largest effect of the crisis was on intra-European migration, which slowed down, while several particularly crisis-hit countries such as Greece, Spain, Portugal and Ireland became net emigration countries again.

This chapter will discuss migratory movements since 1945 within, from and to Europe. This chapter will *not* discuss the long-term impacts of migration on receiving societies, which will be the theme of later chapters, especially Chapters 11, 12 and 13. For better understanding of the data presented in this chapter, see the *Note on Migration Statistics* at the beginning of this book.

Migration in the post-World War II boom

Between 1945 and the early 1970s, two main types of migration led to the formation of new, ethnically distinct populations in advanced industrial countries:

- migration of workers from the European periphery to Western Europe, often through 'guest-worker systems';
- migration of 'colonial migrants' to the former colonial powers.

The precise timing of these movements varied: they started later in Germany and ended earlier in the UK. These two types, which both led to family reunion and other kinds of chain and network migration, will be examined here. There were also other types of migration:

- mass movements of European refugees at the end of World War II (post-1945 refugee movements were most significant in the case of Germany and Poland, for instance);
- return migrations of former colonists to their countries of origin as colonies gained their independence.

One further type of migration became increasingly significant after 1968:

- intra-European Community free movement of workers, which from 1993 was to become intra-European Union free movement of EU citizens.

Map 5.1 gives an idea of some of the main migratory flows of this period.

Foreign workers and 'guest-worker' systems

All the highly industrialized countries of North-Western Europe used temporary labour recruitment at some stage between 1945 and 1973, although this sometimes played a smaller role than spontaneous entry of foreign workers. The rapidly expanding economies were able to utilize the labour reserves of the less developed European periphery: the Mediterranean countries, Ireland and Finland.

105

Map 5.1 *International migration, 1945–1973*

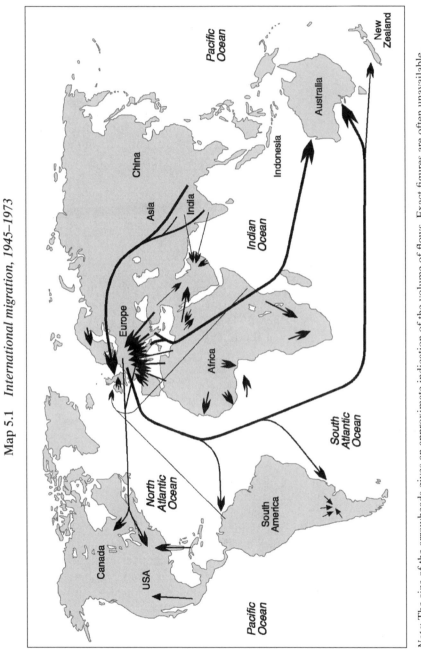

Note: The size of the arrowheads gives an approximate indication of the volume of flows. Exact figures are often unavailable.

Immediately after World War II, the *British* government brought in 90,000 mainly male workers from refugee camps and from Italy through the European Voluntary Worker (EVW) scheme. The scheme was fairly small and only operated until 1951, because it was easier to make use of colonial workers (see below). A further 100,000 Europeans entered Britain on work permits between 1946 and 1951, and some European migration continued subsequently (Kay and Miles, 1992).

Belgium also started recruiting foreign workers immediately after the war. They were mainly Italian men, and were employed in the coalmines and the iron and steel industry. The system operated until 1963, after which foreign work-seekers were allowed to come of their own accord. Many brought in dependants and settled permanently, changing the ethnic composition of Belgium's industrial areas.

France established an *Office National d'Immigration* (ONI) in 1945 to organize recruitment of workers from Southern Europe. Migration was seen as a solution to postwar labour shortages. In view of continuing low birth rates and war losses, massive family settlement was envisaged. ONI also coordinated the employment of up to 150,000 seasonal agricultural workers per year, mainly from Spain. By 1970, 2 million foreign workers and 690,000 dependants resided in France. Many found it easier to come as 'tourists', get a job and then regularize their situation. This applied particularly to Portuguese and Spanish workers, escaping their respective dictatorships, who generally lacked passports. By 1968, ONI statistics revealed that 82 per cent of the foreigners admitted by the ONI came as 'clandestines'.

Switzerland pursued a policy of large-scale labour import from 1945 to 1974. Foreign workers were recruited abroad by employers, while admission and residence were controlled by the government. Job changing, permanent settlement and family reunion were forbidden to seasonal workers until the mid-1960s. Considerable use was also made of cross-frontier commuters. Swiss industry became highly dependent on foreign workers, who made up nearly a third of the labour force by the early 1970s. The need to attract and retain workers, coupled with diplomatic pressure from Italy, led to relaxations on family reunion and permanent stay, so that Switzerland, too, experienced settlement and the formation of permanent migrant communities.

The examples could be continued: the Netherlands brought in 'guest-workers', mainly from Turkey and Morocco. In the 1960s and early 1970s, Luxembourg's industries were highly dependent on foreign labour, and Sweden employed workers from Finland and from Southern European countries. In Italy, migration from the underdeveloped south was crucial to the economic take-off of the northern industrial triangle between Milan, Turin and Genoa in the 1960s: this was internal migration, but rather similar in its economic and social character to foreign worker movements in other European countries. The key case for understanding the 'guest-worker system' was the Federal Republic of Germany (FRG), which set up a highly organized state recruitment apparatus (see Box 5.1).

Box 5.1 The German 'guest-worker system'

The former West-German Government started recruiting foreign workers in the mid-1950s. The Federal Labour Office (*Bundesanstalt für Arbeit*, or BfA) set up recruitment offices in the Mediterranean countries. Employers requiring foreign labour paid a fee to the BfA, which selected workers, testing occupational skills, providing medical examinations and screening police records. The workers were brought in groups to Germany, where employers had to provide initial accommodation. Recruitment, working conditions and social security were regulated by bilateral agreements between the Federal Republic of Germany (FRG) and the sending countries: first Italy, then Spain, Greece, Turkey, Morocco, Portugal, Tunisia and Yugoslavia.

The number of foreign workers in the FRG rose from 95,000 in 1956 to 1.3 million in 1966 and 2.6 million in 1973. This massive migration was the result of rapid industrial expansion and the shift to new methods of mass production, which required large numbers of low-skilled workers. Foreign women workers played a major part, especially in the later years: their labour was in high demand in textiles and clothing, electrical goods and other manufacturing sectors.

German policies conceived migrant workers as temporary labour units, which could be recruited, utilized and sent away again as employers required. To enter and remain in the FRG, a migrant needed a residence permit and a labour permit. These were granted for restricted periods, and were often valid only for specific jobs and areas. Entry of dependants was discouraged. A worker could be deprived of his or her permit for a variety of reasons, leading to deportation.

However, it was impossible to prevent family reunion and settlement. Often officially recruited migrants were able to get employers to request their wives or husbands as workers. Competition with other labour-importing countries for labour led to relaxation of restrictions on entry of dependants in the 1960s. Families became established and children were born. Foreign labour was beginning to lose its mobility, and social costs (for housing, education and healthcare) could no longer be avoided. When the Federal Government stopped labour recruitment in November 1973, the motivation was not only the looming Oil Crisis, but also the belated realization that permanent immigration was taking place.

In the FRG we see, in the most developed form, all the principles – but also the contradictions – of temporary foreign labour recruitment systems. These include the belief in temporary sojourn, the restriction of labour market and civil rights, the recruitment of single workers (men at first, but with increasing numbers of women as time went on), the inability to prevent family reunion completely, the gradual move towards longer stay, and the inexorable pressures for settlement and community formation. The FRG took the system furthest, but its central element – the legal distinction between the status of citizen and of foreigner as a criterion for determining political and social rights – was to be found throughout Europe (see Hammar, 1985).

Sources: Castles and Kosack 1973; Castles *et al.* 1984.

Table 5.1   *Minority population in the main Western European countries of immigration (1950–75) (thousands)*

Country	1950	1960	1970	1975	Per cent of total population 1975
Belgium	354	444	716	835	8.5
France	2,128	2,663	3,339	4,196	7.9
Germany (FRG)	548	686	2,977	4,090	6.6
Netherlands	77	101	236	370	2.6
Sweden	124	191	411	410	5.0
Switzerland	279	585	983	1,012	16.0
UK	1,573	2,205	3,968	4,153	7.8

Notes: Figures for all countries except the UK are for foreign residents. They exclude naturalized persons and immigrants from the Dutch and French colonies. UK data are census figures for 1951, 1961 and 1971 and estimates for 1975. The 1951 and 1961 data are for overseas-born persons, and exclude children born to immigrants in the UK. The 1971 and 1975 figures include children born in the UK, with both parents born abroad.

Source: Castles *et al.* (1984: 87–8), where detailed sources are given.

Multinational agreements were also used to facilitate labour migration. Free movement of workers within the European Economic Community (EEC) which came into force in 1968, was relevant mainly for Italian workers, while the Nordic Labour Market affected Finns going to Sweden. The EC arrangements were the first step towards creating a 'European labour market', which was to become a reality in 1993. However, in the 1960s and early 1970s, labour movement within the Community was actually declining, owing to gradual equalization of wages and living standards within the EC, while migration from outside the Community was increasing. Table 5.1 shows the development of minority populations arising from migration in selected Western European countries up to 1975.

Colonial workers

Migration from former colonies was important for Britain, France, the Netherlands and later also for Portugal. *Britain* had a net inflow of about 350,000 from Ireland, its traditional labour reserve, between 1946 and 1959. Irish workers provided manual labour for industry and construction, and many brought in their families and settled permanently. Irish residents in Britain enjoyed all civil rights, including the right to vote. Immigration of workers from the New Commonwealth (former British colonies in the Caribbean, the Indian subcontinent and Africa) started after 1945 and grew during the 1950s. Some workers came as a result of recruitment by London Transport, but most migrated spontaneously in response to labour demand. By 1951, there were 218,000 people of New Commonwealth origin (including Pakistan, which subsequently left the

Commonwealth), a figure which increased to 541,000 in 1961. Entry of workers from the New Commonwealth declined after 1962, partly due to the introduction of severe restrictions through the Commonwealth Immigrants Act of 1962, and partly as the result of the early onset of economic stagnation in Britain.

However, most of the Commonwealth immigrants had come to stay, and family reunion continued, until it in turn was restricted by the 1971 Immigration Act. The population of New Commonwealth origin increased to 1.2 million in 1971 and 1.5 million in 1981. Most Afro-Caribbean and Asian immigrants and their children in Britain enjoyed formal citizenship (although this no longer applies to those admitted since the 1981 Nationality Act). Their minority status was not defined by being foreign, but by widespread institutional and informal discrimination. Most black and Asian workers found unskilled manual jobs in industry and the services, and a high degree of residential segregation emerged in the inner cities. Educational and social disadvantage became a further obstacle to mobility out of initial low-status positions. By the 1970s, the emergence of ethnic minorities was inescapable.

France experienced large-scale spontaneous immigration from its former colonies in the Maghreb (Algeria, Morocco and Tunisia) as well as from Southern Europe. Smaller numbers of workers came from the former West African colonies of Senegal, Mali and Mauritania. Some of these migrants came before independence, while they were still French citizens. Others came later through preferential migration arrangements, or irregularly. Migration from Algeria was regulated by bilateral agreements which accorded Algerian migrants a unique status. Moroccans and Tunisians, by contrast, were admitted through the *Office National d'Immigration* (ONI). Many people also came from the overseas departments and territories such as Guadeloupe, Martinique and Réunion. All these migrations were initially male-dominated, but with increasing proportions of women as the movement matured. Non-European immigrants in France were relegated to the bottom of the labour market, often working in highly exploitative conditions. Housing was frequently segregated, and very poor in quality; indeed, shanty towns (known as *bidonvilles*) appeared in France in the 1960s. Extreme-right groups began to subject non-European immigrants to a campaign of racial violence: 32 North Africans were murdered in 1973.

The Netherlands had two main inflows from former colonies. Between 1945 and the early 1960s up to 300,000 'repatriates' from the former Dutch East Indies (now Indonesia) entered the Netherlands. Although most had been born overseas and many were of mixed Dutch and Indonesian parentage, they were Dutch citizens. The official policy of assimilation appears to have worked well in this case, and there is little evidence of racism or discrimination against this group. The exception is the roughly 32,000 Moluccans, who wanted to return to their homeland if it could achieve independence from Indonesia. They remained segregated in camps, and rejected integration into Dutch society. In the late 1970s, their disaffection led to several violent incidents. After 1965, increasing numbers of migrants came to the Netherlands from the Caribbean territory of Surinam. In a 'beat the ban' rush, a peak was reached in the years leading up to independence in 1975, and 1980, when visas were introduced. This led to an increase in the number of Surinamese in the Netherlands from 39,000 in 1973 to 145,000 in 1981 (van Amersfoort, 2011).

Comparative perspectives

One common feature in the migratory movements of the 1945–73 period was the predominance of economic motivations on the part of migrants, employers and governments. As we will see in Chapter 6, the same is true of temporary worker recruitment for US agriculture, and Chapter 7 will show that economic motives also played a major part in Australia's postwar migration programme. The colonial workers who migrated to Britain, France and the Netherlands generally had economic reasons, although for the governments, political considerations (such as the desire to maintain links with former colonies) also played a part, while governments of authoritarian origin countries often saw migration as a political 'safety valve' which could relieve unemployment and poverty (see Chapter 3). In the post-1973 period, family migration rose in significance, but fluctuations in labour immigration continued to follow business cycles rather closely.

Another feature of the 1945–73 period was growing diversity of areas of origin, and increasing cultural difference between migrants and receiving populations. At the beginning of the period, most migrants to all main receiving countries came from various parts of Europe. As time went on, increasing proportions came from Asia, Africa and Latin America. This trend was to become even more marked in the following period.

A comparison of the situation of colonial workers with that of guest-workers is instructive. The differences are obvious: colonial workers were citizens of the former colonial power, or had some preferential entitlement to enter and live there. They usually came spontaneously, often following lines of communication built up in the colonial period. Once they came in, they generally had civil and political rights; most (though by no means all) intended to stay permanently. On the other hand, guest-workers and other foreign workers were non-citizens. Their rights were severely restricted. Many were recruited; others came spontaneously and were able to regularize their situation; others came irregularly and worked without documentation. Generally they were seen as temporary workers who were expected to leave after a few years.

There are also similarities, however, especially in the economic and social situations of the two categories. Both became overwhelmingly concentrated in low-skilled manual work, mainly in industry, mining and construction. Both tended to suffer substandard housing, poor social conditions and educational disadvantage. Over time, there was a convergence of legal situations, with family reunion and social rights of foreign workers improving, while the colonial migrants lost many of their privileges. At the same time, both groups were affected by similar processes of marginalization, often (but not always) leading to a degree of separation from the rest of the population and an ethnic minority position.

European migrations in the period of economic restructuring (1974–mid-1990s)

The curbing of organized recruitment of manual workers by West-European countries in the early 1970s was part of a larger process consisting of a fundamental restructuring of the world economy. The subsequent period – often characterized as the epoch of *globalization* (see Chapter 3) – has been marked by:

(a) changes in global investment patterns: increased capital export from developed countries in the 1970s and 1980s led to the establishment of manufacturing industries in some previously underdeveloped areas; in the 1990s and the 2000s new centres of economic dynamism emerged in the Middle East (Gulf oil states and more recently Turkey) and parts of Asia (first South Korea, Taiwan, Singapore, later also Thailand, Malaysia, China and India) and Latin America (e.g., Brazil, Chile);

(b) the micro-electronic revolution, which has reduced the need for manual workers in manufacturing alongside an erosion of traditional skilled occupations in highly developed countries;

(c) expansion of the services sector, with demand for both highly skilled and low-skilled workers;

(d) increasing education and occupational specialization, reinforcing the segmentation of labour markets and declining domestic supply of low-skilled workers;

(e) growing informal sectors in the economies of wealthy countries and casualization of employment, growth in part-time work, increasingly insecure conditions of employment as a consequence of neoliberal economic policies.

These transformations have had profound effects in Africa, Asia and Latin America. In some places, rapid industrialization and social change have taken place. But in other places postcolonial development strategies have had limited success or have entirely failed. Many countries are marked by rapid population growth, rapid urbanization, political instability, falling living standards, persistent poverty and sometimes even famine. The result is an increase in inequality both within and between regions.

Globalization has brought about complementary social and economic transformations in 'North' and 'South' that have increased migration within and to Europe and generated new forms of mobility. The main trends include:

(a)   a decline of government-organized labour migration to Western Europe followed by emergence of a second generation of temporary foreign worker policies in the 1990s;

(b)   family reunion of former foreign workers and colonial workers, and the subsequent formation of new ethnic minorities;

(c)   transition of many Southern and Central European countries as well as Turkey from countries of emigration to countries of transit and immigration;

(d)   growing migration to Western Europe from Eastern Europe (e.g., Poland, Romania, Ukraine) and non-European origin countries located in the Maghreb (e.g. Morocco, Algeria, Tunisia), Latin America (e.g., Ecuador, Bolivia, Brazil) and West Africa (e.g., Senegal, Mali, Ghana and Nigeria);

(e)   large-scale movements of refugees and asylum seekers due to violent conflict and repression; movements have been mostly within conflict regions, but have also led to increasing migration to Europe;

(f)   increasing international migration of high-skilled workers and students, both temporary and long-term;

(g)   proliferation of irregular migration (as a response to increasing entry restrictions) and legalization policies.

Persistence and diversification of migration to Western Europe

The immediate post-1973 period was one of consolidation and demographic 'normalization' of immigrant populations in Western Europe. Active recruitment of foreign workers and colonial workers largely ceased. For colonial migrants in Britain, France and the Netherlands, trends to family reunion continued. The recruitment freeze and immigration restrictions pushed many migrants into permanent settlement, as they feared that they would not to be able to re-emigrate if their return were not successful. Governments initially tried to prevent family reunion, but with little success. In several countries, the law courts played a major role in preventing policies deemed to violate the protection of the family contained in national constitutions. The settlement process, and the emergence of second and third generations born in Western Europe, led to internal differentiation and the development of community structures and consciousness. By the 1980s, colonial migrants and their descendants had become clearly visible social groups.

By the mid-1980s Southern European countries were experiencing migration transitions. Economic growth, combined with a sharp fall in birth rates, led to serious labour shortages. Italy, Spain, Greece, and, to a certain extent,

Portugal, all became countries of immigration, using labour from North Africa, Latin America, Asia and – later – Eastern Europe for low-skilled jobs (King *et al.*, 2000) (see below). Change became even more rapid after the fall of the Berlin Wall in 1989. The collapse of the Soviet Union and the Eastern European socialist states led to instability in Central Europe and undermined many of the barriers that had kept population mobility in check.

The 1985 signature of the Schengen Agreement would lead to a borderless European Area in 1995, which included all then EU members, except for the United Kingdom and Ireland, which opted out. Since then, all new EU members as well as non-EU members Iceland, Norway, Switzerland and Liechtenstein joined the Schengen area, which in 2013 comprised 26 members. Together with the gradual process of EU expansion, this contributed to a growing integration of European migration systems, a radical expansion of the European free migration space, as well as a growing diversification of immigrant populations.

The result of these geopolitical shifts and economic transformations was a growing diversity in the geographical, ethnic, social and cultural backgrounds of European immigrant populations. The combination of the unexpected settlement of former guest-workers and their families after 1973, continued family migration, and the new labour immigration of the 1990s reinforced the politicization of migration.

In the 1990s, although they represented a minority of immigrants, asylum seekers were portrayed by the media as economic migrants and welfare seekers in disguise, and became the target of widespread hostility. Governments vied with each other in introducing tougher asylum rules. They also believed that admission of migrant workers should be avoided since it would inevitably lead to settlement and unpredictable social impacts. Policymakers tightened up national immigration restrictions and attempted to reinforce European cooperation on border control (see Chapters 9 and 10).

Southern European migration transitions

In the 1970s and 1980s, most Southern European countries – the labour reserve for Western Europe, North America, South America and Australia for over a century – underwent migration transitions. Until 1973, Italy, Spain, Portugal and Greece were viewed as lands of emigration. Then, at somewhat different junctures, they started to experience declining emigration and increasing immigration. They have come to share many of the characteristics and concerns of their EU partner states to the north, yet remain demarcated by the key role played by the underground economy in shaping inflows, the preponderance of irregular migration in overall migration and by weak governmental capacity to regulate international migration (Reyneri, 2001).

In *Italy*, numbers of foreigners with residence permits doubled between 1981 and 1991, from 300,000 to 600,000, and then rose to 1.4 million by 2000 and 4.6 million in 2010, representing 7.6 per cent of the total population living in Italy (OECD, 2012; Strozza and Venturini, 2002: 265) (see also Table 5.2). These steep increases are due to a series of regularizations of irregularly resident populations between 1986 and 2009. Entry of non-EU citizens for employment in Italy is officially governed by annual quotas. However, the quotas are very low and do not reflect real labour demand, resulting in substantial rates of overstaying and irregular entry. Romanians form the largest immigrant group. In 2010, their number reached 969,000 and they accounted for almost a quarter of all new registrations of foreign residents. The leading groups of non-EU residents are Albanians (483,000) and Moroccans (452,000) (OECD, 2012: 242).

Spain went through a similar migration transition to Italy. Prior to 1980, Spain was mainly a land of emigration. That status quo began to change with post-Franco democratization after 1975 and membership (alongside Portugal) of the EC in 1986. The 1986–99 period saw rapidly increasing immigration particularly from North Africa, which was boosted by economic growth, the large-scale incorporation of Spanish women into the labour market which generated a demand for reproductive labour (such as domestic work), and regulation of entry through recruitment and regularizations. After 2000, growth consolidated, Latin American migration was encouraged and family migration grew in significance. The registered foreign population in Spain grew from 279,000 in 1990 to 1.3 million in 2000. By 2005, it had shot up to 4.1 million only to increase further to 5.7 million in 2010, which represented 12.4 per cent of its total population (OECD, 2012, see also Table 5.2). As in Italy, a large share of immigrants entered legally and subsequently overstayed visas while a minority entered Spain irregularly. Between 1985 and 2005, Spain authorized 12 legalization campaigns (Plewa, 2006: 247).

Data from municipal registers, which include irregularly resident foreigners, suggested that 896,000 Romanians lived in Spain around 2010. Moroccans were the largest non-EU group of foreigners with a total population of 783,000, followed by an estimated 306,000 Ecuadorians (Instituto Nacional de Estadística, 2011). In line with segmented labour market theory (see Chapter 2), foreign workers are specialized according to their origins. Moroccans and other Africans tend to work in agriculture. Latin American women often work in domestic service and care work, while Latin American men tend to work in construction and services and Europeans in industry (OECD, 2006: 214).

Portugal also went through a predominantly postcolonial, migration transition. From the mid-nineteenth century to the mid-1970s, Portuguese emigrated, leaving a legacy of some 5 million Portuguese and their descendants living abroad (OECD, 2004: 254). The revolution of 1974 and decolonization marked the beginning of significant postcolonial migration from former Portuguese possessions in Africa. As in Spain and Italy, most recent immigrants overstayed visas or arrived irregularly and there have been recurrent legalizations (Cordeiro, 2006: 242; OECD, 2007: 276). Migrants from Eastern Europe, Brazil and former African colonies comprise the bulk of the foreign population. According to official figures, in 2010 the most sizeable immigrant groups were Brazilians (120,000), Ukrainians (50,000), Cape

Verdeans (45,000), Romanians (37,000) and Angolans (24,000) (OECD, 2012: 367). In contrast to Italy and Spain, however, Portugal has never ceased to be an important emigration country, which reflects the relative weakness of its economy compared to other EU countries.

Until 1990, international migration to *Greece* mainly involved repatriation of ethnic Greeks from abroad and arrivals of refugees in transit. After 1990, immigration soared and in 2010 the estimated 810,000 foreigners constituted 7.1 per cent of Greece's population. About a third of Greece's migrants are of Greek ethnic descent: Pontian Greeks from the former Soviet Union (150,000) and ethnic Greeks from Albania (Triandafyllidou and Lazarescu, 2009). In 2010, the largest groups of registered non-EU immigrants came from Albania (491,000), Ukraine (21,500), Georgia (17,000), and Pakistan (16,000). The largest groups of EU nationals in Greece come from Bulgaria and Romania (OECD, 2012:234).

Migration in Central and Eastern Europe

The South-European migration transitions took place at the same time as the integration of Central and Eastern European countries into European migration systems. The post-1989 transition from Communist rule to democracy and market economies has transformed states and societies in Central and Eastern Europe. Migration figured centrally in the crisis and collapse of Communist regimes, and the early 1990s witnessed significant outflows. Initially, this fuelled fears of mass migrations in Western Europe. Populist politicians and sensationalist media spoke of a 'migration crisis' (Baldwin-Edwards and Schain, 1994), and warned that 'floods' of desperate migrants would 'swamp' Western European welfare systems and drag down living standards (Thränhardt, 1996).

But by the mid-1990s it was clear that the 'invasion' was not going to take place. Asylum-seeker entries to European OECD countries peaked at 695,000 in 1992 in response to the Yugoslav civil wars and then declined, although they were to increase again around 2000. East–West movements did increase, although most migrants were members of ethnic minorities moving to so-called ancestral homelands, where they had a right to entry and citizenship: ethnic Germans (*Aussiedler*) to Germany (Levy, 1999; Thränhardt, 1996: 237), Russian Jews to Israel, Bulgarian Turks to Turkey, and Pontian Greeks to Greece.

The bulk of the population, however, did not share the migration opportunities of such minorities – with the exception of former East Germans. Instead, these populations endured transitions to democracy and market economies that often (at least initially) increased unemployment, socioeconomic hardship and interethnic tensions. Movements of Poles, Russians, and other East Europeans to Western Europe in search of work also increased in the 1990s, but did not reach the extreme levels originally predicted.

At the same time, more economically advanced states like Poland, Hungary and the Czech Republic started attracting immigrants in significant numbers. They were generally poorly prepared to regulate international migration, lacking appropriate laws and administrative agencies. Most of the states in the region recorded significant increases in border crossings in the 1990s. Transit migration of third-country nationals moving through Central and Eastern Europe to destinations further west also grew in significance. There were three major migratory movements:

1. Citizens from former Warsaw Pact countries who, until EU Accession in 2004, could enter other such countries legally without a visa and then attempt to migrate on irregularly to the EU. Many Roma ('Gypsies') from South-eastern Europe (especially Romania) participated in such movements.
2. Refugees from conflicts in the Western Balkans, especially in Bosnia and Croatia (1991–3) and Kosovo (1999). Hungary and the Czech Republic received many more refugees than Poland, although most went to Germany.
3. Africans and Asians. With the disintegration of the USSR, its successor states became a relatively easy-to-cross bridge between poles of economic inequality (Stola, 2001: 89).

Ukraine and the Russian Federation have emerged as major source countries for migration to OECD member states since 2000 (OECD, 2006: 34). Millions of people moved within and between the successor states of the former Soviet Union (UNHCR, 1995: 24–5). Russia thus became a major country of immigration, with around 2 million ethnic Russians leaving or being displaced from the Baltic states, Ukraine and other parts of the former Soviet Union (Münz, 1996: 206). Additionally, there were nearly 1 million refugees from various conflicts and some 700,000 ecological displacees, mainly from areas affected by the 1986 Chernobyl nuclear disaster (Wallace and Stola, 2001: 15). During the 1990s, approximately 1 million Russian Jews migrated to Israel.

Migration trends of the new millennium

Migration movements steadied for a while in the mid-1990s mainly due to economic stagnation. But at the beginning of the new millennium, migration movements again increased sharply. Until 2008, Europe experienced renewed economic growth while economic globalization created new employment opportunities, especially for the highly skilled. Many governments introduced preferential entry rules for this category as well as student migrants. Yet many governments continued to ignore or deny the demand for lower-skilled labour migrants, so demand was met through limited temporary and seasonal recruitment schemes, or by irregular migration.

Yet, despite official rhetoric giving priority to economic migration, the largest single immigration category in the great majority of European countries has long remained *family reunion*. However, the relative importance of family reunion from former 'guest-worker' countries is declining. This coincides with a growing importance of labour migration including 'free movement' migration from Central and Eastern Europe to Western and Southern Europe.

On 1 May 2004, 10 new member states gained accession to the EU: the Czech Republic, Cyprus, Estonia, Hungary, Latvia, Lithuania, Malta, Poland, Slovakia and Slovenia (known as the EU10). Most of the existing member states (the EU15) decided to restrict migration from the new Eastern and Central European member states over the seven-year transitional period, but Ireland, the UK and Sweden opted not to. This stimulated major immigration of Poles and of citizens of Baltic republics, especially Lithuanians, to the UK and Ireland, but not to Sweden (partly due to labour market conditions). The enlargement process had a significant legalization effect for EU10 workers employed irregularly in the EU 15 states prior to 1 May 1 2004: several hundred thousand benefited from de facto legalization (Tomas and Münz, 2006). The accession to the EU of Bulgaria and Romania (also known as the EU2) on 1 January 2007 should have had a similar legalization effect (Münz *et al.*, 2007). However, the EU15 countries restricted access to the labour market for workers from Bulgaria and Romania until the end of the transitional period in December 2013.

One million Poles emigrated between 1 May 2004 and April 2007, principally to the UK, Ireland and Germany. By mid-2007, the euphoria that had accompanied accession and the potential for emigration had given way to growing concerns about migration in Poland. The emigration of Polish workers after 1 May 2004 increased employer fears of labour shortages. Poland, like other Eastern and Central European countries, is experiencing low fertility and an ageing population. In the late 2000s, the governments of Central and Eastern European countries were beginning to see themselves as future immigration lands, possibly heralding their migration transitions, and were planning to establish the necessary legal and institutional arrangements. It was in this context that Poland lifted restrictions on short-term workers from Belarus, Georgia, Moldova, Russia and Ukraine.

Asylum entries rose from the late 1990s, peaking at 471,000 for Western Europe in 2001, but had declined to 243,000 by 2005 (OECD, 2006: 253) In 2010, humanitarian migration accounted for 6 per cent of migration into the EU. The declining trend of the 2000s was reversed in 2011 when asylum applications increased because of increasing asylum applications from Afghanistan and from people fleeing violence in Libya and, particularly, Syria in the wake of the Arab Spring (de Haas and Sigona, 2012; OECD, 2012: 39–41, 45-46; see also Box 1.2).

Total inflows into the 24 European OECD countries (that is, the EU27 excluding Bulgaria, Romania, Cyprus, Malta, Latvia, and Lithuania, but plus the non-EU states Iceland, Norway and Switzerland) have been above 2 million for each year since 2000. The long-term trend is upward: from

2.2 million in 2000, the highest recorded year was 2007, with 3.5 million new entrants in the EU (OECD, 2012: 292). While entries to some of the earlier main immigration countries – like France, the UK, Belgium and Scandinavian countries – increased considerably over the 2000s, the biggest increases in the number of legal entries occurred in Southern Europe, which peaked in 2007 at 921,000 in Spain and 515,000 in Italy (OECD, 2012: 292) . France is the only major immigration country where immigration has stagnated over the 2000s.

Migratory consequences of the global economic crisis

Initially, the global economic crisis (GEC) was expected to lead to mass return migration. However, as with the 1973 Oil Crisis, such expectations have not proved correct. The decline in immigration has been relatively modest, and mass returns have not occurred. While total entries into the 24 European OECD countries declined to about 3 million in 2009 and 2010 in response to the GEC, the decline has been much smaller than anticipated by many (see Chapter 11).

In fact, immigration has remained higher than in any year prior to 2007 (OECD, 2012: 28). The economic downturn caused a certain decline in labour migration from outside the EU, but the biggest decreases occurred in overall free-circulation movement within the EU – although migration from Southern Europe increased – and in temporary labour migration, forms of migration which tend to fluctuate strongly with changes in economic conditions (OECD, 2011a: 30). Asylum and family migration have been less affected by the crisis. Return migration has generally been highest for EU migrants who enjoy free mobility, and much lower for immigrants from non-EU states, for whom return often implies giving up their residency rights in the destination country.

So labour migration has continued despite the recession. This reflects persistent labour demand in several sectors and at all skill levels in the highly segmented labour markets of destination countries in North-western Europe. The crisis has most severely hit migrants working in the construction sectors of Southern Europe. Some other sectors have been less affected. For instance, personal-care workers are increasingly demanded by ageing populations. And most European countries continue to welcome and compete for the high-skilled and students.

Obviously, the consequences have been largest for the countries where the crisis hit hardest, particularly Ireland, Southern Europe and some Eastern European countries. The crisis hit Spain particularly hard, and led to rising unemployment among immigrants, particularly in sectors such as construction. The unemployment rate of foreigners climbed to 36 per cent in 2011. This partly explains the decline in immigration from 958,000 in 2007 to 455,000 in 2010. In parallel, outflows have also increased, although more modestly from 227,000 in 2007 to 371,000 in 2011 (Instituto Nacional de Estadistica, 2011), although the real emigration figures are likely to be higher due to underregistration. The crisis has also prompted a new Spanish emigration movement, principally towards the UK, France, Germany and the US, but also to Argentina, Brazil, China and Australia (González Ferrer, 2012).

In Portugal, inflows declined to 30,000 per year in 2010, while emigration has grown to an estimated 70,000 per year, with increasing numbers of Portuguese jobless graduates migrating to Brazil and former colonies in Africa (BBC News, 1 September 2011). In Italy, the crisis has led to a sharp decrease of inflows and increasing emigration. In Greece, immigration has declined since 2010 mainly as a consequence of the economic crisis (OECD, 2012) and increasing return to countries such as Albania (Kerpaci and Kuka, 2012). Increasing numbers of Greek workers have started migrating to the UK, Germany, Turkey, or further afield to Australia or the USA.

In Central and Eastern Europe, consequences for migration have primarily depended on the extent to which the crisis has affected growth and employment. The Polish economy has kept on growing throughout the crisis, and Poland has entered a phase of decreasing emigration and increasing return migration (OECD, 2012: 260), which may herald a future migration transition to a net immigration country. The crisis hit harder in Czech Republic, the Slovak Republic, Hungary, and particularly in the Baltic republics of Estonia, Latvia and Lithuania, leading to decreasing immigration and increasing emigration parallel with steadily worsening labour market conditions (OECD, 2012: 248).

The poorer economies of Romania, Bulgaria and Ukraine have remained emigration countries *par excellence* throughout the crisis. While the worsening economic conditions continued to boost emigration from Bulgaria (primarily to Turkey and Spain), Romania (primarily to Italy, Spain and Hungary) and Ukraine (primarily to Poland, the Russian Federation, Italy and the Czech Republic), return migration has also increased as a result of the crisis affecting Spain and other South-European destinations (OECD, 2012). While the Russian Federation has continued to attract immigrants from former Soviet Union republics (such as Kazakhstan, Uzbekistan, Tajikistan, Ukraine) and China, growing numbers of Russian workers and asylum seekers have been moving to the Czech Republic, Turkey, Poland and Germany (OECD, 2012).

Europe's changing population

Over half a century of immigration has transformed European populations. Table 5.2 gives information on the growth of foreign resident populations in most European countries, while Table 5.3 gives information on foreign-born populations (summarized in Figure 5.1). In 1995 the registered *foreign* resident population of European OECD countries totalled

Table 5.2   *Foreign resident population in European OECD countries (thousands)*

Country	1980	1985	1990	1995	2000	2005	2010	Per cent of total population 2010
Austria	283	272	413	724	702	801	928	11.1
Belgium	–	845	905	910	862	901	1193	10.2
Czech Rep.	–	–	–	159	201	278	424	4.0
Denmark	102	117	161	223	259	270	346	6.2
Estonia	–	–	–	–	253	236	217	16.3
Finland	–	–	–	69	91	114	168	3.1
France	3,714[a]	–	3,597	–	3,263[b]	–	3,769	6.0
Germany	4,453	4,379	5,242	7,174	7,297	6,756	6,754	8.3
Greece	–	–	–	–	305	553	810	7.1
Hungary	–	–	–	140	110	154	209	2.1
Iceland	–	–	–	–	9	14	21	6.6
Ireland	–	79	80	94	126	413[d]	–	9.7
Italy	299	423	781	991	1,380	2,670	4570	7.6
Luxembourg	94	98	–	138	165	189	221	44.0
Netherlands	521	553	692	757	668	691	760	4.6
Norway	83	102	143	161	184	223	369	7.6
Poland	–	–	–	–	49[c]	55[d]	50[e]	0.1[e]
Portugal	–	–	108	168	208	432	448	4.2
Slovenia	–	–	–	–	42	49	83	4.0
Slovak Rep.	–	–	–	22	29	26	68	1.3
Spain	–	242	279	500	1,370	4,144	5,731	12.4
Sweden	422	389	484	532	472	458	611	6.8
Switzerland	893	940	1,100	1,331	1,384	1,512	1,720	22.1
UK	–	1,731	1,875	2,060	2,342	3,035	4,524	7.4

Notes: For the differences between foreign resident population and foreign-born population, see *Note on Migration Statistics* at the front of this book. The figures for the UK in this table are not comparable with the birthplace figures given in Table 5.1. The figures for Germany refer to the area of the old Federal Republic up to 1990, and to the whole of united Germany thereafter.

Key: – data not available; [a] figure for 1982; [b] figure for 1999, for metropolitan France only; [c] figure for 2002; [d] figure for 2006; [e] figure for 2009.

Sources: OECD, 1992: 131; 1997: 29; 2001; 2007: 343; 2012: 356–67.

19.4 million (OECD, 1997: 30). By 2010, this total came to over 34 million. However, the registered *foreign-born* population of these countries by 2010 was 49 million persons. The foreign resident population of the European OECD countries made up about 7.2 per cent of the total population, while the foreign-born population accounted for 10.3 per cent (calculations by authors based on data in OECD, 2012). Significantly, many European countries now have immigrant population shares on a par

Table 5.3   *Foreign-born population in European OECD countries (thousands)*

Country	1995	2000	2005	2010	Per cent of total population 2010
Austria	–	843	1,101	1,316	15.7
Belgium	983	1,059	1,269	1,504[f]	13.9[f]
Czech Republic	–	434	523	661	6.3
Denmark	250	309	350	429	7.7
Estonia	–	287	255	219[f]	16.4
Finland	106	136	177	248	4.6
France	–	4,380	4,926	5,342[g]	8.6[g]
Germany	9,378	10,256	10,399	10,591	13.0
Greece	–	–	1,122[c]	–	10.3[c]
Hungary	284	295	332	451	4.5
Iceland		17	25	35	10.9
Ireland	–	329	487	773	17.3
Italy	–	2,240[c]	–	4,799[f]	8.0[f]
Luxembourg	128	145	152	188	37.6
Netherlands	1,407	1,615	1,735	1,869	11.2
Norway	240	305	380	569	11.6
Poland	–	–	776[d]	–	1.6[d]
Portugal	533	523	661	669	6.3
Slovenia	–	170[d]	–	229	11.2
Slovak Republic	–	119[c]	207[e]		3.9[e]
Spain	–	1,969	4,838	6,660	14.5
Sweden	936	1,004	1,126	1,385	14.8
Switzerland	1,503	1,571	1,773	2,075	26.6
UK[h]	–	4,666	5,557	7,056	11.5

Notes: For the differences between foreign resident population and foreign-born population, see *Note on Migration Statistics* at the front of this book.

Key: – data not available; [c] figure for 2001; [d] figure for 2002; [e] figure for 2004; [f] figure for 2009; [g] figure for 2008; [h] estimates.

Sources: OECD, 2006: 262; 2007: 330; 2012: 336–7.

with the USA – historically viewed as the most significant immigration country – where foreign citizens represent 7.0 per cent and the foreign born represent 12.9 per cent of the total population.

Such trends have important demographic and economic implications. Demographers compare total fertility rates (TFR) – the rate needed to reproduce a population at its current size is a lifetime average of 2.1 babies per woman. EU countries are characterized by a low TFR: 1.6 children per woman in 2010 (compared to 2.1 in the USA). Life expectancy is increasing, and populations are ageing, so that fewer people of working age will in future have to support more elderly people. The share of the total EU27 population aged 65 years or over is projected to increase from

Figure 5.1   *Foreign-born and foreign population in European OECD countries, 2010*

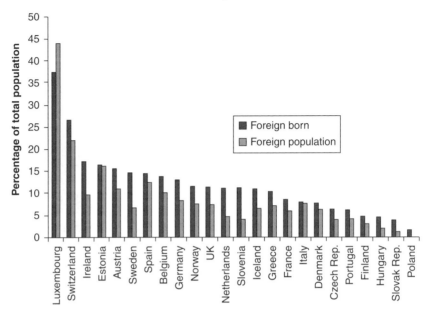

Sources: See Tables 5.1 and 5.2.

17.1 per cent in 2008 to 23.5 per cent in 2030. Consequently, the old age dependency ratio is expected to rise from 25.4 per cent in 2008 to 38.0 per cent in 2030. This means that in 2030, 100 persons of working age are projected to support 38 aged persons (Giannakouris, 2010). While international migration alone will not reverse the ongoing trend of population ageing, continuing demand in particular sectors of the segmented labour markets of Europe is likely to continue to fuel immigration.

Migration has been the main driver of population growth in many European countries. For instance, in 2008 the EU27 population increased by 2.1 million. Two thirds of that increase, or 1.5 million was the result of net immigration, and 600,000 was the result of natural increase (Marcu, 2011). In some European countries such as Italy, where natural growth has become negative, migration has even counterbalanced the otherwise declining population (Lanzieri, 2011).

The total population of the EU27 in 2010 was 501 million, of whom more than 48 million were legally resident foreign-born persons. Recent analyses by Eurostat showed that the population of the EU27 is projected to rise by 5 per cent between 2008 and 2030. Nevertheless, there is considerable variation between regions, with particularly Eastern Europe and Germany projected to have a lower population (Giannakouris, 2010). Such projections of future population growth are based on the assumption of continued immigration. According to one projection by Lanzieri (2011), the EU27 population in 2061 would be 505 million with migration and 414 million without migration. Although such projections should not be taken as predictions, they do illustrate the demographic salience of migration in European societies.

Conclusions

This overview of international migrations within, to and from Europe since 1945 can lay no claim to completeness. The upsurge in migratory movements in the post-1945 period, and particularly since the mid-1980s, indicates that large-scale immigration has become an intrinsic part of European societies. This represents an important historical shift: Europe went from an area of mass emigration in the nineteenth and early twentieth centuries, to an area of large-scale inflows from all over the world and even greater movements within Europe. Moreover, this immigration increasingly concerns the whole of Europe – not just the older industrial areas of North-western Europe as in the past. This has had significant implications for European society and politics, as will be discussed in later chapters.

This increasing immigration is linked to decolonization, economic growth and sustained labour demand, the expansion of the EU, 'neoliberal' economic policies as well as the internationalization of production, distribution and investment. The end of the Cold War and the collapse of the Soviet bloc added new dimensions to global restructuring. One was increased investment in Eastern Europe. Another dimension was the growth of East–West migration, with previously more isolated countries becoming firmly embedded into broader European migration systems.

Many large-scale migrations have been primarily economic in their motivations. Labour migration was particularly significant in the 1945–73 period. In the following years, other types of migration, such as family reunion and refugee and asylum-seeker movements, took on greater importance. Since the mid-1980s, labour migration has become increasingly important again. The lack of legal migration channels for lower-skilled workers has contributed to increasing family and irregular migration. Even migrations in which non-economic motivations have been predominant have had significant effects on the labour markets and economies of both sending and receiving areas. Furthermore, the effect on both sending and receiving societies is always more than just economic: immigration changes demographic and social structures, affects political institutions and helps to reshape cultures.

While there has been a structural trend of rising immigration over the past five decades, there are clear cycles of increasing and decreasing immigration rates, which are strongly related to economic cycles and changes in labour market structure. Rapid economic growth in the late 1980s and early

1990s led to unprecedented immigration rates. Migration slowed down in the mid-1990s, to soar again with economic recovery in the 2000s. However, underlying these overall fluctuations are important geographical shifts. EEC expansion to the south in the 1980s and rapid economic growth transformed Southern Europe from an emigration area into a major destination area in its own right. The fall of Communist regimes around 1990, the creation of the borderless Schengen Area in 1995 and EU expansion in 2004 and 2007 further stimulated migration within an expanding and increasingly integrated European migration system. In addition, economic growth combined with demographic ageing enlarged the group of European immigration countries and therefore boosted immigration from outside Europe.

This chapter showed the relevance of several of the theories discussed in Chapter 2. Dual or segmented labour market theory is particularly useful to understand why labour migration within and to Europe has continued even in times of economic crisis and rising unemployment. Decades of immigration has led to the formation of ethnic minorities and the 'racialization' of particular sectors in the labour markets, particularly with regards to low-skilled and often informal jobs in agriculture, construction, catering, cleaning and care that natives increasingly shun. Migration transition theories are useful to understand how the former labour reserves of the European periphery (Southern Europe, Ireland and Finland) as well as Central and Eastern European countries have transformed from net emigration to net immigration countries, which has led to the outward expansion of the European 'labour frontier' (see also Skeldon, 1997 and Chapter 2). Network and migration systems theories help us to understand why migration has continued or even increased despite attempts by government to curb immigration, particularly of the lower skilled.

Irregular immigration and employment is one of the biggest public issues in European migration today. Irregular migration is largely explained by the labour market demand for lower-skilled workers which remains unmatched by possibilities for legal labour migration (Düvell, 2006). However, the volume of irregular migration should not be exaggerated. It has been estimated that in 2008 there were between 1.9 and 3.8 million irregular residents in the EU27, representing between 0.4 and 0.8 per cent of the total population and between 7 and 13 per cent of the foreign population (Vogel, 2009). Extensive media attention to irregular border crossing has not only led to a 'myth of invasion' (de Haas, 2007b) but it also obscures the fact that the majority of irregular immigrants in the EU have entered legally, on some sort of a visa, and then overstayed (Düvell, 2006). In a striking parallel with the US–Mexico border (see Chapter 6), strict border controls, the building of fences and walls and increased marine surveillance in the Mediterranean and the Atlantic seem to have done little to stop inflows of irregular and regular migrants as long as labour demand persists in the segmented and increasingly 'deregularized' labour markets of Europe. This conflict between migration dynamics and state measures will be the theme of Chapter 10.

The GEC has slowed down inflows and led to a revival of emigration from Southern Europe and Ireland, but has not led to a massive return. It is impossible to predict future migration trends, but *if* economic growth resumes, immigration is also likely to pick up again, while the ageing societies of Europe are likely to generate demand for both unskilled and skilled migrant labour. This perhaps explains why, in spite of the GEC, European countries continue to vie with each other to attract skilled migrants as well as students.

Guide to further reading

tra resources at www.age-of-migration.com

The Age of Migration website includes text 5.1, which provides some additional detail on migration to Greece. The website material related to Chapter 11, on Germany, the Netherlands and Sweden, is also useful for understanding migration patterns to these countries.

For current data on migration flows, it is best to consult the online sources listed at the end of Chapter 1. For a general overview and analysis for developed countries, the annual *International Migration Outlook* of the OECD is invaluable. The *World Migration Reports* of the IOM and the regularly updated material provided by the *Migration Information Source* are also highly recommended. Many national statistical offices now provide data online (often in English), while reports from interior ministries and other government authorities are also often available.

Castles and Kosack (1973) is a comparative study of immigrant workers in France, Germany, Switzerland and the UK from 1945 to 1971, while Miller (1981) provides an early analysis of the political effects of migration. Castles *et al.* (1984) continue the story for the period following the ending of recruitment in 1973–4.

The recent increase of literature on migration to developed countries makes it hard to single out reading. A useful global comparative study on migration policy is Hollifield *et al.* (2013). Geddes (2003) is good on politics of migration, and Boswell and Geddes (2011) analyse post-Cold War European migration patterns and their relation to political and policy making processes. Schierup *et al.* (2006) examine the 'European dilemma' of migration and increasing diversity. Düvell (2006) provides a good overview of irregular migration and Düvell (2012) and Collyer *et al.* (2012) give critical analyses of transit migration. Dancygier (2010) questions the idea that the presence of immigrants necessarily leads to conflict. Givens and Maxwell (2012) give an overview of ethnic minority and migrant political participation in Western Europe. Other useful books include, for Western Europe, Messina (2002); for Central Europe, Wallace and Stola (2001); and for Southern Europe, Baganha and Fonseca (2004), Luso-American Development Foundation (1999), King *et al.* (2000) and King (2001).

Chapter 6

Migration in the Americas

The nations of North, Central and South America and the Caribbean (which together make up 'the Americas') have been made and re-made by the migrations of the last half-millennium. Immigration and settlement was a crucial component of the process of colonization that began in the late fifteenth century when Spain, Portugal, England and France fought to gain control over the 'New World'. The fifteenth to the nineteenth centuries were marked by conquest and resource extraction, at first from gold and silver mines and then from sugar, tobacco and other plantations (Galeano, 1973). While the indigenous population decreased due to the diseases, massacres and forced labour brought by colonization, the arrival and settlement of European migrants and African slaves, along with the consequent process of *mestizaje* (mixing of racial groups), produced deep and lasting changes, which helped create the contemporary face of this continent.

The Americas have continued to be strongly affected by changing patterns of migration throughout modern history. Between about 1850 and 1960, millions of Europeans migrated to the 'New World'. They came not only to the USA and Canada, but also to South America, especially to Argentina and Brazil. While more than 23 million Europeans migrated to the United States between 1880 and 1930 (USINS, 1999), 4 million arrived in Brazil during the same period (Amaral and Fusco, 2005). In Latin America this was a time of colonial liberation struggles and the emergence of Creole ruling elites. These elites quickly became linked to the emerging corporations of the USA, which achieved economic dominance throughout the region. Labour emigration from Mexico to the USA and from the Caribbean to Europe and the USA began at this time, albeit on a small scale.

The early post-1945 period was one of a tentative move to democratic governance and economic resurgence in Latin America, with significant growth through local industrialization under policies of import substitution. However, in the 1970s and 1980s, such initiatives were stifled by US-backed military regimes, which generally opened the door to neoliberal approaches based on privatization, deregulation and export orientation. These policies were championed by US economic advisors (see Klein, 2007, on neoliberalism in Latin America) and enforced through the structural adjustment policies of the IMF, the World Bank and the Inter-American Development Bank. The result was a vast growth in inequality in the continent (ECLAC, 2010). Together with fast demographic growth and rapid urbanization, leading to the emergence of huge slum areas (Davis, 2006), this provided a strong motivation for South–North migration.

Thus the USA and Canada remained major immigration areas, while the rest of the region experienced substantial emigration. A few Southern countries (such as Venezuela) remained primarily countries of immigration, but others have become countries of transit, emigration or a mixture of all of these. In addition, the Americas experienced the forced displacement of thousands of people who fled civil wars and political prosecution under military regimes during the 1970s and the 1980s. At the same time, increasing political and economic instability has resulted in an upsurge of irregular migration of mostly low-skilled workers. While the best known case is that of Mexican workers in the USA, irregular status is suffered by countless workers migrating from and within the region (Connor and Massey, 2010). Finally, it is important to mention a form of 'return migration' that has developed in recent decades. An increasing number of Latin Americans have relocated to their ancestors' countries of origin in Europe or Asia, often under preferential agreements (IOM, 2005).

New trends are emerging in the Americas. Military regimes have fallen and democratic governments have come to power in many countries. Analyses of the 'lost decade' of the 1980s has led to a questioning of the neoliberal economic paradigm (ECLAC, 2010), and nations like Brazil, Argentina, Ecuador, Bolivia and Venezuela are pursuing new development paths. At the same time, US preoccupation with Islam and its military involvement in Iraq and Afghanistan, together with the economic crisis which started in 2008, led to a decline in capacity for political and economic control in Latin America. During the global economic crisis (GEC), South–North migration declined, while movements between Latin America countries grew.

At present, there are over 57 million international migrants in the Americas. This represents just over a quarter of the world's migrant population (IOM, 2010). Migrant flows and numbers vary considerably within the region. The Americas can be portrayed as consisting of five principal subregions. While a number of countries do not fit neatly into these five areas, the classification serves to underscore how immigration and emigration has differentially affected the area as a whole:

1. The USA and Canada have traditionally had substantial populations of European origin due to large influxes of European migrants, which, however, have decreased since the 1970s. The USA also has a large minority population of African-Americans, who are mostly descendants of slaves. In recent times, both countries have remained major countries of immigration drawing migrants from all regions of the world.
2. Mexico and Central American societies largely comprise persons of *mestizo* and indigenous background. Although in geographical and

political terms Mexico forms part of North America, this country's experience of high levels of emigration to the USA and its position as a country of transit migration, draws it closer to its Central American counterparts. Mexico–US migration is the world's largest migration corridor, and dominates public debates on migration in both countries.

3. Caribbean countries display a mixed population resulting from the impact of colonization, slave trafficking and labour migration. This area has sizable populations of African origin, but there are also many of European and Asian descent. In the period of decolonization after 1945 there were substantial flows to former colonial powers: Jamaica and other islands to the UK, Surinamese to the Netherlands, Guadeloupe to France and so on. In recent years, countries such as Cuba, the Dominican Republic, Haiti and Jamaica have all experienced considerable emigration towards the United States.

4. The Andean area in the north and west of South America comprises Ecuador, Peru, Colombia, Bolivia and Venezuela and has a population of *mestizo* and indigenous background. Immigration from Europe during the nineteenth and twentieth centuries to this area was less significant than to others in the region. In recent decades, the Andean area has been characterized by significant migration flows from Ecuador to Spain, and from Colombia to the United States and to Venezuela.

5. The Southern Cone includes Brazil, Argentina, Chile, Uruguay and Paraguay. These countries have substantial populations of European origin due to massive immigrant settlement from Europe. There were also inflows from elsewhere: for example, Brazil received African slaves into the nineteenth century and Japanese workers from the late nineteenth century until the 1960s. In recent decades, Brazil, Argentina and Chile have experienced complex migration patterns: emigration to Europe increased up to the GEC, but since 2009 new movements from Europe have been observed, while immigration from other parts of Latin America has grown.

Migration from 1945 to the 1970s

While the scale of European immigration after 1945 was substantially lower than that of previous times, the Americas experienced more significant levels of intra-regional flows with well-defined migration corridors developing between neighbouring countries. Spontaneous or irregular migration was the predominant form of migration in Latin America, and was not viewed as a problem until the late 1960s (Lohrmann, 1987). The later part of this period also witnessed the beginning of significant emigration movements from Mexico and Central America, the Caribbean countries, the Andean region and the Southern Cone to the industrialized countries of North America and Europe.

The USA and Canada

Large-scale post-1945 immigration to the USA developed later than in Western Europe due to the restrictive legislation enacted in the 1920s. Intakes averaged 250,000 persons annually in the 1951–60 period, and 330,000 annually during 1961–70: a far cry from the average of 880,000 immigrants per year from 1901 to 1910. The 1970 Census showed that the number of overseas-born people had declined to 9.6 million (only 4.7 per cent of the population) (Briggs, 1984) compared with 13.9 million (13.2 per cent of the population) in 1920. The 1965 amendments to the Immigration and Nationality Act were seen as part of the civil rights legislation of the period, designed to remove the discriminatory national-origins quota system. They were not expected or intended to lead to large-scale non-European immigration (Borjas, 1990). In fact, the amendments created a system of worldwide immigration, in which the most important criterion for admission was kinship with US citizens or residents. The result was a dramatic upsurge in migration from Asia and Latin America. At the same time, migration potential from Europe was declining due to the increased prosperity of Western Europe and migration prohibitions in the Soviet Bloc.

US employers, particularly in agriculture, also recruited temporary migrant workers, mainly men, in Mexico and the Caribbean. Trade unions were highly critical, arguing that domestic workers would be displaced and wages held down. Government policies varied: at times, systems of temporary labour recruitment, such as the '*Bracero* Program' (see below), were introduced. In other periods, recruitment was formally prohibited, but tacitly tolerated, leading to the presence of a large number of irregular workers.

Canada followed policies of mass immigration after 1945. At first only Europeans were admitted. Most entrants were British, but Eastern and Southern Europeans soon played an increasing role. The largest immigrant streams in the 1950s and 1960s were of Germans, Italians and Dutch. The introduction of a non-discriminatory 'points system' for screening potential migrants after the 1966 White Paper opened the door for non-European migrants. The main source countries in the 1970s were Jamaica, India, Portugal, the Philippines, Greece, Italy and Trinidad (Breton *et al.*, 1990). Throughout the period, family entry was encouraged, and immigrants were seen as settlers and future citizens.

Mexico and Central America

Migration flows from Mexico during this period were unidirectional to the USA. In an initial phase of 'dissuasion' in the early years of the twentieth century, the Mexican government aimed at attracting home citizens who remained in the territories lost to the USA during the mid-nineteenth century, as well as dissuading potential emigrants from answering the calls of US labour recruiters to move north for work. Later on, there was a phase of negotiation after the outbreak of World War II leading to the so called *'Bracero* Program' (1942–64) that mobilized 4.5 million young men to work as temporary migrants in US agriculture and railway track maintenance (Alba, 2010; Durand, 2004). Mexico received few immigrants during these years. A significant exception was the more than 20,000 Spanish refugees fleeing the Spanish Civil War (Salazar Anaya, 2010).

During this period, Central American countries were characterized by seasonal internal and intra-regional migration. For instance, Guatemalan agricultural workers travelled every year to the south of Mexico to labour on coffee plantations; while Salvadorians went to work in the cotton growing areas of Guatemala and Nicaragua and the banana plantations of Honduras (Castillo, 2006; Hamilton and Stoltz Chinchilla, 1991). Migration flows outside the region, in particular to the USA, only reached significant levels with the outset of military conflicts in the 1960s. Migration to the USA, caused by both economic motivations and the need to seek protection from violence has continued to increase significantly since then (USINS, 1999).

The Caribbean

Intra-regional migration has a long tradition in the Caribbean. For instance, by 1930 there were an estimated 100,000 Haitians and 60,000 Jamaicans in Cuba (Portes and Grosfoguel, 1994). There were also outflows towards former colonizer countries. Britain recruited thousands of men from the Caribbean for military service in both World Wars, with many of these men eventually settling in the UK. The post-1945 period saw a labour shortage in the UK that led to a further influx of labourers from the Caribbean, in particular Jamaica and Barbados (Glennie and Chappell, 2010). During the 1950s and 1960s there were also significant movements of migrants from Dutch overseas provinces and former colonies in the Caribbean towards the Netherlands (Ferrer, 2011).

Caribbean migration to the USA increased significantly in the second part of the twentieth century. The initial upsurge was driven by the movement of Puerto Ricans, yet Cuban migration became very significant in the 1960s following the Cuban revolution (Portes and Grosfoguel, 1994). Cuban immigration remains significant today, with thousands of Cubans being granted asylum and residency status under the 'wet-foot, dry-foot' policy (Migration Dialogue, 2008). This 1995 rule allows any Cuban who manages to enter the USA to stay and to apply for residency after a year, while those apprehended at sea are sent back to Cuba or to a third country.

The Andean area

Migration flows in the Andean area were for the most part intra-regional and on a small scale up to 1970. In the case of Ecuador for instance, there were small migrant flows to Venezuela and to the USA from the 1940s (Jokisch, 2007). Bolivian migration flows to Argentina started in the mid-1930s and lasted for decades until mechanization reduced labour needs. Most Andean countries did not attract large-scale European immigration. Colombia attempted to implement immigration programs after World War II, but failed due to political instability (Bérubé, 2005). Venezuela was an exception in the region, after the military regime of Perez Jiménez established a policy of 'open doors', which successfully attracted a large influx of European immigrants between 1949 and 1958. About 332,000 persons, mainly of Italian origin, settled in Venezuela (Álvarez de Flores, 2006–7; Picquet *et al.*, 1986). Venezuela also experienced high levels of intra-regional immigration – particularly from neighbouring Colombia – beginning in the second half of the 1960s. The growth of migration to Venezuela was linked to the economic boom created by the expansion of the oil industry (Álvarez de Flores, 2006–7).

The Southern Cone

Mass immigration from Europe declined sharply by the 1930s (Barlán, 1988) and thereafter the number of persons born in Europe began to decline in the region. Argentina and Uruguay encouraged immigration until the interwar period, when the economic depression of the 1930s brought significant changes in policies. In the case of Brazil, Japanese migration became significant in the aftermaths of World War I and World War II. Japanese migrants arrived in Brazil in two waves: the first, between 1925 and 1936 and the second one between 1955 and 1961 (Amaral and Fusco, 2005). But as inflows from Europe waned, intra-continental migrations developed. For instance, Paraguayan and Chilean labour migrants began to find employment, especially in agriculture, in North-eastern Argentina and Patagonia in the 1950s and 1960s respectively (Jachimowicz, 2006). Foreign workers also spread from agricultural areas to major urban centres. Single – mostly male – migrants were soon joined by their families, creating neighbourhoods of irregular immigrants in some cities. Argentina also witnessed its first significant outflow of emigrants: between 1960 and 1970, an estimated 185,000 Argentines – mostly high skilled – relocated to countries such as the USA, Spain and Mexico (Jachimowicz, 2006).

Migration since the 1970s

This period was dominated by massive northward flows of both regular and irregular migrants from all areas in Latin America towards the industrialized countries of North America and Europe (see Map 8.1). Two main factors were behind the rise in emigration. The first was increasing demand for foreign labour in the USA, Europe and Japan.

Map 6.1   *Contemporary migrations within and from Latin America*

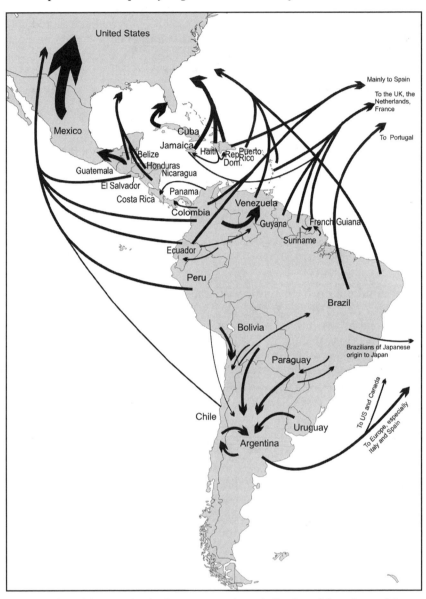

Note: The size of the arrowheads gives an approximate indication of the volume of flows. Exact figures are often unavailable.

The importance of economic restructuring in creating a demand for migrant workers can be seen most clearly in the relationship between the US and Mexican economies: the establishment of the North American Free Trade Agreement (NAFTA) in 1994 accelerated economic integration between the two countries through the growth of *maquiladoras* (mainly US-controlled factories in northern Mexico), as well as labour migration, allowing reduction of labour costs and increased profits for US corporations as well as smaller-scale agricultural and service enterprises (this complex process is analysed in Cypher and Delgado Wise, 2011; Delgado Wise and Covarrubias, 2009).

The second factor was the economic woes of Latin America. GDP per capita in Latin America declined sharply in the 1980s, which some called the 'decade lost to debt' (Fregosi, 2002: 443). Democratic renewal and a trend toward liberalization in the early and mid-1990s briefly buoyed Latin American economies before a succession of economic crises ravaged the area again. The number of people living below the poverty line had increased from 136 million in 1980 to 215 million in 1999 (ECLAC, 2011). Increasing levels of social and economic inequality exacerbated the lack of opportunities for significant sectors of the population, fuelling out-migration. These two factors are interconnected, since the economic problems of Latin America were closely connected with US economic dominance and the introduction of neoliberal policies.

The USA and Canada

Migration to the USA grew steadily after 1970. Total immigrant numbers, i.e. the stock of foreigners (called 'aliens' in the USA) granted legal permanent resident status ('Green Cards'), rose from 4.2 million in the ten-year period 1970–9 to 6.2 million in 1980–9, 9.8 million in 1990–9 and 10.3 million in 2000–9. The decline in the growth rate is due to the impact of the GEC as well as trends towards securitization of migration since 9/11 (see Chapter 9), yet the USA remains the world's number one destination for migrants, and over half of them come from Latin America (OAS, 2011: 58). On average, around 1 million people per year obtained Green Cards in the USA in the first decade of the twenty-first century (OAS, 2011: table B.1.1). Mexicans, Central Americans, Chinese, Indians and Filipinos were the largest groups. In 2010, 620,000 people were naturalized, down from the peak of over 1 million in 2008. Mexicans, Indians, Chinese and Filipinos were the most numerous amongst the new US citizens (UNDESA, 2009).

However, 64 per cent of Green Cards from 2005 to 2009 went to family members of US citizens or permanent residents and 15 per cent to refugees and asylum seekers. Only 15 per cent were employment related, and half of these went to family members of persons admitted as workers. Overall, only 7 per cent of Green Cards went to principal applicants, most of whom were highly skilled workers. This compares poorly with other OECD countries: for example in 2008, 79 per cent of visas issued by Spain, 59 per cent by Germany and 42 per cent by Australia were for work-based immigrants. The US Green Card system is slow and inflexible, with waiting periods of several years, due to numerical and country-of-origin limits (Orrenius and Zavodny, 2010).

In recent years, the US Government has expanded temporary work-related visa schemes, which now bring in far more skilled workers than the Green Cards, but do not provide long-term security of residence. In 2010, 1.7 million temporary workers were admitted – mainly highly skilled personnel. The intake of seasonal agricultural workers (H2A visas) also increased from 28,000 in 2000 to 139,000 in 2010. The main countries of origin for temporary workers were Canada, Mexico and India (UNDESA, 2009).

Refugee admissions plummeted in the wake of the terror attacks of 11 September 2001 due to more stringent security requirements in processing. Middle Eastern and African refugees were particularly adversely affected. However, numbers have since increased again. The Department of Homeland Security (DHS) reported that 73,000 refugees were admitted in 2010. An additional 21,000 persons were granted asylum. Asians formed the largest origin group of both refugees and asylum seekers (UNDESA, 2009) The USA remains by far the world's top resettlement country for refugees, followed by Canada and Australia.

Irregular migration remains significant. As of 2010, there were 10.8 million irregular migrants living in the United States, down from the peak of 11.8 million in 2007 (Hoefer *et al.*, 2011). Irregular migration results from a combination of high labour demand in the USA and the absence of an adequate mechanism for regular entry of low-skilled workers. Increased US border enforcement in recent years has made it more difficult, dangerous and costly for irregular migrants to enter the country (Cornelius, 2001; Jimenez, 2009). One consequence has been an increase in the number of deaths, as migrants take greater risks to reach the USA. Estimates suggest that over the period 1994–2009, between 4,000 and 6,000 migrants died trying to cross the US–Mexico border (Jimenez, 2009). Successive US administrations have failed to implement an immigration reform to address the situation of millions of irregular migrants. Critics point out that the current system has created a 'massive underground of persons' who have lived with an irregular status for years or even decades (Human Rights Watch, 2011). (See Chapter 13 for discussion of the politics of immigration in the USA.)

Canada remains one of the few countries in the world with an active and expansive permanent immigration policy, which aims to admit the equivalent of 1 per cent of its total population of about 34 million each year. In 2010, there were 7.2 million foreign-born residents in Canada, up from 5.5 million in the year 2000. Foreign-born residents made up 21 per cent of the Canadian population – one of the highest shares in any developed country (CIC, 2011). In contrast to earlier European migrants, who settled all over Canada, new arrivals increasingly concentrate in the largest cities: Toronto, Montréal, and Vancouver.

In 2010, Canada recorded 281,000 'landings', to use the Canadian term. Entries from South and East Asia and the Middle East have grown, while entries from Europe have declined. In 2010, the top three countries of origin were the Philippines, India and China. Arrivals from these countries accounted for a third of total arrivals (Challinor, 2011). Two-thirds of arrivals were economic migrants, the majority of whom were skilled; however the category also includes accompanying dependants. This reflects a trend to emphasize skills, education, and language abilities in immigration selection criteria. Yet, there is growing concern regarding high levels of unemployment and underemployment of immigrants despite their impressive credentials (Basok, 2007; Reitz, 2007a; b). Canada granted permanent residency to 25,000 refugees in 2010 (CIC, 2011).

Like the USA, Canada has steadily increased its admissions of temporary foreign workers: in 2010, 182,000 entered Canada, compared with 116,000 in 2000 and 112,000 in 1990. The main countries of origin were the United States, Mexico and France (CIC, 2011). A significant component of Canada's temporary migration programmes is the Seasonal Agricultural Workers Program (SAWP) which, since its inception in 1966, has recruited workers from Mexico and the Caribbean to work in agriculture, particularly in Ontario's tomato industry. While recruitment used to be limited to married men, recently some women have been recruited as well. SAWP is regarded by many as a 'model' for temporary migration programmes due to its high degree of circularity; yet critics point to excessive employer control and workers' restricted mobility and social and political rights (Basok, 2007; Preibisch, 2010).

Increasingly, citizens of Canada and the USA emigrate, often as highly skilled workers but also in search of different lifestyles, especially in retirement. More than 1.1 million Canadians live abroad, primarily in the United States, United Kingdom and Australia (World Bank, 2011b). Similarly, more than 2.4 million US citizens live abroad. Top destination countries for US citizens are Mexico, Canada and Puerto Rico. The magnitude of these diasporas is small in relative terms, however. In the case of the United States, emigrants represent only 0.8 per cent of the total population while immigrants account for 13.5 per cent (World Bank, 2011b).

Mexico and Central America

Millions of Mexicans have left their country of birth in the last four decades. By contrast, immigration to Mexico has been low, with the population share of the foreign born remaining constant at about 0.5 per cent between 1970 and 2000, before reaching 0.9 per cent in 2010 (Instituto Nacional de Estadística y Geografía, 2011). Most Mexican workers have migrated to the USA in 'one of the largest mass migrations in modern history' (Pew Hispanic Centre, 2011). A third of migrants to the USA are Mexican nationals and approximately one tenth of Mexico's population now resides in the USA (Passel and Cohn, 2009). While migration to the USA traditionally originated in the rural areas of the Central Western region of Mexico, it now comes from nearly every part of the country (Alba, 2010), leading to rural depopulation in some areas (Cypher and Delgado Wise, 2011: 146–7). Over half of all Mexican immigrants to the

Box 6.1 Narco-capitalism and the 'ni-nis'

An increasingly important factor in Mexico and the rest of the region is the growth of 'narco-capitalism'; the domination of large areas of Mexico and especially of the border by violent drug cartels. These vie for control of the smuggling routes that link the Central American production areas with the profitable markets for drugs in the USA. Ironically the USA provides weapons for both sides: for the Mexican government forces through military aid and for the gangs through easy purchases in the southern states of the USA. In fact, drug cartels have been intertwined with elements of the government, the police and the army for many years. The recent increase in violence appears to be a result of the attempts of President Calderón since 2006 to meet US demands by cracking down on the cartels. The cartels have diversified into abduction of migrants for purposes of extortion, as well as forcing them to be drug couriers. Migrants who resist are often tortured or murdered. This situation, combined with the US recession and the anti-immigration laws in Arizona and other states, has made it hard for Mexicans to migrate to the USA (Covarrubias *et al.*, 2011; Tetreault, 2011).

The implementation of the free trade provisions of NAFTA after 1994 had already led to the decline of rural employment opportunities in many regions, such as the state of Zacatecas (García Zamora, 2009; García Zamora and Contreras Díaz, 2012). Emigration to the USA became a safety-valve, providing a perspective for young Mexicans who could not find work in agriculture at home. Now this option has been all but closed off by the violence at the border. According to Mexican social scientists, a generation of 'ni-nis' (*ni escuela, ni trabajo* – neither school nor work) has emerged: young people with no prospect of education or long-term employment. Many of them choose the lucrative – but often short – life of the drug-cartel soldier as preferable to a longer life of poverty. By providing a ready source of recruits for the gangs, the presence of the 'ni-nis' helps perpetuate a vicious circle of dependence, poverty, violence and underdevelopment.

Note: in addition to the sources cited, Box 6.1 is based on research by Malena Arias and Stephen Castles in the State of Zacatecas and on analyses by Mexican colleagues.

USA are considered to be irregular (Terrazas, 2010). In 2010, there were estimated to be 6.6 million irregular migrants from Mexico, constituting 62 per cent of the USA's total irregular population (Hoefer *et al.*, 2011).

Mexico has also served as a transit country for migrants seeking to reach the USA and to a lesser extent as a destination for mostly Central American migrants and refugees. While seasonal labour migration from Central America has a long history, Mexico's role as a country of transit and destination increased significantly in the 1980s following the civil wars in Nicaragua, El Salvador and Guatemala which saw thousands of people fleeing to Mexico or travelling through to the country in order to claim asylum in the USA (Ángel Castillo, 2006). The Mexican government has been under constant US pressure to control its southern border in order to reduce transit migration. In 2010, more than 65,000 irregular migrants were deported by Mexican authorities, most of whom were from Central America (Instituto Nacional de Migración, 2010). The risks to migrants trying to reach the USA via its southern neighbour are extreme: kidnapping, extortion and murder are frequent (Comisión Nacional de los Derechos Humanos, 2011).

Several Central American countries have experienced high levels of emigration since the 1970s. Political instability, natural disasters and economic insecurity have contributed to the departure of millions of people (Smith, 2006). The civil wars that devastated many Central American countries from the 1970s to the early 1990s caused many people to flee. Conservative estimates suggest that up a million Central Americans sought refuge in the USA during the 1980s, yet the US administration denied refuge to many for political reasons associated with the Cold War (Gzesh, 2006). As Mahler and Ugrina (2006) argue 'warfare not only killed thousands and displaced millions, it also institutionalized a migration pattern that heretofore had been very minor: emigration to *El Norte*'. Gang violence has become a problem in Central America too. Violent criminal organizations such as the *Mara Salvatrucha*, which were formed in the USA, have been 'exported' to Central America as hundreds of gang members have been deported due to criminal convictions (Migration Dialogue, 2007; Portes, 2010).

The USA is the top destination country for Central Americans, while other destinations include Canada, Mexico and Spain. There are also significant levels of intra-regional migration, with relatively wealthy Costa Rica and Belize attracting migrants from neighbouring countries (Mahler and Ugrina, 2006). The top emigration countries in the region are El Salvador, Guatemala, Nicaragua and Honduras. The significance of emigration for the region is demonstrated by three important facts (World Bank, 2011a). First, emigrants represent a large percentage of the population of many Central American countries. Second, the emigration rate of the tertiary-educated population is 66 per cent for Belize, 31 per cent for El Salvador, 30 per cent for Nicaragua, and 24 per cent for Honduras and Guatemala. Finally, remittances play an important role for the economies of this area. For Honduras and El Salvador for instance, remittances are equivalent to, respectively, 19 and 16 per cent of GDP. However,the experience of Panama and Costa Rica diverges from the rest of Central America. Whether it is due to the absence of armed conflicts or the existence of relative economic and social security, both countries have not experienced nearly as much out-migration as other countries.

The Caribbean

Since the 1970s, the USA and Canada have been the top destination countries for Caribbean migrants, particularly from Anglophone countries (Ferrer, 2011). The number of Caribbean immigrants in the USA grew from 194,000 in 1960 to 3.5 million in 2009. Half of all Caribbean immigrants in the USA came from Cuba and the Dominican Republic (McCabe, 2011). In Canada there were over half a million people of Caribbean origin in 2001, with the largest group coming from Jamaica (Lindsay, 2001).

Several Caribbean countries experience both significant emigration and immigration (Ferrer, 2011; World Bank, 2011a: 59). High two-way mobility reflects lack of economic opportunities at home, return migration of former emigrants and lifestyle migration of middle-class people from rich countries. Haiti experienced a considerable exodus of migrants in the aftermath of the severe earthquake of 2010. An estimated 500,000 Haitians moved to the neighbouring Dominican Republic. Yet many of those fleeing to the Dominican Republic have been victims of discrimination and deportations (Migration Dialogue, 2011).

The experience of Caribbean countries is rather similar to that of Central America: migration is characterized by its magnitude, selectivity, and economic significance. While the absolute number of emigrants coming from Caribbean countries is fairly small, the migrant stock as a percentage of the population is very high. Grenada, St. Kitts and Nevis, Guyana, Antigua and Barbuda, and Barbados are all among the world top-ten emigration countries in terms of percentage of population (Ferrer, 2011; World Bank, 2011a: 4). Caribbean migration is further defined by its selectivity, with much higher average skill levels than for Latin American emigrants. Eight out of the world's top-ten emigration countries of tertiary-educated people are Caribbean countries, and Guyana, Grenada, Jamaica, St. Vincent and the Grenadines and Haiti have the highest levels of skilled emigration in the world (Ferrer, 2011; World Bank, 2011a: 9). This massive loss of skilled workers has created a situation in which many countries have seen their capacity to provide social services curtailed and have become increasingly reliant on remittances.

The Andean area

An increasing number of Andeans have migrated outside the area since the 1970s, traditionally to the USA and more recently to Spain. Yet Venezuela remains a significant country of destination. A number of factors lie behind the increase in migration rates in this area. In Colombia for instance, political, economic and social problems led to an increase in the number of emigrants. Estimates suggest that one in ten Colombians is currently living abroad, the majority of them residing in either the USA or Venezuela (Bérubé, 2005). A significant issue in Colombia is internally displaced persons (IDPs) as a result of the long-term conflict between government forces, left-wing guerrillas, paramilitaries and drug cartels By mid-2010, approximately 3.4 million people were officially registered as IDPs (UNHCR, 2011a).

Economic instability in Ecuador in the 1980s and the 1990s generated two emigration movements. Most participants in the first movement travelled to the USA, with the population of the Ecuadorian-born increasing from 8,000 in 1960 to 143,000 by 1990 (Gibson and Lennon, 1999). In contrast, most of the second migratory movement went to Spain, which had less restrictive entry requirements and offered jobs for low-skilled workers in the informal economy (Jokisch, 2007). Spain became one of the main destinations for Andean migrants up to the GEC, although many have returned home since (Vono de Vilhena, 2011). At the same time Ecuador has experienced an increase in Colombian and Peruvian immigration since 2001 (Jokisch, 2007).

Since the 1990s, Peru, has experienced an increase in migration to Spain and neighbouring countries. In addition, descendants of earlier Japanese immigrants, or *Nikkeijin*, migrated to Japan as workers, following reforms that allowed second- and third-generation persons of Japanese descent easier access to a legal residential status (Kashiwazaki and Akaha, 2006). While the most significant flow of *Nikkeijin* was of Brazilians, many Peruvians also moved (see Chapter 7 for figures).

The experience of Venezuela has been different from that of other Andean countries, with a significant inflow of regional migrants since the 1970s. The reduction of immigration from Europe and oil-related economic growth after 1958 resulted in large-scale immigration from other Latin American countries. In 1979, the Andean Pact was signed, obliging member states to legalize irregular resident nationals from other member states (Picquet *et al.*, 1986). However, despite estimates ranging from 1.2 to 3.5 million irregular residents out of a total Venezuelan population of around 13.5 million, only some 280,000 to 350,000 irregular residents were legalized in 1980 (Meissner *et al.*, 1987). The early twenty-first century was characterized by continued political and economic instability. The unrest encouraged emigration from Venezuela, particularly to the USA (IOM, 2005). Spain also became a major destination country for Venezuelan immigrants, mainly from rural areas. However, Venezuela continued to receive significant migration flows from neighbouring countries (O'Neil *et al.*, 2005: 4).

The Southern Cone

The political and economic transformations of recent decades have resulted in changing migratory patterns. From the late 1960s until the 1980s the rule of military dictatorships forced thousands of people to flee from Argentina, Chile and Uruguay (Pellegrino, 2000). Many found refuge in countries such as Australia, Sweden and Mexico. The coming to power of military regimes also signified a transition to more restrictive immigration policies and fewer entries. Economic woes, particularly during the 1980s, further encouraged emigration from the Southern Cone.

Figure 6.1   *Foreign-born populations in selected American countries*

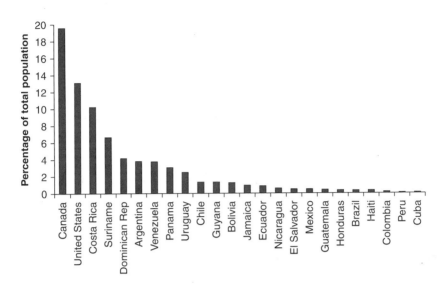

Source: World Development Indicators database, based on United Nations Population Division data, 2005 estimates.

Brazilians migrated to Paraguay in the late 1980s, where they worked in agriculture, while emigration to the USA also increased. By 2000, there were over 1.8 million Brazilians living abroad. Of these, 442,000 lived in Paraguay, 225,000 in Japan and 799,000 in the USA (Amaral and Fusco, 2005). Similarly, hyperinflation in 1989 and economic crises during the late 1990s and early 2000s encouraged emigration from Argentina. Estimates suggest that while in 1960 there were 95,000 Argentinean emigrants, this figure had increased to 603,000 by 2000 and to 806,000 by 2005 (Courtis, 2011).

The Southern Cone has, however, experienced a period of increased political and economic stability in recent years. Argentina and Chile have increasingly attracted intra-regional migrants. Over 65 per cent of the foreign-born population of Argentina are from other South American countries, notably from Paraguay, Bolivia and Chile (Jachimowicz, 2006). Chile has also become a pole of attraction for immigrants from Argentina, Bolivia, Ecuador and Peru. While Chile's 2002 Census reported 38,000 Peruvian immigrants, estimates suggest that by 2009 there were 131,000 – a four-fold increase (Altamirano Rúa, 2010; Courtis, 2011). An increasing proportion of Peruvian migrants are women, many of whom are employed as domestic workers by middle-class Chilean families (Doña and Levinson, 2004). Yet immigrants remains a low percentage of the total population of the countries in the Southern Cone (World Bank, 2011a).

Regional trends and policy developments

The global economic crisis (GEC)

The GEC that started in 2008 had important consequences for Latin America, particularly because the two main destination countries for migrants from the region, the USA and Spain were severely affected by the recession (see also Chapter 11). Spain has one of Europe's highest unemployment rates. (Mohapatra *et al.*, 2011a). The crisis has also led to pressure to further tighten immigration controls. As a result of the GEC, remittances to Latin America fell by 12 per cent in 2009 and remained almost flat in 2010. While remittances flows grew in 2011, this growth was lower than expected (Mohapatra *et al.*, 2011a).

Many migrants in the USA have opted for moving away from depressed sectors and geographical areas in order to increase their employment chances (Mohapatra *et al.*, 2011a). The decline in migration from Mexico to the USA is strongly linked to the US recession, which particularly hit sectors that employ many migrants, such as construction and manufacturing (Ruiz and Vargas-Silva, 2009). While already established migrants are not returning home, prospective migrants are more hesitant to move in a climate of recession (IOM, 2010).

Feminization of migration

Migration flows in the Americas have become increasingly *feminized.* This follows a general pattern of change in the gender composition of international migration flows in recent decades, with the most significant rise being that in women moving as labour migrants rather than as family members. In the case of Latin America, women are now as likely as men to migrate both regionally and intercontinentally: the share of female migrants as percentage of all international migrants has grown from 44.2 per cent in 1960 to 50.1 in 2010 (IOM, 2010). Women make up 50 per cent of all immigrants in the USA and 52 per cent in Canada (UNDESA, 2009). This trend is accentuated in the Southern Cone and the Andean area where women represent a majority of the migrant population. The same applies to Latin American migrants in Spain (Rico, 2006). Domestic work is the predominant occupation for Latin American migrant women. This is a precarious form of employment, as domestic workers are often denied basic guarantees such as minimum wages, safe working conditions and employee benefits. At the same time, the employment of migrant domestic helpers allows middle-class women in destination countries to enter the labour market, often at high-skill levels (Orrenius and Zavodny, 2010, 10). Other sectors which employ significant numbers of migrant women include services and healthcare (Escobar Latapí *et al.*, 2010).

Trafficking and forced labour

Countries in Latin America often serve as origin or transit points for trafficking, mainly to the USA and Canada and, with increasing frequency,
to Europe. The Dominican Republic is a major source and transit point of
trafficked women for the sex trade. Trafficking also exists within various
sub-regions. According to the UN Office on Drugs and Crime, Bolivian
and Paraguayan victims of trafficking have been identified in Argentina,
while Central American victims have been identified in Mexico (UNODC,
2009). Migrants – particularly those with an irregular status – have at times
been subjected to conditions of forced labour. Migrants employed in small
clothing firms or agriculture are among those most at risk. According to
the ILO (2009) the most common form of forced labour in the region is
debt bondage, which occurs both within and across national borders. A
well-documented case is that of Bolivian migrants who are forced to work
in the garment industry in Argentina. This issue came to public attention
following a fire in a factory in 2006 in which several Bolivians died. In the
USA and Canada, both regular and irregular migrants have been found in
debt bondage (ILO, 2009).

Policy initiatives

By the end of 2011, only 17 out of the 35 states that make up the Americas
had ratified the UN International Convention on the Protection of the Rights
of All Migrant Workers and Members of Their Families. Neither the USA
nor Canada, two of the world's top destination countries, have ratified the
Convention (UN Treaty Collection, 2011). However, most countries in the
region, with the exception of a number of Caribbean states, are signatories
to the 1951 United Nations Convention relating to the Status of Refugees
(United Nations Treaty Collection, 2011).

The post-Cold War period in Latin America and the Caribbean has been
marked by efforts to reinvigorate and expand the many regional integration organizations such as MERCOSUR (the Southern Common Market)
(Derisbourg, 2002). MERCOSUR includes Argentina, Brazil, Paraguay,
Uruguay, and Venezuela and encompasses a total population of over
250 million. MERCOSUR has introduced a series of immigration reforms
in the Southern Cone designed to bring about free movement of people as
part of broader sub-regional integration strategies (Perez Vichich, 2005).
In the Caribbean, policies regarding migration in the area fall mostly under
the responsibility of the Caribbean Community (CARICOM), which seeks
to advance the integration of Caribbean nations and allows for the free
movement of certain – mostly skilled – migrants (Ferrer, 2011). Other
regional bodies have taken similar initiatives, but coordination and implementation has been generally poor.

Countries in the region have also adopted more informal modes of cooperation with each other and with international organizations in migration-
related matters. The Puebla Process, which began in 1996, is a multilateral
regional forum on international migration. It is one of 11 regional consultative
processes (RCPs) monitored by the IOM. RCPs seek to bring together representatives of states and international organizations to foster informal dialogue
and the exchange of information on issues of common interest. The catalyst
for the Puebla Process was a growing concern over irregular migration affecting North and Central America (Regional Conference on Migration, 2011).

Irregular migration

Much policy attention has been given to the issue of irregular migration.
However, bilateral and regional cooperation remains problematic. Memo-
randa of understating (MoU) have been signed between North and Central
American countries to enhance border control and reduce irregular migration. In 2004 Mexico signed a MoU with the USA facilitating the deportation of an annual average of 570,000 Mexicans from the USA. In 2006
Mexico signed a similar MoU with Guatemala, Honduras, El Salvador
and Nicaragua. This scheme has seen an annual average of 59,000 Central
American irregular migrants deported from Mexico since 2007 (GMFD,
2010). However, such schemes have done little to curtail irregular migration, nor to reduce stocks of irregular residents in destination countries.

By contrast, regularization programmes have been conducted in the
Southern Cone. Argentina implemented a large regularization programme
between 2006 and 2010 aimed at migrant workers from the MERCOSUR
residing irregularly in the country. As of 2010, the *Patria Grande* programme had benefited an estimated 222,000 migrants by granting them
legal residence in Argentina, while there were more than 400,000 pending
applications (GMFD, 2010). A similar, though smaller programme was
conducted in Chile in 2007–8, attracting 49,000 applications, primarily
from Peruvian migrants (OAS, 2011). A further significant development
was the promulgation of a new Migration Law in Mexico in 2011. This
law formally recognizes the rights of migrants – irrespective of their legal
status – to basic services such as health, education and access to justice
(Honorable Congreso de la Unión, 2011). However, critics point out that
the law by itself may not ensure an end to the violation of migrant rights in
practice (Sin Fronteras, 2011).

Remittances and development

Money sent home by migrants continues to play an important role in
many of the region's economies. The World Bank estimates that Latin
America received US$58.1 billion in remittances in 2010, up from

US$20.2 billion in 2000. Mexico received US$22.6 billion in remittances, the highest amount in the region. Brazil and Guatemala – the second and third recipient – received an estimated US$4.3 billion each (World Bank, 2011a). While the magnitude of flows may not be as large as for Mexico, remittances represent a very significant proportion of the GDP of many Central American and Caribbean countries. Most remittances came from the USA, but there were also significant inflows from Spain, Canada, and Italy (World Bank, 2011a), (See Chapter 3 above on the relationship between remittances and development.)

Growth of social movements concerned with migration

The move towards democratic – and in some cases left-of-centre – governments in Latin America has helped to open the political space for mobilization of migrant association and human rights groups calling for better conditions and rights for migrants. Such social movements have been particularly important in the Americas, and attempts at coordination have been linked to the World Social Forum and the Civil Society Days of the Global Forum on Migration and Development (GMFD), but also to religious groupings like the Catholic Scalabrini Order. One of the most important mobilizations was the mass demonstrations all over the USA in 2006, when Mexican and other migrants in the USA protested against proposed laws, which would have criminalized irregular migrants. On 10 April, millions of people demonstrated in 102 cities, with the largest single gathering of around half a million in Los Angeles (Gelatt, 2006). Further huge protests followed on 1 May (Newman, 2006). The National Alliance of Latin American and Caribbean Communities (NALACC) emerged as an important coordination body, which continued to organize protests, for instance against the anti-immigrant legislation of March 2010 in Arizona (NALACC, 2010).

An important international coalition of migrant and human rights organizations is the People's Global Action on Migration, Development and Human Rights (PGA). The PGA seeks – as its name indicates – to add human rights to the debates on migration and development pursued by the GMFD. The PGA's meeting in Mexico City in 2010 took the initiative to call for a new system of statistical indicators that would reflect all aspects of the costs and benefits of migration for all the parties involved (Castles, 2011; Puentes *et al.*, 2010).

Conclusions

While the USA remains the world's number one international migration destination, the growth of its migrant stock has slipped back in recent years. The USA's economic dominance of the Americas appears to be in decline, and new democratic governments have emerged which are unwilling to toe the neoliberal line. Although South–North movements remain the main feature of migration for the region, their relative importance is waning, as both the USA and Europe face a prolonged economic crisis, while migrations within Latin America to poles of economic growth like Argentina, Chile, Brazil and Venezuela are on the increase. In an unexpected reversal of long-term trends, young and mainly highly educated Europeans are now seeking to escape growing unemployment in Spain, Portugal and Italy by moving to Latin America.

A key question is whether such shifts are just temporary effects of the GEC or instead are indicative of long-term structural changes in the regional political, demographic and economic patterns which shape migration. Clearly, it is too early to answer this question at present. In any case, it must be stressed that the Americas remains a region with high levels of migration driven primarily by stark inequality. The need to migrate to make a decent living is a daily reality for millions of people, even though the risks involved are often very severe. Governments in both the South and North of the continent continue to struggle to improve legal frameworks and policies relating to migration. Often narrowly understood national interests are put above long-term collaborative approaches, which have made little progress, despite efforts by international organizations. No wonder then the issue of migration has become increasingly politicized, especially in immigration countries like the USA, where exclusionary approaches appear as sure vote-getters to many politicians.

The growth of national and international debates on migration has opened the political space for the growth of migrant associations and coalitions of these with human rights groups. One important trend of recent years is that critical voices have grown louder, and people seen hitherto as powerless – like irregular migrants and migrant women – have been willing to make sacrifices and take risks to claim their human rights. The active involvement of migrant organizations in struggles for migration in conditions of safety, dignity and legality may prove a major factor for change in the future. This is a global trend, but may prove especially significant in the Americas, where governments of major immigration countries publicly endorse principles of human rights, while ever-more emigration countries are undergoing democratization.

To what extent do the patterns examined in this chapter on the Americas reflect the various theoretical positions on international migration and its meaning for both origin and destination societies discussed in Chapters 2 and 3? The accounts given here do illustrate how international migration is very much part of the contemporary processes of development and social transformation that are taking place. The Americas includes some of the richest countries of the world as well as some of the poorest and some that are making the breakthrough to economic growth and middle-income status. Human mobility is driven both by inequality and by perceptions of opportunities for improvement elsewhere. The underdevelopment of much of the Americas helps provide labour for the richer parts, confirming key ideas of historical–structural approaches. Yet for those who have the necessary resources and agency, mobility can be a key aspect of individual freedom and of human development. A key question for the future remains whether migration will perpetuate underdevelopment and inequality by shifting human resources to rich areas, or whether it can help provide the capital and skills needed for development and convergence.

Guide to further reading

Good studies of migration to the USA include Borjas (2001); Portes and Rumbaut (2006); and Zolberg (2006). Information on Mexico–US migration can be found in the 2011 Report of Amnesty International (2011) and in Massey *et al*. (2002). The works on the political economy of migration edited by Munck *et al*. (2011) and Phillips (2011b) include studies on the Americas. The website of the Economic Commission for Latin America and the Caribbean (ECLAC) http://www.cepal.org/default.asp?idioma=IN is a valuable source for information on the political economy of Latin America.

A detailed overview of migration concerning the Americas is provided by the *First Report of the Continuous Reporting System on International Migration in the Americas* (Organisation of American States, 2011). For a recent analysis of emergent patterns at sub-regional levels see Martínez Pizarro (2011).

The *International Migration Outlook* of the OECD is an invaluable source for a number of countries in the region, as is the *World Migration Report* of the IOM. *Migration News,* the *Migration Information Source* and the International Network on Migration and Development are good online sources on migration-related issues for the region (see list of websites and URLs at the beginning of the book). The Pew Research Centre provides up-to-date information on a number of migration-related issues in the USA.

Chapter 7

Migration in the Asia–Pacific Region

Well over half the world's population lives in the Asia–Pacific region: 4.2 billion (or 60 per cent) of the world total of 6.9 billion in 2010 (UNDESA, 2011). Yet in 2010, Asia hosted just 27.5 million immigrants – 13 per cent of the world total of 214 million (UNDESA, 2009), India (9 million emigrants), Bangladesh (7 million) and China (6 million) are among the world's main emigration countries in *volume*, although emigration *rates* are low, relative to the vast size of their populations. Pakistan, the Philippines, Afghanistan, Vietnam, Indonesia, South Korea and Nepal are also important origin countries. Top receiving countries for Asian migrants in 2000 were the USA (8 million), India (6 million), Saudi Arabia (2 million), Pakistan (3 million), Hong Kong SAR (2.5 million), Iran (2 million), Canada (2 million) and Malaysia (2 million (IOM, 2010: 166–7) (see Figure 7.1).

In the 1970s and 1980s, international migration from Asia grew rapidly. The main destinations were North America, Australia and the Middle

Figure 7.1   *Foreign-born populations in selected Asia–Pacific countries*

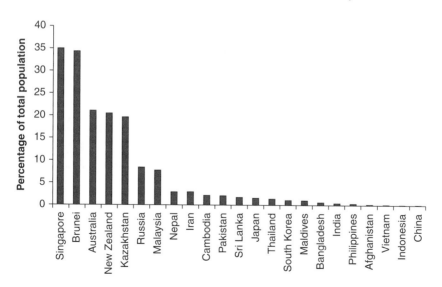

Source: World Development Indicators database, based on United Nations Population Division data, 2005 estimates.

147

East. Since the 1990s, the major growth has been in migration *within* Asia, particularly from less-developed countries like Bangladesh, Indonesia, Vietnam and the Philippines to fast-growing industrializing countries. In view of its great diversity and complexity, it makes little sense to speak of a single 'Asia–Pacific migration system'. According to the UN classification, the Asia–Pacific region includes the Gulf oil states, Turkey and the rest of the Middle East. However, that area is covered in Chapter 8, so this Chapter will be concerned mainly with the sub-regions South Asia (the Indian subcontinent), East Asia (China, Taiwan, Korea and Japan) and South-East Asia (the Indo-Chinese peninsula, Malaysia, Brunei, Singapore and Indonesia), and Oceania (which comprises Australia, New Zealand and many Pacific Islands).

Asia's sub-regions differ greatly in history, culture, religion, economy and politics. At the same time, within each sub-region and even within each country, there is enormous diversity. Generalizations are very difficult, and our account cannot hope to cover all the variations in migratory patterns and experiences. This chapter presents snapshots that illustrate some of the key trends and issues. A section near the end deals with Oceania, where experiences are rather distinct from the rest of the region, due to specific patterns of colonization and settlement. Oceania is in the region but not typically of it, most notably because its dominant nations have been the result of European colonization and large-scale immigration.

The links between internal and international migration are highly complex (Skeldon, 1997; 2006a). India is experiencing large-scale internal migration and urbanization. In China, massive flows from rural areas in the centre and west to the industrial areas of the east (especially Beijing, Shanghai and the Pearl River Delta) have created a 'floating population' estimated at 210 million in 2010 (China Daily, 2010). Indonesia's *transmigrasi* programme shifted about 1.7 million families from densely populated Java to more sparsely populated islands like Sumatra, Sulawesi and Irian Jaya between 1969 and 1998 (Tirtosudarmo, 2001: 211). After the fall of the Suharto regime, *transmigrasi* was scaled down but not stopped. Other countries in the region are experiencing similar internal movements. Forced internal displacement, as a result of conflict, violence, human rights abuses, natural disasters and development projects (such as dams), is also a major issue in Asia. Internal migration will not be dealt with here, but it is important to realize that it is often the first step in a process that leads to international movement.

The development of Asian migration

Westward movements from Central Asia helped shape European history in the Middle Ages, while Chinese migration to South-East Asia goes back centuries (Wang, 1997). In the colonial period, millions of indentured workers were recruited, often by force (see Chapter 4). Chinese settlers in South-East Asian countries (Sinn, 1998) and South Asians in Africa became trading minorities with an important intermediary role for colonialism. In the nineteenth century there was considerable migration from China and Japan to the USA, Canada and Australia. In all three countries, discriminatory legislation was enacted to prevent these movements.

Migration from Asia was low in the early part of the twentieth century owing to restrictive policies by immigration countries and colonial powers. However, movements within Asia continued, often connected with political struggles. Japan recruited 40,000 workers from its then colony, Korea, between 1921 and 1941. Japan also made extensive use of forced labour in World War II. Some 25 million people migrated from densely populated Chinese provinces to Manchuria between the 1890s to the 1930s, with about 8 million staying on 'to reaffirm China's national territory in the face of Japanese expansionism' (Skeldon, 2006a: 23). In the often violent mass population transfers following Indian Independence in 1947, about 5 million Hindus and Sikhs left Pakistan for India and about 6 million Muslims moved into Pakistan from India (Khadria, 2008).

External movements started to grow from the 1960s. The reasons were complex (Fawcett and Carino, 1987; Skeldon, 1992: 20–2). Discriminatory rules against Asian entries were repealed in Canada (1962 and 1976), the USA (1965) and Australia (1966 and 1973). Increased foreign investment and trade helped create the communicative networks needed for migration. The US military presence in Korea, Vietnam and other Asian countries forged transnational links, as well as directly stimulating movement in the shape of brides of US personnel. The Vietnam War caused large-scale refugee movements. The openness of the USA, Canada and Australia to family migration meant that primary movements, whatever their cause, gave rise to further entries of permanent settlers. The huge construction projects in the Gulf oil countries caused mass recruitment of temporary contract workers. Rapid economic growth in several Asian countries led to movements of both highly skilled and unskilled workers.

Asia's massive entry onto the world migration stage in the mid-twentieth century can be seen as the result of the opening up of the continent to economic and political relationships with the industrialized countries in the postcolonial period. Western penetration through trade, aid and investment created the material means and the cultural capital necessary for migration. As we pointed out in Chapters 2 and 3 above, the dislocation of existing forms of production and social structures through industrialization, the 'green revolution' and wars (often encouraged by major powers as part of the Cold War) compelled people to leave the countryside in search of better conditions in the growing cities or overseas. Later on, the rapid industrial take-off of some areas and the continuing stagnation or decline of others created new migration flows. For example industrialization in Malaysia from the 1970s pulled in migrant workers from neighbouring Indonesia.

The early twenty-first century has been a period of growing diversity in Asian and Pacific migration. Economic migrants can be found at all skill

Map 7.1 *Contemporary Migrations within and from the Asia–Pacific region*

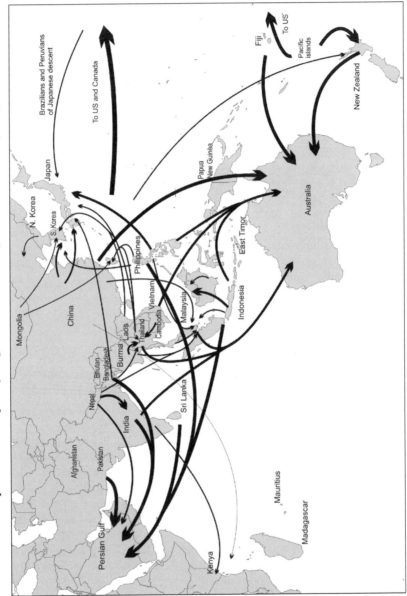

Note: The size of the arrowheads gives an approximate indication of the volume of flows. Exact figures are often unavailable.

levels: the lower-skilled still migrate out of the region but increasingly also within it; many highly skilled people move to highly developed countries, but increasing numbers go to other Asian countries, while highly skilled migrants from other world regions are attracted to areas of economic growth. In 2005 it was estimated that there were some 6.1 million Asians employed outside their own countries within the Asian region, and about 8.7 million in the Middle East. Hugo estimated that there could be over 20 million Asian migrant workers worldwide (Hugo, 2005). Emigration for employment from countries within the region has grown at about 6 per cent a year over the last two decades, with about 2.6 million people leaving their homes in search of work each year (ILO, 2006: 37). The Asian financial crisis of 1997–9 caused only a temporary slow-down (Abella, 2002). Similarly the GEC that started in 2008 led to initial reductions in migration, but these were quickly overcome, as new flows got under way (see Chapter 11).

All countries in the region experience both significant emigration and immigration (and often transit migration too), but it is possible to differentiate between predominantly immigration countries (Brunei, Hong Kong, Japan, Singapore, South Korea, Taiwan), countries with both significant immigration and emigration (Malaysia, Thailand), and mainly emigration countries (Bangladesh, Burma, Cambodia, China, India, Indonesia, Laos, Nepal, Pakistan, Philippines, Sri Lanka, Vietnam) (Hugo, 2005: 8). All of today's predominantly immigration countries (except perhaps Brunei and Singapore) experienced significant emigration in the post-1945 period, and have gone through recent migration transitions, while Malaysia and Thailand appear to be in the middle of such transitions (see Chapter 2 on transition theories).

Four of the world's top ten migration corridors include Asian countries: Bangladesh–India (3.5 million migrants in 2005), India–United Arab Emirates (2.2 million), Philippines–USA (1.6 million) and Afghanistan–Iran (also 1.6 million) (IOM, 2010: 167). This list also helps reveal the diversity and complexity of Asian migration: the Bangladesh–India movement is intra-regional and driven mainly by differences in employment opportunities (and sometimes also by environmental factors); India–UAE is mainly a contract labour flow; Philippines–USA is diverse and includes many permanent settlers; while the Afghanistan–Iran movement is a mix of migrant workers and refugees (see Map 7.1).

Asian migration to Western Europe, North America and Oceania

Three European countries experienced large Asian migrations connected with decolonization: the Netherlands from the former Netherlands East Indies (Indonesia); France from Vietnam; and Britain from the Indian subcontinent and Hong Kong. There were also some smaller movements, like those from Goa, Macau and East Timor to Portugal. Such movements had declined considerably by the late 1970s. In the 1980s, Vietnamese workers were recruited by the Soviet Union and the German Democratic Republic. After German reunification in 1990, many stayed on, often moving into small business, sometimes initially in illicit cigarette trading, and then in more mainstream enterprises.

In the past, many Asian migrants moved to the 'classical immigration countries' (USA, Canada, Australia and New Zealand), but a recent trend is the growth of Asian migration to Europe from China, India, Japan, the Philippines, Vietnam and Thailand (OECD, 2007; see also OECD, 2011a: 46–52). The migrants include medical and information technology personnel, female domestic workers, and manual workers (often moving irregularly). The largest Asian movement was that to the USA after the 1965 Immigration Act: most Asians came through the family reunion provisions of the Act, though refugee or skilled worker movements were often the first link in the migratory chain. Since 1992, Asia has been the source of about one-third of all immigrants, and by 2008 there were over 10 million residents of Asian origin – 27 per cent of the total immigrant population (IOM, 2010: 152). In 2009, China was the second largest source of new immigrants, with 64,200 (following Mexico with 164,900). Philippines came third with 60,000, while India, Vietnam, Korea and Pakistan were also among the top ten source countries. However, Asian entry figures were considerably down on previous years, presumably due to the US recession (OECD, 2011a: table B.1.1) and the earlier recovery from the GEC in some Asian countries.

In Canada, it was the 1976 Immigration Act, with its non-discriminatory selection criteria and its emphasis on family and refugee entry, which opened the door to Asian migration. Since 1993, over half of all immigrants have come from Asia. In 2009, the top three source countries for new entrants were China, India and the Philippines, followed by the USA (OECD, 2011a: table B.1.1). By the 2006 Census, the 2.7 million residents born in Asia made up 41 per cent of the total immigrant population of 6.5 million. The main Asian groups were Chinese (719,000), Indians (455,000), Filipinos (320,000) and Vietnamese (162,000) (Statistics Canada, 2010).

Asian immigration to Australia rapidly increased after the repeal of the White Australia Policy, with additional stimulus from the Indo-Chinese refugee movement at the end of the 1970s. Similarly, after New Zealand abandoned its traditional racially selective entry policies, there have been considerable inflows from the Pacific Islands and from Asia. These trends are dealt with in more detail in section on Oceania below.

Migrations from Asia to North America and Oceania have certain common features. Unexpectedly large movements have developed mainly through use of family reunion provisions. The countries of origin have become more diverse. Vietnamese and other Indo-Chinese refugees were a dominant flow in the 1970s and 1980s; Hong Kong became a major source in the run-up to incorporation into China in 1997, although there has been some return migration since. Recent flows come from the Philippines, India, Japan and Korea. The most important trend is the growth in migration from China. A global labour market for highly skilled personnel has emerged, with Asia as the main source – but increasingly the fast-growing economies of East and South-East Asia are also competing to attract skilled workers themselves.

Contract labour migration to the Middle East

Labour migration from Asia to the Middle East developed rapidly after the oil price rises of 1973. Labour was imported by oil-rich countries first from India and Pakistan, then from the Philippines, Indonesia, Thailand and Korea, and later from Bangladesh and Sri Lanka. Governments of countries like India, Pakistan and the Philippines actively marketed their labour abroad, and concluded labour-supply agreements with Gulf countries, and also allowed private agencies to organize recruitment (Abella, 1995).

By 2010, migrants made up 87 per cent of the total population of Qatar, 70 per cent in the UAE, 69 per cent in Kuwait, 39 per cent in Bahrain, 28 per cent in Oman and 28 per cent in Saudi Arabia (UNDESA, 2009). Asian migration to the Middle East has become more diverse over time. While many migrants remain low-skilled labourers, others have semi-skilled or skilled jobs as drivers, mechanics or building tradesmen. Others went with professional or para-professional qualifications (engineers, nurses and medical practitioners). Many managerial and technical posts are filled by Asians, although sometimes they come second in job hierarchies to senior personnel recruited in Europe or North America.

There has also been an upsurge in demand for domestic workers, nurses, sales staff and other service personnel, leading to a feminization of migrant labour flows, with Sri Lanka and Indonesia as the main sources. In later years, other countries in the Middle East – Lebanon, Jordan and Israel – also became labour-importing countries, especially for domestic workers (Asis, 2008). Overall, there were 10.2 million migrant women in the Middle East in 2010, 38 per cent of all migrants (IOM, 2010; UNDESA, 2009). Asian migration to the Middle East will be dealt with in detail in Chapter 8.

Labour migration within Asia

Since the mid-1980s, rapid economic growth and declining fertility have increased labour demand in the new industrial economies of East and South-East Asia. At the same time, economic stagnation, high fertility and lack of employment in other Asian countries encourage emigration.

Labour migration within Asia grew exponentially in the first half of the 1990s. While flows from Bangladesh, Indonesia and the Philippines continue, new source countries like Vietnam, Cambodia, Laos and Burma have become more significant. In all the 'tiger economies', migrant workers are doing the '3D jobs' (dirty, dangerous and difficult – or just low-skilled and poorly paid) that nationals can increasingly afford to reject.

Despite the increase in intra-Asian labour migration, the contribution to labour forces in receiving countries is still relatively low: migrant workers make up only about 4 per cent of labour forces in East and South-East Asia. However, the situation is different in Singapore and Malaysia, where migrants make up 35 and 19 per cent of the workforces respectively (Department of Statistics Malaysia, 2009; Ministry of Manpower Singapore, 2011). While early flows were mainly low-skilled, highly skilled migration has recently increased throughout the region, particularly because demand for health and care workers is increasing.

Feminization of migration

There was little female labour migration in Asia before the late 1970s, after which the demand for female domestic workers surged, first in the Middle East, and, from the 1990s, within Asia. In 2004, 81 per cent of registered new migrant workers leaving Indonesia were women (ILO, 2007). The female share among first-time migrant workers from the Philippines rose from 50 per cent in 1992 (Go, 2002: 66) to 72 per cent by 2006 (ILO, 2007).

Most migrant women are concentrated in jobs regarded as 'typically female': domestic work, entertainment (often a euphemism for prostitution), restaurant and hotel staff and assembly-line workers in clothing and electronics. These jobs generally offer poor pay, conditions and status, and are associated with patriarchal stereotypes of female docility, obedience and willingness to give personal service. Demand for care-givers is likely to be a major factor in the future, due to population ageing in many destination countries. The increase in domestic service reflects the growth of dual-career professional households in Asia's new industrial countries. Married women have to leave their children in the care of others, and long absences affect relationships and gender roles (Lee, 2010).

Another form of female migration is for marriage. Asian women moved as brides of US servicemen from the 1940s – first from Japan, then Korea and then Vietnam. From the 1980s, a new phenomenon emerged: so-called 'mail order' brides to Europe and Australia (Cahill, 1990). Since the 1990s, foreign brides have been sought by farmers in rural areas of Japan, Taiwan and South Korea, due to the exodus of local women to more attractive urban settings. By the early twenty-first century, marriage migration to East Asian countries was increasing. The Chinese one-child policy and the preference for male children in India have led to large male surpluses in those countries, and brides are being recruited for Indians in Bangladesh and for Chinese farmers in Vietnam, Laos and Burma (IOM, 2005: 112).

Over 90 per cent of international marriages in East Asia are between a foreign-born woman and a native-born man, and many of the foreign brides are recruited through agents. In 2008 Taiwan received 413,000 marriage migrants, while South Korea received 150,000 (11–13 per cent of all marriages in the 2003–8 period). In Japan some 5–6 per cent of all marriages involved foreign partners (Lee, 2010). Many women migrating for marriage come from South-East Asia (Vietnam, Laos, Thailand, Philippines) and China. The receiving countries all have very low total fertility rates (in 2005: Taiwan 1.12; South Korea, 1.24 and Japan 1.29) (Lee, 2010: 7).The high proportion of foreign mothers is regarded by some as a threat to national identity. The Korean and Taiwanese governments have carried out major surveys to help understand the consequences of marriage migration (Bélanger *et al.*, 2010) and implemented policies to tackle abusive match-making businesses and to support marriage migrants and their children (Lee, 2010).

Migration agents and irregular migration

An important feature of Asian labour migration is the major role played by the 'migration industry' (see Chapters 2 and 10). Many movements include substantial irregular migration. This often takes the form of tourist visa holders overstaying their permits, but smuggling and trafficking of people are also frequent. Hugo quotes estimates of irregular migrants in SE Asia countries in the early 2000s totalling about 3.8 million (Hugo, 2005: 22), although this figure is very approximate. Migration agents and labour brokers organize most recruitment of Asian migrant workers to the Gulf and within Asia, while match-makers organize marriage migration. While some agents carry out legitimate activities, others deceive and exploit migrants. Although countries like the Philippines and Vietnam seek to regulate such agencies, this has proved difficult in practice (Kim *et al.*, 2007).

Irregular (or undocumented) migration has grown rapidly and affects many countries in the region. Labour flows from Indonesia to Malaysia have been largely undocumented. Thai workers move irregularly to Malaysia and other countries for work, while Thailand itself hosts up to 1.7 million undocumented workers, mainly from Burma (IOM, 2005: 110-12). Hugo points to the complexity of irregular migration, arguing that there is a continuum from voluntary individual movement, through use of middlemen, to trafficking and bonded labour (Hugo, 2010b: 29). The growth of irregular migration is linked to the unwillingness of governments to allow legal entries and the desire of employers for easily available and exploitable workers. Spontaneous undocumented migration can meet labour needs effectively, but can create situations of insecurity and rightlessness for workers. Moreover, they can become easy scapegoats for social problems like crime, disease and unemployment.

Temporary migration

The majority of Asian governments seek to control migration strictly, and migrants' rights are often very limited. Labour migration is seen as a temporary necessity, which should not lead to permanent settlement or to changes in the culture and identity of destination countries. This matches the initial intentions of key actors. Some employers want low-skilled workers to meet immediate labour needs. Many migrant workers wish to work abroad for a limited period to improve the situation of their families at home. Sending-country governments do not want to lose nationals permanently.

Ideas from Europe, North America or Oceania on the benefits of multiculturalism are unpopular in most Asian societies, which have difficulties with the idea of immigrants turning into citizens. Immigration is seen as a threat to the nation-state and should therefore only be temporary (Castles, 2004c; Hugo, 2005). A key question for the future is whether this exclusionary model can be sustained. Employer demand is important: once employers invest in training migrant workers, their initial ideas may change, and they may want to retain experienced workers. If labour requirements are due to long-term economic and demographic changes, the recruitment of temporary workers does not seem to provide an adequate solution.

East Asia

In East Asia the combination of rapid economic growth, fertility decline, ageing and growing undocumented migration has led to serious contradictions, most evident in Japan, but also emerging in South Korea, Hong Kong, Taiwan and China.

Japan has experienced considerable labour immigration since the mid-1980s. The registered foreign population increased from 817,000 in 1983 to 2.1 million in 2009 (1.7 per cent of the total population) (OECD, 2012: table A5). In 2010, 27 per cent of foreigners were considered 'general permanent residents' and another 19 per cent were 'special permanent residents'. The latter are mainly descendants of Koreans who were recruited (sometimes by force) as workers during the Japanese colonial domination of Korea from 1910 to 1945. In 2010, 687,000 Chinese and 566,000 Koreans were registered (Statistics Bureau Japan, 2012). Many recent migrants are *Nikkeijin*: descendants of past Japanese emigrants now admitted as labour migrants. This category included 231,000 Brazilians and 55,000 Peruvians in 2009 (OECD, 2012: table B5). Japanese government policies and public attitudes remain opposed to recruitment of foreign labour and to long-term stay, for fear of diluting the perceived ethnic homogeneity of the population. In view of the ageing population and projected future labour needs, especially for elder care, such policies may be hard to sustain.

South Korea's foreign resident population has risen rapidly since the early 1990s to 1 million (2 per cent of population) in 2012 (OECD, 2012: table A5). There is considerable public discussion of multiculturalism and the challenges of immigration for a society which is very concerned about ethnic homogeneity. South Korea experienced long-term emigration to the USA and Australia after the Korean War, and exported labour to the Gulf in the 1970s and 1980s, but with rapid economic growth labour emigration had fallen sharply by the mid-1990s. In 1994, the government introduced the 'Industrial Trainee System' – a disguised framework for import of low-skilled labour (Hur and Lee, 2008; Seol, 2001). This scheme failed to reduce irregular migration and was replaced by the 'Employment Permit System' (EPS) in 2004, which gave temporary migrants the same labour market rights as Koreans, but did not permit family reunion.

The EPS restricts the sectors for foreign employment to manufacturing, construction, agriculture and fishery (Ministry of Employment and Labor, 2010), where employers often prefer male employees. Women who wish to go to Korea therefore often have to seek other options, such as marriage migration (Kim *et al.*, 2007; Lee, 2008). Unmatched expectations, unequal relationships and difficulties in communication often cause conflicts between couples or with the wider family. Marriage migrants cannot apply for visa renewal or for citizenship without the endorsement of their spouses. Currently, one in four new marriages is an international marriage, and the number of marriage migrants increased from 25,000 in 2001 to 142,000 in 2011 (Korean Immigration Service, 2002; 2012). Many of the brides are ethnic Koreans from China, but others come from Vietnam, Cambodia and the Philippines.

Between the 1950s and reunification with China in 1997, *Hong Kong* was transformed from a labour-intensive industrial economy to a post-industrial economy based on trade, services and investment. Highly qualified temporary immigrant ('expat') workers from North America, Western Europe and India were recruited for finance, management and education. Unskilled workers from China entered illegally in large numbers. After reunification with China in 1997, Hong Kong became a Special Administrative Region (SAR) with its own laws and institutions. Low-skilled workers from Mainland China are not admitted to Hong Kong, but some 380,000 mainlanders were allowed in from 1997–2004 through family reunion provisions – nearly all women and children. Most of the women are employed as cleaners and restaurant workers (Sze, 2007). In 2010, there were 285,000 foreign domestic helpers in Hong Kong, 48 per cent from the Philippines, 49 per cent from Indonesia and 1 per cent from Thailand. Employers may employ maids for two years and renew the contract, but may also terminate the contract before it expires (HKSARG, 2011).

While foreign nationals may obtain permanent residency after working in Hong Kong for seven years, immigration rules exclude domestic helpers from seeking permanent residence.

Taiwan introduced a foreign labour policy in 1992, permitting recruitment of migrant workers for occupations with severe labour shortages. Duration of employment was limited to two years. Workers came mainly from Thailand, the Philippines, Malaysia and Indonesia. Most recruitment was carried out by labour brokers. Many workers stayed on illegally after two years, or changed jobs to get higher wages and to escape repayments to brokers (Lee and Wang, 1996). In 2011 there were 461,000 registered foreign residents of whom 365,000 were workers (National Immigration Agency Taiwan, 2012). In 2007, the Taiwanese government set up a 'Direct Hiring Joint Service Center' to assist employers in hiring foreign workers without paying high fees to recruitment agencies. The government signed an MOU with the Philippines government for direct hiring in 2011 and launched an online 'Direct Cross-border Hiring Management Service' system in 2012 (Council of Labor Affairs Taiwan, 2012; Wei and Chang, 2011).

South-East Asia

South-East Asia is characterized by enormous ethnic, cultural and religious diversity, as well as by considerable disparities in economic development. Governments of immigration countries are concerned about maintaining ethnic balances, and combating possible threats to security.

Singapore is a country lacking in natural resources, which has successfully built a first-world economy through specialization in modern service industries. It relies heavily on the import of labour at all skill levels. In 2010, the population was 5.1 million (UNDESA, 2011), of whom nearly 2 million were immigrants (IOM, 2010: 170). Between 1990 and 2010, the non-resident workforce grew from 248,000 to 1,089,000 and is now more than a third of the total workforce (Ministry of Manpower Singapore, 2011). The government imposes a foreign worker levy for employing unskilled workers and a 25 per cent 'dependency ceiling' (quota) for employing skilled workers to encourage employers to invest in new technology (Ministry of Manpower Singapore, 2011; Yue, 2011).However, this has led to downward pressure on migrants' wages, rather than reductions in foreign employment. Unskilled workers are not permitted to settle or to bring in their families. About 85 per cent of the foreign workforce are classified as lower-skilled (Abella and Ducanes, 2009). They come from Malaysia, Thailand, Indonesia, the Philippines, Sri Lanka, India and China. Foreign men work in construction, shipbuilding, transport and services; women mainly in domestic and other services. Due to the rule that ties the unskilled workers to a specific job, employers often use the threat of cancelling the visa to force migrants to accept unlawful work conditions (Human Rights Watch, 2011).

Malaysia is another industrializing economy in South-East Asia that has become heavily dependent on immigration. Due to the complex ethnic composition, immigration has been controversial, and successive governments have struggled to find appropriate approaches. Rapid economic growth since the 1980s has created labour shortages, especially in the plantation sector. The official record shows there were 2.1 million registered foreign workers in 2010 – a slight decrease from the peak of 2008. Official estimates of irregular migrants vary from 500,000 to 1.8 million, although employers' associations and trade unions put the figure much higher (Kassim and Zin, 2011: 2). The Malaysian government manages labour migration through three categories: expatriate with an executive post or high skills, foreign worker and foreign domestic worker. The government imposes levies and quotas, and limits the employment of migrant workers to specific sectors (manufacturing and plantations) and from specific countries of origin (Indonesia, Cambodia, the Philippines) (Immigration Department of Malaysia, 2012). Both regular and irregular migrant workers in Malaysia often face exploitive labour conditions and abusive policing (Amnesty International, 2011).

Thailand became a major exporter of workers to the Gulf in the 1980s and then to Taiwan, Malaysia, Japan and Singapore in the early 1990s. Fast economic growth in the 1990s initiated a migration transition. With falling fertility and fast economic growth, many Thais are no longer willing to do '3D jobs' (Skeldon, 2006b: 285). Construction, agricultural and manufacturing jobs have attracted many workers from Burma, Cambodia, Laos and Bangladesh. Many of the Burmese are fleeing violence in their homeland and it is hard to distinguish clearly between migrant workers and refugees. Most of the migrants are irregular. Thai immigration law gives a period of grace (during which they can stay in Thailand) to migrants who enter irregularly but register to be deported. Before deportation, migrants are allowed to work temporarily in unskilled jobs. The government has carried out registrations of migrant workers several times – the last round was in 2009, when about 900,000 migrants (80 per cent from Burma) obtained new work permits, and 380,000 renewed their work permits. Meanwhile, out-migration from Thailand still continues: in 2007, 162,000 workers were officially deployed, for instance to South Korea and Malaysia – 85 per cent male (IOM, 2008: 93–5). Trafficking of Thai women for the sex industry also remains a problem (Hugo, 2005: 24–5).

Countries of emigration

Just as the Mediterranean periphery fuelled Western European industrial expansion up to the 1970s, industrializing Asia has its own labour reserve areas: China, the South Asian countries (Bangladesh, Pakistan, India, Sri Lanka), and many South-East Asian countries (the Philippines, Indonesia, Vietnam, Cambodia, Laos and Burma) have all become major labour providers for the region and indeed for the rest of the world. Asian sending-country governments have set up special departments to manage recruitment and to protect workers, such as Bangladesh's Bureau of Manpower, Employment and Training (BMET) and India's Ministry of Overseas Indian Affairs. The governments of labour-sending countries see migration as economically vital, partly because they hope it will reduce unemployment and provide training and industrial experience, but mainly because of the worker remittances (see Chapter 3 and Hugo, 2005: 28–33). However, by the early twenty-first century, with industrial development spreading to new regions, migration patterns were gaining in complexity. Some sending countries were also increasingly attracting migrants – such as highly skilled personnel or spouses – to make up for demographic imbalances.

China is a vast country with major internal migration. With regard to international migration, China is still mainly an area of emigration, with flows to North America, Europe and – most recently – Africa. The latter is strongly linked to China's emerging trading interests in countries like Mozambique, Zambia, Zimbabwe and Sudan. However, it must be noted that 'the era of cheap labour in China is ending' (Skeldon, 2006b: 282). The rapid economic expansion and the sharp decline in fertility due to the one-child policy mean that China's rural labour reserves are being depleted. Labour shortages have been reported in the industrial cities of the East coast, especially for highly skilled personnel (Pieke, 2011), and internal migration to the coast is slowing down with the growth of regional cities. Professional mobility from Hong Kong, Taiwan and other countries is helping to fill the gap, while emigration of workers from China continues. In the long run China may well become a significant immigration destination for economic migrants as well as for brides.

India too has experienced large-scale emigration, and today the 'Indian diaspora' is estimated at over 20 million persons (including persons of Indian origin now holding other citizenships) across 110 countries (Ministry of Overseas Indians Affairs, 2011). Indians still go in large numbers to the Gulf as manual workers, and to the USA and other developed countries as highly skilled personnel (IT professionals, medical practitioners etc.). However, export of the highly skilled has been increasingly matched by return flows of skills and capital, which are contributing to the development of modern manufacturing and service industries in some parts of India (Khadria, 2008). India is indeed both an emigration and an immigration country, with inflows of mainly lower-skilled workers from Nepal and Bangladesh, as well as refugees from the many conflicts in the region (e,g, in Nepal, Bhutan, Tibet and Sri Lanka). The government reports that there were 352,000 foreigners registered in 2007. The 2001 census shows, however, there were more than 6 million overseas born residents (including Indian citizens), and among them 5.7 million were from neighbouring countries (Naujoks, 2009).

The Philippines is a major emigration country. 10.5 million Filipinos were abroad in 2011, more than 10 per cent of the country's people. About half were seen as permanent emigrants and the other half as temporary Overseas Contract Workers (OCWs). The most popular destinations were the USA (3.4 million), Saudi Arabia (1.6 million), Canada (843,00), United Arab Emirates (680,00), Malaysia (570,000) and Australia (385,000), but Filipinos are to be found all over the world (Commission on Filipino Overseas, 2013). Labour export has been an official policy since the 1970s, when it was seen by the Marcos regime as a political and economic 'safety valve' to reduce discontent. A 'culture of emigration' (see Chapters 2 and 3) has developed: going abroad to work and live has become a normal expectation for many people. The Philippines has developed strong institutions to manage labour export like the Philippine Overseas Employment Administration (POEA) and to maintain links with the diaspora like the Commission on Filipinos Overseas (CFO). Nonetheless, migration is a topic of controversy within the Philippines, and it is far from clear that it has contributed to the economic and social development of the country (Asis, 2008), or whether it has instead exacerbated development stagnation.

Highly qualified migrants and students

Most Asian migration is of low-skilled workers, but mobility of professionals, executives, technicians and other highly skilled personnel is growing. Since the 1960s, university-trained people have been moving from Asia to take up jobs – and often to settle permanently – in North America, Oceania and Europe. This 'brain drain' can mean a serious loss of human capital in medicine, science, engineering, management and education, and be a major obstacle to development. Country studies show substantial skill losses for Asian countries in the 1980s and 1990s. In the case of the Philippines, 40 per cent of permanent emigrants had a college education, and 30 per cent of IT workers and 60 per cent of physicians emigrated. For Sri Lanka, academically qualified professionals comprised up to one-third of outflows (Lowell *et al.*, 2002). India, the Philippines and Pakistan are among the top ten countries from which physicians have emigrated (World Bank, 2011a: 10).

The opposite side of the coin is reliance on highly skilled immigrants in rich countries. Indian and Chinese IT experts played a key role in the rise of Silicon Valley. The 2000 US Census showed that 4.3 million foreign-born persons were college graduates, making up 13 per cent of all college graduates in the USA. Half of the graduates who arrived in the 1990s were from Asia, with India and China as the largest sources. Almost one-third worked in natural and social sciences, engineering and computer-related occupations (Batalova, 2005). In the past, it was mainly the classical immigration countries of North America and Oceania that relied on immigrant professionals. Today, European countries including the UK, Germany and France are making strong efforts to attract them as well.

An important emerging trend is the growth of highly skilled mobility within Asia. Regional migration flows are becoming far more diverse and India, Japan, Singapore, Taiwan, Korea and Malaysia are all seeking overseas professionals – either on a temporary or permanent basis. Like older immigration countries, they have introduced privileged immigration and residence regimes for the highly skilled. In the ten years to 2005, highly skilled immigration increased by 40 per cent in Japan and more than tenfold in Korea (Dumont and Lemaître, 2005: 16). Skilled emigrants may come back to their homelands if opportunities present themselves. The return of Indian IT professionals from the USA and other destinations has been a crucial factor in the rise of the Indian IT industry. Governments seek to encourage such returns through diaspora policies (see below).

Another form of highly qualified migration concerns executives and experts transferred within multinational enterprises, or officials posted abroad by international organizations. China had more than 400,000 foreign specialists employed through the National Foreign Experts Bureau in 2010 (Pieke, 2011), while Malaysia had 32,000 and Vietnam about 30,000 in 2000. They came from other Asian countries, but also from the USA, Europe and Australia (Abella, 2002). Capital investment from overseas is a catalyst for socio-economic change and urbanization, while professional transients are not only agents of economic change, but also bearers of new cultural values. The links they create may encourage people from the developing country to move to the investing country in search of training or work. The returning professional transients bring new experiences and values with them, which can lead to significant changes at home.

The changing face of skilled migration is a reflection of the major shifts taking place in Asia. The annual number of Chinese travelling abroad (for both business and tourism) shot up from less than a million in 1990 to about 15 million by 2003 (Hugo, 2005: 11). Another study estimates that the Chinese overseas tourist market grew to 22 million in 2009 (Li *et al.*, 2010). A corresponding change is the increasing quality of tertiary education within the region, with Japan, China and Korea all competing for foreign students. Although China is still the number one origin country for international students (16.5 per cent of the world's international students in 2009), more foreign students are now coming to China. Japan and Korea have also experienced substantial growth in foreign students (OECD, 2011b). North America, Oceania and Europe are beginning to lose their dominant position within the international education industry.

Diaspora policies

In recent years, perceptions of skilled migration have changed through awareness of the development of diasporas, and the idea they can be a source of remittances and investment for countries of origin, and help homeland producers gain new markets abroad. We still know relatively little about the extent to which migrants of various origins actually feel that they belong to a diaspora with strong homeland links – this is certainly not the case for all migrants. Where significant groups do perceive such connections. they can transmit knowledge and skills, and facilitate temporary or permanent return of experts (see Hugo, 2005: 33–7). Many Asian governments are seeking to reach skilled emigrants and keep in contact with them (Kuznetsov, 2006). Taiwan has been especially successful in maintaining contacts with emigrants and drawing them back as industrialization progressed (Hugo, 2005: 35–7), and other countries are now trying to follow this example. The Chinese diaspora has been a crucial source of capital and expertise in the Chinese economic take-off. Since the early 2000s, China has changed its policy concerning its emigrants from 'permanent migration' to 'flexible mobility'. An important change has been that the idea of migration contributing to development is no longer linked to return. The Chinese diaspora is no longer expected to return permanently, but instead is encouraged to maintain close contact with the homeland.

The Commission on Filipinos Overseas (CFO), established in 1980, has encouraged Filipinos overseas to establish businesses in the Philippines. As a symbol of recognition and appreciation for them, the Philippines President himself has welcomed them at Christmas in *Pamaskong Handog sa OFWs* (Welcome Home Overseas Foreign Workers) ceremonies at Manila airport (Martin, 2008: 17). Similar institutions maintaining close contacts with diasporas have been established in other countries. India's Ministry of Overseas Indian Affairs has the explicit purpose of addressing the needs of diaspora populations. The Sri Lankan Ministry of Foreign Employment Promotion also attempts to reach out to Sri Lankan migrant workers abroad. But one major constraint for most diaspora institutions is obtaining adequate funding (Agunias, 2010: 6). It is hard to assess the success of such efforts: return is more likely to be the result of growing economic opportunities than of symbolic actions.

Refugees

At the end of 2010, UNHCR counted 4 million refugees in the Asia–Pacific, 38 per cent of the global total of 10.5 million (UNHCR, 2011d: 11–13). Refugee numbers declined after 2000, when there were 5.4 million refugees in Asia (44 per cent of the global total), going down to 3.4 million in 2004 (33 per cent of the global total) (UNHCR, 2006: 213). The decline reflected a temporary political stabilization following the violent turmoil arising from colonial liberation struggles and the Cold War. The subsequent increase was the result of renewed conflicts in Afghanistan, Sri Lanka, Burma and elsewhere.

In the wider sense of forced migration (see Chapter 10), millions of people are displaced by conflict, violence, and human rights abuses, but remain in their own countries. The number of people displaced internally by violence was estimated at 4.6 million in South and South-East Asia at the end of 2010 (IDMC, 2011). Millions more are displaced by development projects, such as large dams, while others flee natural disasters, like volcanoes and floods (Cernea and McDowell, 2000). In some places, vulnerable groups (especially indigenous peoples or ethnic minorities) may experience several types of displacement, as in Sri Lanka, where people have been repeatedly displaced by large dam projects, civil war and the 2004 tsunami.

In 2010, Afghanistan remained the biggest global source of refugees, with 3.1 million (29 per cent of the global refugee population) in 75 different asylum countries. Iraq came second with 1.7 million refugees (see Box 7.1). Some 416,000 refugees came from Burma, 339,000 from Vietnam and 185,000 from China (UNHCR, 2011d). However, East Asia and the Pacific were relatively peaceful compared with the Middle East and Central Asia. Pakistan was host to the largest number of refugees worldwide (1.9 million), followed by Iran (1.1 million) and Syria (1 million) (UNHCR, 2011d).

Looking back, Asia's three largest refugee emergencies resulted from the 1947 Partition of India, and from the wars in Indo-China and Afghanistan. Over 3 million people fled from Vietnam, Laos and Cambodia following the end of the Vietnam War in 1975. Many left as 'boat people', sailing long distances in overcrowded small boats, at risk of shipwreck and pirate attacks. Over the next 20 years, 2.5 million found new homes elsewhere, while 0.5 million returned. Over a million were resettled in the USA, with smaller numbers in Australia, Canada and Western Europe. China accepted about 300,000 refugees, mainly of ethnic Chinese origin. (UNHCR, 2000: 79–103).

Apart from these huge refugee movements, there have been many exoduses smaller in numbers, but no less traumatic for those concerned. After the failure of the democracy movement in 1989, thousands of Chinese sought asylum overseas. Conflicts linked to the break-up of the former Soviet Union led to mass displacements in the 1990s affecting many new states, including Georgia, Chechnya, Armenia, Azerbaijan and Tajikistan. At least 50,000 North Koreans have fled to China, often continuing on to South Korea if possible. Other long-standing refugee populations include Tibetans and Bhutanese in India and Nepal, and Burmese in Thailand and Bangladesh. The 26-year civil war in Sri Lanka led to mass internal displacement as well as refugee outflows. The war ended with appalling bloodshed in May 2009, and by 2010, there were an estimated 274,000 IDPs in Sri Lanka, while 141,000 persons had left as refugees (UNHCR, 2011f).

The Asian experience shows the complexity of refugee situations at times of rapid change: they are hardly ever a simple matter of individual political persecution. Almost invariably, economic and environmental pressures play a major part. Refugee movements, like mass labour

Box 7.1 Afghanistan's long refugee emergency

Up to a third of Afghanistan's 18 million people fled the country following the Soviet military intervention in 1979. The overwhelming majority found refuge in the neighbouring countries of Pakistan (3.3 million in 1990) and Iran (3.1 million) (UNHCR, 2000: 119). For political, humanitarian, religious and cultural reasons, Pakistan and Iran were willing to provide refuge for extended periods. Pakistan received substantial military, economic and diplomatic support from the USA. Iran, on the other hand, received very little external assistance (UNHCR, 2000: 118). The different handling of the Vietnamese and Afghan cases show how refugee movements can become part of wider foreign policy considerations for major powers (Suhrke and Klink, 1987).

With the end of the Soviet intervention in 1989, about 1.5 million Afghan refugees returned home. However, the seizure of power by the fundamentalist Taliban, a four-year drought and the devastated condition of the country delayed the return of the rest. To help fund the costs of rebuilding their villages, increasing numbers of Afghans went to work in the Gulf states, while others sought asylum in Western countries (UNHCR, 1995: 182–3).

The events of 11 September 2001 made the world aware of the consequences of protracted situations of conflict. Afghanistan had become the centre of the global Al-Qaeda terrorist network. It was also the world's leading producer of heroin. The US-led invasion of Afghanistan was designed to destroy Al-Qaeda and the Taliban, establish a legitimate government and permit the return of the refugees. By July, more than 1.3 million Afghans had returned. This put severe strain on UNHCR finances (UNHCR, 2002), but Western countries – willing to spend billions on armed intervention – were not ready to top up relief funds. Meanwhile, the governments of Western countries began sending back Afghan asylum seekers, even though it was far from clear that conditions were safe in Afghanistan. The intensification of hostilities between the US-led forces and the Taliban from 2005 hindered further returns.

In 2013, the war dragged on, and, there was no sign of improvement in the humanitarian situation. The Western military coalition was planning to withdraw its troops by mid-2014, and members of vulnerable groups such as the Hazara ethnic minority, as well as many people involved in public services and education, were leaving for fear of a renewed Taliban take-over.

migration, are the result of the massive social transformations currently taking place in Asia (Van Hear, 1998). Long-standing ethnic and religious differences exacerbate conflicts and often motivate high levels of violence. Resolution of refugee-producing situations and the return home of refugees are hampered by scarcity of economic resources and lack of guarantees for human rights in weak and despotic states. Western countries have often become involved in struggles about state and nation formation in Asia, and responses to asylum seekers have been conditioned by such experiences.

Oceania

Oceania is the world-region with the highest proportion of migrants: 16.8 per cent of the population. The great majority of migrants are in Australia (4.7 million in 2010) and New Zealand (962,000) (IOM, 2010: 219–21). The largest permanent migration flow in Oceania today is that between New Zealand and Australia – over 30,000 persons a year. The complex patterns of migration affecting the many nations of the Pacific sub-regions of Melanesia, Polynesia and Micronesia like Papua New Guinea, Fiji, Tonga and Vanuatu will not be examined here (see IOM, 2010: 219–35). Instead, we focus on the two major immigration countries, Australia and New Zealand.

Australia

Since 1945, 7 million immigrants have come to Australia, of whom 700,000 were refugees or displaced persons (DIAC, 2010a). The population has trebled from just 7.6 million in 1947 to an estimated 22.8 million in 2012 (ABS, 2012). Following British conquest in the late eighteenth century, the indigenous population was dispossessed and marginalized, with many people dying as a result of massacres, poor living conditions and imported illnesses. However, there has been some recovery in numbers in the twentieth century: the 2011 Census showed an Aboriginal and Torres Strait Islander population of 550,000 – just 2.4 per cent of the total population. By contrast one Australian in four is an immigrant, and an additional fifth of the population has at least one immigrant parent. Yet immigration and asylum remain highly controversial.

Australia initiated a mass immigration programme after 1945, with the aim of adding the equivalent of 1 per cent of population each year (Collins, 1991). The policy, summed up in the popular slogan 'populate or perish', was one of permanent, family immigration. The aim was to bring immigrants mainly from Britain, but as this source dried up due to postwar recovery, Australia began recruiting refugees from the Baltic and Slavic countries, and then labour migrants from southern Europe. Non-Europeans were not admitted at all, as the White Australia Policy was still in force. From 1947 to 1973 immigration provided 50 per cent of labour force growth, but by the late 1960s, it was becoming hard to attract Southern European migrants. The response was further liberalization of family reunions and recruitment in Yugoslavia and Latin America. The White Australia Policy was abandoned in 1973 and significant Asian immigration began in the late 1970s with the arrival of Indo-Chinese refugees.

Australia has become one of the world's most diverse countries, with people from close to 200 origin areas. Nearly a quarter of the population are immigrants, while some 20 per cent have immigrant parents. From the mid-1970s to the early 1990s, there was a consensus between the major political forces on a non-discriminatory immigration policy and multicultural policies towards ethnic communities. The Australian Labor Party (ALP) government's 1989 *National Agenda for a Multicultural Australia* (OMA, 1989) emphasized the need to recognize cultural diversity as a basis for Australian social policy, citizenship and identity. However, anti-immigration and anti-minority sentiments began to grow. When John Howard became Prime Minister in 1996, leading a Coalition of the Liberal and National Parties, Australian immigration policy entered a new era, with strong emphasis on recruitment of skilled personnel, cuts in family reunion, draconian measures against asylum seekers and a shift away from multiculturalism (see Chapter 12).

Despite the anti-immigration rhetoric, by 2010–11 (figures are for financial years) the total number of permanent entrants to Australia had increased to 183,000 – the highest figure for many years and quite close to the old 1 per cent of population annual target. Permanent immigration has two components, the Migration Program and the Humanitarian Program. All permanent immigrants (including refugees) have the right to family reunion. The Humanitarian Program (refugees and other people in need of protection) has been fairly stable, ranging from around 11,000 to 16,000 per year. Within the Migration Program the various categories have shown rather different trends. The Family category has fluctuated between a low of 31,310 in 1997–8 and a high of over 79,500 in 1987–8, with recent levels around 55,000 a year. By contrast, the Skill category has grown steadily from just 10,100 in 1984–5 to a peak of 114,777 in 2008–9 – just before the effects of the global economic crisis began to bite (DIAC, 2012a; Phillips *et al.*, 2010).

The big change in Australia is the growth of temporary migration. The numbers of temporary work or business visa holders have grown to around 100,000 a year. Many temporary migrants work in the fast-growing mining sector, while others are to be found in Australia's manufacturing and service industries. The number of overseas students entering Australia has grown even faster, reaching a peak of 320,368 in 2008–9. In order to pay high university fees and living costs, many students work up to 20 hours a week, providing a ready labour source for retail and catering businesses. The main origin countries have been China, India and South Korea (DIAC, 2010c). The difference between temporary and permanent migration is blurred in practice, as both temporary work visa holders and students often change status to permanent residence after some years.

Australia has a voluntary resettlement programme for refugees selected in overseas camps, yet its response to asylum seekers has become increasingly hostile. Asylum seekers who arrive from countries like Iraq, Afghanistan and Sri Lanka by boat – usually via Indonesia – are detained for long periods in camps, and are labelled as 'queue-jumpers' and 'security threats' by politicians and the media. Although asylum seeker numbers in

Australia are relatively low, the recent growth is politically controversial because it is seen as undermining the tradition of strict government control of entries. In 2012, the government decided to send asylum seekers who arrived by boat to await processing in camps on the islands of Nauru and Papua New Guinea (Castles *et al.*, 2013).

Emigration has also increased steadily in recent years, rising from around 88,000 in 1981–2 to roughly 326,000 in 2008–9 (Productivity Commission, 2010: 36). It has become an important part of professional or personal experience to live and work abroad. Many Australians go to the UK, the USA and New Zealand, but numbers in newer business centres like Hong Kong, Singapore, Shanghai and Mumbai are also growing.

New Zealand

New Zealand encouraged 'kin immigration' from the UK, with between 9,000 and 16,000 arriving each year through the 1950s and 1960s. Some white foreigners were admitted too, mainly from the Netherlands or displaced persons from Eastern Europe. Entry of Pacific Islanders gradually increased, but many of these came from New Zealand territories and were not considered foreigners. The economic boom of the early 1970s led to government efforts to increase immigration, with a record influx of 70,000 persons in 1973–4 (McKinnon, 1996).

In recent years, there have been trends towards growth in migration, increasing diversity of origins and more temporary migration. Many settlers have come from Asia, especially China and India. Flows from the Pacific Islands have also been significant. The five main origin countries in 2009 were the UK, China, South Africa, Philippines and Fiji. Temporary migrants, including workers, students and working holidaymakers, numbered 161,800 in 2009 (OECD, 2011a: 306–7 and table B.1.1.). The foreign-born population had increased to one million by 2010 (23 per cent of New Zealand's total population), compared with 763,600 in 2004 (18.8 per cent of the total population) (OECD, 2012). The largest origin groups according to the 2006 Census were UK (245,100), China (78,100), Australia (62,700), Samoa (50,600) and India (43,300) (OECD, 2011a: table B.1.4).

Migration has had important consequences for culture, identity and politics. The country has gone from a white settler colony with an indigenous Maori minority to a much more complex multi-ethnic society in which about three-quarters are white people of European origin, while around a quarter are Maori, Asians, Pacific people and others. By 2026, the white European share is projected to fall to 70 per cent (Ministry of Social Development, 2010). Ethnic diversity has become an issue of concern for both government and non-governmental organizations, although the priority of official policy is still on its biculturalism based on the historical relationship between indigenous Maori and British settlers.

Conclusions: perspectives for Asian migration

In Australia and New Zealand, there is widespread recognition that migration has been a major factor shaping society over the last half-century. This is not the case elsewhere in the Asia–Pacific region. Most Asian governments still see migration primarily in economic terms – receiving countries emphasize the importance of temporary labour supplies, while sending countries look at the potential economic benefits of remittances and diaspora investments. But Asian migration does not only have economic impacts: it is becoming a major element of demographic, social and political change.

The early twenty-first century has been a period of growing diversity in Asian migration. Virtually all Asian countries experience simultaneous in- and outflows of varying types, and many have transit flows as well. Economic migrants can be found at all skill levels: the lower-skilled still migrate out of the region but increasingly also within it; many highly skilled people move to Northern countries, but increasing numbers move within Asia, while immigrants from other world regions are attracted to areas of economic growth. Asian women are in increasing demand in many occupations, while migration for the purpose of marriage is growing fast. Refugee and other forced migrant populations still remain large and vulnerable.

New transport and communication technologies have opened the way for increased temporary and circular migration. Often government migration categories do not correspond with social realities. People may visit a country as tourists before deciding to migrate. Those who move as permanent settlers may decide to return home, or may move back and forth between the country of origin and the destination. Temporary migrants may stay permanently, or move repeatedly in both directions, or go elsewhere in search of opportunities. New media and ways of communicating facilitate transnational consciousness, with many migrants having affiliations and a sense of belonging in more than one country.

Again it is important to link the regional experiences to the migration theories reviewed in Chapters 2 and 3. Neoclassical ideas on individual economic motives seem to fit well for highly skilled and student migration and possibly also for lower-skilled labour migration. But even here, family and community decision-making processes are often relevant, and these are better explained by the new economics of labour migration approach. In a broader perspective, it is clear that the rapid growth of Asian migration can only be understood in the context of the rapid social transformations taking place in the region, along with the uneven nature of these shifts.

Many areas have gone through turbulent processes of decolonization, violent conflict and nation-building. Some countries have moved in a short time from low-productivity agricultural economies with traditional social and cultural values, to modern industrial societies. Employment growth has often been linked to rapid demographic shifts, with East Asian countries now exhibiting fertility rates as low as Southern European countries. Others have changed much more slowly, and still have low average income levels, high fertility and high levels of unemployment or underemployment. Such transformations give rise both to strong demand for migrant labour in economic growth areas and availability of labour reserves in areas of slower economic growth. Improvements in transport and communications through globalization provide the means for migration but also for the growth of transnational communities.

At the same time, the experiences of several Asian countries seem to confirm migration transition theories. Some of the labour-surplus countries of a generation ago – like South Korea, Thailand and Malaysia – are now poles of attraction. Some former source countries of highly skilled migrants – notably Taiwan, but also South Korea and incipiently China – have successfully reversed the brain drain and are profiting from the skills of their returnees.

As we suggested in Chapter 3, migration can be a challenge to fundamental ideas on ethnicity, national identity and culture. Asian governments and public opinion often perceive immigration as a threat to their models of the nation-state. The weakness of migration control in some countries contrasts with the dominant Asian model of migration, based on the principles of strict control of foreign workers, prohibition of settlement and family reunion, and denial of worker rights. East Asian authorities emphasize the importance of maintaining ethnic homogeneity, while South-East Asian governments wish to safeguard existing ethnic balances. Yet the globalization of migration is bringing about rapid changes and it is far from clear that Asian governments will be able to prevent unforeseen shifts.

When Western European governments tried to reduce immigration and settlement of foreign populations in the 1970s, they found it difficult: their economies had become structurally dependent on foreign labour, employers wanted stable labour forces, immigrants were protected by strong legal systems, and the welfare state tended to include non-citizens. Such pressures are beginning to make themselves felt in Asia too. There are signs of increasing dependence on foreign workers for the '3D jobs' as labour force growth slows in industrializing countries and local workers reject menial tasks. In these circumstance employers seek to retain 'good workers', migrants prolong their stays, and family reunion or formation of new families in the receiving country takes place. This applies particularly when migrants have scarce skills – the privileged entry and residence rules for the highly skilled may well become a factor encouraging permanent settlement and greater cultural diversity.

The feminization of migration is likely to have important long-term effects on demographic patterns and cultural values. The increase of marriage migration has led to intense public debates on multiculturalism and the integration of permanent migrants in South Korea and Taiwan. Trends towards democracy and the rule of law also make it hard to ignore human rights. The growth of NGOs working for migrants' rights in Japan,

Malaysia and the Philippines indicates the growing strength of civil society. It therefore seems reasonable to predict that settlement and increased cultural diversity will affect many Asian labour-importing countries; yet Asian governments are just beginning to think about the need for plans to deal with long-term effects of migration.

Despite the rapid growth, movements are still quite small in comparison with Asia's vast population. Migrant workers make up a far smaller proportion of the labour force in countries like Japan and South Korea than in European countries (although the proportion is large in Singapore and Malaysia). However, the potential for growth is obvious. The GEC led only to temporary reductions in migration, and did not affect structural trends. The fundamental economic and demographic causes of Asian migration remained strong, and migratory flows quickly resumed. Fast-growing Asian economies seem certain to attract large numbers of migrant workers in the future. This may have far-reaching social and political consequences.

Guide to further reading

Extra resources at www.age-of-migration.com

The Age of Migration website includes additional text (7.1) on the situation of foreign maids in Singapore and provides brief case studies of the migration experiences of Japan (7.2), Malaysia (7.3) and the Philippines (7.4). Website text 12.5, minorities in the Republic of Korea, relates mainly to Chapter 12, but is also relevant here.

Literature on Asian migration has grown exponentially in the last few years, yet there still seems to be no single work that provides a comprehensive treatment. We advise readers to follow up the references given in the text for specific areas. Overview articles by Asis (2005), Hugo (2005) and Skeldon (2006b) are a useful beginning, and the IOM *World Migration Reports* (e.g. IOM, 2010) provide regional overviews. The website of the Colombo Process (http://www.colomboprocess.org) gives summaries on migration in Asian countries. The publications of the Scalabrini Migration Center (Quezon City, Philippines) http://www.smc.org.ph/ provide information and analysis.

Huang *et al.* (2012; 2005) are very useful on domestic work and more generally on female migration. On Japan, Komai (1995), Mori (1997) and Weiner and Hanami (1998) provide good studies in English. The chapters on Japan and Korea in Hollifield *et al.* (2013) present useful summaries. For most other countries, journal articles are still the best sources, while national statistical offices provide important data. The websites of organizations like Amnesty International and Human Rights Watch give critical perspectives.

Chapter 8

Migration in Africa and the Middle East

Africa and the Middle East are regions that have gone through profound political and economic transformations since the end of World War II. Virtually all their societies have experienced decolonization, the often tumultuous formation of new nation-states, conflicts related to access to oil reserves and other natural resources, alongside more general processes of social transformation and globalization. Some countries, particularly oil-rich countries in the Gulf region, have become extraordinarily wealthy while other countries, such as those of the Horn of Africa and the Great Lakes regions have been confronted with frequent violence, high poverty and sustained underdevelopment. Other countries, such as Turkey and those of North Africa occupy more intermediate positions, with modest levels of development and relatively less violence.

These divergent developments have also shaped divergent migration trends. While the Maghreb and Turkey have evolved into prime sources of labour migrants towards Europe, the oil-rich Gulf region has become a global magnet for migrants from poorer countries in the Middle East and North Africa (MENA), sub-Saharan Africa and an increasingly diverse array of Asian countries (see also Chapter 7). The frequent focus on such intercontinental migration flows obscures considerable migration *within* Africa and the Middle East. This particularly applies to sub-Saharan Africa, where the bulk of movement is intra-regional. While the images of crossings by African migrants in boats across the Mediterranean may give the misleading impression of massive migration, only a small fraction of international migration originating in Africa results in journeys to Europe, the Gulf, the US and beyond (Bakewell and de Haas, 2007). African countries such as Côte d'Ivoire, Nigeria, Ghana, Gabon, Libya, Kenya, and South Africa have been important migration destinations in their own right.

In the post-1945 period, Africa and the Middle East have also been major sources of asylum seekers, refugees and internal displacement as a consequence of political oppression and violent conflict. Upheavals leading to forced migration have included the Israeli–Palestinian conflict, the various wars involving Iraq and Afghanistan, the conflict around the Western Sahara since 1975, the Somali civil war, the wars between North and South Sudan, the West African civil wars in Sierra Leone and Liberia in the 1990s and early 2000s, the recurrent conflicts in the Great Lakes regions, and violent conflicts in Libya and Syria in the wake of the Arab

Spring. Contrary to some popular belief, most refugees stay in the region, and only a minority ends up in Europe, North America or other overseas destinations.

As a consequence of demographic shifts as well as social and political transformations, these patterns are currently changing. While still very modest compared to intercontinental migrations from Asia and Latin America, migration from sub-Saharan Africa to Europe, the Middle East, North America, China and other industrialized states is growing. This is linked to infrastructure improvements, globalization and, in some African countries, economic growth, which is enhancing connections with the wider world. Libya and, to a lesser extent, other Maghreb states, have emerged as destination and transit countries for sub-Saharan migrants. Since the 1980s, the Gulf states and Israel have come to increasingly rely on non-Arab labour from Asian and, more recently, sub-Saharan countries. This migration is gaining a (semi-) permanent character, and the settlement of Asian and sub-Saharan migrant groups are creating increasing diverse societies.

What has made many countries in Africa and the Middle East stand out is the dominance of authoritarian regimes and the slow pace of democratization, if any, although the 2011 Arab Spring may mark the onset of more rapid, and possibly violent, political transformations. The fall of Tunisian president Ben Ali in January 2011 marked the start of a series of pro-democratic uprisings throughout the Arab world. This has led to the fall of autocratic rulers in Egypt and Libya in 2011, but also to violent conflicts in countries such as Yemen, Syria, Bahrain, and indirectly also Mali. However, although the Libyan and Syrian conflicts have generated major refugee movements, the Arab Spring has not created mass population movements to Europe as some had predicted (see Box 1.2 and also de Haas and Sigona, 2012; Fargues and Fandrich, 2012). In fact, migration to Europe slowed down, which was mainly a response to the global economic crisis (GEC) and rising unemployment in destination countries (see also Chapter 5).

In this chapter we will discuss migration affecting Africa and the Middle East. Although North Africa and sub-Saharan Africa are often analysed separately, our analysis will emphasize that both regions are strongly linked through political and economic relationships, which have fostered mobility across the Sahara (de Haas, 2006d; McDougall and Scheele, 2012; Scheele, 2012). Throughout known history, there has been intensive population mobility between both sides of the Sahara through the trans-Saharan (caravan) trade, conquest, pilgrimage, and religious education (cf. Berriane, 2012). The Maghreb countries have deep historical ties with West African countries such as Mali and Senegal. The Sahara itself is a huge transition zone, and the diverse ethnic composition of Saharan oases — with their blend of sub-Saharan, Berber, Arab and Jewish influences – testifies to this long history of population mobility (Bakewell and de Haas, 2007: 96; Lightfoot and Miller, 1996: 78; McDougall and Scheele, 2012; Scheele, 2010). Today, ancient caravan routes are once again migration routes for Africans crossing the Sahara (cf. Brachet, 2012; de Haas, 2007b).

Historical and colonial roots of contemporary migrations

The Middle East and large parts of Africa have historically been regions of high non-migratory mobility. The existence of large arid and semi-arid areas encouraged the persistence of nomadic and semi-nomadic ways of life, while the presence of numerous holy places led to pilgrimages (Chiffoleau, 2003). A long history of large empires and ill-defined borders fostered the exchange of goods and knowledge (Laurens, 2005: 25–7), but has also led to displacement. Such migrations were often temporary or circular in nature. More permanent migrations were often driven by warfare, population growth and economic factors. One of the greatest migrations in human history was that of the Bantu people, who left the area now encompassing Nigeria and Cameroon and formed settlements throughout the entire southern half of the continent, bringing their languages and joining with indigenous groups along the way.

Beginning in the sixteenth century, over three centuries of the Atlantic slave trade resulted in upwards of 12 million forced migrants from the continent (Lovejoy, 1989), and the legacies of European colonialism would lay the groundwork for many of the migration patterns that followed. During the nineteenth and twentieth centuries, free mobility decreased due to colonization, the drawing of formal state borders, and increased state regulation. Nomadic populations became the primary victims as states implemented forced sedentarization policies in order to control and tax such groups. Likewise, states regulated the movement of pilgrims and traders. For example, Saudi Arabia limits the number of pilgrims travelling to Mecca and Medina by means of country of origin quotas (Chiffoleau, 2003).

Contemporary African and Middle-Eastern mobility has been shaped in many ways by colonial practices. The nineteenth- and early twentieth-century division of the African and Middle-Eastern 'cake' into politico-administrative entities often imposed arbitrary borders, sometimes dividing established nations. As a result, members of a single ethnic group could become citizens of two or more states and many new countries included members of several ethnic groups. Many individuals continued to regularly cross colonial boundaries. Today, many sub-Saharan African states have very porous borders. The colonial period brought European administrators, farmers and other settlers throughout Africa, as well as Syro-Lebanese merchants to West Africa (*cf.* Leichtman, 2005), and merchants and labourers from the Indian subcontinent to East and Southern Africa. In the post-independence period, these populations generally became privileged but vulnerable minorities, often with a key role in trade.

In Africa, colonialism was always concerned with control of mobility, in order to provide labour for European-owned plantations, industry, infrastructure works and mines (Bakewell, 2008; Cohen, 1987). Colonial labour recruitment was often based on temporary migration, since permanent concentrations were seen as a potential threat to order. Yet colonial administrators could not prevent permanent settlement, and colonialism in fact started processes of rapid urbanization that continue today. Patterns of colonization would also strongly influence postcolonial migrations to Europe, with most migrations oriented towards former colonial powers, such as Congolese emigrating to Belgium, Maghrebians and Senegalese to France or Nigerians, Ghanaians and South Africans to the UK.

Postcolonial migration within Africa

As Map 8.1 illustrates, the bulk of African migrants move within the continent. In fact, Africa has the lowest intercontinental migration rate of all world regions. The usual focus of policy and the media on refugee flows has created a false image of African migration being mainly driven by war, hunger and other forms of human misery. According to UNHCR data, refugees and 'people in refugee-like situations' represented 2.4 million or 14 per cent of international migrants in Africa (UNHCR, 2011b). Although this is a higher proportion than in other world regions, this means that still about 86 per cent of international migration within Africa is *not* primarily related to conflict. However, in situations of stress and conflict, it is often hard to differentiate between refugees escaping violence and migrants who move because their livelihoods are threatened (Akokpari, 2000: 3–4).

During the period of colonial liberation, millions of people fled brutal conflicts with colonial powers reluctant to relinquish control (Algeria, Kenya, Congo, etc.) or with white settler groups determined to cling to their privileges (e.g. Zimbabwe, South Africa). Yet, the defeat of old-style colonialism and the establishment of independent states often did not mean a return to peaceful conditions. During the Cold War, East and West fought proxy wars in Africa. Political and economic pressures, arms supplies, mercenaries and even direct military intervention were factors contributing to new conflicts or the continuation of old ones (Zolberg *et al.*, 1989). Struggles for domination in Angola, Mozambique and Ethiopia involved massive external involvement, with great human costs for local populations.

Over half of Africa's refugees have originated from the Horn of Africa and East Africa (Bakewell and de Haas, 2007: 100; Oucho, 2006: 132). The Horn of Africa has been an area of turbulence, with protracted and repeated armed struggles concerning Ethiopia, Eritrea and Somalia. Large numbers of Somalis have fled to Kenya, Yemen, Europe and North America, and remittances have become crucial to the survival of many Somalis (Horst, 2006; Lindley, 2009). The Great Lakes Region has also been particularly violent: long-drawn-out civil wars in Rwanda, Burundi, Uganda and DRC have led to millions of deaths and mass displacement. Sudan has lived through over 30 years of warfare and massive internal and

Map 8.1 *Contemporary migrations within and from Africa*

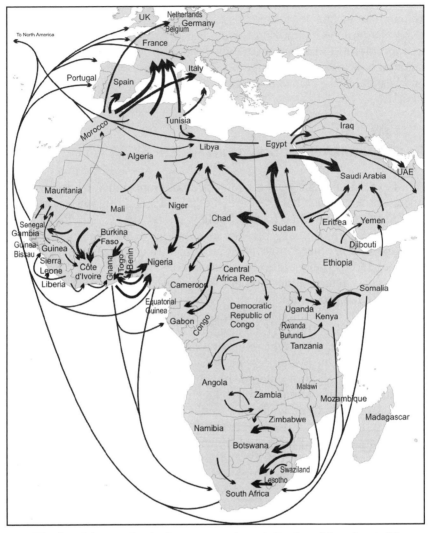

Note: The size of the arrowheads gives an approximate indication of the volume of flows. Exact figures are often unavailable.

international displacement. In 1975, a violent conflict broke out between Morocco and the Polisario independence movement over control of the Western Sahara. This led to the forced migration of thousands of Sahrawis to Algerian refugee camps. Since a United Nations-sponsored ceasefire agreement in 1991, the Western Sahara has been under Moroccan control, and the conflict has remained unresolved so far.

The great majority of African refugees stay within the region. Many African countries have received refugees, often in the middle of their own conflicts: Uganda has admitted Rwandans, Burundians and Sudanese; Eritreans and Ugandans have gone to Sudan; and Burundians, Rwandans, Congolese and Somalis to Tanzania. However, there have also been significant conflict-related long-distance movements of refugees and migrant workers, such as from the Horn of Africa (Somalia, Eritrea, and Ethiopia) to Yemen and growing numbers of Sudanese, Somalis and other Africans have been moving to Egypt, Syria, Jordan and Israel.

Despite the relatively high incidence of conflict-related migration, economic migration predominates in Africa. Important regional migration systems have evolved in recent decades, centring on areas of economic growth such as Libya in the North, Côte d'Ivoire, Ghana and Gabon in the West, Kenya and Mozambique in the East, and Angola, Botswana and South Africa in the South (cf. Bakewell and de Haas, 2007: 96).

Since the mid-twentieth century and after decolonization, the tendency towards urbanization continued, which led to increasing spontaneous migration to the cities. This would led to a fundamental reconfiguration of pre-modern migration patterns and the emergence of new migration systems centred around fast-growing urban clusters, often located in or close to urban areas, capital cities or mining regions. For instance, intra-regional mobility in West Africa has been dominated by a movement from landlocked countries of Sahel West Africa (Mali, Burkina Faso, Niger and Chad) to the relatively more prosperous plantations, mines and cities of coastal West Africa (predominantly Côte d'Ivoire, Liberia, Ghana, Nigeria, Senegal and The Gambia) (Arthur, 1991; Findley, 2004; Kress, 2006). There was also considerable transversal international migration *within* the coastal zone of mostly seasonal workers to the relatively wealthy economies of Côte d'Ivoire, Ghana (before the 1970s) and Nigeria (since the 1970s).

Such coast-bound migration patterns have often been reproduced inside African countries, with people moving from arid and underdeveloped inland zones to the more humid and prosperous agricultural and urbanized zones, generally located in coastal areas. Some inland cities such as Kano in Nigeria or the new, centrally located capitals of Yamoussoukro (Côte d'Ivoire) and Abuja (Nigeria) have also become migration destinations in their own right. Also mining areas such as the goldmines of Witwatersrand near Johannesburg in South Africa, the Copperbelt in Zambia, the southern Katanga province of the Democratic Republic of the Congo and the diamond mines of Sierra Leone have attracted settlers and migrants from distant places.

International migration in Africa has largely been spontaneous. Following patterns elsewhere in the world, in periods of rapid growth, governments have often welcomed labour migrants, while in times of economic crisis migrants have often been expelled in large numbers. One scholar has enumerated 23 mass expulsions of migrants conducted by 16 different African states between 1958 and 1996 (Adepoju, 2001). For instance, in the 1950s and 1960s many West African migrants moved to Ghana. After the 1966 coup in Ghana and the subsequent economic

Figure 8.1   *Foreign-born populations in selected sub-Saharan African countries*

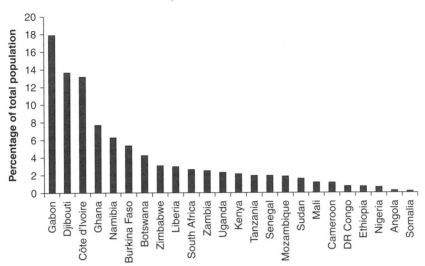

Source: World Development Indicators database, based on United Nations Population Division data, 2005 estimates.

decline, the immigrant community became a scapegoat. In 1969 the Ghanaian government enacted the Aliens Compliance Order, leading to a mass expulsion of some 200,000 migrants, mainly from Nigeria, Togo, Burkina Faso and Niger (Van Hear, 1998: 73–4). With Nigeria's new oil wealth after 1973, millions of Ghanaians and other West Africans sought work there. But corruption and misguided economic policies precipitated a crisis, and in 1983–5 an estimated 2 million low-skilled West Africans were deported from Nigeria, including over one million Ghanaians (Bakewell and de Haas, 2007: 104; Van Hear, 1998: 73–4) (see also Figure 8.1).

Intercontinental migration to Europe and the Gulf States

While most migration from sub-Saharan countries has remained within the continent, since the 1960s many countries in North Africa and the Middle East have witnessed increasing levels of intercontinental emigration to Europe and the Gulf regions. In 2005, it was estimated that the Mediterranean MENA countries (Algeria, Egypt, Israel, Jordan, Lebanon, Morocco, the Palestinian Territories, Syria, Tunisia and Turkey) counted at least 10 million first-generation emigrants (Fargues, 2005). This reflects increasing labour migration to Europe since the 1960s and migration to the Gulf region and Libya since the 1970s.

Initially, the main extra-regional destination was Europe, which now has about 6 million migrants of MENA origin (Fargues, 2005). Main movements since the 1960s have been from Turkey, Morocco and, to a lesser extent, Algeria and Tunisia to Germany, Belgium, Netherlands and France and, since the 1980s, to Italy and Spain. Also after the 1973 Oil Crisis and the subsequent recessions in Europe, migration continued, mainly as a consequence of family migration (see also Chapter 5). In recent years, migration from Turkey to Europe has declined rapidly. After having been the main source of non-EU migration in the EEC between 1960 and 1990, Turkey has entered a migration transition. As a consequence of relatively high political stability and rapid economic growth, Turkey has transformed from a net emigration into a net immigration country (Kirişçi, 2007). Since the mid-1990s, Morocco has taken over Turkey's position as Europe's prime source of non-EU migrant labour.

The 1973 Oil Crisis had a substantial long-term impact on international migration patterns because of the emergence of a new global migration magnet in the oil-rich Gulf region. The sudden rise in the price of oil generated financial resources to undertake major construction and infrastructure projects, requiring the hiring of thousands of foreign workers. The booming Gulf economies initially attracted migrants from Egypt, Sudan, Palestine, Syria, Jordan, and Yemen. These countries were located in the proximity of the Gulf region and had not become integrated in Euro-Mediterranean migration systems since the 1960s like the Maghreb states and Turkey, from which migration to the Gulf would remain much more limited. The Gulf economies also started to attract migrants from nearby sub-Saharan African countries such as Somalia, Eritrea and Ethiopia. In parallel, a sub-regional migration system evolved in North Africa around oil-rich Libya.

During the 1970s, the Gulf monarchies grew increasingly worried about the possible political repercussions of their growing Arab migrant populations. Palestinians, in particular, were viewed as subversive. They were involved in efforts to organize strikes in Saudi oil fields and in civil strife in Jordan and Lebanon. Yemenis were implicated in various anti-regime activities in Saudi Arabia (Halliday, 1985: 674). Non-Saudi Arabs were involved in the bloody 1979 attack on Mecca. One result was the increased recruitment of workers from South and South-East Asia, who were seen as less likely to get involved in politics and easier to control. In most Gulf countries, the use of the Kafala system (see Box 8.1) reinforces the vulnerability of migrants (Lavergne, 2003). The share of women among immigrants has also increased. This feminization of migration primarily reflects increasing inflows of Asian women working as care workers and domestic servants.

The politicization of migration came to a head during the First Gulf War (1990–1), when large numbers of Arab workers were sent home (see also Chapter 7). This contributed to an increasing share of Asian and, to a lesser extent, also sub-Saharan African workers in Gulf immigrant populations. Particularly in the smaller Gulf states, unprecedented levels of immigration have made migrants outnumber native inhabitants. For instance, the United Arab Emirates (UAE) have an estimated combined population of

Box 8.1 The system of sponsorship (Kafala) in the Gulf

The sponsorship system has been a central feature of immigration policy in Gulf countries. Originally, the sponsorship system was based on an agreement between the local *emir* (king) and foreign oil companies in which a *kafil* (sponsor) would find trustworthy men (usually Bedouins) to work on the oil sites. With the oil industry taking off and the national workforce insufficient to fulfil the needs for manpower, the *kafils* had to recruit men from abroad. With time, recruiting and 'sponsoring' foreign workers became the main activities of the *Kafala*. Today, in order to enter a Gulf country, each migrant must find a sponsor. This requirement applies to various forms of migration including construction workers, domestic servants, foreign tradesmen and businessmen. The *kafil* is the official intermediary between the foreigner and the administration, authorities and local society. The *Kafala* system structures the relationship between the state, national *kafils*, and foreigners. Granting *kafil* status to nationals permits the state to delegate some administrative work, to control the foreign population and to reward nationals for their services. But *kafils* often exploit migrants by denying them proper wages and conditions, and retaining their passports, or threatening to report them to the police. Employment contracts are often illegally sold on to other employers. However, Gulf states have begun to abandon the *Kafala* system in order to gain more control over foreign populations.

Source: Rycs, 2005.

over 3 million, of whom at least 70 per cent are migrants (see also Figure 8.2). Three-fifths of migrants are from South Asia while approximately one-quarter are from the MENA (Rycs, 2005, see also Chapter 7).

The trends towards the (partial) replacement of Arab workers by Asian workers, the feminization of labour migration, the vulnerability and exploitation of migrants and structural economic dependency upon immigrant labour are also relevant to labour migration to non-oil-producing states in North Africa and the Middle East, such as Lebanon, Jordan and Israel. In Jordan during the mid-1970s, approximately 40 per cent of the domestic workforce was employed abroad, primarily in the Gulf (Seccombe, 1986: 378). This outflow prompted a replacement migration of foreign workers into Jordan, including inflows of unskilled Egyptians and Syrians.

On the other side of the Jordan River, the Israeli labour market was opened up to workers from Gaza and the West Bank after the 1967 war, as part of a strategy to integrate the occupied territories into the Israeli economy (Aronson, 1990). Most of the workers had to commute daily to work in Israel and were required to leave each evening. Palestinians found jobs primarily in construction, agriculture, hotels, restaurants and domestic services (Semyonov and Lewin-Epstein, 1987). A wave of attacks by Palestinians on Jews in Israel during the first *Intifada* (the uprising of Palestinians in the West Bank and Gaza that began in 1987), and the First Gulf

Figure 8.2   *Foreign-born populations in the Middle East and North Africa*

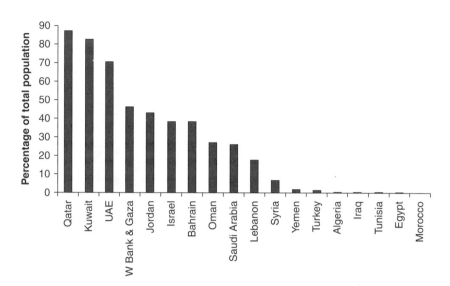

Source: World Development Indicators database, based on United Nations Population Division data, 2005 estimates.

War (1990–1) in response to Iraq's invasion of Kuwait, heightened tension. Israeli authorities introduced restrictive regulations aimed at weakening the *Intifada*. As a result, there was a sharp decline in Palestinian employment.

By 1991, immigration from the former Soviet Union prompted the Israeli government to replace Palestinian labour in construction and agriculture, yet its efforts to employ Soviet Jewish immigrants met with little success, since many of them wanted different jobs or found the pay and working conditions unsatisfactory (Bartram, 1999: 157–61). Increasingly, foreign workers from Romania, the Philippines and Thailand were recruited to replace Palestinian labour. Concurrently, the increasing closure of Gulf state labour markets to Palestinians worsened the economic plight of Palestinians. Reports of precarious conditions, absence of rights, mass expulsions, violence and abuse are regularly made in Gulf countries such as Abu Dhabi, Bahrain and Israel. The feminization of migration resulting from the growth of foreign domestic servant employment is also contributing to the vulnerable position of labour migrants (Baldwin-Edwards, 2005; Jureidini, 2003).

Forced migration in the Middle East

The Middle East has become a major region for all sorts of in- and out-migrations (see Map 8.2). While the oil-rich countries of the Middle East have attracted large numbers of labour migrants, political oppression and

182

Map 8.2 *Migrations within, from and to the Middle East*

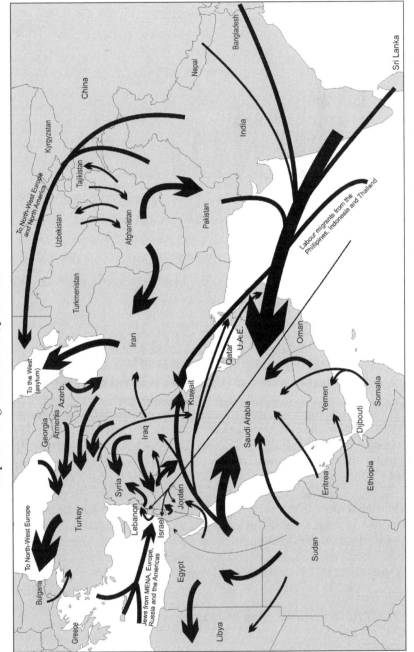

Note: The size of the arrowheads gives an approximate indication of the volume of flows. Exact figures are often unavailable.

warfare, often triggered and sustained by support or intervention from external powers, have accounted for large refugee movements within, to and from the region. After the Islamic revolution 1979, *Iran* generated one of highest rates of brain drain in the world while simultaneously being a major refugee haven for Afghans and Iraqis. In 2000, the number of Iranian emigrants was estimated at 1 million. The majority of them live in the USA, followed by Germany, the United Arab Emirates, Canada, Sweden, the UK, Israel and various West European countries (Hakimzadeh, 2006). Since the 1979 revolution, Iran has also become host to one of the largest long-term refugee populations in the world. At its peak in 1991, the refugee population exceeded over 4 million, among whom were 3 million Afghan refugees who fled the Soviet invasion of Afghanistan in 1979, and 1.2 million Iraqis (Hakimzadeh, 2006). Despite significant return, UNHCR estimated that Iran still hosted 1.1 million refugees in 2012.

Between 1990 and 2002, some 1.5 million Iraqis left their country due to the First Gulf War and Saddam Hussein's repressive regime. In the following years, about 500,000 Iraqis left Iraq through Turkey and Jordan, and tens of thousands left through Iran and Syria. The US-led invasion of Iraq in 2003 and its aftermath have triggered a second wave of Iraqi displacement. The UNHCR reports that in 2012 there were 3 million displaced Iraqis around the world, including 1.3 million displaced within Iraq and 1.5 million abroad, primarily in neighbouring countries (UNHCR, 2012a).

In the Middle East, current refugee issues remains centred on the Palestinians. According to the United Nations Relief and Works Agency for Palestine (UNRWA), Palestinian refugees numbered 4.8 million at the end of 2011 (UNHCR, 2012d: 1). They are scattered throughout the region and the world. Negotiations concerning refugees, repatriation, compensation, reparations and access to the territory have remained largely unresolved. With the Palestinian population of the West Bank and Gaza in dire economic straits, prospects appear bleak for the mass repatriation of Palestinian refugees from Lebanon and Syria. Since the beginning of the second *Intifada* in 2000, roughly 100,000 Palestinians have fled from the West Bank and Gaza Strip. Additionally, most Palestinian refugees living in Iraq had to flee in 2006 after many refugees were killed (Fargues, 2007), while at the time of writing (early 2013) many Palestinians are fleeing from Syria.

Turkey and Egypt have evolved into a central crossroads for refugee flows. Egypt has become host to many Palestinian and Sudanese refugees (Zohry and Harrell-Bond, 2003). Turkey received substantial flows of Balkan (Danış and Perouse, 2005: 97; Içduygu, 2000: 362–3), Iraqi, Iranian and Central Asian populations, while Turkey is also a country of origin for the many Kurdish refugees who have fled to Greece, Germany, Sweden and other countries to escape ethnic conflicts. From 2012, the violent conflict between opposition and government forces in Syria led to the mass flight of citizens, mainly towards Turkey, Jordan and Lebanon (see Box 1.2).

Changing intra-African migrations after 1989

Since 1989, a number of political processes, most notably the end of the Cold War and the 1990–1 Gulf War, coincided with significant changes in migration patterns in Africa and the Middle East. In the above sections, we have already seen that labour migration to the Gulf and other countries in the Middle East has become increasingly Asian. In sub-Saharan Africa, the intensity of conflicts in Africa decreased somewhat and there has been a certain trend towards more democratic modes of governance. We have also seen the rise of new intra-African migration poles such as South Africa and Libya.

Declining levels of conflict led to a decrease in refugee migration in some parts of Africa. From 1994, the end of the apartheid regime in South Africa removed a major cause of conflict. In Mozambique, South Africa had funded and armed the RENAMO rebel movement, and by the early 1990s there were an estimated 5.7 million uprooted Mozambicans, including 1.7 million refugees and 4 million internally displaced persons. By 1996, most had returned home (USCR, 2001). The twenty-first century has also seen the end of brutal conflicts in Angola, Liberia, Sierra Leone, and the Great Lakes Region. However, in some regions new conflicts have broken out, while other conflicts, such as in Somalia, persisted. From 2003, violence in the Western Sudanese province of Darfur, where an estimated 400,000 Sudanese have died, led to massive displacement. By 2012, 500,000 Sudanese refugees lived in other countries, while 2.4 million were internally displaced (UNHCR, 2012b). In Zimbabwe, hundreds of thousands of people have fled deteriorating economic conditions and political repression since 2000, with the majority seeking work and refuge in South Africa (Crush, 2008).

As a partial consequence of the improving security situation, the number of refugees recorded by UNHCR has declined from 6.8 million in 1995 (UNHCR, 1995) to 2.4 million in 2010 (UNHCR, 2011b). The peace agreement between Northern and Southern Sudan in 2005, which ended 22 years of civil war, led to independence of South Sudan in July 2011. An estimated 700,000 Southern Sudanese lived in Sudan, many of whom returned to South Sudan in 2011 and 2012 (UNHCR, 2012b).

Where peace agreements have been successfully implemented, large-scale repatriations of refugees and resettlements of internally displaced persons (IDPs) have occurred. However, most return occurs spontaneously, outside official repatriation schemes. Many of those remaining are in what UNHCR calls 'protracted refugee situations' (UNHCR, 2004) – that is, they have been living in camps or elsewhere for five years or more, and have little hope of returning home (see Chapter 10). Other refugees voluntarily opt not to return or have successfully integrated in receiving societies. For instance, in 2010 the Tanzanian government decided to naturalize more than 162,000 Burundian refugees who had been living in the country since 1972 (UNHCR, 2012c). Also in post-conflict situations, the line between economic and forced migration can be blurred. Based on case studies of Angolans in Zambia, Bakewell (2000) observed that those who are seen as repatriating refugees by the government and UN bodies actually see themselves as villagers moving in search of better livelihoods.

Post-apartheid *South Africa* is the economic powerhouse of sub-Saharan Africa, and draws in migrants from all over the continent, although primarily from Southern Africa. The roots of migration go back to the mine labour system developed between 1890 and 1920 to provide workers for the gold and diamond mines (Cohen, 1987). Workers were recruited during the apartheid period from Mozambique, Botswana, Lesotho, Swaziland and Malawi. Since the end of apartheid in 1994, South Africa has attracted migrants from an increasingly diverse array of African countries. In the post-apartheid era, Africans from as far away as Ghana, Nigeria, Kenya and DR Congo have migrated to South Africa. Many brought with them qualifications and experience in medicine, education, administration and business. Others joined the informal economy as hawkers, street food-sellers or petty traders.

As part of its transition from apartheid, South Africa adopted a new constitution which gives strong guarantees of migrant rights. However, the government has often failed to provide migrants with access to their immigration status, healthcare and education. Corruption and abuse has further complicated the enforcement of immigration laws (Vigneswaran, 2012). Xenophobia has become a major problem (cf. Landau and Freemantle, 2009). The government introduced heavy penalties for unauthorized immigration and, since 1994, 1.7 million undocumented migrants have been deported to neighbouring states like Mozambique, Zimbabwe, and Lesotho (Crush, 2008). While this has failed to significantly curb migration, it has made migrants more vulnerable to abuse and racist violence.

West African labour migration patterns changed due to economic decline in the 1980s and civil wars in Sierra Leone (1991–2001), Liberia (1989–96 and 1999–2003), Guinea (1999–2000) and Côte d'Ivoire (since 2002) (Bakewell and de Haas, 2007). Large-scale movements of refugees and internally displaced people (IDPs) took place, and labour migration patterns were partly disrupted. In Côte d'Ivoire, West Africa's most important migration destination until the 2000s, instability and the launch of an anti-foreigner campaign resulted in over 365,000 persons returning from Côte d'Ivoire to Burkina Faso in 2006 and 2007 (Kress, 2006). However, many migrants have stayed in Côte d'Ivoire, either because they had integrated into local society or had no real options for return. These crises partly contributed to increasing West African migration to Southern Africa, North Africa and, to some extent, Europe. Although most migration remains within the region, increasing numbers of West Africans, both highly skilled and less-skilled, now seek work elsewhere. Many are attracted by the new migration poles in the north (Libya) and south (South Africa, Botswana) of the continent.

Growing interconnectivity between African countries also involved more migration across the Sahara to North Africa. From the early 1990s, the Libyan leader Gaddafi positioned himself as an African leader and actively encouraged entry of African workers. Consequently, Libya became a major destination for sub-Saharan migrants (Boubakri, 2004; Hamood, 2006; HRW, 2006). In the early 1990s, most migrants came from Libya's neighbours Sudan, Chad and Niger, which then developed into transit countries for migrants from further afield (Bredeloup and Pliez, 2005). Since 2000, sub-Saharan Africans in Libya increasingly suffered from xenophobia, violent anti-immigrant riots and expulsions. This prompted some African workers to move on to other North African states and Europe in search of better opportunities although Libya continued to be an important destination in itself (Bakewell and de Haas, 2007: 98–9; Hamood, 2006). Violent conflict in 2011 between Gaddafi militia and rebel groups caused the mass return of migrant workers to sub-Saharan African countries such as Niger, Mali, and Chad (de Haas and Sigona, 2012, see also Box 1.2). The return of many Tuareg from Libya to Mali in 2011 seems to have emboldened the Tuareg rebellion in the North of Mali.

Not only Libya but, to a lesser extent, other North African countries have evolved into destinations for West-African migrants. An increasing number of workers and students consider North Africa as a destination in its own right. Some go to North Africa with the intention to move on to Europe. Those failing or not venturing to enter Europe often prefer to stay in North Africa as a second-best option rather than to return to their often more unstable, unsafe, and substantially poorer home countries.

Migration and settlement along the migration routes have thus helped revitalize ancient trans-Saharan (caravan) trade routes and desert oases in Mali, Niger, Chad, Libya, Algeria, and Mauritania (Bensaad, 2003; Boubakri, 2004; Bredeloup and Pliez, 2005; McDougall and Scheele, 2012; Spiga, 2005). Desert towns and several oases now house significant resident sub-Saharan populations. Similarly, major North African cities, such as Rabat, Oran, Algiers, Tunis, Tripoli, Benghazi, and Cairo, now host sizeable communities of sub-Saharan migrants as a result of their voluntary and less voluntary settlement (Boubakri, 2004: 4; Bredeloup and Pliez, 2005: 11–12; Collyer and de Haas, 2012). The presence of growing immigrant communities confronts North African societies with an entirely new set of social and legal issues typical for immigration countries, issues that do not resonate with their self-image as emigration countries (de Haas, 2007b).

Research on international migration in the Horn of Africa, East Africa and the Great Lakes Region has focused on conflict-related refugee migration. This obscures significant labour migration within and towards these regions. For instance, the southern Katanga province of the Democratic Republic of the Congo has attracted West African migrants. In East Africa, Djibouti, Uganda, Kenya and Sudan have significant immigrant populations. Over recent decades, Kenya has evolved into an important regional migration destination as well as an origin and transit country for migrants aspiring to move to South Africa. Djibouti is another regional migration destination as well as a port for irregular migration to Yemen and the Gulf (Bakewell and Jónsson, 2011; Horwood, 2009; IMI and RMMS, 2012; Okoth, 2003).

New African migrations to Europe, the Middle East and China

While most migration remains within the continent, globalization has created the conditions for growing movements from sub-Saharan Africa to Europe, the Middle East and beyond. The increased role of global capital and reduced state intervention in sub-Saharan Africa has led to greater inequality and a real income decline for many – both in absolute terms for many and relative to the rest of the world in general (Akokpari, 2000), while unemployment soared, particularly among the higher skilled. The structural adjustment polices of the IMF and the World Bank have not brought the expected stimulus to industry and trade, but have often reduced middle-class employment in the health, education and administrative sectors (Adepoju, 2006). At the same time, improved infrastructure, cheaper air transport, the rapid diffusion of telecommunication techniques such as mobile phones (cf. de Bruijn *et al.*, 2009; Schaub, 2012), and improved education are likely to have increased awareness of opportunities outside the continent and, hence, people's migration aspirations.

Much migration, particularly from sub-Saharan Africa to Europe and North America, used to be an elite affair. For instance, in the USA, Africans possess the highest average level of education of any immigrant group (JBHE, 2000). This is because international migration entails significant costs, which are generally out-of-reach for poorer groups (see Chapter 2). However, since 1990, African emigration has seen increased participation of people from less privileged backgrounds. Increasing numbers of women are migrating independently, for instance, as domestic workers from Ethiopia to the Gulf and Yemen (De Regt, 2010; Fernandez, 2010). While regular and irregular migration to Europe used to be a predominantly Maghrebi affair, the share of sub-Saharan Africans has been steadily increasing since the 1990s (de Haas, 2007b). This is linked to increasing trans-Saharan migration of sub-Saharans looking for work in Libya and elsewhere in North Africa, or wishing to move on to Europe from there (see previous section).

The areas receiving the most international attention include those closest to the African Mediterranean coast – namely Spain (including the Canary Islands), Italy, and Malta. Tighter control measures and naval patrols by EU countries have forced irregular migrants to take longer sea routes, increasing the risks and the death rate (Carling, 2007). An estimated 31,000 irregular migrants arrived in the Canary Islands in

2006, a 600 per cent increase from 2005. In an effort to stop boats before they start, Frontex, the EU's border control agency, has been patrolling the shores of Senegal and Mauritania, but this has mainly led to a diversion of routes to other crossing points. African nationals who successfully reach Europe often face unemployment, racism, and homelessness, but these are risks they are willing to take to escape the lack of opportunity at home.

In the media, African migration to Europe is commonly seen as a massive exodus of desperate people fleeing poverty and warfare at home. However, such apocalyptic views hugely exaggerate the limited magnitude of this migration and are based on flawed assumptions about its causes. First, irregular migration from Africa to Europe has probably remained limited to several tens of thousands per year, which is a small fraction of total EU immigration. Second, it is a myth that irregular migration is the main source of African migration to Europe. The vast majority of African migrants in Europe possess valid residency permits, and most irregular migrants have entered Europe legally and subsequently overstayed their visas (de Haas, 2007b; see also Chapter 5). Third, migration to Europe requires significant resources, which explains why most migrants are not among the poorest and most destitute. Finally, dominant discourses on 'combating irregular migration' ignore that this migration has been primarily fuelled by a structural demand for cheap migrant labour in informal sectors.

African migrants are also increasingly attracted to fast-growing economies beyond the traditional destinations in Europe, where economic stagnation, restrictive immigration policies and racism may deter migrants. Some Africans have gone as far afield as Russia, Turkey, Japan, India and China, and even Brazil and Argentina (Andres Henao, 2009) in search of work, education and business opportunities. Migration from Africa to China has been growing fast. China's emergence as a global economic superpower and the relative ease of getting temporary visas has also made it a desired destination for African migrants (Ghosh, 2010). Although numbers are still relatively small, they are growing and this may possibly mark a future shift in *global* migration patterns, away from traditional destinations in Europe and North America, and towards the fast-growing economies of Asia.

Initially most African migrants to China were students, but since 2000, growing numbers of West African (particularly Nigerian and Ghanaian) traders have been reported in China (*cf.* Bakewell and Jónsson, 2011). Although most came with no intention to stay, an increasing number are settling and significant African immigrant communities are appearing. The increase of African immigration accelerated after China's accession to membership of the World Trade Organization in 2001 and about 200,000 Africans were believed to be living in China in the late 2000s. Most Africans are concentrated in Guangdong, a prosperous province in southern China. The majority come from Nigeria, although other origin countries include Senegal, Democratic Republic of Congo, The Gambia, Somalia, South Africa, Cameroon, Niger, and Liberia. According to official estimates, 77 per cent of undocumented foreigners in the Guangdong province in 2009 were Africans (Ghosh, 2010).

As part of the growing Chinese influence in Africa, the number of Chinese migrants in African societies has also been increasing. While in colonial times Africa had seen significant settlement of Europeans and other groups such as merchants and workers from the Indian subcontinent and Syro-Lebanese merchants (see above), Africa has recently emerged as an important destination for Chinese and, to a certain extent, also European migrants. Several fast-growing African countries attract migrants from crisis-hit European countries (see Chapter 5) while North African countries such as Morocco and Tunisia have seen increasing settlement of Europeans retirees, investors and the middle-class seeking more relaxed and exotic lifestyles (cf. Berriane *et al.*, 2010).

However, the major recent trend has been rising Chinese migration to Africa, which is still relatively small, but growing fast. This migration may be seen as part of China's bid to secure raw materials and export markets, but migrants also create their own economic opportunities (BBC News, 2007). Most are temporary migrants who come to Africa as employees of Chinese state-owned enterprises and Chinese companies and are expected to return after the completion of two- or three-year contracts (Jung Park, 2009). However, increasing numbers of independent Chinese migrants come to start their own businesses across the continent (Jung Park, 2009).

Tens of thousands of Chinese migrants are settling in rural and urban areas in Africa, and are involved in agriculture, construction and trade. For many poor Chinese farmers, Africa presents an inviting opportunity and Chinese authorities encourage them to migrate by giving support to investment, project development and the sale of products (BBC News, 2007). Total estimates range from 580,000 to over 800,000 Chinese on the African continent in the late 2000s. By far the largest number of Chinese (200,000–400,000) live in South Africa, followed by Nigeria. Sudan, Angola, Algeria, and Mauritius also host significant Chinese populations, and their numbers are growing in many other countries (Jung Park, 2009).

The political salience of migration

For centuries, the various empires of the Middle East and North Africa used migration and population displacement as strategic tools to stabilize and control newly conquered lands. For instance, as the Ottoman Empire expanded, the government ordered Muslim subjects to settle in recently acquired lands, a process known as '*surgun*' (Tekeli, 1994: 204–6). During the last century of the Ottoman Empire from the 1820s to the 1920s, approximately 5 million people sought refuge in the Empire while several million people fled from it (McCarthy, 1995). With the contraction of the Ottoman Empire and the creation of new nation-states in its wake, policies of national preference developed. The concurrent expulsion of 'non-nationals' and welcoming of 'nationals' reflected a national approach to migration which resulted in population transfers such as the 1923–4 population exchange between Greece and Turkey that resettled hundreds of thousands of displaced people (Mutluer, 2003: 88–94).

The tendency to view migration along national lines became particularly institutionalized in the immigration policies of states. The creation of the Turkish Republic out of the ashes of the Ottoman Empire in the early 1920s already brought in the use of migration as a means of building national identity: ethnic groups accepted as part of the multi-ethnic Ottoman Empire, like the Greeks and the Armenians, were expelled or persecuted, while people of Turkish ethnicity and Sunni Muslim religion were welcomed as settlers (Kirişçi, 2007). In 1934, Turkey promulgated the Law of Resettlement, which authorized ethnic Turks from areas formerly comprising the Ottoman Empire to emigrate to and settle in the Turkish Republic (Tekeli, 1994: 217). This policy continues to the present: as recently as the 1980s, 310,000 ethnic Turks from Bulgaria fled to Turkey to avoid persecution, though many of them later returned to Bulgaria.

Turkey is certainly not the only country in the region to apply national-ethnic criteria to its immigration policy. Israel's Law of Return (1950) encourages the 'return' of Jewish populations to Israel. Overall, Israel's population grew from 800,000 in 1947 to 7.4 million in 2010, with immigration accounting for a large share of population growth. During the 1990s, Israel received approximately 1 million new immigrants from the former Soviet Union. This wave of immigration by the 'Russians,' as they are commonly called, has had important demographic and political effects. Also many Ethiopians of Jewish faith have migrated to Israel, the most notable flows being in 1984–5 and 1991 when the Israeli government encouraged and supported such migration (IMI and RMMS, 2012; Kaplan and Salamon, 2004).

In 2002, the Israeli government 'declared war' on the illegal employment of foreigners, but measures like employer sanctions and deportation appeared to have little deterrent effect. The sharp contrast between the governmental generosity afforded to Jewish immigrants and the lot of foreign workers in Israel prompted soul-searching and calls for a phase-out of foreign worker recruitment (Kop and Litan, 2002: 108). Faced with the day-to-day reality of coping with issues like the education of the children of undocumented migrants, some municipal governments, such as Tel Aviv, took steps to foster integration of the growing non-Jewish, non-Arab immigrant populations (Bartram, 2005).

Like Turkey and Israel, many Arab states in the Middle East and North Africa have adopted national preference policies. In general, Arab countries have exclusively granted the right to settle and to gain citizenship to persons with historic or ethnic ties to the country. The large and recurrent influxes of refugees, especially Palestinians but also Kurds, Iraqis and Syrians, as well as the semi-permanent settlement of Arab, Asian and African immigrants have challenged the immigration and naturalization policies of Arab countries, and there are some signs of change.

In Africa, numerous international organizations have been created for the purpose of removing barriers to trade and the free movement of goods, capital, and people. The Arab Maghreb Union (AMU), the Economic Community of West African States (ECOWAS), the South African Development Community (SADC), the East African Community (EAC) and the Common Market for East and Southern Africa (COMESA) have all introduced rules for free movement of nationals between their member states. Generally, these agreements have been poorly implemented or contradicted by the restrictive policies and practices of member states (Adepoju, 2001; Ricca, 1990).

Despite the existence of zones in which there is nominally freedom of movement, these rights are not always protected, and particularly in times of economic crisis, migrants are often scapegoated and mass deportations have regularly occurred. In the 1970s, Ugandan residents of Indian origin were expelled by the Idi Amin regime, eventually finding refuge in the UK. In Sierra Leone, people of Lebanese descent are still not allowed to vote because they are not African by bloodline (USDS, 2006). South Africa still restricts migration from other SADC states. ECOWAS did not prevent mass deportations when governments deemed it expedient (Akokpari, 2000: 77). Corruption often poses an important challenge for implementation. For instance, in the ECOWAS zone, migrants are vulnerable to harassment, extortion and bribery by border guards and other state officials (Brachet, 2012; de Haas, 2006b), and they therefore engage smugglers to protect them from such abuse.

Migration has also affected international relations. Migrants have been used by destination or origin country governments to further political agendas, leading to shifts in regional migration patterns. Libya provides an extreme example. For instance, in the 1970s and 1980s, Libya admitted large numbers of Egyptians, Tunisians and Palestinians, but then expelled thousands of Egyptians when diplomatic relations soured as a result of Egyptian President Anwar al-Sadat's reorientation of foreign policy towards the West (Farrag, 1999: 74). Nevertheless, Egyptians soon returned and have continued to form the dominant immigrant population in Libya.

There has been an increase of migration through Middle-Eastern and North and West African countries towards Europe, such as from sub-Saharan Africa through Mauritania, Morocco, Algeria and Libya (cf. de Haas, 2008a), and from Central Asia through Turkey (cf. İçduygu and Yükseker, 2012), or from the Horn of Africa through Yemen towards the Gulf region. Such 'transit migration' is a source of considerable tension. European states pressure countries in North Africa and the Middle East to control their borders and to curb irregular migration, but these countries are often reluctant to play the role of Europe's border guard.

In Southern European countries such as Spain, Italy and Malta, growing public and political concern about irregular migration from Africa has led to an increase in land and maritime border controlling by EU countries since the late 1990s. In an effort to stop boats reaching the Canary Islands from West Africa, Frontex, the EU's border control agency, has even started patrolling the shores of Senegal and Mauritania. European countries increased pressure on North and West African countries to collaborate in curbing irregular migration. In return, Spain has provided African countries with several million euros in aid and authorized some recruitment of skilled and unskilled African labourers. Italy has intensively assisted Libya in border patrol, and the detention and deportation of irregular migrants including asylum seekers (Hamood, 2006; Paoletti, 2010).

However, such controls have failed to curb migration because the demand for migrant labour in agriculture, construction and service sectors in Europe persisted. It seems virtually impossible to control Saharan and Mediterranean borders due to their huge length, corruption and the facilitating role of migration networks and transportation workers (Brachet, 2012; Mechlinski, 2010). The main effect of increased border patrolling has therefore been the diversion of overland and maritime migration routes, in which migrants are compelled to take longer and more dangerous itineraries (de Haas, 2008a).

Despite lip service being paid to 'combating illegal migration', neither European nor African states seem to have much genuine interest in curbing migration. What remains largely unspoken behind the belligerent rhetoric is that the economies of receiving and sending countries have become structurally dependent on immigrant labour and money remittances, respectively. In receiving countries, there has been a growing discrepancy between restrictive migration policies and the demand for migrant labour in Europe's segmented and informal labour markets (de Haas, 2008a) (see Chapter 11). For African governments, emigration has been a political-economic safety valve, while money sent back by migrants (remittances) have increased awareness about the potential contribution of migration to poverty alleviation and development (see Chapter 3). Many African states therefore seem to adopt a strategy of formally adhering to Europe's 'fight against illegal immigration', while using the migration issue as a bargaining chip in negotiating aid, economic relations and immigrant quota.

The perception that transit migration through North African and Middle-Eastern countries has grown in recent years, may in fact reflect the increasing political salience of this issue rather than an increase in migration as such (Collyer *et al.*, 2012; Düvell, 2006). In a powerful critique, Düvell (2012) argues how the concept of transit migration was constructed by international organizations such as IOM and Frontex to problematize the phenomenon and justify huge spending and efforts to 'control' it. Although precise figures are lacking, the spectacular numbers reported in the press tend to be politically motivated exaggerations. For instance, over the 2000s the former Libyan leader Gaddafi and Italian politicians have repeatedly suggested that the 1–1.5 million sub-Saharan migrant workers in Libya would be on their way to Europe if they could. In reality, the majority of them came to Libya to work, and the actual number of migrants 'transiting' to Europe is rather small (de Haas, 2008a).

Although high-skilled emigration is still raising concerns about the brain drain, particularly in the healthcare sector (see Chapter 3), most African and poorer Middle-Eastern governments have abandoned the largely unsuccessful attempts of the past to stop emigration and have instead developed policies to maintain ties with emigrant population and to encourage remittances, investments and the circulation or return of migrants. This is part of a wider global trend in which migrant-sending states increasingly try to engage diasporas for development (see Chapter 3 and Gamlen, 2008).

With the exception of the Gulf countries, public policies to regulate immigration have been less developed in the Middle East and Africa. Many countries lack refugee policies, and not all are party to the 1951 Geneva Refugee Convention. There are few domestic laws concerning the right of asylum, and this often remains unclear and discretionary. Particularly in the Middle East and North Africa, the relationship between the UNHCR and local authorities often remains tense (Zaiotti, 2005).

An important future issue is likely to be the integration of migrants into destination countries. As already pointed out, many Middle-Eastern and African countries have a very strict, often national or ethnic understanding of citizenship. The trend of immigrants remaining for longer periods and emerging patterns of semi-permanent settlement renders discussion of increased societal diversity and multiculturalism urgent (Fargues, 2006). Greater protection and the granting of basic rights to migrants have entered the national discourse of countries even if such reforms have yet to be achieved. Granting of citizenship to foreigners is rejected by most governments, but may become a significant issue, especially in Gulf oil states, where migrants outnumber nationals and have become an intrinsic component of society, culture and economy.

Conclusions

This chapter has dealt with vast and diverse regions that are undergoing rapid change. This makes generalization difficult. Yet for all the differences, migration trends in Africa and the Middle East do reflect the general trends in global migration mentioned in Chapter 1. Many countries in Africa and the Middle East show trends towards globalization of migration – that is, more countries are affected more profoundly by significant flows of migrants, to and from an increasing variety of destinations and origins. Growing sub-Saharan migration to North Africa and the Middle East and the recent proliferation of migration to and from China are the most salient examples of this trend. African countries have been increasingly incorporated in international and global migration systems. Since the 1970s, migration has partly shifted away from postcolonial patterns, with the rise of the Gulf countries and Libya as new destinations for migrants from poorer MENA countries and, increasingly, from Asian and sub-Saharan countries. While sub-Saharan migration remains overwhelmingly intra-regional, since the 1990s, migration from Africa to Europe, North America, Asia and Latin America has been growing.

While the oil-rich Gulf countries and Libya host large immigrant populations, other countries in the Middle East and Africa cannot be seen simply as origin regions, and several countries are going through migration transitions (see Chapter 2). While countries such as Nigeria, Côte d'Ivoire, and South Africa have historically attracted large numbers of migrants, several new migration poles such as Angola, Mozambique and Ghana have emerged more recently. North African countries too have witnessed increasing transit and settlement migration. In the Middle East, Turkey has gone through a full migration transition, attracting migrants from an increasingly diverse array of European, Asian and African countries.

The analysis of African migration trends also highlights the need to go beyond stereotypes of African migration being mainly driven by extreme poverty and violent conflict. Most migration is economically motivated and particularly those moving out of the continent may perhaps be poor in Western eyes but can be relatively well-off by origin country standards. This also seems to confirm the theoretical idea that increasing education, better access to media as well as modest increases in income and better infrastructure has the tendency to increase not only people's aspirations but also capabilities to move (see Chapter 3).

The analysis of migration in Africa and the Middle East also questions the usefulness of official migration categories, which often do not correspond to the human realities. A pilgrimage to Mecca can also be the opportunity to foster contact with trading partners or to overstay and become a labour migrant; Palestinian migrants in the Gulf can be both refugees and labour migrants; Angolan refugees in Zambia may see themselves as villagers moving in search of better livelihoods (cf. Bakewell, 2000) and many African migrant workers in Libya became refugees when violent conflict broke out in 2011. Although it is common to distinguish 'receiving states' from 'sending states', such distinctions are often difficult to maintain in practice, as many 'sending states' receive significant numbers of immigrants or transit migrants (Collyer and de Haas, 2012; Fargues, 2007). This questions simple divisions of Africa and, more generally, the world into emigration and immigration countries. Most countries are both.

The analysis in this chapter has also shown the usefulness of dual or segmented labour market theory (see Chapter 2) for understanding the continuation of migration despite the persistence of poverty and unemployment in many African and Middle-Eastern destination countries. As elsewhere in the world, migrant workers tend to concentrate in particular sectors, where natives increasingly refuse to work, or where employers prefer immigrant labour.

Although many governments in Africa and the Middle East have attempted to prevent permanent settlement, in practice, migration is gaining an increasingly permanent character. This echoes a general observation we make in Chapters 3 and 12 that temporary migration almost always leads to permanent settlement of at least a proportion of migrants, despite official policies stressing that migration is only temporary. Immigration has become a key issue in both popular mobilization and political discourses everywhere in the region. This shows the dangers of the usual casting of poor areas in Africa and the Middle East as regions of out-migration: many countries host significant immigrant communities and deal with similar issues of settlement, integration and diversity as most other immigration countries in the world. This seems to coincide with an increasing emphasis on national identity, the politicization of migration, and rising hostility towards immigrants in many African and Middle-Eastern countries (cf. Mitchell, 2012).

In a long historical perspective, it is possible to see that most migratory movements in Africa and the Middle East have common roots. Western penetration triggered profound changes, first through colonization and ambiguous border drawing, then through military involvement, political links, the Cold War, and trade and investment. This exemplifies the relevance of historical–structural and world systems theories in explaining migration. While capitalist economic development and urbanization were entangled with massive rural-to-urban migration within and across national boundaries, colonial and postcolonial conflict created very large refugee movements.

This exemplifies the predictions of migration systems theory discussed in Chapter 2, that increasing flows of capital, goods, and ideas are also likely to stimulate flows of people in both directions. Thus the entry of African countries into the global migration arena may be seen as an inevitable consequence of the increasing integration of these areas into the world economy and into global systems of international relations and cultural interchange. The growing trade, investment and migration links between Africa and China are a case in point.

It is impossible to predict the future of migration in the region, but it is likely that current patterns will undergo fundamental transformation. Whatever its long-term outcome, the Arab Spring is indicative of the coming of age of a better educated, more aware and more *aspiring* generation. This generation no longer accepts conditions of economic stagnation, stark inequality, corruption and political oppression, thus increasing pressures for political and economic reform. If reform is successful, many youngsters may prefer to build a future in their own land. If reform fails, and situations of autocracy and economic stagnation persist, high levels of emigration are likely to continue. An important factor of change is the demographic transitions taking place in much of the Middle East and North Africa. These have led to plummeting birth rates and declining rates of population growth. In the coming decades, the slowing down of the growth of young adult populations may decrease unemployment, particularly if political reform creates conditions for equitable economic growth. In that case, other middle-income countries in North Africa and the Middle East may follow the Turkish scenario and experience declining emigration and increasing immigration.

However, if reform fails, this aspiring generation is also more likely to migrate away to seek better economic, cultural and political opportunities, in which case, emigration may plateau at high levels. At the same time, we may expect increasing migration from and to sub-Saharan Africa as a consequence of globalization and the associated further incorporation in international migration systems. The population growth rate is still at very high levels in most sub-Saharan countries, and economic and other opportunity gaps with industrialized countries remain huge. In this context, increasing levels of education, income and connectivity are likely to fuel emigration to increasingly distant lands. More generally, African development is unlikely to curb migration as it will probably enable and inspire more people to migrate.

Guide to further reading

Extra resources at www.age-of-migration.com

The Age of Migration website includes additional text on 'Migrations Shaping African History' (4.2), 'Remittances to Somalia' (8.1) and 'The Gulf War Crisis of 1990–1991' (8.2).

Useful overviews of African migration include Adepoju (2006), Bakewell and de Haas (2007), Cross *et al.* (2006), Curtin (1997), Mafukidze (2006), Manuh (2005) and Zlotnik (2004). De Bruijn *et al.* (2001) provides a compelling analysis of the complexity and variety of contemporary mobility in sub-Saharan Africa and questions the common notion of mobility as a supposedly rupturing phenomenon. Schielke and Graw (2012) is a collection of interesting anthropological studies from across Africa on the topic of migration expectations and aspirations. Whitehouse's (2012) study on Malians in Congo Brazzaville is an interesting analysis of transnationalism and 'diaspora' within the African continent. Berriane and de Haas (2012) is a (free to download) collection of studies on new African migrations with a focus on innovative methodological approaches. Bakewell and Jónsson (2011) is an insightful synthesis of a study on migration to and from cities in Morocco, Ghana, Nigeria and the Democratic Republic of Congo, highlighting the high rates of intra-African mobility. See www.imi. ox.ac.uk for information and links on African migration.

Collyer *et al.* (2012) is a special issue of *Population, Space and Place* containing articles which critically discuss the concept of transit migration in the context of migration towards Europe. Concerning the MENA, a very useful website is www.carim.org. Baldwin-Edwards' 2005 report to the GCIM is still extremely useful and has an extensive bibliography. De Haas (2008b) provides an overview of the evolution of North African migration systems. On Turkey, see İçduygu and Yükseker (2012), Kirişci (2006) and Mutluer (2003) On Israel, see Bartram (2005).

Chapter 9

Migration, Security and the Debate on Climate Change

One of the most important migration-related developments in the Age of Migration has been the linking of migration to security, a process of social construction termed *securitization*. This has not occurred everywhere and an important priority for future scholarship is to better elucidate why securitization takes place in some regions, contexts, and eras but not in others. The period between 1945 and roughly 1970 in Western Europe was notable for the prevalent pattern of migration not being viewed as germane to security. International migration into and from most Latin American and Iberian countries generally has not been viewed as an important national security concern, save for the exceptional cases of Haiti–Dominican Republic, Cuba and several cases of Central American refugee flows.

The outpouring of scholarship about migration and security, particularly since 2001, has advanced understanding of how securitization, and its opposite, *desecuritization*, take place. Key actors include government employees, political leaders, reporters, editors, migrants and their allies, and the general public as well. In many instances, the role of media coverage of migration appears crucial to outcomes. It follows that there are varying degrees of securitization and diverse processes of social construction of securitization and desecuritization.

Securitization has a mass psychological dimension. Securitization connects migration to meta-issues that comprise symbolic politics. Migration is well-suited for meta-politics, 'because multitudinous phenomena connect to physical mobility of persons'. 'Demonizing the migrant' as a potential 'terrorist' creates fear and a perception of threat to ontological security far exceeding actual developments' (Faist, 2006: 613).

This chapter will feature an overview of the securitization of migration policies in the OECD area between 1970 and 2012. Since its origins in the Allied cooperation during World War II, this assemblage of the world's richer states has become deeply interdependent through trade and joint membership in security alliances and international organizations. The contemporary states comprising this area confront similar challenges in regulation of international migration.

The following three sections provide an overview of the key dimensions of the migration and security nexus, an assessment of migration and security in the transatlantic area and an analysis of the War on Terrorism and its aftermath. The focus will be on the putative security threat arising from the growing presence of Muslims, most of whom are of immigrant background or are the offspring of post-1945 migrants to the West. Subsequent sections will examine several significant cases of diasporas influencing the foreign policy of Middle East and North African states (MENA) states embroiled in geo-strategically significant conflicts and the growing concern over the implications of climate change for migration.

Key dimensions of the international migration and security nexus

Traditionally, security has been viewed through the prism of state security. As a result, relatively few scholars have sought to conceptualize what may be termed the migration and security nexus (Miller, 2000; Tirman, 2004). However, the scope of security concerns is much broader than state security, and is inclusive of human security (Poku and Graham, 1998). Human security is defined in a UNDP report as:

> an analytical tool that focuses on ensuring security for the individual, not the state... In line with the expanded definition of human security, the causes of insecurity are subsequently broadened to include threats to socio-economic and political conditions, food, health, and environmental, community and personal safety … Human security is therefore: people-centred, multidimensional, interconnected, universal. (Jolly and Ray, 2006: 5)

Much migration from poorer countries is driven by the lack of human security that finds expression in impoverishment, inequality, violence, lack of human rights and weak states. Such political, social and economic underdevelopment is linked to histories of colonialism and the present condition of global inequality (see Chapters 2 and 4). Where states are unable to create legal migration systems for necessary labour, many migrants are also forced to move under conditions of considerable insecurity. Smuggling, trafficking, bonded labour and lack of human and worker rights are the fate of millions of migrants. Even legal migrants may have an insecure residence status and be vulnerable to economic exploitation, discrimination and racist violence. Sometimes legal changes can push migrants into irregularity, as happened to the *sans papiers* (undocumented migrants) in France in the 1990s. The frequent insecurity of the people of poorer countries is often forgotten in discussions of state security, yet the two phenomena are closely linked.

Frequently, such migrant insecurity is linked to perceived threats, an aspect of the aforementioned mass psychological dimension, which can be divided into three categories: cultural, socio-economic and political

(Lucassen, 2005). The first perceived threat, the perception of migrant and migrant-background populations as challenging the cultural status quo, may contribute most to migrant insecurity. Such perceptions have been commonplace in Europe since the 1980s. Mexican and other 'Hispanic' migrants to the USA have also been viewed as posing a cultural threat (Huntington, 2004). Often, the religious identity and linguistic practices of migrants loom large in perceived threats. In recent years, Muslims have come to be regarded as a cultural threat in many Western countries.

Examples of the second perceived threat – migrant populations as socio-economic threats – include Italians in Third Republic France, ethnic Chinese diasporas in much of South-East Asia, Syro-Lebanese communities in West Africa, and Chechen and other populations from the Caucasus in the post-Soviet Russian Federation.

The third perceived threat – migrants as potentially politically disloyal or subversive – includes migrant populations such as Palestinians residing in Kuwait prior to the first Gulf War, Yemenites living in Saudi Arabia at the same juncture, ethnic Chinese in Indonesia suspected of political subversion on behalf of Communist China in the 1960s and ethnic Russian populations stranded in Baltic Republics after the collapse of the Soviet Union.

The perceived threats of international migration to national identity and the maintenance of cultural cohesiveness are important aspects of the challenges posed by international migration to the sovereign state (Adamson, 2006). But sometimes international migration is seen as increasing state power. It can facilitate economic growth and is frequently viewed as indispensable to a state's economic wellbeing. Additionally, many immigrants serve as soldiers, and intelligence services can tap immigrant expertise and knowledge of languages. If effective public policies are pursued, international migration can enhance rather than detract from state power (Adamson, 2006: 185).

A state's immigration policies can also contribute to its 'soft power', its ability to achieve foreign policy and security objectives through political and cultural relations without recourse to military or economic coercion. The large body of foreign students studying in the USA can be seen as an important source of soft power, because they help build positive long-term linkages (Nye, 2004). Similarly, treatment of immigrants can affect a state's reputation abroad, a not inconsequential matter for diplomacy and 'smart power', influence that arises from investing in global goods that better enable states to address global issues (Graham and Poku, 2000; National Commission on Terrorist Attacks Upon the United States, 2004)

International migration has also had a significant impact on violent conflicts. Migration flows can interact with other factors to foment violent conflict in several ways such as by providing resources that fuel internal conflicts or by facilitating networks of organized crime (Adamson, 2006: 190–1). Migrant and diasporic communities often provide financial aid and recruits to groups engaged in conflicts in origin states. Kosovar Albanian communities in Western Europe and North America, for instance, provided much of the financing and many recruits for the Kosovo Liberation Army which, in the late 1990s, engaged in heavy fighting with Serbian forces in the former Serbian republic. Similarly, Tamil Sri Lankans in Europe, Canada, India and elsewhere have aided the Tamil Tigers' insurrection in Sri Lanka, an insurgency crushed in 2009. In some instances, organizations viewed by states as engaging in terrorism, such as the Kurdistan Workers' Party (PKK), have simultaneously been involved in human trafficking and drugs and arms smuggling.

From a non-problem to an obsession: migration and security in the OECD area, 1945–2012

The end of World War II witnessed mass population movements in Central and Eastern Europe and elsewhere which generally fell under the rubrics of forced migration and ethnic cleansing (Snyder, 2010: 313–37). It has been estimated that 18.5 million persons were displaced, not including the five million Jews deported to concentration camps (Kulischer, 1948). All of these developments involved massive suffering and loss of life. This underscores the observation that mass human displacements constitute a characteristic outcome of warfare. Nevertheless, the revulsion against Nazi war crimes served to delegitimize extreme right parties and other radical movements that typically view immigration and foreigners as threatening to security.

The Cold War soon ensued and with it a perception of the threat of nuclear warfare. Mainstream study of security largely reflected the tenets of *realism*, a school of thought about international relations that traditionally assumed that only sovereign states were germane to analysis of questions of war and peace. In this perspective, migration seemed of marginal significance for security. In Western Europe, the prevalent assumption characterizing the guest-worker era that post-war migrations would be mainly temporary in nature also contributed to this perception.

The status quo that prevailed after 1945 endured until 1970. A harbinger of change came with the politicization of migration policies that generally took place in the 1970s and 1980s, although in some national contexts earlier. Politicization need not engender securitization, which is the linking of migration to perceptions of existential threats to society. However, politicization brings migration issues into the public arena and thereby increases the likelihood of broader involvement of political agents including those hostile to prevailing policies. The 'hyper-securitization' of migration after 9/11 resulted from incremental processes of increasing securitization of migration that had already evolved in the 1980s and 1990s (Chebel d'Appollonia, 2012: 49–76). A key dynamic involved a blurring of counter-terrorism measures with immigration policy measures.

The construction of an Islamic 'threat'

While there were Islamic fundamentalist movements active in Western Europe in the 1970s, they were not seen as posing much of a threat. The success of the Islamic Revolution in Iran in 1979 began to change that perception. In many Arab states and Turkey, secular-oriented governments felt threatened by Islamic fundamentalist movements. Such governments came to be viewed by some of the more radical Islamic fundamentalists as the 'near enemy' that had to be overthrown and replaced with truly Islamic governance (Gerges, 2005).

Thus, by the 1980s, the growth of Islamic fundamentalism came to affect the transatlantic area in a variety of ways. A massacre of Syrian army cadets led to the brutal repression of Syrian fundamentalists. Many of the survivors ended up as refugees in Germany. The Israeli invasion of Lebanon in 1982 prompted Iranian intervention in the conflict and the creation of Hezbollah, the Party of God. American and French troops deployed to the Beirut area as part of the Multinational Force in 1982 suffered grievous losses in suicide bomb attacks thought to have been perpetrated by Hezbollah or its allies. The war in Afghanistan between the Soviet Union and its Afghan allies and the Mujahadeen, Afghans who fought the Soviets, began to attract non-Afghan Muslim volunteers, some of whom came from Europe and North America. This marked the genesis of what would later become Al-Qaeda (Roy, 2003). A US-led coalition of states, including Pakistan and Saudi Arabia, armed and aided the Mujahideen. Following the defeat of the Soviet Union in Afghanistan, the Pakistani Inter-Services Intelligence agency helped create the Taliban, which recruited heavily amongst the Afghan refugees in Pakistan, another case of refugee-soldiers. By 1996, the Taliban had seized control of most of Afghanistan.

The 1993 attack on the World Trade Center in New York City underscored the vulnerability of the United States even as it demonstrated the efficacy of existing law enforcement arrangements in punishing the individuals involved in the attack. The adoption of the Anti-terrorism and Effective Death Penalty Act and the Illegal Immigration Reform and Individual Responsibility Act in 1996 were complementary and reflected a significant hardening of US Federal Government anti-terrorism and anti-irregular migration policies as well as the issue linkage between migration and terrorism. Yet such measures were not sufficient to prevent the later escalation of violence through the attacks of 11 September 2001, which led to the Bush Administration's 'War on Terrorism' (see below).

There are strong parallels between migration and security developments on both sides of the Atlantic in the 1980s and 1990s. The 1985 signature of the Schengen Agreement can be seen as the birthdate of a European policy on migration and security (White, 2011: 66). By the 1990s, there were growing concerns over the political activities of Islamic and other Middle Eastern radicals on West European soil. The spill over of Algerian violence

Box 9.1 Spillover of insurgency in Algeria to France

In 1992, an offshoot of the Islamic Salvation Front, the Armed Islamic Group (GIA), pursued an insurgency against the Algerian government. Tens of thousands died in a war of terrorism and counterterrorism. France provided military and economic support to the Algerian government, which led to the extension of GIA operations to French soil. A network of militants waged a bombing campaign, principally in the Paris region in 1995, before being dismantled. Some French journalists and scholars believed that the GIA had been penetrated by Algerian agents who then manipulated GIA militants into attacking targets in France in order to bolster French support for the Algerian government (Aggoun and Rivoire, 2004) .

French authorities undertook numerous steps to prevent bombings and to capture the bombers. Persons of North African appearance were routinely subjected to identity checks. Most French citizens and resident aliens of North African background accepted such checks as a necessary inconvenience. Indeed, information supplied by such individuals greatly aided in the neutralization of the terrorist group, several of whom were killed in shootouts with French police. Nevertheless, French police rounded up scores of suspected GIA sympathizers on several occasions as nervousness over attacks remained high.

Such fears appeared warranted in the aftermath of 11 September 2001. Scores of GIA and Al-Qaida-linked individuals, mainly of North African background, were detained for involvement in various plots, including one to attack the US embassy in Paris. Several of those arrested were French citizens of North African background, like Zacarias Moussaoui, who was accused of plotting with the perpetrators of the 9/11 attacks. Algerians and other individuals of North African Muslim background with links to the GIA figured prominently in the hundreds of arrests in the transatlantic area. The anti-Western resentment of some of those arrested was linked to perceived injustices endured by migrants and their families. Despite increased vigilance, several French citizens were involved in a series of suicide bombings of Western targets in Casablanca in 2003. Several of the bombers had been recruited into a fundamentalist network in the Parisian suburbs and their involvement was deeply disturbing to the French population, including most of the Islamic community.

Despite an amnesty offer from the Algerian government to Islamic militants who laid down their arms in 2006, some continued to fight. In 2007, these militants renamed themselves Al-Qaida in the Islamic Maghreb and launched a murderous bombing campaign in Algiers. French and other European intelligence officials continue to worry about the potential for spillovers to Europe (see also Chapter 1). The meagre participation in the 2012 national elections in Algeria reflected widespread disaffection and alienation. Yet, as attested by the Arab Spring of 2011 in nearby states, aspirations for reforms and democratic governance suggest that Al-Qaida-style politics holds scant appeal among the Arab masses.

to mainland France and of Kurdistan Workers' Party (PKK) protests and other political activities to Germany became central national security preoccupations of the respective states. Box 9.1 and AOM Website Text 9.1 provide greater detail.

Following the 1993 attacks in Manhattan, a succession of Federal commissions in the USA investigating terrorism warned that additional countermeasures were needed, but the warnings were largely not heeded (National Commission on Terrorist Attacks Upon the United States, 2004). By 2001, a number of US officials feared a catastrophic attack by Al-Qaida upon a target or targets in the USA, but failed to prevent the attacks on New York and Washington on 11 September 2001 (Shenon, 2008). Perhaps the focus on 'terrorism' as 'irrational violence' hindered understanding of the deep-rooted resentment of many Muslims, in the light of Western support for authoritarian regimes in their own countries (such as Egypt, Saudi Arabia and Tunisia). Moreover, many Muslims perceived Israeli actions (supported by US military aid), such as air raids and arbitrary imprisonment of Palestinians, as forms of state terrorism that could legitimately be resisted. The subsequent difficulties of the US-led interventions in Iraq and Afghanistan illustrate the Western failure to understand the sources of malaise in the Muslim world.

Following the invasion of Iraq in 2003, some European Muslims volunteered to fight the USA in Iraq and many died or were captured. Thousands of European Muslims received military training in camps in the Middle East and North Africa (MENA) and subsequently returned to Europe (Scheuer, 2008). The terrorist attacks in Madrid and London and the numerous planned attacks thwarted by European police and security agencies increased public concern about Muslims in Europe.

Assessing the threat posed by Islamic radicals in the West

The profiles and histories of Islamic populations in North America and Europe are quite divergent. Muslims living in North America are generally more prosperous and well educated than Muslims in Europe, many of whom were recruited as unskilled labour (CSIS, 2006). However, even within Western Europe, Muslim populations are highly heterogeneous. For example, among Muslims of Turkish background, there are Sunnis and Alevis (orthodox Muslims and a non-orthodox Shíite offshoot respectively), as well as ethnic Arabs, Kurds and Turks.

It is important to stress that religious extremism has only appealed to a minority of migrants from the Middle East and North Africa, and that many are quite secular in orientation. It is true that many Muslim immigrants and their descendants confront incorporation barriers in housing, education and employment and endure prejudice and racism. However, the gist of the huge body of social science research on the incorporation of Muslim immigrants and their offspring suggests that most are slowly but steadily incorporating, much like previous waves of immigration in the transatlantic space that have been viewed as problematic or threatening in the past (Lucassen, 2005).

In France, for instance, empirical evidence reveals the widespread use of French in migrant households and decreasing use of Arabic and other mother tongues (Tribalat, 1995). Furthermore, the evidence showed a decline in traditional arranged marriages and a rising intermarriage rate with French citizens and adoption of French social practices. The major problem areas were high unemployment, perceived discrimination and educational problems. However, Tribalat (1995) found that some communities did not fit the general pattern. Persons of Algerian background tended to be less religious and more secular than persons of Moroccan background. Furthermore, the Turkish community in France exhibited a lower proclivity to French usage at home, interacted less with French society and rarely intermarried with French citizens.

The key insight of Tribalat's study is that France's Muslims were incorporating and becoming French like earlier waves of immigrants to France. France's top experts on radical Islam, Gilles Kepel (2002; 2005) and Olivier Roy (2003), doubted that extremists would find much support in immigrant-background populations in Europe. Their assessments appear borne out by research on public opinion in the Middle East and North Africa and other predominantly Muslim areas of the world, which evidence scant support for terrorism (Esposito and Mogahed, 2007).

The attacks of 9/11 as well as those in Madrid and London transformed the decades-old, indeed centuries-old, question of migrant incorporation in Western countries into an acute security issue, not only in Europe but also in North America and Australia. In recent years much has been written about the susceptibility of migrant-background Muslims to mobilization into terrorist movements. For the most part, such articles and books appear inadequately based upon social scientific insights on migrant incorporation. Greatly exaggerated perceptions of the threat posed by Muslim immigrants in the West became commonplace.

The utterances and political beliefs of a relatively small coterie of radical Islamists attracted inordinate attention, especially in the media. Hence it was that extremely marginal parties such as Hizb ut-Tahrir in Great Britain could provoke such a moral panic, way out of proportion to the real threat posed (Husain, 2009). The origin society-oriented preoccupations that prevailed amongst the Islamist radicals profoundly reflected their socialization and upbringing in Europe's Islamic periphery. Nevertheless, their political orientations were taken to reflect profound dysfunctions and failures of immigrant incorporation in West Europe. In fact, their presence was largely due to the existence of refugee and asylum-seeking policies that afforded residency and protection.

Pargenter (2008) stresses the widespread revulsion felt by most Muslims, including those in the West, for the wanton violence against innocent civilians exercised by Al-Qaeda itself or confederates like the late

Abu Musab Al-Zarqawi's group in Iraq and the Armed Islamic Group in Algeria. Numerous credible sources concur that the vast majority of Muslims worldwide view Al-Qaida with contempt and utterly reject its politics and goals (Esposito and Mogahed, 2007; Kepel, 2002; 2004). A study in 2009 found that only 15 per cent of people killed in Al-Qaida attacks between 2004 and 2008 were Westerners and that the vast majority of victims were Muslims (Schmidt and Shanker, 2011: 155).

Public opinion research consistently reveals that European Muslims support and respect European democracies (Boswell and Geddes, 2011: 38; Jackson and Doerschler, 2012). Unfortunately, public opinion surveys also reveal growing negative opinion and prejudice against Muslims and Islam, particularly in the US (Gerges, 2011: 20–2). There subsists an egregious disconnect between perceptions of Muslims and Islam and the values, ideals and aspirations of most Muslims. This state of affairs suggests an urgent need for better education about world affairs and Islam.

Migration, security and the 'War on Terrorism'

What was termed the 'War on Terrorism' by the George W. Bush Administration involved calculated exaggeration and misleading simplification. After largely ignoring the threat posed by Al-Qaida in its first months in office, the Administration then declared a war and likened it to World War II (Clarke, 2004; Shenon, 2008). In doing so, the Administration exaggerated the threat posed by radical Muslims at a time when overall support for achievement of Islamic fundamentalist goals through political violence had declined significantly and mainstream Islamic fundamentalist movements had rejected violence while embracing incremental reform (Gerges, 2005; Roy, 1994). It then compounded the error by linking the government of Iraq to Al-Qaeda and then using that and an unwarranted claim concerning weapons of mass destruction as a pretext to invade Iraq.

The invasion of Iraq proved counterproductive to the campaign against Al-Qaeda and its allies, like the Taliban in Afghanistan, since it increased support for them among some Muslims (Ricks, 2007). Nevertheless, the US-led attack on Afghanistan, later supported by a NATO deployment, badly damaged Taliban and Al-Qaeda forces in Afghanistan without eliminating them (Miller, 2007). With the killing of Osama Bin Laden in 2011, perhaps a remnant of only several hundred militants remained (Schmidt and Shanker, 2011: 242–5).

Al-Qaeda probably played some role in the mounting of the attack in Madrid in 2004 and the attacks in London in 2005 and 2007, although these attacks were initially viewed as home-grown but inspired by Al-Qaeda (Benjamin and Simon, 2005). In early 2008, French and Spanish authorities thwarted a planned series of attacks in Western Europe, apparently timed again to precede general elections in Spain. Most of the suspects were Pakistani migrants, several of whom had recently arrived from the frontier area of Waziristan in Pakistan. Hence, the US Secretary of Defence claimed that the outcome of the war in Afghanistan directly affected European security (Shanker and Kulish, 2008).

Soon after entering office in 2009, US President Obama declared the end of the War on Terrorism. By 2012, US forces in Iraq had been greatly reduced and those remaining were mostly deployed in non-combat missions. Meanwhile, in Afghanistan, US and NATO troop levels were also being drawn down with an endpoint for US and NATO combat missions foreseen for July 2014. Prospects for both Iraq and Afghanistan did not bode well and fears over possible future civil wars appeared warranted. One much discussed scenario foresaw a Taliban role in a future Afghan coalition government (and perhaps) federal state (Green, 2012).

Migration and security in the Middle East and North Africa (MENA)

Comparisons to other areas of the world reveal important contrasts with the dominant pattern of what might be termed hyper-securitization in the transatlantic area since the 1990s. Nevertheless, migration and security represents a salient concern in many areas outside the OECD. Instead of comprehensive examination of all such areas, only a handful of country and regional cases can be considered here.

Geo-strategically, due to its proximity to Europe in the transatlantic space, the MENA assumes enormous significance. The analysis in previous sections revealed important connections between migration and security in the transatlantic area and the MENA. The origin country-orientation of many MENA-background migrants in the West attests to the enduring significance of migration and security-related developments in the MENA for the transatlantic area. A related concern arises from the growing significance of diasporas to understanding of migration and security, particularly in the MENA.

Diaspora refers to a transnational population linked by ethnicity to a traditional, symbolic or historic origin country (see Chapter 2). Diasporas constitute non-state actors although states increasingly promote ties to diasporic populations abroad, especially to spur economic development. Such populations increasingly loom large in all regions of the world, but particularly so in the MENA with its many conflicts. An important analytical question arises about the role of diasporas in conflicts and their settlement or non-resolution. Studies suggest that diasporas can either contribute to democratization and stability or exacerbate or perpetuate conflicts as witnessed in the Azeri–Armenia conflict (Shain and Barth, 2003: 449–50). Box 9.2 analyses the role of the Armenian diaspora in the strife over Nagorno-Karabakh. AOM Website Text 9.2 considers the role played by diaspora Jewry in the Arab–Israeli conflict.

Box 9.2 The Armenian diaspora and the conflict over Nagorno-Karabakh

The Armenian diaspora comprises communities around the world. The two largest ethnic Armenian populations are found in the USA, where an estimated one million Armenians reside, principally in California, New Jersey, and Massachusetts, and in France, where an estimated 500,000 Armenians live, principally in the Marseille and Paris areas (Shain and Barth, 2003: 468).

Soon after the implosion of the Soviet Union, the area of the former semi-autonomous Armenian Soviet Socialist Republic, became an independent state in 1991. Similarly, the neighbouring former Soviet area became the internationally recognized state of Azerbaijan. The territory of the new Azeri state encompassed an area with mixed populations of ethnic Armenians and Azeris called Nagorno-Karabakh. A conflict ensued and Armenian forces seized Nagorno-Karabakh and other Azeri territories. Volunteers from the Armenian diaspora played a key role in the fighting which resulted in the creation of hundreds of thousands of Azeri refugees, most of whom lost their homes and livelihoods and subsist as IDPs in areas still controlled by the Azeri government or found safe haven in neighbouring Iran which has a large ethnic Azeri minority population.

The conflict over Nagorno-Karabakh and other Azeri territories now under Armenian military occupation has largely remained frozen since the early 1990s. However, the first democratically elected president of the new Armenia, Ter-Petrossian, opposed recognition of the self-declared Karabakh. This put Ter-Petrossian at odds with influential elements of the Armenian diaspora which favoured both recognition and annexation and generally a hard line towards both Azerbaijan and Turkey.

Ter-Petrossian's disfavour increased with Armenia's economic collapse. The downturn made Armenians all the more dependent on assistance from the Armenian diaspora. In the USA, the pro-Armenian lobby succeeded in increasing US foreign assistance to Armenia and in instituting a ban on aid to Azerbaijan (Shain and Barth, 2003: 471). The recovery of Armenia's sovereignty and independence led to significant inflows of ethnic Armenians from the diaspora who established political parties in Armenia. Among these was the Dashnak Armenia Revolutionary Federation which fiercely criticized Ter-Petrossian's policies. Eventually, by 1998, Ter-Petrossan was forced to resign and diasporic opposition figured centrally in this outcome. His successor Kocharian embraced an Armenian foreign policy orientation which was much more pleasing to hard-line elements in the Armenian diaspora. According to Shain and Barth (2003: 472), the weight of the diaspora '...manifests itself most powerfully regarding the possibility of a peace settlement with Azerbaijan'.

Both the behaviour of the Armenian and Jewish diasporas may be viewed as a challenge to state-centric analysis and, in a sense, to the state itself. However, comparison of the Israeli and Armenian cases suggests that the abilities of diaspora populations to influence politics and policies in homelands vary a great deal. The economic plight of Armenia compared to that of Israel, meant that the Armenian diaspora was much more influential than the Jewish diaspora in the formulation of Armenia's and Israel's respective foreign policies (Shain and Barth, 2003). The two cases also differ in that Israel long enjoyed an aura bordering on deference amongst Jews that Armenia lacks among Armenians. However, the Israeli–Jewish diaspora relationship may be evolving as emigration of Israel's Jews, particularly its most affluent and well-educated citizens, increases and prospects for a two-state solution to the Arab–Israeli conflict fade (Lustik, 2011).

A growing concern: environment, climate change and migration

In Chapter 2, we drew attention to push–pull models that assume that population growth and environmental degradation directly cause migration. We showed that such deterministic approaches ignore the interaction between these and the many other factors that influence decisions to migrate or to stay put. We stressed the need for a multi-pronged understanding of migration that takes account of the many aspects of change that affect societies and communities, as well as the role of individual and collective agency in shaping migratory behaviour.

In recent years, increasing attention has been paid to the relationship between climate change and migration. This can be seen as a special case of environmental drivers of migration, but as one of growing current significance. Concerns about climate change-induced migration have emerged in the context of debates on global warming and the inability of states to take effective action to mitigate it through regulation of carbon emissions. Environmentalists have claimed that the effects of global warming, especially on sea-levels and rainfall patterns, will lead directly to massive population displacements. They call for action to prevent such migrations as well for the broadening of the definition of refugees to include people displaced by climate change. The underlying assumption seems to be that migration is intrinsically negative and should be stopped where possible.

Migration scholars, by contrast, have pointed out that migration is driven by many interacting factors, and can rarely be reduced to the effects of just one form of change, such as climate change. Moreover, they have argued that migration itself can be one of the most effective ways of responding to change and building better livelihoods.

The state of knowledge on climate change and migration

In the 1980s and 1990s, some environmentalists claimed that predicted climate-change-induced developments (such as sea-level rise, drought or desertification) could be mapped onto settlement patterns to predict future human displacement. In other words, if climate change models predicted a sea-level rise of (say) 50 centimetres, it would be possible to map all coastal areas affected by this and work out how many people lived in such areas. The assumption then was that all these people would have to move (for an example of this approach see Myers and Kent, 1995). No consideration was given to possible adaptation strategies, such as flood defences, changes in livelihood patterns or short-distance mobility. Others put forward scenarios of mass displacements as a cause of future global insecurity (Homer-Dixon and Percival, 1996), while certain NGOs even escalated forecasts of future population displacements up to one billion by 2050 (Christian Aid, 2007).

By contrast, migration and refugee scholars argued that climate change in itself was not a major cause of migration, and that people's decisions to move were always shaped by multiple factors (Black, 2001; Castles, 2002). They therefore called for micro-level research on actual experiences of how communities coped with modifications in their living conditions and economic opportunities resulting from climate change.

The knowledge base has since developed a great deal. Researchers have begun to carry out studies at the local and regional levels, and the empirical basis for understanding the relationship between climate change and migration is much enhanced. Findings of studies have been published in books which cover a range of conceptual, normative and descriptive topics (for example see McAdam, 2010; Piguet and de Guchteneire, 2011). Information and research centres have issued reports and working papers analysing experiences of climate change and the strategies adopted by affected populations (e.g. Hugo, 2008; Massey *et al.*, 1998; Piore, 1979). Important debates on methodology are taking place (Kniveton *et al.*, 2008), and significant empirical studies are beginning to appear in scientific journals (e.g. Pratikshya and Massey, 2009). A doctoral thesis has analysed the politicization of the climate change displacement debate (Gemenne, 2009).

The current state-of-the-art in understanding the climate-change-migration nexus is summed up in a study published by the Foresight programme of the British Government Office for Science (Foresight, 2011) The *Foresight Report* focuses on the environmental effects of climate change resulting from human activity – notably the global warming caused by increased use of fossil fuels. The Government Chief Scientist commissioned over 80 reports and papers covering drivers of migration, the state of science, case studies of relevant experiences, models for analysing change and policy development. The authors include migration researchers, economists, demographers, geographers, environmentalists and social scientists from 30 countries worldwide. The *Foresight Report* starts by arguing that estimates of the numbers of environmental/climate change migrants are:

> Methodologically unsound, as migration is a multi-causal phenomenon and it is problematic to assign a proportion of the actual or predicted

number of migrants as moving as a direct result of environmental change. A deterministic approach that assumes that all or a proportion of people living in an 'at risk' zone in a low-income country will migrate neglects the pivotal role that humans take in dealing with environmental change and also ignores other constraining factors which influence migration outcomes. (Foresight, 2011: 11)

It is impossible to summarize the many important findings of the *Foresight Report* here. Attention may be drawn to some key points. First, migration is likely to continue regardless of environmental change, because it is driven by powerful economic, political and social processes. Many people will migrate into areas of greater environmental vulnerability, such as cities built on floodplains in Asia and Africa. Second, environmental change is equally likely to make migration less possible as more probable. Where people are impoverished by such factors as drought or desertification, they may lack the resources to move, and may have to stay in situations of extreme vulnerability. Third, attempts at preventing migration may lead to increased impoverishment, displacement and irregular migration in the long run. Migration can represent a transformational adaptation to environmental change, and may be an effective way to build resilience.

Finally, and perhaps most important, environmental change will influence the volume, directions and characteristics of migration in the future – even if it is not possible to disentangle environmental and other drivers. This means that: 'Giving urgent policy attention to migration in the context of environmental change now will prevent a much worse and more costly situation in the future' (Foresight, 2011: 10).

As a result of the Foresight project and the other studies carried out in recent years, it is now possible to go beyond some of the simplistic statements of the past. It is still too early to speak of scientific consensus about the causes, extent and impacts of climate change, but certain ideas seem to be gaining acceptance as pointers for further research and action.

To start with, climate-change-induced migration should not be analysed in isolation from other forms of movement – especially economic migration and forced migration. Forced migration results from conflicts, persecution and the effects of development projects (such as dams, airports, industrial areas and middle-class housing complexes). Such development-induced displacement is actually the largest single form of forced migration, predominantly leading to internal displacement of 10–15 million people per year, and mainly affecting disempowered groups such as indigenous peoples, other ethnic minorities and slum-dwellers (Cernea and McDowell, 2000).

Possible climate-change-related migration is often closely linked to other aspects of environmental change. The effects of changing farming practices (e.g. mechanization, use of fertilizers and pesticides, mono-cultures, irrigation, concentration of land ownership) on the environment may be hard to distinguish from cyclical weather variations and long-term climate change. Rural–urban migration and the growth of cities are key social-change processes of our times. All too often, this means that people leaving the land end up in urban slums (Davis, 2006) that are highly vulnerable to disasters and climatic factors, such as storms, landslides, water insecurity and flooding. Migration scholars now recognize that environmental factors have been significant in driving migration throughout history and have often been neglected in the past. In other words, we should generally look for *multiple and interacting causes* when studying migration and include climate change as one of the factors to be analysed.

Further, recent research indicates that there is little evidence that climate change will cause massive migration movement. It is very difficult to identify groups of people already displaced by climate change alone. There are certainly groups which have been affected by climatic (or broader environmental) *variability*, but these need to be distinguished from long-term climate change. In addition, other economic, political, social and cultural factors are also at work. Even the cases portrayed in the media as most clear-cut become more complex when looked at closely. For instance, Bangladesh is often seen as an 'obvious example' of mass displacement due to sea-level rise, but an analysis by Findlay and Geddes (2011) questions this conventional view, showing that longer-term migration is related to differential patterns of poverty, access to social networks, and household and community structures.

But the absence of the displaced millions predicted by Myers and others just a few years ago should not be taken as a reason for complacency. It seems probable that the forecast acceleration of climate change over the next few decades will have major effects on production, livelihoods and human security. A study of the Asia–Pacific region identifies a number of 'hot spot areas which will experience the greatest impact': these include densely settled delta areas, low-lying coastal areas, low-lying atolls and coral islands, some river valleys, and semi-arid low-humidity areas. The largest populations likely to be affected are in mega-cities built on average only a few metres above sea-level, like Shanghai, Tianjin, Tokyo, Osaka and Guangzhou (Hugo, 2010a). It has been estimated that the number of people living in floodplains of urban areas in East Asia may rise from 18 million in 2000 to 45–67 million by 2060 (Foresight, 2011: 13). Such areas are experiencing massive growth through rural–urban migration. Significant changes in peoples' ability to earn a livelihood in specific locations will lead to a range of adaption strategies, many of which will not involve migration. However, certain families and communities are likely to adapt through temporary or permanent migration of some of their members, while in extreme cases it may become impossible to remain in current home areas, so that forced displacement will ensue.

To sum up: migration is not an inevitable result of climate change, but one possible adaptation strategy out of many. It is crucial to understand the factors that lead to differing strategies and varying degrees of vulnerability and resilience in individuals and communities. Moreover, migration should not generally be seen as negative: people have always moved in search of better livelihoods, and this can bring benefits both for origin and destination areas (UNDP, 2009). Migrants should not be seen as passive victims; they have some degree of *agency*, even under the most difficult conditions. Strategies that treat them as passive victims are counterproductive, and protection of rights should also be about giving people the chance to deploy their agency. The objective of public policy should not be to prevent migration, but rather to ensure that it can take place in appropriate ways and under conditions of safety, security and legality (Zetter, 2010).

Conclusions

The post-9/11 period witnessed a reinforcement of the securitization of migration policies that had developed from the 1980s, particularly after the end of the Cold War, and the emergence of a new security agenda. Analysis of climate change and its implications for security occupies a key place on that agenda. There has been a parallel proliferation of books about securitization of migration, but mainly about the transatlantic space. A scholarly consensus has emerged that migrant populations were the most adversely affected by the pattern of securitization.

Nevertheless, migrant populations have proven resilient in the face of adversity. Radical Islam has elicited scant support in the transatlantic zone and political incorporation of growing Muslim populations is ongoing. Securitization of migration has not taken place in some regions such as most of Latin America and Iberia. Important priorities for future scholarship are to better understand the implications of non-state actors like diasporas for security matters and to compare securitization processes in the transatlantic region with security in other regions.

Guide to further reading

Extra resources at www.age-of-migration.com

The Age of Migration website includes additional Text 9.1 'Spillover of the Kurdistan Workers' Party (PKK) Insurgency to Germany' and Text 9.2 'The Role of Diaspora Jewry in the Arab–Israeli Conflict'.

There has been a remarkable outpouring of scholarship about migration and security since 1990. To a certain extent, this evolution parallels the expansion of terrorism research, a social science growth industry well analysed by Jackson, Jarvis, Gunning and Smyth (2011) who provide an important critique of what may be termed the terrorism industry that has propagated undue fear and vastly exaggerated the threat posed by terrorism. A number of books and articles about Muslims in the West appear skewed by related biases and exaggerations (Vaisse, 2010).

Notable more recent contributions about migration and security include Paoletti (2011), Dancygier (2010), Greenhill (2010), Bourbeau (2011) and Chebel d'Appollonia (2012). On Muslims in Europe, see Glazer (2009), Laurence (2012), Pargenter (2008), Gerges (2011), Kurzman (2011) and Jackson and Doerschler (2012). On the complex security and theoretical implications of transnational and diasporic populations, see Adamson and Demetriou (2007) and Shain and Barth (2003).

For climate change, the key reading is the Foresight Report. All the papers along with the main report are available for free download at http://www.bis.gov.uk/foresight.

Chapter 10

The State and International Migration: The Quest for Control

International migration to highly developed states entered a new phase during the global economic recession of the early 1970s. To prevent unwanted migration, post-industrial democracies, such as France, Germany and the USA, embarked on what can be termed a 'quest for control' over cross-border movements. This quest entailed sustained efforts to prevent unauthorized migration and the abuse or circumvention of immigration regulations and policies.

This chapter appraises key components of governmental strategies designed to regulate immigration flows. Although focusing on transatlantic states, many of the issues addressed in this chapter are relevant to, and have implications for, other regions. The policies examined include employer sanctions enforcement, legalization or amnesty programmes (also called regularizations), temporary foreign-worker admission programmes, asylum and refugee policies, regional integration approaches, and measures against human smuggling and trafficking. Testifying to the growing political salience of migration, cooperation on such issues has become a central feature of international politics.

Employer sanctions

Since the 1970s, the USA and most European states have implemented laws punishing employers for the unauthorized hiring of undocumented foreigners. Known as employer sanctions, they are often coupled with legalization programmes which give work and residence permits to undocumented workers who meet certain criteria. These carrot-and-stick measures, it is argued, remove the motivation for undocumented work since employers may be punished for unlawful hiring of foreigners while formerly undocumented workers will regularize their legal status. However, in practice, these programmes have met resistance as employers often had the political clout to prevent effective enforcement of employer sanctions while many migrant workers failed to regularize due to fear of losing their job or being unable to find a new one.

Despite the political consensus behind many of these policies, effective enforcement was often lacking due to insufficient personnel, poor coordination between various agencies, inadequate judicial follow-up and the adaptation of employers and irregular employees to enforcement measures. Symptomatic of the progressive regionalization of immigration policies in Europe, in May 2007, the European Commission adopted a directive on employer sanctions designed to decrease the demand for irregular migrant labour (CEC, 2007: 24). The directive's aim was to provide minimum standards and to harmonize preventive measures, employer sanctions, and enforcement policies across EU member states.

The measures included employer verification of the identity and employment authorization of third-country nationals, as well as compulsory notification to competent governmental authorities of the intention to hire prior to the actual hiring of employees. Those employers who did not follow these measures would expose themselves to heavy fines and other costs including deportation costs and the repayment of wages, unpaid taxes and social security. Furthermore, other administrative penalties included the possibility of being barred from EU subsidies and business for a period of five years. Nevertheless, disagreements over the directive between EU member states persisted.

Unlike many Western European states, the USA lacked an employer sanctions policy prior to 1986. The termination of the *Bracero* guest-worker programme with Mexico in 1964 led to growing concerns over irregular migration to the USA during the 1960s and 1970s. Continued irregular migration led to the appointment in 1978 of the Select Committee on Immigration and Refugee Policy (SCIRP). In 1981, SCIRP recommended the implementation of an employer sanctions policy and a legalization programme, as well as the introduction of a counterfeit-resistant employment identification document (SCIRP, 1981). In 1986, President Reagan signed into law the Immigration Reform and Control Act (IRCA) which made the hiring of unauthorized foreigners a punishable offence. The IRCA permitted an assortment of documents to prove employment eligibility, many of which could be easily forged or fraudulently obtained. The Commission for Immigration Reform concluded by 1994 that the employer sanctions system adopted in 1986 had failed because many unauthorized foreign workers could simply present false documents to employers (Martin and Miller, 2000a: 46).

The enforcement of employer sanctions was further hampered by political opposition within the USA. Several Hispanic advocacy groups alleged that employer sanctions would increase employment discrimination of minorities, while business interests viewed the restrictions as another government-imposed burden. Others feared that enforcement would disrupt entire industries, such as labour-intensive agriculture, which would result in crops rotting in the fields and higher food costs. Even the AFL-CIO, the major confederation of unions, which had been a proponent of punishing the irregular employment of undocumented foreigners since the early 1980s, announced in 2000 that it no longer supported enforcement of employer sanctions. The AFL-CIO was under new leadership, which emerged from unions with large numbers of immigrant members including many undocumented workers. This faction had close ties to the US Conference of Catholic Bishops, which supported a broad legalization of the millions of irregular resident foreigners. This diverse opposition ensured that there would be no political consensus in support of the enforcement of employer sanctions in the USA.

The overall record of employer sanctions enforcement has not been strong. In 1999, the US government announced that it was suspending enforcement, which resulted in a reduction of the number of INS employer investigations from 7,537 cases completed and 17,552 arrests in 1997 to 3,898 cases completed and 2,849 arrests in 1999 (INS, 2002: 214). Such figures indicate that only a small proportion of the millions of irregular workers in the USA were affected, even before suspension of enforcement. The events of 11 September 2001 and the successive reorganization of the INS under the Department of Homeland Security (DHS) in 2003 signified a substantial shift in the mission of worksite inspectors. Enforcement took on a 'National Security focus', which resulted in the diversion of funds and resources from workplaces lacking security relevance to employers in key strategic areas, such as airports (Brownell, 2005).

The continued growth of the irregular foreign population triggered the divisive immigration debate that has been at the forefront of US politics since 2004. Several proposals sought the establishment of a counterfeit-resistant identification card, the participation of employers in an electronic-based verification system, an increase in fines for contravening employers, an increase in border controls, the creation of a guest-worker programme, and the possibility for most migrants to benefit from a legal pathway to residency through earned legalization.

In 2007, the Bush Administration announced a major enforcement initiative centred on so-called 'no-match letters'. Such letters are sent by the Social Security Administration to employers advising them that an employee's name or social security number do not match the agency's records. In response to a no-match letter, employers have 14 or 90 days to resolve the discrepancy or to fire the unauthorized worker or risk fines up to US$10,000. Prior to 2007, such no-match letters generally had not been followed-up with enforcement; however, a Department of Homeland Security spokesman has declared, '[w]e are tough and we are going to be even tougher' (Preston, 2007). The initiative appeared to confirm that the US never truly had a credible employer sanctions regime due, in part, to the ease of circumventing the 1986 law. Enforcement of employer sanctions increased under the Obama Administration. Its significance, however, paled in comparison to other enforcement measures, most notably deportations which soared to record levels. Overall estimates of the irregularly employed population simultaneously declined. But this may have resulted from the economic recession rather than from stepped up enforcement.

218 The Age of Migration

Legalization programmes

Prior to the 1970s, many national migration policies used 'back door' rather than 'front door' immigration to remedy labour or demographic shortages. During the *Bracero* policy era, nearly 87,000 Mexicans working without authorization were legalized in the USA. In France, foreigners who took up employment irregularly after 1947 were routinely legalized and, between 1945 and 1970, legalization comprised the major mode of legal entry into France (Miller, 1999: 40–1). Thereafter, the French government declared that legalization would be exceptional, but there were recurrent legalizations throughout the 1970s and 1980s (Miller, 2002).

In 1981, the election of a Socialist President and a Leftist majority in the National Assembly set the stage for a new French approach to legalization to counter irregular migration and employment. Unlike previous legalizations, trade unions and immigrant associations participated in the legalization effort and additional governmental personnel were mobilized to facilitate the processing of applications. As a result, approximately 120,000 of 150,000 applicants were legalized. (Miller, 1999: 40–1) Although the legalization benefited its participants, it did not alter the underlying labour-market dynamics fostering irregular migration and employment. Application deadlines were repeatedly extended and the criteria for eligibility evolved. But for French government officials the legalization of 1981–3 constituted a major success, one fit for emulation elsewhere.

The legalization provisions in the US IRCA of 1986 differed in several key respects from its French counterpart. First, the IRCA had a five-year period between the cut-off date for eligibility (1 January 1982) and the effective starting date of the general programme (4 May 1987) known as I-687. The general programme was open to all foreigners who could prove residency prior to 1 January 1982. Almost 1.7 million foreigners applied for legal status under I-687 and 97 per cent were approved. A congressional bid to extend the deadline for application was defeated. The IRCA also had a programme for Special Agricultural Workers (SAW), which targeted foreigners who could demonstrate evidence of seasonal employment for 90 days between 1 May 1985 and 1 May 1986. A total of 1.3 million foreigners applied, but widespread fraud contributed to a much lower approval rate than the I-687 programme. In all, approximately 2.7 million undocumented migrants underwent legalization under IRCA provisions (GAO, 2006; Kramer, 1999: 3; OECD, 2006).

The second major difference between the French and US legalization programmes involved the treatment of immediate family members of successful applicants. After prodding by the US Conference of Catholic Bishops, the US government promulgated a 'family fairness doctrine', empowering INS district commissioners to grant temporary, protected legal status to irregularly resident dependants of legalizing foreigners out of humanitarian considerations. This doctrine was further developed under the Immigration Act of 1990, which enabled the spouses and children of legalized foreigners to become permanent residents (Miller, 1989: 143–4).

The migration transition of Southern European states during the 1980s led to a wave of mass legalizations from which more than 3.2 million foreigners benefited. Since 1986, Italy has had six legalization programmes resulting in the regularization of about 1.4 million migrants (see Chapter 5). Between 1985 and 2005, Spain authorized 12 legalizations (Plewa, 2006: 247). However, many migrants reverted to irregular status due to expired visas and administrative backlogs.

In 2000, Switzerland enacted a legalization programme to regularize approximately 13,000 foreigners (mostly Sri Lankans) who had entered the country prior to 31 December 1992 (OECD, 2001: 251). Similarly, legalization advocacy grew in Germany where authorities had long viewed legalization as a policy likely to backfire and encourage further irregular migration. In 2007, the lower house of the German parliament adopted legislation granting the possibility of legalization to employed foreigners who had been denied refugee status but who could not be repatriated.

As a new generation of European countries embraced mass legalizations, France, once Europe's leading advocate of legalization, began to shun such policies. In 2006, then Minister of the Interior Nicolas Sarkozy introduced a procedure to process the irregularly resident parents of children in French schools on an individual basis. This measure, along with an increase in deportation orders and the cancelling of a provision granting undocumented migrants legal status after 10 years of residency, marked a tightening of French immigration policy. Nevertheless, France recorded a 55 per cent increase in the number of migrants legalized from 2005 to 2006 (*Le Monde*, 6 April 2007).

The debate concerning the wisdom of legalization as sound immigration policy also resonated across the Atlantic. In 2006 and 2007, several proposals emerged to meet the challenges posed by the growing undocumented population in the USA. Several of these proposals advocated 'earned legalization' which would permit undocumented migrants to benefit from a legal pathway to citizenship upon demonstration of English proficiency, uninterrupted employment, payment of taxes, and a clean criminal record. However, such legislation faced opposition across the political spectrum and was defeated by 2007. This postponed any chance of comprehensive immigration reform in the USA until after the 2008 general election.

The US Congressional stalemate over comprehensive immigration reform continued into the Obama era. Despite considerable Congressional and public support for the proposed legislation, dubbed the Dream Act, which would have enabled the legalization of certain categories of young migrants in irregular status, the hopes proved illusory. This prompted President Obama to issue an executive order in 2012 which granted a kind of semi-legalization for younger migrants in irregular status.

Assessments of legalization programmes have varied. Legalizations can be interpreted as evidence of governmental inability to prevent irregular migration or as evidence that sovereign states can adapt to, and cope with, international population movements in the era of globalization. Opponents of legalization typically contend that such policies undermine the rule of law. Proponents of legalization point out that legalized foreigners generally experience improvements in their overall socio-economic and employment prospects.

Temporary foreign-worker admission programmes

The post-Cold War era has witnessed the re-emergence of temporary foreign worker (TFW) programmes, which had been curtailed in Western Europe after 1973. This has occurred in states with a history of guest-worker programmes, such as Germany and the Netherlands, as well as in states with little or no previous guest-worker experience, such as Italy. Post-Cold War TFW programmes have differed in many respects from their predecessors in the 1960s and 1970s. For one thing, the number of admitted foreign workers has declined. Other major differences include the separate treatment of highly skilled and low-skilled foreign labour (Castles, 2006: 741).

Germany's resumption of TFW admissions was, in part, an effort to support the new democratic governments in Central and Eastern Europe and to secure their cooperation on stemming irregular migration and human trafficking. Since the mid-1970s, representatives of influential German employer groups such as hotels, restaurants and agriculture had supported the adoption of a seasonal worker programme similar to the Swiss programme of the 1960s and 1970s. However, the Swiss government had changed its policy by the 1980s, as former seasonal workers and their families had come to comprise the single largest component of resident foreigners in Switzerland. By 1999, only 10,000 seasonal workers were admitted to Switzerland, as compared with over 200,000 in 1964 (Miller, 1986: 71; OECD, 2001: 50). Like France, which admitted only 7,612 seasonal workers in 1999 as compared to a past average of 100,000 per year, the Swiss had largely phased out their seasonal foreign-worker policy (Tapinos, 1984: 47). Hence, the German advocacy of emulation of Swiss seasonal foreign-worker policy reflected a lapse in historical memory.

In Southern Europe, guest-worker programmes remained essentially marginal policies (Castles, 2006: 754; Reyneri, 2003). In Spain, many of the visas initially allotted for the recruitment of foreign workers were granted instead to irregular foreigners undergoing legalization (Lopez-Garcia, 2001: 114–15). To complicate matters, some employers preferred irregular foreigners to legal foreign workers in order to avoid social security payments (Lluch, 2002: 87–8). By 2002, most foreigners were required to return home in order to obtain a visa (Plewa and Miller,

2005: 73). Nevertheless, backdoor immigration continued, resulting in the 2005 *Normalisation* programme (see above). The recurring possibility of achieving long-term residence through mass legalization weakened the viability of TFW policies in Spain and other Mediterranean countries (Castles, 2006: 754; Plewa and Miller, 2005).

In the USA, temporary foreign-worker proposals have been championed as an effective way to legalize millions of irregularly employed foreigners. However, it is doubtful that a TFW programme would reduce the employment of irregular foreigners, as evidenced by the failure of such programmes in Europe. A Pew Hispanic poll revealed that, while showing strong support for a proposed guest-worker programme, more than half of the Mexicans surveyed expressed a desire to remain permanently in the USA and most would likely stay upon the expiration of their proposed six-year renewable visa (Martin, 2005: 47).

The re-emergence of TFW programmes in the last decade has led to a dualistic approach to migration. Many states seek to attract and encourage settlement of highly skilled workers into their societies while restricting the length of stay of unskilled labourers. States have also placed greater emphasis on attracting international students and researchers with ties to the host country since such individuals constitute a pool of readily available (and desirable) migrants (OECD, 2006: 80–1).

Refugees and asylum

The number of refugees worldwide has risen in the early twenty-first century following a decline since the mid-1990s. Asylum seeker numbers are still lower than in the 1990s, but asylum has remained a major political issue in many countries. Sensationalist journalists and right-wing politicians map out dire consequences such as rocketing crime rates, fundamentalist terrorism and overstretched welfare systems. Calls for strict border control, the detention of asylum seekers and the deportation of irregular foreigners abound. The public appeal of such polemics is obvious: right-wing electoral successes in many countries can be linked to fears of mass influxes from the South and East. Yet the reality is that 80 per cent of refugees remain in poor countries in Africa, Asia, the Middle East and Latin America (UNHCR, 2012d: 1).

Defining forced migration

Refugees and asylum seekers are *forced migrants* who flee their homes to escape persecution or conflict, rather than *voluntary migrants* who move for economic or other reasons. Although this distinction is commonplace, we have pointed out in Chapter 2 that 'voluntary' migrants also face constraints and that many 'forced' migrants do have a certain level of agency, for instance in the form of resources which allow them to leave in the first place. Popular usage tends to refer to all kinds of forced migrants as 'refugees', but most forced migrants flee for reasons not recognized by international refugee law, often remaining within their country of origin. Here we are mainly concerned with those who cross international borders, but all forms of forced migration are connected in both causes and effects (for more detail see Castles and Van Hear, 2005) At the end of 2011, the official total of people displaced by violence or persecution worldwide was 42.5 million. (UNHCR, 2012d: 1).

A *refugee* (or Convention refugee) is defined by the 1951 *United Nations Convention Relating to the Status of Refugees* as a person residing outside his or her country of nationality, who is unable or unwilling to return because of a 'well-founded fear of persecution on account of race, religion, nationality, membership in a particular social group, or political opinion' (UNHCR, 2011a: 3). By 2010, 148 of the UN's 193 member states had signed the Convention or its 1967 Protocol (Li and Batalova, 2011). Signatories undertake to protect refugees and to respect the principle of *non-refoulement* (not to return them to a country where they may be persecuted). Such commitments are not always carried out in practice.

Resettlement refers to refugees permitted to move from countries of first asylum to countries able to offer long-term protection and assistance. Such persons are usually selected by United Nations High Commissioner for Refugees (UNHCR) in cooperation with the governments of resettlement countries. Until recently, the main resettlement countries have been the USA, Canada, Australia, New Zealand and Scandinavian countries. In the last few years, several new countries have been added, albeit with rather small programmes (see below).

Asylum seekers are people who have crossed an international border in search of protection, but whose claims for refugee status have not yet been decided. Determination procedures may take many years. Host countries offer varying types of protection – typically full refugee status for those who fulfil the 1951 Convention criteria, temporary protection for war refugees, and humanitarian protection for people not considered refugees, but who might be endangered by return. In some European countries up to 90 per cent of asylum applications are rejected, yet many rejected applicants stay on. Without any clear legal status, they lead a marginalized existence.

Internally displaced persons (IDPs) 'have been forced to flee their homes because their lives were in danger, but unlike refugees they have not crossed an international border. Many IDPs remain exposed to violence, hunger and disease during their displacement and are subject to a multitude of human rights violations' (IDMC, 2007: 9).There are no international legal instruments or institutions specifically designed to protect IDPs, although they are covered by general human rights conventions. As it became harder for people displaced by violence to cross frontiers, IDP numbers grew worldwide to a total of 27.5 million people in 2010. IDPs are to be found in over 50 countries (UNHCR, 2011b).

Development displacees are people compelled to move by large-scale development projects, such as dams, airports, roads and urban housing. The World Bank – which funds many development projects – estimates that development projects displace 10–15 million people per year. Many development displacees experience permanent impoverishment and social marginalization (Cernea and McDowell, 2000).

Environmental and disaster displacees are people displaced by environmental change (desertification, deforestation, land degradation, rising sea levels), natural disasters (floods, volcanoes, landslides, earthquakes), and man-made disasters (industrial accidents, radioactivity). This category is controversial: while some environmentalists claim that there are already tens of millions of 'environmental refugees' and that, with global warming, hundreds of millions may eventually be at risk of displacement (Myers, 1997; Myers and Kent, 1995), migration experts have questioned such alarmist views, noting that, while environmental factors may play a certain part in forced migration, displacement is always closely linked to other factors, such as social and ethnic conflict, weak states, poverty, inequality and abuse of human rights (McAdam, 2010; Piguet and de Guchteneire, 2011). This topic is discussed in detail in Chapter 9.

Finally, the concept of *persons of concern* to the UNHCR includes Convention refugees plus all persons who receive protection or assistance from UNHCR: asylum seekers, some IDPs, returnees and stateless persons.

Global forced migration trends

The global *refugee* population grew from 2.4 million in 1975 to reach a peak after the end of the Cold War with 18.2 million refugees in 1993 (UNHCR, 1995). By 2005, the global refugee population covered by the UNHCR mandate, which does not include Palestinian refugees, had declined to 8.7 million – the lowest figure since 1980. But the trend then reversed in 2006 with refugee numbers jumping to 9.9 million, mainly due to the flight of 1.2 million Iraqis to Jordan and Syria (UNHCR, 2007a: 5). Refugee numbers continued to increase, reaching 10.4 million by the end of 2011. In 2011, 800,000 people were newly displaced across international borders – the highest figure in more than a decade. (UNHCR, 2012d:1). Figures for 2012 and 2013 may be even higher, due to the war in Syria.

The number of *persons of concern to the UNHCR* peaked at 27.4 million in 1995, but had decreased to 17.5 million by 2003. It appeared that global violence was declining, but then the number of persons of concern rose to a new record of 33 million in 2006. Most of the increase was due to UNHCR's enhanced responsibility for IDPs and stateless persons, but some 3 million persons were newly displaced (UNHCR, 2007a). By 2011 the figure had reached 35.4 million (UNHCR, 2012d:7). Table 10.1 shows which countries produced and which countries hosted the most refugees in 2011.

Table 10.1   *The world's main refugee-origin and refugee-receiving countries,*
end 2011

Top-ten refugee-origin countries		*Top-ten refugee-receiving countries*	
Afghanistan	2,644,000	Pakistan	1,702,000
Iraq	1,428,000	Iran	886,000
Somalia	1,077,000	Syria	755,000
Sudan	500,000	Germany	572,000
Dem. Rep. of Congo	492,000	Kenya	567,000
Myanmar (Burma)	414,000	Jordan	451,000
Colombia	396,000	Chad	367,000
Vietnam	338,000	China	301,000
Eritrea	252,000	Ethiopia	289,000
China	205,000	USA	265,000

Source: UNHCR (2012d: 15).

Refugees come from areas hit by war, violence and chaos. It is noteworthy that the two top refugee producers, Afghanistan and Iraq, were countries that had experienced US-led invasions as part of the 'war on terror'. Many of the main refugee-receiving countries are very poor: refugee flows are generated in regions of poverty and conflict, and mostly remain within these regions.

However, UNHCR does not cover most Palestinian refugees, who still constitute the world's largest exile population. Palestinian refugees come under the mandate of the United Nations Relief and Works Agency for Palestine (UNRWA). They numbered 4.8 million at the end of 2011 (UNHCR, 2012d: 1).

Yet even though four out of five refugees (UNHCR, 2012d: 1) remain in developing countries, Western Europe, North America and Australia have been gripped by panic about asylum since the 1980s. Annual asylum applications in these areas rose from 90,000 in 1983 to 323,000 in 1988, and then surged again with the end of the Cold War to 829,000 in 1992 (UNHCR, 1995: 253). Applications fell sharply after this, mainly due to changes in refugee law in Germany, Sweden and the Netherlands. Asylum applications began to increase again from 1997. For OECD countries as a whole, asylum seeker inflows increased to 596,000 in 2001 and then declined to 286,000 by 2006, before increasing again to 429,000 in 2011 (OECD, 2012: table A3). At the end of 2011, UNHCR recorded 876,000 asylum seekers worldwide (UNHCR, 2012d).

Forced migration and global politics

Forced migration has become a major factor in global politics (Loescher, 2001). This is reflected in the changing nature of the *international refugee regime*. This term designates a set of legal norms based on humanitarian

and human rights law, as well as a number of institutions designed to protect and assist refugees. The core of the regime is the 1951 Convention, and
the key institution is the United Nations High Commissioner for Refugees
(UNHCR), but many other organizations also play a part: intergovernmental agencies like the International Committee of the Red Cross (ICRC),
the World Food Programme (WFP) and the United Nations Children's
Fund (UNICEF); as well as hundreds of non-governmental organizations
(NGOs) such as OXFAM, CARE International, *Médecins sans Frontières*
(MSF) and the International Rescue Committee (IRC).

The refugee regime was shaped by two major international conflicts:
World War II and the Cold War (Keely, 2001). Many of the 40 million
displaced persons who left Europe in 1945 were resettled in Australia,
Canada and other countries, where they made an important contribution to
post-war economic growth. During the Cold War, offering asylum to those
who 'voted with their feet' against communism was a powerful source
of propaganda for the West. Since the 'non-departure regime' of the Iron
Curtain kept the overall asylum levels low, the West could afford to offer
a warm welcome to those few who made it. Asylum levels remained relatively low with occasional spikes following events like the 1956 Hungarian
Revolution and the 1968 Prague Spring.

Different refugee situations were developing elsewhere. The colonial
legacy led to weak undemocratic states, underdeveloped economies and
widespread poverty in Asia, Africa and Latin America. Western countries
sought to maintain their dominance by influencing new elites, while the
Soviet Bloc encouraged revolutionary movements. The escalation of struggles against white colonial or settler regimes in Africa from the 1960s,
resistance against US-supported military regimes in Latin America in the
1970s and 1980s, and long-drawn-out political and ethnic struggles in the
Middle East and Asia – all led to vast flows of refugees (Zolberg *et al.*, 1989).
From the 1980s profound social transformations and increased inequalities,
linked to economic globalization as well as the end of the Cold War, fuelled
conflicts, which led to renewed refugee flows (see also Chapter 3).

Western states and international agencies responded by claiming that
such situations were qualitatively different from the individual persecution
for which the 1951 Convention was designed (Chimni, 1998). The solution
of permanent resettlement in developed countries was not seen as appropriate, except for Indo-Chinese and Cuban refugees who fitted the Cold War
mould. In 1969, the Organization of African Unity (OAU, now the African Union) introduced its own Refugee Convention, which broadened the
refugee definition to include people forced to flee their countries by war,
human rights violations or generalized violence. A similar definition for
Latin America was contained in the Cartagena Declaration of 1984. Today,
UNHCR follows this broader approach and has taken on new functions as
a humanitarian relief organization. It helps run camps and provides food
and medical care around the world (Loescher, 2001). This expanding role
has made it one of the most powerful UN agencies.

By the 1980s, asylum seekers were coming directly to Europe and North America from conflict zones in Latin America, Africa and Asia. Numbers increased sharply with the collapse of the Soviet Bloc. The most dramatic flows were from Albania to Italy in 1991 and again in 1997, and from former Yugoslavia during the wars in Croatia, Bosnia and Kosovo. Many of the 1.3 million asylum applicants arriving in Germany, France and Italy between 1991 and 1995 were members of ethnic minorities (such as Roma) from Romania, Bulgaria and elsewhere in Eastern Europe. The situation was further complicated by ethnic minorities returning to ancestral homelands (such as the German *Aussiedler*) as well as undocumented workers from Poland, Ukraine and other post-Soviet states (see Chapter 5).

The early 1990s were a period of politicization of asylum. Extreme-right mobilization, arson attacks on asylum-seeker hostels and assaults on foreigners were threatening public order. Rather than countering racist attacks, European states reacted with a series of restrictions, which seemed to herald the construction of a 'Fortress Europe' (Keely, 2001; UNHCR, 2000):

- Changes in national legislation to restrict access to refugee status.
- Temporary protection regimes instead of permanent refugee status for people fleeing the wars in former Yugoslavia.
- 'Non-arrival policies' to prevent people without adequate documentation from entering Western Europe. Citizens of an increasing number of states were required to obtain visas before departure. 'Carrier sanctions' compelled airline personnel to check documents before allowing people to embark.
- Diversion policies: by declaring countries bordering the EU to be 'safe third countries'. Western European countries could return asylum seekers to these states, if they had used them as transit routes.
- Restrictive interpretations of the 1951 UN Refugee Convention, for instance, excluding persecution through 'non-state actors' (such as the Taliban in Afghanistan).
- European cooperation on asylum and immigration rules, through the Schengen Convention, the Dublin Convention of 1990 and its replacement, the Dublin Regulation of 2003, and EU agreements.

The US experience was similar: refugee admissions began to decline in the late 1990s as traditional flows from communist countries tailed off with the end of the Cold War. Then the events of 11 September 2001 precipitated a sharp fall in admissions. Such restrictive measures in receiving countries contributed to the decrease in refugee flows and asylum applications. However, a recent quantitative study found that a decline in violence and terrorism explained most of the reduction in asylum seeking in developed countries, and that tougher policies accounted for only about a third of the decline in applications since 2001 (Hatton, 2009).

The refugee regime of Western countries has been fundamentally transformed over the last 30 years. It has changed from a system designed to welcome Cold War refugees from the East and to resettle them as permanent exiles in new homes, to an exclusionary regime, designed to keep out asylum seekers from the South.

Refugees and asylum seekers in Western countries

Relatively few countries in the world allow resettlement from countries of first asylum, the main ones that have in the past have been the USA, Canada, Australia, New Zealand and Scandinavian countries. Since 2007, eleven new resettlement programmes have been added, in Bulgaria, the Czech Republic, France, Germany, Hungary, Japan, Paraguay, Portugal, Spain, Romania, and Uruguay. However, the numbers admitted to these countries are quite small (Nicholson, 2012). Resettlement countries also experience entries of asylum seekers, who apply for refugee status. Many other countries around the world also have significant entries of asylum seekers.

Between 1975 and 2000, the USA provided permanent resettlement to over 2 million refugees, including some 1.3 million people from Indochina. The USA accepted more people for resettlement during this period than the rest of the world combined (UNHCR, 2000). Inflows from Central America and the Caribbean were also important. The open door policy towards Cubans, which had been in place since 1959, was restricted in the 1980s, and interdiction at sea commenced in the 1990s. Many Haitians attempting to come to the USA during the 1980s and 1990s were prevented from doing so.

After the terrorist attacks of 11 September 2001, the USA temporarily halted its refugee resettlement programme. Stronger detention powers were introduced for non-citizens suspected of terrorist activities. In 2006, the US government 'held 2,000 to 3,000 asylum seekers in detention on any given day, often in remote areas with limited access to legal counsel' (USCRI, 2007). Refugee admission fell from an average of 76,000 a year in the 1997–2001 period, to fewer than 29,000 in both 2002 and 2003. However, from 2008 onwards, the annual ceiling for refugee admissions (set by the US President) has been 80,000. In 2010, 73,000 refugees came to the USA through the resettlement programme – two-thirds of them from Iraq, Burma and Bhutan. A further 21,000 persons already in the USA were granted asylum in 2010 (UNHCR, 2011d).

Canada, like the USA, accepted large numbers of people from Indochina, some 200,000 between 1975 and 1995. By 1998, resettlement admissions had fallen to under 9,000 (UNHCR, 2000). In 2010, Canada resettled 12,000 refugees in collaboration with UNHCR (UNHCR, 2011d). In addition, in 2010, 22,500 new asylum applications were received (Li and Batalova, 2011) and 51,000 asylum applications were pending at the end of the year (UNHCR, 2011d).

Australia's Humanitarian Programme has admitted between 12,000 and 16,000 persons per year since the early 1990s. Admissions under the programme totalled 13,750 in 2009–10, and the planning figure for 2010–11 was the same. About half the entrants under the Humanitarian Programme are refugees resettled with UNHCR) (Phillips *et al.*, 2010). This positive approach to resettlement contrasts with a very hostile attitude towards asylum seekers. Those who arrive from countries like Iraq, Afghanistan, Iran and Sri Lanka on boats from Indonesia are detained for long periods in camps, and are labelled as 'queue-jumpers' and 'security threats' by politicians and the media. The Liberal-National Coalition government of 1996–2007 introduced laws 'excising' Australia's northern islands from its 'migration zone'. In the 'Pacific solution', asylum seekers arriving by boat from Indonesia were to be sent to small Pacific islands like Nauru. Other asylum seekers (including children) were kept in grim detention centres in remote areas, often for several years.

The Labor Government elected in 2007 closed the offshore camps but maintained mandatory detention. Since then, the government and the Liberal-National Opposition have outdone each other in tough language against boat arrivals. In 2012, following an increase in boat arrivals and amid heated political debates, the government re-introduced offshore detention on the Pacific islands of Nauru and Papua New Guinea. The public polemic against the fairly small number of asylum applicants (8,250 in 2010) (UNHCR, 2011g) is a curious contrast to Australia's large and fast-growing immigration programme (for more detail see Castles *et al.*, 2013; Crock and Saul, 2002; Phillips and Spinks, 2011)

Until recently, Europe took little part in refugee resettlement – the only significant exceptions being Sweden and Norway. However, direct asylum-seeker entries are a major issue. In the EU, the top five countries of origin for asylum seekers during the 1990–2000 period were the Federal Republic of Yugoslavia (836,000 persons), Romania (400,000), Turkey (356,000), Iraq (211,000) and Afghanistan (155,000). The two peaks of asylum seekers from Yugoslavia coincided with the wars in Croatia and Bosnia in 1991–3 and in Kosovo in 1998–9 (Castles *et al.*, 2003: 14). Asylum applications declined in the latter part of the 1990s before increasing again. The UK had had relatively few asylum applicants earlier, but by 1999 new applications were running at over 90,000 a year, with a peak of 103,000 in 2002. The British government put forward a 'new vision' for refugee protection. A key idea was to set up protection areas for refugees in their region of origin, so that asylum seekers could be safely removed from the EU. Another was to set up 'transit processing centres' outside EU borders: asylum seekers who arrived in the EU would be sent to camps in countries like Libya and Ukraine for determination of status (Castles and Van Hear, 2005: 118–19). These proposals raised serious human rights concerns and were not implemented, but they helped create a climate in which asylum seekers were seen as a security threat, justifying ever-tighter legal procedures, and increased use of detention and deportation.

Berlusconi's Italian government actually did start returning boats to Libya, where asylum seekers were detained and denied access to legal process. In 2012, the European Court of Human Rights ruled that Italy must pay compensation of €15,000 (US$18,700 at the time) to 24 Somali and Eritrean asylum seekers who were on three boats carrying 200 people pushed back to Libya in 2009 (Needham, 2012). Britain tightened up entry procedures and legal processes, and denied welfare to entrants who did not immediately apply for asylum upon arriving, making many of them homeless and destitute. Other EU countries followed suit.

As a result of the combination of policy restrictions and the decreased number of violent conflicts in origin countries, new asylum applications in the EU15 fell sharply from 393,000 in 2002 to 180,000 in 2006. However, by 2006, the effects of the invasion of Iraq were becoming obvious: asylum applications by Iraqis rose 80 per cent to 19,375 persons – the largest asylum inflow to the EU (UNHCR, 2007b). Asylum applications continued to rise. By 2010, the EU25 (that is including the Accession States of 2004, but not Bulgaria and Romania) plus Norway and Switzerland received 254,180 asylum applications. France (47,800) and Germany (41,300) had the most, followed by Sweden (31,800), UK (22,100) and Belgium (19,900) (OECD, 2011a: table A.1.3.).

A key issue for Europe in 2011–12 was the effects of the 'Arab Spring'. The flight of people from oppressive regimes was portrayed by some politicians and media as an invasion. But in fact numbers remained fairly small: the main arrival points, Italy and Malta, together received only about 4 per cent of all people fleeing Libya (27,465 persons out of 790,000) (see Box 1.1).

Protracted refugee situations

Clearly, flight from violence remains a major international challenge. Efforts for prevention of conflicts and for protection and assistance of forced migrants are far from adequate, since conflict and impoverishment often go together. This can make it difficult to distinguish clearly between economic and forced migration, so that UNHCR and other agencies seek to develop new approaches for 'mixed flows' (Crisp, 2008). While rich countries become less and less willing to admit asylum seekers, many are seeking refuge in new destinations like South Africa, Kenya, Egypt, Malaysia and Thailand. In 2009, South Africa received over 220,000 asylum seekers, four times as many as the USA. In 2010, 25,600 asylum claims were lodged in UNHCR's Malaysia office and 19,300 in the Kenya office (UNHCR, 2011d).

The great majority of refugees remain in poor countries, which may lack the capacity to protect them and the resources to provide adequate material assistance. Refugees may spend many years living on subsistence rations in isolated camps or communities with few resources. UNHCR applies the term 'protracted refugee situation' to refugee populations of 25,000 persons or more in exile for five or more years, while the US Committee on Refugees and Immigrants speaks of 'warehoused refugees' (USCR, 2004). Such refugees have few opportunities for work and education, and no prospect of return home to countries still torn by war or ethnic violence. The hopelessness of long years in exile can take a heavy toll: depression, other mental illnesses and interpersonal violence are frequent consequences.

UNHCR estimated that some 7.1 million refugees were in a protracted situation by the end of 2011. Protracted refugee situations existed in 26 countries (UNHCR, 2012d: 12) Resettlement to a 'third country' is the only hope for many, but the chances are slim. During 2011, a total of 79,800 refugees were admitted by 22 resettlement countries, including the USA (51,500), Canada (12,900), Australia (9,200), Sweden (1,900) and Norway (1,300). This figure represents a decline of nearly 20,000 from the previous year (UNHCR, 2012d: 19). The decline was mainly due to a sharp fall in refugees admitted to the USA, which nonetheless remains the world's leading resettlement country (UNHCR, 2012d: 19). At the current rate, it would take over 80 years to resettle all the refugees in protracted exile – assuming that no new refugees arrived in that time! Politicians often talk about a 'queue' for resettlement, and accuse those who seek asylum by going directly to potential host countries of being 'queue-jumpers'. But a queue that takes up to 80 years is not a realistic life prospect. The inability of the international community to provide realistic solutions to protracted refugee situations is the root cause of spontaneous asylum-seeker movements.

Regional integration

States have sought to regulate international migration either through bilateral treaties or through regional agreements. The latter option could only prove to be a viable solution provided that member states of regional organizations committed themselves to the long-term goal of evening out national economies (Castles, 2006: 749) A question remains as to whether regional integration in the post-Cold War period in Europe and North America helped or hindered the quest for migration control. Transatlantic comparisons need to be grounded in history, as the evolution of the two regional integration processes proved quite dissimilar. The European project is much older and more far-reaching than the North American Free Trade Agreement (NAFTA), and there is no inevitable logic that NAFTA will follow the same path as the European Union.

The European Union's governance structure

Stretching back to the European Coal and Steel Community (ECSC) of the early 1950s and the European Community (EC) up to 1992, the EU and its predecessors have comprised a federalist project with an explicit commitment to eventually supersede member-state sovereignty through the creation of European institutions and governance. The project has always been security-driven, as economic and, eventually, political integration was above all a strategy to prevent the recurrence of war between member states.

The Single European Act (SEA) of 1986 aimed to achieve a genuine common market and paved the way for signature of the 1992 Treaty on European Union (TEU, also known as the Maastricht Treaty), which resulted in the reinforcement and expansion of federalist European institutions within the then 15-member-state area. The TEU created three pillars related to the single market, Justice and Home Affairs, and the Common Foreign and Security Policy respectively. Governance procedures in the pillars varied, with the first pillar being the most supranational – that is, controlled by decisions at the EU level rather than by member states. The TEU left immigration and asylum matters in the third pillar, that is, in the hands of the member states.

Aiming to secure an 'area of freedom, security, and justice', the 1997 Treaty of Amsterdam integrated into the EU body of law all decisions made by the member states of the Schengen Agreement (see below). Issues concerning 'visas, asylum, immigration, and other policies related to free movement of persons' were brought under the first pillar of the Union. This common immigration and refugee policy introduced a progressive transfer of decisions pertaining to free movement (external border control, asylum, immigration, and rights of third-country nationals) from intergovernmental to supranational authority. The Lisbon Treaty which was signed in 2007 and ratified in 2009 marked the complete inclusion of migration and asylum within the framework of European treaties. Hence, migration and asylum were to become normal issues in EU governance.

Freedom of movement within the European Communities and the European Union

Migration has always figured in the history of European integration. The 1957 Treaty of Rome envisaged the creation of a common market between the six signatory states. Under Article 48, workers from member states were to enjoy freedom of movement if they found employment in another member state. In the 1950s, Italy pushed for regional integration in order to foster employment opportunities for its many unemployed citizens (Romero, 1993). By 1968, when Article 48 came into effect, Italy's unemployment problem had eased, due in part to economic development spurred by the infusion of EC structural funds. Relatively little intra-EC labour migration occurred (Werner, 1973). It was firmly established that the freedom of labour movement applied only to citizens of EC member states, not to third-country nationals from outside the EC.

The planned accession of Spain and Portugal in the mid-1980s sparked an important debate over the likely effects on labour mobility. Some feared the rest of the enlarged EC would be flooded with Portuguese and Spanish workers. However, at the end of a seven-year transition period, the predicted massive inflow did not occur. Instead, after their accession to the EC in 1986, Spain and Portugal became significant lands of immigration in their own right. Meanwhile, intra-European labour mobility remained behind expectations, partly because intra-European capital mobility substituted for labour mobility (Koslowski, 2000: 117; see also Chapter 5).

France, Germany, Belgium, Luxembourg, and the Netherlands signed the Schengen Agreement in 1985. They committed themselves to hasten the creation of a border-free Europe in which EC citizens could circulate freely internally with harmonized external frontier controls. The SEA (Single European Act) of 1986 defined the single market as 'an area without internal borders in which the free movement of goods, persons, services, and capital is ensured within the provision of this treaty' (Geddes, 2000: 70). Many Europeans, including the governments of several EU member states, balked at the idea of eliminating internal boundaries, fearing that it would lead to further irregular migration and loss of governmental control over entry and stay foreigners.

In March 1995, the Schengen Agreement finally came into force for those signatory states which had established the necessary procedures: Germany, Belgium, Spain, France, Portugal, Luxembourg, and the Netherlands. Border elimination was, however, compensated for by the creation of the Schengen Information System (SIS), a network of information designed to enhance cooperation between states on judicial matters such as transnational crime and terrorism. Effectively, the Agreement created a new class of 'Schengen citizens' to be added to the existing categories of EU citizens and 'third-country' (i.e. non-EU) citizens. Austria joined the Schengen Agreement in 1995, followed by Denmark, Finland, and Sweden in 1996 (Denmark was able to opt out of certain sections). At first, the UK and Ireland refused to join the Schengen Agreement, insisting on their own stricter border controls of people coming from the continent, but eventually agreed to take part in some aspects of the Agreement.

Labour-mobility restrictions were placed on the workers of Central and Eastern European states (the 'A8'), which joined the EU in 2004, by most of the 15 states already comprising the EU, with the exception of the UK, Ireland and Sweden. By 2011, 669,000 A8 citizens were working in the UK, despite a temporary drop in numbers during the GEC (Migration Observatory, 2012). The magnitude of the migration surprised the British government but also reflected a legalization effect as a substantial number of those who were registered had been living in the UK prior to 2004 (Boswell and Geddes, 2011: 181–7).

As part of the agreed transition period for other EU countries, Germany limited free movement and access to its labour market for another two years following the 2009 deadline. In July 2007, the Merkel government announced its decision to lift the restrictions, most likely as a result of the

February 2006 report on transitional procedures released by the European Commission. The document stressed the positive effects of free movement on the economies and labour markets of the countries that had already relaxed labour movement restrictions. Spain and Portugal also removed restrictions.

Comparable fears surrounded Turkey's candidacy bid. Following a favourable vote of the European Parliament, EU leaders decided to initiate accession talks with Turkey in October 2005 despite the reservations held by several governments. Unlike previous enlargements in which periods of adjustment were established, permanent mechanisms were considered to control the additional migration of Turkish workers expected after accession to the EU.

European citizenship

Under the Treaty on European Union (TEU), resident foreigners from other EU states are enfranchised to vote in their country of residence (in local and European, but not national, elections), an important aspect of EU citizenship. Nevertheless, provisions protect EU countries in which the proportion of foreign nationals is greater than 20 per cent, such as Luxembourg. By 2006, 13.2 million residents (2.7 per cent of the total population) of the 27 EU member states were from other EU states (Münz *et al.*, 2007: 2–4).

More problematic has been the status of third-country nationals, who do not benefit from freedom of movement. Instead, member states largely retain their prerogatives over entry, stay, and removal of non-EU citizens. Nevertheless, under the Schengen Agreement of 1985 (which came into force in 1995), third-country nationals are permitted short-term stays of up to three months in the Schengen area. A 2003 directive defined 'long-term' residents to be resident foreigners who had resided in a signatory state for five years or more. And it stipulated that such resident foreigners could live in another member state for more than three months if employed or self-employed but also for purposes of education and vocational training (Boswell and Geddes, 2011: 197).

The overall effect of European regional integration in recent years may have made the European quest for control more credible, as EU states participating in the Schengen group have been able to externalize control functions through the creation of a buffer zone in Central and Eastern Europe and a common border in Southern Europe. The EU remains open to legal migration and porous to irregular migration.

The North American Free Trade Area (NAFTA)

The origins of NAFTA had much to do with the sudden progression of regional integration in Europe in the mid-1980s. Rightly or wrongly, many countries that traded with the EC feared that Schengen and the

Single European Act (SEA) would lead to a Fortress Europa, a zone less accessible to imports from outside the EC. This perception helped hasten the signature of a US–Canadian free-trade agreement in 1988. Later, Mexican President Carlos Salinas approached the US administration with the idea of enlarging the US–Canadian free-trade pact to include Mexico. The NAFTA treaty came into effect on 1 January 1994. Unlike the EU, NAFTA only created a free-trade area. Nevertheless, this much less ambitious project met with considerable political opposition in the USA and in Mexico, where it helped spark the Zapatista revolt.

Paradoxically, concerns over international migration figured centrally in NAFTA's genesis but such concerns were barely mentioned in the treaty text. US and Mexican views on irregular migration were sharply opposed. To Mexicans, migration to the USA was driven by US labour-market demands. For the USA, much migration was in contravention of its laws and was spurred by the failure of the Mexican economy to generate sufficient growth and jobs to employ its growing population. Restrictions on mobility remained largely unaltered by the treaty as only certain categories of professionals could move freely across borders.

During the run-up to NAFTA, both President Clinton and President Salinas hailed the pact as a way to reduce irregular migration. Salinas warned that the US would either get Mexican tomatoes or Mexican migrants to pick them in the US (Delano, 2011: 136–40). Such presidential optimism belied the key research finding of several studies, namely that trade liberalization would diminish irregular migration only over the long term, and that even successful liberalization would initially create dislocations in the economy, leading to an at least temporary upsurge in emigration. Philip L. Martin later refined this finding into his theory of a 'migration hump' (Martin, 1993, see also Chapter 2). Irregular migration from Mexico to the USA in fact grew significantly in the wake of NAFTA. Liberalization of the Mexican economy in the 1990s hit the poor and middle-class very hard. Farmers and their families in the *Ejido* sector (in which collective ownership and state subsidies had formerly acted as barriers to neoliberal reforms for one-third of Mexico's population), were adversely affected and many moved northwards, just as Martin had predicted. Overall, NAFTA has led to significantly expanded trade between the signatory states and greater socio-economic interdependence.

The election of Vincente Fox as President of Mexico in 2000 ushered in a new era. President Fox and his newly elected American counterpart, President Bush, sought a fresh departure in US–Mexico relations, specifically on bilateral migration issues. President Fox and his foreign minister repeatedly referred to the European experience and called for freedom of migration within NAFTA. However, the two regional integration projects differed markedly due to the US dominance of the North American economy and the huge economic gap between Mexico and the USA (OECD, 1998: 7).

Curiously, there was little public discussion of what might be the most important European referent to NAFTA, namely possible North American emulation of structural and regional funds, which have had the effect of levelling the socio-economic playing field within the European space. In European regional integration history, an aspect of the commitment to a federalist project involved the use of European funds to aid less developed areas. Italy and later Ireland, Spain and Portugal were all major beneficiaries. The contrast with the North American situation was stark (Miller and Gabriel, 2008).

Regional integration in North America and Europe has had important implications for governmental control strategies. The historical and institutional contexts of the two projects vary greatly but they comprise a salient dimension of overall strategies to reduce irregular and otherwise unwanted migration. The results of NAFTA were a significant increase in irregular migration from Mexico to the USA, which only tapered off with the recession of 2007/2008.

The 'migration industry'

The migration-facilitating role of migrant networks is an important factor in understanding why migration often becomes partly self-perpetuating and can be so difficult to control (see Chapter 2). Another, related, factor is the emergence of the so-called 'migration industry'(see also Boswell and Geddes, 2011: 39–41; 43–50). This term embraces a broad spectrum of people and institutions who have an interest in migration or earn their livelihood by organizing migratory movements. Such people include travel agents, labour recruiters, brokers, interpreters, housing agents, immigration lawyers, human smugglers (like the 'coyotes' who guide Mexican workers across the Rio Grande, or the Moroccan fishermen who ferry Moroccans and other Africans to Spain), and even counterfeiters who falsify official identification documents and passports. Banking institutions have become part of the 'migration industry' as well, as many banks have established special transfer facilities for remittances.

Migration agents also include members of migrant communities such as shopkeepers, priests, teachers and other community leaders who help their compatriots on a voluntary or part-time basis. Others are criminals, out to exploit migrants or asylum seekers by charging them extortionate fees for often non-existent jobs. Yet others are police officers or bureaucrats who seek to make money on the side by showing people loopholes in regulations or issuing false documents. One major impediment to efforts aimed at curbing irregular migration has been that smugglers are often viewed as 'social bandits,' if not heroes, rather than as criminals (Kyle and Liang, 2001: 1).

The development of the 'migration industry' is an inevitable aspect and an extension of the social networks and transnational linkages which are part of the migratory process (see Chapter 2). Once a migratory movement is established, a variety of needs for special services arise. Even governments which initiate labour recruitment rarely provide all of the necessary services. While some countries use bilateral treaties, others, as exemplified by the UK, have tended to utilize 'third-party entities' or private operators to contract guest-workers (GAO, 2006: 21–3). East Asian states (Japan, Taiwan and South Korea) have made considerable use of brokers for migrant labour and (in South Korea) for marriage migration (Surak, 2013). In spontaneous or irregular movements, the need for agents and brokers is all the greater. There is a broad range of entrepreneurial opportunities, which are seized upon by both migrants and non-migrants alike. The role of the agents and brokers is vital: without them, few migrants would have the information or contacts needed for successful migration.

In time, the 'migration industry' can become the primary motive force in a migratory movement. In such situations, governmental policies aimed at curtailing migration run counter to the economic interests of the migration agents, who have an interest in and foster the continuation of the migration. This can make migration notoriously difficult to control. One observer has characterized migration agents as 'a vast unseen international network underpinning a global labour market; a horde of termites ... boring through the national fortifications against migration and changing whole societies' (Harris, 1996: 135).

Human smuggling and trafficking

Increased border controls and the tightening of immigration policies increase the reliance of migrants on smuggling. If dependence on smugglers and other migration facilitators becomes very high, this can evolve in exploitative forms of migration which are also known as trafficking. An increasingly salient feature of the migration industry has been the rise of organizations devoted to the smuggling and trafficking of migrants. It is important to distinguish between people-trafficking and people-smuggling. Formal definitions are embodied in two international treaties, known as the 'Vienna Protocols', adopted by the UN General Assembly in 2000. According to Ann Gallagher (2002) of the UN High Commission for Human Rights: 'Smuggled migrants are moved illegally for profit; they are partners, however unequal, in a commercial transaction ... [b]y contrast, the movement of trafficked persons is based on deception and coercion whose purpose is exploitation'.

These definitions are useful, although the line between such categories is often blurred. This particularly applies to trafficking, as research indicates that trafficked migrants are not necessarily coerced and have a certain level of agency. Furthermore, non-trafficked migrants can also be exploited: it is impossible to accurately measure the number of people affected by trafficking and smuggling. Clients of smuggling gangs include not only economic migrants, but also refugees unable to make an asylum claim because restrictive border rules prevent them from entering countries of potential asylum (Gibney, 2000). İçduygu's study highlights the scope of the smuggling industry in Turkey. As a gateway to the European Union, an average 200,000 irregular migrants passed through Turkey every year between 1997 and 2003 at an estimated cost of $1,600 per person paid to smugglers, amounting to a $300 million annual business. A quarter of migrants were known to have used the services of smugglers to enter Turkey and to cross over to Europe. About 400,000 migrants were apprehended while crossing Turkey between 1997 and 2003 (İçduygu, 2004: 302).

A US government report revealed that the percentage of foreigners smuggled increased from 9 per cent of all border patrol apprehensions in 1997 to 14 per cent in 1999. Estimates of the numbers involved in trafficking range from 4 to 27 million persons. One study estimated that as many as 50,000 women were trafficked to the USA each year (Richards, 1999: 3). Human trafficking may generate profits of US$ 5 to 10 billion per year (Martin and Miller, 2000b: 969). An ILO report estimated the number of victims of any form of forced labour to be 12.3 million at any given time (USDS, 2007: 8). The wide variation in such estimates indicates the unreliability of the data.

Women and young girls are particularly vulnerable to trafficking and constitute 80 per cent of all victims (minors make up approximately 50 per cent of all victims) (UNODC, 2006: 33; USDS, 2007: 8). Seventy per cent of sources in the UN human trafficking database reported cases involving women, 33 per cent children, and only 9 per cent men. Of these cases, 87 per cent involved sexual exploitation while 28 per cent involved forced labour. In a context of increased entry restrictions and border controls, prospective migrants sometimes accept the services of traffickers of their own free will. However, many are deceived by promises of good jobs and salaries into accepting traffickers' services (UNODC, 2006).

Imprisonment, deportation and even death are the risks faced by irregular migrants, while the leaders of smuggling and trafficking organizations are rarely apprehended. British women's minister Harriet Harman pointed out in July 2007 that 85 per cent of women in British brothels came from outside the UK, compared with only 15 per cent 10 years earlier. The sex industry had been transformed by global trafficking, yet only 30 men had been prosecuted in Britain for trafficking women for prostitution, and no man had ever been prosecuted for paying for sex with a trafficked woman (Branigan, 2007).

Some observers have contended that increased restrictive measures in the EU created greater demand for traffickers' services (Morrison, 1998). The clientele of traffickers and smugglers often include persons who might have valid claims for refugee status, such as Kurds fleeing Iraq (Kyle and Koslowski, 2001: 340). Similar unintended outcomes were witnessed in the USA (Cornelius, 2001; Skerry and Rockwell, 1998). By disrupting the *modus operandi* and traditional routes of smugglers, increased border enforcement has contributed to rising fees. Underscoring the false dichotomy that sometimes exists between smuggling and trafficking, insolvent migrants have, upon arrival, been forced into a condition of debt bondage until they reimburse the smuggler. Additionally, increased border enforcement has resulted in mounting deaths as smugglers take greater risks to achieve their mission (see Chapter 6).

The People's Republic of China (PRC) has instituted very harsh measures to counter human trafficking, including life imprisonment and capital punishment for convicted criminals. Studies of smuggled and trafficked Chinese revealed complex global networks which were difficult to dismantle through law enforcement. Lower-echelon 'snakeheads' might be apprehended and punished but higher-echelon criminals were more elusive (Chin, 1999: 200).

Conclusions: a quixotic or credible quest for control?

Assessment of the capacity of nation-states to regulate international migration seems both important and difficult. Western states intervene more now than in the past to regulate immigration. Increased openness towards high-skilled workers has coincided with greater restrictiveness towards entry of low-skilled workers The quest for control characteristically included imposition of employer sanctions, phasing in and out of temporary foreign-worker admissions policies, legalizations, tightening of admission rules concerning refugees and asylum seekers, increased border controls and measures against irregular immigration, human smuggling and trafficking. More restrictiveness has increased the reliance of prospective migrants importance on transnational networks and the 'migration industry'.

The overall assessment that emerges is mixed. Persisting levels of irregular immigration throughout the world should by no means be interpreted as the general failure of states to control their borders. What states do *does* matter a great deal. First, many debates on irregular migration exaggerate the magnitude of the phenomenon and obscure the fact that the vast majority of migrants do move in accordance with the law. Second, most irregular migrants entered destination countries legally, and only become irregular after their visas expired.

Third, there is often a considerable gap between tough discourses of politicians who incessantly repeat belligerent statements about 'combating illegal migration' and 'fighting trafficking' and the often much more lenient policy *practices*. Politicians are influenced by employers' lobbying to (temporarily or permanently) allow more legal immigration or to turn a blind eye (e.g., not enforce laws on illegal labour) to illegal practices. Fourth, looking at policy practices, there is even reason to question the very assumption that there has been a generic increase in immigration policy restrictiveness. Analyses of policy changes have found that levels of restrictiveness have tended to oscillate in accordance with economic cycles and political-ideological shifts, while immigration policies have increasingly been about selection (e.g., favouring the high-skilled), rather than about curbing volumes as such (Czaika and Haas, 2011; de Haas, 2011; Ortega and Peri, 2009).

Nevertheless, in a context of continuous demand for low-skilled migrant labour, there seems to be a direct relation between the decreasing possibilities for the low-skilled to migrate legally and what seems to be an increase in irregular migration and residency. In the USA alone, the population of irregularly resident foreigners stood at nearly 11 million in 2010, further fuelling the scepticism that has prevailed over the last three decades about the willingness and capacity of democratic governments to regulate international migration.

Guide to further reading

Extra resources at www.age-of-migration.com

Text 10.1 on the *Age of Migration* website summarizes the French approach to irregular employment. Text 10.2 provides a summary of major legalization programmes in the transatlantic area. Text 5.1 (listed earlier) assesses the evolution up to 2007 of legalizations in Greece, which like Italy and Spain, became a land of immigration after 1990.

Concerning laws punishing irregular employment of foreigners, many governments issue yearly or periodic reports on enforcement. The French government, for instance, began to publish reports from the mid-1970s. The title of the report has evolved from time to time with governmental changes: see Martin and Miller (2000a).

On temporary foreign-worker policies, see Castles (2006), Plewa and Miller (2005), Plewa (2007), and Martin, Abella and Kuptsch (2006). Analyses of legalization policies have proliferated in the twenty-first century, especially in France. See De Bruycker (2000) and Levinson (2005). Comparison of international migration and regionalization processes constitutes an increasingly important area of inquiry. See Miller and Stefanova (2006) and Boswell and Geddes (2011).

Laczko and Gozdziak (2005) examine data problems and issues in research on human trafficking. The IOM and the International Centre for Migration Policy Development engage in extensive research on human trafficking, which is reported on in their publications. Valuable annual reports on human trafficking include the US Department of State's *Trafficking in Persons Report*.

Chapter 11

Migrants and Minorities in the Labour Force

People migrate for many reasons. Although government policies often focus on economic migration, a big share of migration is not primarily for economic purposes. The largest entry category for many countries is family reunion. Other people move to seek refuge from war and persecution. The increased ease of mobility is also leading to more movement for education, marriage, retirement or simply in search of new lifestyles. But many people do migrate for explicitly economic reasons: in search of higher incomes, better employment chances or professional advancement. Moreover, all international migration has an economic dimension: origin countries look to remittances, investments and technology transfer by migrants as resources for economic growth, while destination countries are concerned with the role of migrants in meeting demand for labour and skills.

This chapter focuses on the position of migrants and minorities in the labour force. It concentrates on lower-skilled migrants and their descendants in advanced economies. We start by looking at the factors that drive demand for migrant labour in advanced economies, and how migrants meet this demand. The next section presents information on the labour market situation of migrants, paying attention to both foreign-born workers themselves and their descendants: the 'second generation'. Then we will look at the consequences of the global economic crisis (GEC), which started in 2007, for migrants and migration. A final section examines the dynamics of labour market change, and links these to the 'new political economy' of globalization and social transformation in both North and South.

Labour demand in advanced economies

It is often claimed that labour migration from poor to rich countries meets *mutual needs* (see CEC, 2005; GCIM, 2005). Poor countries have too many young labour market entrants for their weak economies to employ, so they 'need' to export surplus workers. Rich countries, by contrast, have declining numbers of young people entering their labour markets and cannot fill the growing numbers of jobs, so they 'need' to import labour. But it is important to realize that such needs are socially constructed. The 'need' for low-skilled labour in richer countries is the result of poor wages, conditions and social status in certain sectors. A European study showed that 'immigration plays an important role in improving labour market efficiency', because some jobs are avoided by natives:

> dirty, difficult and dangerous jobs, low-paid household service jobs, low-skilled jobs in the informal sector of the economy, jobs in sectors with strong seasonal fluctuation, e.g. farming, road repairs and construction, hotel, restaurant and other tourism-related services. (Münz *et al.*, 2007: 7)

If the conditions and status of such jobs were improved, local workers might be more willing to take them while marginal employers might go out of business. The result might be that certain types of work would be relocated to lower-wage economies. Such 'offshoring' or 'outsourcing' has in fact been common since the 1970s in the manufacturing sector, where much of the production has been moved to new industrial economies. In many cases, 'global commodity chains' (Gereffi, 1996) or 'global value chains' (Ponte and Gibbon, 2005) have been developed, in which routine manufacturing tasks are carried out by low-paid workers in poor countries, while higher-paid activities such as design, management and marketing initially remained in the rich countries. More recently, the 'back office' jobs of banks and insurance firms have also been outsourced, and this process is even beginning to affect some research and development work, which can be done more cheaply in emerging hi-tech areas within low-wage economies like India.

Agriculture also seems an obvious choice for outsourcing, since productivity is low, especially in fruit and vegetable production. However, both local farm employers and local farm workers would be hurt by moving production offshore, and they have had the political clout to prevent this happening. This explains the persistence of trade protection and US farm subsidies as well as the EU's Common Agricultural Policy, both of which are costly to taxpayers, disadvantageous to consumers and highly damaging to agriculture in poor countries.

Rather than a *need* for migrant labour, we should therefore be analysing a *demand*, which is portrayed as a need by powerful economic and political interests. Government policies in receiving countries have responded to this demand either by creating recruitment and management systems for legal foreign labour or by tacitly permitting (and sometimes regularizing) irregular employment of migrants, or, often, by allowing a mix of regular and irregular migrant employment (Castles *et al.*, 2012).

Recognition of the demand for migrant labour in post-industrial economies represented an important shift in the early twenty-first century. As described in Chapter 5, foreign labour employment in Europe stagnated or declined after 1973 in a period of recession and restructuring. Many European countries adopted 'zero immigration policies', but were unable to prevent family reunion and permanent settlement. The USA changed its immigration rules in 1965, but did not expect a significant increase in entries from non-traditional sources. However, the early 1990s saw an upsurge of migration to developed countries, driven by both economic and political factors.

The reaction of policy-makers was to tighten up national immigration restrictions and to increase international cooperation on border control. An important reason for this restrictiveness (especially in Europe) was the fear that temporary migrants might again turn into new ethnic minorities. There was a further reason: in view of increased demand for highly skilled personnel and offshoring of low-skilled jobs, governments stated or believed that low-skilled migrant workers were no longer needed.

In the early 2000s there was a gradual shift in official views. What led to this change? A major *economic factor* was the realization that developed countries could not export all low-skilled work to low-wage countries. The manufacture of cars, computers and clothing could be shifted to countries such as China, Brazil or Malaysia, but the construction industry, hotels and restaurants, hospitals and aged-care had to be where their consumers were. Moreover, Southern European countries that had been major sources of migrant workers in the past had now become important immigration areas.

A major *demographic factor* was the realization that fertility rates had fallen sharply and that the proportion of older people in the population of highly developed countries was rising fast (see also Chapter 5). If there are fewer young people, they will expect better opportunities, and few of them will accept low-skilled jobs. European labour market experts now forecast that manual jobs in manufacturing and agriculture may further decline, but that there is likely to be a growth in unmet demand for low-skilled service workers in household and care jobs (Münz *et al.*, 2007: 9). To respond to this demographic challenge, the European Commission (EC) called for measures to encourage higher fertility, flexible employment, longer working lives and greater productivity – but also stressed the need for 'receiving and integrating immigrants' (Europa, 2008). New industrial countries in Asia also have low fertility and ageing populations, which will lead to major future challenges with regard to welfare and aged-care. For instance, the total fertility rate in South Korea has fallen rapidly to 1.2 – similar to that in Italy and Spain.

Migrants in the labour market

In this section we examine how migrant workers became incorporated into the labour markets of advanced industrial countries up to about 2007, when boom turned to bust. The employment situation of migrants during the boom is often the key to understanding their experience in the subsequent recession.

The contribution of migrant workers to expansion before the GEC

Some economists have argued that migrant labour made a crucial contribution to the post-war boom (e.g. Kindleberger, 1967). Migrants replaced local workers, who were able to obtain more highly skilled jobs. Without the flexibility provided by immigration, bottlenecks in production and inflationary tendencies would have developed. However, other economists have argued that immigration reduced the incentive for rationalization, keeping low-productivity firms viable and holding back the shift to more capital-intensive forms of production . Such observers also claim that capital expenditure on housing and social services for immigrants reduced the capital available for productive investment (see for instance, Borjas, 2000; Jones and Smith, 1970).

Overall there is little doubt that the high net immigration countries, like West Germany, Switzerland, France and Australia, had the highest economic growth rates in the 1945–73 period. Countries with relatively low net immigration (like the UK and the USA at this time) had much lower growth rates (see Castles *et al.*, 1984: chapter 2; Castles and Kosack, 1973: chapter 9). However, one can also argue that the dominant direction of causality was the other way around: fast-growing and low-unemployment economies attracted more migrants. Immigration boosted growth and profits of industries and corporations by keeping labour costs down and undermining the power of trade unions. Thus, labour immigration primarily benefited corporations and the relatively well-to-do, while non-migrant low-skilled workers felt more threatened.

Most empirical studies show that the effect of immigration on the wages of local workers may be slightly positive or negative, but the high-skilled generally benefit more than the low-skilled (Smith and Edmonston, 1997). Where the skills of immigrant workers complement those of non-migrant workers, both groups will benefit. For instance, the availability of migrant domestic workers and child-carers enables non-migrant women to work (UNDP, 2009). Migrants are often willing to accept work that locals are no longer prepared to undertake, such as care, domestic, agricultural and catering jobs. Negative effects on wages are most likely if new migrants compete with the existing workforce. Therefore, the workers most negatively affected by the entry of new migrants tend to be earlier migrants (UNDP, 2009). However, the most important conclusion from empirical studies is that the effects of immigration on employment and wages are *very small*. This should preclude exaggerated claims about the positive or negative effects of migration.

Despite oscillations in immigration policies and attempts to restrict entry of lower-skilled workers, the number of foreign workers in OECD countries has shown a clearly increasing trend over the past decades. By 2005, foreign-born workers made up a substantial share of the labour force: 25 per cent in Australia and Switzerland, 20 per cent in Canada and around

15 per cent in the USA, New Zealand, Austria and Germany. The figure for other Western European countries was around 12 per cent. (OECD, 2007: 63). Migrants made up between one-third and two-thirds of new employees in most Western and Southern European countries (OECD, 2007: 67).

New immigrants often bring skills with them: the old stereotype of the unskilled migrant coming in to take the least qualified positions is no longer valid (Collins, 2006; Portes and Rumbaut, 2006). In Belgium, Luxembourg, Sweden and Denmark, over 40 per cent of the employed migrants who arrived from 1995 to 2005 had tertiary education. In France the figure was 35 per cent and in the Netherlands 30 per cent. In many cases, migrant workers had higher qualification profiles than local-born workers. Only in Southern European countries did low-skilled labour migration predominate (OECD, 2007: 67–8).

Migrant employment patterns: the migrant generation

High migrant workplace concentrations for men in the 1970s were found in factories, building sites, or services such as garbage collection and street cleaning. Women were also to be found in factories (especially textiles and clothing, engineering and food processing) and in services such as cleaning and health. By the mid-2000s, migrants could be found right across the economy, but remained overrepresented in manufacturing and construction – sectors deserted by many nationals. In the services sector, the foreign-born were overrepresented in hotels and restaurants, and the healthcare and social services sector (OECD, 2007: 72–3). In 2005, more than 50 per cent of cleaning jobs were held by migrants in Switzerland, and more than 30 per cent in Austria, Germany, Sweden, Italy, Greece and the USA. They were also overrepresented as waiters or cooks, and domestic carers. These were typically jobs with poor pay and conditions, and little security.

However, foreign-born persons were also overrepresented in some service occupations requiring high-skill levels, such as teachers (in Switzerland and Ireland), doctors and nurses (in the UK) and computer experts (USA). Migrant employment in the tertiary sector was 'dualistic' with concentration at low and high-skill levels and a gap in between (see also OECD, 2007; Bauder, 2006). Overall, migrants still tended to have lower occupational status and higher unemployment rates than non-migrant workers. Yet the labour market positions of migrant workers were much more varied than they had been 20 or 30 years earlier. New migrants often came with higher qualifications and sometimes gained access to better jobs than their predecessors, although older migrant workers often seemed to have got stuck in the manual manufacturing sectors for which they were originally recruited.

The labour market advantage of 'new' immigrants compared with the 'old' should not be overstated. In general, migrants experienced a 'poor return on education' (Reyneri and Fullin, 2010: 45). A research project carried out in six European countries emphasized the varying experiences of migrants. They had lower unemployment levels but less qualified jobs in Southern European countries, while they tended to have more qualified jobs but a higher risk of unemployment in North-Western Europe, indicating a 'trade-off between the risk of unemployment and the access to highly qualified jobs' (Reyneri and Fullin, 2010: 43).

But overview studies cannot fully reveal the complex national patterns of differentiation based on ethnicity, gender and legal status. The general picture in the UK, for example, was of a labour force stratified by ethnicity and gender and with a high degree of youth unemployment. Generally, people of Indian, Chinese, or Irish background tended to have employment situations as good as or sometimes better than the average for white British (Dustmann and Fabbri, 2005). By contrast, other groups were worse off, with a descending hierarchy of black Africans, black Caribbeans, Pakistanis, and – at the very bottom – Bangladeshis. Gender distinctions varied: young women of black African and black Caribbean ethnicity seemed to perform better in both education and employment than men of these groups, while the opposite appeared to be the case for Pakistanis and Bangladeshis (ONS, 2004).

The second generation

Most labour migrants to OECD countries up to the 1970s were workers with low skill levels. In the meantime, a new *second generation* (native-born persons with both parents foreign-born) has emerged. These young people have generally received their education in the destination country. In most OECD countries *persons with a migration background* (foreign-born persons plus the second generation) made up a large proportion of young adults by 2005 – the highest share was in Australia (45 per cent of persons aged 20–29), followed by Switzerland and Canada (30–35 per cent), and then Sweden, USA, the Netherlands, Germany, France and the UK (20–30 per cent) (OECD, 2007: 79).

In general, the research shows that the second generation has better average educational outcomes than the migrant parent generation. They also do better than young migrants of the same age group (20–29). However, the outcomes of the second generation tend to lag behind those of native-born young people without a migration background. This may be partly explained by the low educational and socio-economic levels of their parents, since such factors tend to be transmitted across generations. The OECD's Programme for International Student Assessment – PISA) examined performance of 15-year-olds in mathematics, science, reading and cross-curricular competencies. The study showed that, even after allowing for parental background, second-generation students remained at a substantial disadvantage. This applied particularly to former guest-worker-recruiting countries, like Germany, Belgium, Switzerland and Austria.

Second-generation education disadvantage was found to be insignificant in the cases of Sweden, France, Australia and Canada (OECD, 2007: 79–80). This indicates that the original mode of labour market incorporation can have effects that cross generations (see also Portes and Rumbaut, 2006: 92–101). The OECD research also revealed substantial gender differences. In all OECD countries studied (except the USA), second-generation young women did better than their male counterparts at school. Schooling in host countries thus seems to have an important emancipatory effect for second-generation women.

The most important question for the second generation is whether they can get decent jobs in the host country. The OECD found that young second-generation members had a higher employment probability than immigrants in the same age group, but still suffered significant disadvantage compared with young people without a migration background. The disadvantage seemed greatest at the top end of the qualification scale, indicating the persistence of a 'glass ceiling' for minorities. Native-born children of immigrants from African countries seemed to have the greatest labour market difficulties: in Europe they were up to twice as likely to be unemployed as young people without a migration background. Possible explanations included lack of access to informal networks that help in job-finding; lack of knowledge of the labour market; and discrimination on the basis of origin or class (OECD, 2007: 81–5).

Migrant entrepreneurs

Up to the 1970s, migrants in some countries were seen as wage-workers, and rarely became entrepreneurs. In Germany, Switzerland and Austria their work permits prohibited self-employment. The situation was different in the USA, Australia, the UK and France, where migrants began to run small shops and cafés early on. Since the 1980s, migrant self-employment has become far more common everywhere. An OECD study found 12.6 per cent of working-age migrants were involved in non-agricultural entrepreneurship in OECD countries in 2007–8, compared with 12 per cent of non-migrants. Migrants were overrepresented in self-employment in Australia, UK, France, Belgium, Denmark, Sweden, Norway, USA and Central and Eastern Europe. but underrepresented in Southern Europe, Ireland, Israel, Germany, Austria and Switzerland (OECD, 2011a: 142–3). Probable explanations are that past exclusion from entrepreneurship in the former guest-worker-recruiting countries has had a long-term effect, while in Southern Europe the recentness and the often irregular nature of migration have not been conducive to business formation.

Although ethnic businesses initially often cater for the needs of ethnic communities, they rapidly expand across the economy. Typical initial migrant-owned businesses are ethnic restaurants, 'mom and pop' food stores and convenience stores (Waldinger *et al.*, 1990). Immigrant-owned businesses frequently employ family members from the country of origin, holding costs low. For instance, Light and Bonacich (1988) traced the origins of the Korean business community in Los Angeles to the Korean War, which led to extensive migration between Korea and the USA. More recently, Ness (2005: 58–95) has shown how Korean entrepreneurs came to dominate the New York greengrocery business, at first employing co-ethnics, then replacing them with Mexican workers at lower wages – and then re-employing Koreans when the Mexicans demanded better pay and conditions (see also Waldinger, 1996).

Some scholars stress the economic dynamism of immigrant entrepreneurs with their positive effects upon economic growth and quality of life for consumers (Fix and Passel, 1994: 53). A more critical viewpoint stresses the suffering entailed by intense competition, long hours of work, and exploitation of family labour and of illegally employed migrants (Collins *et al.*, 1995; Light and Bonacich, 1988) The growth of small business in Europe is linked to neoliberal policies of economic deregulation, which have made it easier to start businesses and to employ workers on a casual basis. In many such businesses, both the employers and the workers are migrants or members of ethnic minorities. Studies show complex patterns of ethnic and gender segmentation, with some ethnic minority groups doing quite well while others are disadvantaged and impoverished. There is no clear status distinction between the employed and the self-employed – the former can include high-status managers as well as low-paid service workers, while the latter range from medical professionals to cab drivers and food-stall operators.

Migrant workers in the global economic crisis (GEC)

The patterns of migrant labour force participation established in the boom years were profoundly affected by the GEC, although it has not led to a massive return or reversal of migration flows predicted by some. This has been discussed for various regions in Chapters 5–8. Here we can only summarize some main trends and provide a few examples.

Effects of the GEC on migrant employment and unemployment in OECD countries

The immediate impacts of the GEC were felt most strongly in the richer economies (Phillips, 2011a). Overall *unemployment* in the OECD grew by 55 per cent between December 2007 and January 2012 – an increase of nearly 14 million in the number of unemployed people. The largest increases were in Ireland, Spain, Greece, Iceland and Estonia (OECD, 2012: 60). In most OECD countries migrants have been more affected by unemployment than the native-born (the only exceptions were Switzerland, the Czech

Box 11.1 Why migrant unemployment and employment rose at the same time

It seems paradoxical that both foreign unemployment and employment grew at the same time. To understand why this was the case requires looking at both short-term factors (what economists call 'conjunctural' issues like interest rates, consumer behaviour and entrepreneurs' propensity to invest), and longer-term structural factors (like changes in underlying economic and demographic patterns). Conjunctural factors led to a sharp decline in some types of production, especially of consumer goods and therefore also of the steel and plastics needed to make them. Yet structural changes like the shift away from manufacturing to the services and the demographic decline in the domestic labour forces of European countries continued. Migrants working in declining sectors lost their jobs, but other migrants were able to gain jobs in emerging sectors.

The gender aspects of employment change are important: migrant men were far more affected by job losses than migrant women. This is because migrant men tended to be employed in the sectors hardest hit by the downturn, especially manufacturing and construction, while migrant women were more concentrated in less-affected sectors, notably social services, care work and domestic work. As fertility rates fell and the populations of developed countries aged, there has been increased demand for migrant women to fill such positions. In fact, 643,000 new jobs were created in 'residential care activities' from 2008 to 2011, and more than half were taken by foreign-born workers. Immigrants (especially women) also filled 193,000 new jobs as domestic workers (OECD, 2012: 67). At the same time, the GEC has reinforced the trend towards part-time, temporary and causal employment, with women more likely to enter such employment relationships than men (OECD, 2011a: 78–81). The growth in employment of migrant women does not necessarily represent a gain, since many of the new jobs are part-time, badly paid and precarious, and women often have to work long hours to make up for the loss of male migrants' earnings.

Republic and Luxembourg) (OECD, 2012: 63). Yet foreign *employment* in European OECD countries actually increased by 5 per cent from early 2008 to the third quarter of 2010, while the employment of native-born persons declined by over 2 per cent (OECD, 2011a: 74–5). In other words, foreign unemployment increased, but so did foreign employment! (See Box 11.1.)

The crisis is also putting additional pressure on already disadvantaged youth (OECD, 2012: 73). In late 2010, 44 per cent of young migrants aged 15–24 were jobless in Spain, 35 per cent in Sweden and Belgium and 33 per cent in France. On average in European OECD countries in 2010, a quarter of young migrants were unemployed, compared with to a fifth of young native-born persons. Youth unemployment of both migrants and nationals has certainly grown since in some countries, notably Spain. In many OECD countries, youth unemployment for the foreign-born was twice as high (or more) than that of locally born youth in 2011 (OECD, 2012: 75). The OECD classifies many young people as NEET; 'neither in employment, nor in education nor training' (OECD, 2012: 75), which sounds strikingly similar to the *'ni-nis'* (*ni escuela ni trabajo*) – Mexico's marginalized youth – mentioned in Box 6.1 above.

Long-term unemployment is also a major problem: in 2011 more than half of foreign-born unemployed had been jobless for at least a year in Ireland, Germany and some Central European countries. In most OECD countries, 30–50 per cent of the foreign-born unemployed had been out of work for at least a year. Increasing numbers had been unemployed for at least two years (OECD, 2012: 68). Unemployment rates varied by area of origin: in Europe, migrants from Africa were worst affected (25 per cent unemployed in 2010); in the USA, Africans, Mexicans, other Central Americans and South Americans and Caribbeans all had unemployment rates of 11–12 per cent. In Australia, migrants from the Middle East and North Africa were most affected (OECD, 2011a: 84).

Decline and recovery in new labour migration

New labour migration fell globally in 2008 and 2009, but has partially recovered since, albeit unevenly. In the USA, both overall employment and migrant employment fell sharply in 2008–9 (IOM, 2011: 55), but with the hesitant return to growth in 2010–11, migrant employment grew faster than employment of natives (Mohapatra *et al.*, 2011b: 5–6). The number of unemployed Mexican migrants had fallen to about 720,000.

In South America, the picture is mixed. In view of importance of migration to the USA and the relative stagnation of labour demand there, migratory flows to the North have been much reduced. Emigration to Spain from Ecuador and other Latin American countries has also fallen, and there has been significant return migration. However, the emergence of new migration poles (such as Brazil, Chile and Argentina) within Latin America has also led to a growth of migration within the continent.

In early 2009, the sharp economic downturn was causing some governments in South-East and East Asia to close their borders to new migrant workers (Abella and Ducanes, 2009). But by 2011 it was becoming clear that the effects of the GEC on Asian migration were moderate and short-lived (IOM, 2011: 68). Migrant departures from Bangladesh, for example, which had fallen by 20 per cent in 2010, grew by 37 per cent in the first three-quarters of 2011. Deployments of Overseas Contract Workers (OCWs) from the Philippines grew by 20 per cent from 2008–10 despite the GEC, and by a further 7 per cent in the first three-quarters of 2011. This growth was due to the high demand for labour in the Gulf Cooperation Council (GCC) countries are well as in Russia, which in turn was linked to the high price of oil. Recruitment of Filipino seafarers, who sail the oceans under many flags, also increased (Mohapatra *et al.*, 2011b: 9).

Similarly, in 2008–9 there were sharp falls in migrant labour flows from the poorer countries of the former Soviet Union in Central Asia like Tajikistan and Kazakhstan to Russia (Canagarajah and Kholmatov, 2010). But in 2011, flows recovered considerably, as labour demand increased again in Russia and other destination countries. Many African economies rebounded relatively quickly from the GEC, although the Arab Spring negatively affected growth in North Africa from 2011. However, the economic outlook remains optimistic particularly for sub-Saharan Africa, and various countries among which Ghana, South Africa, Mozambique and Angola continue to attract migrations, primarily from within the continent but also from China and even Southern Europe (see also Chapters 5 and 8).

Fall in irregular migration

Irregular migration is highly sensitive to labour market demand in destination countries (e.g. McCabe and Meissner, 2010: 7). Irregular employment is particularly common in low-skilled jobs in low-productivity sectors of the economy, such as agriculture, construction, catering and certain services. These jobs – which often have insecure and exploitative conditions – may be strongly affected by economic downturns. Since irregular migrants move through networks and tend to rely on information and support from previous migrants (see Chapter 2), potential migrants quickly learn of the lack of work opportunities in recessions. Moreover, irregular migrants generally lack entitlements to welfare support, and have little motivation to come to a destination country if work is not available.

The, at least, temporary decline of migrant employment in areas as diverse as the USA, Russia, Spain, the Gulf States and Malaysia has been linked to concentration in the crisis-sensitive construction industry. In the USA, the failure of attempts at immigration reform and creation of a path to 'earned citizenship' for irregular migrants in 2006–7 opened the way for the 'Secure Fence Act' of 2006, designed to prevent Mexican migrants entering across the South-West border (McCabe and Meissner, 2010: 5). In any case, the tightening of border control that started in 1994 with 'Operation Gatekeeper' had already had the effect (unexpected by policymakers if not by researchers) of transforming much Mexican migration from short-term cyclical flows to permanent settlement (Alba, 2010: 2; see also Chapter 6).

Little return migration

Although the GEC has led to some return migration, the mass return flows predicted by some observers at the beginning of the crisis have not taken place. This strikingly resembles migration trends after the 1973 Oil Crisis, when the predicted massive return did not occur either, and many migrants decided to stay on the relatively safe side of the border. Since their families at home are often dependent on remittances, migrants 'adopt several strategies to cope with the recession, such as lowering spending, looking for a new or second job, moving to a cheaper house, refinancing mortgage, drawing down savings, selling possessions, mortgaging property, or declaring bankruptcy' (Jha *et al.*, 2009: 3). Many migrants stayed on, partly because the situation in origin countries was often even worse than in destination countries (IOM, 2011: 55).

In some cases, governments took measures to compel unemployed migrants to leave. This has often been coupled with campaigns to remove irregular workers. Malaysia, Singapore and some of the Gulf States announced such approaches. However, they were hard to implement in practice, due to lack of institutional capacity is some places, employer concerns that unemployed nationals would not be willing to take 'migrant jobs', and the efforts of migrants to remain.

On the other hand, there is evidence of departures of Polish and other Central and Eastern European workers from Britain and Ireland. Lack of jobs in the destination countries is certainly one reason, but improving prospects and the gain in value of home-country currencies relative to the UK Pound (Mohapatra *et al.*, 2011b: 11) may also have played a role. In addition, these migrants, as EU citizens, have the right to return to Britain, Ireland or other EU countries once employment prospects pick up. The right to return means there is no reason to sit out the crisis in the destination country. This illustrates that free migration regimes may, paradoxically, lead to less semi-permanent immigration of workers than restrictive policies, which often tend to push workers into permanent settlement.

Little or no decline in migrant stocks

Overall therefore, it seems clear that new labour migration – and especially irregular migration – has fallen, while other forms of migration are less affected. Return migration is quite limited. The result is that migrant stocks in destination countries have declined little or not at all. This is an important finding. However, it still represents the interruption of the trend to rapid increases in migrant flows and steady increases in stocks in many regions over the 1990s and the early 2000s.

In previous recessions (such as that following the 1973 Oil Crisis), there was some initial decline in migrant stocks due to the fact that many migrants had always intended to stay a few years only, and were ready to return home. Often this return was selective: those with the best prospects at home left, while migrants from countries strongly affected by the recession tried to stay. The decline in numbers associated with return labour migration was quickly made up by family reunion, family formation and settlement of those who stayed. This led to a demographic normalization of migrant populations, which in turn resulted in increased needs for housing and for public services such as education, health, welfare and recreation amenities. It is too early to say at present whether this has happened again following the GEC.

Remittances: decline in growth rates, but no sharp falls in transfers

As pointed out in Chapter 3 above, economic remittances – the money sent home (mainly to their families) by migrants – have become a crucial economic factor in many less-developed countries. The ability to support families through remittances is a key motivation for migration. Although many observers predicted a sharp decline in remittances as a consequence of the GEC, after an initial decline, remittances recovered. Indeed some countries, such as Pakistan and Bangladesh, actually experienced an increase in remittances in early 2009, partly because migrants were trying hard to compensate for difficult conditions at home, and partly because of the repatriation of savings by returning unemployed migrants (Jha *et al.*, 2009).

Remittance flows are not directly related to migration flows, but rather to the stock of migrants in a specific country (Ratha *et al.*, 2009: 4). Since migrant stocks have not declined much (if at all), remittances levels have on the whole been maintained: although some migrants have lost their jobs or experienced wage cuts, reducing their capacity to remit. However, this has sometimes been made up by migrants' willingness to make sacrifices in order to continue to provide support for their families and communities at home.

Latin America, especially Mexico, seemed to be more severely affected than other world regions. The initial decline in money flows to Mexico was linked to the downturn in the US housing construction industry (Ruiz and Vargas-Silva, 2009). Remittances to Mexico grew again in 2011, although the volume was still 11 per cent down on the December 2007 level (BBVA, 2012). However, in 2012 remittances declined again, albeit by only 1.6 per cent, due to job losses by Mexicans in the USA as well as exchange rate fluctuations (BBVA, 2013).

Long-term prospects: still unclear

It will be some years before the full significance of the GEC for migration becomes evident. The immediate effects appear to have been less than predicted in 2008 and 2009. One of the key findings to emerge from the many studies is the unexpected degree of resilience of migrant employment. Although migrant workers did play a 'buffering role in the labour market both during expansion and contraction phases of the business cycle' (OECD, 2010: 85), they also continued to be a structural part of destination-country economies, with migrant employment actually growing in some cases during the crisis. Nonetheless, hardships have often been severe for many migrants and for their dependents. Origin countries have had to face serious financial consequences. Another consequence has been the rise of hostility to migrants in many destinations countries, giving rise to dangerous outbursts of racism and, in some cases, motivating exclusionary action by authorities.

A return to economic growth is likely to lead to new migratory flows to dynamic economic areas, just as in the past. The intriguing question is whether these dynamic economic areas will be the same as before. The GEC may be a symptom of a long-term underlying shift in economic power away from the USA and the other older industrial economies to the emerging BRICS economies (Brazil, Russia, India, China and South Africa). All of those countries (except perhaps China) are already poles of attraction for international migrants. China still mainly relies on internal migration, although it is beginning to recruit overseas professionals, while some immigration of Arab and African traders and migrants is also occurring. In ten years' time, we may well look back at the 2007–12 GEC as a turning-point to the emergence of important new migration systems, just as we do today with regard to the post-1973 recession. In any case, the experience of migrant workers in the GEC is a reflection of the specific part they have come to play in the new global political economy, as will be discussed in the next section.

The new political economy: making the global labour market

The information in this chapter indicates the continuing importance of migrant labour for advanced economies. This confirms the various theories reviewed in Chapter 2 which argue that the demand for both low- and high-skilled immigrant labour has become a structural feature of advanced economies. Migrant workers meet special types of labour demand, and often experience economic and social disadvantage. But changes in the work situation and social position of workers in advanced economies can only be fully understood through analysis of the global restructuring of investment, production and trade, and the way this has changed economic and social conditions in migrant-origin and destination countries. In this section we examine the development of the global labour market, and link this to shifts in the characteristics of welfare states and the meaning of citizenship.

The dynamics of labour force change

A main argument for neoliberal globalization has been the claim that it would lead to faster economic growth in developing countries, and thus, in the long run, to poverty reduction and convergence with advanced industrial countries. The claim of reducing inequality has been crucial in underpinning ideologies of 'open borders' and 'a level playing field'. Flows across borders – of commodities, capital, technology and labour – were meant to secure optimal allocation of resources, to ensure that production factors could be obtained at the lowest possible cost, and to promote increased productivity everywhere. Yet global inequality by the mid-2000s was 'probably the highest ever recorded' (Milanovic, 2007: 39). Within-country inequality appears to be greatest in the countries which have most completely espoused neoliberal economic policies (Wilkinson and Pickett, 2010).

Liberalization of flows was never complete – for instance rich countries protected their own agriculture while demanding the removal of barriers for others. But the contradiction was greatest with regard to flows of people, where control of cross-border movements was seen as a crucial aspect of nation-state sovereignty. Economists argued that the removal of restrictions on human mobility would lead to large increases in global income (Bhagwati, 2003; Nayar, 1994), but politicians in labour-importing countries were aware of popular suspicion of immigration, and responded with a rhetoric of national interests and control.

For example, the British Conservative Party has adopted tough-sounding anti-immigration rhetoric. This is attractive to anti-immigration groups (like Britain's 'Migration Watch'), but antagonizes the business groups, which traditionally support the Conservative Party yet urgently need migrant workers. Gamlen (2013) therefore argues that the Conservative policy is designed to fail: by doing so it will simultaneously satisfy the apparently incompatible demands of both right-wing exclusionists and economic liberals. Similarly, one may argue that restrictive immigration policies serve the interests of certain employers, because it does not so much stop migration as create an often undocumented, cheap and rightless labour force. Many employers may actually prefer irregular workers, because their lack of rights makes them easier to exploit (Ness, 2005).

In fact, the interplay between market forces demanding freedom of movement and political forces demanding control can be seen as highly effective in creating a global labour market stratified not only according to 'human capital' (possession of education, training and work skills), but also according to gender, race, ethnicity, origins and legal status. The new global labour market is thus an expression of a global class hierarchy, in which people with high human capital from rich countries have almost unlimited rights of mobility, while others are differentiated, controlled, and included or excluded in a variety of ways (Bauman, 1998).

To understand recent changes and the impact of the crisis, it is necessary to sketch out the development of global class relations (see Schierup *et al.*, 2006; Veltmayer, 2010). A *first phase* of expansion in core industrial economies from 1945 to about 1973 was marked by mass production in large factories. Migrant workers – mainly from areas geographically and culturally fairly close to the core industrial countries – played a vital part in the economic boom (Kindleberger, 1967). Many were employed in unionized factories and enjoyed the benefits of reasonable wages and welfare safety nets.

In the 1970s, economic recession helped initiate a *second phase,* in which capital investment in labour-intensive production was moved to low-wage economies, while migrant labour recruitment was stopped. Many manufacturing plants closed, and blue-collar unions lost members. But, against official expectations, not only colonial immigrants but also many former guest-workers stayed on, and were joined by spouses and children. From the late 1970s, the governments of the Reagan/Thatcher era promoted labour-market restructuring. Many migrant workers were pushed out of regular employment, some getting insecure casual jobs, others setting up marginal small business, with yet others becoming dependent on welfare benefits. At the same time, new migrations to emerging industrial areas developed, such as the movement of workers from slower-growing Asian economies to Japan, Taiwan, South Korea and Malaysia, and the recruitment of Asian contract workers by Gulf oil states.

However, the very success of neoliberal globalization led to a new *third phase* by the 1990s: the growth of precarious employment and exploitative work in the advanced economies. As discussed in Chapters 2 and 3 above, social transformation in poor countries created economic conditions conducive to emigration of both highly skilled and unskilled workers to post-industrial economies. This corresponded with the new demand for migrant workers due to the economic, demographic and social shifts outlined above. The 'contexts of reception' (Portes and Rumbaut, 2006: 92–3) for new migrants were quite different from those of their predecessors in the 1960s and 1970s: a state that offered reduced protection to workers; weak unions and more fragmented labour markets which opened the door for exploitative employment practices; and the existence of ethnic communities with varying capacity to help newcomers in the job search.

In this new phase, migrants and minorities have been particularly vulnerable to high unemployment and social exclusion. At the same time, the racialization (see Chapter 3) of exclusion and poverty has been crucial in the shift away from welfare universalism and social redistribution. The presence of immigrants and minorities has helped legitimate the restructuring of welfare states and has played an important role in strategies to divide the 'deserving' from the 'undeserving' poor (Schierup and Castles, 2011). Migrants and ethnic minorities are among the chief victims of weakened welfare states and deregulated labour markets. Yet precarious jobs are not simply there in advance waiting to be taken up by migrants. Migrants and ethnic minorities can often be exploited as a 'reserve army of labour' due to their exclusion from citizenship and labour rights, and their lack of access to established institutions and networks of power (Goldring and Landolt, 2011). This makes workers available for deregulated sections of the labour market, leaving them no choice but to accept sub-standard wages and conditions (e.g. Bauder, 2006).

Thus the equality of worker and human rights laid down in instruments of international law does not exist in social reality, where a new hierarchy of citizenship prevails (Castles, 2005). All people may have certain rights on paper, but many lack the opportunities and resources to actually enjoy these rights. The relativity of citizenship is particularly clear with regard to the right to cross national borders, and to work and take up residence in destination countries. Rich states compete with each other to attract highly skilled workers, but take drastic measures to restrict legal entry of lower-skilled workers. Since there is a continuous demand for lower-skilled workers in agriculture, construction, manufacturing and the services, millions of migrants have irregular status.

The transformation of work

The neoliberal globalization of production since the late 1970s has reshaped the world of work. Global commodity chains, polarization of labour markets, devaluation of old skills and the decline of job security have affected workers everywhere, but migrants have often been most vulnerable to change.

New employment forms: subcontracting, temporary work and casualization

A key element of neoliberal employment practices has been the drive to turn wage-workers, who previously enjoyed the protection of labour law and collective agreements, into independent 'contractors', who have no guarantee of work, have to buy their own tools and equipment, and bear all the risks of accident, sickness or lack of jobs (Schierup *et al.*, 2006: chapter 9). Often, these 'contractors' are immigrants. The pressure to become independent contractors has affected occupations as diverse as building tradesmen, truck drivers, graphic designers and architects. A striking example from the USA concerns the New York 'black-car drivers', who take executives and tourists to and from the airports. Once paid employees, they now have to buy the expensive luxury vehicles (on credit) and bear all operating costs, with no guarantee of work. The result is low income and extreme working hours. Most of the drivers are South Asians (Ness, 2005: 130–80).

Employing migrants on a temporary basis is another way of enhancing employer control and reducing demands for better wages and conditions. In 2007, the OECD found that migrants were more likely to be employed in temporary jobs than natives in all European immigration countries (except Austria and Switzerland). In Spain, 56 per cent of the foreign-born had temporary jobs compared with less than 30 per cent of locals (OECD, 2007: 75–6) – which may help explain the rapid rise in unemployment of migrants in Spain during the GEC. In Europe's partial economic recovery of 2010, migrant workers were overrepresented in new hirings, mainly because of a shift to temporary contracts (OECD, 2011a: 86).

Economic deregulation has led to the removal of many legal controls on employment and the reduction of work-site inspections by labour market authorities. This allowed a big expansion in casual employment: that is, hiring by the hour or for specific tasks, especially of migrants, young people and women. Casual jobs are typical for cleaning, catering, and other service occupations, but also for the construction, textile and garment industries. Many big firms no longer engage directly in production, but subcontract it to smaller firms in sectors of the labour market with a high degree of informality and scant regulation of working conditions. Through outsourcing to subcontractors they strive for a maximum of flexibility. The frequent celebration of the rise of 'ethnic entrepreneurship' needs to be seen in the context of such trends.

Migrant women workers

In Chapter 3 we summarized some theoretical discussions on gender and migration. As early as 1984, Morokvasic argued that migrant women from peripheral zones living in Western industrial democracies:

> represent a readymade labour supply which is, at once, the most vulnerable, the most flexible and, at least in the beginning, the least demanding work force. They have been incorporated into sexually segregated labour markets at the lowest stratum in high technology industries or at the 'cheapest' sectors in those industries which are labour intensive and employ the cheapest labour to remain competitive. (Morokvasic, 1984: 886)

Gender-segregated labour markets have become a crucial feature of the new global division of labour. International financial institutions have celebrated the feminization of labour migration, partly on the basis of the (not entirely uncontested) assumption that women are more reliable remittance-senders than men, and therefore make a positive contribution to the development of their origin-areas. However, this supposed benefit is predicated on the principle of temporary migration as well as the growth of temporary employment, especially for women (Rosewarne, 2012).

As the demand for male labour has fallen due to declines in manufacturing and construction employment, migrant women have increasingly entered the labour force. As noted above, migrant women in OECD countries were less affected than men by unemployment during the GEC, due to their concentration in services jobs. However, they had to make up family-income losses when men lost their jobs (OECD, 2011a: 80). The new growth sectors (such as domestic and care work) are linked to traditional female roles, and the informalization of such work has dragged down pay and conditions, leading to 'a regrowth of inequalities and insecurities' (Piper, 2011: 65).

Migrant women are disadvantaged by two interlocking sets of mechanisms. On the one hand – like all women – they face gender-specific factors such as employers' assumptions that they are not primary breadwinners, but rather temporary workers who will leave to get married (Schrover *et al.*, 2007). In addition, migrant women are disadvantaged by stereotypes of specific ethnic and racial groups, and often also by weak legal status (Browne and Misra, 2003: 489).

Contrary to neoliberal theories of the labour market, which argue that variations in employment status are due to differing levels of human capital, many studies show the importance of race, gender, class and sexual orientation in allocating positions. The disadvantaged position of migrant women is crucial to sectors such as the garment industry. A US study revealed that 'women of colour are differentially situated in local labour markets compared with white women and co-ethnic men, so that economic restructuring affects each group uniquely' (Browne and Misra, 2003: 497). An analysis of European labour market statistics found:

> There are sharp differences in pay between men and women, which can be explained in part by women's disproportionate representation in low pay sectors, such as cleaning and domestic work, the casual or part-time nature of many female jobs and their concentration in the informal sector. (Ayres and Barber, 2006: 30)

Migrant women domestic workers form a category of gendered and racialized labour that has expanded remarkably in virtually all advanced industrial economies (Anderson, 2000; 2007; Cox, 2006). Domestic work can become a niche for migrant women (Schrover *et al.*, 2007: 536–7): however bad the conditions, it does offer a chance of a job, often combined with live-in conditions that are perceived by migrant women's families as sheltered. Domestic work is marked by a hierarchy of work tasks, of formal and informal modes of employment, and of groups with varied statuses. For instance, Filipina domestic workers are preferred in some places due to their better education and English, but rejected in others because they are seen as too active in defending their rights.

Domestic work by migrant women can be the result of increased opportunities of professional or white-collar employment for majority-group women: hiring foreign maids can free women in Italy, the USA or Singapore from housework and childcare (Huang *et al.*, 2005; Iredale *et al.*, 2002). Such transnational care hierarchies sometimes go a stage further, when migrant domestic workers hire a maid in the home country to look after their own children. Such 'global care chains' may mean higher living standards and better education, but at a high emotional cost.

The growth of the informal economy

One of the most significant – and perhaps surprising – trends of the last 30 years has been the growth of informal economies in advanced countries, and this trend has been a major explanation of the continuation of low-skilled, frequently irregular labour migration. Neoliberalism and economic deregulation have led to a burgeoning of informal work in formerly highly regulated labour markets. All the trends already mentioned – subcontracting, temporary work, casualization, and gendered and racialized work situations – can be summed up through the concept of informalization, defined by Ness (2005: 22) as: 'referring to a redistribution of work from regulated sectors of the economy to new unregulated sectors of the underground or informal economy'.

Informal employment has been a major driver of undocumented migration. This is particularly obvious in the USA, with its officially estimated irregular population of about 11 million (Passel and Cohn, 2011). Most of them are Mexican and other Central American and Caribbean migrants in low-skilled jobs. In Europe, irregular residents made up less than 1 per cent of the EU's total population (Clandestino, 2009; table 1; see also Chapter 5) – far less than is often suggested in the media. Some politicians argue that irregular immigration is the cause of informalization, but several researchers have argued that the main causality is the other way round: economic deregulation and employer practices have created informal sector jobs, drawing in irregular migrants (Reyneri, 2003). This applies most obviously in Southern Europe, but informal work is widespread, for instance in British agriculture, cleaning and catering, but also in the cases of traffic wardens and security work – both services devolved by public authorities to subcontractors.

From labour market segmentation to precarious work

Taken together, the various forms of labour force restructuring add up to a process labelled as *labour market segmentation* by economists (see also Chapter 2). This means that people's chances of getting jobs depend not only on their human capital (i.e. their education and skills) but also on gender, race, ethnicity and legal status. More recently, social scientists have begun to talk about *precarious work* and to analyse the processes which push certain categories of workers – and particularly migrants – into insecure and exploitative jobs.

Labour market segmentation is not new. In Western Europe in the 1960s, the discrimination inherent in guest-worker policies funnelled immigrants into specific economic sectors and occupations (Castles and Kosack, 1973). Similarly, a US Department of Labor report found that: 'Newcomers arrive in the United States ... with distinct legal statuses. In turn, this proliferation of legal statuses may become a new source of social and economic stratification' (US Department of Labor, 1989: 18). However, labour market segmentation is changing in complex ways, linked to a new global social geography. This reflects Sassen's (1988) argument that foreign investment and displacement of manufacturing jobs abroad had fostered new migratory streams to the USA, and that the casualization of labour and growing illegal alien employment were characteristic of global cities.

Twenty years on, Ness examined the transformation of the social geography of New York City (Ness, 2005: chapter 2). In the early twentieth century, immigrant labour from Southern and Eastern Europe had been crucial to the emergence of the garment, printing, meatpacking, construction and transportation industries. Industry was concentrated in 'ethnic neighbourhoods' and immigrants came to form the backbone of the city's strong labour movement. In the late twentieth century, these traditional industries were restructured, with most production jobs being moved to non-unionized 'sunbelt' states or offshore to the Caribbean, Latin America and Asia. Many new jobs were created in retailing, personal services, and business services (see also Waldinger, 1996). The new economy was heavily stratified on the basis of ethnicity, with US-born white people getting high-skilled jobs in the services sector, African Americans and US-born Latinos getting public sector jobs and immigrants often getting low-wage jobs in such areas private transportation, catering, delivery, security and building maintenance (Ness, 2005: 17). Parallels to the changes in New York City can be found everywhere. For example, the garment industry provides many national examples of hierarchies based on race and gender (Rath, 2002).

A study of the Toronto labour market by Goldring and Landolt (2011) brings together work status and citizenship rights through a 'work–citizenship matrix'. This matrix links indicators of precarious work, such as level of unionization, contract type, terms of employment, and payment in cash. The level of precariousness is related to explanatory factors based on individual and human capital, households and networks, contextual and policy factors, and macro-economic and labour market conditions. The study found that a transition from irregular to legal status did not lead to significantly improved labour market outcomes. Labour markets were becoming stratified according to migratory status, and precarious status became 'a source of vulnerability in the short run as well as a long-term trap because low-wage and precarious jobs become a "sticky" web for people with precarious status' (Goldring and Landolt, 2011: 336).

Conclusions

Economic migration is vital for advanced economies. Migrant workers – both highly skilled and less skilled – provide *additional labour* at a time of high demand resulting from economic, demographic and social shifts. They also provide *special types of labour* to fill gaps that native workers are incapable or unwilling to fill. Migration thus helps to maintain labour market flexibility, encouraging investment and economic growth. In the GEC, migrants served as a *buffer* which somewhat mitigated the effects of the crisis on domestic labour forces. However, the economic and demographic forces that drive migration remained active even in the crisis, with migrants taking a growing share of jobs as economies began to recover.

During the post-1945 boom, migrant workers were steered into subordinate jobs: 'guest-workers' had strictly limited labour market rights, while colonial migrants were often subject to racial discrimination. In addition, many migrants lacked education and vocational training, and therefore entered the labour market at low levels. A key question was whether long-term residence in developed countries could lead to upward mobility. Even more crucial was the question whether the initial disadvantaged position would be carried over to the migrants' descendants, the second generation.

Labour market data show that migrants' work situation has become much more diverse, partly as a result of the shift to service-based economies. But some migrants have tended to get stuck in manufacturing jobs with poor prospects. High unemployment rates – often twice the average for natives – and low activity rates reveal that migrant workers often still have a disadvantaged position. Many migrant workers now have service jobs, some of them in high-skilled positions (like doctors, nurses and teachers), but overwhelmingly in such areas as cleaning, catering, domestic work and care.

As for the second generation, the picture is even more mixed, with important variations by ethnic group and host country. On the whole, children of migrants have done better than their parents, but have generally been less successful in both education and the labour market than young people without a migration background. Moreover, even those young second-generation members who have done well in education sometimes fail to get commensurate jobs.

One reaction of migrants to this rather negative labour market experience has been to establish their own businesses. However it is not clear that this always represents a better situation: some migrant or ethnic entrepreneurs do gain higher incomes and status, but others establish businesses in marginal sectors, and can only keep going through long hours, poor working conditions and exploiting the labour of other migrants (including family members).

The key finding of this chapter is that, over the last 40 years, economic restructuring in rich countries has been linked to a new international division of labour, in which migrant workers play important but varied roles. The shift to neoliberal economic policies has reshaped the conditions under which migrant workers are employed. Deregulation of the economy has gone hand-in-hand with the decline of trade unions and the erosion of welfare state protection. Formal employment within large-scale enterprises has in many cases been replaced by a variety of work arrangements that differentiate and separate workers along ethnic, class, education and gender lines. Temporary and causal employment, chains of subcontracting, informalization and new forms of labour market segmentation affect both native and migrant workers. However, it is the disadvantaged and vulnerable groups of workers – migrant women, irregular workers, ethnic and racial minorities – who end up in the most precarious positions. Deprivation of human and worker rights for groups that lack legal status and market power seems to be an integral aspect of all advanced and emerging industrial economies today.

The patterns of labour market disadvantage and differentiation established in earlier years had profound effects during the GEC. Migrants were particularly hard hit by unemployment and decline in earnings. Some groups have suffered more than others: irregular migrants play a crucial role in some economic sectors yet lack entitlement to social benefits. Irregular migration declined fast during the crisis, and many irregulars returned home. Migrant men working in construction and manufacturing were hard hit by unemployment, while women – more concentrated in care work and other services – were less likely to lose their jobs. Yet this did not mean an improved situation for women, for the new jobs that were created were overwhelmingly temporary or casual, reducing job security yet more.

Yet the overall lesson of the GEC was that migrant workers were essential to the economies of industrial countries, especially in Europe and some Asian countries, where demographic change is leading to a declining local labour force. In most places, migrant stocks have not fallen, and there is little doubt that new migrations will evolve where economic conditions improve. Moreover, as new industrial areas emerge in Asia, Latin America and Africa, migrant workers will play a part there too, and the differentiation of labour crucial to existing global commodity chains will become important in new contexts.

Guide to further reading

Extra resources at www.age-of-migration.com

In this chapter, we were able to look only at a limited range of studies on the labour market experience of migrants and the economic effects of migration. It would be important to look at other indicators, like wage levels (and how they change over time), income levels, poverty, employment rates and participation rates. Readers are recommended to use the further reading and to follow up the sources we cite for more on these issues.

The Age of Migration website includes an additional text on the educational and occupational success of the 'second generation' in Germany (11.1), as well as a summary of discussion between economists about whether migration is good or bad for destination-country economies and for specific groups of the population. This includes the debate between US economists George Borjas and David Card on whether labour immigration is bad for US workers (11.2). The website also includes an analysis of labour market segmentation in the French car and building industries in the 1970s and 1980s (11.3).

Hatton and Williamson's two books (1998; 2005) provide useful overviews of the economics of migration. For developed countries in general see the OECD's annual *International Migration Outlook*. For the USA see:Borjas (2001); Daniels (2004); Portes and Rumbaut (2006); and Smith and Edmonston (1997). European studies include: Dustmann and Fabbri (2005); and Münz *et al.* (2007). For Australia see: Castles *et al.* (1998); Collins (1991; 2006); Lever-Tracey and Quinlan (1988) and Wooden (1994). On Canada see Reitz (1998). Older but still relevant texts on the political economy of migrant labour include Piore (1979) and Sassen (1988; 2001). Useful newer collections are Phillips (2011b) and Munck *et al.* (2011).

Studies on ethnic entrepreneurs include: Kloosterman and Rath (2003); Light and Gold (1999); Rath (2002); Waldinger (1996); and Waldinger and Lichter (2003). Gender and migrant labour are examined in: Anderson (2000); Browne and Misra (2003); Pessar and Mahler (2003); Phizacklea (1990, 1998); and Schrover *et al.* (2007). On irregular migration and the informal sector see: Düvell (2006); Ness (2005); and Reyneri (2003).

Chapter 12

New Ethnic Minorities and Society

Migration since 1945 has led to growing cultural diversity and the formation of new ethnic groups in many countries. Such groups are visible through the presence of different-looking people speaking their own languages, the development of ethnic neighbourhoods, and the establishment of ethnic associations. In this chapter we will examine the experience of a range of societies. The topic would really require detailed description of developments in each immigration country – including emerging ones in Africa, Latin America and Asia. That is not possible here, and the chapter focuses mainly (though not exclusively) on Western Europe, North America and Oceania. Accounts of diversity and minorities in selected countries – the USA, Australia, the UK, France, Germany and Italy – are presented in Boxes 12.1 – 12.6. The *Age of Migration website* provides further material on some other immigration countries: Canada, the Netherlands, Sweden and South Korea.

The aim of the chapter is to analyse similarities and differences in the migratory process, and to discuss why ethnic group formation and growing diversity have been relatively easily accepted in some countries, while in others the result has been marginalization and exclusion. In some cases, outcomes differ for various immigrant groups. We examine the consequences for the ethnic groups concerned and for society in general. Our argument is that the migratory process works in a rather similar way everywhere with respect to settlement, labour market segmentation, residential patterns and ethnic group formation. The main differences are to be found in public attitudes and government policies on immigration, settlement, education, housing, citizenship and cultural pluralism.

This chapter uses a range of statistical concepts. For better understanding of these, please consult the Note on Migration Statistics at the beginning of the book.

Incorporation: how immigrants become part of society

A crucial question is how immigrants and their descendants can become part of receiving societies and nations. A second question is how the state and civil society can and should facilitate this process. Answers have varied in different countries. The process is most commonly referred to as 'integration', but this can imply a specific idea of where the process should lead, so we prefer the more neutral term 'incorporation'. In newer immigration countries, for instance the Gulf oil states and North-East Asia, there is a widespread belief that immigrants are only temporary and should not be integrated at all. In older immigration countries the key issue is whether immigrants should be incorporated as *individuals* – that is, without taking account of cultural difference or group belonging – or as *communities* – that is, ethnic groups which tend to cluster together and maintain their own cultures, languages and religions.

The starting point for understanding incorporation is historical experiences of nation-state formation: in Europe and its settler colonies (such as Canada, Argentina or Australia) this refers to the ways in which emerging states handled difference when dealing with internal ethnic or religious minorities, conquering new territories, incorporating immigrants, or ruling subjugated peoples (see Chapter 4). Differing ideas about citizenship developed from these experiences (see Chapter 3). 'National models' for dealing with ethnicity and cultural difference emerged (see Bertossi, 2007; Brubaker, 1992; Favell, 1998), and these models affected how states and the public later reacted to immigrants (Castles and Davidson, 2000). In other world regions, the main concern has often been with building a new national identity following decolonization, and how immigrants do or do not fit into this identity.

For example, the British history of conquering Wales, Scotland and Ireland and of dealing with religious diversity led to a politically integrated state that accepted difference: the United Kingdom required political loyalty, but a person's group identity could be Welsh or Scottish, Protestant or Catholic. In France, the 1789 Revolution established principles of equality and the rights of man that rejected group cultural identity, and aimed to include individuals as equal political subjects. In both Britain and France, however, it was the expansion of the state that created the nation – political belonging came before national identity. Germany was different: it was not united as a state until 1871, and the nation came before the state. This led to a form of ethnic or folk belonging that was not consistent with incorporation of minorities as citizens. These differing approaches imply different relationships between society and nation, and between civic belonging and national identity. In Britain a person could be a full member of the society and political nation and yet belong to a distinct cultural or religious group. In France, civic identity required a unitary national identity. In Germany, national identity came first, and was the precondition for belonging as a citizen.

By contrast, the white settler societies of the New World were built through the dispossession of indigenous peoples, and through immigration from Europe. Incorporation of immigrants as citizens was part of their national myths. This led to models of assimilation, such as the US image of the 'melting pot'. In the settler societies, civic belonging was thought to lead to national identity, so that differing identities were acceptable as a passing phase on the way to 'Americanization' (or the equivalent). Of course, it was thought that only white people could be assimilated: Australia, New Zealand, Canada and the USA all had racially selective immigration laws.

In North-East Asia, emerging immigration countries like Japan and South Korea have strong beliefs in ethnic homogeneity, and find it very hard to incorporate people of different backgrounds. South-East Asian countries like Malaysia have culturally mixed populations, but the public and politicians often fear that incorporating newcomers could upset existing ethnic balances. Similarly, in post-apartheid South Africa, immigration from other African countries is often seen as a threat, and has led to violent clashes. In North Africa, increasing presence of sub-Saharan migrants is largely seen as an undesirable phenomenon.

When immigration to highly developed countries started to gain ground in the post-1945 boom, incorporation of the newcomers was not a major issue. The numbers were not expected to be large, and there was a strong belief in the 'controllability of difference'. The 'classical immigration countries' (the USA, Canada, Australia etc.) only wanted white settlers from their 'mother countries' or other North-Western European countries, and saw no problem in assimilating them. Britain, France and the Netherlands also expected to be able to assimilate fairly small groups of immigrants from their colonies and from other European countries such as Spain and Italy. Germany and other 'guest-worker' importers (e.g. Austria and Switzerland) did not anticipate family reunion or settlement, and therefore pursued polices of temporary admission to the labour market – like many emerging immigration countries today. (See Chapter 3 for 'ideal-types' of citizenship, which are important contexts for the varying incorporation models.)

Assimilation meant that immigrants were to be incorporated into society through a one-sided process of adaptation. They were to give up their distinctive linguistic, cultural or social characteristics and become indistinguishable from the majority population. The 'guest-worker' model can be described as *differential exclusion*: migrants were to be temporarily incorporated into certain areas of society (above all the labour market) but denied access to others (especially citizenship and political participation) (Castles, 1995).

But the belief in the controllability of difference proved misplaced in all these cases. In the post-war boom, labour migration grew in volume and became a structural feature of Western economies. Racially selective immigration rules broke down, and migrants increasingly came from more distant or culturally different countries. When the economic boom faltered in the 1970s, family reunion took place – even in 'guest-worker' countries. Then the end of the Cold War and globalization brought new migrations from ever more diverse origins.

Box 12.1 Minorities in the USA

US society is a complex ethnic mosaic deriving from five centuries of immigration. The white population is a mixture of the original mainly British colonists and later immigrants who came from all over Europe. Assimilation of newcomers is part of the 'American creed', but this process has always been racially selective. Native American societies were devastated by white expansion westwards, while millions of African slaves were brought to America to labour in the plantations of the South.

The USA is becoming ever more culturally diverse. The foreign-born population grew by 8.8 million between 2000 and 2010, to reach an estimated 40 million. The foreign-born share in population rose from only 5 per cent in 1970 to 13 per cent in 2010. By then, 53 per cent of the foreign-born were from Latin America, 28 per cent from Asia and only 12 per cent from Europe. Ethnic minorities now make up over a quarter of the population – and are especially strongly represented in younger age cohorts.. Hispanics are the descendants of Mexicans absorbed into the USA through its south-western expansion, as well as recent immigrants from Latin America. The Asian population is also growing fast.

US population by race and Hispanic origin, 2010

	Millions	*Per cent*
Total population	308.7	100.0
Hispanic or Latino origin (of any race)	50.5	16.3
One race;	299.7	97.1
White	223.6	72.4
Black or African–American	38.9	12.6
American Indian and Alaskan Native	2.9	0.9
Asian	14.7	4.8
Native Hawaiian and other Pacific Islander	0.5	0.2
Some other race	19.1	6.2
Two or more races	9.0	2.9

Note: Data are for 'household population' (excluding people in institutions like prisons). Race is based on self-identification.

Source: US Census Bureau (2011b).

The movement of European immigrants and African–Americans into low-skilled industrial jobs in the early twentieth century contributed to labour market segmentation and residential segregation. In the long run, many 'white ethnics' achieved upward mobility, while African–Americans became increasingly ghettoized. Despite the rise of a black middle class after the Civil Rights Movement of the 1960s, distinctions between the majority of African–Americans and whites in income, unemployment rates, social conditions and education are still extreme. Members of some recent immigrant groups, especially from Asia, have high educational and occupational levels.

→

Incorporation of immigrants into the 'American dream' has been largely left to market forces. Nonetheless, government has played a role by making it easy to obtain US citizenship, and through compulsory public schooling. Irregular migration and the costs of welfare for immigrants have been major political issues since the 1990s. The construction of fences and surveillance systems along the US–Mexico border did not cut migration but made it more dangerous and expensive: many migrants lost their lives trying to cross the deserts of California, Arizona and Texas. In view of the high risks and costs, many Mexican workers decided to stay on in the US and to bring their families. Thus border control measures turned temporary labour movement into permanent settlement.

Today immigration reform is a central issue in US politics. In 2010, just over one-third of the 40 million foreign-born residents were naturalized US citizens (37 per cent), another third were legal residents or legal temporary migrants (35 per cent), and just under a third (28 per cent) were irregular residents. However, reform efforts at the federal level have stalled over the last decade. In response, there has been an increase in state initiatives. While some states have enacted tougher laws relating to work authorization verification and immigration enforcement (such as the Arizona Senate Bill 1070), other states (such as California and Maryland) have adopted more immigrant-friendly laws.

Sources: Chishti and Bergeron (2011); Feagin (1989); Gargis (2011); Migration Information Source (2011); MPI Data Hub (2012); Navarro (2012); OECD (2011a); Passel and Cohn (2011); Portes and Rumbaut (2006); Roberts (2010); Singer *et al.* (2008); Tavernise and Gebeloff (2010); US Census Bureau (2011a, 2011b); Wasem (2007).

In the classical immigration countries, migrants from non-Western European backgrounds (Southern and Eastern Europe, Latin America, Asia and Africa) tended to have disadvantaged work situations and to become concentrated in specific neighbourhoods. While patterns of residential segregation differed across countries, in many places, immigrants settled initially in inner-city areas. This led to community formation and the maintenance of minority cultures, languages and religions. Assimilation had failed for many immigrant groups and new approaches were needed. Even in the European 'guest-worker' countries, settlement was taking place despite official denials. The absence of measures to assist incorporation often led to social exclusion, and an enduring link between class and ethnic background.

Governments replaced assimilation (initially at least) with the principle of *integration*, which meant recognizing that adaptation was a gradual process that required some degree of mutual accommodation. Acceptance of cultural maintenance and community formation might be a necessary stage, but the final goal was still absorption into the dominant culture – integration was often simply a slower and gentler form of

Box 12.2 Minorities in Australia

Australia has pursued a programme of planned immigration since 1947: 7 million new settlers have arrived. Immigration has helped treble the population from 7.6 million in 1947 to 22.8 million by 2012. Australia is home to nearly 5 million overseas-born people, nearly a quarter of the population. A similar proportion is Australian-born with at least one parent born overseas. In 2011 there were 550,000 Aboriginal and Torres Strait Islander people (2.4 per cent of total population).

Historically, Australians have been fearful of migration from Asia, and a 'white Australia policy' was introduced in 1901. Post-1947 migration was designed to be mainly from Britain, with a gradual broadening to the rest of Europe. But the white Australia policy proved unsustainable, and Asian entries grew rapidly from the 1970s. By 2009, an estimated 74 per cent of the total population was born in Australia followed by 11 per cent from Europe, Asia (8.5 per cent) Oceania (3 per cent), Middle East and Northern Africa (1.5 per cent), Sub-Saharan Africa (1.3 per cent) and the Americas (1.1 per cent).

Australia – like the USA and Canada – has seen immigration as vital for nation-building. Family migration has been the norm. In the 1950s and 1960s, immigrants were expected to quickly assimilate. However, non-British immigrants (especially Eastern and Southern Europeans) tended to get low-paid manual jobs. This in turn meant clustering in low-income areas, providing the basis for ethnic community formation.

By the 1970s, a policy of multiculturalism had been adopted. The Australian approach emphasizes the duty of the state to combat racism and to ensure that minorities have equal access to government services, education and jobs. Public support for immigration and multiculturalism waned in the 1990s. Disaffection with multiculturalism increased following 9/11 and the Bali bombing of 2002, in which 88 Australians were killed. Between 1996 and 2007, the Liberal–National Coalition dismantled many multicultural institutions and promoted principles of integration and social cohesion around 'core cultural values'. This was linked to a tough line on asylum, including mandatory detention of irregular entrants and the 'Pacific Solution' in which asylum seekers were sent to camps in Nauru and Papua New Guinea. At the same time the Coalition increased immigration, particularly of high-skilled workers.

The Australian Labor Party (ALP) Government elected in 2007 introduced changes to asylum policy including ending the Pacific Solution. However, 'border protection' was a central issue in the 2010 federal election, with both major parties treating boat arrivals as a threat to national sovereignty and security. Yet this public concern with the small number of asylum seekers – 6200 in 2009 – obscured much bigger changes: economic immigration soared (108,000 in 2008–9), while the number of temporary workers (101,000 in 2008–9) and international students (320,000 in 2008–9) grew even faster. However, despite this emphasis on temporary migration, Australian immigration policy provides clear pathways to permanent residency, dependent on labour market performance.

Sources: Castles *et al.* (2013); Collins (1991); DIAC (2010a; b; 2012b); Jupp (2002); Karlsen *et al.* (2010); Markus *et al.* (2009); Vasta (1999).

assimilation. Today, of all the highly developed immigration countries, France comes closest to the assimilationist model (see Box 12.4 and Chapter 13). Elsewhere, however, there was a shift to approaches that recognized the long-term persistence of group difference. In some countries, such models were referred to as 'multiculturalism'; in other places terms like 'minorities policy', 'equality and freedom of choice' were used.

Multiculturalism meant that immigrants (and sometimes non-migrant minority groups) should be able to participate as equals in all spheres of society, without being expected to give up their own culture, religion and language, although usually with an expectation of conformity to certain key values. There have been two main variants. In the USA, cultural diversity and the existence of ethnic communities are officially accepted, but it is not seen as the role of the state to work for social justice or to support the maintenance of ethnic cultures. The second variant is multiculturalism as a public policy. Here, multiculturalism implies both the willingness of the majority group to accept cultural difference and state action to secure equal rights for minorities. Multiculturalism originated in Canada, and was taken up under various labels between the 1970s and the 1990s in Australia, the UK, the Netherlands, Sweden and elsewhere.

All of the different approaches to incorporation have proved problematic in one way or another, so that by the early twenty-first century there appeared to be a widespread 'crisis of integration'. In recent years, immigrant incorporation has been overshadowed by concerns about security (see Chapter 9) and national identity. The pendulum has swung back from celebrating diversity to insisting on forms of 'civic integration' based on often rather unclear ideas about social cohesion and national values.

Immigration policies and minority formation

We can distinguish three groups amongst the highly developed immigration countries with regard to their immigration and integration policies. The 'classical immigration' countries encouraged family reunion and permanent settlement and treated most legal immigrants as future citizens. The second group includes France, the Netherlands and the UK, where immigrants from former colonies were often citizens at the time of entry. Permanent immigration and family reunion have generally been permitted (though with some exceptions). Immigrants from other countries have had a less favourable situation, although settlement and naturalization have often been allowed. The third group consists of those countries which tried to cling to 'guest-worker' models, above all Germany, Austria and Switzerland. Such countries tried (but failed) to prevent family reunion, were reluctant to grant secure residence status and had highly restrictive naturalization rules until recently.

The distinctions between these three categories are neither absolute nor static. Some countries do not fit the categories: for example, Sweden admitted both migrant workers and refugees, but always accepted family reunion. The USA tacitly permitted irregular farmworker migration from Mexico, but denied rights to such workers. France had very restrictive rules on family reunion until the 1970s. Germany and Switzerland gradually improved family reunion rules and access to long-term residence status. The Netherlands had both colonial immigrants and 'guestworkers'. One important change has been the erosion of the privileged status of migrants from former colonies. Making colonized people into subjects of the Dutch or British crown, or citizens of France, was a way of legitimating colonialism, and after 1945 it also seemed a convenient way of bringing in low-skilled labour. All three countries removed citizenship from most former colonial subjects and put them on a par with foreigners. The Netherlands government pushed for Surinamese independence in 1975 primarily because it was seen as a way to prevent migration, although the actual result proved to be counterproductive in the form of a large pre-independence migration wave (van Amersfoort, 2011).

There has been some convergence: former colonial countries have become more restrictive with regard to citizenship, while former 'guestworker' countries have become less so. But this has gone hand-in-hand with a new differentiation, most importantly through the creation of a privileged status for intra-Community migrants in the European Community (and later EU) countries from 1968 onwards (see Chapter 10).

Immigration policies have consequences for immigrants' future status. Policies designed to keep migrants in the status of temporary mobile workers make it likely that settlement will take place under discriminatory conditions. Moreover, official ideologies of temporary (or more recently 'circular') migration create expectations within the receiving population. If a temporary sojourn turns into settlement, then it is the immigrants who tend to be blamed for problems. Visible differences – for instance dark skin colour or Islamic dress – can attract suspicion and social exclusion. Immigration policies also shape the consciousness of migrants themselves. In countries where permanent immigration is accepted and the settlers are granted secure residence status and civil rights, a long-term perspective is possible. Where the myth of short-term sojourn is maintained, immigrants' perspectives are inevitably contradictory. Return to the country of origin may be difficult or impossible, but permanence in the immigration country is doubtful. Such immigrants settle and form ethnic groups, but they find it more difficult to plan a future as part of the wider society. The result is often isolation, separatism and emphasis on difference. Thus discriminatory immigration policies cannot stop the completion of the migratory process, but they can be the first step towards the marginalization of the future settlers.

Labour market position

As we argued in Chapter 11, labour market segmentation based on ethnicity, race, legal status and gender has developed in all immigration countries. This was intrinsic in the type of labour migration practised until the mid-1970s in older immigration countries, and which is still widespread in emerging labour importing areas. However, today's migrants are much more diverse in educational and occupational status. States have increasingly encouraged highly skilled personnel and business people to migrate to industrial countries, and these are an important factor in skill upgrading and technology transfer. Many refugees bring skills with them, although they are not always allowed to use them. Low-skilled migrants are officially unwelcome, but enter through family reunion, as asylum seekers or irregularly. Their contribution to low-skilled occupations, small business and households (e.g., childcare, cleaning) is of great economic importance, but is officially unrecognized.

Labour market segmentation is part of the migratory process. When people come from poor to rich countries, without local knowledge or networks, lacking proficiency in the language and unfamiliar with local ways of working, then their entry point into the labour market is likely to be at a low level. The question is whether there is a fair chance of later upward mobility. This partly depends on state policies. Some countries (including

---

Box 12.3 Minorities in the United Kingdom

The UK uses three classifications for its population of immigrant origin:

In 2010, there were 4.1 million *foreign citizens* (6.6 per cent of the total population of about 62 million) – twice the 1993 figure.

The *foreign-born population* numbered over 6 million in 2010 (about 10 per cent of total population), compared with 4 million in 1993 (7 per cent). The main countries of origin for the *foreign-born* were: India (9 per cent), Poland (8 per cent), Pakistan (6 per cent), Ireland (5 per cent) and Germany (4 per cent).

The *ethnic minority population* are mostly British-born descendants of New Commonwealth immigrants who arrived from the 1950s to the 1970s (see Chapter 5). In 2010–11 about 7 million people (11 per cent of the UK population) identified themselves as having a 'non-white ethnicity'. Nearly 90 per cent of UK residents identified themselves as White; 5 per cent as Asian or Asian British; 3 per cent as Black or Black British; and 3 per cent as members of another ethnic group.

Commonwealth immigrants who came before 1971 were British subjects and enjoyed all citizenship rights. The 1971 Immigration Act and the

$\longrightarrow$

→

1981 British Nationality Act put Commonwealth immigrants on a par with foreigners in most respects. Citizens of other EU states have employment and social rights, and can vote in local and European elections, but not in parliamentary elections.

The *race relations approach* which emerged in the late 1960s and the 1970s meant recognizing the existence of distinct groups, defined primarily on the basis of race. Acceptance of cultural and religious diversity was officially labelled as *multiculturalism*. Race Relations Acts outlawed discrimination in public places, employment and housing. However, racism remained a major problem. Minority youth rioted in inner-city areas in the 1980s and 1990s. The government responded with measures to reduce youth unemployment, improve education, rehabilitate urban areas and change police practices. But the 1999 Stephen Lawrence Inquiry (set up to analyse the poor police response after the murder of a young black man by a white gang) revealed the continued strength of institutional racism. In 2001, riots broke out involving youth of Asian origin in several northern cities.

In the early twenty-first century, the main immigration issue was asylum. Five new asylum laws were introduced between 1993 and 2006, successively tightening up entry rules, and introducing detention and restrictions on welfare. By the mid-2000s public attention had shifted to the perceived threat of Islam. The London bombings of July 2005 precipitated concern about the loyalty of young Muslims. Government policies under the Labour Government emphasized 'social cohesion'. Citizenship tests for immigrants were introduced, based on ideas of 'Britishness' and 'core values'.

Another new issue was the rapid and unexpected growth in labour migration from Poland and other Central and Eastern European countries – known collectively as the 'A8' – which joined the EU in 2004. A8 migrants often found work in agriculture and food-processing industries, leading to migrant concentrations in areas which had previously had little experience of immigration. The Conservative–Liberal Democrat Government elected in 2010 attempted to cut immigration, as well as welfare programmes. Labour flows from the A8 declined and earlier migrants left – partly because of lack of jobs in the UK as a consequence of the GEC, and partly because of new opportunities at home.

Members of ethnic minorities were hard hit by rising unemployment. Worst affected were black people, with 48 per cent unemployment in 2009. The urban riots of 2011, which involved young people of all backgrounds, seem to have been triggered by a growing feeling of hopelessness.

Such findings highlight the contrast between the formal equality enjoyed by ethnic minorities and their frequent experiences of inequality, social exclusion and racism. The UK experience shows that citizenship is not necessarily a protection against social disadvantage and racism. Yet it also shows that in the long run groups that have initial negative experiences do become incorporated into society and can experience upward mobility.

Sources: Athwal *et al.* (2010); IPPR (2010); Layton-Henry (2004); Migration Observatory (2011; 2012); ONS (2004); Solomos (2003); Somerville *et al.* (2009).

Australia, Canada, Sweden, the UK, France and Netherlands) have active policies to improve the labour market position of immigrants and minorities through language courses, basic education, vocational training and anti-discrimination legislation. Other countries (including the USA, Japan, Malaysia and the Arab Gulf states) seem content to exploit the labour of immigrants, either through maintaining them in a situation of irregularity or by setting up discriminatory contract labour arrangements.

Residential segregation, community formation and the global city

Some degree of residential segregation is to be found in many immigration countries, though nowhere is it as extreme as in the USA, where in certain areas there is almost complete separation between blacks and whites, and sometimes Asians and Hispanics too. In other countries there are city neighbourhoods where immigrant groups are highly concentrated, though they rarely form the majority of the population. Residential segregation arises partly from immigrants' situation as newcomers, lacking social networks and local knowledge. Equally important is their low social status and income. Another factor is discrimination by landlords: some refuse to let to immigrants, while others make a business of charging high rents for poor accommodation.

Institutional practices may also encourage residential segregation. Many migrant workers were initially housed by employers or public authorities. There were migrant hostels and camps in Australia, barracks provided by employers in Germany and Switzerland, and hostels managed by the government *Fonds d'Action Sociale* (FAS, or Social Action Fund) in France. These generally provided better conditions than private rented accommodation, but led to control and isolation. Hostels also encouraged clustering: when workers left their initial accommodation they tended to seek housing in the vicinity.

In countries where racism is relatively weak such as Australia, immigrants often move out of inner-city areas to better suburbs as their economic position improves. Thus, ethnic clustering can be understood in such contexts as a transitory phenomenon. However, where racism and social exclusion are strong, concentration persists or may even increase. Segregation increases when members of the majority population move out of inner-city areas to the suburbs (a phenomenon also known as 'white flight'). The departure of better-off immigrants can lead to increased concentration by social class as well as ethnicity.

Residential segregation is a contradictory phenomenon. In terms of the theory of ethnic minority formation (see Chapter 3), it contains elements of both other-definition and self-definition. Immigrants cluster together for economic and social reasons, and are often kept out of certain areas by racism. But they also frequently *want* to be together, in order to provide mutual support and protection, to develop family and neighbourhood networks and to maintain their languages and cultures. Ethnic neighbourhoods allow the establishment of small businesses and agencies which cater for immigrants' needs, as well as the formation of associations of all kinds.

Global reorganization of finance, production and distribution have reinforced the dominant position of 'global cities' (Sassen, 2001) which attract immigrants, both for highly specialized activities and for low-skilled service jobs which service the luxurious lifestyles of the elites (see Chapter 2). Ethnic clustering and community formation may be seen as necessary products of migration to the global cities. They may lead to conflicts, but they can also lead to renewal and enrichment of urban life and culture – although paradoxically, this can in turn lead to gentrification and displacement of ethnic minorities. Specific ethnic groups can never be completely isolated or self-sufficient in modern cities. Much of the energy and innovative capacity within the cities lies in the cultural syncretism of the multi-ethnic populations, as Davis (1990) has shown in the case of Los Angeles. Just as there can be no return to mono-ethnic populations (which was always a myth in any case), so there is no way back to static or homogeneous cultures (equally a myth). The global city with its multicultural population is a powerful laboratory for change.

Box 12.4 Minorities in France

France, like Britain, has a confusing array of statistical classifications for its immigrant population. The category of *immigrés* (*immigrants*) has recently been introduced to give information on people born abroad of non-French parents. In 2007, *immigrés* numbered about 5.3 million (8 per cent of total population) (see table below). In addition there are about half a million *French citizens of Overseas Departments and Territories,* mostly of African, Caribbean and Pacific Island origin. France's immigrant population has changed from one of mainly Southern European origins in the 1970s to a majority of non-Europeans today: predominantly North and West Africans but with a substantial Asian component.

Reticence about the use of ethnic categories is based on France's 'republican model', which lays down principles of civic citizenship and equal individual rights for all. Recognition of cultural difference or ethnic communities is unacceptable. The idea is that immigrants should become citizens, and will then enjoy equal opportunities. The reality is different. People of non-European birth or parentage (whether citizens or not) face social exclusion and discrimination. Minorities have become concentrated in inner-city areas and in large high-rise estates on the periphery of the cities (*les banlieues*). The work situation of ethnic minorities is marked by low-status, insecure jobs and high unemployment rates, especially for youth: in 2010, 43 per cent of young men in officially designated 'sensitive urban zones' (ZUS, *zones urbaines sensibles)* were jobless.

→

⟶

France: immigrant population 2009 by origins

	Per cent	Numbers (thousands)
Europe	**38.4**	**2,046**
European Union (27 states)	**34.1**	**1,814**
Spain	4.7	252
Italy	5.8	311
Portugal	11.0	584
UK	2.8	151
Other EU 27	9.7	516
Other Europe	4.4	232
Africa	**43.2**	**2,303**
Algeria	13.5	721
Morocco	12.5	664
Tunisia	4.4	236
Other Africa	12.8	682
Asia	**14.4**	**768**
Turkey	4.5	242
Cambodia, Laos, Vietnam	3.0	161
Other Asia	6.9	365
Americas, Oceania	**3.9**	**208**
Total	**100**	**5,325**

Note: figures are for Metropolitan France (excluding Overseas Departments).
Source: INSEE (2012).

The position of immigrants in French society has become highly politicized, with the emergence of both an anti-immigrant right-wing party, the *Front National* (FN) and movements of citizens of North African origin. Major riots, notably in 2005 and 2007, concentrated political attention on the long-term effects of immigration. These trends are examined in detail in Chapter 13.

President Sarkozy's Centre-Right government from 2007 to 2012 used anti-immigrant measures as a populist electoral tool. These included more restrictive family reunion policies, deportations of Roma, (largely symbolical) border controls to keep out Tunisian immigrants in 2011, attacks on religious slaughter, and public claims about the incompatibility of Islam and French identity. In the run-up to the Presidential Election of 2012, Sarkozy called for the halving of immigration and claimed that France was threatened by Islamic terrorists. Nonetheless, Sarkozy was defeated by the Socialist candidate François Hollande, indicating perhaps that immigration was less important to electors than other issues, such as unemployment.

Sources: Body-Gendrot and Wihtol de Wenden (2007); Hargreaves (2007); INSEE (2012); Simon (2008); Wihtol de Wenden (1988); Wihtol de Wenden and Leveau (2001).

Empirical research suggests that, in general, levels of residential segregation in Europe are more moderate compared to the USA, although there are big differences across immigrant groups, cities and countries (Musterd, 2005). Contrary to popular belief, overall segregation levels do not appear to increase, partly because the effects of new immigration may be counterbalanced by the integration and upward residential mobility of long-term settlers (Musterd and Van Kempen, 2009). Particularly in countries such as Germany, Sweden and the Netherlands, immigrants often live in social housing of relatively high quality. Empirical analyses of ethnic clustering suggest that upward steps in migrants' residential careers (e.g., an onward move to a non-immigrant neighbourhood) reflect broader integration processes (Musterd and De Vos, 2007). This suggests that promoting education and labour market access are more effective integration policies than 'spatial social engineering projects' such as the promotion of mixed neighbourhoods (Musterd and Ostendorf, 2009).

Social policy

As migrants moved into the inner cities and industrial towns, they were often blamed for rising housing costs, declining housing quality and deteriorating social amenities. In response, a whole set of social policies were developed. Sometimes policies designed to reduce ethnic concentrations and ease social tensions achieved the opposite.

Nowhere were the problems more severe than in France: in the 1960s *bidonvilles* (shantytowns) occupied by migrant workers and their families emerged. After 1968, measures were taken to eliminate *bidonvilles* and make public housing more accessible to immigrants. The concept of the *seuil de tolérance* (threshold of tolerance) was introduced, according to which the immigrant presence should be limited to a maximum of 10 or 15 per cent of residents in a housing estate or 25 per cent of students in a class (MacMaster, 1991: 14–28; Verbunt, 1985: 147–55). The implication was that immigrant concentrations presented a problem, and that dispersal was the precondition for assimilation. Subsidies to public housing societies (*habitations à loyer modéré,* or HLMs) were coupled to quotas for immigrants. To minimize the perceived risk of conflicts with local residents, immigrant families were concentrated in specific estates. The HLMs could claim that they had adhered to the quotas – on an average of all their dwellings – while in fact creating new ghettos (Weil, 1991b: 249–58).

By the 1980s, the *banlieues* were rapidly turning into areas of social problems and ethnic conflicts. Social policies focused on urban youth, and the Socialist government developed a range of programmes to improve housing and social conditions, and to boost educational outcomes and unemployment. Such policies had little effect: today the *banlieues* remain hotspots of segregation, youth unemployment and violence. The ethnic youth uprisings of 2005 and 2007 reflected the deep feelings

Box 12.5 Minorities in Germany

Until the late 1990s, politicians declared that Germany was 'not a country of immigration'. Yet, with over 20 million newcomers since 1945 (many of them 'ethnic Germans' from the former Soviet Union, Poland and Romania), it has in fact had more immigration than any other European country, and has the second largest foreign-born population of all countries in the world, after the USA. In 2009, Germany had 10.6 million *foreign-born persons* – 13 per cent of its total population of 82 million. The largest groups were people from Turkey (1.5 million), Poland (1.1 million), Russian Federation (1 million), Kazakhstan (628,000) and Italy (518,000 (OECD, 2011a: 390).

Children born to foreign citizen parents remain foreign citizens, though they can (under certain conditions) opt for German citizenship at maturity. Roughly one of every five foreigners living in Germany was born there, and is thus a second- or third-generation immigrant. In 1961, Germany's *foreign resident population* was just 0.7 million (1 per cent of total population). By 2010, there were 7.2 million foreigners, ten times as many (9 per cent) (see table below).

Foreign resident population in Germany by main nationalities (1995 and 2010)

Nationality	1995 thousands	2010 thousands	2010 per cent of foreign population
Turkey	2,014	1,629	24.1
Italy	586	517	7.7
Poland	277	419	6.2
Serbia	798	335	5.0
Greece	360	276	4.1
Croatia	185	220	3.3
Russian Federation	–	191	2.8
Austria	185	175	2.6
Bosnia & Herzegovina	316	152	2.3
Netherlands	113	136	2.0
Other	2300	2704	39.9
Total	**7,134**	**6,754**	**100**
EU (older members)		1,623	24.0
EU (post-2004 members)		820	12.1

Notes: Serbia includes persons recorded under the former country names 'Yugoslavia', 'Serbia-Montenegro' and 'Serbia or Kosovo'.

Sources: OECD (1997; 2012: 361).

Most of the 'guestworkers' who came from Southern Europe and Turkey between the 1950s and the early 1970s were initially employed as manual workers in manufacturing industries, leading to residential concentration in industrial areas and city central districts. Later economic restructuring

$\longrightarrow$

→

eliminated many of the jobs held by immigrants, leading to unemployment rates of 20 per cent or more – nearly twice the national average (see Chapter 11). Lack of school programmes to address the problems faced by children of immigrants meant that they too tended to have poor labour market chances.

Following reunification in 1990, there was a wave of racist violence against immigrants and asylum seekers. The reality of permanent settlement and the dangers of creating an underclass became obvious. Attention focused on the Turkish minority, with its mainly Islamic background. Municipal authorities set up special offices to ensure appropriate service provision for minorities. In Frankfurt am Main this was called the Office for Multicultural Affairs, but at the national level multiculturalism was rejected as threatening to national unity.

The Citizenship Law of 1999 marked a major change. It was designed to make it easier for immigrants and their children to become Germans, but it stopped short of recognizing dual citizenship – a key demand of Turkish immigrants. Germany's first Immigration Law was passed in 2004. This was designed to establish a modern system for planning and managing migration intakes. It also established integration courses providing German language teaching as well as an introduction to the country's laws, history and culture. Such courses are compulsory for certain categories of new entrants and existing foreign residents.

Migration to Germany has declined in recent years, with both inflows and outflows between 600,000 and 700,000 annually, so that net migration is very low (under 100,000). Since the German population is ageing and declining, due to low fertility, successive governments have been keen to attract highly skilled immigrants. At the same time restrictions on low-skilled labour migrants have been maintained, with some limited temporary labour schemes for agriculture, construction and the hospitality sector.

Germany is an important example of the unforeseen effects of migration. Labour recruitment was designed to bring in temporary workers who would not stay, but in the long run it led to permanent settlement and the emergence of a multi-ethnic society. Official denial made things worse, because it exacerbated the exclusion of migrants from society. In the long run public attitudes and policy approaches had to change. This is now happening, but it is a difficult and lengthy process.

Sources: Green (2004); OECD (1999; 2011); Schierup *et al.* (2006); Süssmuth (2001).

---

of discrimination and exclusion felt by the inhabitants of the *banlieues* (Body-Gendrot and Wihtol de Wenden, 2007).

The extent to which the state should introduce special social policies to facilitate immigrant integration is controversial. On the one hand, special policies for immigrants can reinforce tendencies to segregation. Up to the 1980s, German education authorities pursued a 'dual strategy', designed to provide skills needed for life in Germany while at the same time maintaining homeland cultures to facilitate return. This led to special classes for foreign children, contributing to social isolation and poor educational performance (Castles *et al.*, 1984, ch. 6). Housing policies in the UK were intended to be non-discriminatory, yet they sometimes led to the emergence of 'black' and 'white' housing estates. Sweden's special public housing schemes for immigrants led to a high degree of ethnic concentration and separation from the Swedish population (Andersson, 2007).

On the other hand, multicultural social policies are based on the idea that immigrants need services that address their special needs with regard to education, language and housing. The absence of such measures can put immigrants and their children at a disadvantage, and deny them opportunities for upward mobility. The key assumption of multiculturalism is that specific policies do not lead to separatism but, on the contrary, are the precondition for successful integration.

It is possible to suggest a rough classification of social policy responses to immigration and minority formation. From the 1970s, Australia, Canada, the UK, Sweden and the Netherlands pursued active social policies targeting immigrants and minorities. In the first three, the label 'multicultural' was used. Britain also spoke of 'race relations policy', while Sweden used the term 'immigrant policy' and the Netherlands 'minorities policy'. In all these countries, social policies that specifically target immigrants and minorities have been heavily criticized in recent years. As a result, multicultural policies have in some cases been replaced by an emphasis on 'integration', 'social cohesion' and 'shared citizenship values'. However, some of the social policies have been maintained under new labels. Some scholars have therefore contested the view that multicultural policies are in general retreat (cf. Banting and Kymlicka, 2012).

A second group of countries rejects special social policies for immigrants. US authorities regard special policies for immigrants as unnecessary government intervention. Nonetheless, the equal opportunities, anti-discrimination and affirmative action measures introduced after the Civil Rights Movement of the 1960s benefited immigrants, and special social and educational measures are to be found at the local level. However, access to social benefits and education by non-citizens (especially irregular immigrants) has been under attack since the 1980s. French governments have rejected special social policies on the principle that immigrants should become citizens, and that any special treatment would hinder this. Yet despite this there have been programmes, such as Educational Priority Zones or, more generally, *la politique de la ville* (urban policy), which target areas of disadvantage, without special mention of immigrants.

The third group of countries consists of those that have recruited migrant labour, particularly through 'guest-worker' systems. Germany has pursued rather contradictory policies. In the 1960s, the government commissioned charitable organizations (linked to the churches and the labour movement) to provide special social services for foreign workers. Foreign workers also had equal rights to work-related social benefits, but could be deported in the event of long-term unemployment or disability. After recruitment stopped in 1973, migrants (supported by labour unions and NGOs) won landmark court cases on welfare rights and family reunion. As settlement became more permanent, welfare, health and education agencies began to take account of the needs of immigrants – despite the official claim that 'Germany was not a country of immigration'. The experience in Austria, the Netherlands and Belgium was similar: while national-level politicians rejected long-term integration, city authorities recognized the real diversity of urban populations by providing special services for minorities. Switzerland, by contrast, leaves social provision to individual initiative and the private sector.

In the early twenty-first century there seems to have occurred some convergence in social policy, fuelled by concerns about social exclusion or what a report into the 2001 riots in Northern England referred to as 'parallel lives' (Cantle, 2001). Political leaders have questioned multicultural approaches, and have introduced such measures as citizenship tests and integration contracts. Nonetheless, special programmes to combat the social disadvantages faced by immigrants and their descendants can also be found almost everywhere, despite differences in rhetoric. The recession that started in 2008 has reduced the funding available for such measures. The future of integration policies is thus uncertain at present (for comparative evaluation of integration policies see MIPEX, 2012).

While there is a vast literature on 'integration policies', empirical evidence on the effectiveness of these policies is surprisingly limited (cf. Ersanilli, 2010). One comparative study found that access to citizenship has positive effects on socio-cultural integration of Turkish immigrants in France and Germany, countries which require some degree of assimilation, but not in the Netherlands (Ersanilli and Koopmans, 2010). Based on a comparison of eight European countries, Koopmans (2010) argued that the effects of multicultural policies have been generally negative. However, others have questioned such views (e.g. Barting and Kymlicka, 2012). The existing evidence is scarce and inconclusive, and results seem to vary across specific migrant groups and the different social, economic and cultural dimensions of 'integration' (cf. EFFNATIS, 2001), and more research is clearly needed.

However, the most salient insight seems that the effects of various 'integration policies', whether positive or negative, are generally rather small (cf. Ersanilli and Koopmans, 2011), and that their importance should therefore not be exaggerated. To a large extent, modes of migrant incorporation are determined by skills, class and the social ties of migrants as well as structural factors such as access to education and labour markets (Fokkema and de Haas, 2011; van Tubergen *et al.*, 2004), which often lie beyond the scope of specific 'integration policies'. Portes and Zhou (1993) introduced the term 'segmented assimilation' to describe the diverse possible outcomes of adaptation processes. Based on a review of the 'second generation' in the USA, Portes *et al.* stressed that while the second generation assimilates in the sense of learning English and American culture, 'it makes a great deal of difference whether they do so by joining the mainstream middle class or the marginalized, and largely racialized, population at the bottom' (Portes *et al.*, 2005: 1000).

Racism and minorities

Here too, varying patterns may be distinguished, although this classification is based more on the characteristics of immigrants than the types of immigration countries mentioned in the previous section. First, some settlers have merged into the general population and *do not constitute separate ethnic groups*. These are generally people who are culturally and socio-economically similar to the majority of the receiving population: for instance British settlers in Australia or Austrians in Germany.

Second, some settlers form *ethnic communities*: they tend to cluster in certain neighbourhoods and to maintain their original languages and cultures, but they are not excluded from citizenship, political participation and opportunities for economic and social mobility. The ethnic community may have developed partly due to initial discrimination, but the principal reasons for its persistence are cultural and psychological. Examples are Italians in Australia, Canada or the USA; Irish in the UK; and people of Southern European background in France, Belgium or the Netherlands. Such communities are likely to decline in saliency over time, as later generations intermarry with other groups, and move out of initial areas of concentration.

Third, some settlers form *ethnic minorities*. Like ethnic communities, they tend to live in certain neighbourhoods and to maintain their languages and cultures. But, in addition, they may have a disadvantaged socio-economic position and be partially excluded from the wider society by one or more of such factors as weak legal status, refusal of citizenship, denial of political and social rights, ethnic or racial discrimination, and racist violence and harassment. Examples are some Middle Eastern and Asian immigrants in Australia, Canada or the USA; Hispanics in the USA; Afro-Caribbeans and Asians in the UK; North Africans and Turks in most Western European countries; and asylum seekers of non-European background just about everywhere. However, it is important to emphasize that, despite discrimination and exclusion, ethnic minorities often succeed in improving their socio-economic situation over two or three generations, enabling them to become more fully incorporated into society. So, ethnic minorities may often become ethnic communities in the longer run.

All the countries examined have settlers from all three categories, but our concern here is with the second and third categories. It is important to examine why some immigrants in time take on the character of ethnic communities, while others remain ethnic minorities. A further important question is why more immigrants take on minority status in some countries than in others. Two groups of factors appear relevant: those connected with the characteristics of the settlers themselves, and those connected with the social structures, cultural practices and ideologies of the receiving societies.

Looking at the settlers, it is clear that visible or phenotypical difference (skin colour, appearance) is a main marker for minority status. This applies even more to non-immigrant minorities, such as aboriginal peoples in the USA, Canada and Australia, or African–Americans in the USA and the Roma in Europe. They often make up the most marginalized groups in Western countries. Visible difference is also often a marker for exclusion in non-Western societies, for example of native black populations and sub-Saharan African immigrants in North Africa, Asian workers in the Gulf oil countries, and South-East Asians in Korea and Japan. There are four possible explanations for this: visible difference may coincide with recent arrival, with cultural distance or with socio-economic position, or, finally, it may serve as a target for racism.

The first explanation is partly correct: in many cases, black, Asian or Hispanic settlers are among the more recently arrived groups. Historical studies reveal examples of racism and discrimination against white immigrants quite as virulent as against non-whites today (see Chapter 4). Recent arrival may make a new unknown group appear more threatening, and new groups tend to compete more with local low-income groups for jobs and housing. But recent arrival cannot explain why indigenous populations are victims of exclusionary practices, nor why African–Americans and other long-standing minorities are discriminated against. Neither can it explain why racism against white immigrant groups tends to disappear in time, while that against non-whites continues over generations.

What about cultural distance? Some non-European settlers come from rural areas with pre-industrial cultures, and may find it hard to adapt to industrial or post-industrial cultures. But many Asian settlers in North America and Australia are of urban background and highly educated. This does not protect them from racism and discrimination. Many people perceive culture mainly in terms of language, religion and values, and see non-European migrants as very different. This applies particularly to Muslims. Fear of Islam has a tradition going back to the medieval crusades. In recent years, concerns about terrorism have led to increased Islamophobia (fear of and hostility to Islam and Muslims), even though only a very small minority of Muslims actually support extremist ideologies.

As for the third explanation, phenotypical difference does frequently coincide with socio-economic status. Some immigrants from less developed countries lack the education and vocational training necessary for upward mobility in industrial economies. But even highly skilled immigrants may encounter discrimination. Many immigrants discover that they can only enter the labour market at the bottom, and that it is hard to move up the ladder later. Thus low socio-economic status is as much a result of processes of marginalization as it is a cause of minority status.

We therefore conclude that the most significant explanation of minority formation lies in practices of exclusion by the majority populations and the states of the immigration countries. We refer to these practices as racism and to their results as the racialization of minorities (see Chapter 3). Traditions and cultures of racism are strong in all European countries and former European settler colonies (Essed, 1991; Goldberg, 1993; Murji and Solomos, 2005). The salience of racism and racist violence since the late 1970s can be linked to growing insecurity for many people resulting from rapid economic and social change.

Racist violence

All over Europe, racist violence became widespread by the 1980s (Björgo and Witte, 1993: 1). German reunification in 1990 was followed by outbursts of racist violence. Neo-Nazi groups attacked refugee hostels and foreigners on the streets, sometimes to the applause of bystanders. Racist violence persists today: in 2012 a gang of neo-Nazis were found to have murdered nine people of Turkish and Greek descent as well as a German policewoman between 2000 and 2006. The perpetrators attacked Turkish fast-food stalls at random. The police failed to investigate properly, publicly blaming Turkish criminals for the attacks. A study found that Turkish immigrants in Germany had lost much of their confidence in the German state, with the majority afraid there would be further racially motivated killings (Witte, 2012).

The USA has a long history of white violence against African–Americans. Despite the anti-racist laws secured by the Civil Rights Movement of the 1960s, the Ku Klux Klan, neo-Nazi and white supremacy groups remain a threat. According to a 2008 study, the highest levels of violent hate crime continue to be directed toward members of the African–American community and others of African origin, while hate crimes targeting people of Hispanic or Latino origin rose nationwide by one third since 2003. Racist violence also targeted people of Asian origin. These included attacks on persons of South Asian origin, who were sometimes targeted in the belief they were Muslims and from the Middle East (Human Rights First, 2008). However, conflicts between minority groups also arises, as shown by the violence of African–Americans towards Koreans in Los Angeles during the 'Rodney King riots' of 1991.

In the UK, 89 people lost their lives through racial violence from 1993 to 2010. Taxi drivers, takeaway workers and shop workers – many of whom work alone and at night – were at particular risk. An analysis of 660 cases of racial violence found that 80 per cent of victims were men. Where the ethnicity of victims was known, just over 45 per cent were Asian, 18 per cent black and 10 per cent white British. Eighty-nine per cent of all perpetrators of racial violence were white (Athwal *et al.*, 2010: 5).

Even countries that pride themselves on their tolerance, like Canada, Sweden and the Netherlands, report a high incidence of racist attacks.

Box 12.6 Minorities in Italy

Since the 1980s, Italy has experienced a dramatic migration transition. From 1945 to 1975, 7 million Italians emigrated to escape economic stagnation and poverty. Large Italian communities remain in the USA, Argentina, Brazil, Australia, France, Germany, Belgium and Switzerland. But, rapid economic growth and declining fertility have reversed former patterns. Italy's legally resident foreign population rose from just 0.4 million in 1985 to 4.6 million in 2011. Foreign residents make up 7 per cent of Italy's total population of 60 million. Many lower-skilled migrants are irregular on arrival, but may achieve legalization later (see Chapter 10) . The table shows the diversity of the immigrant population.

Italy: legal foreign residents by main nationalities 1999 and 2009

Nationality	1999 thousands	2009 thousands	2009 per cent of foreign population
Romania	61	888	21.0
Albania	133	467	11.0
Morocco	156	432	10.2
China	57	188	4.4
Ukraine	7	174	4.1
Philippines	67	124	2.9
Tunisia	47	104	2.5
Serbia and Montenegro	41	–	–
Ecuador	11	86	2.0
India	28	106	2.5
Poland	30	106	2.5
Moldova	–	106	2.5
Other countries	704	1,456	34.4
Total	**1,341**	**4,235**	**100.0**

Source: ISTAT, 2010b.

Immigrants are important in sustaining agriculture and industry. Irregular workers are concentrated in the 'underground economy', which comprises about a quarter of Italy's economic activity. Legal immigrants are important as workers – both skilled and unskilled – in the industries of Northern Italy and also in services throughout the country. Several indicators show the trend to permanent settlement: increased family reunion (31 per cent of entrants in 2009), a higher female share (53 per cent of foreign residents in 2010), more births to foreign women (11 per cent of all births in 2004) and increasing numbers of children entering Italian schools.

The right-wing parties campaign against immigration as a threat to law and order, and there has been considerable violence, especially against non-Europeans. Trade unions, left-wing parties, church organizations and

$\longrightarrow$

→

advocacy groups support migrant rights and call for interculturalism, while employers' associations campaign for increased labour migration.

Italy had no immigration law until 1986, and it was not until 1998 that the Centre–Left Government tried to create a broadly based regulatory system, including a long-term residence permit (*carta di soggiorno*). In 2001 the Centre–Right Berlusconi coalition used claims that immigrants were a threat to the country as a major electoral argument. A year later it passed the Bossi-Fini Law, which repealed many of the 1998 measures. It favoured recruitment of seasonal workers and introduced tough measures against irregular immigration, including detention and deportation. But the Berlusconi government also introduced a legalization campaign, which led to a big increase in the legal foreign population. The Centre–Left Prodi government, elected in May 2006, promised a new approach, but the planned reforms were not implemented.

In 2008, the third Berlusconi coalition government introduced the 'Security Package' (*Pachetto Sicurezza*). This included: fines of 5,000–10,000 euros and immediate expulsion for irregular migrants, as well as confiscation of property and severe fines for landlords letting to irregular migrants. The government's anti-immigrant stance included the expulsion of Roma and Sinti migrants in 2008 despite many being EU citizens, a move that was criticized by the EU. In January 2010, the Ministry of Education introduced a 30 per cent ceiling on the enrolment of foreign-born non-Italian students in classrooms. In this hostile climate, racist attacks on immigrants ensued, including the burning down of migrant shacks by mobs in Naples. In 2010 the unemployment of seasonal workers in Southern Italy led to social tensions and anti-migrant riots.

Sources: Calavita (2004); Einaudi (2007); IOM (2011); ISTAT (2007; 2010a; b); King (2000); Mahony (2010); Merrill (2011); OECD (2010; 2011a); Pastore (2007); PICUM (2010); Reyneri (2003); Rusconi (2010); Statewatch (2010); *The Economist* (2010).

In Australia in 2009 and 2010 there was a series of attacks on Indian students – many of them working part-time in shops, fast-food outlets or as taxi drivers. Matters came to a head with a number of murders of Indians, especially in Melbourne. The Australian police denied that racism was involved, while the Indian media were convinced that this was the case (Soutphommasane, 2010).

In its 2006 Report, (EUMC, 2006) the EU's European Monitoring Centre on Racism and Xenophobia (EUMC) pointed out that key targets for racism included Europe's 8 million Roma, as well as Muslims and Jews. The Report also identified high levels of discrimination in employment, housing and education. In early 2007, the EU member states' justice and interior ministers finally agreed on a set of rules for combating racism and xenophobia. However, these were considerably weaker than the initial proposal by the European Commission. The rules set only minimum standards and allowed member states to opt out if they wished (Brand, 2007).

Racist violence has not gone unchallenged. Anti-racist movements have developed in most immigration countries, often based on coalitions between minority organizations, trade unions, left-wing parties, churches and welfare organizations. Such organizations have helped to bring about equal opportunities and anti-discrimination legislation, as well as policies and agencies designed to curb violence. However, as long as politicians are eager to make electoral capital out of anti-immigrant or anti-Muslim sentiments, racism will continue to be a problem. Racist campaigns, harassment and violence are important factors in the process of ethnic minority formation. By isolating minorities and forcing them into defensive strategies, racism may lead to self-organization and separatism, and even encourage religious extremism. Conversely, anti-racist action may help overcome the isolation of minorities, and facilitate their social and political incorporation into mainstream society.

Minorities and citizenship

Becoming a citizen is a crucial part of the incorporation process (see Chapter 3). *Citizenship* is a formal legal status (often referred to as *nationality*), designating membership of a nation-state. But it is also important to consider the contents of citizenship. These are usually defined in terms of civil, political and social rights, but linguistic and cultural rights are also very important for immigrants.

Historically, laws on citizenship or nationality derive from two competing principles: *ius sanguinis* (literally: law of the blood), which is based on descent from a national of the country concerned, and *ius soli* (law of the soil), which is based on birth in the territory of the country. *Ius sanguinis* is often linked to an ethnic or folk model of the nation-state (typical of Germany and Austria, but also common in Asia), while *ius soli* generally relates to a nation-state built through incorporation of diverse groups on a single territory (such as France and the UK), or through immigration (the USA, Canada, Australia, Latin American countries) (see Chapter 3). In practice, all modern states have citizenship rules based on a combination of *ius sanguinis* and *ius soli,* although one or the other may be predominant.

Acquisition of nationality by immigrants

Table 12.1 shows trends in acquisition of nationality. Acquisition includes naturalizations and other procedures, such as declarations on the part of descendants of foreign immigrant parents or conferral of nationality through marriage. The absolute number of acquisitions was high in the *ius soli* countries Australia, Canada and the USA, but it is not possible to calculate acquisition rates due to lack of data on the foreign population. However, these 'classical immigration countries' see citizenship for newcomers as

Table 12.1 Acquisition of nationality in selected OECD countries (1988, 1995, 2005 and 2009)

Country	1988		1995		2005		2009	
	Thousands	Rate Per cent	Thousands	Rate Per cent	Thousands	Rate Per cent	Thousands	Rate Per cent
Australia	81	na	115	na	99	na	99	na
Belgium	8	1.0	26	2.8	32	3.6	33	3.2
Canada	59	na	228	na	199	na	156	na
Czech Rep	na	na	na	na	3	1.0	2	0.4
France	46	1.3	na	na	155	*4.8	136	**3.7
Germany	17	0.4	72	1.0	117	1.7	96	1.4
Italy	12	1.2	7	1.1	19	0.8	40	1.0
Japan	6	0.6	14	1.0	15	0.8	15	0.7
Korea (S)	na	na	na	na	17	3.5	***15	1.9
Netherlands	9	1.4	71	9.4	28	4.1	30	4.1
Spain	na	na	7	1.5	43	1.1	***84	1.6
Sweden	11	4.3	32	6.0	36	7.8	29	5.1
Switzerland	11	1.1	17	1.3	38	2.6	43	2.7
UK	65	3.5	41	2.0	162	5.7	204	4.9
USA	242	na	488	na	604	na	744	na

Notes: The statistics cover all means of acquiring the nationality of a country. The acquisition rate gives the number of persons acquiring the nationality of a country as a percentage of the stock of the foreign population at the beginning of the year.

Key: n.a., data is not available. *The 2005 rate for France is an estimate based on the 1999 foreign population figure. **The 2009 rate for France is an own estimate. ***Figures for 2008.

Sources: For 1988: own calculations based on OECD (1997). For 1995, 2005 and 2009: OECD (2006: table A.1.6; 2007: table A.1.6; 2011a: table A.1.6).

essential for national identity. In 2005 alone, the USA plus Canada granted citizenship to 800,000 immigrants, compared with 687,000 for all 25 EU countries.

Trends are hard to interpret, because special factors (like legal changes) may play a part. Also a saturation effect may apply, where immigration has slowed down and most immigrants have already become citizens. Nonetheless, it seems clear that between 1988 and 1995 there was an upward trend in acquisitions in several European countries. Sweden and the Netherlands had the greatest increases, due to conscious efforts to encourage immigrants to become citizens. This trend continued from 1995 to 2005 for Sweden (after which the saturation effect probably became relevant), but not for the Netherlands, where policies became more restrictive, although saturation may also have been a factor. Germany moved away from its traditionally restrictive approach to citizenship for immigrants in the late 1990s, so acquisitions increased. Southern European countries remain restrictive, which is partly due to the relative recentness of most immigration. Japan has maintained its very restrictive regime, while the Czech Republic is included to show the low naturalization rates typical of Central and Eastern Europe.

The rules for becoming a citizen in various countries are complex and have undergone considerable change in recent years (see Aleinikoff and Klusmeyer, 2000; 2001). In Europe, the distinction between *ius soli* and *ius sanguinis* countries was eroded by a trend towards more liberal rules in the 1990s (Bauböck *et al.*, 2006a; b). However, in the early twenty-first century rules again became more restrictive, especially in Denmark, France, Greece, the Netherlands, the UK and Austria. Rules have remained or become relatively less restrictive in Belgium, Finland, Germany, Luxembourg and Sweden (Bauböck *et al.*, 2006b: 23).

Legal requirements for naturalization (such as 'good character', regular employment, language proficiency, evidence of integration) are quite similar in various countries, but actual practices vary sharply. Switzerland, Austria and (until recently) Germany impose long waiting periods and complex bureaucratic practices, and treat naturalization as an act of grace by the state. Conversely, classical immigration countries encourage newcomers to become citizens. The act of becoming American (or Australian or Canadian) is seen as an occasion for celebration of the national myth. The introduction of citizenship ceremonies in some European countries such as the Netherlands is motivated by the desire to pass on 'national values', yet could have positive effects by providing a symbolic welcome into the nation.

Status of the second generation

The transmission of citizenship to the children of immigrants and subsequent generations is the key issue for the future. National variations parallel those found with regard to naturalization. In principle, *ius soli* countries confer *birthright citizenship* on all children born in their territory. *Ius sanguinis* countries confer citizenship only on children of existing citizens. However, most countries actually apply models based on a mixture of the two principles. Increasingly, entitlement to citizenship grows out of long-term residence in the country: the *ius domicili*.

Ius soli is applied most consistently in Australia, Canada, New Zealand, the USA and the UK. A child born to immigrant parents in the USA or Canada becomes a citizen, even if the parents are visitors or illegal residents. In Australia, New Zealand and the UK, the child obtains citizenship if at least one of the parents is a citizen or a legal permanent resident. Such countries use the *ius sanguinis* principle to confer citizenship on children born to their citizens while abroad (Çinar, 1994: 58–60; Guimezanes, 1995: 159). A combination of *ius soli* and *ius domicili* emerged in France, Italy, Belgium and the Netherlands in the 1990s. Children born to foreign parents in the territory obtained citizenship, providing they had been resident for a certain period and fulfilled other conditions. Since 2000, Germany, Finland and Spain have adopted similar arrangements. France, Belgium, the Netherlands and Spain also introduced the so-called double *ius soli*: children born to foreign parents, at least one of whom was also born in the country, acquire citizenship at birth. This means that members of the 'third generation' automatically become citizens, unless they specifically renounce this right upon reaching the age of majority (Bauböck *et al.*, 2006a; Çinar, 1994: 61).

Where *ius sanguinis* is still applied strictly (Austria, Switzerland, Japan and South Korea), children who have been born and grown up in a country may be denied not only security of residence, but also a clear national identity. They are formally citizens of a country they may never have seen, and can even be deported there in certain circumstances. Other *ius sanguinis* countries (notably Germany) have taken cautious steps towards *ius domicili*. This means giving an option of facilitated naturalization to young people of immigrant origin.

Dual citizenship

Trends are rather different with regard to dual or multiple citizenship (acquiring the nationality of a host country without renouncing the nationality of the country of origin). This is a way of recognizing the multiple or transnational identities of migrants and their descendants and is also seen as an effective policy to encourage naturalization. Dual citizenship can be seen as a form of 'internal globalization' through which 'nation-state regulations implicitly or explicitly respond to ties of citizens across states' (Faist, 2007: 3). This represents a major shift, since the idea of singular national loyalties has been historically central to state sovereignty. One reason for change is the trend towards gender equality. In the past, nationality in binational marriages used only to be transmitted through the father. Nationality rules in European countries were changed in the 1970s and 1980s. Once mothers obtained the same right to transmit their nationality as fathers, binational marriages automatically led to dual citizenship.

Australia, Canada and the USA have long permitted dual citizenship for immigrants. By contrast, most European countries signed the 1963 Strasbourg Convention on the Reduction of Cases of Multiple Nationality. However, attitudes and laws have changed: by 2004 only five of the EU15 states required renunciation of the previous nationality (Bauböck *et al.*, 2006a: 24). The Netherlands introduced the right to dual citizenship in 1991, but withdrew it again in 1997 (Entzinger, 2003). Germany introduced measures to facilitate acquisition of nationality for immigrants and their children in 2000, but maintained its ban on dual citizenship. In both countries, however, there are important exceptions and many people do hold dual citizenship. In addition, many emigration countries have changed their nationality rules to allow emigrants to hold dual citizenship, as a way of maintaining links with their diasporas. Laws imposing singular citizenship are also difficult to enforce, particularly if emigration countries (such as Morocco) do not give their citizens the right to relinquish their nationality.

Linguistic and cultural rights

Many of the associations set up in the process of ethnic community formation are concerned with language and culture: they teach the mother tongue to the second generation, organize festivals and carry out rituals. Language and culture not only serve as means of communication, but take on a symbolic meaning which is central to ethnic group cohesion. In most cases, language maintenance applies in the first two to three generations, after which there is a rapid decline. The significance of cultural symbols and rituals may last much longer.

Many non-migrants see cultural difference as a threat to a supposed cultural homogeneity and to national identity. Migrant languages, religions and cultures become symbols of otherness and markers for discrimination, as shown particularly by the growth in hostility to Islam and its visible symbols – such as women's clothing. Majority groups often see renouncing such practices as essential for success in the country of immigration. Failure to do so is regarded as indicative of a desire for separatism. Hostility to different languages and cultures is rationalized with the assertion that the official language is essential for economic success, and that migrant cultures are inadequate for a modern secular society. The alternative view is that migrant communities need their own languages and cultures to develop identity and self-esteem.

Policies and attitudes on cultural and linguistic maintenance vary considerably. Some countries have histories of multilingualism. Canada's policy of bilingualism is based on two 'official languages', English and French. Multicultural policies have led to limited recognition of – and support for – immigrant languages, but they have hardly penetrated into mainstream contexts, such as broadcasting. Switzerland has a multilingual policy for its founding languages, but does not recognize immigrant languages. Australia and Sweden both accept the principle of linguistic and cultural maintenance, and have multicultural education policies. They provide language services (interpreting, translating, mother-tongue classes), funding for ethnic media and support for ethnic community cultural organizations. However, such measures have been reduced in recent years.

In the USA, language has become a contentious issue. The tradition of monolingualism is being eroded by the growth of the Hispanic community: in major cities like Los Angeles and Miami, the number of Spanish speakers is overtaking that of English speakers. This led to a backlash in the 1980s, in the form of 'the English-only movement', which called for a constitutional amendment to declare English the official language. Most states passed legislation to introduce this measure, but it proved extremely hard to implement, and public agencies and private companies continued to provide multilingual material and services. *Monolingualism* is the *basic* principle applied to immigrants in France, the UK, Germany and the Netherlands (even where regional languages are accepted, such as Welsh in the UK and Frisian in the Netherlands). Nonetheless, all these countries have been forced to introduce language services to take account of migrant needs in communicating with courts, bureaucracies and health services.

Conclusions: the integration challenge

The reality in each country is much more complex and contradictory than our brief accounts can show. Incorporation of migrants into society does take place, particularly in the longer term, often leading to processes of upward social mobility and dispersal of initial ethnic clusters. Civil society may play a greater role than the state in incorporation: educational opportunities, labour markets, and housing and neighbourhood relationships can be decisive, while state policies have sometimes been inflexible, unrealistic and inappropriate.

Nonetheless, comparison of national experiences and policies provides some useful conclusions. The first is that temporary migrant labour recruitment almost always leads to permanent settlement of at least a proportion of migrants. The second is that the character of future ethnic groups will be influenced by what the state does in the early stages of migration. Policies which deny the reality of immigration encourage social marginalization, minority formation and racism. Third, in order to cope with the difficult experience of settlement in a new society, immigrants and their descendants need their own associations and social networks, as well as their own languages and cultures. Fourth, the best way to prevent marginalization and social conflicts is to grant permanent immigrants full rights in all social spheres. This means making citizenship easily available, even if this leads to dual citizenship.

The approaches of states and the public in host countries towards the incorporation of immigrants have varied considerably. Starting in the 1990s, but especially from the early 2000s, policies on incorporation of immigrants and minorities have been questioned and revised. The inescapable reality of permanent settlement has led to the abandonment of the differential exclusionary approach in Germany. Immigration and citizenship laws have been reformed. While multiculturalism is increasingly rejected at the national level, local provision of special social and educational services for minorities is widespread. However, there are limits to change: Germany still rejects dual citizenship and has introduced compulsory integration measures. Austria and Switzerland still cling to exclusionary policies, although these are modified by local integration efforts. However, differential exclusion remains the dominant approach to foreign workers in many of the new industrial countries of Asia and the Gulf.

By the early 1990s, assimilation seemed to be on the way out everywhere, except in France. Democratic civil societies were thought to have an inherent trend towards multiculturalism (Bauböck, 1996). That is no longer the case: there has been a widespread backlash against multiculturalism. Canada has maintained its multicultural principles, but watered down their implementation, and Australia has gone even further in this direction. Sweden, the Netherlands and the UK have all relabelled policies with much greater emphasis on 'integration', 'social cohesion' and 'core national values'. The Netherlands has had perhaps the most dramatic turnaround and seems to be on the way to a new assimilationism (Vasta, 2007). Several scholars have sought to explain and theorize this return to an assimilation rhetoric (Alba and Nee, 1997; Brubaker, 2003; Joppke, 2004). Others have pointed out that assimilation does not take place in the same way for all migrant groups, but is linked to complex patterns of differentiation on the basis of race and class (Portes and Rumbaut, 2006: 60–3, 271–80; Zhou, 1997).

The backlash against multiculturalism has a number of causes. One is the growing awareness of the enduring social disadvantage and marginalization of many immigrant groups – especially those of non-European origin. A frequent official approach is to claim that ethnic minorities are to blame by clustering together and refusing to integrate. Another factor is the growing fear of Islam and terrorism (see Chapter 9). Events like 9/11, the bombings in Madrid and London, and the murder of film-maker Theo van Gogh by an Islamic extremist in the Netherlands in 2004 are seen by some as evidence of the incompatibility of Muslim values with modern European societies.

In this interpretation, recognition of cultural diversity has had the perverse effect of encouraging ethnic separatism and the development of 'parallel lives'. This is summed up in French academic Kepel's caricature of 'Londonistan' as a haven for Islamic ideologists (Kepel, 2005).

A model of individual integration – based if necessary on compulsory integration contracts and citizenship tests – is thus seen as a way of achieving greater equality for immigrants and their children. The problem for such views, however, is that the one country that has maintained its model of individual assimilation is also experiencing serious problems. The minority youth riots of 2005 and 2007 in France showed that the republican model of individual integration has largely failed to overcome inequality and racism.

All the varying policy approaches to incorporation of immigrants thus seem problematic: differential exclusion is useless once settlement takes place; multiculturalism appears to lead to separatism, and assimilation can perpetuate marginalization and conflict. In our view, this situation actually reflects the unwillingness of host societies to deal with two issues. The first is the deep-seated cultures of racism that are a legacy of colonialism, imperialism, anti-Semitism and other forms of intolerance. In times of stress, such as economic restructuring, recession or international conflict, racism can reinforce social exclusion, discrimination and violence against minorities. The second issue is the trend to greater inequality resulting from globalization, economic restructuring, deregulation and privatization. Increased international competition puts pressure on employment, working conditions and welfare systems. At the same time neoliberal economic policies encourage greater pay differences and reduce the capacity and willingness of states to redistribute income to alleviate poverty and social disadvantage.

Taken together, these factors have contributed to a racialization of ethnic difference (see Chapter 3). Minorities may have poor employment situations, low incomes and high rates of impoverishment. This in turn leads to concentration in low-income neighbourhoods and growing residential segregation. The existence of separate and marginal communities is then taken as evidence of failure to integrate, and this in turn is perceived as a threat to the host society. The result for Europe, as Schierup *et al.* (2006) argue, is a 'dual crisis' of national identity and the welfare state. Attempts to resolve the crisis through discrimination against minorities do not provide a solution. Rather, they threaten the fundamental values upon which democratic societies are based.

Guide to further reading

Extra resources at www.age-of-migration.com

In earlier editions of *The Age of Migration*, we provided a detailed comparison of two very different immigration countries, Australia and Germany. For reasons of space, this chapter could not be included in this edition, but it is available as Text 12.1 on *The Age of Migration* website. The website also includes short accounts of the situation of migrants and minorities in Canada (12.2), Netherlands (12.3), Sweden (12.4) and South Korea (12.5).

It would take up too much space to give further reading for individual countries here – instead we refer readers to the sources used for the country boxes. The annual OECD *International Migration Outlook* provides up-to-date statistics and policy information for many countries, while the Migration Information Source contains data and good short country studies: http:// www.migrationinformation.org/.

Useful comparative studies include Reitz (1998), which covers Canada, the USA and Australia, and (Hollifield *et al.*, 2013), which covers North America, Europe, Australia and some Asian countries. King *et al.* (2000) provides studies of Southern European immigration countries. Good comparative studies on citizenship include: Aleinikoff and Klusmeyer (2000; 2001) and Bauböck *et al.* (2006a; b). Useful works on multiculturalism include Parekh (2000; 2008), Modood (2007) and Kymlicka (1995). Kymlicka has also co-edited a book on *Multiculturalism in Asia* (Kymlicka and He, 2005). Banting and Kymlicka (2006) and Schierup *et al.* (2006) are good on the relationship between multiculturalism and the welfare state.

Chapter 13

Immigrants and Politics

The most lasting significance of international migration may well be its effects upon politics. This is not inevitably the case. Much depends on how immigrants are treated by governments, and on the origins, timing, nature and context of a particular migration. It makes a difference whether migrants were legally admitted and permitted to naturalize or whether their entry (legal or irregular) was seen as merely temporary but they then stayed on permanently. On the one hand, immigrants can quickly become citizens without a discernible political effect, save for the addition of more potential voters. On the other hand, international migration may lead to an accretion of politically disenfranchised populations whose political marginality is compounded by various socio-economic problems. Migrants have a major stake in the nature of public policies affecting them, particularly in the immigration policies of receiving states but also in the much less studied emigration policies of origin states (Delano, 2011: 14–22; Green and Weil, 2007: 1).

The universe of possible political effects of international migration is wide and characteristically intertwines the political systems of origin and receiving societies and sometimes one or more transit countries as well. The political significance of international migration can be active or passive. Immigrants can become political actors in their own right or manifest apoliticism, which itself can be important to maintenance of the status quo. On the other hand, immigrants often become the object of politics: allies for some and foes for others. Chapter 12 has already dealt with one key political issue: the extent to which immigrants and their descendants can become citizens with full rights of political participation. Naturalization in democratic settings enables new citizens to vote and sometimes to decisively affect electoral outcomes and immigration policy content (Zolberg, 2006: 92, 96–8).

This chapter will analyse migration-related political phenomena, which include the following themes: origin countries and expatriates, extra-parliamentary forms of migrant participation and representation, non-citizen voting, immigrant and ethnic voting blocs, anti-immigrant parties and movements as well as the politics of immigration policy-making. This chapter deals mainly with North America and Europe, but events there in today's very interconnected world often have repercussions outside the two areas.

Origin countries and expatriates

Mercantilist European states in the seventeenth and eighteenth centuries sought to discourage or bar emigration as the loss of subjects was thought to detract from state economic and military power (Green and Weil, 2007). After the French Revolution and its proclamation of a human right to emigrate, the ability of European states to deter emigration began to erode. Concurrently, factors like decreasing economic barriers to transatlantic travel and, in some instances, state assistance to emigration resulted in massive emigration by Europeans between 1820 and 1920 (see also Chapter 4).

In the twenty-first century a category of states did persist in endeavouring to prevent most emigration. This was notably the case of Communist states like North Korea which employed draconian means to prevent emigration. Nevertheless, tens of thousands of North Koreans succeeded in escaping northward, some by sea but most by land, to the People's Republic of China. Many such migrants sought to reach Bangkok, Thailand and from there points elsewhere, including the Republic of Korea (Greenhill, 2010: 227–61). Since the end of the Cold War, a number of states that remain governed by Communist parties have reformed formerly stringent systems of internal control, most notably the People's Republic of China, with major implications for both internal and external migration (Torpey, 2007: 25–8).

In many other cases, especially in lesser developed countries after World War II, emigrants were not viewed positively by governments even though they signed bilateral accords authorizing recruitment of their subjects or citizens for employment abroad. These origin country governments often proclaimed that emigration would be temporary and that migrants would return home. These blandishments sometimes masked de facto policies of neglect of expatriate populations abroad. However, some governments – as was notably the case of the newly created Italian Republic – did take active steps to support their citizens' welfare and rights in destination countries as early as the latter part of the nineteenth century. Indeed, protection of migrants and prevention of exploitation of Italian emigrants figured importantly in Italian politics and fostered Italian nationalism. Some states viewed Italian policies towards emigrants as emblematic and studied them (Douki, 2007).

In the twenty-first century, most states have significant populations of citizens or subjects living abroad. For many, if not most, expatriates, the country of origin and its politics remain the foremost concern (Ögelman, 2003). Likewise, governments of migrant-sending societies now increasingly nurture a relationship with emigrants through so-called Diaspora engagement policies (see Gamlen, 2006, 2008 and Chapter 3). This is often driven by economic concerns such as facilitating the sending of remittances, but it is of broader political and theoretical significance as examined in Chapter 10 (Adamson and Demetriou, 2007: 503). For example, emigration of Jews from Israel has long been viewed as posing an existential threat to the Israeli state although the traditional hostility of Israel towards the estimated 500,000 Israelis who reside abroad has given way to a more solicitous stance, motivated in part by the hope of facilitating returns of expatriates to Israel (Lustik, 2011).

The world's states vary widely in their political institutions. Migration taking place between two authoritarian or non-democratic states differs from that taking place between two states that possess democratic institutions. Often, emigrants arrive in democratic settings from states with authoritarian governments. Migrants to non-democratic settings are unlikely to participate much in political life in receiving states. The millions of mainly South Asian and Arab-origin migrants in the Gulf-area monarchies are largely politically quiescent, although the growing political activism of Arab migrants in Kuwait by 1974 played a role in subsequent Kuwaiti recourse to South Asian-origin workers (Stanton-Russell, 2006: 254–5). Strikes and protests by mainly South Asian migrants in 2006 and 2007 did achieve some reforms (DeParle, 2007; Surk and Abbot, 2008). In such cases, diplomatic representation in support of migrants' interests by origin country governments takes on particular significance. But the track record of origin country governments defending the interests of expatriate compatriots is, at best, uneven.

For instance, both the Philippines and India tried to mandate minimum wages for their expatriates working in the Gulf states in 2007 and 2008 respectively. Bahraini companies resisted paying higher wages, thereby sparking strikes by Indian workers. The Bahraini Minister of Labour held that India had no authority to enforce the measure in the Gulf. The Filipino effort to secure a minimum wage for expatriate maids resulted in a drop in employer demand for them. The steps taken by India and the Philippines to better the lives of their expatriates were undercut by the ability of employers in the Gulf states to find labour elsewhere (Surk and Abbot, 2008).

International migration often takes place in bilateral relationships characterized by domination and subordination, with origin countries occupying the latter role. This disadvantage can adversely affect the ability of origin county governments to protect migrant interests through diplomatic means. Moreover, origin country governments sometimes collude with the governments of receiving states in maintenance of the status quo unfavourable to, if not oppressive of, migrants. Such would appear to be the case of at least some of the governments of the many millions of migrants in the Gulf monarchies. The acquiescence of origin country governments is linked to views that emigration is a safety valve that relieves unemployment, generates remittances, that may promote development and, hence, decrease political tensions (see Chapter 3). But the costs paid by migrants often are very high in terms of work accidents, exploitative employment conditions and highly regimented, segregated housing arrangements, usually devoid of family life.

The governments of emigration countries such as Algeria, Turkey and Mexico similarly strove to defend the interests of expatriate populations abroad. Many origin countries have developed extensive consular services to this end (Delano, 2011). A corollary to this is the efforts of origin country governments to maintain the political loyalties and allegiance of expatriate populations (Smith, 2003). This is particularly significant in bilateral contexts involving emigration from authoritarian origin countries to democratic settings, such as the movement of Algerians to France (view Text 13.1 of the *Age of Migration* website).

Another policy to maintain ties with emigrants is to allow their participation in origin country elections. The modalities for expatriate voting vary considerably. Some origin countries, like Turkey and Italy, require emigrants to return home to vote. Other states, like Algeria, Venezuela and Israel permit consular voting. Still others permit absentee voting, as in the USA. Indeed, absentee balloting by Floridians abroad played a key role in the contested outcome of the 2000 US presidential election.

Mexicans living abroad became eligible to cast absentee ballots from abroad in the 2006 Mexican presidential election (Box 13.1 provides more detail). The Venezuelan Government's 2012 decision to close the Venezuelan consulate in Miami appeared related to the electoral propensities of Venezuelans living in Florida as President Chávez won only 2 per cent of the 10,799 votes cast in Miami in the 2006 presidential election. Consequently, thousands of Venezuelans in the Florida area planned to take charter flights or buses to New Orleans in order to vote in the highly polarized 2012 presidential election which was won by Chavez (Zabludovsky, 2012: A7).

By 2007, 115 countries and territories allowed citizens to vote from abroad (Gutierrez *et al.*, 2012: 2). In the 1996 presidential elections in Armenia, eligible voters outside Armenia may have outnumbered voters residing in Armenia (Earnest, 2008: 2). Electoral campaigning increasingly reflects the weight of voters abroad. Ecuadorian and Dominican Republic presidential candidates campaign for votes in New York City, just as Italian and Portuguese parties have campaigned for votes in Paris (Lee *et al.*, 2006; Miller, 1978; 1981). Some sending countries have created legislative districts to solely represent citizens living abroad (Earnest, 2008: 2) Nevertheless, the potential for emigrants to influence electoral outcomes at home does not necessarily translate into effective representation of their interests by origin country governments.

Finally, the power imbalance that often characterizes relations between migrant-sending and migrant-receiving states does not mean that less powerful states are powerless. To the contrary, states such as Libya under the late Colonel Gaddafi skilfully exploited Libya's role as a destination and transit state for African migrants desirous of entry into Italy and Europe as a kind of diplomatic resource to achieve other goals sought by Libya (Paoletti, 2011). Libya managed to shed its rogue state status in part by agreeing to cooperate with Italy and the EU on migration control

Box 13.1 The decade-long path to Mexican absentee voting rights

The government of Mexico moved to strengthen ties with its citizens abroad by extending their political rights, most notably the right to vote in Mexican elections. A constitutional reform to this effect was passed in August 1996, but the first absentee voting took place in 2006. The delay arose from a clause requiring the Mexican Congress to reform Mexican Federal Election regulations which established the rules under which voting takes place. It took until June 2005 for the Mexican Congress to pass such legislation.

However, in April 2004, the Mexican Foreign Ministry had voiced fears that instituting absentee voting might lead to anti-immigrant reactions in the USA and warned against placing of voting booths and issuance of voting cards in the USA. Hence, when the Mexican Congress passed the long awaited reform on 28 June 2005, it was the most conservative of all the options. There would be no voting booths abroad, no voting cards issued abroad (rather they would be mailed) and the absentee voting would be limited to the presidential election.

Only 32,632 absentee ballots were received in the 2006 Mexican presidential election, most of which came from the USA. Factors affecting the disappointing results included lack of familiarity with the absentee-voting process, inability or unwillingness to pay for the certified postage required to mail the ballots to Mexico and the unwillingness of unauthorized Mexicans to return to Mexico to obtain the required voter identification document. In the 2012 Mexican presidential election, only 40,714 absentee ballots were received by the 30 June deadline. As in the 2006 election, the conservative *Partido Acción Nacional* (PAN) presidential candidate received most of the votes.

Nevertheless, despite the meagre voting by expatriates in the 2006 and 2012 elections, the introduction of absentee voting was regarded as a milestone. It reflected a profound change in policy towards Mexicans abroad (Delano, 2011: 218–22).

matters. The complex diplomacy surrounding migration issues resulted in important gains for Libya such as major investments in highway construction projects that became moot with the outbreak of civil strife in Libya in 2011 that led to NATO's intervention, Gaddafi's death and an uncertain Libyan future.

Similarly, the reversal of Cuba's longstanding policy of discouraging emigration of Cubans in 1994 led to a significant flow of Cubans to the USA. Greenhill (2010: 75–130) regards such cases as examples of coercive diplomacy by a weaker state against a much more powerful neighbour. She contends that liberal democracies are particularly vulnerable to such coercive diplomacy involving international migrants. Democracies embrace democratic values which makes them more vulnerable to shaming and allegations of hypocrisy than authoritarian states.

Extra-parliamentary forms of migrant participation and representation

The act of emigration usually results in disenfranchisement of emigrants in their new setting, whether democratic or authoritarian. Larger scale migration, thus, can create big populations which are not entitled to vote in the democratic states in which they have taken up residency and often pay taxes. Naturalization rates which result in political enfranchisement of foreigners vary greatly across countries. Since the 1970s, immigrants in Europe have increasingly articulated political concerns, participated in politics and sought representation. Immigrant protest movements became part of the tapestry of Western European politics and frequently affected decision-making. Persistent hunger strikes by undocumented immigrants and their supporters, for example, brought pressure to bear on French and Dutch authorities to liberalize rules regarding legalization.

The protracted rioting in France in 2005 and 2007, (see Box 13.2) was foreshadowed by events in the preceding decades, in which clashes with the police became almost routinized, scripted events. A largely peaceful

---

Box 13.2 The unrest in France in 2005 and 2007

The riots of October/November 2005 in the peripheral housing projects (*banlieues*) of Paris and other big cities resulted in the destruction of approximately 9,200 vehicles, one accidental death, 2,888 arrests and a cost of more than 200 million euros. The unrest revealed the scope of the social malaise inherent in France's inability to incorporate its disaffected youths of migrant background. The roots of the unrest were to be found in socio-economic and ethnic exclusion experienced by many youths, who have pervasive feelings of anguish and hopelessness concerning their lives and their uncertain futures. French youths of migrant background, primarily Maghrebi and Turkish, were confronted with endemic forms of discrimination in the job market, with unemployment rates in some heavily immigrant areas reaching 40 per cent, nearly four times the national average. Police conducting routine identification regularly used racial profiling, while owners of clubs and bars denied entrance to their establishments to non-whites.

Moreover, episodes of police violence tended to aggravate the strained relationship between migrant youths and the police which resulted in further alienation from the institutions of the Republic. Following a process of ghettoization, certain areas became exclusion zones in which poverty, high unemployment, and an absence of upward social mobility coexisted with petty crime and delinquency. Isolated from the inner cities due to the high cost and relative lack of public transportation, such environments fostered the development of a distinct male-dominated urban culture characterized

→

by unique and creative forms of artistic and musical expression including graffiti and rap music.

Furthermore, this seclusion led to a sense of territorial appropriation by rival bands of youngsters who felt a need to defend their territory against outsiders. In this context, violence and regular skirmishes with the police became an outlet to escape the idleness and monotony of their lives. Gangs provided many youths with a sense of belonging, giving meaning to their lives. Group dynamics of emulation and competition among members and between rival groups appeared to have played a crucial role in the incendiary attacks on cars. Additionally, the presence of the media helped to foster a kind of destructive competition between various youth gangs.

The immediate causes of the unrest consisted of several incidents which occurred in a relatively short period of time sparking angry outbursts. First, the fatal fire at the hotel Paris-Opera in April 2005 resulted in the deaths of 25 persons, most of whom were immigrants who were paying relatively high rent, and had been waiting for years to benefit from more social housing. This incident exposed the precarious and bleak living conditions of many immigrant families. Various associations, whose membership largely consisted of persons of African descent, the same as the fire victims, organized demonstrations.

Second, the French government cancelled several social programmes and subsidies that had been in place since the 1990s including a neighbourhood policing programme which had helped to maintain a relationship of trust between youths and law enforcement officers. Immediately prior to the riots, then Interior Minister Nicolas Sarkozy vowed to 'clean up the suburbs', starting with La Courneuve (where a boy of 11 years had been tragically gunned down during the spring of 2005) and harshly rebuked the youth of Argenteuil, another Parisian suburb, following an incident on October 25, referring to them as scum. Two days later, the deaths of two teenagers, who were electrocuted in a power substation while trying to hide from the police, triggered the riots.

The riots had no religious connotation. No religious demands were made and the rioters ignored appeals by officials of Muslim organizations to end the rioting. The majority of the participants were not delinquents, but were normal youths angered by their situations and constant harassment. The riots were a spontaneous and genuine movement of disaffected youths aimed at showing their frustration with the French government and a society which they felt had forsaken them. Ironically, the violent protests of the largely immigrant-background youths constituted classically French political participation and mainly involved French citizens.

By 2007, the situation in the suburbs was as before and another spate of rioting ensued. In 2008, newly elected President Sarkozy announced another plan to improve life in heavily immigrant suburbs, the sixteenth in 31 years. But by the end of his presidency in 2012, little had changed and periodic rioting similar to that of 2005 ensued, although these incidents were localized and of short duration.

rent strike in SONACOTRA housing for migrant workers began in 1975 and was sustained for years, despite the deportation of some strike leaders. Tens of thousands of migrants and their French allies repeatedly rallied and marched (Miller, 1978). In the late 1970s and early 1980s, repeated strikes by mainly migrant and migrant-background workers disrupted the French automobile industry where foreigners comprised one-quarter of employees (Miller, 1984). (See case study 11.3 on *The Age of Migration website*.)

Also during the 1980s, a country-wide movement of *beur* activists emerged. *Beur* means Arab in the *verlan* slang used especially by migrant and migrant-background youths in urban areas. *Beur* activists repeatedly organized mass rallies and participated in marches to protest against socio-economic conditions and police-community relations as well as to affirm their identity and place in French society (Bouamama, 1994; Jazouli, 1986). The marches and rallies of 1983 and 1984 involved tens of thousands of mainly migrant youths. Many of the heavily migrant neighbourhoods that were the focus of *beur* activists in the 1980s would be rocked by riots in October/November, 2005.

The twilight years of the twentieth century and the early years of the twenty-first century in the USA witnessed growing activism of migrants and migrant-background populations on US immigration policy issues. Largely Mayan Indian-background Guatemalan citizens working in poultry-processing plants in Delaware and Maryland regularly descended upon Washington, DC by the thousands to march in support of legalization policies. Mexican migrants organized relays of runners carrying the statue of Our Lady of Guadaloupe in the hope of securing divine intervention in the form of a legalization policy. The spring of 2006 witnessed massive rallies and marches around the USA in opposition to a restrictive House bill and in support of a Senate bill that, if adopted, would have authorized a legalization.

Non-citizen voting rights: a global issue

The anomaly of foreign nonitizens living in democratic societies without political rights has long been viewed as problematic. Naturalization rules and practices vary from state to state and are sometimes unavailable to foreigners. Consequently, many democratic states have authorized non-citizens to vote in local and, less frequently, in national elections. The perceived legitimacy or illegitimacy of non-citizen exclusion or enfranchisement in elections can spark conflict as in the case in Côte d'Ivoire.

Overall, 65 of the world's nearly 200 states permit some form of non-citizen voting, and in 36 of the 65 the voting is available to all foreigners regardless of origin (Andrès, 2007: 80). Of the 65 states, 35 are non-European. In many respects, the USA established a precedent for electoral enfranchisement of non-citizens. Between 1776 and 1926, at least 40 US federal states and territories authorized some form of non-citizen voting, including voting in state wide and US national elections. Indeed, the 1928 national elections marked the first time that non-citizens did not vote (Andrès, 2007: 68). In Western Europe, the question of non-citizen voting rights emerged as an important issue in the 1970s. Immigrants often sought participation and representation in local government. In several countries, advisory councils were instituted to give immigrants a voice in local government. Experiences with these advisory councils varied and some were discontinued. Some people contested them as efforts to co-opt foreigners, while others saw them as illegitimate interference by foreigners in the politics of the host society (Earnest, 2008: 11). In certain countries, foreigners were accorded a right to vote in local and regional elections.

Sweden was the pacesetter in this regard, but migrant participation in Swedish local and regional elections declined over time. The Netherlands was the second country to accord qualified foreigners voting rights. However, the results of migrant voting there also were somewhat disappointing (Rath, 1988: 25–35). Proposals to grant local voting rights to legally resident foreigners became important domestic political and constitutional issues, particularly in France and Germany. However, the pattern of weak migrant participation in local elections persisted even as more and more European states authorized such voting (Oriol and Vianna, 2007: 40–4).

By the 1980s, the stakes involved in the granting of voting rights were quite high in many Western democracies. However, many immigrants were already politically enfranchised, particularly in the UK. This did not prevent the eruption of riots involving immigrants and their British-born children (Dancygier, 2010). The granting of local voting rights was thus not in itself a panacea for the problems facing immigrants in Western Europe.

The Treaty on European Union (TEU) was signed in 1992 (see Chapters 5 and 10), making citizens of European Union member states eligible to vote, or to be elected to office, in European and municipal elections if they resided anywhere within the Union. Foreigners from other EU states became eligible to vote in, and stand for elections, as of 1994 and subsequently in the 1999 and 2004 European elections. France was the last of the then 15 EU member states to implement the TEU: EU citizens became eligible to vote and to run in French municipal elections by 2001. Participation by foreigners in European elections has been weak. In France, for instance, only 4 per cent of non-French EU citizens voted in 1994, but this share doubled in each subsequent European election (Oriol, 2007: 41). Broadly similar patterns of weak to modest participation by non-national EU citizens in European elections have been observed in Finland, Luxembourg and Belgium (Dervin and Wiberg, 2007; Dubajic, 2007; Zibouh, 2007).

Since 1992, there has been a growing movement in support of granting Third Country Nationals voting rights within member states of the EU and at the level of EU institutions. The European Parliament has voted several times in favour of extending European citizenship to all long-term non-EU residents within member states (Oriol, 2007 :95). However, opposition within the European Council has thwarted such initiatives. Some EU member states hold that the grant of voting rights to Third Country Nationals would depreciate the importance of naturalization.

Elsewhere, half of the 23 states comprising the Caribbean and Central and North America authorize some form of non-citizen voting and/or electability as of 2007. Most South American countries permit foreign residents to vote in municipal elections. Only Suriname and Ecuador reserve voting exclusively to nationals. Brazil allows Portuguese residents to vote on the basis of a bilateral treaty. Eight out of 53 African states allow non-citizens to vote often on the basis of British Commonwealth ties or reciprocity agreements (Andrès, 2007).

Several Asian states also allow non-citizen voting, including the Republic of Korea, which permits foreign residents after three years on permanent residence permits to vote in municipal elections – however, very few foreigners are accorded permanent residency. People who migrated from the UK and Ireland to Australia prior to 1984 remain eligible to vote even if they have not obtained Australian citizenship, but this does not apply to more recent migrants. New Zealand allows all permanent resident foreigners to vote in all elections, but not to stand for office (Andrès, 2007). Since 1950, Israel has allowed resident foreigners to vote in local elections, but only those residents who come to Israel under the Law of Return but who refuse Israeli citizenship. This suggests that Israel discriminates in the allocation of voting rights based on religion (Earnest, 2008: 28).

The new wave of democratization since 1990 has only served to heighten the saliency of non-citizen voting issues around the world. One of the paradoxes of this period of globalization is the growing number of politically disenfranchised persons living in the same democratic societies that are held up for emulation elsewhere.

Migrants and ethnic voting blocs

The politics of the state of Israel, created in 1948, remain heavily influenced by Jewish immigration, although, from a Zionist perspective, such migration constitutes 'return' (Bartram, 2008: 303–4). As a result of the inflow of Sephardic Jews primarily from largely Muslim societies in North Africa and the Middle East during the 1950s and 1960s, the Sephardic-origin Jewish population surpassed that of European-origin Ashkenazi Jews in the mid-1970s. This demographic shift benefited the right-wing Likud bloc led by Menachem Begin, who was elected prime minister in 1977 with the support of Sephardic-origin Jews. In 1990, a new wave of Ashkenazi Soviet Jewish immigration began, again affecting the balance between Ashkenazi and Sephardic Jews as well as Arab Israelis.

Now comprising about 15 per cent of the Israeli electorate, the Soviet Jewish or 'Russian' vote importantly affected the outcomes of general elections beginning in 1992. By the 1996 election, an immigrant party led by the former Soviet dissident Natan Sharansky won seven seats in the Knesset (parliament) and joined the coalition government dominated by the Likud. In the 2001 Israeli election, there were several predominately Soviet Jewish parties competing for votes, with Sharansky's again receiving the most. A number of Soviet Jewish political leaders called for mass expulsion of Israeli Arabs and Palestinians from the West Bank and Gaza. Polls revealed growing support for 'transfer', the Israeli euphemism for ethnic cleansing of Palestinian Arabs. By 2007, the leader of a party espousing transfer, Israel Beitenu, which was strongly supported by Soviet Jews in the 2006 election, became a member of the Israeli cabinet. Avigdor Lieberrman would later become Foreign Minister under Prime Minister Netanyahu.

The Israeli case illustrates in the extreme the potential impact of an immigrant voting bloc upon electoral outcomes. Immigrants generally are not such an important factor as in Israel and immigrants do not necessarily vote in ethnic blocs. Yet immigration is clearly affecting electoral politics across Western democracies as growing numbers of foreigners naturalize, and as immigrant-origin populations are mobilized to vote.

In the 1996 referendum over the future of Quebec and the Canadian Federation, Quebec's immigrant voters overwhelmingly voted against separation from the rest of Canada and for maintenance of the status quo. They decisively affected the outcome, prompting angry anti-immigration remarks by Quebecois leaders. In the close 2002 German elections, the 350,000 Germans of Turkish background emerged as a potentially decisive voting bloc whose backing may have enabled the Social Democratic–Green coalition to scrape through to victory. Although only one per cent of the electorate in 2002, the Turkish–German voting bloc was expected to double in size by 2006 as a consequence of naturalization (Johnson and Gugath, 2002). Naturalized German citizens from Eastern Europe, on the other hand, strongly favour conservative parties, which prevailed in the 2006 elections that brought Angela Merkel to the Chancellorship (Wüst, 2000; 2002).

There seems to be a broad long-term trajectory towards increasing representation of immigrants and immigrant-background minorities in local and national governments in many democracies. The growing numbers of immigrant voters has made political parties and their leaders more sensitive to migration-related concerns and issues. It has also sparked interest in the representatives of minority background who are elected to public office. In general, political parties on the left side of the political spectrum appear to take the lead in appealing to immigrant voters by defending their rights and are generally rewarded for their efforts (Messina, 2007). Conservative parties often benefit electorally from an anti-immigrant backlash. However, a number of conservative parties have begun to compete in earnest for the immigrant-origin electorate, particularly in Great Britain, Canada and the USA.

In the USA, the Latino population, which counts over 50 million, constitutes an increasingly important electorate at the state and federal levels. Following the 1996 US elections, some Republicans felt that President Clinton and the Democrats had outmanoeuvred the Republicans by encouraging a naturalization campaign while several Republican presidential candidates embraced anti-immigrant positions. Subsequently, George W. Bush ran a campaign in 2000 that courted Hispanic voters, and electoral concerns drove his immigration initiative towards Mexico in 2001. Bush's narrow and much contested victory in the 2000 election reflected the heightened appeal of Bush and the Republican Party to Latino voters, who had generally voted Democratic in the past. The strongly Republican preferences of Cuban–Americans in Florida may have been critical to the outcome. The stronger showing by Bush and Republican candidates led to speculation about possible Latino re-alignment away from the Democrats. But the results of the 2006 mid-term elections and 2008 presidential election suggested that such re-alignment had not happened. (See the case study on Latino voters in the 2006 mid-term elections on the website.) The support of two-thirds of the Latino vote was a key factor in Barack Obama's 2008 election to the presidency and his re-election in 2012. In the run-up to the 2012 election, President Obama and his challenger, Mitt Romney, courted Hispanic voters and President Obama's executive decision with regard to young irregular resident foreigners clearly was motivated by a desire to shore up support for the President among Hispanics (see Box 1.1 for more detail).

Many naturalized immigrants do not register to vote or exercise their voting rights. DeSipio's review of studies of naturalized American participation in the 1996 election led him to conclude that the naturalized participate less than other Americans, even with controls for socio-economic differences in place (DeSipio, 2001). More recently, DeSipio estimated that 20 per cent of Latino immigrants and a few in the second generation engage in the civic and political life of the sending country after emigration. But he found that such transnational engagement has little effect on US politics. Latino immigrants who belong to origin country-oriented associations tend to become *more* active than most immigrants in US politics. But this reflects political socialization rather than transnationalism. People who are organizationally active are likely to be active in many areas (DeSipio, 2006). This exemplifies that transnational political engagement and political integration in receiving countries can be complementary and do not have to be substitutes.

Anti-immigrant movements and parties

Anti-immigrant sentiments are not a monopoly of political conservatives. There are many conservatives who embrace pro-immigration and pro-immigrant public policies. And there are many on the political left who criticize immigration and public policies concerning immigrants for many reasons, and much the same can be said about political centrists. In fact, left-wing parties have historically been opposed to recruitment of low-skilled workers, which they saw as undermining the position of native workers and undermining the negotiation position of trade unions. 'Guest-worker' and other temporary immigration schemes have often been backed by right-wing parties and powerful business lobbies. In the Netherlands, for instance, the Christian Democratic Party supported extension of the rights to family reunion for immigrants in the 1960s while this was also favoured by the conservative-liberal VVD (People's Party for Freedom and Democracy) in order to ensure that the Netherlands remained competitive in its ability to attract workers (Bonjour, 2008). Indeed, the complicated politics of immigration often make for uncustomary political alliances. Hence, there is a need to define carefully what is meant by anti-immigrant movements and parties.

Political parties are organizations which regularly put up candidates to run for public offices contested in elections. An example is the *Front National* (FN) in France. Anti-immigrant parties such as the FN do not necessarily oppose all facets of French immigration policies. Some FN leaders and supporters endorse admission of seasonal foreign workers who mainly come from Morocco and Tunisia for employment in labour-intensive French agriculture, which is particularly important in the southern-French area of Provence, an important base of support for the FN. But the FN is appropriately termed an anti-immigrant party because the major thrust of its activities is directed against immigration policies and against immigrants, especially irregular migrants and immigrants from North Africa. It favours sharp curtailment of legal immigration to France and the exit of France from the EU.

Movements are more diffuse networks of individuals and groups that embrace similar political views and values. An example of a movement is the English Defence League (EDL) which emerged in 2009 and which comprises local chapters in a number of English cities and has like-minded homologues in other Western societies with which the EDL has links. The EDL is not anti-immigrant per se, rather it is selectively anti-immigrant in that it opposes immigration of Muslims to the UK because its adherents view Muslims and Islam as a security threat and as incompatible with Western democracy and values. Hence, the EDL also attempts to appeal to non-Muslim immigrant groups in the UK. The EDL has to date has not openly embraced authoritarian policies, although some EDL members have been associated with violence at demonstrations and made death threats against Leftists (Wikipedia, 2013). However, movements can become parties: some EDL members work closely with the anti-immigrant British National Party and the EDL leader Robinson announced in October 2012 that the EDL would become a party and field candidates in the future (Rawlinson, 2012).

Radical right is a term sometimes used interchangeably with anti-immigrant. Radical right refers to political movements and political parties that share characteristics of nativism (the practice or policy of favouring native-born citizens as distinguished from immigrants), authoritarianism and populism. Authoritarianism is the practice or policy of unquestioning obedience to the authority of a political leader or small group of leaders. Populism refers to diverse grassroots movements attuned to the needs of common people, especially farmers, which are critical of the role of large money interests in politics (Safire, 1993: 595–6). Populism can be both left- and right-wing.

Anti-immigrant politics in the transatlantic area is scarcely without historical precedent (see Chapter 4). Nevertheless, after World War II with a few exceptions, anti-immigrant politics remained marginal until the 1980s. In both the UK and Switzerland, politicization of immigration issues by the late 1950s and the mid-1960s respectively led to curtailment of migrant worker admissions. In the following years, immigration became a major political issue and remains so today. (See the case study on the 1964 Revision of the Italo-Swiss bilateral accord on the website.)

Certainly, support for anti-immigrant parties in Europe involved an element of protest voting. While 15 per cent of the electorate voted for the FN in France in the 1980s and one-third of all voters sympathized with FN positions on immigration (Weil, 1991a), it was also clear that the FN was picking up part of the protest vote traditionally received by the French Communist Party. The FN did particularly well in areas with concentrations of *Pieds-Noirs*, literally black feet, the name given to European background French citizens of Algeria, most of whom repatriated to mainland France in 1962. FN opposition to the European institutions was also a major point of attraction to some of its electorate (Marcus, 1995).

By 1997, the FN dominated municipal governments in four southern cities and nearly 4 million French citizens voted for FN candidates in the first round of legislative elections that year, and candidate Le Pen achieved the second-place in the 2002 presidential elections. Support for the FN decreased in the 2007 elections, when former Minister of Interior Sarkozy campaigned for election as President with a law and order line, which included strong measures against irregular migration. However, the FN, now under the leadership of Marine Le Pen, the daughter of the original party leader, remained a potent force in the 2012 elections. Presidential candidate Marine Le Pen won 18 per cent of the vote in the first round but refused to endorse incumbent President Sarkozy in the runoff election won by Socialist candidate François Hollande. Only two FN candidates obtained seats in the national legislative elections won by the Socialists.

Belgium became the scene of urban unrest in 1991, when youths who were largely of Moroccan origin clashed with police following a rumour that the *Vlaams Blok* (Flemish Bloc), traditionally a party seeking independence for Flanders, would stage a rally in a heavily immigrant-populated area. By 1990, the Flemish Bloc had become both a regionalist party and an anti-immigrant party, a combination seen in several other European states, especially in Northern Italy. A core plank of the party's platform called for repatriation of immigrants. The Flemish Bloc won 12 seats in the National Assembly in the 1991 general elections as compared with two in the previous elections. It improved upon the 1991 results in the 1999 and 2003 elections, winning over 11 per cent of the vote in 2003. However, due to a Belgium Supreme Court ruling in 2004 that the party was racist, it dissolved itself and became the Flemish Interest (Messina, 2007: 63). The Flemish Interest took 12 per cent of the vote in the 2007 elections and 7.8 per cent in 2008 (Mudde, 2012).

Similarly, in the 1991 Austrian municipal and regional elections, the anti-immigrant Freedom Party scored an important breakthrough by increasing its share of the vote to almost one-quarter. Eventually, the Freedom Party achieved a rough parity with the Austrian Socialist Party and the People's Party and formed a government with the latter. This precipitated a crisis in EU–Austria relations, as other EU member states regarded the Freedom Party's positions on immigration as unacceptable. The Freedom Party's leader, Jörg Haider, resigned as chairman in 2000. After the Freedom Party's share of the vote slumped to 10 per cent in the 2002 national elections as compared with nearly 22 per cent in the 1995 elections, Haider left the party to form the Union for the Future of Austria. Most Freedom Party parliamentarians followed him in joining the new party (Messina, 2007: 61). However, Haider died in an accident and his new party won 10.7 per cent of the votes in the 2008 national election as compared to the Freedom Party's 17.5 per cent. The two Austrian radical right parties both numbered among the only five such parties that succeeded in joining governments in Western Europe.

In neighbouring Switzerland, the Swiss People's Party won 28.9 per cent of the vote in 2007, making it the most popular Swiss party. It joined the coalition government and was instrumental in adoption of more restrictive legislation on asylum and supported the referendum banning construction of minarets in 2009 (Mudde, 2012: 5,17).

In Italy, a backlash against immigration has become a major political force. In the 1990s, the regionalist Northern League, *Forza Italia* (led by entrepreneur Silvio Berlusconi) and the neo-fascist National Alliance attacked immigration. Meanwhile, the politically influential Catholic clergy and the Pope himself voiced support for humanitarian initiatives such as legalization. Many Italian voters supported right-wing parties and protested against the deeply embedded corruption of the Christian Democrats and the Socialists. Protest voting against a discredited *partitocrazia* party machine was far more prevalent than anti-immigrant voting. But the second Berlusconi government announced a crackdown on irregular immigration in 2002. In the general elections of 1996 the Northern League gained 10 per cent of the vote, but its support declined to less than 5 per cent in 2006, when Berlusconi's centre-right coalition was forced out of government (Messina, 2007: 62–3). However, Berlusconi was soon back with an increased majority in early 2008. His election campaign relied heavily on stirring up anti-immigrant resentment and the Northern League's posters exhorted voters: 'Defend your future: oust illegal immigrants'. In the 2009 elections, the Northern League received 8.3 per cent of the vote (Mudde, 2012).

By 2007, anti-immigrant political movements had developed virtually across Europe, also in formerly Communist states like the Czech Republic and Bulgaria, where the Attack Party won 9 per cent of the vote in the 2009 elections. Many of these movements had historical precedents. Immigration issues have served as an entrée for extreme right-wing parties into mainstream politics across Europe, even in Scandinavia. However, the Bulgarian Attack Party principally targeted Roma and ethnic Turks with its slogan 'Let us give back Bulgaria to the Bulgarians' (Stefanova, 2007).

Some scholars have suggested that the emergence of right-wing parties has had anti-immigrant effects across the political spectrum, especially in European Countries with multiparty representative parliamentary systems. In her study on the impact of anti-immigration parties on mainstream parties' immigration positions in the Netherlands, Flanders and the UK between 1987 and 2010, Davis (2012) describes how the entire political spectrum in the Netherlands and Flanders has moved to the right in response to the rise of far-right anti-immigrant parties since the 1980s. Interestingly, she also observed that, when the far-right threat (temporarily) falls away, an opposite movement occurs, with parties adopting less restrictive positions. Her study also shows how such strategies are largely ineffective or can even be counterproductive. This is not only because as anti-immigrant voters tend to opt for the 'original' instead of the 'copycats' as Jean-Marie Le Pen, former leader of the French Front National, once argued, but also because their zigzagging or flip-flopping on immigration issues undermines their long-term credibility in the eyes of many voters.

In the two-party systems of the UK and the USA, anti-immigration parties seem to do less well. The National Front in the UK, for example, appeared to be gaining strength in the mid-1970s before the Conservative Party, under the leadership of Margaret Thatcher, pre-empted it by adopting key parts of its programme (Layton-Henry and Rich, 1986: 74–5). Britain's two-party system and its 'first past the post' electoral law make it very difficult for any new party to win seats in the House of Commons. In the USA too, the two-party system and a single-member district winner-take-all electoral law make it very difficult for any third party to compete, but strongly anti-immigrant opinions can be found within the mainstream parties. In Canada, aside from previously noted complaints about immigrant voting results in Quebec, political opposition to immigration per se is virtually non-existent.

In Australia the situation is rather different. More than two in five Australians are immigrants or children of immigrants, and attitudes towards immigration are generally positive. However, since the mid-1990s, there has been considerable politicization of asylum issues, with the major parties seeking to outdo each other with their rhetoric of getting tough on 'queue-jumpers'. This preoccupation with the quite small number of asylum-seekers (see Chapter 7) has obscured public engagement with the major shifts that have taken place in the much larger migration programme, notably the increasing economic focus in selection and the growth of temporary migration (Castles *et al.*, 2013).

Although most research concentrates on anti-immigrant movements and parties in Europe and North America, anti-immigrant politics has also figured importantly elsewhere. Over the 2000s, the increasing numbers of sub-Saharan migrants living and working in Libya and other Maghreb countries have regularly been exposed to racist attacks, discrimination in the labour market and arbitrary arrests, imprisonment and deportation. In 2012, a crackdown on irregular migration, raids on immigrant neighbourhoods, and arrests of leaders of immigrant associations seemed part of a strategy of the Moroccan government to shift the blame for the economic crisis, crime and mass youth unemployment onto the shoulders of the several thousands of sub-Saharan migrants living in Morocco.

Anti-immigrant politics at times has proved deadly for Palestinians and Syrians living and working in Lebanon, such as during the 2005 crisis which led to the retreat of Syrian troops long stationed in Lebanon. In neighbouring Israel, anti-immigrant politics reached a fever pitch when arsonists burned apartments housing African migrants in Jerusalem in 2012. This followed several earlier arson attempts and protests against the growing number of Africans, around 60,000, who have entered Israel in recent years. Most hail from Eritrea and Sudan or South Sudan and many claim to be refugees. Prime Minister Netanyahu pledged speedy construction of a 150 mile, 16 foot tall steel fence along the Israeli-Egyptian border (Kershner, 2012). Other countries in the Middle East and North Africa that have witnessed anti-immigrant politics, sometimes involving violence and killings, include Egypt, Libya, Kuwait, Saudi Arabia, Iran and pre-1990 Iraq.

Anti-immigrant politics has figured importantly in several African states, including the Republic of South Africa and the Côte d'Ivoire, and Nigeria and Ghana, which share a history of mass expulsions of immigrant workers (see Chapter 8). In Latin America and the Caribbean, anti-immigrant politics flares up chronically in the Dominican Republic and to a lesser extent in Costa Rica. In Asia, and the Pacific, anti-immigrant parties and movements have been important in Malaysia, Singapore, South Korea, Taiwan, Fiji and certain regions of India, notably Assam and along the border with Bangladesh where Indian authorities have constructed a wall somewhat similar to the wall built along the US–Mexican border.

The politics of immigration policy-making

Ultimately, the political dimension of international migration matters the most because the modern world has been structured by a nation-state system that renders international migration inherently problematic, because international migrants, by definition, cross from one sovereign jurisdiction to another (Zolberg, 1981). In this sense, international migration is intrinsically political and is almost inevitably an imagined or real challenge to the state sovereignty. A major debate surrounding formulation of immigration policies, particularly in the most developed, democratic states, arises from disagreements over the autonomy of national states and continuities and discontinuities in the nature of the nation-state system in an era of globalization. This debate has influenced scholarship that seeks to elucidate why states adopt immigration policies and why certain migration policy outcomes occur.

Freeman (1995) has argued that a gap in immigration policy preferences between the political elite and the general public prevailed in Western democracies. Political elites favoured 'expansive' (more liberal), immigration policies generally opposed by the mass of the public. He hypothesized that immigration produced concentrated benefits, especially to employers and investors, and diffuse costs borne by the general public, especially over the medium and long term. The insulation of pro-immigration political elites from electorates generally less supportive of liberal immigration policies led to a general pattern of expansive immigration policies in Western democracies. However, he observed significant variations between traditional immigration lands like the USA, Canada and Australia, Northern European states and Southern European states. Freeman's views ran decidedly counter to those analysts who viewed OECD-area immigration policies as draconian and restrictive.

For Hollifield (1992), liberal democracies face embedded constraints, which limit their prerogatives in formulation of immigration policies. International migrants are human beings with rights, and immigration policies are thereby constrained, particularly in democratic societies. The classic illustration of this came in France in 1977, when a Council of State ruling invalidated the government's effort to prevent family reunification. The French government declared a zero immigration policy, but could not translate that declaration into policy because France had a bilateral treaty with Portugal that granted legally admitted Portuguese workers a right to family reunification. Hence, the 'expansive' nature of immigration policies towards more liberal regimes in many Western democracies reflects underlying, diffuse liberal values, such as notions of elementary human rights, but this should not be construed as an erosion of the sovereign state.

Soysal (1994) viewed the emergence of an embryonic international regime concerning migrant rights as effectively constraining the immigration policy-making of European democracies. Multilateral and bilateral treaties and the influence of international organizations such as the ILO and the Council of Europe empowered international migrants and shaped immigration policy-making. Joppke (1998; 1999) disagreed, viewing such constraints as largely self-imposed by national legal systems or as resulting from past policies. In his view, states need to regulate immigration, but by making commitments, such as signing the Geneva Convention on refugees, they impose limitations on what they can do. Joppke does not view these limitations as external constraints.

Other important perspectives include the globalization thesis, which views democratic states as increasingly unable to control migration between countries due to underlying socio-economic and political transformations that are eroding governmental capacity to regulate international migration. This thesis is explicitly rejected by scholars who affirm that, over the medium to long term, immigration policies reflect state interests (Messina, 2007: 239–45). The path dependency perspective views immigration policy outcomes as due to entrenched institutional arrangements that delimit policy options and shape decision-making (Messina, 2007: 102–5). Hence, the French propensity for recourse to legalization in the 1970s and 1980s had much to do with earlier decisions taken to legalize foreigners (Miller, 2002). Recent scholarship about the EU and immigration policy-making suggests that member states are pooling sovereign prerogatives in order to better achieve immigration policy goals that can be achieved more readily at the regional level (Boswell and Geddes, 2011; Geddes, 2003; Lahav, 2004). Menz (2009) explains that the shift to 'managed migration' as a new immigration paradigm in the six European states he has studied, reflects the imprint of the varying political economy traditions of the respective states but also the growing influence of the EU in immigration policy-making.

Concerning the USA, Zolberg (2006) contends that immigration policy has always been central to the development of the American state and society. It is a 'nation by design'. He views US immigration policy history as composed of expansive and restrictionist eras in which a policy status quo, once achieved, is difficult to alter, due in part to the institutional nature of the American state, characterized by a division of powers between the judicial, legislative and executive branches of government. Tichenor (2002: 294) identified four interlocking processes affecting US immigration law-making: (1) changing institutional opportunities and constraints; (2) the shifting views of immigration experts; (3) perceived international threats and the lack thereof and; (4) the changing nature of interest group coalitions. Together these processes determine US immigration law and policy outcomes.

Conclusions

International migration is and has always been inherently political, which makes it all the more puzzling that the branch of the social sciences most concerned with politics, political science, came to it very slowly and belatedly compared to disciplines like history and sociology (Hollifield, 2000). Migration can dramatically affect electorates, as witnessed in the Israeli and US cases, and immigrants can influence politics through non-electoral means as well. Immigrants have fostered transnational politics linking origin-country and host-society political systems in fundamental ways.

Migrants and minorities are both subjects and objects of politics. A recent anti-immigrant backlash has strengthened the appeal of certain right-wing parties in Western Europe. One way in which migration has fundamentally altered the Western European political landscape is through the constitution of increasingly significant Islamic organizations, which some suggest present a dilemma for democratic political systems: refusal to accept their role would violate democratic principles, yet some people see their aims and methods as intrinsically anti-democratic. Others see Western states as facilitating Muslim emancipation reminiscent of Jewish emancipation in nineteenth century Europe (Laurence, 2012). International migration has fostered new constituencies, new parties and new issues. Many of Western Europe's newer political parties feature anti-immigrant themes. Violence against immigrants is also a factor in ethnic minority formation and political mobilization. For example, experiences of racist violence from the 1960s onwards was a major factor in the emergence of black and Asian organizations in the UK.

In the USA, Canada and Australia, immigrant political participation and representation is less of an issue, partly because in these countries immigration has been part of nation building and the partly because of the traditional preponderance of family-based permanent immigration. However, family-based admissions have declined relative to other categories of immigrant admissions in all three and temporary admissions of skilled migrants and students have increased. Disenfranchisement of legally resident foreigners and irregularly resident foreigners in major US cities increasingly troubles authorities. Much of New York City's population cannot vote, either because they are not naturalized or because they are irregularly resident. Virtually everywhere, international migration renders politics more complex. Ethnic mobilization and ethnic voting blocs are becoming important issues in many countries. Another new issue may be seen in the politics of naturalization. One or two decades ago, virtually no one knew naturalization law or considered it important. The changing nature of international migration and its politicization have changed that.

Immigrant politics are in a continual state of flux because of the fundamental changes in migration patterns as well as the broader transformations in political patterns, which often lag behind. Demographic changes in the USA since the 1960s has resulted in major changes in the American electorate and voting by 2012. The re-election of President Obama in 2012 bore mute testimony. As migratory movements mature – moving through the stages of immigration, settlement and minority formation – the character of political mobilization and participation changes. This often coincides with a shift from concern with origin country politics to mobilization around the interests of ethnic groups in the immigration country.

If political participation is denied through refusal of citizenship and failure to provide channels of representation, immigrant politics is likely to take on militant forms. This applies particularly to the descendants of immigrants born in the countries of immigration. If they are excluded from political life through non-citizenship, social marginalization or racism, they are likely to present a major challenge to existing political structures in the future. At the same time, we can observe a long-term historical pattern of intergenerational incorporation of migrants, inclusive of those groups once viewed as a threat to social cohesion and security. This pattern tends to augur well for the future.

Guide to further reading

Extra resources at www.age-of-migration.com

The Age of Migration website contains the following: Text 13.1 '*The Amicale des Algériens en Europe 1962–1992*'; and Text 13.2 'Non-Citizen Voting in US History'.

Classic contributions on migrants and politics include Castles and Kosack (1973); Miller (1981); Baldwin-Edwards and Schain (1994); Freeman (1979; 1986; 1995); Hammar (1990); Hollifield (1992); Layton-Henry (1990); Ireland (1994); and Soysal (1994). Cohen and Layton-Henry (1997) provide a valuable collection of contributions to the study of the politics of migration prior to 1995.

Important more recent scholarship includes Lahav (2004); Motomura (2006); Bloemraad (2006) Schierup, Hansen and Castles (2006); Green and Weil (2007); Earnest (2008); Schain (2008); Menz (2009); Boswell (2009); Givens and Maxwell (2012); Boswell and Geddes (2011); Laurence (2012).

Chapter 14

Conclusion: Migration in the Twenty-First Century

This book has argued that international migration is a constant, not an aberration, in human history. Population movements have always accompanied demographic growth, economic transformations, technological change, political conflict and warfare. Over the last five centuries, migration has played a major role in colonialism, industrialization, nation-state formation and the development of the capitalist world market. However, international migration has never been as pervasive, or as socio-economically and politically significant, as it is today. Never before have political leaders accorded such priority to migration concerns.

The hallmark of the age of migration is the global character of international migration: the way it affects more and more countries and regions, and its linkages with complex processes affecting the entire world. This book has endeavoured to elucidate the principal causes, processes and effects of international migration. Contemporary patterns, as discussed in Chapters 5, 6, 7 and 8, are rooted in historical relationships and shaped by a multitude of political, demographic, socio-economic, geographical and cultural factors. These flows result in greater ethnic diversity within countries and deepening transnational linkages between states and societies. International migrations are greatly affected by governmental policies and may, in fact, be precipitated by decisions to recruit foreign workers or to admit refugees.

Yet, international migrations may also possess a relative autonomy and be impervious to governmental policies. Official policies often fail to achieve their objectives, or even bring about the opposite of what is intended. People as well as governments shape international migration. Decisions made by individuals, families and communities – often with imperfect information and constrained options – play a vital role in determining migration and settlement. The social networks which arise through the migratory process help shape long-term outcomes, and defy attempts by governments to regulate migration. The agents and brokers who make up the burgeoning 'migration industry' have their own interests and aims. At the same time, significant sections of the populations of receiving countries may oppose immigration. As seen in Chapter 10, governments sometimes react by adopting strategies of denial, hoping that the problems will go away if they are ignored. In other instances, mass deportations and repatriations have been carried out. Governments vary greatly in their capacities to regulate international migration and in the credibility of their efforts to regulate unauthorized migration.

317

In Chapter 2, we provided some theoretical perspectives on the reasons why international migrations take place and in Chapter 3 we discussed how they often lead to permanent settlement and the formation of distinct ethnic groups in the receiving societies and have considerable potential to contribute to social and economic development in origin societies. We argued that migration should be understood as an intrinsic part of broader processes of development, social transformation and globalization, instead of a problem to be solved. This is why migration is inevitable, irrespective of political preferences. The migratory process needs to be understood in its totality as a complex system of social interactions with a wide range of institutional structures and informal networks in sending, transit and receiving countries, and at the international level. Certainly in a democratic setting, legal admission of migrants will almost inevitably result in some settlement, even when migrants are admitted temporarily. But even for authoritarian states such as those of the Arab Gulf it is increasingly difficult to prevent settlement taking place.

Acceptance of the seeming inevitability of migration, as well as of permanent settlement and formation of ethnic groups, as part of the way contemporary societies are changing is the necessary starting point for any meaningful consideration of desirable public policies. The key to adaptive and effective policy-making in this realm (as in others) is understanding of the causes and dynamics of international migration. Policies based on misunderstanding or mere wishful thinking are virtually condemned to fail. Hence, if governments decide to admit foreign workers, they should from the outset make provision for the legal settlement of that proportion of the entrants that is almost sure to remain permanently: a consideration that needs to be taken to heart by the governments of countries as diverse as Japan, Malaysia, South Korea, Brazil, Turkey, Saudi Arabia, Spain, Italy and Greece at present.

Today governments and peoples have to face up to some very serious dilemmas. The answers they choose will help shape the future of their societies, as well as the relations between the rich countries of the North and the developing countries of the South. Central issues include:

- future perspectives for global migration and mobility;
- improving international cooperation and governance in the migration arena;
- policies towards irregular migration;
- regulating legal immigration and integrating settlers;
- the role of ethnic diversity in social and cultural change, and the consequences for the nation-state.

Future perspectives for global migration and mobility

When the first edition of *The Age of Migration* was published in 1993, its central concern was with immigration and its effects on advanced industrial economies. We showed how the labour migrations of the post-1945 period had led to (often unexpected) settlement and minority formation processes, which were challenging ideas on national identity and citizenship. We also showed how migration within and from Africa, the Middle East, Latin America and Asia was growing in volume and significance. Since 1993, the globalization of migration has progressed rapidly with the integration of an increasing number of countries into international migration systems. Its patterns and its consequences for societies of origin, transit and destination are changing constantly. This fifth edition has tried to reflect these trends, but inevitably can only cover a fraction of the massive shifts occurring.

A first key shift concerns the growing connectivity between processes of globalization, social transformation and migration. Chapters 2 and 3 explored these links, showing that processes of economic, political and cultural change and development transform social relationships in both rich and poor countries, creating the conditions for greater human mobility. The combination of increased North–South inequality, improved transport and communication technologies, and rising transnational consciousness facilitates movement and greater diversity in migration patterns and outcomes.

A second, closely connected shift has been the rapid demographic transition to low mortality and fertility and greater longevity in developed countries. Declining cohorts of young labour market entrants and increasing age-dependency ratios make future labour demand at all skill levels seem likely. According to the medium variant of the UN's *2010 Revision* of *World Population Prospects*, the world population is expected to increase from 6.9 billion in mid-2011 to 9.3 billion in 2050 and to then grow more slowly to reach 10.1 billion by 2100 (UNDESA, 2011). Virtually all of the expected 2.4 billion additional human beings in the coming 20–30 years will be born in the developing world. Like it or not, Europeans and North Americans are likely to have to continue to rely on newcomers from Africa, Asia and Latin America. Industrializing Asian countries like South Korea are undergoing amazingly fast demographic transitions, and China appears fated to undergo the same process. Some areas that constituted important zones of emigration in the twentieth century, like North Africa and Mexico, may become zones of immigration if future reforms stimulate growth and prosperity. By the middle of the twenty-first century, prosperous countries may be competing not just for highly skilled personnel – as they already do today – but also for low-skilled workers to build their houses, run their services and look after the elderly.

A third important shift relates to labour force dynamics. We touched on this theme for developing regions in Chapters 5, 6, 7 and 8, and explored it in more detail for advanced economies in Chapter 11. Migration has played a crucial role in labour force growth in industrialized countries. Migrant labour market positions and outcomes have become more diverse than in the past, yet many migrant workers still experience disadvantage. This is linked to a new political economy of labour, in which much of manufacturing employment has been outsourced to low-wage economies. As a partial result of neoliberal economic policies, today's advanced economies are characterized by the resurgence of exploitative and poorly regulated, often irregular work in agriculture, services and manufacturing sweatshops. Patterns of labour market segmentation by gender, ethnicity, race, origins and legal status force many migrants into precarious forms of employment, characterized by subcontracting, spurious self-employment, temporary and casual work, and informalization, with immigrants typically picking up jobs that natives shun. Today, such labour market segmentation is proliferating all around the world, and partly explains why also poorer countries in Africa and Asia also attract significant numbers of labour immigrants.

A fourth major shift results from the emergence of a multipolar world of regions, characterized by disparate and distinctive regionalization patterns. At the same time, the growing political and economic influence of emerging powers like China, India, Turkey, South Africa, Brazil and Mexico will change the global landscape of migration as they increasingly attract and compete for lower- and high-skilled migrant labour.

A fifth shift is the emergence of more flexible types of international mobility: changes in transportation, technology and culture are making it normal for people to think beyond national borders and to cross them frequently for all types of reasons. While the share of international migrants on the world population has not significantly increased over the past half century, short-term mobility has soared. Mobility for study, tourism, marriage and retirement is assuming greater significance and is also affecting ideas on migration. Mobility implies an opening of borders for at least some kinds of movement, as well as more flexible types of movement, for a variety of purposes, which do not necessarily lead to long-term stay. For the foreseeable future, the world will experience both migrations in the traditional sense and new types of mobility.

Improving international cooperation and governance

These trends are likely to increase the economic importance of international migration for many countries, thus reinforcing its potential to bring about cultural and social change. That in turn may further increase the political saliency of migration. This raises the question of whether this might give rise to improved international cooperation and governance, as has happened with finance (IMF and World Bank), trade (WTO) and many other forms of global connectivity (Held *et al.*, 1999). International migration constitutes the most important facet of the international political economy not covered by a global regime for cooperation and governance.

However, achievement of real change through international cooperation remains elusive despite three important developments: the creation of the Global Commission on International Migration and publication of its influential report (GCIM, 2005), the convening of a High Level Dialogue on Migration and Development at the UN in 2006, and its follow-up through an annual Global Forum on Migration and Development since

2007. For all their merits, these consultative démarches have not resulted in concrete measures towards a regime for international cooperation on migration. The unwillingness of states to move forward in this area is also seen in the very poor ratification record of the 1990 *International Convention on the Protection of the Rights of All Migrant Workers and Members of their Families*, passed by the UN General Assembly on 18 December 1990. As mentioned in Chapter 1, only 46 states (out of 193 UN member states) had ratified it by 2013. These were mainly countries of emigration; immigration countries have not been willing to support measures designed to protect migrants.

There are at least four reasons not to expect a global migration regime to emerge anytime soon. First, at least for the next few decades, there will remain a significant supply of foreign labour at the global level. This creates a disincentive to multilateral cooperation between origin and destination countries, as individual states can sign bilateral agreements to recruit foreign labour or (tacitly or openly) tolerate irregular entry of foreign labour. However, this situation may change in the long-term with the predicted coming stabilization of population in many world regions.

Second, there is no inherent reciprocity of interests between workers in more socio-economically advanced states and those in less developed states. The rich countries perceive little benefit in reciprocity. Their workers generally will not benefit from facilitated entry to less developed states. Labour movements would be largely unidirectional, from less developed areas to the more developed areas. Why would the most developed states cede sovereign prerogatives to regulate international migration to establish an international regime?

Third, as Koslowski (2008) has argued, leadership is vital to regime formation. US leadership since 1945 has helped forge liberal international trade regimes in many areas. Neither the USA nor any of the other most powerful states have evidenced much leadership in forging a global regime concerning international migration. To the contrary, the USA has been very sceptical about international fora on international migration, something already clearly evident in 1986 when the OECD convened the first major multilateral conference on international migration since World War II (Miller and Gabriel, 2008). More generally, the influence of the USA is still large but declining in an increasingly multipolar world. Perhaps emerging powers such as Brazil, which have recently experienced high emigration and have been critical towards immigration regimes of OECD countries, may play such a leadership role in the future, but that remains to be seen.

Fourth, political leaders and public debates in immigration countries still generally treat migration as something fundamentally abnormal and problematic. The overwhelming concern seems to be to stop or reduce migration, as if it were inherently bad. This is very clear in debates on migration and development (see Chapter 3). Even well-meaning initiatives, like attempts to address the 'root causes' of emigration from poor countries through efforts to achieve 'durable solutions' to impoverishment and violence, are driven by the idea that migration should be reduced (Castles and Van Hear, 2012). Political leaders still seem to believe that development will curtail migration from poorer countries, although evidence points clearly to the contrary (de Haas, 2007c). In general, development facilitates migration through increasing people's aspirations and capabilities to migrate.

As we have shown in this book, migration has taken place throughout history and is stimulated by economic change and growth. One sign of this is the growth of highly skilled mobility between advanced economies. Another is the realization that rich countries like the USA, UK and Australia have large diasporas, which make important contributions to both sending and receiving countries. Rather than reducing migration, we suggest, the aim should be to work for greater economic and social equality between rich and poor countries and better protection of migrant rights, so that migration will take place under better conditions and will enrich the experiences and capabilities of migrants and communities. This will also increase the capability of migrants to contribute to development in origin countries (UNDP, 2009). Thus reducing 'unwanted migration' is a valid aim only if it is coupled with the understanding that this may well mean greater mobility overall – but mobility of a different and more positive kind. This would require measures that go well beyond the usual range of migration-related policies.

Genuine reform of trade policies, for instance, could encourage economic growth in less developed countries. A key issue is the level of prices for primary commodities as compared with industrial products. This is linked to constraints on world trade through tariffs and subsidies. Reforms could bring important benefits for less developed countries. But trade policies generally operate within tight political constraints: few politicians are willing to confront their own farmers, workers or industrialists, particularly in times of economic recession. Reforms favourable to the economies of the less developed countries will only come gradually, if at all (Castles and Delgado Wise, 2008).

Regional integration – the creation of free-trade areas and regional political communities – is sometimes seen as a way of diminishing 'unwanted' migration by reducing trade barriers and spurring economic growth, as well as by legalizing international movement of labour. This can be a potentially effective strategy to stimulate circular mobility. After all, the evidence on past and contemporary migration dynamics reveals a crucial paradox: the more migration is subject to regulation and restrictions, the less circular migration tends to take place. This is because where migration entails high costs and risks, migrants find it hard to return home for fear they will not be able to migrate again; they therefore tend to remain for longer periods or even permanently in destination countries.

Both in the USA and in the EU, more immigration restrictions have pushed supposedly temporary immigrants into permanent settlement. So, while restrictive immigration policy encourages more permanent types of migration, free migration policies tend to encourage mobility and circular movement. The effect of free mobility regimes on migration dynamics depends on specific economic, political and historical conditions. For instance, when Spain joined the EEC in 1986, the predicted mass emigration did not occur. Instead, many migrants returned. The EU enlargements of 2004 and 2007 did lead to large-scale emigration from Eastern Europe, but this migration is generally more temporary in character than migration from outside the EU.

Restrictive policies and border controls have failed to significantly curb immigration to wealthy countries. Rather, they have led to greater reliance on increasingly risky and costly irregular migration and have paradoxically encouraged permanent settlement. A commonly presented 'smart solution' to curb immigration is to address the perceived root causes of migration through increasing development aid. A fundamental reason to be sceptical about the idea of 'aid instead of migration' is that available evidence strongly suggests that economic and human development tends to coincide with an increase rather than a decrease in emigration and overall mobility. Trade, aid and remittances tend to be complements to, rather than substitutes for, migration. At the same time, demand for both skilled and unskilled migrant labour is likely to persist. In fact, the focus on origin country development creates a false suggestion that migration is mainly driven by poverty, diverting the attention away from the demand-driven nature of much labour migration.

The initial effect of development and integration of less developed countries into the world market is to increase internal and international migration. This is because the early stages of development lead to rural–urban migration and the acquisition by many people of the financial and cultural resources needed for international migration. Reaching the advanced stage of the 'migration transition' – through which emigration declines, and is eventually replaced by a more balanced relationship between in- and out-migration – requires demographic and economic conditions which generally take generations to develop. Neither restrictive measures nor development strategies can stop international migration, because there are such powerful forces stimulating population movement. These include the increasing pervasiveness of a global culture and the growth of cross-border movements of ideas, capital and commodities. The world community will have to learn to live with large-scale migration for the foreseeable future.

Responding to irregular immigration

A major trend since the 1980s has been the emergence of a new generation of temporary foreign worker policies often touted as a way to better manage and substitute for irregular migration. Recently, international organizations have used the more positive label of 'circular migration'. There are many reasons to doubt that such policies will succeed.

In European countries such as Germany some observers have suggested a need for increased immigration to compensate for low birth rates and an ageing population: foreign workers might provide the labour for age-care and other services as well as the construction industry. But immigration cannot effectively counteract the demographic ageing of Western societies unless it is substantially increased. Political constraints will not permit this. Public opinion may accept entry programmes for highly skilled labour, family reunification and refugees, but not a resumption of massive recruitment of foreign labour for low-level jobs. Most industrial democracies have to struggle to provide adequate employment for existing populations of low-skilled citizen and resident foreign workers. In addition, in view of global demographic ageing and the emergence of new economic powers which increasingly attract migrants from all over the world, it should not be taken for granted that there will always be a quasi-unlimited pool of unskilled and skilled labour ready to migrate to the West.

One of the most pressing challenges for many countries today, therefore, is to find ways of responding to irregular or 'unwanted' migratory flows. Irregular immigration is a somewhat vague blanket term, which embraces:

- legal entrants who overstay their entry visas or who work without permission, which is the most important form of irregular migration;
- illegal border-crossers;
- family members of migrant workers, prevented from entering legally by restrictions on family reunion;
- asylum seekers not regarded as genuine refugees.

Most such migrants come from poor countries and seek employment, but often lack recognized work qualifications. They may compete – or at least be perceived to compete – with lower-qualified local people for unskilled jobs, and for housing and social amenities. Many regions throughout the world have experienced an increase in such immigration in the last 35 years or so. Of course, the migration is not always as 'unwanted' as is made out: employers often benefit from cheap workers who lack rights, and some governments (especially those of the USA and Southern European countries) tacitly permit such movements. Often there is a significant contradiction between government policy statements and actual implementation on the ground.

Appearing to crack down on 'unwanted immigration' is increasingly regarded by governments as essential for safeguarding social peace. In several regions of the world, the result has been a series of agreements designed to secure international cooperation in stopping irregular entries, to increase border control and to speed up the processing of applications for asylum. Several African and Asian countries have carried out quite draconian measures, such as mass expulsions of foreign workers (for example, Nigeria, Libya, Malaysia), building fences and walls along borders (South

Africa), severe punishments for illegal entrants (corporal punishment in Singapore) and sanctions against employers (South Africa, Japan and other countries). In addition, non-official punishments such as beatings by police are routinely meted out in some countries.

The exact impact of these measures is hard to assess, but as long as labour markets continue to generate a demand for migrant workers, the effectiveness of such controls seems to be limited. They also seem to fulfil an important symbolical function. In fact, 'elected leaders and bureaucrats increasingly have turned to symbolic policy instruments to create an *appearance* of control' (Massey *et al.*, 1998: 288). Yet harsh political discourse on immigration which obscures the real demand for migrant labour can be a catalyst for the very xenophobia and apocalyptic representations of a massive influx of migrants to which they claim to be a political–electoral response. The killing spree by Anders Breivik in July 2011 in Norway (see Chapter 1) shows how far such responses can go.

The difficulty in achieving effective control is not hard to understand. Barriers to mobility contradict the powerful forces of globalization which are leading towards greater economic and cultural interchange. In an increasingly international economy, it is difficult to open borders for movements of information, commodities and capital and yet close them to people. Global circulation of investment and know-how always means movements of people too. Moreover, flows of highly skilled personnel tend to encourage flows of less-skilled workers. The instruments of border surveillance cannot be sufficiently fine-tuned to let through all those whose presence is officially wanted, but to stop all those who are not. Nevertheless, there should be no mistaking that measures like enforcement of employer sanctions have a deterrent effect where there exists the genuine political will to punish unauthorized employment of undocumented foreign workers. However, such political will is often absent despite the usually tough rhetoric through which politicians proclaim their desire to 'crack down' on irregular migration and unauthorized unemployment.

The matter is further complicated by a number of factors (see Castles *et al.*, 2012): the contradiction between state and market – or more precisely between government rules that refuse entry to low-skilled workers and labour market demand for them; the eagerness of employers to hire foreign workers (whether documented or not) for menial jobs, when nationals are unwilling to take such positions; the difficulty of adjudicating asylum claims and of distinguishing economically motivated migrants from those deserving of refugee status; and the inadequacies and inflexibility of immigration law. The trend towards economic and labour market deregulation since the 1980s and the weakening of organized labour and declining trade union membership in many Western democracies has also tended to increase unauthorized foreign employment. Policies aimed at reducing labour market rigidities and enhancing competitiveness may result in expanded employer hiring of authorized and unauthorized foreign workers (see Chapter 11). Social welfare policies may also have unintended consequences, making employment of unauthorized foreign workers more propitious, since this allows employers to avoid paying social insurance contributions.

Thus, despite the claimed desire of governments to stop irregular migration, many of the causes are to be found in the very political and social structures of the immigration countries, and their relations with less developed areas. Yet in the current political climate there is no doubt that receiving countries will continue to regulate migration and attempt to curb irregular immigration. How successful such measures can be remains to be seen.

Legal migration and integration

Virtually all democratic states and many not-so-democratic states have growing foreign populations. As shown in Chapters 5, 6, 7 and 8, the presence of these immigrants is either the result of conscious labour recruitment or immigration policies, or occurs more spontaneously due to the existence of various linkages between sending and receiving countries. In some cases (especially in North America and Oceania), policies of large-scale immigration still exist. They are selective: economic migrants, family members and refugees are admitted according to quotas which are politically determined. In other regions, especially Western Europe and East Asia, migration systems tend to be driven mainly by employer demand, with governments often playing a facilitating role. In many cases, such demand-driven migration policies favour temporary labour migration over permanent settlement migration. In recent years, 'classical immigration countries' like Australia, New Zealand, Canada and (to a lesser extent) the USA have increased their temporary intakes, although sometimes with built-in pathways to permanent status.

Planned entries are conducive to acceptable social conditions for migrants as well as to relative social peace between migrants and local people. Countries with immigration quota systems generally decide on them through political processes which permit public discussion and the balancing of the interests of different social groups. Participation in decision-making increases the acceptability of immigration programmes. At the same time, this approach facilitates the introduction of measures to prevent discrimination and exploitation of immigrants, and to provide social services to support successful settlement. There is therefore a case for advocating that all countries that continue to have immigration should move towards planned immigration policies. However, recent trends have been more towards the growth of demand-driven temporary migration programmes. This shows the need for introducing measures to safeguard the rights of temporary migrants too. Pathways to permanence can be an important aspect of this.

As Chapters 10 and 13 showed, governmental obligations towards immigrant populations are shaped by the nature of the political system in the receiving society, as well as the mode of entry of the newcomers. Governments possess an internationally recognized right to regulate entry of foreigners, a right that may be voluntarily limited through governmental signature of bilateral or multilateral agreements (for example, in the case of refugees and family migrants). Clearly it makes a difference whether or not a foreigner has arrived on a territory through legal means of entry. In principle, the proper course for action with regard to legally admitted foreign residents in a democracy is straightforward. They should be rapidly afforded equality of socio-economic rights and a large measure of political freedom, for their status would otherwise diminish the quality of democratic life in the society. However, this principle is frequently ignored in practice. Unauthorized immigration, residence and employment make immigrants especially vulnerable to exploitation. The perceived illegitimacy of their presence can foster conflict and anti-immigrant violence.

'Guest-worker'-style restrictions on the employment and residential mobility of legally admitted foreigners appear difficult to reconcile with prevailing market principles, to say nothing of democratic norms. The same goes for restrictions on political rights. Freedom of speech, association and assembly should be unquestionable. The only restriction on the rights of legally admitted foreigners which seems compatible with democratic principles is the reservation of the right to vote and to stand for public office to citizens. This is only justifiable if resident foreigners are given the opportunity of naturalization, without daunting procedures or high fees. But, even then, some foreign residents are likely to decide not to become citizens for various reasons. A democratic system needs to secure their political participation too. This can mean setting up special representative bodies for resident non-citizens, or extending voting rights to non-citizens who fulfil certain criteria of length of stay (as in Sweden, the Netherlands and, in the nineteenth century, much of the USA).

The global character of international migration results in the intermingling and cohabitation of people from increasingly different physical and cultural settings. Older immigration countries have developed approaches to incorporate newcomers into their societies, with a view to making them into citizens in the long run. Some newer immigration countries, for instance in the Middle East (see Chapter 8), and East and South-East Asia (see Chapter 7), reject the idea of permanent settlement, and treat migrants as temporary sojourners, however long they stay, and despite the fact that many of these countries have become *de facto* settlement countries. The long-term presence of new ethnic minorities may eventually compel those countries to change their immigration policies and to accommodate permanent settlement, for instance through facilitating naturalization.

Chapter 12 analysed incorporation models in Europe, North America and Oceania, showing that there are important variations, ranging from 'exclusionary' approaches that keep migrants as a separate (and usually disadvantaged) part of the population, through 'assimilationist' approaches that offer full membership but at the price of abandoning migrants' original languages and cultures, to 'multicultural' approaches that offer both full membership and recognition of cultural difference. We argued that a trend away from exclusionary and assimilationist models and towards multicultural approaches could be discerned from the 1970s to the 1990s. Changes in citizenship laws to offer easier naturalization for migrants and birth right citizenship for their children were an important sign of change.

However, this trend has been questioned and to some extent reversed in recent years. Critics of multiculturalism argue that it is detrimental to the economic integration and success of minorities, and that it can lead to permanent cultural and political divisions. There is a new emphasis on 'national values' and loyalty. The result is a call to replace multicultural policies with measures to strengthen 'social cohesion'. Symptomatic of this trend has been the tightening up of naturalization rules, restrictions on dual citizenship in some places, and the introduction of citizenship tests in Australia and several European countries. Yet, at the same time, many countries have maintained the multilingual services and anti-discrimination rules typical of multicultural societies. In some places the rhetoric on multiculturalism seems to have changed more than the reality. At the time of writing, the picture is confused, indicating the persistence of important struggles in the public arena.

Ethnic diversity, social change and the nation-state

The age of migration has already changed the world and many of its societies. Many highly developed countries and many less developed ones have become far more diverse than they were even a generation ago. In fact, few modern nations have ever been ethnically homogeneous. However, the nationalism of the last two centuries strove to create myths of homogeneity. In its extreme forms, nationalism even tried to bring about such homogeneity through expulsion of minorities, ethnic cleansing and genocide. But the reality for most countries today is that they have to contend with a new type of pluralism, and that – even if migration were to stop tomorrow – this will affect their societies for generations.

One reason why immigration and the emergence of new ethnic groups have had such an impact is that these trends have coincided with the crisis of modernity and the transition to post-industrial societies. The labour migration of the pre-1973 period appeared at the time to be reinforcing the economic dominance of the old industrial nations. Today we can interpret it as part of a process of capital accumulation which preceded a seminal change in the world economy. Growing international mobility of capital, the electronic revolution, the decline of old industrial areas and the rise of new ones are all factors which have led to rapid change in advanced economies. The erosion of the old blue-collar working class, labour market segmentation and the increased polarization of the labour force have led to a social crisis in which immigrants find themselves doubly at risk: many of them suffer unemployment and social marginalization, yet at the same time they are often inaccurately portrayed as the cause of the problems. That is why the emergence of the 'two-thirds society', in which the top strata are affluent while the bottom third is impoverished, is often accompanied by ghettoization of the disadvantaged and the rise of racism.

Nowhere is this more evident than in today's global cities: New York, Los Angeles, Toronto, Paris, London, Tokyo, Istanbul, Johannesburg, Bangkok and Sydney – to name just a few – are crucibles of social change, political conflict and cultural innovation. They are marked by great gulfs: between the corporate elite and the informal sector workers who service them; between the well-guarded suburbs of the rich and the decaying inner cities or peripheral slum areas of the poor; between citizens of democratic states and 'illegal' non-citizens; between dominant cultures and minority cultures. The gulf may be summed up as that between inclusion and exclusion. The included are those who fit into the self-image of a prosperous, technologically innovative and democratic society. The excluded are the shadow side: those who are needed to do the menial jobs in industry and the services, but who do not fit into the ideology of the model.

Both groups include nationals and immigrants, though the immigrants are more likely to belong to the excluded and to be made into scapegoats. But the groups are more closely bound together than they might like to think: the corporate elite need the irregular immigrants, the prosperous suburbanites need the slum-dwellers they find so threatening. It is out of this contradictory and multilayered character of the global city that its enormous energy, its cultural dynamism and its innovative capability emerge. But these coexist with potential for social breakdown, conflict, repression and violence (as shown by the 2005 and 2007 riots in France or the 2011 riots in the UK).

The new ethnic diversity affects societies in many ways. Amongst the most important are issues of political participation, cultural pluralism and national identity. Immigration and formation of ethnic groups have already had major effects on politics in most developed countries. The importance of minority voting in the US Presidential Elections of 2012 (see Chapters 1 and 13) has been widely discussed. The effects of growing immigrant populations and increased ethnic diversity are potentially destabilizing, if long-term residents find themselves excluded from politics. The only resolution appears to lie in broadening political participation to embrace immigrant groups, which in turn may mean rethinking the form and content of citizenship, and decoupling it from ideas of ethnic homogeneity or cultural assimilation.

This leads on to the issue of cultural pluralism. Processes of marginalization and isolation of ethnic groups have gone so far in many countries that culture has become a marker for exclusion on the part of some sections of the majority population, and a mechanism of resistance by the minorities. Even if serious attempts were made to end all forms of discrimination and racism, cultural and linguistic difference would persist for generations, especially if migration continues, as seems probable. That means that majority populations will have to learn to live with cultural pluralism, even if it means modifying their own expectations of acceptable standards of behaviour and social conformity. Majorities as well as minorities need to be incorporated in diverse societies.

If ideas of belonging to a nation have been based on myths of ethnic purity or of cultural superiority, then they are threatened by the growth of ethnic diversity. Whether the community of the nation has been based on belonging to an ethnic group (as in Germany or Japan) or on a unitary culture (as in France), ethnic diversity inevitably requires major political and psychological adjustments. The shift is smaller for countries that have seen themselves as nations of immigrants, for their political structures and models of citizenship are geared to incorporating newcomers. However, these countries too have historical traditions of racial exclusion and cultural homogenization which still need to be worked through.

Citizens of immigration countries may have to re-examine their understanding of what it means to belong to their societies. Monocultural and assimilationist models of national identity are no longer adequate for the new situation. Immigrants may be able to make a special contribution to the development of new forms of identity. It has always been part of the migrant condition to develop multiple identities, which are linked to the cultures both of the country of origin and of the destination. Such personal identities possess complex new transcultural elements, manifest in growing transnationalism and expanding diasporic populations around the world. The strength of transnational social, economic and cultural ties also reinforces the potential of migrants to contribute to development processes in origin countries through sending money, investing, cultural exchange and political participation.

Immigrants are not unique in this; multiple identities are becoming a widespread characteristic of contemporary societies. But it is above all migrants who are compelled by their situation to have multilayered socio-cultural identities, which are constantly in a state of transition and renegotiation. Moreover, migrants frequently develop a consciousness of their transcultural position, which is reflected not only in their artistic and cultural work, but also in social and political action. Despite current conflicts about the effects of ethnic diversity on national cultures and identity, immigration does offer perspectives for change. New principles of identity may emerge, which may be neither exclusionary nor discriminatory, and may provide the basis for better intergroup cooperation.

Inevitably transcultural and transnational identities will affect fundamental political structures. The democratic nation-state is a fairly young political form, which came into being with the American and French revolutions and achieved global dominance in the nineteenth century. It is characterized by principles defining the relationship between people and government which are mediated through the institution of citizenship. The nation-state was an innovative and progressive force at its birth, because it was inclusive and defined the citizens as free political subjects, linked together through democratic structures. But the nationalism of the nineteenth and twentieth centuries turned citizenship on its head by equating it with membership of a dominant ethnic group, defined on biological, religious or cultural lines. In many cases the nation-state became an instrument of exclusion and repression.

National states, for better or worse, are likely to endure. But global economic and cultural integration and the establishment of regional agreements on economic and political cooperation are undermining the exclusiveness of national loyalties. The age of migration could be marked by the erosion or at least the challenging of nationalism and the weakening of divisions between peoples. Admittedly there are countervailing tendencies, such as racism, the rise of extreme-right organizations and the resurgence of nationalism in many countries. Coming transformations are likely to be uneven, and setbacks are possible, especially in the event of economic or political crises. But the inescapable central trends are the increasing ethnic and cultural diversity of most countries, the emergence of transnational networks which link emigration and immigration societies, and the growth of cultural interchange. The age of migration may yet be a period of greater unity in tackling the pressing problems that beset our small planet.

Bibliography

Abadan-Unat, N. (1988) 'The socio-economic aspects of return migration to Turkey', *Revue Européenne des Migrations Internationales*, 3, 29–59.

Abella, M.I. and Ducanes, G. (2009) *Technical Note: The Effect of the Global Economic Crisis on Asian Migrant Workers and Governments' Responses* (Bangkok: ILO Regional Office for Asia and the the Pacific). www.age-of-migration.com/uk/financialcrisis/updates/1d.pdf.

Abella, M.I. (1995) 'Asian Migrant and Contract Workers in the Middle East' in Cohen, R. (ed.) *The Cambridge Survey of World Migration* (Cambridge: Cambridge University Press) 418–23.

Abella, M.I. (2002) 'Complexity and Diversity of Asian Migration' (Geneva: unpublished manuscript) 1–19.

ABS (2012) *Population Clock* (Canberra: Australian Bureau of Statistics). www.abs.gov.au/ausstats/abs%40.nsf/94713ad445ff1425ca25682000192af2/164750 9ef7e25faaca2568a900154b63?OpenDocument, accessed 31 October 2012.

Adams, R.H. (1991) 'The Economic uses and Impact of International Remittances in Rural Egypt', *Economic Development and Cultural Change*, 39, 695–722.

Adams, R. H. (2003) *International Migration, Remittances, and the Brain Drain: A Study of 24 Labor-Exporting Countries* (Washington, DC: World Bank).

Adams, R.H. (2011) 'Evaluating the Economic Impact of International Remittances On Developing Countries Using Household Surveys: A Literature Review', *Journal of Development Studies*, 47:6, 809–28.

Adamson, F.B. (2006) 'Crossing borders: International Migration and National Security' *International Security*, 31:1, 165–99.

Adamson, F.B. and Demetriou, M. (2007) 'Remapping the boundaries of "state" and "national identity": incorporating diasporas into IR theorizing', *European Journal of International Relations*, 13:4, 489–526.

Adepoju, A. (2001) 'Regional integration, continuity and changing patterns of intra-regional migration in Sub-Saharan Africa' in Siddique, M.A.B. (ed.) *International Migration into the 21st Century* (Cheltenham/Northampton, MA: Edward Elgar).

Adepoju, A. (2006) 'Leading issues in international migration in sub-Saharan Africa' in Cross, C., Gelderblom, D., Roux, N. and Mafukidze, J. (eds) *Views on Migration in Sub-Saharan Africa* (Cape Town: HSRC Press) 25–47.

Adler, S. (1981) *A Turkish Conundrum: Emigration, Politics and Development, 1961–1980.* (Geneva: ILO).

Aggoun, L. and Rivoire, J.B. (2004) *Francalgerie, Crimes et Mensonges d'Etats* (Paris: La Découverte).

Aghazarm, C., Quesada, P. and Tishler, S. (2012) *Migrants caught in crisis: The IOM experience in Libya* (Geneva: International Organization for Migration).

Agunias, D.R. (2006) *Remittances and Development: Trends, Impacts, and Policy Options* (Washington, DC : Migration Policy Institute).

Agunias, D.R. (2010) *The Future of Diaspora Policy.* Background Paper for the World Migration Report (Geneva: International Organization for Migration).

Aït Hamza, M. (1988) 'L'émigration, Facteur d'Intégration ou de Désintégration des Régions d'Origine' *Le Maroc et La Hollande. Actes de la Première Rencontre Universitaire* (Rabat: Université Mohammed V) 161–75.

Akokpari, J.K. (2000) 'Globalisation and migration in Africa', *African Sociological Review,* 4:2, 72–92.

Alba, F. (2010) 'Mexico: a crucial crossroads' (Washington, DC: Migration Information Source) www.migrationinformation.org/Profiles/display.cfm?ID=772, accessed 01 June 2011.

Alba, R. and Nee, V. (1997) 'Rethinking assimilation theory for a new era of immigration', *International Migration Review,* 31:4, 826–74.

Aleinikoff, T.A. and Klusmeyer, D. (eds) (2000) *From Migrant to Citizens: Membership in a Changing World* (Washington, DC: Carnegie Endowment for International Peace).

Aleinikoff, T.A. and Klusmeyer, D. (eds) (2001) *Citizenship Today: Global Perspectives and Practices* (Washington, DC: Carnegie Endowment for International Peace).

Altamirano Rúa, T. (2010) *Migration, Remittances and Development in Times of Crisis* (Lima: Pontificia Universidad Católica del Perú).

Álvarez de Flores, R. (2006–7) 'Evolución Histórica de las Migraciones en Venezuela: Breve Recuento', *Aldea Mundo,* 11:22, 89–93.

Amaral, E. and Fusco, W. (2005) *Shaping Brazil: the Role of International Migration.* www.migrationinformation.org/Profiles/display.cfm?ID=311, accessed 19 September 2011.

Amin, S. (1974) *Accumulation on a World Scale* (New York: Monthly Review Press).

Amnesty International (2011) *Amnesty International Annual Report 2011: The State of the World's Human Rights.* www.amnesty.org/en/annual-report/2011, accessed 24 January 2012.

Andall, J. (2003) *Gender and Ethnicity in Contemporary Europe* (Oxford: Berg).

Anderson, B. (1983) *Imagined Communities* (London: Verso).

Anderson, B. (2000) *Doing the Dirty Work: The Global Politics of Domestic Labour* (London: Zed Books).

Anderson, B. (2007) 'A Very Private Business: Exploring the Demand for Migrant Domestic Workers', *European Journal of Women's Studies,* 14:3, 247–64.

Andersson, R. (2007) 'Ethnic residential segregation and integration processes in Sweden' in Schönwälder, K. (ed.) *Residential Segregation and the Integration of Immigrants: Britain, the Netherlands and Sweden* (Berlin: Wissenschaft-szentrum) www.wzb.eu, 61–91.

Andrès, H. (2007) 'Le droit de vote des étrangers : une utopie déjà réalisée sur les cinq continents', *Migrations sociétés,* 19:114, 65–81.

Andrès Henao, L. (2009) 'African immigrants drift toward Latin America' *Reuters.* www.reuters.com/article/2009/11/16/us-latinamerica-africans-idUSTRE5AF0AG20091116, 15 November, accessed 24 July 2012.

Ángel Castillo, M. (2006) *Mexico: Caught Between the United States and Central America* www.migrationinformation.org/Feature/display.cfm?ID=389, accessed 11 November 2011.

Anthias, F. and Yuval-Davis, N. (1989) 'Introduction' in Anthias, F. and Yuval-Davis, N. (eds) *Woman-Nation-State* (Basingstoke and London: Macmillan) pp. 1–15.

Appleyard, R. (1989) 'Migration and Development: Myths and Reality', *International Migration Review,* 23:3, 486–99.

Archdeacon, T. (1983) *Becoming American: An Ethnic History* (New York: The Free Press).

Aronson, G. (1990) *Israel, Palestinians and the Intifada: creating facts on the West Bank* (London: Kegan Paul International).

Arthur, J.A. (1991) 'International Labor Migration Patterns in West Africa', *African Studies Review,* 34:3, 65–87.

Asis, M.M.B. (2005) 'Recent Trends in International Migration in Asia and the Pacific', *Asia-Pacific Population Journal,* 20:3, 15–38.

Asis, M.M.B. (2008) 'How international migration can support development: a challenge for the Philippines' in Castles, S. and Delgado Wise, R. (eds) *Migration and Development: Perspectives from the South* (Geneva: International Organization for Migration). www.imi.ox.ac.uk/pdfs/migration-and-development-perspectives-from-the-south.

Athwal, H., Bourne, J. and Wood, R. (2010) *Racial Violence: the Buried Issue* (London: Institute of Race Relations) www.irr.org.uk/pdf2/IRR_Briefing_No.6.pdf, accessed 28 February 2012.

Ayres, R. and Barber, T. (2006) *Statistical Analysis of Female Migration and Labour Market Integration in the EU.* Integration of Female Immigrants in Labour Market and Society Working Paper 3. (Oxford: Oxford Brookes University).

Bade, K. (2003) *Migration in European History* (Oxford: Blackwells).

Baeck, L. (1993) *Post-War Development Theories and Practice* (Paris: UNESCO and The International Social Science Council).

Baganha, M.I.B. and Fonseca, M.L. (2004) *New Waves: Migration from Eastern to Southern Europe* (Lisbon: Luso-American Foundation).

Bakewell, O. (2000) 'Repatriation and Self-Settled Refugees in Zambia: Bringing Solutions to the Wrong Problems', *Journal of Refugee Studies,* 13:4, 356–73.

Bakewell, O. (2008) ' "Keeping Them in Their Place": the ambivalent relationship between development and migration in Africa', *Third World Quarterly,* 29:7, 1341–58.

Bakewell, O. and de Haas, H. (2007) 'African Migrations: continuities, discontinuities and recent transformations' in de Haan, L., Engel, U. and Chabal, P. (eds) *African Alternatives* (Leiden: Brill) 95–118.

Bakewell, O. and Jónsson, G. (2011) 'Migration, mobility and the African city' (Oxford: International Migration Institute (IMI), University of Oxford) www.imi.ox.ac.uk/pdfs/imi-working-papers/wp-11-50-migration-mobility-and-the-african-city, accessed 22 July 2013.

Baldwin-Edwards, M. (2005) *Migration in the Middle East and the Mediterranean* (Switzerland: Global Commission on International Migration Geneva).

Baldwin-Edwards, M. and Schain, M.A. (eds) (1994) *The Politics of Immigration in Western Europe* (Ilford: Frank Cass).

Balibar, E. (1991) 'Racism and Nationalism' in Balibar, E. and Wallerstein, I. (eds) *Race, Nation, Class: Ambiguous Identities* (London: Verso) 37–67.

Banting, K.G. and Kymlicka, W. (eds) (2006) *Multiculturalism and the Welfare State: Recognition and Redistribution in Contemporary Democracies* (New York and Oxford: Oxford University Press).

Banting, K.G. and Kymlicka, W. (2012) *Is There Really a Backlash Against Multiculturalism Policies? New Evidence from the Multiculturalism Policy Index.* GRITIM working paper series No. 14. (Barcelona: Universitat Pompeu Fabra).

Barlán, J. (1988) 'A System Approach for Understanding International Population Movement: The Role of Policies and Migrant Community in the Southern Cone'. IUSSP Seminar. (Genting Highlands, Malaysia).

Bartram, D. (1999) *Foreign Labor and Political Economy in Israel and Japan* (Madison: University of Wisconsin).

Bartram, D. (2005) *International Labor Migration: Foreign Workers and Public Policy* (New York: Palgrave Macmillan).

Bartram, D. (2008) 'Immigrants and natives in Tel Aviv: What's the difference?' in Price, M. and Benton-Short, L. (eds) *Migrants to the Metropolis* (Syracuse: Syracuse University Press).

Basch, L., Glick-Schiller, N. and Blanc, C.S. (1994) *Nations Unbound: Transnational Projects, Post-Colonial Predicaments and Deterritorialized Nation-States* (New York: Gordon and Breach).

Basok, T. (2007) *Canada's Temporary Migration Program: A Model Despite Flaws.* www.migrationinformation.org/Feature/display.cfm?ID=650, accessed 30 September 2011.

Batalova, J. (2005) *College-Educated Foreign Born in the US Labor Force.* (Washington DC: Migration Information Source) www.migrationinformation. org/USfocus/print.cfm?ID=285, accessed 23 July 2007.

Bauböck, R. (1991) 'Migration and Citizenship' *New Community,* 18:1.

Bauböck, R. (ed.) (1994a) *From Aliens to Citizens: Redefining the Status of Immigrants in Europe* (Aldershot: Avebury).

Bauböck, R. (1994b) *Transnational Citizenship: Membership and Rights in International Migration* (Aldershot: Edward Elgar).

Bauböck, R. (1996) 'Social and cultural integration in a civil society' in Bauböck, R., Heller, A. and Zolberg, A.R. (eds) *The Challenge of Diversity: Integration and Pluralism in Societies of Immigration* (Aldershot: Avebury) pp. 67–131.

Bauböck, R. and Rundell, J. (eds) (1998) *Blurred Boundaries: Migration, Ethnicity, Citizenship* (Aldershot: Ashgate).

Bauböck, R., Ershøll, E., Groenendijk, K. and Waldrauch, H. (eds) (2006a) *Acquisition and Loss of Nationality: Policies and Trends in 15 European States, Volume I: Comparative Analyses*, IMISCOE Research (Amsterdam: Amsterdam University Press).

Bauböck, R., Ershøll, E., Groenendijk, K. and Waldrauch, H. (eds) (2006b) *Acquisition and Loss of Nationality: Policies and Trends in 15 European States, Volume II: Country Analyses*, IMISCOE Research (Amsterdam: Amsterdam University Press).

Bauder, H. (2006) *Labor Movement: How Migration Regulates Labor* (Oxford: Oxford University Press).

Bauer, T. and Zimmermann, K. (1998) 'Causes of International Migration: A Survey' in Gorter, P., Nijkamp, P. and Poot, J. (eds) *Crossing Borders: Regional and Urban Perspectives on International Migration* (Aldershot: Ashgate) pp. 95–127.

Bauman, Z. (1998) *Globalization: the Human Consequences* (Cambridge: Polity).

BBC News (26 November 2007) *China in Africa: Developing ties.* http://news. bbc.co.uk/1/hi/world/africa/7086777.stm, accessed 26 November 2007.

BBC News (September 2011) 'Portugal's jobless graduates flee to Africa and Brazil' by Lucy Ash, BBC News, Lisbon, see http://www.bbc.co.uk/news/ world-14716410, accessed 23 July 2013.

BBC News (22 March 2012) *Obituary: Toulouse gunman Mohamed Merah.* www. bbc.co.uk/news/world-europe-17456541, accessed 22 March 2012.

BBVA (2012) *Hispanic jobs in the U.S. increase, as do remittances to Mexico, Mexico Migration Flash* (Mexico City: Bancomer Foundation). www.bbvaresearch.com/ KETD/ketd/esp/index.jsp, accessed 3 August 2012.

BBVA (2013) *Mexico Migration Flash* (Mexico City: Fundación BBVA Bancomer) www.bbvaresearch.com/KETD/fbin/mult/130201_FlashMigracionMexico_26_ eng_tcm348-372244.pdf, accessed 15 February 2013.

Bélanger, D., Lee, H.-K. and Wang, H.-Z. (2010) 'Ethnic diversity and statistics in East Asia: "foreign brides" surveys in Taiwan and South Korea' *Ethnic and Racial Studies,* 33:6, 1108–30.

Bell, D. (1975) 'Ethnicity and Social Change' in Glazer, N. and Moynihan, D.P. (eds) *Ethnicity – Theory and Experience* (Cambridge, MA: Harvard University Press).

Ben Ali, D. (1996) 'L'Impact de Transferts des Résidents Marocains à l'Etranger (RME) sur l'Investissement Productif', *Séminaire sur 'La Migration Internationale', 6-7 juin 1996.* (Rabat: Centre d'Etudes et de Recherches Démographiques (CERED)).

Benjamin, D. and Simon, S. (2005) *The Next Attack* (New York: Times Book/H. Holt).

Bensaad, A. (2003) 'Agadez, carrefour migratoire sahélo-maghrébin'. *Revue Européenne des Migrations Internationales,* 19:1.

Berriane, J. (2012) 'Ahmad al-Tijani and his Neighbors. The Inhabitants of Fez and their Perceptions of the Zawiya ' in Desplat, P. and Schulz, D. (eds) *Prayer in the City. The Making of Sacred Place and Urban Life* (Bielefeld: Transcript Verlag) 57–75.

Berriane, M. and de Haas, H. (2012) *African Migrations Research: Innovative Methods and Methodologies* (Trenton, NJ: Africa World Press) www.imi.ox.ac. uk/pdfs/research-projects-pdfs/african-migrations-workshops-pdfs/rabat-workshop-2008/african-migrations-innovative-methods-and-methodologies.

Berriane, M., Aderghal, M., Janati, M.I. and Berriane, J. (2010) *New mobilities around Morocco: A case study of the city of Fes.* Final Report for the MacArthur-Funded Project on 'African Perspectives on Human Mobility' (Oxford/Rabat: International Migration Institute (IMI)/Université Mohammed V Agdal Rabat). www.imi.ox.ac.uk/pdfs/research-projects-pdfs/aphm-pdfs/ morocco-english-2011-report.

Bertossi, C. (2007) *French and British models of integration: public philosophies, policies and state institutions.* Working Paper 46. (Oxford: Centre on Migration, Policy and Society). http://compas.ox.ac.uk/, accessed 15 April 2007.

Bérubé, M. (2005) *Colombia: in the Crossfire.* www.migrationinformation.org/ Profiles/display.cfm?ID=344, accessed 01 November, 2011.

Bhagwati, J. (2003) 'Borders Beyond Control', *Foreign Affairs,* 82:1, 98–104.

Björgo, T. and Witte, R. (eds) (1993) *Racist Violence in Europe* (London: Macmillan).

Black, R. (2001) 'Environmental refugees: myth or reality?', *UNHCR Working Papers*: 34, 1–19.

Blackburn, R. (1988) *The Overthrow of Colonial Slavery 1776–1848* (London and New York: Verso).

Bloemraad, I. (2006) *Becoming a Citizen: Incorporating Immigrants and Refugees in the United States and Canada* (Berkeley: University of California Press).

Böcker, A. (1994) 'Chain Migration over Legally Closed Borders: Settled Migrants as Bridgeheads and Gatekeepers', *Netherlands' Journal of Social Sciences,* 30:2, 87–106.

Body-Gendrot, S. and Wihtol de Wenden, C. (2007) *Sortir des banlieues. Pour en finir avec la tyrannie des territoires* (Paris: Autrement).

Böhning, W.R. (1984) *Studies in International Labour Migration* (London and New York: Macmillan and St. Martin's).

Bonjour, S. (2008) 'Ambtelijke onmin rond gezinnen van gastarbeiders: Beleids-vorming inzake gezinsmigratie in Nederland, 1955–1970', *Tijdschrift voor Sociale en Economische Geschiedenis,* 5:1, 101–27.

Borjas, G.J. (1989) 'Economic Theory and International Migration', *International Migration Review,* 23:3, 457–85.

Borjas, G.J. (1990) *Friends or Strangers: The Impact of Immigration on the US Economy* (New York: Basic Books).

Borjas, G.J. (2000) *Issues in the Economics of Immigration* (Chicago and London: University of Chicago Press).

Borjas, G.J. (2001) *Heaven's Door: Immigration Policy and the American Economy* (Princeton, NJ and Oxford: Princeton University Press).

Boserup, E. (1965) *The Conditions of Agricultural Growth: The Economics of Agrarian Change under Population Pressure* (Chicago: Aldine).

Boswell, C. (2009) *The Political Uses of Expert Knowledge: Immigration Policy and Social Research* (Cambridge and New York: Cambridge University Press).

Boswell, C. and Geddes, A. (2011) *Migration and Mobility in the European Union* (Basingstoke: Palgrave Macmillan).

Bouamama, S. (1994) *Dix ans de marche des Beurs* (Paris: Desclée de Brouwer).

Boubakri, H. (2004) 'Transit migration between Tunisia, Libya and Sub-Saharan Africa: study based on Greater Tunis'. Paper presented at the Regional Conference on 'Migrants in transit countries: sharing responsibility for management and protection. (Istanbul, 30 September – 1 October 2004, Strasbourg: Council of Europe)

Bourbeau, P. (2011) *The Securitization of Migration* (New York: Routledge).

Bourdieu, P. (1979) 'Le Capital Social: Notes Provisoires' *Actes De La Recherche En Sciences Sociales,* 31:1, 2–3.

Bourdieu, P. (1985) 'The forms of capital' in Richardson, J.G. (ed.) *Handbook of Theory and Research for the Sociology of Education* (New York: Greenwood) 241–58.

Brachet, J. (2012) 'From one Stage to the Next: Transit and Transport in (Trans) Saharan Migrations' in Berriane, M. and de Haas, H. (eds) *African Migrations Research: Innovative Methods and Methodologies* (Trenton, NJ: Africa World Press) pp. 109–32. www.imi.ox.ac.uk/pdfs/research-projects-pdfs/african-migrations-workshops-pdfs/rabat-workshop-2008/african-migrations-innovative-methods-and-methodologies.

Brand, C. (2007) *EU agrees on weakened anti-racism rules* (New York: ABC News) http://abcnews.go.com/International/wireStory?id=3056841, accessed 14 August 2007.

Branigan, T. (2007) 'Crackdown pledged on sex with trafficked women', *The Guardian,* 18 July (London).

Bredeloup, S. and Pliez, O. (2005) 'Editorial: Migrations entre les deux rives du Sahara', *Autrepart,* 4:36, 3–20.

Breton, R., Isajiw, W.W., Kalbach, W.E. and Reitz, J.G. (1990) *Ethnic Identity and Equality* (Toronto: University of Toronto Press).

Brettell, C.B. and Hollifield, J.F. (eds) (2007) *Migration Theory: Talking Across Disciplines*, 2nd edn (New York and London: Routledge).

Briggs, V.M. (1984) *Immigration Policy and the American Labor Force* (Baltimore and London: Johns Hopkins University Press).

Browne, I. and Misra, J. (2003) 'The intersection of gender and race in the labor market' *Annual Review of Sociology*, 29:487–513.

Brownell, P. (2005) 'The declining enforcement of employer sanctions' *Migration Information Source* (Washington, DC: Migration Policy Institute).

Brubaker, R. (1992) *Citizenship and Nationhood in France and Germany* (Cambridge, MA: Harvard University Press).

Brubaker, R. (2003) 'The return of assimilation? changing perspectives on immigration and its sequels in France, Germany and the United States' in Joppke, C. and Morawaska, E. (eds) *Towards Assimilation and Citizenship: Immigration in Liberal Nation-States* (Basingstoke: Palgrave Macmillan)

Cahill, D. (1990) *Intermarriages in International Contexts* (Quezon City: Scalabrini Migration Center).

Calavita, K. (2004) 'Italy: immigration, economic flexibility, and policy responses' in Cornelius, W., Hollifield, J.F. and Martin, P.L. (eds) *Controlling Immigration: A Global Perspective* (Stanford, CA: Stanford University Press).

Calmes, J. and Thee-Brenan, M. (2012) 'Electorate Routes to a Familiar Partisan Divide?' *New York Times*, 7 September.

Canagarajah, S. and Kholmatov, M. (2010) *Migration and remittances in CIS countries during the Global Economic Crisis* (Washington, DC: World Bank). www.worldbank.org/eca.

Cantle, T. (2001) *Community Cohesion: A Report of the Independent Review Team* (London: Home Office).

Carling, J. (2002) 'Migration in the age of involuntary immobility: theoretical reflections and Cape Verdean experiences', *Journal of Ethnic and Migration Studies*, 28:1, 5–42.

Carling, J. (2007) 'Migration control and migrant fatalities at the Spanish-African borders'. *International Migration Review*, 41, 316–43.

Castells, M. (1996) *The Rise of the Network Society* (Oxford: Blackwell).

Castells, M. (1997) *The Power of Identity* (Oxford: Blackwell).

Castells, M. (1998) *End of Millennium* (Oxford: Blackwell).

Castillo, M.Á. (2006) *Mexico: Caught Between the United States and Central America,* www.migrationinformation.org/Feature/display.cfm?id=389, accessed 30 September 2011.

Castles, S. (1995) 'How nation-states respond to immigration and ethnic diversity'. *New Community,* 21:3, 293–308.

Castles, S. (2002) *Environmental Change and Forced Migration: Making Sense of the Debate.*New Issues in Refugee Research, Working Paper No. 70 (Geneva: UNHCR).

Castles, S. (2004a) 'The factors that make and unmake migration policy', *International Migration Review,* 38:3, 852–84.

Castles, S. (2004b) 'Why migration policies fail', *Ethnic and Racial Studies,* 27:2, 205–27.

Castles, S. (2004c) 'The myth of the controllability of difference: labour migration, transnational communities and state strategies in the Asia-Pacific region' in Yeoh, B.S.A. and Willis, K. (eds) *State/Nation/Transnation: Perspectives on Transnationalism in the Asia-Pacific* (London and New York: Routledge) pp. 3–26.

Castles, S. (2005) 'Nation and empire: hierarchies of citizenship in the new global order', *International Politics*, 42:2, 203–24.

Castles, S. (2006) 'Guestworkers in Europe: A Resurrection?', *International Migration Review*, 40:4, 741–66.

Castles, S. (2011) 'Bringing human rights into the migration and development debate', *Global Policy*, 2:3, 248–58.

Castles, S. and Davidson, A. (2000) *Citizenship and Migration: Globalisation and the Politics of Belonging* (Basingstoke: Macmillan).

Castles, S. and Delgado Wise, R. (eds) (2008) *Migration and Development: Perspectives from the South* (Geneva: International Organization for Migration) www.imi.ox.ac.uk/pdfs/migration-and-development-perspectives-from-the-south.

Castles, S. and Kosack, G. (1973) *Immigrant Workers and Class Structure in Western Europe* (London: Oxford University Press).

Castles, S. and Van Hear, N. (2005) *Developing DFID's Policy Approach to Refugees and Internally Displaced Persons.* Report to the Conflict and Humanitarian Affairs Department (Oxford: Refuge Studies Centre).

Castles, S. and Van Hear, N. (2012) 'Root causes' in Betts, A. (ed.) *Global Migration Governance* (Oxford: Oxford University Press) pp. 287–306.

Castles, S., Arias Cubas, M., Kim, C. and Ozkul, D. (2012) 'Irregular migration: causes, patterns and strategies' in Omelaniuk, I. and National Institute for Migration Mexico (INAMI) (eds) *Reflections on Migration and Development* (Berlin and Geneva: Springer and International Organization for Migration).

Castles, S., Booth, H. and Wallace, T. (1984) *Here for Good: Western Europe's New Ethnic Minorities* (London: Pluto Press).

Castles, S., Foster, W., Iredale, R. and Withers, G. (1998) *Immigration and Australia: Myths and Realities* (Sydney: Allen & Unwin).

Castles, S., de Haas, H., Van Hear, N. and Vasta, E. (2010) 'Special issue: Theories of Migration and Social Change', *Journal of Ethnic and Migration Studies*, 36:10.

Castles, S., Crawley, H. and Loughna, S. (2003) *States of Conflict: Causes and Patterns of Forced Migration to the EU and Policy Responses* (London: Institute of Public Policy Research).

Castles, S., Ozkul, D and Vasta, E. (2013) 'Australia: a classical immigration country in transition' in Hollifield, J., Martin, P.L. and Orrenius, P. (eds) *Controlling Immigration: a Global Perspective* (Stanford, CA: Stanford University Press)

CEC (2005) *Green Paper on an EU Approach to Managing Economic Migration* COM (2004) 811 final (Brussels: Commission of the European Communities).

CEC (2007) *Proposal for a Directive of the European Parliament and of the Council Providing for Sanctions against Employers of Illegally Staying Third-country Nationals* (Brussels: Commission of the European Union).

Cernea, M.M. and McDowell, C. (eds) (2000) *Risks and Reconstruction: Experiences of Resettlers and Refugees* (Washington, DC: World Bank).

Challinor, A.E. (2011) *Canada's Immigration Policy: a Focus on Human Capital*, www.migrationinformation.org/Profiles/display.cfm?ID=853, accessed 26 September 2011.

Chami, R., Barajas, A., Cosimano, T., Fullenkamp, C., Gapen, M. and Montiel, P. (2008) *Macroeconomic Consequences of Remittances*: International Monetary Fund Occasional Paper, 259.

Chebel d'Appollonia, C. (2012) *Immigration and Insecurity in the United States and Europe* (Ithaca: Cornell University Press).

Chiffoleau, S. (2003) 'Un champ à explorer : le rôle des pèlerinages dans les mobilités nationales, régionales et internationales du Moyen-Orient', *Revue Européenne Des Migrations Internationales*, 19:3, 285–89.

Chimni, B.S. (1998) 'The geo-politics of refugee studies: a view from the South', *Journal of Refugee Studies*, 11:4, 350–74.

Chin, K.-l. (1999) *Smuggled Chinese: Clandestine Immigration to the United States* (Philadelphia: Temple University Press).

China Daily (2010) 'China's 'floating population' exceeds 210m' (Beijing, 27 June). www.chinadaily.com.cn/china/2010-06/27/content_10024861.htm.

Chishti, M. and Bergeron, C. (2011) *Supreme Court Upholds Legal Arizona Workers Act with Limited Implications for Other State Immigration Laws*: Migration Policy Institute). www.migrationinformation.org/USFocus/display.cfm?ID=843, accessed 23 February 2012.

Chiswick, B.R. (2000) 'Are immigrants favorably self-selected? An economic analysis' in Brettell, C.B. and Hollifield, J.F. (eds) *Migration Theory: Talking Across Disciplines* (New York and London: Routledge) pp. 61–76.

Christian Aid (2007) *Human Tide: The Real Migration Crisis* (London: Christian Aid). www.christianaid.org.uk/Images/human-tide.pdf.

CIC (2011) *Facts and Figures 20010 – Immigration Overview: Permanent and Temporary Residents* in Canada, C.a.I. (ed.) (Ottawa: Citizenship and Immigration Canada,) www.cic.gc.ca/english/resources/statistics/facts2010/index.asp, accessed 30 September 2011.

Cinanni, P. (1968) *Emigrazione e Imperialismo* (Rome: Riuniti).

Çinar, D. (1994) 'From aliens to citizens: a comparative analysis of the rules of transition' in Bauböck, R. (ed.) *From Aliens to Citizens* (Aldershot: Avebury) pp. 49–72.

Clandestino (2009) *Comparative Policy Brief – Size of Irregular Population* (Hamburg: Clandestino Research Project). http://clandestino.eliamep.gr.

Clarke, R.A. (2004) *Against All Enemies* (New York: Free Press).

Clemens, M.A. (2007) 'Do visas kill? Health effects of African health professional emigration' (Washington, DC: Center for Global Development).

Cohen, P. and Bains, H.S. (1988) *Multi-Racist Britain* (Basingstoke and London: Macmillan).

Cohen, R. (1987) *The New Helots: Migrants in the International Division of Labour* (Aldershot: Avebury).

Cohen, R. (1991) 'East-West and European Migration in a Global Context', *New Community*, 18:1, 9–26.

Cohen, R. (1995) 'Asian Indentured and Colonial Migration' in Cohen, R. (ed.) *The Cambridge Survey of World Migration* (Cambridge: Cambridge University Press).

Cohen, R. (1997) *Global Diasporas: An Introduction* (London: UCL Press).

Cohen, R. and Kennedy, P. (2000) *Global Sociology* (Basingstoke: Palgrave Macmillan).

Cohen, R. and Layton-Henry, Z. (1997) *The Politics of Migration* (Cheltenham: Edward Elgar).

Collins, J. (1991) *Migrant Hands in a Distant Land: Australia's Post-war Immigration,* 2nd edn (Sydney: Pluto Press).

Collins, J. (2006) 'The changing political economy of Australian immigration'. *Tijdschrift voor Economische en Sociale Geografie,* 97:1, 7–16.

Collins, J., Alcorso, C., Castles, S., Gibson, K. and Tait, D. (1995) *A Shop Full of Dreams: Ethnic Small Business in Australia* (Sydney: Pluto Press).

Collyer, M. (2005) 'When do social networks fail to explain migration? Accounting for the movement of Algerian asylum-seekers to the UK' *Journal of Ethnic and Migration Studies,* 31:4, 699–718.

Collyer, M. and de Haas, H. (2012) 'Developing dynamic categorisations of transit migration', *Population Space and Place,* 18:4, 468–81.

Collyer, M., Düvell, F. and de Haas, H. (2012) 'Critical approaches to transit migration', *Population Space and Place,* 18:4, 407–14.

Comisión Nacional de los Derechos Humanos (2011) *Informe Especial Sobre Secuestro de Migrantes en México,* www.cndh.org.mx/#, accessed 6 July, 2011.

Commission on Filipino Overseas (2013) *Stock Estimates of Filipinos Overseas* (Manila: Department of Foreign Affairs Philippine Overseas Employment Administration) http://www.cfo.gov.ph/index.php?option=com_content&view=article&id=1340:stock-estimate-of-overseas-filipinos&catid=134, accessed 29 May 2013.

Connor, P. and Massey, D. (2010) 'Economic Outcomes among Latino Migrants to Spain and the United States: Differences by Source Region and Legal Status', *International Migration Review,* 44:4, 802–29.

Cordeiro, A. (2006) 'Portugal and the immigration challenge' in Majtczak, O. (ed.) *The Fifth International Migration Conference* (Warsaw: Independent University of Business and Government).

Cornelius, W. (2001) 'Death at the Border: Efficacy and Unintended Consequences of US Immigration Control Policy', *Population and Development Review,* 27:4, 661–85.

Council of Labor Affairs Taiwan (2012) *Foreign Labor (in Chinese),* www.cla.gov.tw/cgi-bin/siteMaker/SM_theme?page=4aadd21a, accessed 22 January, 2012.

Courtis, C. (2011) 'Marcos Institucionales, Normativos y de Políticas sobre Migración Internacional en Argentina, Chile y Ecuador' in Martínez Pizarro, J. (ed.) *Migración Internacional en América Latina y el Caribe - Nuevas Tendencias, Nuevos Enfoques* (Santiago de Chile: CEPAL) pp. 99–206.

Covarrubias, H.M., Tetreault, D.V., Soto Esquivel, R. and Záyago Lau, E. (2011) 'México en el desfiladero: profundización del subdesarrollo bajo el modelo neoliberal' in Covarrubias, H.M., Soto Esquivel, R. and Záyago Lau, E. (eds) *El Desarrollo Perdido: Avatares del Capitalismo Neoliberal in Tiempos de Crisis* (Mexico City: Miguel Angel Porrua) pp. 247–80.

Cox, R. (2006) *The Servant Problem: Domestic Employment in a Global Economy* (London and New York: I.B. Tauris).

Crisp, J. (2008) *Beyond the nexus: UNHCR's evolving perspective on refugee protection and international migration,* New Issues in Refugee Research 155. (Geneva) www.unhcr.org/research/RESEARCH/4818749a2.pdf, accessed 5 February 2009.

Crock, M. and Saul, B. (2002) *Future Seekers: Refugees and the Law in Australia* (Sydney: Federation Press).

Cross, C., Gelderblom, D., Roux, N. and Mafukidze, J. (eds) (2006) *Views on Migration in Sub-Saharan Africa* (Cape Town: HSRC Press).

Cross, G.S. (1983) *Immigrant Workers in Industrial France: The Making of a New Laboring Class* (Philadelphia: Temple University Press).

Crush, J. (2008) *South Africa: Policy in the Face of Xenophobia.* (Washington, DC: Migration Information Source), www.migrationinformation.org/Profiles/display.cfm?ID=689, accessed 24 July 2012.

CSIS (2006) *Currents and Crosscurrents of Radical Islam* (Washington, DC: CSIS)

Curtin, P.D. (1997) 'Africa and Global Patterns of Migration' in Wang, G. (ed.) *Global History and Migrations* (Boulder, CO: Westview) pp. 63–94.

Cypher, J. M. and Delgado Wise, R. (2011) *Mexico's Economic Dilemma* (Lanham MD: Rowan & Littlefield).

Czaika, M. and de Haas, H. (2011) *The Effectiveness of Immigration Policies: a Conceptual Review of Empirical Evidence,* IMI/DEMIG Working Paper No 33. (Oxford: International Migration Institute (IMI), University of Oxford). www.imi.ox.ac.uk/publications/working_papers.

Dancygier, R.M. (2010) *Immigration and conflict in Europe* (New York and Cambridge: Cambridge University Press).

Daniels, R. (2004) *Guarding the Golden Door* (New York: Hill and Wang).

Danış, D. and Perouse, J. (2005) 'La Politique Migratoire Turque: vers une Normalisation?', *Migrations et Société,* 19:98, 93–106.

Davis, A. (2012) *The Impact of Anti-Immigration Parties on Mainstream Parties' Immigration Positions in the Netherlands, Flanders and the UK 1987–2010: Divided electorates, left-right politics and the pull towards restrictionism* (Florence: PhD thesis, EUI, Department of Political and Social Sciences). http://hdl.handle.net/1814/21719.

Davis, M. (1990) *City of Quartz: Excavating the Future in Los Angeles* (London: Verso).

Davis, M. (2006) *Planet of Slums* (London and New York: Verso).

de Bruijn, M., Brinkman, I. and Nyamnjoh, F. (eds) (2009) *Mobile Phones: the New Talking Drums of Everyday Africa* (Leiden/Bamenda: African Studies Centre/Langaa).

de Bruijn, M., van Dijk, R. and Foeken, D. (2001) *Mobile Africa: changing patterns of movement in Africa and beyond* (Leiden and Boston: Brill).

De Bruycker, P. (ed.) (2000) *Regularisations of Illegal Immigrants in the European Union* (Belgium: Bruylant).

de Haan, A. (1999) 'Livelihoods and Poverty: The Role of Migration', *Journal of Development Studies,* 36:2, 1–47.

de Haan, A., Brock, K., Carswell, G., Coulibaly, N., Seba, H. and Toufique, K.A. (2000) *Migration and Livelihoods: Case Studies in Bangladesh, Ethiopia and Mali,* IDS Research Report 46 (Brighton: Institute of Development Studies).

de Haas, H. (1998) 'Socio-Economic Transformations and Oasis Agriculture in Southern Morocco' in de Haan, L. and Blaikie, P. (eds) *Looking at Maps in the Dark.* (Utrecht/Amsterdam: KNAG/FRW UvA) pp. 65–78.

de Haas, H. (2003) *Migration and Development in Southern Morocco: The Disparate Socio-Economic Impacts of Out-Migration on the Todgha Oasis Valley.* (Nijmegen: PhD thesis Radboud University).

de Haas, H. (2006a) *Engaging diasporas: How governments and development agencies can support diasporas' involvement in development of origin countries* (A study for Oxfam Novib; Oxford: International Migration Institute (IMI), University of Oxford). www.imi.ox.ac.uk/publications/reports.

de Haas, H. (2006b) *International migration and national development: Viewpoints and policy initiatives in countries of origin – The case of Nigeria* (Nijmegen and The Hague: Radboud University and DGIS, Ministry of Foreign Affairs). www.imi.ox.ac.uk/publications/reports.

de Haas, H. (2006c) 'Migration, remittances and regional development in Southern Morocco' *Geoforum,* 37:4, 565–80.

de Haas, H. (2006d) 'Trans-Saharan Migration to North Africa and the EU: Historical Roots and Current Trends' *Migration Information Source* (Washington, DC: Migration Policy Institute). www.migrationinformation.org/feature/display.cfm?id=484.

de Haas, H. (2007a) *Remittances and social development: A conceptual review of the literature* (Geneva: UNRISD).

de Haas, H. (2007b) *The Myth of Invasion: Irregular migration from West Africa to the Maghreb and the European Union* (Oxford: International Migration Institute (IMI), University of Oxford). www.imi.ox.ac.uk/publications/reports.

de Haas, H. (2007c) 'Turning the tide? Why development will not stop migration', *Development and Change* 38:5, 819–41.

de Haas, H. (2008a) 'The Myth of Invasion – The Inconvenient Realities of African Migration to Europe', *Third World Quarterly* 29(7), 1305–22.

de Haas, H. (2008b) 'North African migration systems: evolution, transformations and development linkages' in Castles, S. and Delgado Wise, R. (eds) *Migration and Development: Perspectives from the South* (Geneva: International Organization for Migration). www.imi.ox.ac.uk/pdfs/migration-and-development-perspectives-from-the-south.

de Haas, H. (2009) *Mobility and Human Development* (New York: UNDP).

de Haas, H. (2010a) 'Migration and development: a theoretical perspective', *International Migration Review,* 44:1, 227–64.

de Haas, H. (2010b) 'The internal dynamics of migration processes: A theoretical inquiry', *Journal of Ethnic and Migration Studies,* 36:10, 1587–617.

de Haas, H. (2010c) *Migration transitions: a theoretical and empirical inquiry into the developmental drivers of international migration.* IMI/DEMIG Working Paper No 24. (Oxford: International Migration Institute (IMI), University of Oxford). www.imi.ox.ac.uk/publications/working_papers.

de Haas, H. (2011) *The Determinants of International Migration,* IMI/DEMIG Working Paper No 32 (Oxford: International Migration Institute (IMI), University of Oxford). www.imi.ox.ac.uk/publications/working_papers.

de Haas, H. (2012) 'The Migration and Development Pendulum: A Critical View on Research and Policy', *International Migration,* 50:3, 8–25.

de Haas, H. and Fokkema, T. (2010) 'Intra-Household Conflicts in Migration Decisionmaking: Return and Pendulum Migration in Morocco', *Population and Development Review,* 36:3, 541–61.

de Haas, H. and Sigona, N. (2012) 'Migration and revolution', *Forced Migration Review,* June 2012:39, 4–5. www.fmreview.org/en/north-africa/dehaas-sigona.pdf.

de Haas, H. and Vezzoli, S. (2010) *Migration and development: Lessons from the Mexico–US and Morocco–EU experiences.* IMI Working Paper No 24 (Oxford: International Migration Institute (IMI), University of Oxford). www.imi.ox.ac.uk/publications/working_papers.

de Lepervanche, M. (1975) 'Australian Immigrants 1788–1940: Desired and Unwanted' in Wheelwright, E.L. and Buckley, K. (eds) *Essays in the Political Economy of Australian Capitalism, vol. 1* (Sydney: Australia and New Zealand Book Co.)

De Mas, P. (1978) *Marges marocaines: limites de la coopération au développement dans une région périphérique: Le cas du Rif* ('s-Gravenhage: NUFFIC/ IMWOO/Projet Remplod).

De Regt, M. (2010) 'Ways to Come, Ways to Leave: Gender, Mobility, and Il/ legality among Ethiopian Domestic Workers in Yemen', *Gender & Society,* 24:2, 237–60.

Decloîtres, R. (1967) *The Foreign Worker* (Paris: OECD).

Delano, A. (2011) *Mexico and Its Diaspora in the United States* (Cambridge: Cambridge University Press).

Delgado Wise, R. and Covarrubias, H.M. (2009) 'Capitalist restructuring, development and labour migration: the Mexico-US case' in Munck, R. (ed.) *Globalisation and Migration: New Issues, New Politics,* (London and New York: Routledge) pp. 130–45.

DeParle, J. (2007) 'Fearful of Restive Foreign Labor, Dubai Eyes Reforms', *New York Times*. 6 August.

Department of Statistics Malaysia (2009) *Selected Social Statistics: iii. Labour and Human Resource Statistics – Series 10* Selected Social Statistics. www. statistics.gov.my/portal/index.php?option=com_content&view=article&id=36 3&Itemid=149&lang=en#9.

Derisbourg, J.P. (2002) 'L'Amérique latine entre Etats-Unis et Union européenne', *Politique Etrangère,* 67:2.

Dervin, F. and Wiberg, M. (2007) 'Présence absente des électeurs étrangers en Finlande', *Migrations Société,* 19:114, 99–113.

DeSipio, L. (2001) 'Building America, one person at a time: Naturalization and political behavior of the naturalized in contemporary American politics' in Gerstle, G. and Mollenkopf, J. (eds) *E Pluribus Unum* (New York: Russell Sage Foundation).

DeSipio, L. (2006) 'Transnational Politics and Civic Engagement: Do Home-Country Political Ties Limit Immigrant Pursuit of U.S. Civic Engagement and Citizenship?' in Lee, T., Ramakrishnan, S.K. and Ramirez, R. (eds) *Transforming Politics, Transforming America: The Political and Civic Incorporation of Immigrants in the United States* (Charlottesville: University of Virginia Press).

DeWind, J., Kim, E.M., Skeldon, R. and Yoon, I.-J. (2012) 'Korean Development and Migration' *Journal of Ethnic and Migration Studies,* 38:3, 371–88.

DFID (2007) *Moving Out of Poverty – Making Migration Work Better for Poor People* (London: Department for International Development).

DIAC (2010a) *Fact Sheet No 2: Key Facts in Immigration* (Canberra: Department of Immigration and Citizenship). www.immi.gov.au/media/fact-sheets/02key. htm, accessed 29 May 2013.

DIAC (2010b) *Fact Sheet No 4: More than 60 Years of Post-war Migration* (Canberra: Department of Immigration and Citizenship).

DIAC (2010c) *Fact Sheet No 50: Overseas Students in Australia* (Canberra: Department of Immigration and Citizenship).

DIAC (2012a) *2010–11 Migration Program Report* (Canberra: Department of Immigration and Citizenship). www.immi.gov.au/media/statistics/pdf/report-on-migration-program-2010-11.pdf, accessed 5 July 2012.

DIAC (2012b) *Temporary Entrants and New Zealand Citizens in Australia* (Canberra: Department of Immigration and Citizenship). www.immi.gov.au/media/ statistics/pdf/temp-entrants-newzealand-mar12.pdf, accessed 5 July 2012.

Dohse, K. (1981) *Ausländische Arbeiter und bürgerlicher Staat* (Konistein/ Taunus: Hain).

Doña, C. and Levinson, A. (2004) *Chile: Moving Towards a Migration Policy.* www. migrationinformation.org/Profiles/display.cfm?ID=199, accessed 5 December 2011.

Douki, C. (2007) 'The Liberal Italian States and Mass Emigration' in Green, N. and Weil, F. (eds) *Citizenship and Those Who Leave* (Urbana: University of Illinois Press) pp. 91–113.

DRC (2006) *Skilled migration: healthcare policy options* (Brighton: Development Research Centre (DRC) on Migration, Globalisation and Poverty, University of Sussex).

Dubajic, N. (2007) 'Le vote des étrangers au Luxembourg: evolution de 1999 à 2005', *Migrations Société,* 19:114, 129–40.

Dumont, J.-C. and Lemaître, G. (2005) *Counting Immigrants and Expatriates in OECD Countries: A New Perspective.* Social, Employment and Migration Working Papers No. 25 (Paris: OECD).

Durand, J. (2004) *From Traitors to Heroes: 100 Years of Mexican Migration Policies.* (Migration Information Source) www.migrationinformation.org/feature/ display.cfm?ID=203, accessed 1 May 2011.

Dustmann, C. and Fabbri, F. (2005) 'Immigrants in the British Labour Market', *Fiscal Studies,* 26:4, 423–70.

Düvell, F. (ed.) (2006) *Illegal Immigration in Europe: Beyond Control* (Basingstoke: Palgrave Macmillan).

Düvell, F. (2012) 'Transit Migration: A Blurred and Politicised Concept', *Population, Space and Place,* 18:4, 415–27.

Earnest, D. (2008) *Old Nations, New Voters* (Albany, NY: State University of New York Press).

ECLAC (2010) *Time for Equality: Closing Gaps, Opening Trails* (Santiago: Economic Commission for Latin America and the Caribbean). www.eclac.cl/ publicaciones/xml/1/39711/100604_2010-115-SES-33-3-Time_for_equality_ doc_completo.pdf.

ECLAC (2011) *Briefing Paper.* Social Panorama of Latin America 2011 (Santiago de Chile: Economic Commission for Latin America and the Caribbean).

EFFNATIS (2001) *Effectiveness of National Integration Strategies Towards Second Generation Migrant Youth in a Comparative European Perspective, final report of the EFFNATIS project* (European Forum for Migration Studies, University of Bamberg). http://www.efms.uni-bamberg.de/pdf/finalreportk.pdf, accessed 2 April 2013.

Einaudi, L. (2007) *Le Politiche dell'Immigrazione in Italia dall'Unità a oggi* (Rome: Editori Laterza).

Engels, F. (1962) 'The Condition of the Working Class in England' in Marx, K. *Engels on Britain* (Moscow: Foreign Languages Publishing House).

Entzinger, H. (1985) 'Return Migration in Western Europe: Current policy trends and their implications, in particular for the second generation', *International Migration,* XXIII:2, 263–90.

Entzinger, H. (2003) 'The rise and fall of multiculturalism: the case of the Netherlands' in Joppke, C. and Morawaska, E. (eds) *Towards Assimilation and Citizenship: Immigration in Liberal Nation-States* (Basingstoke: Palgrave Macmillan).

Escobar Latapí, A., Pedraza, L. and Massini, M. (2010) *The Future of Migration Policies in the Americas.* Background Paper WMR 2010 (Geneva: International Organization for Migration).

Ersanilli, E. (2010) *Comparing Integration. Host culture adoption and ethnic retention among Turkish immigrants and their descendants in France, Germany and the Netherlands* (PhD thesis. Amsterdam: Vrije Universiteit) http://hdl.handle.net/1871/19217

Ersanilli, E. and Koopmans, R. (2010) 'Rewarding Integration? Citizenship Regulations and the Socio-Cultural Integration of Immigrants in the Netherlands, France and Germany', *Journal of Ethnic and Migration Studies,* 36:5, 773–91.

Ersanilli, E. and Koopmans, R. (2011) 'Do Immigrant Integration Policies Matter? A Three-Country Comparison among Turkish Immigrants', *West European Politics,* 34:2, 208–34.

Esposito, J. and Mogahed, D. (2007) *Who Speaks for Islam?What a Billion Muslims Really Think.* (New York: Gallup Press).

Essed, P. (1991) *Understanding Everyday Racism* (Newbury Park, London and New Delhi: Sage).

EUMC (2006) *The Annual Report on the Situation regarding Racism and Xenophobia in the Member States of the EU* (Vienna: European Monitoring Centre on Racism and Xenophobia). http://eumc.europa.eu/eumc/material/pub/ar06/AR06-P2-EN.pdf.

Europa (2008) *Summaries of EU legislation: employment and social policy: social and employment situation in Europe* (Brussels: Europe Direct). http://europa.eu/legislation_summaries/employment_and_social_policy/situation_in_europe/c10160_en.htm#, accessed 19 December 2011.

Faini, R. and Venturini, A. (1994) *Migration and Growth: The Experience of Southern Europe* (London: CEPR).

Faist, T. (2000) 'Transnationalization in international migration: implications for the study of citizenship and culture', *Ethnic and Racial Studies,* 23:2, 189–222.

Faist, T. (2006) 'Extension du domaine de la lutte: International Migration and Security before and after 11 September 2011' in Messina, A. and Lahav, G. (eds) *The Migration Reader* (Boulder and London: Lynne Rienner Publishers) pp. 609–15.

Faist, T. (ed.) (2007) *Dual Citizenship in Europe* (Aldershot: Ashgate).

Fargues, P. (2005) *How Many Migrants from, and to, Mediterranean Countries of the Middle East and North Africa?* (San Domenico Fiesole: European University Institute, RSCAS). www.carim.org/Publications/CARIM-AS05_16-Fargues.pdf.

Fargues, P. (2006) 'Afrique du Nord et Moyen-Orient: des migrations en quête d'une politique', *Politique Etrangère*: 4, 1017–29.

Fargues, P. (ed.) (2007) *Mediterranean Migration: 2006–2007 Report* (San Domenico Fiesole: European University Institute, RSCAS).

Fargues, P. and Fandrich, C. (2012) *Migration after the Arab Spring* (San Domenico di Fiesole: European University Institute, RSCAS).

Farrag, M. (1999) 'Emigration dynamics in Egypt' in Appleyard, R. (ed.) *Emigration dynamics in developing countries, Vol. IV: The Arab Region* (Aldershot: Ashgate).

Favell, A. (1998) *Philosophies of Integration: Immigration and the Idea of Citizenship in France and Britain* (London: Macmillan).

Fawcett, J.T. (1989) 'Networks, Linkages, and Migration Systems', *International Migration Review,* 23, 671–80.

Fawcett, J.T. and Carino, B.J. (1987) *Pacific Bridges: The New Immigration from Asia and the Pacific Islands* (New York: Center for Migration Studies).

Feagin, J.R. (1989) *Racial and Ethnic Relations* (Englewood Cliffs, NJ: Prentice-Hall).

Fernandez, B. (2010) 'Cheap and disposable? The impact of the global economic crisis on the migration of Ethiopian women domestic workers to the Gulf' *Gender & Development,* 18:2, 249–62.

Ferrer, M. (2011) 'Marcos Institucionales, Normativos y de Políticas sobre Migración Internacional: el Caso de El Salvador y una Exploración en Costa Rica y el Caribe' in Martínez Pizarro, J. (ed.) *Migración Internacional en América Latina y el Caribe – Nuevas Tendencias, Nuevos Enfoques* (Santiago de Chile: CEPAL) pp. 333–417.

Findlay, A. and Geddes, A. (2011) 'Critical views on the relationship between climate change and migration: some insights from the experience of Bangladesh' in Piguet, É., Pécoud, A. and De Guchteneire, P. (eds) *Migration and Climate Change* (Cambridge: Cambridge University Press) pp. 138–59.

Findley, S.E. (2004) 'Mali: Seeking Opportunity Abroad' *Migration Information Source* (Washington, DC: Migration Policy Institute).

Fishman, J.A. (1985) *The Rise and Fall of the Ethnic Revival: Perspectives on Language and Ethnicity* (Berlin, New York and Amsterdam: Mouton Publishers).

Fix, M. and Passel, J.S. (1994) *Immigration and Immigrants: Setting the Record Straight* (Washington, DC: The Urban Institute).

Fokkema, T. and de Haas, H. (2011) 'Pre- and Post-Migration Determinants of Socio-Cultural Integration of African Immigrants in Italy and Spain' *International Migration* (see http://onlinelibrary.wiley.com/doi/10.1111/j.1468-2435.2011.00687.x/abstract).

Foot, P. (1965) *Immigration and Race in British Politics* (Harmondsworth: Penguin).

Foresight (2011) *Migration and Global Environmental Change. Final Project Report* (London: The Government Office for Science). www.bis.gov.uk/assets/foresight/docs/migration/11-1116-migration-and-global-environmental-change.pdf, accessed 22 March 2012.

Fox-Genovese, E. and Genovese, E.D. (1983) *Fruits of merchant capital: Slavery and bourgeois property in the rise and expansion of capitalism* (New York: Oxford University Press).

France 24 (2012) *Socialist Hollande triumphs in French presidential poll.* 7 March, www.france24.com/en/20120506-socialist-hollande-triumphs-french-presidential-election.

Frank, A.G. (1966) *The Development of Underdevelopment* (New York: Monthly Review Press).

Frank, A.G. (1969) *Capitalism and Underdevelopment in Latin America* (New York: Monthly Review Press).

Franz, J.G. (1939) 'Review: Cityward Migration: Swedish Data. by Jane Moore', *Sociometry,* 2:1, 109.

Freeman, G. (1979) *Immigrant Labor and racial Conflict in Industrial Societies: the French and British Experience, 1945–1975* (Princeton: Princeton University Press).

Freeman, G.P. (1986) 'Migration and the political economy of the welfare state', *Annals AAPSS*: 485, 51–63.

Freeman, G.P. (1995) 'Modes of Immigration Politics in Liberal Democratic States', *International Migration Review,* 24:4, 881–902.

Fregosi, R. (2002) 'Au-delà de la crise financière et institutionnelle, l'Argentine en quête d'un véritable projet', *Politique Etrangère,* 67:2, 435–54.

Froebel, F., Heinrichs, J. and Kreye, O. (1980) *The New International Division of Labour* (Cambridge: Cambridge University Press).

Galeano, E.H. (1973) *Open Veins of Latin America : Five Centuries of the Pillage of a Continent* (New York: Monthly Review Press).

Gallagher, A. (2002) 'Trafficking, smuggling and human rights: tricks and treaties', *Forced Migration Review*, 12, 25–8.

Gamlen, A. (2006) *Diaspora Engagement Policies: What are they, and what kinds of states use them?* (Oxford: Centre on Migration, Policy and Society (COMPAS), University of Oxford).

Gamlen, A. (2008) 'The Emigration State and the Modern Geopolitical Imagination', *Political Geography,* 27:8, 840–56.

Gamlen, A. (2013) *Tory immigration policy is not doomed to fail - it is designed to do so.* (London: Guardian) www.guardian.co.uk/commentisfree/2013/jan/14/immigration-policy-designed-to-fail, accessed 15 February 2013.

Gammage, S. (2004) 'Exercising exit, voice and loyalty: A gender perspective on transnationalism in Haiti', *Development and Change,* 35:4, 743–71.

Gammage, S. (2006) 'Exporting people and recruiting remittances – A development strategy for El Salvador?', *Latin American Perspectives,* 33:6, 75–100.

GAO (2006) *Foreign Workers-Information on Selected Countries Experiences* (Washington, DC: US Governmental Accountability Office).

García Zamora, R. (2009) 'Migración internacional y desarrollo, Oppotunidades y desafios para Mexico' in Garcia Zamora, R. (ed.) *Desarrollo económico y migración: los desafíos de las politcas publicas en Mexico* (Mexico City: Ángel Migrante) pp. 115–49.

García Zamora, R. and Contreras Díaz, F.J. (eds) (2012) *Seminario Estatal de Universitarios: por una Nueva Estrategia de Deasrollo Integral para Zacatecas, Vol I: Economía, Demografía, Migracíon y Desarrollo* (Mexico City: Universidad Autónoma de Zacatecas, Unidad Académica de Economía, Unidad Académica de Estudios del Desarrollo).

Gargis, P. (2011) 'Alabama Gov. Signs Nation's Toughest Immigrant Law' *Reuters*, 10 June 2011. http://uk.reuters.com/article/2011/06/09/usa-immigration-alabama-idUSN0911157920110609, accessed 30 March 2013.

Garrard, J.A. (1971) *The English and Immigration: A Comparative Study of the Jewish Influx 1880–1910* (London: Oxford University Press).

GCIM (2005) *Migration in an Interconnected World: New Directions for Action: Report of the Global Commission on International Migration* (Geneva: Global Commission on International Migration).

Geddes, A. (2000) *Immigration and European Integration: Towards Fortress Europe?* (Manchester and NY: Manchester University Press).

Geddes, A. (2003) *The Politics of Migration and Immigration in Europe* (London: Sage).

Geertz, C. (1963) *Old Societies and New States - the Quest for Modernity in Asia and Africa* (Glencoe, IL: Free Press).

Gelatt, J. (2006) *Senate Debates Temporary Worker Program and Path to Legal Status for the Unauthorized.* (Washington, DC: Migration Information Source). www.migrationinformation.org/USFocus/print.cfm?ID=391, accessed 11 June 2010.

Gellner, E. (1983) *Nations and Nationalism* (Oxford: Blackwell).

Gemenne, F. (2009) 'Environmental Changes and Migration Flows: Normative Frameworks and Policy Responses' *Institut d'Etudes Politiques de Paris and Doctoral School in Social Science of the French Community of Belgium* (Paris and Liège: Sciences Po Paris and University of Liège).

Gereffi, G. (1996) 'Global commodity chains: new forms of coordination and control among nations and firms in international industries', *Competition and Change,* 1:4, 427–39.

Gerges, F.A. (2005) *The far enemy: why Jihad went global* (Cambridge and New York: Cambridge University Press).

Gerges, F.A. (2011) *The Rise and Fall of Al-Qaeda* (New York: Oxford University Press).

Ghosh, P.R. (2010) 'African immigrants gravitating to China' *International Business Times* (see http://m.ibtimes.co.uk/china-africa-immigration-43475.html).

Giannakouris, K. (2010) 'Most EU regions face older population profile in 2030', *Eurostat Statistics in Focus,* 1, 1–20.

Gibney, M.J. (2000) *Outside the Protection of the Law: The Situation of Irregular Migrants in Europe* (Oxford: Refugee Studies Centre, University of Oxford).

Gibson, C. and Lennon, E. (1999) *Historical Census Statistics on the Foreign-born Population of the United States: 1850–1990* Population Division Working Paper 29 (Washington, DC: US Census Bureau). www.census.gov/population/www/documentation/twps0029/twps0029.html.

Gibson, J. and McKenzie, D.J. (2011) 'Eight Questions about Brain Drain', *Journal of Economic Perspectives,* 25:3, 107–28.

Giddens, A. (2002) *Runaway World : How Globalisation is Reshaping our Lives,* 2nd edn (London: Profile).

Givens, T.E. and Maxwell, R. (2012) *Immigrant Politics : Race and Representation in Western Europe* (Boulder, CO: Lynne Rienner Publishers).

Glazer, N. and Moynihan, D.P. (1975) 'Introduction' in Glazer, N.A. and Moynihan, D.P. (eds) *Ethnicity: Theory and Experience* (Cambridge, MA: Harvard University Press).

Glazer, S. (2009) 'Radical Islam in Europe' in Global Issues: 2009 (ed.) (Washington, DC: CQ Press) pp. 81–113.

Glennie, A. and Chappell, L. (2010) *Jamaica: From Diverse Beginning to Diaspora in the Developed World.* www.migrationinformation.org/Profiles/display.cfm?ID=787, accessed 30 September, 2011.

Glick-Schiller, N. (1999) 'Citizens in transnational nation-states: the Asian experience' in Olds, K., Dicken, P., Kelly, P.F., Kong, L. and Yeung, H.W.-c. (eds) *Globalisation and the Asia-Pacific: Contested Territories* (London: Routledge) pp. 202–18.

GMFD (2010) *Joint Strategies to Address Irregular Migration.* Background Paper (Puerto Vallarta Mexico,: Global Forum on Migration and Development). www.gfmd.org/en/documents-library/mexico-2010.html.

Go, S.P. (2002) 'Detailed case study of Philippines' in Iredale, R., Hawksley, C. and Lyon, K. (eds) *Migration Research and Policy Landscape: Case Studies of Australia, the Philippines and Thailand* (Wollongong: Asia Pacific Migration Research Network) pp. 61–89.

Goldberg, D. (1993) *Racist Culture: Philosophy and the Politics of Meaning* (Oxford: Blackwell).

Goldberg, D.T. and Solomos, J. (eds) (2002) *A Companion to Racial and Ethnic Studies* (Malden MA and Oxford: Blackwell).

Goldin, I., Balarajan, M. and Cameron, G. (2011) *Exceptional People: How Migration Shaped Our World and Will Define Our Future* (Princeton and Oxford: Princeton University Press).

Goldring, L. and Landolt, P. (2011) 'Caught in the work-citizenship matrix: the lasting effects of precarious legal status on work for Toronto immigrants', *Globalizations,* 8:3, 325–41.

González Ferrer, A. (2012) '¿Se van los españoles? Sí. Y deberíamos preocuparnos' *El Diario,* 8 October (www.eldiario.es/piedrasdepapel/crisis-emigracion_6_55704437.html.

Gore, C. (2000) 'The rise and fall of the Washington consensus as a paradigm for developing countries', *World Development,* 28:5, 789–804.

Graham, D. and Poku, N. (eds) (2000) *Migration, Globalization and Security* (London: Routledge).

Green, D. (2012) 'Transition to the Endgame: The Challenge of U.S. Policy toward Afghanistan' in Ragee, B. and Miller, M. (eds) *National Security under the Obama Administration* (New York: Palgrave Macmillan).

Green, N. and Weil, P. (2007) *Citizenship and Those Who Leave* (Urbana: University of Illinois Press).

Green, S. (2004) *The Politics of Exclusion: Institutions and Immigration Policy in Contemporary Germany* (Manchester: Manchester University Press).

Greenhill, K.M. (2010) *Weapons of Mass Migration : Forced Displacement, Coercion, and Foreign Policy* (Ithaca, NY: Cornell University Press).

Guarnizo, L.E., Portes, A. and Haller, W. (2003) 'Assimilation and transnationalism: determinants of transnational political action among contemporary migrants', *American Journal of Sociology,* 108:6, 1211–48.

Guimezanes, N. (1995) 'Acquisition of nationality in OECD countries' in OECD (ed.) *Trends in International Migration: Annual Report* (Paris: OECD) pp. 157–79.

Gurak, D.T. and Caces, F. (1992) 'Migration networks and the shaping of international migration systems' in Kritz, M.M., Lim, L.L. and Zlotnik, H. (eds) *International Migration Systems: A Global Approach* (Oxford: Clarendon Press) pp. 150–76.

Gutierrez, D., Batalova, J. and Terrazas, A. (2012) *The 2012 Mexican Presidential Election and Mexican Immigrants of Voting Age in the United States* (Washington, DC: Migration Policy Institute).

Gzesh, S. (2006) *Central Americans and Asylum Policy in the Reagan Era.* www.migrationinformation.org/Feature/display.cfm?id=384, accessed 11 November 2011.

Habermas, J. and Pensky, M. (2001) *The Postnational Constellation: Political Essays* (Cambridge: Polity in association with Blackwell Publishers).

Hage, G. (1998) *White Nation: Fantasies of White Supremacy in a Multicultural Society* (Sydney and New York: Pluto Press and Routledge).

Hakimzadeh, S. (2006) 'Iran: A Vast Diaspora Abroad and Millions of Refugees at Home '*Migration Information Source* (Washington, DC: Migration Policy Institute) www.migrationinformation.org/Profiles/display.cfm?id=424.

Halliday, F. (1985) 'Migrations de main d'oeuvre dans le monde arabe: l'envers du nouvel ordre économique', *Revue Tiers Monde,* 26:103.

Hamilton, N. and Stoltz Chinchilla, N. (1991) 'Central American Migration: A Framework for Analysis', *Latin American Research Review,* 26:1, 75–110.

Hammar, T. (ed.) (1985) *European Immigration Policy: a Comparative Study* (Cambridge: Cambridge University Press).

Hammar, T. (1990) *Democracy and the Nation-State: Aliens, Denizens and Citizens in a World of International Migration* (Aldershot: Avebury).

Hamood, S. (2006) *African Transit Migration through Libya to Europe: The Human Cost* (Cairo: FMRS, The American University in Cairo).

Hardt, M. and Negri, A. (2000) *Empire* (Cambridge, MA: Harvard University Press).

Hargreaves, A.C. (2007) *Multi-Ethnic France: Immigration, Politics, Culture and Society* (New York and London: Routledge).

Harris, J.R. and Todaro, M.P. (1970) 'Migration, unemployment and development: A two-sector analysis', *American Economic Review*, 60, 126–42.

Harris, N. (1996) *The New Untouchables: Immigration and the New World Worker* (Harmondsworth: Penguin).

Hatton, T.J. (2009) 'The Rise and Fall of Asylum: What Happened and Why?', *Economic Journal*, 119:535, F183–F213.

Hatton, T.J. and Williamson, J.G. (1998) *The Age of Mass Migration: Causes and Economic Effects* (Oxford and New York: Oxford University Press).

Hatton, T.J. and Williamson, J.G. (2005) *Global Migration and the World Economy* (Boston: MIT Press).

Heering, L., van der Erf, R. and van Wissen, L. (2004) 'The role of family networks and migration culture in the continuation of Moroccan emigration: A gender perspective', *Journal of Ethnic and Migration Studies*, 30:2, 323–37.

Heinemeijer, W.F., van Amersfoort, J.A., Ettema, W., De Mas, P. and van der Wusten, H. (1977) *Partir pour rester, une enquête sur les incidences de l'émigration ouvrière à la campagne marocaine* (Den Haag: NUFFIC).

Held, D., McGrew, A., Goldblatt, D. and Perraton, J. (1999) *Global Transformations: Politics, Economics and Culture* (Cambridge: Polity).

Henry, S., Schoumaker, B. and Beauchemin, C. (2004) 'The impact of rainfall on the first out-migration: A multi-level event-history analysis in Burkina Faso', *Population and Environment*, 25:5, 423–60.

HKSARG (2011) *Foreign Domestic Helpers* (Hong Kong: Immigration Department, The Government of the Hong Kong Special Administrative Region) www.immd.gov.hk/ehtml/faq_fdh.htm#9, accessed 22 January 2012.

Hoefer, M., Rytina, N. and Baker, B. (2011) *Estimates of the Unauthorized Immigrant Population Residing in the United States: January 2010* (Washington, DC: US Department of Homeland Security).

Hoerder, D. (2002) *Cultures in Contact: World Migrations in the Second Millennium* (Durham: Duke University Press).

Hollifield, J.F. (1992) *Immigrants, Markets and States: The political Economy of Postwar Europe* (Cambridge, MA: Harvard University Press).

Hollifield, J.F. (2000) 'The politics of international migration: how can we "bring the state back in"?' in Brettell, C.B. and Hollifield, J.F. (eds) *Migration Theory: Talking Across Disciplines* (New York and London: Routledge) pp. 137–85.

Hollifield, J.F., Martin, P.L. and Orrenius, P. (eds) (2013) *Controlling Immigration: a Global Perspective*, 3rd ed (Stanford, CA: Stanford University Press).

Homer-Dixon, T. and Percival, V. (1996) *Environmental Security and Violent Conflict: Briefing Book* (Toronto: University of Toronto and American Association for the Advancement of Science).

Homze, E.L. (1967) *Foreign Labor in Nazi Germany* (Princeton, NJ: Princeton University Press).

Honorable Congreso de la Unión (2011) *Ley de Migración*. Leyes Federales de México. www.diputados.gob.mx/LeyesBiblio/index.htm, accessed 6 July 2011.

Horst, C. (2006) *Transnational Nomads : How Somalis Cope with Refugee Life in the Dadaab Camps of Kenya* (New York and Oxford: Berghahn).

Horwood, C. (2009) *In Pursuit of the Southern Dream: Victims of Necessity, Assessment of the irregular movement of men from East Africa and the Horn to South Africa* (Geneva: International Organization for Migration).

HRW (2006) *Libya: Stemming the Flow. Abuses Against Migrants, Asylum Seekers and Refugees* (London: Human Rights Watch).

Huang, S., Thang, L.L. and Toyota, M. (eds) (2012) *Global Networks Special Issue: Transnational Mobilities for Care: Rethinking the Dynamics of Care in Asia* (Oxford and Malden, MA: Blackwell).

Huang, S., Yeoh, B. and Rahman, N.A. (2005) *Asian Women as Transnational Domestic Workers* (Singapore: Marshall Cavendish Academic).

Hugo, G. (2005) *Migration in the Asia-Pacific Region* (Geneva: Global Commission on International Migration).

Hugo, G. (2008) *Migration, Development and Environment*. IOM Migration Research Series (Geneva: International Organization for Migration).

Hugo, G. (2010a) 'Climate change-induced mobility and the existing migration regime in Asia and the Pacific' in McAdam, J. (ed.) *Climate Change and Displacement: Multidisciplinary Perspectives* (Oxford and Portland, OR: Hart) pp. 9–35.

Hugo, G. (2010b) *The Future of Migration Policies in the Asia-Pacific Region*. Background Paper for the World Migration Report (Geneva: International Organization for Migration). http://publications.iom.int/bookstore/free/WMR2010_migration_policies_asia-pacific.pdf.

Human Rights First (2008) *Violence based on racism and xenophobia*. (New York: Human Rights First) www.humanrightsfirst.org/our-work/fighting-discrimination/2008-hate-crime-survey/usa/ii-violence-based-on-racism-and-xenophobia/, accessed 9 March, 2012.

Human Rights Watch (2011) *World Report 2011: Events of 2010* (New York: Human Rights Watch) www.hrw.org/sites/default/files/reports/wr2011.pdf.

Huntington, S.P. (2004) *Who Are We* (New York: Simon & Schuster).

Hur, J.J. and Lee, K. (2008) 'Demographic Change and International Labor Mobility in Korea' *PECC-ABAC Conference on 'Demographic Change and International Labor Mobility in the Asia Pacific Region: Implications for Business and Cooperation'*. (Seoul, Korea: 25–6 March, www.pecc.org/.

Husain, E. (2009) *The Islamist* (Harmondsworth: Penguin).

İçduygu, A. (2000) 'The Politics of International Migratory Regimes', *International Social Science Journal*, 357–66.

İçduygu, A. (2004) 'Transborder crime between Turkey and Greece: Human smuggling and its regional consequences', *Southeast European and Black Seas Studies*, 4:2, 294–311.

İçduygu, A. and Yükseker, D. (2012) 'Rethinking transit migration in Turkey: reality and re-presentation in the creation of a migratory phenomenon', *Population, Space and Place*, 18:4, 441–56.

IDMC (2007) *Internal Displacement: Global Overview of Trends and Developments in 2006* (Geneva: Internal Displacement Monitoring Centre and Norwegian Refugee Council).

IDMC (2011) *Internal Displacement: Global Overview of Trends and Development in 2010* (Geneva: Internal Displacement Monitoring Centre).

ILO (2006) *Realizing Decent Work in Asia: Fourteenth Asian Regional Meeting: Report of the Director-General* (Geneva: International Labour Office).

ILO (2007) *Labour and Social Trends in ASEAN 2007* (Bangkok: International Labour Office Regional Office for Asia and the Pacific).

ILO (2009) *The Cost of Coercion: 2009 Global Report on Forced Labour* (Geneva: International Labour Organization,)

IMI and RMMS (2012) *Global Migration Futures. Using scenarios to explore future migration in the Horn of Africa & Yemen* (Oxford and Nairobi: International Migration Institute, University of Oxford and Regional Mixed Migration Secretariat). www.imi.ox.ac.uk/pdfs/research-projects-pdfs/gmf-pdfs/global-migration-futures-using-scenarios-to-explore-future-migration-in-the-horn-of-africa-yemen, accessed November 2012.

Immigration Department of Malaysia (2012) *Foreign Worker*. www.imi.gov.my/, accessed 24 January 2012.

INS (2002) *Statistical Yearbook of the Immigration and Naturalization Service, 1999* (Washington, DC: US Government Printing Office).

INSEE (2012) *Répartition des immigrés par pays de naissance* (Paris: Institut national de la statistique et des études économiques) www.insee.fr/fr/themes/tableau.asp?reg_id=0&ref_id=immigrespaysnais, accessed 6 March 2012.

Instituto Nacional de Estadística (2011) *Población Nacida en el Exterior, por Año Llegada a Venezuela, Según Pais de Nacimiento, Censo 2001.*

Instituto Nacional de Estadística y Geografía (2011) *Extranjeros residentes en México - 1950 a 2010.*

Instituto Nacional de Migración (2010) *Boletín Mensual de Estadísticas Migratorias 2010* (México DF: SEGOB).

IOM (2005) *World Migration 2005: Costs and Benefits of International Migration* (Geneva: International Organization for Migration).

IOM (2008) *Regional Thematic Working Group on International Migration including Human Trafficking: Situation Report on Internationla Migration in East and South-East Asia* (Bangkok: International Organization for Migration) www.colomboprocess.org/images/stories/situationreport.pdf.

IOM (2010) *World Migration Report 2010: The Future of Migration: Building Capacities for Change* (Geneva: International Organization for Migration).

IOM (2011) *World Migration Report 2011: Communicating Effectively about Migration* (Geneva: International Organization for Migration).

IPPR (2010) *Recession leaves almost half of young black people unemployed, finds IPPR.* (London: Institute for Public Policy Research North) www.ippr.org/press-releases/111/2419/recession-leaves-almost-half-young-black-people-unemployed-finds-ippr, accessed 28 February 2012.

Iredale, R., Guo, F. and Rozario, S. (eds) (2002) *Return Skilled Migration and Business Migration and Social Transformation* (Wollongong: Centre for Asia Pacific Social Transformation Studies).

Ireland, P. (1994) *The Policy Challenge of Ethnic Diversity* (Cambridge, MA: Harvard University Press).

ISTAT (2007) *Demografia in cifre* (Rome: Istituto Nazionale di Statistica) http://demo.istat.it/, accessed 16 August 2007.

ISTAT (2010a) *Demographic Indicators 2009* (Rome: Italian National Institute of Statistics). www3.istat.it/salastampa/comunicati/in_calendario/inddemo/20100218_00/demographicindicators.pdf, accessed 8 February 2012.

ISTAT (2010b) *The foreign population resident in Italy* (Rome: Italian National Institute of Statistics) http://en.istat.it/salastampa/comunicati/non_calendario/20101012_00/Foreign_residents.pdf, accessed 8 February 2012.

Jachimowicz, M. (2006) *Argentina: A New Era of Migration and Migration Policy*. www.migrationinformation.org/USfocus/display.cfm?ID=374, accessed 5 December 2011.

Jackson, J.A. (1963) *The Irish in Britain* (London: Routledge & Kegan Paul).

Jackson, P.I. and Doerschler, P. (2012) *Benchmarking Muslim Well-Being in Europe: Reducing Disparities and Polarizations* (Bristol: Policy Press).

Jackson, R., Jarvis , L., Gunning, J. and Smyth, M.B. (2011) *Terrorism: A Continual Introduction* (Basingstoke: Palgrave MacMillan).

Jazouli, A. (1986) *L'action collective des jeunes maghrébins en France* (Paris: Editions Harmattan).

JBHE (2000) 'African Immigrants in the United States are the Nation's Most Highly Educated Group (1999–2000)' *The Journal of Blacks in Higher Education*: 26, 60–1.

Jha, S., Sugiyarto, G. and Vargas-Silva, C. (2009) *The Global Crisis and the Impact on Remittances to Developing Asia*. ADB Economics Working Paper Series (Manila: Asian Development Bank) www.adb.org/Documents/Working-Papers/2009/Economics-WP185.pdf.

Jimenez, M. (2009) *Humanitarian Crisis: Migrant Deaths at the U.S.–Mexico Border* (San Diego: American Civil Liberties Union of San Diego and Imperial Counties & Comisión Nacional de los Derechos Humanos).

Johnson, I. and Gugath, B. (2002) 'Turkish voters are transforming political landscape in Germany', *The Wall Street Journal*, 29 September.

Jokisch, B. (2007) *Ecuador: Diversity in Migration*. www.migrationinformation.org/USfocus/display.cfm?ID=575, accessed 01 November 2011.

Jolly, R. and Ray, D.B. (2006) *The Human Security Framework and National Human Development Reports* (New York: United Nations Development Programme (UNDP)). http://hdr.undp.org/en/media/NHDR_Human_Security_GN.pdf, accessed 7 November 2012

Jones, K. and Smith, A.D. (1970) *The Economic Impact of Commonwealth Immigration* (Cambridge: Cambridge University Press).

Jones, R.C. (1998a) 'Introduction: The Renewed Role of Remittances in the New World Order', *Economic Geography,* 74:1, 1–7.

Jones, R.C. (1998b) 'Remittances and Inequality: A Question of Migration Stage and Geographical Scale', *Economic Geography,* 74:1, 8–25.

Joppke, C. (1998) *The Challenge to the Nation-State: immigration in Western Europe and the United States* (New York: Oxford University Press).

Joppke, C. (1999) *Immigration and the Nation-State: the United States, Germany and Britain* (Oxford: Oxford University Press).

Joppke, C. (2004) 'The retreat of multiculturalism in the liberal state: theory and policy', *British Journal of Sociology,* 55:2, 237–57.

Jung Park, Y. (2009) *Chinese Migration in Africa* (Johannesburg: South African Institute of International Affairs (SAIIA)).

Jupp, J. (ed.) (2001) *The Australian People: an Encyclopedia of the Nation, Its People and Their Origins* (Cambridge: Cambridge University Press).

Jupp, J. (2002) *From White Australia to Woomera: The History of Australian Immigration* (Melbourne: Cambridge University Press).

Jureidini, R. (2003) 'L'échec de la protection de l'État: les domestiques étrangers au Liban', *Revue Européenne Des Migrations Internationales*, 19:3, 95–127.

Kaplan, S. and Salamon, H. (2004) 'Ethiopian Jews in Israel: A part of the people or apart from the people?' in Rebhun, U. and Waxman, C.I. (eds) *Jews in Israel: Contemporary Social and Cultural Patterns* (Hanover [u.a.], Brandeis University Press: University Press of New England).

Kapur, D. (2003) *Remittances: the new development mantra?* Paper prepared for the G-24 Technical Group Meeting, 15–16 September (New York and Geneva: United Nations). unctad.org/en/Docs/gdsmdpbg2420045_en.pdf.

Karlsen, E., Phillips, J. and Koleth, E. (2010) 'Seeking asylum: Australia's humanitarian program' (Canberra: Australian Parliamentary Library)

Kashiwazaki, C. and Akaha, T. (2006) *Japanese Immigration Policy: Responding to Conflicting Pressures.* www.migrationinformation.org/Profiles/display.cfm?ID=487, accessed 19 September 2011.

Kassim, A. and Zin, R.H.M. (2011) *Policy on Irregular Migrants in Malaysia: An Analysis of its implementation and Effectiveness.* Discussion Paper Series No. 34. www3.pids.gov.ph/ris/dps/pidsdps1134.pdf.

Katseli, L.T., Lucas, R.E.B. and Xenogiani, T. (2006) *Effects of Migration on Sending Countries: What do we know?* Working Paper No. 250. (Paris: OECD).

Kay, D. and Miles, R. (1992) *Refugees or Migrant Workers? European Volunteer Workers in Britain 1946–1951* (London: Routledge).

Keely, C.B. (2001) 'The international refugee regimes(s): the end of the Cold War matters', *International Migration Review,* 35:1, 303–14.

Kenny, M. (1962) 'Twentieth-Century Spanish Expatriates in Mexico: An Urban Sub-Culture', *Anthropological Quarterly,* 35:4, 169–80.

Kepel, G. (2002) *Jihad: the trail of political Islam* (Cambridge, MA: Belknap of Harvard University).

Kepel, G. (2004) *The War for Muslim minds: Islam and the West* (Cambridge, MA: Belknap Press.

Kepel, G. (2005) *Europe's Answer to Londonistan* (London: Open Democracy) www.opendemocracy.net/conflict-terrorism/londonistan_2775.jsp, accessed 25 February 2008.

Kerpaci, K. and Kuka, M. (2012) 'Identity in the Narratives of Albanian Return Migrants from Greece', *Journal of Educational and Social Research,* 2:6, 51–7.

Kershner, I. (2012) 'Israeli Leader Pledges Hard Line on Migrants' *New York Times* (4 June, New York). www.nytimes.com/2012/06/05/world/middleeast/netanyahu-vows-crackdown-on-african-asylum-seekers.html?_r=0.

Khadria, B. (2008) 'India; skilled migration to developed countries, labour migration to the Gulf' in Castles, S. and Delgado Wise, R. (eds) *Migration and Development: Perspectives from the South* (Geneva: International Organization for Migration) www.imi.ox.ac.uk/pdfs/migration-and-development-perspectives-from-the-south.

Kim, H.M., Kim, G.-D., Kim, M.-J., Kim, J.S. and Kim, C. (2007) *Research on Labour and Marriage Migration Process from Mongolia and Vietnam to Korea and the Impact on Migrant Rights (in Korean)* 2007 Joint Project of Inter-Asian NIs on Current Human Rights Issues (Seoul: National Human Rights Commission).

Kindleberger, C.P. (1967) *Europe's Postwar Growth - the Role of Labor Supply* (Cambridge, MA: Harvard University Press).

King, R. (2000) 'Southern Europe in the changing global map of migration' in King, R., Lazaridis, G. and Tsardanidis, C. (eds) *Eldorado or Fortress? Migration in Southern Europe* (London: Macmillan) pp. 3–26.

King, R. (ed.) (2001) *The Mediterranean Passage: Migration and New Cultural Encounters in Southern Europe* (Liverpool: Liverpool University Press).

King, R. and Skeldon, R. (2010) "Mind the Gap!' Integrating Approaches to Internal and International Migration', *Journal of Ethnic and Migration Studies,* 36:10, 1619–46.

King, R. and Vullnetari, J. (2006) 'Orphan pensioners and migrating grandparents: the impact of mass migration on older people in rural Albania', *Ageing & Society,* 26:783–816.

King, R., Lazaridis, G. and Tsardanidis, C. (eds) (2000) *Eldorado or Fortress? Migration in Southern Europe* (Basingstoke: Palgrave Macmillan).

King, R., Fielding, T., Thomson, M. and Warnes, T. (2006) 'Time, generations and gender in migration and settlement' in Penninx, R., Berger, M. and Kraal, K. (eds) *The Dynamics of International Migration and Settlement in Europe* (Amsterdam: Amsterdam University Press) pp. 233–67.

Kirişci, K. (2006) 'National Identity, asylum and immigration: the EU as a vehicle of post-national transformation in Turkey' in Kieser, H.L. (ed.) *Turkey Beyond Nationalism:Toward Post-Nationalist Identities* (London: I.B. Tauris).

Kirişçi, K. (2007) 'Turkey: A Country of Transition from Emigration to Immigration'. *Mediterranean Politics,* 12:1, 91-97.

Kiser, G. and Kiser, M. (eds) (1979) *Mexican Workers in the United States* (Albuquerque: University of New Mexico Press).

Klein, N. (2007) *The Shock Doctrine: the Rise of Disaster Capitalism* (London: Allen Lane).

Kloosterman, R. and Rath, J. (2003) *Immigrant Entrepreneurs : Venturing Abroad in the Age of Globalization* (Oxford: Berg).

Klug, F. (1989) ' "Oh to be in England": the British case study' in Yuval-Davis, N. and Anthias, F. (eds) *Woman–Nation–State* (London: Macmillan)

Kniveton, D., Schmidt-Verkerk, K., Smith, C. and Black, R. (2008) *Climate Change and Migration: Improving Methodologies to Estimate Flows*. IOM Migration Research Series (Geneva: International Organization for Migration) www.iom.int/jahia/webdav/site/myjahiasite/shared/shared/mainsite/published_docs/serial_publications/MRS-33.pdf.

Komai, H. (1995) *Migrant Workers in Japan* (London: Kegan Paul International).

Koopmans, R. (2010) 'Trade-Offs between Equality and Difference: Immigrant Integration, Multiculturalism and the Welfare State in Cross-National Perspective', *Journal of Ethnic and Migration Studies,* 36:1, 1–26.

Kop, Y. and Litan, R.E. (2002) *Sticking Together: The Israeli Experiment In Pluralism* (Washington, DC.: Brookings Institute Press).

Korean immigration service (2002) *Immigration Statistics 2001 (in Korean).* Ministry of Justice, Korea, http//www.immigration.go.kr, accessed 20 January 2012.

Korean Immigration Service (2012) *Immigration Statistics, December 2011 (in Korean).* Ministry of Justice, Korea, www.immigration.go.kr, accessed 20 January 2012.

Koslowski, R. (2000) *Migrants and Citizens* (Ithaca, NY: Cornell University Press).

Koslowski, R. (2008) 'Global Mobility and the Quest for an International Migration Regime', *Conference on International Migration and Development: Continuing the Dialogue-Legal and Policy Perspectives* (New York:17–18 January, CMS and IOM).

Kramer, R. (1999) *Developments in International Migration to the United States* (Washington, DC: Department of Labor).

Kress, B. (2006) 'Burkina Faso: Testing the Tradition of Circular Migration' *Migration Information Source,* March (Washington, DC: Migration Policy Institute).

Krissman, F. (2005) 'Sin Coyote Ni Patrón: Why the "Migrant Network" Fails to Explain International Migration' *International Migration Review,* 39:1, 4–44.

Kritz, M.M., Lim, L.L. and Zlotnik, H. (eds) (1992) *International Migration System: A Global Approach* (Oxford: Clarendon Press).

Kubat, D. (1987) 'Asian Immigrants to Canada' in Fawcett, J.T. and Cariño, B.V. (eds) *Pacific Bridges: The New Immigration from Asia and the Pacific Islands* (New York: Center for Migration Studies).

Kulischer, E.M. (1948) *Europe on the Move: War and Population Changes* (New York: Columbia University Press).

Kureková, L. (2011) *The role of welfare systems in affecting out-migration: the case of Central and Eastern Europe,* IMI/DEMIG Working Paper No 46 (Oxford: International Migration Institute (IMI), University of Oxford) www.imi.ox.ac.uk/publications/working_papers.

Kurzman, C. (2011) *The Missing Martyrs* (Oxford and New York: Oxford University Press).

Kuznetsov, Y. (ed.) (2006) *International Migration of Skills and Diaspora Networks: How Countries Can Draw on Their Talent Abroad* (Washington, DC: World Bank).

Kyle, D. and Koslowski, R. (2001) *Global Human Smuggling* (Baltimore and London: Johns Hopkins University Press).

Kyle, D. and Liang, Z. (2001) 'Migration merchants: human smuggling from Ecuador and China' in Guiraudon, V. and Joppke, C. (eds) *Controlling a New Migration World* (London and New York: Routledge).

Kymlicka, W. (1995) *Multicultural Citizenship: A Liberal Theory of Minority Rights* (Oxford: Clarendon).

Kymlicka, W. and He, B. (eds) (2005) *Multiculturalism in Asia* (Oxford: Oxford University Press).

Laczko, F. and Gozdziak, E. (2005) *Data and research on human trafficking: A global survey* (Geneva: International Organization for Migration). www.eldis.org/cf/rdr/rdr.cfm?doc=DOC19255.

Lahav, G. (2004) *Immigration and Politics in the New Europe: Reinventing Borders* (New York: Cambridge University Press).

Landau, L.B. and Freemantle, I. (2009) 'Tactical Cosmopolitanism and Idioms of Belonging: Insertion and Self-Exclusion in Johannesburg', *Journal of Ethnic and Migration Studies,* 36:3, 375–90.

Lanzieri, G. (2011) *Fewer, older and multicultural? Projections of the EU populations by foreign/national background* (Luxembourg: Publications Office of the European Union: Eurostat Methodologies and Working Papers).

Laurence, J. (2012) *The Emancipation of Europe's Muslims: The State's Role in Minority Integration* (Princeton, NJ: Princeton University Press).

Laurens, H. (2005) 'Les Migrations au Proche-Orient de l'Empire ottoman aux Etats-nations. Une perspective historique.' in Jaber, H. and Métrai, F. (eds) *Mondes en mouvements. Migrants et migrations au Moyen-Orient au tournant du XXIe siècle* (Beyrouth: Institut Français du Proche Orient IFPO)

Lavergne, M. (2003) 'Golfe arabo-persique: un système migratoire de plus en plus tourné vers l'Asie', *Revue Européenne Des Migrations Internationales,* 19:3, 229–41.

Layton-Henry, Z. (ed.) (1990) *The Political Rights of Migrant Workers in Western Europe* (London: Sage).

Layton-Henry, Z. (2004) 'Britain: from immigration control to migration management' in Cornelius, W., Hollifield, J.F., Martin, P.L. and Tsuda, T. (eds) *Controlling Immigration: A Global Perspective,* 2nd edn (Stanford, CA: Stanford University Press) pp. 294–333.

Layton-Henry, Z. and Rich, P.B. (eds) (1986) *Race, Government and Politics in Britain* (London: Macmillan).

Lee, E.S. (1966) 'A Theory of Migration' *Demography,* 3:1, 47–57.

Lee, H.K. (2008) 'International marriage and the state in South Korea: focusing on governmental policy', *Citizenship Studies,* 12:1, 107–23.

Lee, H.K. (2010) *Family Migration Issues in North-East Asia.* Background Paper for the World Migration Report 2010 (Geneva: International Organization for Migration) http://publications.iom.int/bookstore/free/WMR2010_family_ migration_neasia.pdf.

Lee, J.S. and Wang, S.-W. (1996) 'Recruiting and managing of foreign workers in Taiwan', *Asian and Pacific Migration Journal,* 5, 2–3.

Lee, T., Ramakrishnan, S.K. and Ramirez, R. (eds) (2006) *Transforming Politics, Transforming America: The Political and Civic Incorporation of Immigrants in the United States* (Charlottesville: University of Virginia Press).

Leichtman, M.A. (2005) 'The legacy of transnational lives: Beyond the first generation of Lebanese in Senegal', *Ethnic and Racial Studies,* 28:4, 663–86.

Lever-Tracey, C. and Quinlan, M. (1988) *A Divided Working Class* (London and New York: Routledge & Kegan Paul).

Levinson, A. (2005) *The Regularisation of the Unauthorized Migrants: Literature Survey and Case Studies* (Oxford: Centre on Migration, Policy and Society).

Levitt, P. (1998) 'Social remittances: migration driven local-level forms of cultural diffusion', *International Migration Review,* 32:4, 926–48.

Levitt, P. and Glick-Schiller, N. (2004) 'Conceptualising simultaneity: a transnational social field perspective on society', *International Migration Review,* 38:3, 1002–39.

Levy, D. (1999) 'Coming home? Ethnic Germans and the transformation of national identity in the Federal Republic of Germany' in Geddes, A. and Adrian, F. (eds) *The Politics of Belonging: Migrants and Minorities in Contemporary Europe* (Aldershot: Ashgate).

Lewis, J.R. (1986) 'International Labour Migration and Uneven Regional Development in Labour Exporting Countries', *Tijdschrift voor Economische en Sociale Geografie,* 77:1, 27–41.

Lewis, M. and Lyall, S. (2012) 'Norway Mass Killer Gets the Maximum: 21 Years', *New York Times,* 24 August 2012.

Lewis, W.A. (1954) 'Economic Development with Unlimited Supplies of Labour', *Manchester School of Economic and Social Studies,* 22, 139–91.

Li, M. and Batalova, J. (2011) *Refugees and Asylees in the United States* (Washington, DC: Migration Information Source) www.migrationinformation.org/ USfocus/display.cfm?id=851. Accessed: 16 March 2012.

Li, X.R., Harrill, R., Uysal, M., Burnett, T. and Zhan, X. (2010) 'Estimating the size of the Chinese outbound travel market: A demand-side approach' *Tourism Management,* 31, 250–9.

Lieten, G.K. and Nieuwenhuys, O. (1989) 'Introduction: Survival and Emancipation' in Lieten, G.K., Nieuwenhuys, O. and Schenk-Sandbergen, L. (eds) *Women, Migrants and Tribals: Survival Strategies in Asia* (New Delhi: Manohar).

Light, I. and Bonacich, E. (1988) *Immigrant Entrepreneurs* (Berkeley, CA: University of California Press).

Light, I.H. and Gold, S.J. (1999) *Ethnic Economies* (San Diego, CA and London: Academic).

Lightfoot, D.R. and Miller, J.A. (1996) 'Sijilmassa: The rise and fall of a walled oasis in medieval Morocco', *Annals of the Association of American Geographers,* 86:1, 78–101.

Lindley, A. (2009) 'The Early-Morning Phonecall: Remittances from a Refugee Diaspora Perspective', *Journal of Ethnic and Migration Studies,* 35:8, 1315–34.

Lindley, A. (2012) *The Early Morning Phonecall: Somali Refugees' Remittances* (New York and Oxford: Berghahn).

Lindsay, C. (2001) *The Caribbean Community in Canada: Profiles of Ethnic Communities in Canada* (Ottawa: Social and Aboriginal Statistics Division).

Lipton, M. (1980) 'Migration from the rural areas of poor countries: The impact on rural productivity and income distribution', *World Development,* 8: 1–24.

Lluch, V.A. (2002) 'Apartheid sous plastique – El Ejido', *Le Monde Diplomatique, Histoires d'Immigration,*85–9.

Loescher, G. (2001) *The UNHCR and World Politics: A Perilous Path* (Oxford: Oxford University Press).

Lohrmann, R. (1987) 'Irregular Migration: A Rising Issue in Developing Countries', *International Migration,* 25:3, 253–66.

Lopez, M. and Taylor, P. (2012) *Latino Voters in the 2012 Election.* Pew Hispanic Research Center http://www.pewhispanic.org/2012/11/07/latino-voters-in-the-2012-election/, accessed 7 November 2012.

Lopez-Garcia, B. (2001) 'La régularisation des Maghrébins sans papiers en Espagne' in Leveau, R., Wihtol de Wenden, C. and Mohsen-Finan, K. (eds) *Nouvelles citoyennetées: réfugiés et sans-papiers dans l'espace européen* (Paris: IFRI) p. 113.

Lovejoy, P.E. (1989) 'The Impact of the Atlantic Slave Trade on Africa: A Review of the Literature', *Journal of African History,* 30:3, 365–94.

Lowell, B.L., Findlay, A.M. and International Migration Branch (2002) *Migration of Highly Skilled Persons from Developing Countries : Impact and Policy Responses: Synthesis Report International Migration Papers, 44* (Geneva: International Labour Office -ILO).

Lucas, R.E.B. and Stark, O. (1985) 'Motivations to Remit: Evidence from Botswana', *Journal of Political Economy,* 93, 901–18.

Lucassen, J. (1995) 'Emigration to the Dutch colonies and the USA' in Cohen, R. (ed.) *The Cambridge Survey of World Migration* (Cambridge: Cambridge University Press).

Lucassen, L. (2005) *The Immigrant Threat: the Integration of Old and New Migrants in Western Europe since 1890* (Urbana and Chicago: University of Illinois Press).

Lucassen, L., Feldman, D. and Oltmer, J. (2006) 'Immigrant integration in Western Europe, then and now' in Lucassen, L., Feldman, D. and Oltmer, J. (eds) *Paths of Integration: Migrants in Western Europe (1880–2004)* (Amsterdam: Amsterdam University Press) pp. 7–23.

Luso-American Development Foundation (1999) 'Metropolis International Workshop Proceedings' (Lisbon: Luso-America Development Foundation).

Lustik, I.S. (2011) 'Israel's Migration Balance: Demography, Politics and Ideology', *Israel Studies Review,* 26:1, 33–65.

Lutz, H., Phoenix, A. and Yuval-Davis, N. (eds) (1995) *Crossfires: Nationalism, Racism and Gender in Europe* (London: Pluto Press).

Mabogunje, A.L. (1970) 'Systems Approach to a Theory of Rural-Urban Migration', *Geographical Analysis,* 2:1, 1–18.

MacMaster, N. (1991) 'The "seuil de tolérance": the uses of a "scientific" racist concept' in Silverman, M. (ed.) *Race Discourse and Power in France* (Aldershot: Avebury).

Mafukidze, J. (2006) 'A discussion of migration and migration patterns and flows in Africa' in Cross, C., Gelderblom, D., Roux, N. and Mafukidze, J. (eds) *Views on Migration in Sub-Saharan Africa* (Cape Town: HSRC Press) pp. 103–29.

Mahler, S. and Ugrina, D. (2006) *Central America: Crossroads of the Americas.* www.migrationinformation.org/Feature/display.cfm?ID=386, accessed 30 September 2011.

Mahony, H. (2010) 'Italy to Raise EU Citizen Expulsion Policy at September Meeting'. euobserver.com. http://euobserver.com/9/30657 accessed 8 January 2012.

Manning, P. (2005) *Migration in World History* (New York: Routledge).

Manuh, T. (ed.) (2005) *At Home in the World? International Migration and Development in Contemporary Ghana and West Africa* (Accra, Ghana: Sub-Saharan Publishers).

Marcu, M. (2011) 'The EU-27 population continues to grow', *Eurostat Statistics in Focus,* 31/2009, 1–11.

Marcus, J. (1995) *The National Front and French Politics: The Resistible Rise of Jean-Marie Le Pen* (New York: New York University Press).

Markus, A., Jupp, J. and McDonald, P. (2009) *Australia's Immigration Revolution* (Sydney: Allen & Unwin).

Martin, D. (2005) *The US Refugee Program in Transition* (Washington, DC: Migration Information Source) www.migrationinformation.org/Feature/display.cfm?id=305, accessed 1 August 2007.

Martin, P.L. (1991) *The Unfinished Story: Turkish Labour Migration to Western Europe* (Geneva: International Labour Office).

Martin, P.L. (1993) *Trade and Migration: NAFTA and Agriculture* 30 (Washington, DC: Institute for International Economics).

Martin, P.L. (2008) 'Another Miracle? Managing Labour Migration in Asia'. *United Nations Expert Group Meeting on International Migration and Development in Asia and the Pacific* (Bangkok: United Nations Economic and Social Commission for Asia and the Pacific) www.un.org/esa/population/meetings/EGM_Ittmig_Asia/P01_Martin.pdf.

Martin, P.L. and Miller, M.J. (2000a) *Employer Sanctions: French, German and US Experiences* (Geneva: ILO).

Martin, P.L. and Miller, M.J. (2000b) 'Smuggling and Trafficking: A conference report', *International Migration Review,* 34:3, 969–75.

Martin, P.L. and Taylor, J.E. (1996) 'The anatomy of a migration hump' in Taylor, J.E. (ed.) *Development Strategy, Employment, and Migration: Insights from Models* (Paris: OECD, Development Centre) pp. 43–62.

Martin, P.L., Abella, M. and Kuptsch, C. (2006) *Managing Labor Migration in the Twenty-first Century* (New Haven and London: Yale University Press).

Martínez Pizarro, J. (ed.) (2011) *Migración Internacional en América Latina y el Caribe – Nuevas Tendencias, Nuevos Enfoques* (Santiago de Chile: CEPAL).

Martiniello, M. (1994) 'Citizenship of the European Union: a critical view' in Bauböck, R. (ed.) *From Aliens to Citizens* (Aldershot: Avebury) pp. 29–48.

Marx, K. (1976) *Capital* I (Harmondsworth: Penguin).

Massey, D.S. (1990) 'Social Structure, Household Strategies, and the Cumulative Causation of Migration', *Population Index,* 56 (1): 3-26.

Massey, D.S. (2000a) 'Book Review – The Age of Mass Migration: Causes and Economic Impact by Timothy J. Hatton and Jeffrey G. Williamson', *Journal of Modern History* 72:2, 496–7.

Massey, D.S. (2000b) 'To study migration today, look to a parallel era', *Chronicle of Higher Education* 46:50, 5.

Massey, D.S., Alarcón, R., Durand, J. and González, H. (1987) *Return to Aztlan: the Social Process of International Migration from Western Mexico* (Berkeley, CA: University of California Press).

Massey, D.S., Arango, J., Hugo, G., Kouaouci, A., Pellegrino, A. and Taylor, J.E. (1993) 'Theories of international migration: A review and appraisal', *Population and Development Review,* 19:3, 431–66.

Massey, D.S., Arango, J., Hugo, G., Kouaouci, A., Pellegrino, A. and Taylor, J.E. (1998) *Worlds in Motion: Understanding International Migration at the End of the Millennium* (Oxford: Clarendon Press).

Massey, D.S., Durand, J. and Malone, N.J. (2002) *Beyond Smoke and Mirrors: Mexican Immigration in an Era of Economic Integration* (New York: Russell Sage Foundation).

Mazzucato, V., Kabki, M. and Smith, L. (2006) 'Locating a Ghanaian funeral: Remittances and Practices in a Transnational Context', *Development and Change,* 37:5.

McAdam, J. (ed.) (2010) *Climate Change and Displacement: Multidisciplinary Perspectives* (Oxford: Hart Publishing).

McCabe, K. (2011) *Caribbean Immigrants in the United States.* www.migration-information.org/USfocus/display.cfm?ID=834, accessed 11 November 2011.

McCabe, K. and Meissner, D. (2010) 'Immigration the United States: recession affects flows, propsects for reform' (Washington, DC: Migration Information Source) www.migrationinformation.org/Profiles/display.cfm?ID=766. accessed 9 March 2010.

McCarthy, J. (1995) *Death and Exile: The Ethnic Cleansing of Ottoman Muslims 1821–1922* (Princeton: Darwin Press).

McDougall, J. and Scheele, J. (eds) (2012) *Saharan frontiers: space and mobility in Northwest Africa* (Bloomington: Indiana University Press).

McDowell, C. and de Haan, A. (1997) *Migration and Sustainable Livelihoods: A Critical Review of the Literature* (University of Sussex: Institute of Development Studies).

McKenzie, D.J. (2006) 'Beyond Remittances: The Effects of Migration on Mexican Households' in Özden, Ç. and Schiff, M. (eds) *International Migration, Remittances, and the Brain Drain* (Washington, DC: World Bank).

McKinnon, M. (1996) *Immigrants and Citizens: New Zealanders and Asian Immigration in Historical Context* (Wellington, NZ: Institute of Policy Studies).

Mechlinski, T. (2010) 'Making Movements Possible: Transportation Workers and Mobility in West Africa' *International Migration* (online version).

Meissner, D., Papademetriou, D. and North, D. (1987) *Legalization of Undocumented Aliens: Lessons from Other Countries* (Washington, DC: Carnegie Endowment for International Peace).

Menz, G. (2009) *The Political Economy of Managed Migration* (Oxford: Oxford University Press).

Merrill, H. (2011) 'Migration and Surplus Populations: Race and Deindustrialisation in Northern Italy', *Antipode,* 43:5, 1542–72.

Messina, A.M. (2007) *The Logics and Politics of Post-World War II Migration to Western Europe* (Cambridge: Cambridge University Press).

Messina, A.M. (ed.) (2002) *West European Immigration and Immigrant Policy in the New Century* (Westport, CT and London: Praeger).

Migration Dialogue (2007) *Migration News: Latin America.*

Migration Dialogue (2008) *Migration News: Latin America.*

Migration Dialogue (2011) *Migration News: Latin America.*

Migration Information Source (2011) *Heading into the 2012 Elections, Republican Presidential Candidates Walk the Immigration Policy Tightrope* (Washington DC: Migration Policy Institute) www.migrationinformation.org/Feature/print.cfm?ID=867, accessed 23 February, 2012.

Migration Observatory (2011) *Migrants in the UK: an Overview.* (Oxford: The Migration Observatory, University of Oxford) http://migrationobservatory.ox.ac.uk/briefings/migrants-uk-overview, accessed 28 February 2012.

Migration Observatory (2012) *Migration Flows of A8 and Other EU Migrants to and from the UK.* (Oxford: The Migration Observatory, University of Oxford) http://migrationobservatory.ox.ac.uk/briefings/migration-flows-a8-and-other-eu-migrants-and-uk, accessed 28 February 2012.

Milanovic, B. (2007) 'Globalization and inequality' in Held, D. and Kaya, A. (eds) *Global Inequality: Patterns and Explanations* (Cambridge and Malden, MA: Polity) pp. 26–49.

Miles, R. (1989) *Racism* (London: Routledge).

Miller, M.J. (1978) *The Problem of Foreign Worker Participation and Representation in France, Switzerland and the Federal Republic of Germany* (Madison: University of Wisconsin).

Miller, M.J. (1981) *Foreign Workers in Western Europe : An Emerging Political Force* (New York: Praeger).

Miller, M.J. (1984) 'Industrial policy and the rights of labor: the case of foreign workers in the French automobile assembly industry', *Michigan Yearbook of International Legal Studies.*

Miller, M.J. (1986) 'Policy ad-hocracy: The Paucity of Coordinated Perspectives and Policies', *The Annals,* 485, 65–75.

Miller, M.J. (1989) 'Continuities and Discontinuities in Immigration Reform in Industrial Democracies' in Entzinger, H. and Carter, J. (eds) *International Review of Comparative Public policy, 1* (Greenwich, CT and London: JAI Press).

Miller, M.J. (1999) 'Prevention of unauthorized migration' in Bernstein, A. and Weiner, M. (eds) *Migration and Refugee Policies: An Overview* (London and New York: Pinter).

Miller, M.J. (2000) 'A durable international migration and security nexus: the problem of the Islamic periphery in transatlantic ties' in Graham, D. and Poku, N. (eds) *Migration, Globalization and Human Security* (London: Routledge).

Miller, M.J. (2002) 'Continuity and change in postwar French legalization policy' in Messina, A. (ed.) *West European Immigration and Immigrant Policy in the New Century* (Westport, CT and London: Praeger).

Miller, M.J. (2007) 'Disquiet on the Western Front:Sleeper Cells, Transatlantic Rift and the War in Iraq' in Miller, M.J. and Stefanova, B. (eds) *The War on Terror in Comparative Perspective* (Basingstoke: Palgrave Macmillan).

Miller, M.J. and Gabriel, C. (2008) 'The US-Mexico Honeymoon of 2001:A Retrospective' in Gabriel, C. and Pellerin, H. (eds) *Governing International Labour Migration: Current Issues, Challenges and Dilemmas* (New York: Routledge) pp. 147–62.

Miller, M.J. and Stefanova, B. (2006) 'NAFTA and the European Referent: Labor Mobility in European and North American Regional Integration' in Messina, A. and Lahav, G. (eds) *The Migration Reader: Exploring Politics and Policies* (Boulder, CO: Lynne Reiner).

Ministry of Employment and Labor (2010) *Introduction of Industry, Employment Permit System* (Seoul: Ministry of Employment and Labor) www.eps.go.kr/en/index.html, accessed 5 July 2011.

Ministry of Manpower Singapore (2011) *Singapore Yearbook on Manpower Statistics, 2011.* www.mom.gov.sg/Documents/statistics-publications/yearbook11/mrsd_2011YearBook.pdf.

Ministry of Overseas Indians Affairs (2011) *Facts on Indian Diaspora* (Overseas Indian Facilitation Centre) www.oifc.in/Facts/Facts-on-Indian-Diaspora, accessed 26 January 2012.

Ministry of Social Development (2010) *The Social Report* (Wellington: New Zealand Ministry of Social Development) www.socialreport.msd.govt.nz/people/ethnic-composition-population.html, accessed 31 August 2011.

MIPEX (2012) *Migrant Integration Policy Index* (London and Brussels: British Council and Migration Policy Group) www.mipex.eu/, accessed 29 February 2012.

Mitchell, M.I. (2012) 'Migration, citizenship and autochthony: strategies and challenges for state-building in Côte d'Ivoire', *Journal of Contemporary African Studies,* 30:2, 267–87.

Moch, L.P. (1992) *Moving Europeans: Migration in Western Europe since 1650* (Bloomington: Indiana University Press).

Moch, L.P. (1995) 'Moving Europeans: historical migration practices in Western Europe' in Cohen, R. (ed.) *The Cambridge Survey of World Migration* (Cambridge: Cambridge University Press).

Modood, T. (2007) *Multiculturalism: A Civic Idea* (Cambridge: Polity).

Mohapatra, S., Ratha, D. and Silwal, A. (2011a) *Outlook for Remittance Flows 2011–13.* Migration and Development Brief 16 (Washington, DC: World Bank).

Mohapatra, S., Ratha, D. and Silwal, A. (2011b) *Outlook for Remittance Flows 2012–14.* Migration and Remittances Unit Migration and Development Brief (Washington, DC: World Bank).

Mori, H. (1997) *Immigration Policy and Foreign Workers in Japan* (London: Macmillan).

Morokvasic, M. (1984) 'Birds of passage are also women' *International Migration Review,* 18:4.

Morrison, J. (1998) *The Cost of Survival: The Trafficking of Refugees to the UK* (London: British Refugee Council).

Motomura, H. (2006) *Americans in Waiting* (Oxford: Oxford University Press).

MPI Data Hub (2012) *American Community Survey 2010 Migration Information Source* (Washington, DC : Migration Policy Institute) www.migrationinformation.org/DataHub/acscensus.cfm, accessed 23 February 2012.

Mudde, C. (2012) *The Relationship between Immigration and Nativism in Europe and North America* (Washington, DC: Migration Policy Institute) www.migrationpolicy.org/pubs/Immigration-Nativism.pdf.

Munck, R., Schierup, C.-U. and Delgado Wise, R. (eds) (2011) *Globalizations: Special Issue: Migration, Work and Citizenship in a Global Era, 8: 3* (London: Routledge).

Münz, R. (1996) 'A continent of migration: European mass migration in the twentieth century', *New Community,* 22:2, 201–26.

Münz, R., Straubhaar, T., Vadean, F. and Vadean, N. (2007) *What are the Migrants' Contributions to Employment and Growth? A European Approach.* HWWI Policy Papers 3-3. (Hamburg: Hamburg Institute of International Economics), accessed 29 May 2013.

Murji, K. and Solomos, J. (eds) (2005) *Racialization: Studies in Theory and Practice* (Oxford: Oxford University Press).

Musterd, S. (2005) 'Social and ethnic segregation in Europe: Levels, causes, and effects', *Journal of Urban Affairs,* 27:3, 331–48.

Musterd, S. and De Vos, S. (2007) 'Residential dynamics in ethnic concentrations', *Housing Studies,* 22:3, 333–53.

Musterd, S. and Ostendorf, W. (2009) 'Residential Segregation and Integration in the Netherlands', *Journal of Ethnic and Migration Studies,* 35:9, 1515–32.

Musterd, S. and Van Kempen, R. (2009) 'Segregation and Housing of Minority Ethnic Groups in Western European Cities', *Tijdschrift voor Economische en Sociale Geografie,* 100:4, 559–66.

Mutluer, M. (2003) 'Les migrations irrégulières en Turquie. Traduit par Stéphane de Tapia', *Revue Européenne Des Migrations Internationales,* 19:3, 151–72.

Myers, N. (1997) 'Environmental refugees', *Population and Environment,* 19:2, 167–82.

Myers, N. and Kent, J. (1995) *Environmental Exodus: an Emergent Crisis in the Global Arena* (Washington, DC: Climate Institute).

Myrdal, G. (1957) *Rich Lands and Poor* (New York: Harper & Row).

NALACC (2010) *Attacks against immigrant communities intensify, while prospects of a worthwhile immigration reform become harder to imagine in 2010* (Chicago: National Alliance of Latin American & Caribbean Communities (NALACC)) www.nalacc.org/fileadmin/Documents/PressReleaseEnglish/NALACC_2010/2010/April_VR/20100419-Analisys_for_VR_dispatch.pdf, accessed 11 June, 2010.

National Commission on Terrorist Attacks Upon the United States (2004) *The 9/11 Commission Report* (New York: W.W.Norton).

National Immigration Agency Taiwan (2012) *Statistics.* www.immigration.gov.tw/lp.asp?ctNode=29986&CtUnit=16677&BaseDSD=7&mp=2, accessed 22 January 2012.

Naujoks, D. (2009) *Emigration, Immigration, and Diaspora Reltions in India Migration Information Source* (Washington, DC : Migration Policy Institute) www.migrationinformation.org/Profiles/display.cfm?ID=745#12, accessed 26 January 2012.

Navarro, M. (2012) 'For Many Latinos, Racial Identity Is More Culture Than Color' *New York Times*, 13 January, www.nytimes.com/2012/01/14/us/for-many-latinos-race-is-more-culture-than-color.html?pagewanted=all.

Nayar, D. (1994) 'International labour movements, trade flows and migration transitions: a theoretical perspective', *Asian and Pacific Migration Journal*, 3:1, 31–47.

Needham, K. (2012) 'Court rules against 'turn back the boats' policy' *Sydney Morning Herald*. (Sydney). www.smh.com.au/national/court-rules-against-turn-back-the-boats-policy-20120224-1tti3.html#ixzz1pFVGppk2, accessed 16 March 2012.

Ness, I. (2005) *Immigrants, Unions and the New U.S. Labor Market* (Philadelphia, PA: Temple University Press).

Newland, K. (2007) *A new surge of interest in migration and development* (Washington, DC: Migration Information Source) www.migrationinformation.org, accessed 6 February 2007.

Newman, M. (2006) 'Immigrants stage protests across US' *New York Times*, 1 May. www.nytimes.com/2006/05/01/us/01cnd-immig.html.

Nicholson, M. (2012) *Refugee resettlement needs outpace growing number of resettlement countries Migration Information Source* (Washington DC: Migration Information Source) www.migrationinformation.org/Feature/display.cfm?ID=912, accessed 2 November 2012.

Noiriel, G. (1988) *Le creuset français: Histoire de l'immigration XIXe–XXe siècles* (Paris: Seuil).

Noiriel, G. (2007) *Immigration, antisémitisme et racisme en France (XIXe–XXe siècle)* (Paris: Fayard).

Nyberg-Sorensen, N., Van Hear, N. and Engberg-Pedersen, P. (2002) 'The migration-development nexus evidence and policy options state-of-the-art overview', *International Migration*, 40:5, 3–47.

Nye, J.P. (2004) *Soft Power: The Means to Success in the World Politics* (New York: Public Affairs).

O'Neil, K., Hamilton, K. and Papademetriou, D. (2005) *Migration in the Americas* (Geneva: Global Commission on International Migration).

OAS (2011) *SICREMI 2011 I: International Migration in the Americas: First Report of the Continuous Reporting System on International Migration in the Americas* (Washington, DC: Organization of American States).

OECD (1987) *The Future of Migration* (Paris: OECD).

OECD (1992) *Trends in International Migration* (Paris: OECD).

OECD (1997) *Trends in International Migration: Annual Report 1996* (Paris: OECD).

OECD (1998) *Trends in International Migration: Annual Report* (Paris: OECD).

OECD (1999) *Trends in International Migration: SOPEMI 1999 Edition* (Paris: OECD).

OECD (2001) *Trends in International Migration: Annual Report 2001* (Paris: OECD).

OECD (2004) *Trends in International Migration: Annual Report 2004* (Paris: OECD).

OECD (2006) *International Migration Outlook: Annual Report 2006* (Paris: OECD).

OECD (2007) *International Migration Outlook: Annual Report 2007* (Paris: OECD).

OECD (2010) *International Migration Outlook: SOPEMI 2010* (Paris: OECD).

OECD (2011a) *International Migration Outlook 2011: SOPEMI* (Paris: OECD).

OECD (2011b) *Education at a Glance 2011: OEDC Indicators.* www.oecd.org/dataoecd/61/2/48631582.pdf.

OECD (2012) *International Migration Outlook 2012* (Paris: OECD).

Ögelman, N. (2003) 'Documenting and Explaining the Persistence of Homeland Politics among Germany's Turks', *International Migration Review,* 37:1, 163–93.

Okoth, K. (2003) 'Kenya: What Role for Diaspora in Development? ' (Washington, DC: Migration Policy Institute) www.migrationinformation.org/feature/display.cfm?ID=150, accessed: 13 August 2003.

OMA (1989) *National Agenda for a Multicultural Australia* (Canberra: AGPS).

ONS (2004) *Focus on Ethnicity and Identity* (London: Office for National Statistics) www.statistics.gov.uk, accessed 15 March 2004.

Organisation of American States (2011) *International Migration in the Americas: First Report of the Continuous Reporting System on International Migration in the Americas [SICREMI]* (Washington, DC: OAS).

Oriol, P. (2007) 'Le droit de vote des résidents étrangers dans l'Union européenne', *Migrations Société,* 19:114, 83–97.

Oriol, P. and Vianna, P. (2007) 'Résidents étrangers et droit de vote', *Migrations Société,* 19:114, 37-46.

Orozco, M. and Rouse, R. (2007) *Migrant Hometown Associations and Opportunities for Development: a Global Perspective* (Washington, DC: Migration Information Source) http://migrationinformation.org, accessed 6 February 2007.

Orrenius, P. and Zavodny, M. (2010) *How Immigration Works for America.* Annual Report: Federal Reserve Bank of Dallas (Dallas: Federal Reserve Bank of Dallas).

Ortega, F. and Peri, G. (2009) *The Causes and Effects of International Migrations: Evidence from OECD Countries 1980–2005* (Cambridge, MA: NBER Working Paper No. 14833).

Oucho, J.O. (2006) 'Migration and refugees in Eastern Africa: a challenge for the East Africa Community' in Cross, C., Gelderblom, D., Roux, N. and Mafukidze, J. (eds) *Views on Migration in Sub-Saharan Africa* (Cape Town: HSRC Press) pp. 130–47.

Özden, Ç. and Schiff, M. (eds) (2005) *International Migration, Remittances, and the Brain Drain* (Washington, DC: The International Bank for Reconstruction and Development / The World Bank).

Paice, E. (2006) *Tip & Run: the Untold Tragedy of the Great War in Africa* (London: Weidenfeld and Nicolson).

Paine, S. (1974) *Exporting Workers: The Turkish Case* (Cambridge: Cambridge University Press).

Paoletti, E. (2010) *The Migration of Power and North-South Inequalities: The Case of Italy and Libya* (Basingstoke: Palgrave Macmillan).

Papademetriou, D.G. (1985) 'Illusions and Reality in International Migration: Migration and Development in post World War II Greece', *International Migration,* 23:2, 211–23.

Papademetriou, D.G. and Martin, P.L. (eds) (1991) *The Unsettled Relationship. Labor Migration and Economic Development* (New York: Greenwood Press).

Parekh, B. (2000) *Rethinking Multiculturalism: Cultural Diversity and Political Theory* (Basingstoke: Palgrave Macmillan).

Parekh, B. (2008) *A New Politics of Identity* (Basingstoke: Palgrave Macmillan).

Pargenter, A. (2008) *The New Frontiers of Jihad* (Philadelphia, PA: University of Pennsylvania Press).

Passaris, C. (1989) 'Immigration and the Evolution of Economic Theory', *International Migration,* 27:4, 525–42.

Passel, J. and Cohn, D.V. (2009) *Mexican Immigrants: How Many Come? How Many Leave?* (Washington, DC: Pew Hispanic Center).

Passel, J.S. and Cohn, D.V. (2011) 'Unauthorized Immigrant Population: National and State Trends 2010' (Washington DC: Pew Hispanic Center) http://pewhispanic.org/reports/report.php?ReportID=133, accessed 15 July 2011.

Pastore, F. (2007) *La politica migratoria italiana a una svolta* (Rome: Centro Studi di Politica Internazionale).

Pellegrino, A. (2000) 'Trends in International Migration in Latin America and the Caribbean', *International Social Science Journal,* 52:165, 395–408.

Penninx, R. (1982) 'A Critical Review of Theory and Practice: The Case of Turkey', *International Migration Review,* 16:4, 781–818.

Penninx, R., Berger, M. and Kraal, K. (eds) (2006) *The Dynamics of International Migration and Settlement in Europe* (Amsterdam: Amsterdam University Press).

Perez Vichich, N. (2005) 'El Mercosur y la Migración Internacional', Expert Group Meeting on International Migration and Development in Latin America and the Caribbean, Mexico City, 30 November–2 December 2005.

Pessar, P. and Mahler, S. (2003) 'Transnational migration: bringing gender in', *International Migration Review,* 37:3, 812–46.

Petersen, W. (1958) 'A General Typology of Migration', *American Sociological Review,* 23:3, 256–66.

Petras, J. and Veltmayer, H. (2000) 'Globalisation or imperialism?', *Cambridge Review of International Affairs,* 14:1, 1–15.

Pew Hispanic Centre (2011) *The Mexican-American Boom: Births Overtake Immigration* (Washington, DC: Pew Research Centre).

Pfahlmann, H. (1968) *Fremdarbeiter und Kriegsgefangene in der deutschen Kriegswirtschaft 1939–45* (Darmstadt: Wehr & Wissen).

Phillips, J. and Spinks, H. (2011) 'Boat arrivals in Australia since 1976' (Canberra: Australian Parliamentary Library).

Phillips, J., Klapdor, M. and Simon-Davies, J. (2010) 'Migration to Australia since federation: a guide to the statistics, Background Note' (Canberra: Australian Parliamentary Library).

Phillips, N. (2011a) 'Migration and the global economic crisis' in Phillips, N. (ed.) *Migration in the Global Political Economy* (Boulder, CO: Lynne Rienner).

Phillips, N. (ed.) (2011b) *Migration in the Global Political Economy* (Boulder, CO: Lynne Rienner).

Phizacklea, A. (1983) *One Way Ticket? Migration and Female Labour* (London: Routledge and Kegan Paul).

Phizacklea, A. (1998) 'Migration and globalisation: a feminist perspective' in Koser, K. and Lutz, H. (eds) *The New Migration in Europe* (London: Macmillan) pp. 21–38.

Phizacklea, A. (1990) *Unpacking the Fashion Industry: Gender, Racism and Class in Production* (London: Routledge).

Picquet, M., Pelligrino, A. and Papail, J. (1986) 'L'immigration au Venezuela', *Revue Européenne des Migrations Internationales,* 2:2.

PICUM (2010) *PICUM's Main Concerns about the Fundamental Rights of Undocumented Migrants in Europe* (Brussels: Platform for International Cooperation on Undocumented Migrants).

Pieke, F.N. (2011) 'Immigrant China' *Modern China,* 38:1, 40–77.

Piguet, E. and de Guchteneire, P. (eds) (2011) *Migration and Climate Change* (Cambridge: Cambridge University Press).

Piore, M. (1979) *Birds of Passage: Migrant Labor and Industrial Societies* (Cambridge: Cambridge University Press).

Piper, N. (2011) 'Towards a gendered political economy of migration' in Phillips, N. (ed.) *Migration in the Global Political Economy* (Boulder, CO: Lynne Rienner) pp. 61–82.

Plewa, P. (2006) 'How have regularization programs affected Spanish governmental efforts to integrate migrant populations' in Majtczak, O. (ed.) *The Fifth International Migration Conference* (Warsaw: Independent University of Business and Government).

Plewa, P. (2007) 'The Rise and Fall of Temporary Foreign Workers Policies: Lessons from Poland', *International Migration,* 45:2, 3–36.

Plewa, P. and Miller, M.J. (2005) 'Postwar and post-Cold War generations of European temporary foreign worker policies: implications from Spain', *Migraciones Internacionales,* 3:2, 58–83.

Poku, N. and Graham, D. (eds) (1998) *Redefining Security* (Westport, CT: Praeger).

Polanyi, K. (1944) *The Great Transformation: The Political and Economic Origins of Our Time* (New York: Farrar & Rinehart).

Polanyi, K. (2001) *The Great Transformation: the Political and Economic Origins of Our Time,* 2nd Beacon Paperback (Boston, MA: Beacon Press).

Ponte, S. and Gibbon, P. (2005) 'Quality standards, conventions, and the governance of global value chains', *Economy and Society,* 34:1, 1–31.

Portes, A. (1998) 'Social Capital: Its origins and applications in modern sociology', *Annual Review of Sociology,* 606–30.

Portes, A. (1999) 'Conclusion: towards a new world - the origins and effects of transnational activities', *Ethnic and Racial Studies,* 22:2, 463–77.

Portes, A. (2010) 'Migration and social change: some conceptual reflections', *Journal of Ethnic and Migration Studies,* 36:10, 1537–63.

Portes, A. and Bach, R.L. (1985) *Latin Journey: Cuban and Mexican Immigrants in the United States* (Berkeley, CA: University of Calfornia Press).

Portes, A. and Böröcz, J. (1989) 'Contemporary immigration: theoretical perspectives on its determinants and modes of incorporation', *International Migration Review,* 28:4, 606–30.

Portes, A. and Grosfoguel, R. (1994) 'Caribbean Diasporas: Migration and Ethnic Communities', *Annals of the American Academy of Political and Social Science,* 533,48–69.

Portes, A. and Rumbaut, R.G. (2006) *Immigrant America: a Portrait,* 3rd edn (Berkeley, CA: University of California Press).

Portes, A. and Zhou, M. (1993) 'The New 2nd-Generation - Segmented Assimilation and Its Variants' *Annals of the American Academy of Political and Social Science,* 53074–96.

Portes, A., Fernandez-Kelly, P. and Haller, W. (2005) 'Segmented assimilation on the ground: The new second generation in early adulthood', *Ethnic and Racial Studies,* 28:6, 1000–40.

Portes, A., Guarnizo, L.E. and Landolt, P. (1999) 'The study of transnationalism: pitfalls and promise of an emergent research field', *Ethnic and Racial Studies,* 22:2, 217–37.

Potts, L. (1990) *The World Labour Market: A History of Migration* (London: Zed Books).

Pratikshya, B. and Massey, D. S. (2009) 'Processes of internal and international migration from Chitwan, Nepal', *International Migration Review,* 43:3, 621–51.

Preibisch, K. (2010) 'Pick-Your-Own Labour: Migrant Workers and Flexibility in Canadian Agriculture', *International Migration Review,* 44:2, 404–41.

Preston, J. (2007) 'U.S. set for a crackdown on illegal hiring', *New York Times.* (New York). 8 August.

Price, C. (1963) *Southern Europeans in Australia* (Melbourne: Oxford University Press).

Productivity Commission (2010) *Population and Migration: Understanding the Numbers* Commission Research Paper (Melbourne: Productivity Commission).

Prost, A. (1966) 'L'immigration en France depuis cent ans' *Esprit,* 34:348.

Puentes, R., Canales, A., Rodríguez, H., Delgado-Wise, R. and Castles, S. (2010) *Towards an Assessment of Migration, Development and Human Rights Links: Conceptual Framework and New Strategic Indicators* (Mexico City: People's Global Action on Migration, Development and Human Rights) http://rimd. reduaz.mx/documentos_miembros/7081PuentesCanalesetal29102010.pdf.

Ranis, G. and Fei, J.H.C. (1961) 'A theory of economic development', *American Economic Review,* 51, 533–65.

Rath, J. (1988) 'La participation des immigrés aux élections locales aux Pays-Bas', *Revue Européenne des Migrations Internationales,* 4:3, 23-36.

Rath, J. (ed.) (2002) *Unravelling the Rag Trade: Immigrant Entrepreneurship in Seven World Cities* (Oxford: Berg).

Ratha, D., Mohapatra, S. and Silwal, A. (2009) *Migration and Remittance Trends 2009.* Migration and Development Brief 11 (Washington, DC: World Bank).

Ratha, D., Mohapatra, S. and Silwal, A. (2011) *Outlook for Remittance Flows 2010–11* (Washington, DC: World Bank).

Ravenstein, E.G. (1885) 'The Laws of Migration', *Journal of the Royal Statistical Society,* 48, 167–227.

Ravenstein, E.G. (1889) 'The Laws of Migration', *Journal of the Royal Statistical Society,* 52, 214–301.

Rawlinson, K. (2012) 'English Defence League to become political party...', *Independent,* 11 October (London) www.independent.co.uk/topic/EnglishDefenceLeague.

Regional Conference on Migration (2011) *Regional Conference on Migration: the Puebla Process* (San Jose Cosat Rica: Virtual Secretariat, Regional Conference on Migration) www.rcmvs.org/Descripcion.htm, accessed 27 January 2011.

Reichert, J.S. (1981) 'The migrant syndrome: Seasonal U.S. labor migration and rural development in central Mexico', *Human Organization,* 40, 56–66.

Reitz, J. G. (1998) *Warmth of the Welcome: The Social Causes of Economic Success for Immigrants in Different Nations and Cities* (Boulder, CO: Westview Press).

Reitz, J.G. (2007a) 'Immigrant employment success in Canada, Part I: Individual and contextual causes', *Journal of International Migration and Integration,* 8:1, 11–36.

Reitz, J.G. (2007b) 'Immigrant Employment Success in Canada, Part II: Understanding the Decline', *Journal of International Migration and Integration,* 8:1, 37–62.

Rex, J. (1986) *Race and Ethnicity* (Milton Keynes: Open University Press).

Rex, J. and Mason, D. (eds) (1986) *Theories of Race and Ethnic Relations* (Cambridge: Cambridge University Press).

Reyneri, E. (2001) *Migrants' Involvement in Irregular Employment in the Mediterranean Countries of the European Union* (Geneva: International Labour Organization).

Reyneri, E. (2003) 'Immigration and the underground economy in new receiving South European countries: manifold negative effects, manifold deep-rooted causes', *International Review of Sociology,* 13:1, 117–43.

Reyneri, E. and Fullin, G. (2010) 'Labour market penalties of new immigrants in new and old receiving West European countries', *International Migration,* 49:1, 31–57.

Rhoades, R.E. (1979) 'From caves to main street: Return migration and the transformations of a Spanish village', *Papers in Anthropology,* 20:1, 57–74.

Ricca, S. (1990) *Migrations internationales en Afrique* (Paris: L'Harmattan).

Richards, A.O. (1999) *International Trafficking in Women to the United States: A Contemporary Manifestation of Slavery and Organized Crime* (Washington, DC: Center for the Study of Intelligence).

Ricks, T.E. (2007) *Fiasco* (New York: Penguin Books).

Rico, M.N. (2006) 'Las Mujeres Latinoamericanas en la Migración Internacional' *II Foro Social Mundial de las Migraciones* (Madrid: 22–24 June)

Roberts, S. (2010) 'Census figures challenge views of race and ethnicity', *New York Times,* 21 January.

Romero, F. (1993) 'Migration as an issue in European interdependence and integration: the case of Italy' in Milward, A., Lynch, F., Renieri, R., Romero, F. and Sorensen, V. (eds) *The Frontier of National Sovereignty* (London: Routledge).

Rosenberg, C.D. (2006) *Policing Paris : the Origins of Modern Immigration Control Between the Wars* (Ithaca, NY and London: Cornell University Press).

Rosewarne, S. (2012) 'Temporary international labor migration and development in South and Southeast Asia', *Feminist Economics,* 18:2, 63–90.

Rostow, W.W. (1960) *The Stages of Economic Growth: a Non-Communist Manifesto* (Cambridge: Cambridge University Press).

Roy, O. (1994) *The Failure of Political Islam* (Cambridge, MA: Harvard University Press).

Roy, O. (2003) 'Euroislam: The Jihad Within?' *The National Interest,*63–73.

Rubenstein, H. (1992) 'Migration. Development and Remittances in Rural Mexico', *International Migration,* 30:2, 1992.

Ruiz, I. and Vargas-Silva, C. (2009) 'Another consequence of the economic crisis: a decrease in migrants' remittances', *Applied Financial Economics,* 20:1, 171–82.

Rusconi, S. (2010) 'Italy's Migration Experience': Migration Citizenship Education. www.migrationeducation.org/38.1.html?&rid=178&cHash=b18ff335ad7 4f6e52754cfcb43318922, accessed 8 February 2012.

Russell, S.S. (1992) 'Migrant Remittances and Development', *International Migration,* 30(3–4), 267–87.

Rycs, J.F. (2005) 'Le "Sponsorship" peut-il encore canaliser les flux migratoires dan les pays du Golfe? Le cas de Emirats Arabes Unis' in Jaber, H. and Métrai, F. (eds) *Mondes en mouvements. Migrants et migrations au Moyen-Orient au tournant du XXIe siècle* (Beyrouth: Institut Français du Proche Orient IFPO).

Safire, W. (1993) *Safire's New Political Dictionary: the Definitive Guide to the New Language of Politics* (New York: Random House).

Safran, W. (1991) 'Diasporas in Modern Societies: Myths of Homeland and Return', *Diaspora,* 1:1, 83–99.

Salazar Anaya, D. (2010) 'Tres Momentos en la Inmigración Internacional en México, 1880–1946' in Rodríguez Chávez, E. (ed.) *Extranjeros en México: Continuidades y Aproximaciones* (México, DF: Instituto Nacional de Migración) 51–87.

Sassen, S. (1988) *The Mobility of Labour and Capital* (Cambridge: Cambridge University Press).

Sassen, S. (2001) *The Global City : New York, London, Tokyo*, 2nd edn (Princeton, NJ: Princeton University Press).

Schain, M. (2008) *The Politics of Immigration in France, Britain, and the United States : A Comparative Study* (New York: Palgrave Macmillan).

Schama, S. (2006) *Rough Crossings: Britain, the Slaves and the American Revolution* (London: BBC Books).

Schaub, M.L. (2012) 'Lines across the desert: mobile phone use and mobility in the context of trans-Saharan migration', *Information Technology for Development,* 18:2, 126–44.

Scheele, J. (2010) 'Traders, saints, and irrigation: Reflections on Saharan connectivity', *Journal of African History,* 51:03, 281–300.

Scheele, J. (2012) *Smugglers and Saints of the Sahara : Regional Connectivity in the Twentieth Century* (Cambridge: Cambridge University Press).

Scheuer, M. (2008) *Marching Toward Hell* (New York: Free Press).

Schielke, S. and Graw, K. (eds) (2012) *The Global Horizon: Migratory Expectations in Africa and the Middle East* (Leuven: Leuven University Press).

Schierup, C.U. and Alund, A. (1987) *Will they still be dancing?* (Stockholm: Almquist and Wiksell International).

Schierup, C.U. and Castles, S. (2011) 'Migration, minorities and welfare' in Phillips, N. (ed.) *Migration in the Global Political Economy* (Boulder and London: Lynne Rienner) pp. 15–40.

Schierup, C.U., Hansen, P. and Castles, S. (2006) *Migration, Citizenship and the European Welfare State: A European Dilemma* (Oxford: Oxford University Press).

Schiff, M. (1994) *How Trade, Aid, and Remittances Affect International Migration* (Washington: World Bank, International Economics Department).

Schmidt, C. and Shanker, T. (2011) *Counter Strike:The Untold Story of America's Secret Campaign Against Al-Qaeda* (New York: Times Books).

Schnapper, D. (1991) 'A host country of immigrants that does not know itself', *Diaspora,* 1:3, 353–64.

Schnapper, D. (1994) *La Communauté des Citoyens* (Paris: Gallimard).

Schrover, M., Van der Leun, J. and Quispel, C. (2007) 'Niches, Labour Market Segregation, Ethnicity and Gender', *Journal of Ethnic and Migration Studies,* 33:4, 529–40.

SCIRP (1981) *Staff Report* (Washington, DC: Select Commission on Immigration and Refugee Policy).

Seccombe, I.J. (1986) 'Immigrant Workers in an Emigrant Economy', *International Migration,* 24: 2.

Semyonov, M. and Lewin-Epstein, N. (1987) *Hewers of Wood and Drawers of Water* (Ithaca, NY: ILR Press).

Sen, A. (1999) *Development as Freedom* (Oxford: Oxford University Press).

Seol, D.H. (2001) 'Situation of and Measures on Undocumented Foreign Workers in Korea (in Korean)', *Shinhak Sasang*:113, 49–75.

Seton-Watson, H. (1977) *Nations and States* (London: Methuen).

Shain, Y. and Barth, A. (2003) 'Diasporas of International Relations Theory', *International Organization,* 57:3, 449–79.

Shanker, T. and Kulish, N. (2008) 'US Ties Europe's Safety to Afghanistan', *The New York Times, 11 February.*

Shaw, M. (2000) *Theory of the Global State: Globality as Unfinished Revolution* (Cambridge: Cambridge University Press).

Shenon, P. (2008) *The Commission* (New York: Hachette Book Group USA).

Shimpo, M. (1995) 'Indentured migrants from Japan' in Cohen, R. (ed.) *The Cambridge Survey of World Migration* (Cambridge: Cambridge University Press).

Simon, P. (2008) 'The choice of ignorance: the debate on ethnic and racial statistics in France', *French Politics, Culture & Society,* 26:1, 7–31.

Sin Fronteras (2011) *Crisis en Política Migratoria Mexicana.* Boletin de Prensa, 25 May (México DF: Sin Fronteras IAP).

Singer, A., Hardwick, S.W. and Brettell, C.B. (2008) 'Twenty-First Century Gateways: Immigrants in Suburban America', *Migration Information Source* (Washington, DC: Migration Policy Institute) www.migrationinformation.org/Feature/display.cfm?ID=680, accessed 23 February 2012.

Sinn, E. (ed.) (1998) *The Last Half Century of Chinese Overseas* (Hong Kong: Hong Kong University Press).

Sjaastad, A.H. (1962) 'The Costs and Returns of Human Migration', *Journal of Political Economy,* 70:5, 80–93.

Skeldon, R. (1990) *Population Mobility in Developing Countries: A Reinterpretation* (London: Belhaven Press).

Skeldon, R. (1992) 'International Migration within and from the East and Southeast Asian Region: A Review Essay', *Asian and Pacific Migration Journal,* 1:1, 19–63.

Skeldon, R. (1997) *Migration and Development: A Global Perspective* (Harlow: Addison Wesley Longman).

Skeldon, R. (2006a) 'Interlinkages between internal and international migration and development in the Asian region', *Population, Space and Place*:12, 15–30.

Skeldon, R. (2006b) 'Recent trends in migration in East and Southeast Asia', *Asian and Pacific Migration Journal,* 15:2, 277–93.

Skeldon, R. (2012) 'Migration Transitions Revisited: Their Continued Relevance for The Development of Migration Theory', *Population, Space and Place,* 18:2, 154–66.

Skerry, P. and Rockwell, S.J. (1998) 'The Cost of a Tighter Border: People-Smuggling Networks', *Los Angeles Times,* 3 May.

Smith, A.D. (1986) *The Ethnic Origins of Nations* (Oxford: Blackwell).

Smith, A.D. (1991) *National Identity* (Harmondsworth: Penguin).

Smith, D.P. and King, R. (2012) 'Special Issue: Re-Making Migration Theory: Transitions, Intersections and Cross-Fertilisations', *Population, Space and Place,* 18:2, i–ii, 127–224.

Smith, J. (2006) *Guatemala: Economic Migrants Replace Political Refugees.* www.migrationinformation.org/Profiles/display.cfm?id=392, accessed 11 November 2011.

Smith, J.P. and Edmonston, B. (eds) (1997) *The New Americans: Economic, Demographic and Fiscal Effects of Immigration* (Washington, DC: National Academy Press).

Smith, R. (2003) 'Migrant Membership as an Instituted Process: Transnationalization, the State and Extra-Territorial Conduct of Mexican Politics', *International Migration Review,* 37:2, 297–343.

Snyder, T. (2010) *Bloodlands:Europe Between Hitler and Stalin* (New York: Basic Books).

Solomos, J. (2003) *Race and Racism in Britain,* 3rd edn (Basingstoke: Palgrave Macmillan).

Somerville, W., Sriskandarajah, D. and Latorre, M. (2009) 'United Kingdom: A Reluctant Country of Immigration' (Washington, DC: Migration Information Source) www.migrationinformation.org/Profiles/display.cfm?ID=736, accessed 28 February 2012.

Soutphommasane, T. (2010) *India confronts Australia over racism* (London: The Guardian) www.guardian.co.uk/commentisfree/2010/jan/07/india-australia-racism-students-murder, accessed 9 March 2012.

Soysal, Y.N. (1994) *Limits of Citizenship: Migrants and Postnational Membership in Europe* (Chicago and London: University of Chicago Press).

Spiga, S. (2005) 'Aménageurs et Migrants dans les Villes du Grand Sud Algérien', *Autrepart,* 36:4, 81–103.

Stalker, P. (2000) *Workers without Frontiers* (Geneva, London and Boulder, CO: International Labour Office and Lynne Rienner Publishers).

Stanton-Russell, S. (2006) 'Politics and Ideology in Policy Formulation: The Case of Kuwait' in Messina, A. and Lahav, G. (eds) *The Migration Reader* (Boulder, CO: Lynne Rienner) pp. 246–66.

Stark, O. (1978) *Economic-Demographic Interactions in Agricultural Development: The Case of Rural-to-Urban Migration* (Rome: FAO).

Stark, O. (1980) 'On the Role of Urban-to-Rural Remittances in Rural Development', *Journal of Development Studies,* 16369–74.

Stark, O. (1991) *The Migration of Labor* (Cambridge and Oxford: Blackwell).

Stark, O. (2009) 'Reasons for Remitting', *World Economics,* 10:3, 147–57.

Stark, O. and Levhari, D. (1982) 'On Migration and Risk in LDCs', *Economic Development and Cultural Change*: 31, 191–6.

Stark, O. and Bloom, D.E. (1985) 'The New Economics of Labor Migration', *American Economic Review,* 75, 173–8.

Stark, O., Helmenstein, C. and Prskawetz, A. (1997) 'A brain gain with a brain drain', *ECOLET,* 55:2, 227–34.

Statewatch (2010) 'Interior Minister to Press for Punishment of EU Nationals Residing Illegally' (Statewatch) www.statewatch.org/news/2010/sep/03italy-eu-nationals.htm, accessed 8 February 2012.

Statistics Bureau Japan (2012) *e-Stat: Portal Site of Official Statistics of Japan (in Japanese)* www.e-stat.go.jp/SG1/estat/eStatTopPortalE.do, accessed 20 January 2012.

Statistics Canada (2010) *Census 2006* (Ottawa: Statistics Canada) www12.statcan.gc.ca/census-recensement/2006/dp-pd/hlt/97-550/Index.cfm?Page=INDX&LANG=Eng, accessed 1 September 2011.

Stefanova, B. (2007) 'Voting a la carte: Electoral Support for the Radical Right in the 2005 Bulgarian Elections', *Politics in Central Europe,* 2:2, 38–70.

Steinberg, S. (1981) *The Ethnic Myth: Race Ethnicity and Class in America* (Boston, MA: Beacon Press).

Stiglitz, J.E. (2002) *Globalization and its Discontents* (Harmondsworth: Penguin).

Stirn, H. (1964) *Ausländische Arbeiter im Betrieb* (Frechen/Cologne: Bartmann).

Stola, D. (2001) 'Poland' in Wallace, C. and Stola, D. (eds) *Patterns of Migration in Central Europe* (Basingstoke: Palgrave Macmillan).

Strozza, S. and Venturini, A. (2002) 'Italy is no longer a country of emigration. Foreigners in Italy: how many, where do they come from' in Rotte, R. and Stein, P. (eds) *Migration Policy and the Economy: International Experiences* (Munich: Hans Seidel Stiftung).

Suhrke, A. and Klink, F. (1987) 'Contrasting patterns of Asian refugee movements: the Vietnamese and Afghan syndromes' in Fawcett, J.T. and Carino, B.V. (eds) *Pacific Bridges: The New Immigration from Asia and the Pacific* (New York: Center for Migration Studies).

Surak, K. (2013) 'The migration industry and developmental states in East Asia' in Gammeltoft-Hansen, T. and Sorensen, N.N. (eds) *The Migration Industry and the Commercialization of International Migration* (London and New York: Routledge) pp. 89–110.

Surk, B. and Abbot, S. (2008) 'India wants oil-rich Emirates to pay workers better wages', *Sunday News Journal* (Wilmington, DE).

Süssmuth, R. (2001) *Zuwanderung gestalten, Integration fördern: Bericht der unabhängigen Kommission 'Zuwanderung'* German Government Report (Berlin: Bundesminister des Innern).

Suzanne, G. (2012) 'US Election: Obama scored big with single women', *Guardian Weekly*.

Sze, L.-S. (2007) *New Immigrant Labour from Mainland China in Hong Kong* (Hong Kong: Asian Labour Update) www.amrc.org.hk/alu_article/discrimination_at_work/new_immigrant_labour_from_mainland_china_in_hong_kong, accessed 23 March, 2007.

Tapinos, G. (1984) 'Seasonal workers in French agriculture' in Martin, P.L. (ed.) *Migrant Labor in Agriculture* (Davis: Gianni Foundation of Agricultural Economics).

Tapinos, G.P. (1990) *Development Assistance Strategies and Emigration Pressure in Europe and Africa* (Washington, DC: Commission for the Study of International Migration and Co-operative Economic Development).

Tavernise, S. and Gebeloff, R. (2010) 'Immigrants Make Paths to Suburbia, Not Cities', *New York Times*, 14 December.

Taylor, E. (1984) 'Egyptian migration and peasant wives', *Merip Reports,* 124, 3–10.

Taylor, J.E. (1999) 'The new economics of labour migration and the role of remittances in the migration process', *International Migration,* 37:1, 63–88.

Taylor, J.E. and Wyatt, T.J. (1996) 'The shadow value of migrant remittances, income and inequality in a household-farm economy', *Journal of Development Studies,* 32:6, 899–912.

Taylor, J.E., Arango, J., Hugo, G., Kouaouci, A., Massey, D.S. and Pellegrino, A. (1996a) 'International migration and national development', *Population Index,* 62:2, 181–212.

Taylor, J.E., Arango, J., Hugo, G., Kouaouci, A., Massey, D.S. and Pellegrino, A. (1996b) 'International migration and community development', *Population Index,* 62:3, 397–418.

Taylor, P., Gonzalez-Barrera, A., Passel, J. and Lopez, M.H. (2012) *An Awakened Giant: The Hispanic Electorate is Likely to Double by 2030* (Washington, DC: Pew Hispanic Center).

Tekeli, I. (1994) 'Involuntary displacement and the problem of the resettlement in Turkey from the Ottoman Empire to the present' in Shami, S. (ed.) *Population Displacement and Resettlement: Development and Conflict in the Middle East* (New York: Center for Migration Studies).

Terrazas, A. (2010) *US in Focus: Mexican Immigrants in the United States*. www.migrationinformation.org/USFocus/display.cfm?ID=767, accessed 10 October 2010.

Tetreault, D.V. (2011) 'Mexican peasant and indigenous movements. Adaptation and resistance to neoliberalism' in Covarrubias, H.M., Soto Esquivel, R. and Záyago Lau, E. (eds) *El Desarrollo Perdido: Avatares del Capitalismo Neoliberal in Tiempos de Crisis* (Mexico City: Miguel Angel Porrua) pp. 281–302.

The Economist (2010) 'Southern misery', *The Economist,* 14 January.

Thiollet, H. (2010) 'Nationalisme d'État et nationalisme ordinaire en Arabie Saoudite: la nation saoudienne et ses immigrés', *Raisons politiques,* 37: février 2010, 89–102.

Thränhardt, D. (1996) 'European migration from East to West: present patterns and future directions', *New Community,* 22:2, 227–42.

Tichenor, D.J. (2002) *Dividing Lines* (Princeton: Princeton University Press).

Tirman, J. (2004) *The Maze of Fear:Security and Migration after 9/11* (New York/London: The New Press).

Tirtosudarmo, R. (2001) 'Demography and security: transmigration policy in Indonesia' in Weiner, M. and Russell, S.S. (eds) *Demography and National Security* (New York and Oxford: Berghahn Books) pp. 199–227.

Todaro, M.P. (1969) 'A model of labor migration and urban unemployment in less-developed countries', *American Economic Review,* 59,138–48.

Todaro, M.P. and Maruszko, L. (1987) 'Illegal migration and US immigration reform: A conceptual framework', *Population and Development Review,* 13:1, 101–14.

Tomas, K. and Münz, R. (2006) *Labour Migrants Unbound? EU Enlargement Transitional Measures and Labour Market Effects* (Stockholm: Institute for Futures Study).

Torpey, J. (2007) 'Leaving: A Comparative View' in Green, N. and Weil, F. (eds) *Citizenship and Those Who Leave* (Urbana: University of Illinois Press) pp. 113–32.

Triandafyllidou, A. and Lazarescu, D. (2009) *The Impacts of the Recent Global Economic Crisis on Migration. Preliminary Insights from the South-eastern Borders of the EU (Greece)* (San Domenico Fiesole: European University Institute, RSCAS).

Tribalat, M. (1995) *Faire France: Une enquête sur les Immigrés et leurs Enfants* (Paris: La Découverte).

UN Population Division (2010) *International Migration 2009: Graphs and Maps from the 2009 Wallchart* (New York: UN Population Division).

UN Treaty Collection (2011) *International Convention on the Protection of the Rights of All Migrant Workers and Members of their Families: Status of Ratification, Declarations and Reservations* (New York: United Nations).

UNDESA (2009) *Trends in International Migrant Stock: The 2008 Revision* (New York: United Nations Department of Economic and Social Affairs, Population Division) http://esa.un.org/migration/index.asp?panel=1.

UNDESA (2011) *World Population Prospects: the 2010 Revision* (New York: United Nations Department of Economic and Social Affairs) http://esa.un.org/unpd/wpp/Analytical-Figures/htm/fig_1.htm, accessed 16 November 2012.

UNDP (2009) *Overcoming Barriers: Human Mobility and Development.* Human Development Report 2009 (New York City: Human Development Report 2009, UNDP) http://hdr.undp.org/en/reports/global/hdr2009/.

UNHCR (1995) *The State of the World's Refugees: In Search of Solutions* (Oxford: Oxford University Press).

UNHCR (2000) *The State of the World's Refugees: Fifty Years of Humanitarian Action* (Oxford: Oxford University Press).

UNHCR (2002) *Afghan Humanitarian Update No. 63* (Geneva: UNHCR).

UNHCR (2004) *Protracted Refugee Situations* (Geneva: UNHCR Executive Committee of the High Commissioner's Programme).

UNHCR (2006) *Refugees by Numbers 2006 Edition.* (Geneva: UNHCR) www.unhcr.org/basics/BASICS/3b028097c.html#Numbers, accessed 31 July 2007.

UNHCR (2007a) *2006 Global Trends: Refugees, Asylum-Seekers, Internally Displaced and Stateless Persons* (Geneva: United Nations High Commission for Refugees: Division of Operational Services) www.unhcr.org/statistics/STATISTICS/4676a71d4.pdf.

UNHCR (2007b) *Asylum Levels and Trends in Industrialized Countries, 2006* (Geneva: UNHCR).

UNHCR (2011a) *2011 UNHCR Country Operations Profile – Colombia.* (Geneva: United Nations High Commissioner for Refugees) www.unhcr.org/cgi-bin/texis/vtx/page?page=49e492ad6&submit=GO, accessed 13 December 2011.

UNHCR (2011b) 'Statistical Yearbook 2010' (Geneva: United Nations High Commissioner for Refugees).

UNHCR (2011c) *Asylum applications in industrialized countries jump 17 per cent in first-half 2011* (Geneva: United Nations High Commissioner for Refugees) www.unhcr.org/4e9d42ed6.html, accessed 14 March 2012.

UNHCR (2011d) *Global Trends 2010* (Geneva: United Nations High Commissioner for Refugees) www.unhcr.org/4dfa11499.html, accessed 6 September 2011.

UNHCR (2011e) *The 1951 Convention Relating to the Status of Refugees and its 1967 Protocol* (Geneva: United Nations High Commissioner for Refugees) www.unhcr.org/4ec262df9.html.

UNHCR (2011f) *UNHCR Statistical Database Online* (Geneva: United Nations High Commissioner for Refugees).

UNHCR (2011g) *Asylum Levels and Trends in Industrialized Countries 2010* (Geneva: United Nations High Commissioner for Refugees).

UNHCR (2012a) *2012 UNHCR Country Operations Profile – Iraq* (Geneva: UNHCR) www.unhcr.org/pages/49e486426.html, accessed 24 July 2012.

UNHCR (2012b) *2012 UNHCR Country Operations Profile – Sudan* (Geneva: UNHCR)www.unhcr.org/cgi-bin/texis/vtx/page?page=49e483b76&submit=GO, accessed 24 July 2012.

UNHCR (2012c) *2012 UNHCR Country Operations Profile – Tanzania* (Geneva: UNHCR) www.unhcr.org/pages/49e45c736.html, accessed 25 July 2012.

UNHCR (2012d) *Global Trends 2011* (Geneva: United Nations High Commissioner for Refugees) www.unhcr.org/4fd6f87f9.html.

United Nations Treaty Collection (2011) *Convention relating to the Status of Refugees: Status of Ratification, Declarations and Reservations.* http://treaties.

un.org/pages/ViewDetailsII.aspx?&src=TREATY&mtdsg_no=V~2&chapter= 5&Temp=mtdsg2&lang=en, accessed 27 December 2011.

UNODC (2006) *Trafficking in Persons: Global Patterns* (Vienna: United Nations Office on Drugs and Crime).

UNODC (2009) *Global Report on Trafficking in Persons* (Vienna: United Nations Office on Drugs and Crime).

US Census Bureau (2011a) *The Foreign Born From Latin America and the Caribbean: 2010* American Community Survey Briefs: US Census Bureau) www. census.gov/prod/2011pubs/acsbr10-15.pdf, accessed 23 February 2012.

US Census Bureau (2011b) *Overview of Race and Hispanic Origins* (Washington, DC: US Census Bureau) www.census.gov/prod/cen2010/briefs/c2010br-02. pdf, accessed 23 February 2012.

US Department of Labor (1989) *The Effects of Immigration on the US Economy and Labor Market* US Government Document (Washington, DC: US Department of Labor).

USCR (2001) *World Refugee Survey 2001* (Washington, DC: US Committee for Refugees).

USCR (2004) *World Refugee Survey 2004* (Washington, DC: US Committee for Refugees).

USCRI (2007) *Country Report: USA* (Washington, DC: US Committee for Refugees and Immigrants) www.refugees.org/countryreports.aspx?subm= &ssm=&cid=1607, accessed 27 April 2007.

USDS (2006) *Sierra Leone: Country Reports on Human Rights Practices 2006* (Washington, DC: US Department of States).

USDS (2007) *2007 Trafficking in Persons Report* (Washington, DC: US Department of States).

USINS (1999) *Statistical Yearbook of the Immigration and Naturalization Service 1997* (Washington, DC: US Immigration and Naturalization Service).

Vaisse, J. (2010) 'Denying Eurabia' *Foreign Policy Magazine* (see http://www. brusselsjournal.com/node/4261).

van Amersfoort, H. (2011) *How the Dutch Government stimulated the unwanted migration from Suriname*, IMI Working Paper 47 (Oxford: International Migration Institute (IMI), University of Oxford) www.imi.ox.ac.uk/publications/ working_papers

Van Hear, N. (1998) *New Diasporas: the Mass Exodus, Dispersal and Regrouping of Migrant Communities* (London: UCL Press).

Van Hear, N. (2004) 'Diasporas, Remittances, Development, and Conflict' *Migration Information Source, June 1, 2003* (Washington, DC: Migration Policy Institute).

van Tubergen, F., Maas, I. and Flap, H. (2004) 'The economic incorporation of immigrants in 18 western societies: Origin, destination, and community effects', *American Sociological Review*, 69:5, 704–27.

Vasta, E. (1993) 'Immigrant women and the politics of resistance', *Australian Feminist Studies,* 185–23.

Vasta, E. (1999) 'Multicultural Politics and Resistance: Migrants Unite?' in Hage, G. and Couch, R. (eds) *The Future of Australian Multiculturalism* (Sydney: RIHSS Sydney University)

Vasta, E. (2007) 'From ethnic minorities to ethnic majority policy: multiculturalism and the shift to assimilationism in the Netherlands', *Ethnic and Racial Studies,* 30:5, 713–40.

Vasta, E. and Castles, S. (eds) (1996) *The Teeth are Smiling: The Persistence of Racism in Multicultural Australia* (Sydney: Allen & Unwin).

Vasta, E., Rando, G., Castles, S. and Alcorso, C. (1992) 'The Italo-Australian community on the Pacific rim' in Castles, S. (ed.) *Australia's Italians* (Sydney: Allen & Unwin).

Vecoli, R.J. (1964) 'Contadini in Chicago: A Critique of The Uprooted', *Journal of American History,* 51:3, 404–17.

Veltmayer, H. (2010) 'The global crisis and Latin America', *Globalizations,* 7:1, 217–33.

Verbunt, G. (1985) 'France' in Hammar, T. (ed.) *European Immigration Policy: A Comparative Study* (Cambridge: Cambridge University Press).

Vertovec, S. (1999) 'Conceiving and researching transnationalism', *Ethnic and Racial Studies,* 22:2, 445–62.

Vertovec, S. (2004) 'Migrant transnationalism and modes of transformation', *International Migration Review,* 38:3, 970–1001.

Vigneswaran, D. (2012) 'Experimental Data Collection Methods and Migration Governance' in Berriane, M. and de Haas, H. (eds) *African Migrations Research: Innovative Methods and Methodologies* (Trenton, NJ: Africa World Press) www.imi.ox.ac.uk/pdfs/research-projects-pdfs/african-migrations-workshops-pdfs/rabat-workshop-2008/african-migrations-innovative-methods-and-methodologies 133-172.

Vogel, D. (2009) 'Size and Development of Irregular Migration to the EU': Comparative Policy brief CLANDESTINO project) http://clandestino.eliamep.gr/wp-content/uploads/2009/12/clandestino_policy_brief_comparative_size-of-irregular-migration.pdf, accessed 17 July 2012.

Vogler, M. and Rotte, R. (2000) 'The effects of development on migration: Theoretical issues and new empirical evidence', *Journal of Population Economics,* 13:3, 485–508.

Vono de Vilhena, D. (2011) 'Panorama Migratorio en España, Ecuador y Colombia a Partir de las Estadísticas Locales' in Martínez Pizarro, J. (ed.) *Migración Internacional en América Latina y el Caribe - Nuevas Tendencias, Nuevos Enfoques* (Santiago de Chile: CEPAL) pp. 27–98.

Waldinger, R.D. (1996) *Still the Promised City? African-Americans and New Immigrants in Postindustrial New York* (Cambridge, MA, and London: Harvard University Press).

Waldinger, R.D. and Lichter, M.I. (2003) *How the Other Half Works: Immigration and the Social Organization of Labor* (Berkeley, CA, and London: University of California Press).

Waldinger, R.D., Aldrich, H. and Ward, R. (1990) *Ethnic Entrepreneurs: Immigrant Business in Industrial Societies* (Newbury Park, CA, London, New Delhi: Sage Publications).

Wallace, C. and Stola, D. (eds) (2001) *Patterns of Migration in Central Europe* (Basingstoke: Palgrave Macmillan).

Wallerstein, I. (1974) *The Modern World System I, Capitalist Agriculture and the Origins of the European World Economy in the Sixteenth Century* (New York: Academic Press).

Wallerstein, I. (1980) *The Modern World System II, Mercantilism and the Consolidation of the European World-Economy, 1600–1750* (New York: Academic Press).

Wallerstein, I. (1984) *The Politics of the World Economy: The States, the Movements, and the Civilisations* (Cambridge: Cambridge University Press).

Wallman, S. (1986) 'Ethnicity and boundary processes' in Rex, J. and Mason, D. (eds) *Theories of Race and Ethnic Relations* (Cambridge: Cambridge University Press).

Wang, G. (1997) *Global History and Migrations* (Boulder, CO: Westview Press).

Wasem, R.E. (2007) *Immigration Reform: Brief Synthesis of Issue* (Washington, DC: Congressional Research Service).

Weber, M. (1968) *Economy and Society* (New York: Bedminister Press).

Wei, Y.-l. and Chang, S.C. (2011) 26 July 'Taiwan, Philippines sign MOU on hiring laborers' *Focus Taiwan*. http://focustaiwan.tw/ShowNews/WebNews_Detail.aspx?Type=aALL&ID=201107260042, accessed 22 January 2012.

Weil, P. (1991a) 'Immigration and the rise of racism in France: the contradictions of Mitterrand's policies', *French Society and Politics,* 93–4.

Weil, P. (1991b) *La France et ses Étrangers* (Paris: Calmann-Levy).

Weil, P. (2002) 'Towards a Coherent Policy of Co-Development', *International Migration* 40:3, 41–56.

Weiner, M. and Hanami, T. (eds) (1998) *Temporary Workers or Future Citizens? Japanese and U.S. Migration Policies* (New York: New York University Press).

Weiss, L. (1997) 'Globalization and the myth of the powerless state', *New Left Review*: 225, 3–27.

Werner, H. (1973) *Freizügigkeit der Arbeitskräfte und die Wanderungsbewegungen in den Ländern der Eurpäischen Gemeinschaft* (Nuremburg: Institut für Arbeitsmarkt-und Berufsforschungl).

White, G. (2011) *Climate Change and Migration* (Oxford: Oxford University Press).

Whitehouse, B. (2012) *Migrants and Strangers in an African City: Exile, Dignity, Belonging* (Bloomington: Indiana University Press).

Wieviorka, M. (1995) *The Arena of Racism* (London: Sage).

Wihtol de Wenden, C. (1988) *Les Immigrés et la Politique: Cent-cinquante Ans d'Évolution* (Paris: Presses de la FNSP).

Wihtol de Wenden, C. and Leveau, R. (2001) *La Beurgeoisie: les trois ages de la vie associative issue de l'immigration* (Paris: CNRS Editions).

Wikipedia (2013) *English Defence League* (USA: Wikipedia Foundation) http://en.wikipedia.org/wiki/English_Defence_League, accessed 13 March 2013.

Wilkinson, R. and Pickett, K. (2010) *The Spirit Level: Why Equality is Better for Everyone* (Harmondsworth: Penguin).

Witte, J. (2012) *Turks in Germany Fear Racially motivated Murders* (Hamburg: Spiegel Online International) www.spiegel.de/international/germany/0,1518,808949,00.html, accessed 9 March 2012.

Wooden, M. (1994) 'The economic impact of immigration' in Wooden, M., Holton, R., Hugo, G. and Sloan, J. (eds) *Australian Immigration: A Survey of the Issues*, 2nd edn (Canberra: AGPS).

World Bank (2006) *Global Economic Prospects 2006: Economic Implications of Remittances and Migration* (Washington, DC: World Bank).

World Bank (2007) *Remittance Trends 2006* (Washington, DC: Migration and Remittances Team, Development Prospects Group, World Bank).

World Bank (2011a) *Migration and Remittances Factbook 2011* (Washington, DC: World Bank).

World Bank (2011b) *Workers' Remittances and Compensation of Employees, Received (% of GDP)* http://data.worldbank.org/indicator/BX.TRF.PWKR.DT.GD.ZS/countries?display=default, accessed 5 December, 2011.

Wüst, A. (2000) 'New Citizens – New Voters? Political Preferences and Voting Intentions of Naturalized Germans: A Case Study in Progress', *International Migration Review,* 34:2, 560–7.

Wüst, A. (2002) *Wie Wählen Neubürger?* (Opladen: Leske & Budrich).

Yang, D. (2011) 'Migrant Remittances', *Journal of Economic Perspectives,* 25:3, 129–51.

Yue, C.S. (2011) *Foreign Labor in Singapore: Trends, Policies, Impacts, and Challenges.* Discussion Paper Series. http://dirp3.pids.gov.ph/ris/dps/pidsdps1124.pdf, accessed 29 May 2013.

Zabludovsky, K. (2012) 'A closed consulate may limit Venezuelan votes in the U.S.', *New York Times,* 2 October.

Zachariah, K.C., Mathew, E.T. and Rajan, S.I. (2001) 'Impact of Migration on Kerala's Economy and Society', *International Migration,* 39:1, 63–88.

Zaiotti, R. (2005) 'From Engagement to Deadlock: A Regional Analysis of Refugee policies in the Middle East Between the Two 'Gulf Crises' (1990–2003)' in Jaber, H. and Métrai, F. (eds) *Mondes en mouvements. Migrants et migrations au Moyen-Orient au tournant du XXIe siècle* (Beyrouth: Institut Français du Proche Orient IFPO).

Zelinsky, Z. (1971) 'The Hypothesis of the Mobility Transition', *Geographical Review,* 61:2, 219–49.

Zetter, R. (2010) 'The conceptual challenges: developing normative and legal frameworks for the protection of environmentally displaced people' in McAdam, J. (ed.) *Climate Change and Displacement: Multidisciplinary Perspectives* (Oxford: Hart Publishing) pp. 131–50.

Zhou, M. (1997) 'Segmented assimilation: issues, controversies, and recent research on the new second generation', *International Migration Review,* 31:4, 975–1008.

Zibouh, F. (2007) 'Le droit de vote des étrangers aux élections municipales de 2006 en Belgique', *Migrations Société,* 19:114, 141–68.

Zlotnik, H. (1999) 'Trends of international migration since 1965: what existing data reveal', *International Migration,* 37:1, 21–62.

Zlotnik, H. (2004) *International Migration in Africa: an Analysis based on Estimates of the Migrant Stock* (Washington, DC: Migration Information source).

Zohry, A. and Harrell-Bond, B. (2003) *Contemporary Egyptian Migration: An Overview of Voluntary and Forced Migration.* Working paper C3 (Sussex: University of Sussex, Development Research Centre on Migration, Globalisation and Poverty) www.migrationdrc.org/publications/working_papers/WP-C3.pdf.

Zolberg, A. (1981) 'International Migration in Political Perspective' in Kritz, M., Keely, C. and Tomasi, S. (eds) *Global Trends in Migration: Theory and Research on International Population Movements* (New York: Center for Migration Studies).

Zolberg, A.R. (2006) *A Nation by Design: Immigration Policy in the Fashioning of America* (Cambridge, MA: London: Harvard University Press).

Zolberg, A.R. and Benda, P.M. (eds) (2001) *Global Migrants, Global Refugees: Problems and Solutions* (New York and Oxford: Berghahn Books).

Zolberg, A.R., Suhrke, A. and Aguayo, S. (1989) *Escape from Violence* (Oxford and New York: Oxford University Press).

Index

Abu Musab Al-Zarqawi   206
advanced economies/societies   47, 63, 253,
   318–21
   'developed countries'   8, 8f, 9f, 31, 50, 125,
   242, 263
   'highly developed countries'   6, 19, 22,
   50, 111
   labour demand   **240–2**
   see also industrial economies
Afghanistan   2, 14, 117, 127, 147, 147f, 163,
   167, 172, 202, 226, 228, 376
   refugees   163, 164
   Soviet intervention (1979)   165b, 183
   US-led invasion   12, 165b, 204,
   206–7
Africa   5, 14, 34, 49, 71, 77, 85, 86, 96, 108,
   110–11, 114, 119, 134, 149, 160, 211,
   221, 226, 246, 249–50, 262, 264, 268,
   305, 319, 320
   see also 'migration in Africa and Middle East'
African-Americans   91–2, 97, 127, 260,
   283–4, 378
Africans   245, 253, 275b, 312
Afro-Caribbeans   61, 109, 128, 282
age   30, 31, 39, 356
   see also ageing population
age of migration   328
   general trends   **1–24**, 193, 203b, 321, 329
ageing population   117–18, 121–2, 124–5,
   154, 156–7, 242, 248b, 279b,
   324, 357
agency   **31**, 36, **37–9**, 45, 46, **51**, 75, 78, 99,
   146, 209, **213**, 221–2
   see also free will
agriculture   3, 48–9, 53, 72, 98, 110, 124,
   129–31, 133, 135, 142, 157, 159, 180,
   181, 189, 192, 211, 216, 234, 242–3,
   254, 256, 259, 273b, 279b, 285b,
   309, 320
   'farming'/'farmers'   34, 39, 90, 92, 95, 97,
   241
   'subsistence agriculture'   89, 95
aid/ODA   71, 74, 149, 323, 371
al-Qaeda   2, 165b, 202, **203b**, 203–5,
   206, 349
Albania   115, 119, 226, 285t, 356
Algeria   70–1, 95, 97, 109, 112, 175–6, 178–9,
   186, 189, 191, 276t, 299, 309
   spillover of insurgency to France   **202–4**

American dream   90, 268b
American Revolution   67, 91, 330, 371
Americas   85–6, 102, 269b, 276t
   migration   21, **126–46**
   migration from 1945 to 1970s   **128–31**
   migration since 1970s   **131–40**
   regional trends and policy
      developments   **141–4**
   see also Central America
Americas: migration from 1945 to 1970s
   128–31
   Andean area   **130–1**
   Mexico and Central America   **129–30**
Americas: migration since 1970s   **131–40**
   Andean area   **138–9**
   Caribbean   **137–8**
   Mexico and Central America   **135–7**
   Southern Cone   **139–40**
   USA and Canada   **133–5**
Americas: regional trends and policy
      developments   **141–4**
   policy initiatives   **142–3**
   remittances and development   **143–4**
Amin, I.   191
Amnesty International   146, 159, 171, 333
Andean countries   21, **128**
   migration (1945–1970s)   128, **130–1**
   migration (since 1970s)   **138–9**
Angola   175, 177, 184, 189, 194, 250
Angolans   115, 185, 194
Annan, K.   18
anthropologists/anthropology   38, 58, 196
anti-Semitism   60, 97, 294, 365
Arab Spring (2011)   2–3, 77, 117, 172–3, 186,
   194–5, 203b, 229, 250, 343, 346
   migration and revolution   **14–15b**
Arab–Israeli conflict   207, 209
Arabs   42, 173, 204, 253
   see also Israeli Arabs
Argentina   14, 21, 55, 119, 127–8, 131,
   139–40, 142, 145, 188, 265, 285b
Arizona   3, 4b, 136b, 144, 268b
Armed Islamic Group (GIA, Algeria)   203b,
   206
Armenia   164, 209
   conflict over Nagorno-Karabakh   207,
   208b
   influence   **208–9**
   see also Chinese diaspora